The Baby Name Wizard

The Baby Name Wizard

A MAGICAL METHOD FOR FINDING THE PERFECT NAME FOR YOUR BABY

LAURA WATTENBERG

broadway books

new york

Broadway Books titles may be purchased for business or promotional use or
for special sales. For information, please write to: Special Markets Department,
Random House, Inc., 1745 Broadway, New York, NY 10019.

PRINTED IN THE UNITED STATES OF AMERICA

BROADWAY BOOKS and its logo, a letter B bisected on the diagonal,
are trademarks of Random House, Inc.

Visit our website at www.broadwaybooks.com

First edition published 2005

Library of Congress Cataloging-in-Publication Data
Wattenberg, Laura.
The baby name wizard : a magical method for finding the perfect name
for your baby / Laura Wattenberg—1st ed.
p. cm.
Includes index.
ISBN 0-7679-1752-9
1. Names, Personal—Dictionaries. I. Title
CS2377.W38 2005
929.4.4.03—dc22   2004057949

20 19 18 17 16 15 14 13 12 11

For Martin, and the daughters we named together.

Contents

✳

Acknowledgments ix

In Search of the Perfect Name: The Wizard's Origins 1

Methods: A Peek Behind the Wizard's Curtain 3

Rules of Thumb for Choosing a Name 6

Family Matters: Namesakes, Traditions, and Conflicts 10

Name Trends: What's New and What's Next 13

Today's Top 25 18

Getting Started: A Quick Guide to the Book 19

Name Snapshots: Girls 21

Name Snapshots: Boys 127

Style Families 217

    African 217

    African-American 218

    Androgynous 221

    Antique Charm 223

    Bell Tones 224

    Biblical 225

    Brisk and Breezy 228

    Celtic 229

    Charms and Graces 231

    Country & Western 232

    English 234

    The -ens 235

    Exotic Traditionals 237

    Fanciful 238

    French 239

    German/Dutch 241

    Greek 242

Guys and Dolls   243
Italian   244
Jewish   245
Lacy and Lissome   247
Ladies and Gentlemen   248
Last Names First   249
Latino/Latina   253
Little Darlings   256
Long Gone   257
Mid-Century   258
Modern Meanings   260
Muslim   261
Mythological   262
Namesakes   263
New Classics   264
Nickname-Proof   265
Nicknames   267
Place-Names   273
Porch Sitters   274
Saints   276
Scandinavian   277
'70s–'80s   278
Shakespearean   280
Slavic   281
Solid Citizens   282
Surfer Sixties   283
Timeless   285
Why Not?   286
Resource List   289
Index   291

Acknowledgments

✳

Everyone has an opinion about names, and I've been grateful for that fact as I've turned to friends, family, and total strangers to help make this book whole.

Jennie Baird was the book's first champion. She instantly saw its potential, and her support helped make it a reality. I'm further indebted to the people who gave me input on the book concept and proposal, and the publishing process: Sarah Blustain, Neil Cronin, Stacy Cronin, Ari Juels, Daniel Max, Judith Miller, Dan Newman, Amey Stone, and Bonnie Wong. Also to Karl Arruda, Andrea Dunn, Catherine Miranda, Alina Plourde, Laura Raymond, Julie Steinberg, and Janine Sullivan, who offered valuable insights on specific name styles.

Thanks to my agent, Stephanie Rostan, whose enthusiasm and practical guidance made a potentially hair-raising process a pleasure. My editor, Tricia Medved, showed unfailing patience, grace, and courage in staring down a book with 1,550 graphs, seven spellings of Kaitlyn, and one first-time author.

Finally, a special thank-you to Julie Miles, Bernard Miller, Ruth Miller, and Karen Richter for reviewing large swaths of the manuscript, and to Martin Wattenberg for doing absolutely all of the above.

The Baby Name Wizard

In Search of the Perfect Name: The Wizard's Origins

✳

When my first daughter was a baby, I noticed a curious phenomenon. It seemed that every baby girl we met in Riverside Park in New York was named either Hannah or Olivia. But every one of their mothers said she had chosen the name to be unusual!

That was my introduction to the mysterious landscape of modern names. Like hairstyles and hemlines, names have fashions that change with each generation. Name fashions, though, are deeper and more expressive. They represent countless nuances of culture, language, and tradition. Each name has meanings that evolve, shaped by the people who bear it and the world that surrounds it.

When the time came to choose a name for my second child, I set out to find a map of the name landscape. Name dictionaries were an obvious place to start, but names are far more than words. Knowing that Olivia comes from the Latin word for olive doesn't tell you whether there will be three other Olivias on your block. And learning that Elmo has the same root as "helmet" doesn't clue you in that Elmo is a furry red Muppet. What I wanted wasn't a dictionary, but a practical guide to name fashions, history, and style.

Over the following years, I compiled a huge database of name information: popularity data from cities and countries around the world. Birth announcements in Ivy League alumni magazines. Lists of Catholic saints. African-American sorority memberships. Soap opera cast lists. Colonial census records. Then I developed computer models to spot trends and pick out names with similar styles. One such model, a "Name Matchmaker," could take any name and suggest others that matched it in style and feeling—for both boys and girls. I knew I was onto something when I told the Matchmaker the names of my two daughters, and the top boy's match it suggested was the very name my husband and I had picked out for a boy.

Consider *The Baby Name Wizard* a field guide to American names. It's designed to help you understand what's out there, identify name styles, and spot trends. But above all, it's designed to guide you to the perfect choice for your own personal taste and style.

I hope the *Wizard* will serve you well as you start your exploration of the world of names. If you have name observations or stories of your own to share, drop me a line at book@babynamewizard.com.

Methods:
A Peek Behind
the Wizard's Curtain

※

You don't need to know what's behind the *Wizard*'s curtain to read this book. But if you're curious about the graphs or skeptical about the "sister and brother" names, here's a peek at the research behind the names.

This book distills a vast database of name information, the result of my years of research into how we name our children. That database includes current and historical popularity data for each name from the United States and around the world. It also tracks names by regional, ethnic, historical, and religious associations, as well as subtler social groupings such as frequent sightings on soap operas or Ivy League campuses.

Most important, the database is more than just a roster of names. It is the platform for computer and statistical models to reveal patterns about name fashion, image, and style. While most of us can identify certain names as "preppy" or "trendy," the computer models validate our intuition, quantify the distinctions, and identify other names with the same properties. They reveal the reason behind the rhyme of naming.

You're here to learn about names, not statistics, but a few examples help illustrate the path from stats to style. For a straightforward application of name data, consider the thousands of graphs of name popularity throughout the book. Unlike many European countries, the United States does not regulate or formally track names given to children. The best historical data we have comes from the Social Security Administration (SSA), which each year receives millions of requests for Social Security numbers for new babies. The SSA now reports a ranking of each year's most popular names from 1 to 1,000.

While name ranks are interesting, they are not useful to graph or to compare across generations. For instance, if you graphed the top-1,000 names by *rank*, the 500th most popular name would appear exactly half as popular as the #1 name—it's halfway down the list. But fashion doesn't work that way. The top hits are vastly more common than other names, so the 500th most common boy's name, Kendall, is actually just 1.6 percent as popular as the top choice, Jacob. Rankings also disguise powerful generational differences. There's always a #1 name, but today's #1s are only a fraction as common as John and Mary were a century ago.

The graphs in this book represent not the ranks but the estimated *frequency of use* of names from 1900 to today. The data is based on raw SSA figures, with error correction and normalization to adjust for flaws and differences among historical samples. The resulting graphs, combined with the peak and current popularity ranks, give you an excellent sense of both the trend and scale of usage of the name. For example, compare these two graphs of the use of the name Mary since 1900—first showing rank, then frequency:

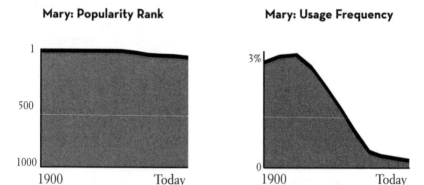

Mary is still a top-100 name, but its usage has dropped 95 percent from a century ago. The *Wizard* graphs are the only place to find that information.

Deeper analysis of the name data shows up in the style categorizations. To help identify styles, I used a variety of statistical techniques to find patterns of names with similar histories and properties. Trends appeared at different levels. Ethnic heritage is one factor: Germanic names were popular a century ago, Celtic names today. Specific sounds and letters are also sensitive to fashion shifts. For instance, clusters of consonants starting with "r" tend to mark a name as old-fashioned. Note how Dillon sounds modern and trendy, Dillard outmoded. Other names defied easy analysis and required Internet-age detection. I spent countless hours cross-referencing name patterns against databases of TV and movie characters, international school rosters, and other fashion cues.

The "Sister and Brother" name suggestions were identified with the help of a custom computer program I call the Name Matchmaker. This program is designed to take any name and pinpoint others with a similar style and feeling, based on dozens of criteria, including history, popularity, structure, origin, and cultural associations. The Matchmaker's judgments can be eerily accurate. When you enter boys' names and ask for the top matching girls' names, the program suggests such couples as John and Mary, Jason and Jennifer, Rhett and Scarlett, and Jagger and Presley.

Of course, as in all phases of the project, it takes a human to interpret the data and make the final judgments. It's my own call to say that a boy named Romeo matches a girl named Valentine. You'll doubtless be surprised at some of my conclusions, and downright peeved at a few. That's half the fun, isn't it? After all, when was the last time you sat around reading a name dictionary and quibbling with its derivations from Old English? The point of all the research and technology is to produce a real-world guide to names, with the kind of information that's worth kibitzing over. A hearty dinnertime debate over the merits of the name Leon is the best compliment the book could receive.

Rules of Thumb for Choosing a Name

Rule #1: Personal taste isn't so personal

Not long ago, I heard an expectant mother beside herself with outrage. She had just learned that another woman in her small town had "stolen" her baby name! No, she admitted, she had never met the woman. But for years now she had been planning to name a baby Keaton, a name she had personally invented, and now there was another little Keaton right across town. Someone must have told that other mother her own secret, special name. Thief!

Chances are this was not really a case of name larceny. That mom had just run into a startling fact of baby-name life: Our tastes, which feel so personal, are communal creations. Keaton? Well, it's a surname ending in "n," a style parents are flocking to for fresh ideas that sound like classic names. K in particular is a hot first letter. And don't forget that almost every parent today grew up watching Alex Keaton on *Family Ties*. So just like that outraged mom, thousands of parents across the country have independently "invented" the name for their kids.

We live in a shared culture with communities and experiences that shape our likes and dislikes. That means overlapping tastes—and as a rule, the closer two people are, the greater the overlap. Many of us have had a long-cherished name "stolen" by friends who had long cherished it themselves. It's frankly unnerving to discover that the quirky name you've always just happened to like is now a chart topper. Whatever happened to individual style?

Before you panic and name your son Aloysius, remember that communal taste is really a good thing. That shared perspective is exactly what gives names their style and nuance. It's also the context that lets you define your own style, meaningfully. Use the backdrop of your social group, your community, and your generation to choose names that make the kind of statement you're looking for. And if you do meet another

Keaton, take it as a positive sign that your son will be fashionable. Parents are the ones who worry about a name standing out; kids are happy to fit in.

Rule #2: All last names are not created equal

I can see a runway model wearing a sheath dress that's so gorgeous I could just melt looking at it. But I know perfectly well that the same dress on my real-world figure would be a train wreck. Similarly, I know that the stylish Irish name Kennedy, paired with my last name Wattenberg, would sound like someone falling down stairs.

In names as in clothes, the key is to choose the styles that flatter you. Run down this basic checklist before you make your final choice.

Length and rhythm: Sullivan and Flanagan match in style, but Sullivan Flanagan is a red-flag name. Watch out for singsong rhythms and tongue twisters.

The "Justin Case" Syndrome: A perfectly reasonable first name can meet a perfectly reasonable last name and create something perfectly ridiculous. When you have a candidate picked out, say the full name out loud repeatedly to look for hidden land mines. Include nicknames, too—Benjamin Dover is one thing, Ben Dover quite another.

Meeting in the middle: Look carefully where the end of one name meets the beginning of another. Jonas Sanders will be heard as Jonah Sanders or Jonas Anders. Alexander Anderson sounds like a stutter.

Special cases: If your last name is a common word, it's especially important to avoid alliteration. Jenny Jumps and Walter Wall sound like characters from a children's picture book. If your last name is a common first name, take special care to choose first names that won't make you sound inside out. Nicholson Thomas, for instance, is asking for trouble. And if your last name just *is* trouble (Rump, Hogg, etc.), you can use the rhythm of a long, rolling first name to draw the emphasis away from it.

Rule #3: All naming is local

America is a sprawling, diverse country, and at any given time many different name trends are operating at once. Money, geography, ethnicity, and education all swirl together to form "microclimates" of style, with local spikes in the use of particular names.

You can look up Oliver and say, "Ah, popularity rank #267, I won't meet many Olivers." But if your friends have kids named Julius, Lucy, and Charlotte, you should expect to see Olivers on your block. Not to say that's a bad thing. In that kind of community Oliver won't risk teasing, whereas he might find it rough going in a sea of Kaydens and Madisyns. Use the sister/brother names and style categories in this book to help gauge how a name will fit into your specific social surroundings.

Rule #4: Other people's opinions matter

As a parent, the choice of a baby name is entirely up to you. Why should you listen to what anybody else has to say, let alone your crazy friends and relatives?

Some food for thought: The choice may be yours, but you are making it for someone else. You are just a trustee in this matter, assigned to handle the affairs of another person who is unable to act because he or she has not yet been born. And those crazy friends and relatives? They are going to be your baby's friends and relatives before long. Don't let them bully you, but don't completely ignore them, either. As a group, they represent the society that's going to be hearing, and judging, your child's name for a lifetime. You don't have to flag down every passing car to ask for opinions, but it's worth choosing a few levelheaded confidantes to air out your ideas.

If you don't want to open the floodgates on a public name debate, this book gives you some middle ground. As you browse through the pages, think of it as a conversation with a friend who has thought an awful lot about names—and who will shut up when you're done with her. For a name you're seriously considering, try reading the listed sister/brother names out loud, too. They will give you the best sense of how the name you like will come across to others.

Rule #5: Choose the name you would like to have yourself

This is the top piece of advice I give expectant parents. We all have many factors in mind when we choose a name. We may want to honor our relatives or our ethnic heritage. We may see baby naming as an opportunity for personal expression. Use whatever criteria you like to narrow down your name choices, but before you fill in the birth certificate, stop and give the name this final test: If you were starting life today, knowing everything you know about the world, is this the name *you* would want to represent you? If so, you can feel confident that you're giving your child the best birthday present possible, one that will last a lifetime.

Family Matters:
Namesakes, Traditions,
and Conflicts

✳

You're about to introduce a new member of your family. This is a special, magical time filled with special, magical dilemmas, conflicts, and frustrations.

Names carry unique significance in a family setting, representing connections with the past as well as a glimpse into the future. We carry reflections of our families with us in our names, as surnames and often as first and middle names as well. Even if you don't directly name your child after relatives, you can still be blindsided by family issues you never thought about before you contemplated parenthood. Here's a primer on some of the top trouble spots:

Namesakes

The simplest namesake is a Junior. Dad is Johann Schmidt, son is Johann Schmidt, Jr., grandson is Johann III. If that's your family tradition and everyone buys into it, you're golden. Skip this section and start concentrating on finding different nicknames to use in each generation.

In most families, though, the ways we honor relatives are more fluid and up to individual discretion. We have first and middle names to play with, nicknames and variations. We may shy away from naming after living relatives, or have beloved relatives with atrocious names. Some common strategies for sticky situations:

The middle name cure-all: Middle names are America's polite dumping ground for outmoded names. We use the middle name to honor Aunt Mildred without actually raising a little Millie. Best of all, as middle names, many of those quirky choices, especially foreign names, start to sound stylish and distinctive. Some parents are tempted to overdo it, stuffing two or three names in the middle to cover all their obligations. Resist this impulse if you can; this is a three-name-max society, and extra names bring practical headaches.

The not-quite namesake: If you don't want two Margarets to create confusion at family gatherings, or just can't bear to name your son after your husband's grandpa Selig, try echoing the namesake with a slightly different choice. Many families just follow the first letter of the name. For a closer match, consider alternate forms from different times and cultures. Margaret would probably be delighted to be honored with a little Margot or Margery. Digging even deeper, you can start with a name root or meaning and derive a new equivalent. Edna, for instance, is believed to come from the same root as Eden. And the Yiddish Selig means happy, same as the Hebrew Asher. If you really want to go all out, consider an anagram. Baseball star Nomar Garciaparra was named for his father Ramon.

The nicknamesake: This favorite trick lets you name your son after great-grandpa Archie while sidestepping his given name Archibald. Many traditional nicknames can arise from multiple given names. So Uncle Don might be a Donald, but nephew Little Don is a Donovan. And Archie? Try the simple, uncommon choice Archer. The Nicknames style section in this book is a great source of ideas for alternate nick-namesakes.

That name is MINE!

You and your siblings were raised together. You share the same heritage, traditions, and life-shaping experiences. Is it any surprise you share the same favorite names?

So out of the thousands of names in the world, you and your sister have both zeroed in on Maeve as the one and only perfect choice for a little girl. The rule is simple here, gals: first come, first served. Unless some previous explicit agreement exists, whoever gives birth to a girl first has dibs on the name. In a small, close family, this dibs system might even extend to cousins or beyond.

Some exceptions: In a really big family, something's gotta give. Among your ten brothers and sisters and thirty nieces and nephews, you may have to accept an occasional duplicate name. Also, try to stay flexible to respect the input of in-law families. Perhaps your husband and your sister's husband both have fathers named Charles. You can both use the name if it's important, but try to hammer out a deal to call one boy Charlie and the other Chaz.

The last frontier: last names

It's old news by now that many parents, married or not, have different last names. Even couples who share a name may choose a hyphenated or combined version, or come up with other creative ways to incorporate the mother's birth name into their new family identity. More and more, those solutions have an impact on given names as well.

The middle maiden name: This is a simple, tried-and-true method to incorporate Mom's family heritage into a child's name. Most any surname sounds fine as a middle name, and the full name spoken aloud will sound like a hyphenated surname.

The last shall be first: Some families take a bolder step and use a family surname as the child's first name. With the current popularity of surname-style names, this option is more appealing than ever. Not that it's a new idea: Family surnames are traditional choices in the South, and you can pick up an Edith Wharton novel to see the same trend in Gilded Age New York. But please do proceed with caution. Try to put aside your emotional attachments and realize that not every surname is destined for a first-name role. (Sorry, Fantuzis and Rosenblatts.)

For the hyphenated child: If your child will be using a double last name, take triple the care in selecting a first name. Choose a name that sounds good with the full hyphenated version *and* with each surname alone. During the course of a lifetime, your child may have reasons to slim the name down: to look good on a theater marquee, to merge names with a spouse, or a dozen other situations we can't yet imagine. A little extra flexibility can't hurt.

Name Trends: What's New and What's Next

Why should you care about trends? You're picking a name because you love it, not because of what everybody else thinks. In fact, you're determined to buck the trends and pick a name off the beaten track! Well if so, you're smack dab in the middle of the hottest naming trend of the twenty-first century.

Each year, hundreds of American babies are named Unique. It reflects a society where individuality has become a cherished virtue. Remember, as a kid, looking for souvenir license plates with your name printed on them? It's tough times now for the souvenir manufacturers, with every family in town inventing its own spelling of names like Alysha and Kayden.

In the 1950s, the top-ten names for boys and girls accounted for a quarter of all babies. Today, it's less than a tenth. Even parents who opt for familiar classics are rejecting the once-standard nicknames. James sounds distinguished; Jim too "ordinary." And "ordinary" is becoming an endangered species: Names like Fred and Joan have completely disappeared.

So how do you stay truly distinctive in a sea of distinctive names? And how do you make sure you're not crossing the line from creative to just plain weird? Your child will be an individual, but you still want him to fit in.

The best way to find your perfect balance is to understand the trends that shape name style. As you read this book, you may end up rethinking whether Madison is really more individual than Martha, and Summer more creative than June. Or you may be emboldened to use a name your parents would never have dreamed of.

To get you started, here are the five most influential trends for the names of the coming generation. Each takes a different path toward individuality. The first four tap existing sources—the past, foreign languages, surnames, and common words—for names that are fresh but familiar. The fifth breaks new ground with completely modern inventions. For each trend you'll find examples that illustrate the current height of fashion, as well as suggestions of undiscovered names that could hit the same style bull's-eye.

Antique Revivals

Some of the hottest "new" names today are the ones that sound oldest. Parents are going hunting for antiques, plucking forgotten gems from the world of candlelight and horse-drawn carriages. These throwbacks come in two flavors: rough-hewn pioneers and refined ladies and gentlemen. On the pioneer side, Old Testament graybeard names like Zachariah and Levi are surprise hits. For the ladies and gents, nineteenth-century favorites like Julian and Annabel are regaining their luster, especially among the new generation of urban sophisticates.

FASHION FAVORITES
Girls: Hannah, Abigail, Madeline, Sophia
Boys: Elijah, Caleb, Oliver, Sebastian

FRESH OPTIONS
Girls: Susannah, Rafaela, Beatrice, Lavinia
Boys: Japheth, Matthias, Phineas, Benedict
See more under: Antique Charm, Biblical, Exotic Traditionals, Ladies and Gentlemen

Foreign Imports

Americans are now selecting from a global smorgasbord of names. In the past, most foreign-born hits were twists on familiar English names, such as the French Danielle and Paulette. Today, exotic roots are a plus. Celtic traditions are the top source of new hits for boys, such as the Irish name Aidan, the Scottish Cameron, and Welsh Dylan. (What's more, Celtic boys' names are equally hot for *girls*: consider Morgan, Brynn, and Kennedy.) Other hot linguistic sources include Arabic, Greek, Italian, Russian, and Swahili.

Girls: Caitlin, Tatiana, Aaliyah, Gianna
Boys: Cameron, Logan, Amani, Giovanni

FRESH OPTIONS
Girls: Emlyn, Katia, Akilah, Chiara
Boys: Cormac, Nikos, Bakari, Dario
See more under: African, Celtic, Greek, Italian, Muslim, Slavic

Surnames

Surnames are now a top source for first names, in a style that recalls the 1900s heyday of names like Ellsworth, Palmer, and Jennings. Unlike that earlier generation, though, today's surnames are used for boys and girls alike. One of the hottest styles for girls is long, masculine-sounding surnames that shorten to familiar girlish nicknames. Emerson (Emmy), Cassidy (Cassie), and Addison (Addie) are all rising. On the flip side, if you're looking for a fresh surname idea for boys that will stay firmly masculine, try rugged tradesman names, or surnames that contract to male nicknames.

FASHION FAVORITES
Girls: Madison, Hailey, Mackenzie, Taylor
Boys: Jackson, Colton, Tyler, Hunter.

FRESH OPTIONS
Girls: Sheridan, Ellery, Connolly, Kimball
Boys: Nicholson, Dennison, Archer, Carver
See more under: Last Names First

Meaning Names

If you want a name that's brand new but still carries meaning, the most direct place to look is your dictionary. Thousands of parents are taking a word or place name with a positive connotation and bestowing it on a child. It's like a name and a dream in one. (The romanticism of the names has made them far more popular for girls than boys.) At their best, these names are alive with energy. At their worst, they pigeonhole a child with narrow or unrealistic expectations. If you're browsing your own dictionary, look for choices flexible enough to inspire your child toward a wide world of different dreams.

FASHION FAVORITES
Girls: Destiny, Trinity, Autumn, Sierra
Boys: Chance, Zion, Justice, Dakota

FRESH OPTIONS
Girls: Amity, Lark, Mercy, Arcadia
Boys: Price, Canyon, Merit, Everest
See more under: Charms and Graces, Modern Meanings, Place Names

Kay-lees

The ultimate in individuality, of course, is to invent a whole new name. Each year, more and more parents tweak sounds and spellings for a custom-crafted product. Even these names, though, make up a distinct style. The sounds that name inventors favor are remarkably consistent: Vigorous starts, long, bright vowels, and smooth endings. Almost any permutation of the top sounds gives you a hit name—Jaden-Kayden-Kayla-Kailey-Jaelyn. If you love these sounds but want deeper roots, promising options include the Irish name Keelin for girls and the Sioux classic Chayton for boys. But if you enjoy mix-and-match creativity, just grab some Scrabble tiles and design your own name, or use the pre-fab building blocks below.

FASHION FAVORITES
Girls: Kayla, Jayla, Makayla, Kylie
Boys: Jayden, Jalen, Brayden, Cayden

Beginning	Middle	End
Am	ber	a
Ay	d	ah
Bai	k	ee
Bry	kay	eigh
Cay	l	en
Hay	n	er
Ja	r	in
Jay	s	lin
Ka	t	ly
Kay		on
Ky		y
La		yn
Ma		
Shay		
Ty		

See more under: Bell Tones, The -ens

Today's Top 25

*

"Mary's only #61? Then what *is* a common name?" Satisfy your curiosity with this rundown of the twenty-five most popular names for boys and girls. This small list accounts for a fifth of all babies born—more than #200 to #1,000 put together.

RANK	BOYS	GIRLS
1	Jacob	Emily
2	Michael	Emma
3	Joshua	Madison
4	Matthew	Hannah
5	Andrew	Olivia
6	Joseph	Abigail
7	Ethan	Alexis
8	Daniel	Ashley
9	Christopher	Elizabeth
10	Anthony	Samantha
11	William	Isabella
12	Ryan	Sarah
13	Nicholas	Grace
14	David	Alyssa
15	Tyler	Lauren
16	Alexander	Kayla
17	John	Brianna
18	James	Jessica
19	Dylan	Taylor
20	Zachary	Sophia
21	Brandon	Anna
22	Jonathan	Victoria
23	Samuel	Natalie
24	Christian	Chloe
25	Benjamin	Sydney

Getting Started: A Quick Guide to the Book

The *Wizard* is designed to guide you to names that fit your own personal taste and style. It's divided into three main sections: Name Snapshots, Style Families, and the Name Index.

NAME SNAPSHOTS

The Name Snapshots are compact profiles of 1,500 names, a big enough range to account for most of the babies named in America plus hundreds of rare and exotic suggestions. (Books that list 20,000 or 40,000 names typically count dozens of variants of each name. The Snapshot approach groups variants together for ease of browsing.)

To get started, look up the Snapshot of a name that you like. You'll find a rundown of all the most pertinent facts about the name, including style designations, nicknames, variants, and a graph charting the popularity of the name over the course of the past century. One special feature, "Sisters and Brothers," is designed to guide you to alternatives that feel similar to your choice. (A custom computer program helped identify the many elements that make up each name's trademark style.) If one of the sisters or brothers strikes your fancy, your search can widen from there. For even more ideas, check out the Style lists for your favorite names.

STYLE FAMILIES

The Style Families are your introduction to the many style threads running through American naming traditions, identified through analysis of name usage, structure, and origin. From biblical classics to modern meaning names, choose the styles that interest you and get background on their history and image, with dozens of name suggestions.

NAME INDEX

The Name Index is the master list which includes page references for every name snapshot, nickname, variant spelling and the unusual names that only appear in the Style Family listings. Use it to track down each occurrence of your favorite choice.

Key: Understanding the Name Snapshots

Each Snapshot is a guide to the name's image and usage—and a starting point for finding new name ideas.

Popularity: Current U.S. popularity rank.

Style: Defines a family of names that share a feeling, from "Country & Western" to "Surfer Sixties." Turn to the Styles section of the book for more background and lists of names in each category.

Nicknames: Nickname options, traditional and creative.

Variants: Popular alternate spellings, international variants, and closely related names.

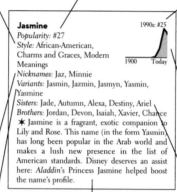

Commentary: Notes on the name's image, usage, and cultural associations.

Peak: The popularity peak is labeled with a national ranking to give you a sense of scale. This name peaked at #25 in the '90s.

Graph: Historical popularity graph, showing the trend in the name's usage from 1900 to today.

Sisters and Brothers: Suggestions of names that match in style and feeling. Not just for sibling naming—check the Sisters and Brothers for alternative ideas, middle names, or just to better understand the image of your favorite name.

Aaliyah
2002: #63

Popularity: #91
Style: African, African-American, Lacy and Lissome
Variants: Aliya, Aliyah, Aleah
Sisters: Ashanti, Taniya, Trinity, Amani, Iyanna
Brothers: Omari, Jabari, Josiah, Mekhi, Elijah
✴ The late R&B artist Aaliyah made this name a household word, and her image remains tied to it. Aaliyah is pure silken smoothness, practically a liquid name. It can be derived from a Swahili word meaning "most exalted," or the Hebrew term for "ascent."

Abigail
2003: #6

Popularity: #6
Style: Antique Charm, Biblical
Nicknames: Abby, Gail
Variants: Abigale, Avigail
Sisters: Hannah, Chloe, Lily, Faith, Isabel
Brothers: Caleb, Ethan, Gabriel, Julian, Isaac
✴ Abigail was once considered a Puritan name, and later became the stereotypical name for a servant or secretary. Today, this biblical classic is getting a well-deserved makeover. It still has its colonial aura of simple purity but has shed its dowdy starch. Now Abby is cute, Gail is sophisticated, and the full Abigail is the mainstream of fashion.

Ada
1900s: #85

Popularity: Rare
Style: Ladies and Gentlemen, Little Darlings, Saints
Variants: Adah
Sisters: Flora, Rhea, Leora, Iva, Alma
Brothers: Leo, Alton, Jules, Sam, Ben
✴ A century ago, three-letter girls' names were the hottest thing going. Most of those names—Oda, Una, Ila—are best left in the past, but Ada is definitely worth a second look. It is one of the simplest, cleanest names for girls. The spelling Adah is biblical, a wife of Esau.

Addison
2003: #192

Popularity: #192
Style: Androgynous, Last Names First
Nicknames: Addie
Sisters: Reagan, Madison, Parker, Connolly, Carson
Brothers: Bryson, Cooper, Tucker, Landon, Drake
✴ A direct descendant of the super hit Madison, Addison has a decidedly masculine sound. Expect to see spelling variants like Addysen taking the name in a girlier direction.

Adela
1910s: #430

Popularity: Rare
Style: Lacy and Lissome, Ladies and Gentlemen, Saints, Why Not?
Variants: Adele
Sisters: Flora, Amalia, Iva, Camilla, Althea
Brothers: Foster, Henry, Merritt, Albin, Jules
✴ Check it out: a quaint, pretty, turn-of-the-century name that nobody's using. Say it out loud a few times; that soft, lilting sound feels nice, doesn't it? A star in waiting.

Adelaide
1900s: #252

Popularity: Rare
Style: Ladies and Gentlemen, Saints
Nicknames: Addie
Sisters: Millicent, Angeline, Winifred, Ida, Henrietta
Brothers: Rupert, Ferdinand, Forest, Casper, Leopold
✴ Adelaide is an adventurous revival option that could make a big impact. It is antique and delicate sounding, though the best-known Adelaide is a cheeky dame from *Guys and Dolls*. Addie is pure cuteness for a little girl.

Adeline

Popularity: #666
Style: Antique Charm, Ladies and Gentlemen
Nicknames: Addie

1910s: #171

Sisters: Estelle, Angeline, Dorothea, Violet, Harriet
Brothers: August, Emory, Clement, Julius, Bertram
✳ Sweet Adeline used to be strictly for barbershop quartets, but the popularity of Madeline has eased her back into style. The name is still old-fashioned, but in an "aw, cute" way.

Adina

Popularity: Rare
Style: Biblical, Jewish, Lacy and Lissome
Nicknames: Addie, Dina

rarely used

Sisters: Aviva, Melia, Elisha, Atara, Dalia
Brothers: Avi, Jonas, Aric, Boaz, Elan
✳ This pretty Old Testament name is extremely unusual, yet feels timeless.

Adriana

Popularity: #107
Style: Italian, Lacy and Lissome, Latino/Latina, Shakespearean
Nicknames: Dree

2003: #107

Variants: Adrianna, Adrian, Adrienne
Sisters: Gabriela, Angelica, Alana, Mirand‐, Liliana
Brothers: Damian, Emmanuel, Marco, Sergio, Quinton
✳ This old feminine form of Adrian is a completely modern hit. It touches all the bases: antique and literary, Italian and sultry. Adriana's the name for a supermodel you can take home to Mom.

Adrienne

Popularity: #635
Style: African-American, French, Nickname-Proof, Timeless

1980s: #189

Variants: Adrianna, Adrian, Adrianne
Sisters: Candace, Justine, Veronica, Christina, Simone
Brothers: Terrance, Geoffrey, Travis, Lance, Noel
✳ Adrienne is an elegant old favorite—French, feminine, and familiar. You probably have some friend who'll shout "Yo! Adrian!" like Rocky Balboa, but that joke is now heading for retirement.

Aeron

Popularity: Rare
Style: Fanciful, Mythological
Sisters: Rhiannon, Electra, Aine, Lotus, Echo

rarely used

Brothers: Triton, Fife, Conan, Rhodri, Sinbad
✳ This name may be best known as a piece of furniture: Herman Miller's skeletal Aeron chair, a staple of stylish dot-com offices. Aeron was, in fact, a battle goddess of early Welsh mythology. It's a strong and unusual name, just barely a realistic choice for a girl.

Agatha

Popularity: Rare
Style: English, Ladies and Gentlemen
Nicknames: Aggie

1900s: #380

Sisters: Philomena, Augusta, Matilda, Adelaide, Louisa
Brothers: Rupert, Horace, Casper, Clement, Basil
✳ Agatha is one of the heavy names long relegated to oil portraits of ancestors. It's still out on the fringes, but inching closer to consideration. As a middle name, it lightens up to sound pleasantly eccentric.

Agnes

Popularity: Rare
Style: Porch Sitters
Nicknames: Aggie, Nessie
Variants: Inez

1900s: #37

Sisters: Ida, Ethel, Myrtle, Thelma, Gladys
Brothers: Lester, Wilbur, Cyril, Floyd, Virgil
✳ It is hard for us to imagine the world in which Agnes was a trendy, glamorous choice for a little girl. Someday, perhaps, this age-old standard will return to style, but for now it's the most unfashionable classic around.

Aida

Popularity: Rare
Style: Exotic Traditional, Nickname-Proof
Sisters: Carmen, Aurea, Luz, Iole, Aurora

1940s: #255

Brothers: Alonzo, Royce, Theron, Regis, Giovanni
✳ Aida (eye-EE-da) was the tragic heroine of Verdi's Egyptian opera, and her name perfectly captures the artful exoticism of the work. In the U.S., Aida has usually been pronounced as two syllables, an alternate spelling of Ida. The operatic pronunciation is splashier and more contemporary.

Aine

Popularity: Rare   rarely used
Style: Celtic, Mythological
Variants: Áine, Anya
Sisters: Niamh, Sian, Aoife,   1900   Today
Alannah, Ciara
Brothers: Niall, Ronan, Oisin, Seamus, Finn
✱ Áine was the queen of the fairies in Celtic mythology, and the name still sounds perfect for a charming sprite. It's a favorite in contemporary Ireland—pronounce it AWN-ya.

Ainsley

2003: #440

Popularity: #440
Style: Bell Tones, Celtic, Last Names First
Variants: Ainslee   1900   Today
Sisters: Ryleigh, Piper, Finlay, Carson, Aubrey
Brothers: Landen, Sullivan, Greyson, Kolby, Reece
✱ Ainsley is taken from an old Scottish surname and was traditionally used more for boys than girls. It has a decorous sound suitable for a butler: "Ainsley, we'll be taking our brandy in the smoking room this evening." Ainsley is ready to soar in the U.S., where, like Audrey and Aubrey, it is exclusively feminine.

Aisha

2003: #613

Popularity: #613
Style: African-American, Muslim
Variants: Iesha   1900   Today
Sisters: Yasmin, Jamila, Shakira, Ayana, Amira
Brothers: Rashad, Jamil, Tariq, Khalid, Raheem
✱ The name of Mohammed's favorite wife, Aisha is a classic throughout the Muslim world. Its sound is the prototype for African-American standards like Lakeisha.

Alana

2003: #200

Popularity: #200
Style: Lacy and Lissome
Nicknames: Lani, Ali, Lana
Variants: Alanna, Alannah,   1900   Today
Alaina, Alayna
Sisters: Alissa, Layla, Alina, Serena, Nadia
Brothers: Colin, Micah, Drew, Lucas, Fabian
✱ This attractive invention is as sweet and fluid as caramel syrup. It has such a natural femininity that it fits in comfortably with older classics. The variant Alannah is especially popular in Ireland, where it is taken from the Gaelic endearment "a leanbh," meaning "O, child."

Alanis

2003: #735

Popularity: #735
Style: Namesakes
Sisters: Annika, Dasia, Sarahi, Calista, Avril   1900   Today
Brothers: Holden, Adriel, Landon, Jagger, Gael
✱ This is a creative name that feels like it must have deep roots. In fact, rocker Alanis Morissette's father, Alan, chose it as a variation on his own name. You can choose it for its New Age allure—it's soft but not too girly.

Alessandra

2003: #587

Popularity: #587
Style: Italian, Lacy and Lissome
Nicknames: Sandra, Sandy, Alex, Allie, Lessa   1900   Today
Variants: Alejandra, Lisandra, Alexandra
Sisters: Giovanna, Eliana, Francesca, Viviana, Christiana
Brothers: Giancarlo, Maximilian, Matteo, Nico, Tristan
✱ This Italian classic is every bit as lush as the familiar Russian form Alexandra. It just swaps out snowy vistas for Mediterranean sunshine. Alejandra is the popular Spanish version.

Alexa

2003: #66

Popularity: #66
Style: Lacy and Lissome
Nicknames: Lexi, Alex
Sisters: Ariana, Gabriela, Maya,   1900   Today
Kylie, Talia
Brothers: Bryce, Xavier, Dalton, Cole, Tristan
✱ Alexa is a twentieth-century invention that's built like a classic. It first popped up in the '40s as a glamorous, Hollywood-style creation akin to Lana. It's still sleek, but powerful, too—more cougar than kitten.

Alexandra

1990s: #28

Popularity: #38
Style: Lacy and Lissome, New Classics, Slavic
Nicknames: Alex, Sandy, Allie,   1900   Today
Lexi, Sandra, Sasha, Xander, Xandra, Shura
Sisters: Angelica, Gabriela, Daniela, Victoria, Miranda
Brothers: Zachary, Lucas, Nathaniel, Dimitri, Adrian
✱ Alexandra is the classic, regal feminine form of Alexander. The name is a relative newcomer to English, and its roots in Russia and Scandinavia add a luxurious hint of fur muffs and winter palaces. The standard nicknames, though, are decidedly American and down-to-earth. If you prefer a Russian style, try Sasha or Shura.

Alexandria 1990s: #81
Popularity: #124
Style: Lacy and Lissome,
Place Names
Nicknames: Alex, Lexi, Andi,
Sandy, Xander
Variants: Alexandrea
Sisters: Anastasia, Savanna, Angelica,
Cassandra, Tatiana
Brothers: Darius, Zachary, Raleigh, Trenton,
Chandler
✶ Riding high on two trends, Alexandria takes
the popular Alexander root and turns it into a
place name. If you choose this five-syllable sen-
sation, be sure to choose a nickname, too.

Alexia 2002: #127
Popularity: #134
Style: Lacy and Lissome
Nicknames: Lexi, Alex, Xia
Variants: Alexea, Alessia
Sisters: Alayna, Valeria, Skylar, Amaya,
Madelyn
Brothers: Jaylen, Kaleb, Landon, Camron,
Ryder
✶ This pretty Alex variant is lighter and more
modern than Alexandra. But the name makes
neurologists cringe, since alexia (like amnesia or
dyslexia) is a neurological condition: loss of the
ability to read. The more common the name
becomes, the less that will matter. In the mean-
time, the Italian version Alessia is one way to
sidestep the issue.

Alexis 2001: #5
Popularity: #7
Style: Androgynous, Saints
Nicknames: Lexi, Alex
Variants: Alexus, Alexys
Sisters: Morgan, Serena, Olivia, Tatiana,
Damaris
Brothers: Cameron, Dylan, Xavier, Darius,
Adrian
✶ It's easy to see the appeal of this name, with
its crackling sound and elegant strength. And it's
not just another derivative of Alexander, but
a traditional Greek name in its own right.
However, if you're looking for an unconvention-
al style statement, it's time to look elsewhere—
this is a monster hit.

Alice 1900s: #10
Popularity: #426
Style: Ladies and Gentlemen
Nicknames: Allie, Elsie, Lisa
Variants: Alys, Alyce, Alix,
Alison
Sisters: Helen, Anne, Ruth, Marian, Eleanor
Brothers: Arthur, Walter, Louis, Henry, Theodore
✶ This plain and simple classic has been sadly
neglected for years. Right now, opinions are
divided. To some, the model Alice is long-suffer-
ing housewife Alice Kramden of *The Honey-
mooners*. To others, it's the girlish enchantment
of *Alice in Wonderland*. Expect to see the name
come back first in the tony urban neighborhoods
where Lucy and Henry are hits.

Alicia 1980s: #45
Popularity: #132
Style: Lacy and Lissome,
Latino/Latina, New Classics
Nicknames: Ali, Licha
Variants: Alisha, Alecia, Alesha,
Alycia, Elisha
Sisters: Andrea, Vanessa, Raquel, Amanda,
Katrina
Brothers: Travis, Derek, Jeremy, Ryan, Bradley
✶ This Spanish form of Alice is decorous and
delicate, but choosing it is a lot like marrying into
a big family. Thousands of sound-alike Aleshas,
Elishas, and Alycias come with the bargain.

Alina 2003: #384
Popularity: #384
Style: German/Dutch, Lacy and
Lissome, Slavic
Variants: Elina
Sisters: Nadia, Daniella, Talia,
Anika, Marina
Brothers: Lukas, Abel, Quinn, Mateo, Dorian
✶ Alina slides smoothly into many guises. In
the right context it can sound sensual, sophisti-
cated, or cheerfully girlish. It's used in several
different languages and can fit in anywhere. A
name on the rise.

Alisa 1970s: #341
Popularity: #695
Style: Lacy and Lissome, New
Classics
Nicknames: Allie, Lise
Variants: Elisa
Sisters: Lara, Andrea, Holly, Felicia, Melanie
Brothers: Marc, Brett, Geoffrey, Darren, Jared
✶ The old standby Alice has many modern
descendants. Alisa is the brightest and cheeriest
of the lot, with a classic sound.

Allegra

Popularity: Rare   rarely used
Style: Jewish, Lacy and Lissome, Ladies and Gentlemen
Nicknames: Allie
Variants: Alegra
Sisters: Althea, Geneva, Leora, Emeline, Rafaela
Brothers: Archer, Hugo, Jasper, Gideon, Garrick
★ Allegra is a dynamic choice, joyously feminine and ready to take on the world. One word of caution, though: It's also the name of an allergy medicine, which could dismay some of the sneezier members of your family.

Allie

1900s: #207

Popularity: #326
Style: Guys and Dolls, Nicknames
Variants: Allie, Ali
Sisters: Josie, Callie, Eliza, Tess, Maggie
Brothers: Jake, Max, Alex, Walker, Andy
★ Allie's a particularly flexible nickname. It can be used as a diminutive for many different names, from offbeat antiques to ultra-modern creations. (Take a peek at the nickname section for ideas.) That gives Allie a timeless style that's not overly girlish. As a given name, it's cheerful and unpretentious.

Allison

1990s: #43

Popularity: #45
Style: New Classics
Nicknames: Allie, Ally
Variants: Alison, Allyson, Alyson
Sisters: Natalie, Erin, Andrea, Lauren, Danielle
Brothers: Eric, Brian, Jared, Jonathan, Evan
★ Allison looks like a surname, but it has always been a girl's given name. It started off centuries ago as a nickname for Alice. Today, with its three popular spellings, it has left Alice in the dust and established itself as an American classic.

Alma

1900s: #57

Popularity: #640
Style: Ladies and Gentlemen, Nickname-Proof
Sisters: Clara, Theda, Viola, Edith, Flora
Brothers: Julius, Louis, Everett, Arthur, Conrad
★ Alma is the Spanish and Italian word for soul, and thinking of it that way helps tip the name's style balance from fusty to warm and compassionate.

Alondra

2003: #128

Popularity: #128
Style: African-American, Latino/Latina
Nicknames: Lonnie
Variants: Alandra
Sisters: Mariana, Amaya, Julissa, Nayeli, Angelia
Brothers: Diego, Omar, Xavier, Mateo, Andres
★ This glossy new hit is Spanish for "lark." It's luxurious to pronounce—the name you want for an intimate evening on a moonlit beach.

Althea

1910s: #402

Popularity: Rare
Style: Ladies and Gentlemen, Mythological, Why Not?
Nicknames: Thea
Sisters: Rhea, Cecile, Geneva, Aurelia, Louisa
Brothers: Jules, Edmond, Benedict, Hugh, Felix
★ A cozy antique with origins in Greek mythology, Althea is avant-garde style for artists and Ph.D.s.

Alyssa

2001: #14

Popularity: #14
Style: Lacy and Lissome
Nicknames: Aly, Lissa
Variants: Alissa, Allyssa, Alysa, Elissa
Sisters: Brianna, Alexis, Ariana, Kayla, Marissa
Brothers: Jordan, Dylan, Austin, Hunter, Chase
★ Alyssa and its many variants are generally described as variants of Alicia. They're better understood as a phenomenon in their own right—an attempt to capture the very essence of lacy femininity in a name. The less traditional the spelling, the lacier.

Amanda

1980s: #3

Popularity: #53
Style: '70s–'80s, Lacy and Lissome, New Classics
Nicknames: Mandy
Sisters: Stephanie, Andrea, Jessica, Danielle, Nicole
Brothers: Jeremy, Derek, Brandon, Joshua, Kyle
★ Amanda is one of the picturesque Latinate names that English writers used to dream up for their heroines. (It's formed from the Latin *amare*, "to love.") These old literary romantics have a double appeal today. They're still ravishing, but by surviving the centuries, they've also developed an air of authority.

Amani

Popularity: #715
Style: African, African-American, Muslim
Sisters: Kenia, Naima, Kamaria, Shani, Aliyah
Brothers: Omari, Khalid, Kwame, Jelani, Tariq

★ Amani was a boy's name in the U.S. during the first wave of Afrocentric names in the '70s. Its delicate sound moved it to the girls' side, where it continues to gain momentum. Amani is taken from the Swahili word for peace.

2002: #681

Amaya

Popularity: #184
Style: Lacy and Lissome, Latino/Latina
Variants: Amya
Sisters: Eliana, Dasia, Arely, Tamia, Anahi
Brothers: Mateo, Adan, Yahir, Emiliano, Jairo

★ Amaya is a Spanish surname with a honey-rich sound that's a natural for a girl's name. An MTV *Real World* cast member helped popularize the name.

2003: #184

Amber

Popularity: #74
Style: '70s–'80s, Charms and Graces, Nickname-Proof
Sisters: Heather, Erica, Danielle, Ashley, April
Brothers: Dustin, Adam, Cory, Ryan, Jared

★ Amber was occasionally heard a century ago when jewel names were in vogue. It really took off decades later thanks to the romantic novel *Forever Amber*, a mid-century sensation. As a result, the name's image is satin-and-lace sensual.

1980s: #13

Amelia

Popularity: #113
Style: Antique Charm, English, Shakespearean
Nicknames: Amy, Mia, Mel, Lia, Millie
Variants: Amélie, Amalia, Emilia
Sisters: Cecilia, Sophie, Annabel, Miriam, Lydia
Brothers: Simon, Max, Edgar, Owen, Pierce

★ Amelia was a shrinking violet for years, but now she's ready for her close-up. Parents are attracted to this gentle charmer as a twist on Emily or kindred spirit to Olivia. The up-and-coming nickname choice is Mia, as in the heroine of Meg Cabot's *Princess Diaries* books.

2003: #113

America

Popularity: #510
Style: Modern Meanings, Place Names
Nicknames: Meri, Amy, Ricki
Sisters: Liberty, Journey, Montana, Haven, Sierra
Brothers: Phoenix, Maverick, Washington, Justice, Dakota

★ A combination of the craze for place names and a surge of patriotism have sent this name back into the mainstream. But the same power that attracts parents to the name makes it problematic. The word *America* carries such a strong image that it's tough to look past it to the girl herself.

2002: #414

Amira

Popularity: #698
Style: Jewish, Lacy and Lissome, Muslim
Sisters: Layla, Mahala, Tamia, Aviva, Dalia
Brothers: Jaron, Amir, Elisha, Tariq, Elan

★ This gentle name is a good global choice, easy to spell and pronounce in many languages. The name in fact has twin origins in Arabic and Hebrew, a peaceful coexistence that is a positive association in its own right.

2003: #698

Amity

Popularity: Rare
Style: Charms and Graces, Why Not?
Nicknames: Ami
Sisters: Verity, Calla, Melody, Lavender, Dahlia
Brothers: Stone, Tobias, Micah, Justus, Aric

★ Amity is rarely used as a name, but it's attractive in both sound and meaning—a pretty expression of goodwill. The one potential negative, the *Amityville Horror*, is blessedly fading from memory.

rarely used

Amy

Popularity: #120
Style: '70s–'80s, Nickname-Proof, Surfer Sixties
Variants: Aimee, Amie
Sisters: Kerry, Heather, Stacy, April, Tara
Brothers: Brian, Chad, Eric, Jeremy, Scott

★ Amy is bright, simple, and cheerily unpretentious. It was a monster hit in the '70s but doesn't sound dated. Think of the name's recent decline as merely a "stock market correction" back to its natural place as a modest, beloved classic. The French Aimée is equally traditional but showier.

1970s: #2

Anaïs 2003: #917
Popularity: #917
Style: Exotic Traditional, French, Namesakes
Sisters: Colette, Simone, Esmé, Bijou, Fleur
Brothers: Valentin, Joaquim, Roc, Régis, Loïc
★ This name is associated with Anaïs Nin, the writer famed for her diaries and erotic stories. For those familiar with Nin, the name projects a sensual feminism. It is currently a hot name in France.

Anastasia 2002: #267
Popularity: #268
Style: Greek, Lacy and Lissome, Saints, Slavic
Nicknames: Ana, Annie, Stasia, Stacy
Sisters: Tatiana, Valentina, Francesca, Liliana, Artemisia
Brothers: Fabian, Dimitri, Maximilian, Dominick, Roman
★ This Greek/Russian enchantress radiates mystery and romance. The legend of the lost Romanov princess Anastasia is a big reason, but the gossamer name is simply a natural for shadowy beauties.

Andrea 1980s: #33
Popularity: #56
Style: Lacy and Lissome, New Classics
Nicknames: Andy, Andi
Variants: Andra
Sisters: Monica, Amanda, Stephanie, Nicole, Melissa
Brothers: Timothy, Sean, Christopher, Jeremy, Aaron
★ Like its male counterpart Andrew, Andrea is a classic that seems to grow stronger with each generation. It's soft and melodic with a serious core. A standard throughout the English-speaking world.

Angel 2002: #114
Popularity: #121
Style: African-American, Modern Meanings
Nicknames: Angie
Sisters: Autumn, Diamond, Alana, Jade, Heaven
Brothers: Chance, Dante, Prince, Justice, Jett
★ After centuries of Angela, Angelica, and Angelina, American parents decided to cut to the chase. "My little girl is an angel, and I'm calling her one!" A loving appellation that walks a line between confident and cutesy.

Angela 1970s: #7
Popularity: #103
Style: Timeless
Nicknames: Angie
Variants: Angelia, Angel
Sisters: Monica, Sonya, Michelle, Tamara, Teresa
Brothers: Scott, Patrick, Bradley, Shawn, Jeffrey
★ For years, Angela was *the* way to name your daughter with a touch of heaven. Today, the options have exploded. Half a dozen different "Angel" names are popular, and Heaven itself is now a popular name. But Angela's still a hit and it remains the most modest, enduring choice.

Angelica 1990s: #99
Popularity: #142
Style: Lacy and Lissome, Latino/Latina
Nicknames: Angie, Ange
Variants: Angelique, Angelika
Sisters: Cassandra, Vanessa, Adriana, Alessandra, Gabriela
Brothers: Emmanuel, Andre, Gabriel, Lucas, Javier
★ Is there such a thing as demure extravagance? If so, you're looking at it. Angelica is a flamboyant name with a modest heart.

Angelina 2003: #71
Popularity: #71
Style: Antique Charm, Lacy and Lissome
Nicknames: Angie, Lina
Variants: Angeline, Angelia
Sisters: Isabella, Madelyn, Annalise, Gabriella, Juliana
Brothers: Sebastian, Elijah, Julian, Leonardo, Dominick
★ This flowery, old-fashioned form of Angela has been popularized by actress Angelina Jolie. Among the younger set it's known as a popular ballet-dancing mouse.

Anita 1960s: #83
Popularity: #947
Style: African-American, Latino/Latina, Solid Citizens
Nicknames: Nita, Ani
Sisters: Roberta, Yvonne, Teresa, Janice, Rita
Brothers: Rodney, Glenn, Dwight, Gerard, Martin
★ This Spanish-accented variant of Anna became an American standard beginning in the 1930s. Parents have since turned to fresher inventions, but Anita's crisp, bright sound is still pleasant and fashionable.

Anna

1900s: #4

Popularity: #21
Style: Antique Charm, Biblical, Timeless
Nicknames: Annie, Nan
Variants: Ana, Anne
Sisters: Julia, Catherine, Lillian, Eva, Grace
Brothers: Joseph, Henry, Charles, Simon, Julian
★ Anna takes the simplicity of Ann, adds an old-fashioned gentleness, and then tops it off with a sophisticated continental sheen. That's an irresistible combination to the affluent, educated parents who have made this name one of their top choices.

Annabelle

2003: #292

Popularity: #292
Style: Antique Charm
Nicknames: Anna, Annie, Belle
Variants: Annabel, Annabella
Sisters: Madeline, Phoebe, Adeline, Arabella, Juliette
Brothers: Solomon, Maxwell, Oliver, Jasper, Harrison
★ Annabelle is decorative but modest. The overwhelming impression is of sweetness. The name has come back from a long period of disuse and is on its way to widespread popularity. For spellings, women seem to prefer Annabel, men Annabelle. See also the discussion under Isabel.

Annalise

2003: #719

Popularity: #719
Style: Antique Charm
Nicknames: Ann, Annie, Lise
Variants: Anneliese
Sisters: Lisbeth, Julianne, Arabella, Mariel, Renata
Brothers: Andreas, Sebastian, Julian, Gunnar, Markus
★ This compound name has an Old World charm that should win it many admirers.

Anne

1910s: #57

Popularity: #325
Style: Timeless
Nicknames: Annie, Nancy
Variants: Ann, Anna
Sisters: Catherine, Rose, Margaret, Ruth, Cecilia
Brothers: Carl, Arthur, John, Paul, Edward
★ Anne is not in the top 300 names? Come on, folks . . . I know we all love the continental forms of girls' names now, but ten times as many Annas as Annes is going a bit too far. For all of you tempted by the likes of Rose and Claire, how about giving this warm, soft, and simple classic another chance?

Annette

1960s: #77

Popularity: #752
Style: French, Mid-Century
Nicknames: Annie, Nettie
Sisters: Yvonne, Paula, Donna, Suzanne, Pamela
Brothers: Dean, Randall, Tony, Douglas, Curtis
★ Thanks to Annette Funicello, this name has one foot back in 1964, nestled on a beach blanket. Its classic femininity still shines through, making it a worthy holdover.

Annie

1900s: #28

Popularity: #339
Style: Antique Charm, Guys and Dolls, Nicknames
Variants: Ani
Sisters: Lucy, Clara, Lillie, Rose, Ruby
Brothers: Charlie, Joe, Leo, Sam, Harry
★ Annie is a fun-loving name, full of life. The classic American Annies are all over the cultural map but linked by a lively unpredictability: Annie Oakley, Annie Hall, Little Orphan Annie. Annie can be a nickname for longer names of every description (see the Nicknames style section). By choosing it as a full name, you're making fun your number-one priority.

Annika

2003: #284

Popularity: #284
Style: Lacy and Lissome, Scandinavian
Nicknames: Annie
Variants: Anika
Sisters: Sofia, Katerina, Dania, Anastasia, Iliana
Brothers: Lukas, Kai, Johan, Anton, Stefan
★ This Swedish pet form of Anna has the sound of a modern invention but the reserved demeanor of a Nordic classic. It's been popularized by golfer Annika Sorenstam, a Stockholm native who is a good model for the name's strength and grace.

Antoinette

1910s: #175

Popularity: Rare
Style: African-American, French, Ladies and Gentlemen
Nicknames: Toni, Netta, Ann
Sisters: Marguerite, Clarice, Evangeline, Genevieve, Eloise
Brothers: Ferdinand, Frederic, Laurence, Napoleon, Armand
★ In America, this name sounds ornate, old-fashioned, and above all French. In France, it sounds . . . exactly the same. The elaborate old French classics are rare on both sides of the Atlantic right now, with simpler choices like Charlotte and Camille taking their place.

Antonia

1900s: #267

Popularity: #731
Style: Italian, Saints, Timeless, Why Not?
Nicknames: Toni, Tonia, Tia, Toña
Sisters: Marcella, Helena, Genevieve, Marina, Louisa
Brothers: Everett, Conrad, Carlo, Francis, Oliver

★ This overlooked classic is a fashion-forward choice. It shares many of the charms of Olivia, but trades in that name's delicate lace for plush velvet. Familiar but uncommon, with an old-world soul.

Anya

2003: #486

Popularity: #486
Style: Lacy and Lissome, Little Darlings, Slavic
Sisters: Dasia, Alina, Hana, Elle, Katia
Brothers: Lukas, Roman, Nico, Jovan, Dimitri

★ Anya offers a lot of punch in a small package. In Russian it's the pet form of Anna, and it makes a gently exotic twist on that popular standard.

April

1970s: #34

Popularity: #281
Style: '70s–'80s, Charms and Graces, Nickname-Proof
Variants: Avril
Sisters: Heather, Tara, Holly, Shannon, Amy
Brothers: Brian, Chad, Shawn, Heath, Jeremy

★ In the '70s and '80s, April was a huge hit name while calendar companions May and June were out of sight. The tide is ready to turn the other way now, but you still won't go wrong with April. Months, seasons, and even days all remain comfortably in style for girls.

Arabella

Popularity: Rare
Style: Lacy and Lissome, Why Not?
Nicknames: Bella, Bell, Ari
Variants: Arabel, Arabelle
Sisters: Rafaela, Araminta, Lisandra, Annalise, Artemisia
Brothers: Griffith, Dennison, Blaise, Broderick, Evander

rarely used

★ A perfectly lovely creation that has been a favorite in literature for centuries. Arabella is similar in feel to Isabella and Annabella, but much less common. (Maribella is an even rarer alternative.) The variant Arabel is trim and elegant.

Aretha

1960s: #726

Popularity: Rare
Style: African-American, Lacy and Lissome, Namesakes, Surfer Sixties
Sisters: Valencia, Corinna, Rolanda, Mahalia, Odetta
Brothers: Baron, Donell, Dedrick, Otis, Wilson

★ This comes close to being a one-woman name for singer Aretha Franklin, but if we can have hundreds of little Elvises, why not a few Arethas? Surely the Queen of Soul deserves namesakes just like the King of Rock and Roll.

Aria

2003: #673

Popularity: #673
Style: Lacy and Lissome, Modern Meanings
Sisters: Amya, Lyric, Sky, Selah, Elle
Brothers: Sage, Quinn, Major, Storm, Blaise

★ In an opera, an aria is an elaborate solo. Translate that into a name and you get a dramatic, artistic image with a simple sound.

Ariadne

Popularity: Rare
Style: Exotic Traditional, Mythological, Saints
Nicknames: Ari
Sisters: Artemis, Hermione, Beatrix, Daphne, Ione
Brothers: Leander, Achilles, Tarquin, Horatio, Phineas

rarely used

★ In Greek myth, Ariadne was the clever heroine who gave her beloved Theseus a thread to find his way out of the Labyrinth. In keeping with the tale, her name sounds both romantic and intelligent. Ariadne was also the one classical deity to be adopted into Celtic mythology, which gives the name a British Isles flavor.

Ariana

2003: #79

Popularity: #79
Style: African-American, Lacy and Lissome
Nicknames: Ari
Variants: Arianna, Aryanna
Sisters: Alexa, Daniela, Alondra, Juliana, Brianna
Brothers: Tristan, Isaiah, Kaleb, Jalen, Andre

★ Ariana belongs to the satin-and-lace world of ultra-feminine names. It's smooth, supple, and surprisingly serious. The name was originally a form of Ariadne; the Italian spelling Arianna is equally popular.

Ariel 1990s: #117
Popularity: #214
Style: Jewish, Namesakes, New Classics, Shakespearean
Nicknames: Ari
Variants: Arielle
Sisters: Miranda, Aviva, Mariah, Raven, Bianca
Brothers: Alec, Spenser, Darius, Levi, Jaron
✶ Ariel is a name with two lives. It is a charming Shakespearean and Hebrew name—and it is the name of Disney's Little Mermaid. Parents who like the first association tend to be turned off by the second, but if you don't mind the mermaids, Ariel remains ethereal and lovely.

Arlene 1930s: #69
Popularity: #842
Style: Solid Citizens
Nicknames: Arly, Arlie
Variants: Arline, Arleen
Sisters: Elaine, Shirley, Norma, Jeanette, Gloria
Brothers: Donald, Gene, Gordon, Eugene, Franklin
✶ Arlene is generations past its fashion prime, but has quietly stuck around through the lean times and may be mounting a modest comeback. The nickname Arlie is cute and spunky.

Armani 2001: #786
Popularity: #932
Style: Fanciful
Sisters: Lexus, Prada, Isis, Unique, Iyanna
Brothers: Gianni, Sincere, Blaze, Maximus, Zenith
✶ Before you dismiss this designer name as an unlikely flight of fancy, remember that Tiffany wasn't a first name fifty years ago, either. Luxury labels are a natural target for glamour seekers, and Armani is now here for girls and boys alike. Its popularity has been boosted by its resemblance to the African name Amani.

Artemisia
Popularity: Rare rarely used
Style: Exotic Traditional, Lacy and Lissome
Nicknames: Artie, Mimi
Variants: Artemesia, Artemis
Sisters: Apollonia, Valentine, Luna, Arabella, Mahalia
Brothers: Thelonius, Montague, Barnabas, Peregrine, Matthias
✶ This ruffled wedding gown of a name hides a serious streak beneath its frills. It's associated with a warrior princess of ancient Greece, and with Italian baroque painter Artemisia Gentileschi. A nickname is a must.

Ashanti 2002: #117
Popularity: #322
Style: African, African-American
Sisters: Nevaeh, Aaliyah, Amari, Trinity, Zaria
Brothers: Malachi, Jaheim, Mekhi, Omarion, Jamari
✶ An overnight sensation, Ashanti follows Aaliyah straight from the the pop charts to the name charts. The name's a natural, with its jazzy sound and echoes of African history.

Ashley 1980s: #4
Popularity: #8
Style: '70s–'80s
Nicknames: Ash
Variants: Ashleigh, Ashlie, Ashlee, Ashly, Ashli
Sisters: Amber, Amanda, Brittany, Jessica, Megan
Brothers: Justin, Brandon, Dustin, Andrew, Ryan
✶ The sudden, immense popularity of Ashley in the '80s ushered in a whole generation of names. School rosters are now packed full of androgynous surnames with a dash of aristocratic hauteur. Yet the grandmomma of them all, Ashley, has been so widely used that it has shed its patrician edge to become the girl next door.

Ashlyn 2003: #141
Popularity: #141
Style: Bell Tones, The -ens
Nicknames: Ash
Variants: Ashlynn
Sisters: Kailyn, Jazmin, Alexa, Emmalee, Camryn
Brothers: Kaden, Kyler, Trenton, Brady, Corbin
✶ This little hit has been cooked up from the top ingredients of the past twenty years. Take a pinch of Ashley, a splash of Kaitlyn, and you've got a familiar-sounding concoction that's easy to digest.

Ashton 2001: #365
Popularity: #474
Style: Androgynous, Last Names First, The -ens
Nicknames: Ash
Variants: Ashtyn
Sisters: Tyler, Payton, Logan, Carson, Aubrey
Brothers: Weston, Keaton, Skyler, Jarret, Keegan
✶ Like a successful TV show, Ashley has generated spin-offs. Androgynous Ashton recaptures Ashley's surname roots in a trendy Madison-like style.

Asia

Popularity: #239
Style: African-American,
Nickname-Proof, Place Names
Sisters: Tyra, India, Aleah,
Tessa, Kiana
Brothers: Dante, Alec, Chance, Deon, Malik

1900　Today

★ Asia is the biggest of places, but a tidy little name. The aura of the continent helps it feel more ambitious than other similarly soft, petite choices.

Aspen

2002: #559

Popularity: #568
Style: Country & Western,
Place Names, The -ens
Sisters: Sierra, Regan, Savanna,
Haven, Sage
Brothers: Colton, Trace, Dayton, Walden, River

1900　Today

★ Aspen has a crisp boyish sound and the popular hook of a place name. Not just any place name, mind you, but a beautiful and glamorous mountain resort. It's certainly not a timeless name, but it's perfect for this moment.

Astrid

2002: #992

Popularity: Rare
Style: Antique Charm, Exotic
Traditional, German/Dutch,
Scandinavian
Sisters: Sigrid, Dagmar, Signe, Greta, Margit
Brothers: Gunnar, Magnus, Lars, Armin,
Torsten

1900　Today

★ A cool and funky classic, Astrid is playfully clunky, like thick-soled clogs.

Athena

2002: #504

Popularity: #520
Style: Exotic Traditional,
Greek, Mythological,
Nickname-Proof
Variants: Athina
Sisters: Isis, Anastasia, Thalia, Justice, Artemis
Brothers: Maximilian, Fabian, Ulysses, Antony,
Orion

★ This is a real power name, as in lightning-bolts-from-the-sky powerful. The Greek goddess of wisdom and victory, Athena is finally getting her overdue consideration as an English given name. You can also try the more reserved Roman equivalent, Minerva.

Atlanta

Popularity: Rare
Style: Place Names, Why Not?
Nicknames: Lani
Sisters: Geneva, Marietta,
Aspen, Laramie, Augusta
Brothers: Richmond, Stratton, Campbell, Coty,
Dennison

rarely used
1900　Today

★ Atlanta may be the capital of Georgia, but when it comes to baby names, it's neighbor Savannah that rules the roost. Why not look a few miles inland and give this less common name a try?

Aubrey

Popularity: #186
Style: Androgynous, Last Names
First, Nickname-Proof
Variants: Aubrie, Aubree
Sisters: Mallory, Peyton, Avery, Autumn, Macy
Brothers: Parker, Brady, Skyler, Ashton,
Brennan

1900　Today

★ Aubrey is oh-so-close to Audrey, which almost persuades you it's a classic girl's name. In fact, it's one of the prissy boys' names that American parents used to associate with British prep school lads. Like many of those names, it's found new life on the girls' side. Next up, Chauncey?

Audra

1970s: #390

Popularity: Rare
Style: '70s–'80s, Ladies and
Gentlemen
Nicknames: Audie
Sisters: April, Carrie, Rosanna,
Tara, Felicia
Brothers: Kurtis, Garrick, Carlo, Brent, Clinton

1900　Today

★ This pretty, old-fashioned name had its revival twenty-five years ahead of the pack. Audra is the only name you'll find in both the Ladies and Gentlemen and '70s–'80s categories. The result is a name that can fit with many different styles, but truly stands alone.

Audrey

1920s: #72

Popularity: #78
Style: Nickname-Proof,
Timeless
Variants: Audry, Audra
Sisters: Claire, Avery, Kathryn,
Caroline, Ava
Brothers: Clayton, Davis, Raymond, Warren,
Jack

1900　Today

★ Back in the '30s, Audrey was a trendy choice alongside kindred spirits Shirley and Beverly. But Audrey had a cleaner, classic sound that never lost its luster. Today, it's a welcome alternative to fading favorites Ashley and Courtney.

Augusta
1900s: #214
Popularity: Rare
Style: Ladies and Gentlemen, Place Names, Saints
Nicknames: Gussie, Gus
1900　Today
Sisters: Louisa, Aurelia, Eugenia, Viola, Delphia
Brothers: Ambrose, Clement, Leopold, Edmund, Julius
✳ Augusta is one of the true grandes dames. You won't have to worry about being taken lightly with this name. In fact, you might worry about scaring people away. Yet Augusta's really not such a big leap from hit names like Amelia and Madeline, and it's awfully handsome. The nickname Gussie was once a big hit in its own right.

Aurea
1930s: #569
Popularity: Rare
Style: Lacy and Lissome, Saints, Why Not?
Sisters: Twila, Elida, Margot, Adela, Lilia
1900　Today
Brothers: Royce, Glynn, Stanton, Glendon, Rex
✳ Seldom used since the '40s, Aurea has the supple flow of a modern hit. It also has a deep history dating back to medieval saints.

Aurelia
1900s: #411
Popularity: Rare
Style: Ladies and Gentlemen, Saints, Why Not?
Nicknames: Lia, Ria
1900　Today
Sisters: Amalia, Eloise, Theodora, Lavinia, Althea
Brothers: Clement, Edison, Rudolph, Edmond, Cornelius
✳ Aurelia is a romantic relic of ancient Rome. The name's ladylike comportment led it to a Victorian-era revival, but it's seldom thought of today. Consider it as an exotic twist on Amelia—proper yet seductive.

Aurora
2003: #372
Popularity: #372
Style: Exotic Traditional, Mythological, Timeless
Nicknames: Rory
1900　Today
Sisters: Catalina, Annabelle, Esperanza, Lydia, Maia
Brothers: Roman, Alfonso, Ivan, Ulysses, Emanuel
✳ Aurora was the Roman goddess of the dawn, and the name sounds the part. Ethereal yet strong, you can picture it equally on a theater marquee and an executive office. Wherever you see it, you're sure to remember it.

Autumn
2001: #73
Popularity: #76
Style: Charms and Graces, Modern Meanings, Nickname-Proof
1900　Today
Sisters: Summer, Sierra, Jade, Meadow, Sage
Brothers: Trevor, Chase, Colin, Brady, Kaleb
✳ The name May was the peak of fashion in 1900, June in 1930, April in 1970. Now those dewy Spring months have given way to Summer and Autumn. With an image of cozy sweaters and falling leaves, Autumn is the warm and wistful season choice.

Ava
2003: #41
Popularity: #41
Style: Antique Charm, Little Darlings, Nickname-Proof
Variants: Eva
1900　Today
Sisters: Lily, Ivy, Mia, Grace, Sofia
Brothers: Owen, Eli, Julian, Miles, Ronan
✳ Most little old names like this sound dowdy, but Ava is voluptuous. Bombshell actress Ava Gardner is the main reason, along with the va-va-voom V sound. The name is suddenly soaring.

Avery
2003: #90
Popularity: #90
Style: Androgynous, Last Names First, Nickname-Proof
Sisters: Aubrey, Peyton, Ava, Mallory, Emory
1900　Today
Brothers: Carson, Riley, Parker, Carter, Landon
✳ Light and nimble as a bird, Avery is a lyrical successor to Ashley and Courtney. Like those names, it took the historical path of surname, to male name, to female name. Unlike them, it remains a popular choice for boys as well.

Avis
1910s: #299
Popularity: Rare
Style: Ladies and Gentlemen, Little Darlings, Nickname-Proof
Sisters: Cleo, Ione, Willa, Iris, Esme
1900　Today
Brothers: Milo, Axel, Felix, Reuben, Wolf
✳ Simple yet surprising, Avis is a contender for the "quirky classic" mantle now that Zoe and Iris have gone mainstream. The Avis car rental company's "We're number two" campaign is one major obstacle.

Aviva

Popularity: Rare
Style: Jewish, Lacy and Lissome, Why Not?
Nicknames: Viv, Avi

rarely used

| 1900 | Today |

Sisters: Adira, Melia, Ilana, Allegra, Tova
Brothers: Lazar, Elkan, Avi, Elan, Raz
★ Aviva is a modern Hebrew favorite that means springtime, and the name fairly bursts with life—forward and backward. It has the grace and vitality to win many new admirers.

Avril

Popularity: Rare
Style: Charms and Graces, French
Variants: April, Averil, Averill

rarely used

| 1900 | Today |

Sisters: Fleur, Amity, Azure, Honoré, Esme
Brothers: Mathias, Bond, Regis, Magnus, Luc
★ This name is now known as the French form of April, associated with Canadian rock star Avril Lavigne. It does, though, have a separate history as an English name. That parallel track gives us Avril as a relative of Averill, a Scottish first and last name.

Ayanna

Popularity: #364
Style: African, African-American, Lacy and Lissome
Nicknames: Yanni
Variants: Ayana, Aiyana

2003: #364

| 1900 | Today |

Sisters: Tamia, Kianna, Amani, Viviana, Aleah
Brothers: Javon, Ahmad, Tariq, Darian, Dante
★ A fluid creation that echoes the sound of classic American names in a modern form. While Ayanna's feminine style sounds universal, the name has African roots and has been used almost exclusively by African Americans.

Bailey

Popularity: #99
Style: Androgynous, Bell Tones, Last Names First
Nicknames: Bay
Variants: Bailee, Baylee

2001: #69

| 1900 | Today |

Sisters: Jordan, Sydney, Shelby, Mikayla, Logan
Brothers: Tanner, Dalton, Parker, Bryce, Brennan
★ In the standard spelling Bailey, this name is boyish in a clear, sunny way. Creative reworkings like Baylee emphasize the prettiness of the sound.

Barbara

Popularity: #628
Style: Solid Citizens
Nicknames: Barb, Barbie, Babs, Bobbie
Variants: Barbra

1940s: #3

| 1900 | Today |

Sisters: Marilyn, Patricia, Joyce, Beverly, Shirley
Brothers: Donald, Richard, Gerald, Larry, Franklin
★ Barbara is a completely familiar name. There's hardly a person in America who has grown up without Barbaras around—relatives, teachers, neighbors. But today, this handsome name is going to be a tough sell. Barbara was so vastly popular for such a short time that it's stubbornly glued to its era.

Beatrice

Popularity: Rare
Style: English, French, Ladies and Gentlemen, Shakespearean
Nicknames: Bea, Tricia
Variants: Beatrix, Beatriz

1900s: #44

| 1900 | Today |

Sisters: Cordelia, Adelaide, Clarice, Dorothea, Marian
Brothers: Jules, Theodore, Alden, Casper, Benedict
★ Beatrice is the properest of proper ladies, the kind of formidable figure who would never show a bare ankle in public. Is it impudent to suggest she could be a real crowd-pleaser? The name is light and pretty, and on a little girl turns positively cute. It's also the name of one of Shakespeare's most modern and appealing heroines.

Beatrix

Popularity: Rare
Style: English, Exotic Traditional, Saints, Why Not?
Nicknames: Trixie, Bea
Variants: Beatrice, Beatriz

rarely used

| 1900 | Today |

Sisters: Elodie, Anthea, Christabel, Portia, Sidony
Brothers: Tarquin, Alistair, Barnaby, Crispin, Phineas
★ Beatrice's exotic sister is just as genteel on the surface but hints at surprises beneath. The nickname Trixie may be an added temptation toward the saucy side.

Belinda

1960s: #165

Popularity: Rare
Style: Lacy and Lissome, Surfer Sixties
Nicknames: Lin, Lindy
Sisters: Angelia, Deirdre, Tabitha, Melody, Roxanna
Brothers: Terence, Roderick, Geoffrey, Brendan, Travis

✱ Belinda hit it big in the '60s at the same time as the rhyming name Melinda. Its roots, though, run deeper. The name has been in steady use since the Renaissance. If you like Belinda's essence but not its '60s overtones, Elodia and Rosalinda are antique alternatives.

Bella

2003: #327

Popularity: #327
Style: Antique Charm
Variants: Belle
Sisters: Golda, Leora, Lilla, Hallie, Eliza
Brothers: Ezra, Eli, Walker, Zack, Jonas

✱ Isabella is a smash, Anabella's on the way up, so why not zippy little Bella? It's making a comeback as parents decide that this old-fashioned sweetie stands nicely on its own.

Belle

1900s: #219

Popularity: Rare
Style: Antique Charm, Why Not?
Variants: Bella
Sisters: Cleo, May, Bess, Maeve, Phoebe
Brothers: Everett, Anton, Ellis, Julius, Reuben

✱ This sweetheart of a name means beautiful and walks with a spring in its step. Despite all its merits, it's still extremely uncommon. Not even the heroine of Disney's *Beauty and the Beast* gave it a boost. You will, though, meet Isabelles and Annabelles with this nickname.

Bertha

1900s: #26

Popularity: Rare
Style: German/Dutch, Porch Sitters
Nicknames: Bertie
Variants: Berta
Sisters: Gladys, Myrtle, Beulah, Agnes, Hilda
Brothers: Waldo, Norval, Lester, Morris, Roscoe

✱ The Germanic classic Bertha was once one of the hottest names in America, but when the phrase "Big Bertha" entered the language in World War I, this poor name was doomed. (The phrase originally referred to the largest German artillery.) If you're looking for a namesake for your beloved Granny Bertha, try Bella or Bethany.

Bess

1900s: #308

Popularity: Rare
Style: Guys and Dolls, Nicknames
Nicknames: Bessie
Sisters: Nell, Evie, Molly, Mabel, Fae
Brothers: Nat, Ike, Archie, Ned, Charley

✱ Yes, it's yet another nickname for Elizabeth, but don't tune out yet. Bess sounds soft and cute, but adult. That puts it in select company, and makes it a great choice to revive as either a full or pet name. The diminutive Bessie was far more common in the past and is associated with blues great Bessie Smith.

Beth

1960s: #69

Popularity: Rare
Style: Jewish, Nicknames, Surfer Sixties
Sisters: Jill, Laurie, Carla, Shari, Michele
Brothers: Jon, Jeffery, Greg, Brad, Todd

✱ Beth is one of the many nicknames of Elizabeth that have broken free to take on lives of their own. It was particularly common during the '60s but holds up much better than other nicknames of that time. Beth has been especially popular with Jewish families, who take it from the Hebrew word for house (as in Bethel, "house of God").

Bethany

1980s: #98

Popularity: #206
Style: Biblical, New Classics
Nicknames: Beth
Sisters: Tabitha, Vanessa, Meredith, Jocelyn, Miranda
Brothers: Derek, Brandon, Zachary, Timothy, Jared

✱ This New Testament place name has the sound and rhythm of a classic girl's name, but remains pleasantly individual.

Betsy

1950s: #270

Popularity: Rare
Style: Mid-Century, Nicknames
Sisters: Kathy, Connie, Pam, Becky, Judy
Brothers: Mickey, Garry, Cliff, Ken, Roger

✱ Betsy is perennially girlish. If you meet a real Betsy, though, chances are she's not a young girl but a mom or a grandma. That disconnect has the name in fashion limbo for now, but its fundamental charm will eventually bring it back.

Betty

Popularity: Rare
Style: Nicknames, Solid Citizens
Nicknames: Bette, Betts
Variants: Bettie, Bettye
Sisters: June, Billie, Rosalie, Jean, Shirley
Brothers: Gene, Donald, Jimmy, Ted, Joe

1930s: #2

✹ From Betty Grable to Betty Crocker, this name is a symbol of wholesome, all-American womanhood. Yet that very symbolism seems to be scaring off today's parents. Even the traditionalists who've dusted off chestnuts like Lucy and Maggie have left this classic by the wayside. Maybe it's a tad too domestic, suggesting a lifetime spent in an apron. Or maybe we're just not quite ready. Look for a new batch of Bettys in fifteen years.

Beverly

Popularity: Rare
Style: Solid Citizens
Nicknames: Bev
Variants: Beverley
Sisters: Marilyn, Phyllis, Constance, Aurea, Rosemary
Brothers: Stanton, Gerald, Richard, Donald, Jerome

1930s: #21

✹ Beverly's a little bit matronly, but it has attractions that make it a contender. With its ladylike sound nestled around that strong "v," it's a worthwhile alternative to powerhouses Evelyn and Olivia.

Bianca

Popularity: #161
Style: Italian, Latino/Latina, Shakespearean
Nicknames: Bibi
Variants: Blanca
Sisters: Angelica, Ariel, Jasmin, Alejandra, Paola
Brothers: Marco, Lorenzo, Rodrigo, Dante, Giovanni

1990s: #112

✹ Bianca is Italian for white, a counterpart to the French Blanche and the Spanish Blanca. It's one of the handsome exotics Shakespeare favored for his plays in Italian settings. In recent years, the name's image has shifted to Latina and glamorous, influenced by Nicaraguan jet-setter Bianca Jagger.

Billie

Popularity: Rare
Style: Androgynous, Guys and Dolls, Nicknames
Sisters: Bobbie, Ruthie, Melba, Patsy, Bettie
Brothers: Benny, Jackie, Joe, Buddy, Doyle

1930s: #117

✹ There were tons of these boyish names in the '20s and '30s—little girl Freddies, Johnnies, Sammies, and Bobbies. The great Billie Holliday helps make this one special. It's not exactly fashionable, but charming nonetheless.

Blair

Popularity: Rare
Style: Androgynous, Brisk and Breezy
Sisters: Brooke, Lacy, Britt, Leigh, Sloane
Brothers: Brant, Drake, Greyson, Lance, Bradley

1980s: #451

✹ Do you consider this the preppiest girl's name around? Perhaps you, too, frittered away hours of your youth watching reruns of *The Facts of Life*. The rich prep school queen on that sitcom is the modern prototype for this familiar but uncommon name.

Blanche

Popularity: Rare
Style: French, Ladies and Gentlemen
Variants: Blanca
Sisters: Estelle, Mae, Beatrice, Viola, Pearl
Brothers: Claude, Emil, Virgil, Luther, Clement

1900s: #58

✹ Blanche could be one of the most formal of names, French and fusty. But the immortal character Blanche DuBois of *A Streetcar Named Desire* turned that image inside out and gave the name a wild Southern spin. The sitcom *The Golden Girls* played off that in naming their saucy belle Blanche Devereaux. Today the name is half wallflower, half diva.

Bonita

Popularity: Rare
Style: Mid-Century
Nicknames: Bonnie, Nita
Variants: Benita
Sisters: Sandra, Merry, Cherie, Bernadette, Danita
Brothers: Roger, Lanny, Butch, Johnny, Jerrold

1940s: #218

✹ Bonita is Spanish for pretty. It became a common given name in the '40s and '50s, thanks to the huge popularity of the name Bonnie. Bonnie is not really a nickname but it sounds like one, so parents seized on Bonita as a more formal given name.

Bonnie

1940s: #34

Popularity: 974
Style: Charms and Graces, Mid-Century
Variants: Bonny
Sisters: Judy, Connie, Gayle, Joy, Vicki
Brothers: Wayne, Allen, Jerry, Jim, Dennis

✱ Bonnie is taken from the Scottish word meaning "pretty." The name's good feelings and cutie-pie style made it a longtime favorite. That kind of genial style is out right now, and the name has quietly drifted off the radar. It's not trendy, but likable.

Brandy

1970s: #79

Popularity: #602
Style: '70s–'80s
Variants: Brandi, Brandie
Sisters: Krista, Aimee, Nikki, Misty, Tasha
Brothers: Dusty, Brent, Chad, Cory, Jerrod

✱ Perhaps the only common English name that comes from an alcoholic beverage. (Sherry is borderline.) The name took off in the '70s on the heels of a popular song ("Brandy, you're a fine girl, what a good wife you would be . . ."). It's now more likely to remind people of the TV and singing star Brandy, but it's still plummeting out of fashion.

Brenda

1950s: #18

Popularity: #228
Style: Celtic, Mid-Century, Nickname-Proof
Sisters: Sheila, Pamela, Cheryl, Kathleen, Paula
Brothers: Barry, Douglas, Ronald, Duane, Darrell

✱ Brenda Starr, Girl Reporter, made her debut in the Sunday funnies in 1940. She was the perfect modern girl, looking like Rita Hayworth and living like Lois Lane. Her fresh Scottish first name fairly bounded from the page. For thirty years, that image of Brenda held, but a name can only stay modern for so long.

Brenna

2003: #301

Popularity: #301
Style: Celtic, Nickname-Proof
Variants: Brynna
Sisters: Emilee, Logan, Tessa, Baylee, Kira
Brothers: Tucker, Quinn, Brody, Lane, Chandler

✱ Brenna is a slimmed-down version of Brenda. Thin is in, and this name's smooth silhouette is likely to keep it rising.

Brianna

2001: #18

Popularity: #17
Style: African-American, Lacy and Lissome
Nicknames: Bree
Variants: Briana, Breanna, Brianne, Breanne, Bryanna
Sisters: Alyssa, Kaitlyn, Savanna, Bailey, Morgan
Brothers: Brennan, Kyler, Trenton, Bryce, Devin

✱ This feminine take on Brian is a smash with several popular spellings. It followed on the heels of Brittany and seems to appeal to the same group of parents—Brittany and Brianna are a popular pairing for sister names. It's worth noting that Brittany is now falling out of favor, so Brianna might not be high-flying much longer.

Bridget

1970s: #151

Popularity: #305
Style: Celtic, New Classics
Nicknames: Bree, Bridie
Variants: Brigid, Brighid, Brigit, Brigitte
Sisters: Shannon, Kelly, Alison, Leslie, Holly
Brothers: Kevin, Bradley, Brian, Casey, Sean

✱ Bridget is a great American success story. In the nineteenth century, a wave of poor Irish immigrants was struggling to gain a foothold in the U.S. Bridget, the classic Irish name, was shunned as a name of the servant class. Generations later, Bridget is still as Irish as you can get, and today parents eagerly seek out that touch of the Emerald Isle. The name has become a beloved modern classic.

Britt

Popularity: Rare — rarely used
Style: Brisk and Breezy, Scandinavian
Variants: Britta
Sisters: Greer, Bryn, Lotte, Sloane, Tova
Brothers: Rune, Piers, Hayes, Leif, Gunnar

✱ This Scandinavian name (a nickname for Birgit) has a brittle style that's icy but enticing. Keep in mind that many people will assume it's short for Brittany. The form Britta might help avoid that confusion.

Brittany

1990s: #6

Popularity: #211
Style: '70s–'80s, Place Names
Nicknames: Britt
Variants: Britany, Brittanie, Brittni, Britny, Britney
Sisters: Chelsea, Whitney, Courtney, Amber, Brianna
Brothers: Brandon, Corey, Taylor, Dustin, Brenton

★ This glittering place name became part of the rhythm of the '80s and '90s. It wasn't just Brittany, but Britney, Brittni, and countless variations. The result was a name that went from fresh invention to overexposure in record time (with a big assist from singer Britney Spears).

Brooke

2003: #43

Popularity: #43
Style: Brisk and Breezy, New Classics
Sisters: Jenna, Paige, Allison, Blake, Sloane
Brothers: Grant, Drew, Trey, Ian, Brandon

★ Brooke started out in high style, thanks to grande dame Brooke Astor. It then hit the mainstream in the late '70s with the double whammy of actress Brooke Shields and a character on *All My Children*. It doesn't have a long history as a name, but it feels like a classic.

Brooklyn

2003: #119

Popularity: #119
Style: Place Names, The -ens
Nicknames: Brook, Lyn
Variants: Brooklynn
Sisters: Jordyn, Payton, Aspen, Skylar, Savanna
Brothers: Trenton, Camden, Gage, Kaden, Dawson

★ Link the familiar names Brooke and Lynn in a trendy Kaitlyn-like rhythm to yield a place name. This one is catching on like crazy, but the one place you won't find lots of little Brooklyns is in New York. Maybe the Brooklyn natives can start naming their daughters Peoria?

Brynn

2003: #294

Popularity: #294
Style: Brisk and Breezy, Celtic
Variants: Bryn, Brynne
Sisters: Maeve, Emlyn, Tyne, Carys, Laney
Brothers: Finn, Griffith, Rohan, Rhys, Baird

★ This Welsh name is poised for a breakthrough in the U.S. Its strength is its swiftness, which leaves competitors like Brianna and Brooklynn looking fussy by comparison. In the U.K., it is primarily a male name.

Cadence

2003: #478

Popularity: #478
Style: Modern Meanings
Nicknames: Cady, Kay
Variants: Kadence, Kaydence
Sisters: Lyric, Harmony, Kaya, Meadow, Kenzie
Brothers: Camron, Jett, Kolby, Phoenix, Konnor

★ A cadence is a rhythmic flow of sounds, as in a poem or a song. Its recent leap from word to name owes much to its fashionable nicknames. K- spellings are equally common and take the name farther from its musical roots.

Caitlin

1990s: #69

Popularity: #145
Style: Bell Tones, Celtic, The -ens
Nicknames: Cait
Variants: Kaitlyn, Katelyn, Kaitlynn, Caitlyn, etc.
Sisters: Megan, Jillian, Courtney, Morgan, Casey
Brothers: Brendan, Colin, Keenan, Garrett, Devin

★ This Irish Gaelic form of Catherine has a chiming-bell quality that parents love. If you want a truly Gaelic aura, though, look elsewhere. If you tally up its many spellings, Caitlin has been one of America's most common baby names for years. Catriona (pronounced Katrina) is a less familiar Irish spin on Catherine. See also: Kaitlyn.

Calista

2001: #702

Popularity: #870
Style: Lacy and Lissome
Nicknames: Callie, Cali
Sisters: Felicity, Sienna, Camilla, Dimitra, Allegra
Brothers: Blaise, Garrison, Magnus, Dominic, Elias

★ This graceful name is from the Greek for "most beautiful" and is worthy of that mantle. Actress Calista Flockhart of *Ally McBeal* fame raised awareness of the name, but it has the goods to fly on its own.

Calla

rarely used

Popularity: Rare
Style: Charms and Graces, Little Darlings, Why Not?
Nicknames: Callie
Sisters: Willa, Mercy, Cassia, Luna, Bay
Brothers: Joah, Carsten, Bram, Forest, Jasper

★ Calla has seldom been used as a name, but oh, is it ever ready. The dewdrop elegance of calla lilies gives the name instant luster. Calla has a chance to modernize the old favorite Callie, much as Jenna did for Jennie and Tessa for Tessie.

Callie

Popularity: #341
Style: Guys and Dolls, Nicknames
Variants: Cali, Caleigh, Kallie, Kali
Sisters: Allie, Josie, Maggie, Bess, Abbie
Brothers: Jake, Simon, Will, Clay, Alex

1900s: #219

★ Callie is a malleable little name that parents arrive at from different angles. Some like it as a cozy traditional nickname, like Josie or Maggie. Others make it a modern full name, with spellings like Kali.

Cameron

Popularity: #306
Style: Androgynous, Celtic
Nicknames: Cammie, Cami
Variants: Camryn, Kameron
Sisters: Kennedy, Logan, Addison, Mckenna, Avery
Brothers: Griffin, Keegan, Donovan, Connor, Quinn

2001: #244

★ Actress Cameron Diaz has single-handedly opened this name to girls, much to the chagrin of thousands of male Camerons. It works nicely as a girl's name but loses the Scottish swagger that makes it such a smash for boys. If you love the nickname Cami, Camilla is another stylish option.

Camilla

Popularity: 883
Style: English, Saints, Timeless, Why Not?
Nicknames: Cami, Millie, Milla
Variants: Camille
Sisters: Adela, Kathryn, Louisa, Rafaela, Charlotte
Brothers: Benedict, Hugh, Laurence, Carleton, Edmund

2003: #883

★ A trendy sound, but a timeless and graceful name. In England, the association with Prince Charles's companion Camilla Parker-Bowles runs strong, but in the U.S., it's the name's own ladylike poise that shines through.

Camille

Popularity: #256
Style: French, Timeless
Nicknames: Cami
Variants: Camilla
Sisters: Noelle, Hope, Tatiana, Elise, Celine
Brothers: Tristan, Marco, Quentin, Miles, Brice

2003: #256

★ Ah, how romantic! The French classic Camille has a creative, artistic image, equal parts flower petals thrown in a stream and cigarettes smoked at a sidewalk café. The name is very popular in contemporary France.

Camryn

Popularity: #311
Style: Bell Tones, The -ens
Nicknames: Cami, Cam
Variants: Kamryn
Sisters: Lauryn, Ashlyn, Keeley, Payton, Madilyn
Brothers: Dawson, Braden, Cade, Corbin, Landon

2001: #207

★ In 1998, actress Camryn Manheim won an Emmy and gave a memorable, much-publicized acceptance speech. Her first name, previously unusual, instantly shot up the charts. Parents sensed the name's potential as a solution to the gender confusion of Cameron and as a match for the style of mega-hit Kaitlyn.

Candace

Popularity: #747
Style: New Classics
Nicknames: Candy
Variants: Candice, Candis
Sisters: Meredith, Holly, Katrina, Adrienne, Cara
Brothers: Geoffrey, Lance, Derek, Terrance, Clint

1980s: #115

★ Candace sounds comfortably modern and American, like Janice, but it has something extra. The name is a little stronger, even regal. Perhaps it's just the classy image of Candice Bergen, but the name also has a long and grand history. Candace was a traditional name for ancient queens of Ethiopia, and mentioned as such in the Bible.

Caprice

Popularity: Rare
Style: Modern Meanings
Sisters: Calla, Amity, Echo, Evening, Lark
Brothers: Finn, Ranger, Eamon, Fox, Saber

rarely used

★ A caprice is a whim, an impulse, a lark. It's shaped conveniently like a classic French name and could be a picturesque choice for a girl. The British model and actress Caprice Bourret may raise the name's profile.

Carissa

Popularity: #459
Style: Lacy and Lissome
Variants: Charissa, Karissa, Charis, Karis
Sisters: Angelica, Arielle, Carina, Larissa, Kassandra
Brothers: Quinton, Jarett, Tristan, Beau, Devin

1990s: #302

★ Carissa is constructed from the Greek root charis ("grace"), on the lacy model of Clarissa. Reflections of the word "caress" give the name a rosewater sweetness. Also consider Charis itself, which, in fact, has a longer history as an English given name.

Carla

Popularity: #424
Style: Italian, Surfer Sixties
Nicknames: Carly
Variants: Karla

1960s: #82
1900 — Today

Sisters: Lisa, Jill, Paula, Gina, Denise
Brothers: Craig, Jon, Randy, Kent, Douglas
★ Carla was a big hit of the '60s, but it doesn't sound like the other breezy names of that time. Its style and strength are more like the classics of earlier generations. That has helped Carla stick around while other, trendier '60s names are vanishing.

Carly

Popularity: #187
Style: Nicknames
Variants: Karli, Carlie
Sisters: Stevie, Justine, Abby, Tessa, Casey

1990s: #139
1900 — Today

Brothers: Drew, Dillon, Alex, Brett, Connor
★ The name Carly started to be heard when Carly Simon topped the pop charts in the '70s. It has held on strong and is now more common than the formal Carla. On the model of Ms. Simon, it's sweet and pretty with a strong independent streak.

Carmen

Popularity: #251
Style: Latino/Latina, Timeless
Variants: Carmel
Sisters: Iris, Luz, Anita, Carolyn, Claudia

1940s: #50
1900 — Today

Brothers: Ramon, Lionel, Jerome, Mario, Ruben
★ This classic has a passionate soul, thanks to Bizet's operatic heroine. Yet the name is too slim and chic to wallow in melodrama. Computer game superstar Carmen Sandiego is a better model for Carmen's modern cross-cultural potential.

Carol

Popularity: #871
Style: Androgynous, Mid-Century, Solid Citizens
Nicknames: Carrie
Variants: Carole, Carroll, Karol

1940s: #5
1900 — Today

Sisters: Janet, Marcia, Barbara, Donna, Joyce
Brothers: Ronald, Larry, Bruce, Roger, Gerald
★ To understand the name Carol, think of it as being to the 1940s what Courtney is to us today. An uncommon male name is embraced as a modern, androgynous choice for women and becomes a runaway hit. By now Carol sounds neither modern nor androgynous and is fading away. More traditional feminine forms of the name, like Caroline and Carolina, have risen to take its place.

Carolina

Popularity: #257
Style: Antique Charm, Country & Western, Latino/Latina, Place Names
Nicknames: Carrie
Variants: Caroline

2003: #257
1900 — Today

Sisters: Michaela, Savannah, Catalina, Liliana, Marietta
Brothers: Colton, Walker, Dallas, Marcos, Porter
★ Usually, adding an "a" to the end of a girl's name makes it frillier. In this case, it makes it sassier. Carolina's a lady, make no mistake, but she's not shy and nobody's fool.

Caroline

Popularity: #67
Style: Antique Charm, Timeless
Nicknames: Carrie, Carol, Callie
Variants: Carolina

2001: #62
1900 — Today

Sisters: Madeline, Claire, Daniela, Victoria, Isabel
Brothers: Nathaniel, Alex, Julian, Clayton, Isaac
★ Elegant Caroline is soaring today. The name is regal, strong, and serene, and appeals to a wide cross section of parents. Compare that with seemingly similar names like Pauline and Francine, which have sunk like stones. The "een" sound, dominant for much of the century, is on its way out and "eye-n" is coming in. Don't be surprised to see Clementines and Emmalines soon.

Carolyn

Popularity: #431
Style: Mid-Century
Nicknames: Carrie, Lyn, Callie
Variants: Caroline, Carolynn

1940s: #12
1900 — Today

Sisters: Judith, Sharon, Patricia, Janet, Kathleen
Brothers: Dennis, Kenneth, Alan, Douglas, Richard
★ Carolyn is an appealingly grown-up name. Neither frilly nor boyish, it sounds like an attractive, responsible woman with a good head on her shoulders. Over the past decade, Carolyn has given way to the older French form Caroline.

Carrie

1970s: #42

Popularity: #749
Style: '70s–'80s, Nicknames
Variants: Karrie, Cari, Kari
Sisters: Christy, Audra, Jessie, Amy, Stacy
Brothers: Jamie, Byron, Ben, Chris, Ross

★ Perhaps you love Carrie because it's a perky turn-of-the-century nickname. Or perhaps you're a little tired of it because of the Carries, Karis, and Kerries who swarmed through the '70s. The latter view seems to be winning out right now. The name is falling out of fashion, despite the influence of style queen Carrie Bradshaw on *Sex and the City*.

Carson

2001: #709

Popularity: #876
Style: Androgynous, Last Names First, The -ens
Nicknames: Cari
Sisters: Hunter, Darby, Logan, Bailey, Cassidy
Brothers: Cullen, Kane, Garrison, Tucker, Sawyer

★ As a boy's name, Carson is rollickingly masculine. It wouldn't be a likely girl's choice save for the model of novelist Carson McCullers (born Lula Carson Smith). That literary model helps make this a chic choice, and gives you a good answer for relatives who moan, "That's a *boy's* name!"

Casey

1980s: #99

Popularity: #318
Style: '70s–'80s, Androgynous, Celtic, Country & Western
Nicknames: Case
Variants: Kacey, Kasey, Kaycee, Kacie
Sisters: Mallory, Ryan, Shea, Carly, Tyler
Brothers: Drew, Brett, Corey, Travis, Dustin

★ Back in the days of train engineer Casey Jones, Casey was pure Irish manliness. But names with a -y ending are all targets for gender crossover, and today a new Casey is as likely to be a girl as a boy. The original spelling is particularly energetic and self-confident.

Cassandra

1990s: #66

Popularity: #144
Style: Lacy and Lissome, Mythological, New Classics
Nicknames: Cass, Cassie, Sandra
Variants: Casandra, Kassandra
Sisters: Vanessa, Miranda, Angelica, Bethany, Sabrina
Brothers: Derek, Jonathan, Andre, Brett, Jason

★ Isn't it amazing what a classical pedigree can do? Most names with this much flounce sound like pure frill. But thanks to its tragic mythological weight, Cassandra is sumptuous and serious. It's one name that your practical mother-in-law and princess-obsessed niece might agree on.

Cassia

Popularity: Rare

rarely used

Style: Charms and Graces, Lacy and Lissome
Nicknames: Cass, Cassie
Variants: Keziah
Sisters: Acacia, Sienna, Chiara, Verity, Arielle
Brothers: Cullen, Stone, Japheth, Antony, Frost

★ Cassia is a spice, a form of cinnamon. Its pretty sound begs for adoption as a girl's name. The original Hebrew version Keziah (keh-ZAI-uh) was the name of one of Job's daughters in the Bible.

Cassidy

2001: #110

Popularity: #153
Style: Country & Western, Last Names First
Nicknames: Cass, Cassie
Sisters: Savanna, Kennedy, Carson, Skyler, Delaney
Brothers: Colton, Tanner, Austin, Donovan, Dillon

★ The cowboy Cassidys (Butch and Hopalong) still enliven this name. A young Cassidy is more likely to be a city gal than a ranch hand, but the energetic, self-assured spirit of the name owes plenty to its cowboy days.

Cassie

1980s: #176

Popularity: #552
Style: Nicknames
Nicknames: Cass
Variants: Cassey

Sisters: Carly, Tia, Jessie, Katie, Candice
Brothers: Drew, Jarrod, Brett, Derek, Travis

★ This extremely popular nickname is cute, but not too cutesy. Clip it even shorter and you have the supremely confident Cass. See also: Cassandra and Cassidy.

Catalina

Popularity: #751
Style: Antique Charm, Exotic
Traditional, Latino/Latina,
Place Names
Nicknames: Cat, Catie
Sisters: Aurora, Annabelle, Marietta, Juliette,
Esperanza
Brothers: Domenic, Romeo, Alfonso, Solomon,
Cruz

2003: #751
1900　Today

✱ This lovely Spanish form of Catherine makes a distinctive and elegant alternative to Caitlin or Katrina. It also meshes nicely with turn-of-the-century favorites like Isabelle.

Catherine

Popularity: #106
Style: Timeless
Nicknames: Cat, Cathy, Cate
Variants: Katherine, Catharine,
Kathryn, Katerina
Sisters: Margaret, Cecilia, Anna, Josephine, Mary
Brothers: Edward, George, Frederick, Charles,
James

1900s: #19
1900　Today

✱ Catherine is the French form of the classic regal name, and the form most used in Britain. This spelling was also the U.S. favorite in the nineteenth century, so it now carries a gently old-fashioned appeal. See also: Katherine.

Cecile

Popularity: Rare
Style: French, Ladies and
Gentlemen, Why Not?
Nicknames: Ceil, Sissy
Variants: Cecilia
Sisters: Eloise, Corine, Josefa, Blanche, Clarice
Brothers: Clement, Jules, Edmond, Frederic,
Luther

1900s: #236
1900　Today

✱ Cecile has the soft grace of comeback queens Lillian and Eleanor, heard through a French translator.

Cecilia

Popularity: #271
Style: Saints, Timeless
Nicknames: Sissy, Ceil, Celia,
Ceci
Variants: Cecily, Cicely
Sisters: Helena, Lydia, Miriam, Amelia, Lillian
Brothers: Oliver, Max, Edgar, Anderson,
George

1900s: #184
1900　Today

✱ Shh . . . this soft, sibilant selection is sentimental yet serious. Some suggest it suffers from a surplus of S sounds, but it's oh so sweet and satisfying.

Cecily

Popularity: Rare
Style: Antique Charm, English,
Saints, Why Not?
Nicknames: Ceil
Variants: Cicely
Sisters: Amalia, Beatrice, Violet, Anthea, Elodie
Brothers: Pierce, Colman, Benedict, Albin,
Alistair

rarely used
1900　Today

✱ This pretty form of Cecilia is especially quaint and delicate, but you wouldn't want to cross a Cecily. That lady's tougher than she looks. The name's rhythm and style make it a great sister for Olivia or Isabella.

Celeste

Popularity: #298
Style: French, Timeless
Nicknames: Lessie
Variants: Celestine
Sisters: Camille, Simone, Noelle, Hope, Giselle
Brothers: Quentin, Spencer, Miles, Noel,
Graham

2001: #287
1900　Today

✱ Celeste is elegant, confident, and womanly. This French-American classic is a fabulous example of a name that sounds mature, but not a bit boring. A high-impact choice.

Celia

Popularity: #657
Style: Shakespearean, Timeless,
Why Not?
Nicknames: Ceil
Sisters: Lena, Helena, Estella, Belle, Nora
Brothers: Ellis, Anton, Sam, Carl, Henry

1900s: #166
1900　Today

✱ Sweet, serious Celia is an attractive name with surprisingly few takers. As a given name, it dates back to Shakespeare, but you can also use it as a nickname for Cecilia.

Celine

Popularity: #792
Style: French
Variants: Céline
Sisters: Giselle, Nathalie,
Camille, Anaïs, Simone
Brothers: Adrien, Brice, Noe, Quentin, Luc

2003: #792
1900　Today

✱ Singer Céline Dion has been both a blessing and a curse to this name. She introduced its silken charms to a whole new audience, but she's so strongly identified with the name that her image is hard to shake.

Chanel

1990s: #498

Popularity: Rare
Style: '70s–'80s, Fanciful
Variants: Chanelle
Sisters: Whitney, Tiffany, Nikita, Soleil, Cristal
Brothers: Marquis, Coty, Bronson, Westley, Paris
✱ A natural sister for Tiffany—your family will be a living stroll down Fifth Avenue. (Prada and Armani update the theme.) Chanel has a sleek French essence inherited from fashion icon Coco Chanel, but it is not used as a first name in France. For an authentic Gallic alternative, try Chantal.

Chantal

1990s: #799

Popularity: Rare
Style: African-American, French, Saints
Variants: Chantel, Chantelle, Shantel
Sisters: Dominique, Simone, Tiana, Nicolette, Camille
Brothers: Marcel, Fabrice, Quentin, Darius, Antoine
✱ This '50s French classic started to catch on in the U.S. in the '80s, but it's still uncommon and maintains a distinctly French character. Alternate spellings shift the style toward African-American.

Charity

1970s: #277

Popularity: #531
Style: Antique Charm, Charms and Graces, Nickname-Proof, Why Not?
Sisters: Harmony, Holly, Willow, Felicity, Mercy
Brothers: Elias, Gideon, Hart, Beau, Barrett
✱ With its generous spirit and girly style, Charity may be the cheeriest of the virtue names.

Charlene

1940s: #114

Popularity: Rare
Style: African-American, Mid-Century
Nicknames: Charlie
Variants: Charline, Charleen, Sharleen, Carlene
Sisters: Marcia, Francine, Jolene, Rosanne, Sherrill
Brothers: Jerald, Roger, Gary, Darrell, Ronald
✱ This feminine form of Charles was a standard through much of the twentieth century. It has now yielded the fashion high ground back to nineteenth-century favorite Charlotte.

Charlotte

1940s: #63

Popularity: #183
Style: Antique Charm, English
Nicknames: Lottie, Lotte, Charlie
Sisters: Georgia, Josephine, Camilla, Claire, Amelia
Brothers: Benjamin, Oliver, Edgar, Samuel, Julian
✱ Charlotte is a high-status name today. Not a showy name, not an aggressive name, but a top choice of the trendsetting elite. Three key traits: warmth, dignity, and the cute old-fashioned nickname Lottie.

Chastity

1970s: #471

Popularity: Rare
Style: Charms and Graces
Nicknames: Chas, Chassie
Variants: Chasity
Sisters: Patience, Serenity, Harmony, Mercy, Verity
Brothers: Honor, Tobias, Peregrine, River, Merit
✱ Of all the virtue names, Chastity may have the most contemporary sound. Parents shy away from it nonetheless, reluctant to include any direct reference to sex (or the lack thereof) in their daughter's name. Charity is an attractive alternative.

Chelsea

1990s: #30

Popularity: #180
Style: '70s–'80s, Nickname-Proof, Place Names
Variants: Chelsey, Chelsie
Sisters: Brittany, Justine, Kelsey, Whitney, Courtney
Brothers: Taylor, Cody, Zachery, Dustin, Drew
✱ Chelsea's an English place name that American and Australian parents flocked to as a kicky, modish creation. As it became popular, though, it lost some of its kick. Chelsea Clinton's high profile helped transform the name into a familiar, respectable standard.

Cherie

1960s: #316

Popularity: Rare
Style: Surfer Sixties
Nicknames: Cher
Variants: Cheri, Sherry, Sherie, Sheree
Sisters: Jeanine, Candy, Suzette, Angelia, Marcie
Brothers: Curt, Robbie, Bart, Dirk, Baron
✱ In the '30s, Cherie was a perfectly ingenious invention. It took the essence of trendy hits like Shirley and gave it a stylish French twist. (Chérie is French for "darling.") The name was perhaps too perfectly a creation of its time. It has yet to make the leap to the twenty-first century.

Cheryl

1950s: #19

Popularity: Rare
Style: Mid-Century
Nicknames: Cher
Variants: Cherryl, Sheryl,
Cheryle, Sherrill, Sherrell
Sisters: Lynn, Brenda, Cathy, Sheila, Vicki
Brothers: Terry, Douglas, Barry, Bruce, Randall
✶ Cheryl was the Kaitlyn of the '50s: a popular sensation that inspired a frenzy of creative spelling. It first appeared in the '20s with a hard "ch" sound like "cherry." Once that softened to a "sh," on the model of the French *chérie*, the name really hit its stride. Like many sudden sensations, Cheryl passed out of fashion in a hurry and is now a rarity in any spelling.

Cheyenne

1990s: #105

Popularity: #135
Style: Country & Western,
Place Names
Variants: Cheyanne, Shyanne
Sisters: Sierra, Cassidy, Savannah, Scarlett, Aspen
Brothers: Dakota, Colton, Shane, Wyatt, Chase
✶ Like Dakota, Cheyenne gives us the mindbender of parents naming their kids after Indians to make them sound like cowboys. Or in this case, cowgirls. In the classic spelling, this is a rare pure Wild West name for girls. Increasingly popular variations like Shyanne morph it into a modern invention.

Chloe

2003: #24

Popularity: #24
Style: Antique Charm, English,
Little Darlings, Nickname-Proof
Sisters: Maia, Zoe, Sophia,
Phoebe, Emma
Brothers: Liam, Gavin, Miles, Carter, Caleb
✶ Chloe has been one of the top girls' names in England for years, and Americans are catching on. The Greek -e ending (as in Zoe and Phoebe) makes a strong but sprightly sound for girls.

Christiana

1990s: #738

Popularity: #922
Style: Lacy and Lissome
Nicknames: Chris, Christie,
Chrissy
Variants: Christiane, Christina
Sisters: Angelica, Celeste, Alexandra, Sabine, Gabriela
Brothers: Spencer, Duncan, Maximilian, Alexis, Remington
✶ A mouthful, but perhaps the most sophisticated of all the Christine variations. The variant Christiane was a big hit in France in the '40s, and Germany in the '60s.

Christina

1980s: #19

Popularity: #112
Style: '70s–'80s, Timeless
Nicknames: Chris, Chrissy,
Christie, Tina
Variants: Christine, Kristina, Christiana
Sisters: Stephanie, Veronica, Rebecca, Adrienne, Amanda
Brothers: Jeremy, Christopher, Patrick, Matthew, Adam
✶ Christina is a survivor of the '70s storm of Christy names. Its timeless elegance is as strong as ever, and a lavish girl's classic like this one will always find takers.

Christine

1960s: #27

Popularity: #332
Style: '70s–'80s, French, Surfer
Sixties
Nicknames: Chris, Christie,
Chrissy
Variants: Christina, Kristine, Kristin
Sisters: Stephanie, Michele, Lisa, Amanda, Kimberly
Brothers: Timothy, Brian, Steven, Matthew, Jeffrey
✶ Before there was Kristin, or Christa, or Kirsten, there was this French/English standard. The Chris craze has now yielded to a Kay craze (Kaitlyn, Kayla, Kaylee), but Christine still sounds sharp. The name's warm, true sound transcends its historical trendiness.

Christy

1970s: #71

Popularity: #960
Style: '70s–'80s, Nicknames
Nicknames: Chris
Variants: Christie, Christi,
Kristi, Kristie, Kristy
Sisters: Kari, Tricia, Melinda, Kelli, Stacy
Brothers: Jamie, Chad, Brian, Toby, Brad
✶ Add up all the spellings, and there were more girls named Christy in the '70s than Sarah or Mary. And that doesn't even count the Kristens, Christines, and Kristas who go by this nickname. Why did parents love Christy so? The name has a sparkle to it, like sunshine on fresh Christmas snow. Unfortunately, that impression is now buried in an avalanche of datedness and the name is close to disappearing.

Cindy

1960s: #48

Popularity: #273
Style: Mid-Century, Nicknames, Surfer Sixties
Variants: Cindi, Cyndi, Cinda
Sisters: Wendy, Tammy, Kim, Tracy, Denise
Brothers: Randy, Troy, Todd, Ricky, Craig

✱ Cindy is a prototype for the perky breed of girls' names. Its femininity is the high-spirited kind, like a cheerleader rather than a damsel or diva. While the name is still rooted in its mid-century prime, it sounds as sunny and pleasant as ever—especially in its traditional role as a nickname for Cynthia or Lucinda.

Claire

2001: #82

Popularity: #95
Style: French, Timeless
Variants: Clare, Clara
Sisters: Elise, Caroline, Isabel, Leah, Hope
Brothers: Grant, Isaac, Julian, Harrison, Samuel

✱ Claire is sweet, pretty, and smart. This classic is now enjoying a burst of popularity, especially among Ivy League parents who appreciate its dressed-for-success strength. The traditional English spelling is Clare, the French Claire.

Clara

1900s: #23

Popularity: #295
Style: Antique Charm, Ladies and Gentlemen, Nickname-Proof
Sisters: Eva, Belle, Esther, Lucy, Rose
Brothers: Louis, Julius, Theo, Arthur, Charles

✱ Clara's trim and cute, but every inch a lady. This name has the sweet heirloom style that has made Emma and Lily smash hits. It's on its way up.

Clarice

1910s: #257

Popularity: Rare
Style: Ladies and Gentlemen, Nickname-Proof
Variants: Clarisse, Clarissa
Sisters: Corinne, Lenora, Estelle, Adele, Marguerite
Brothers: Roland, Maurice, Conrad, Bertrand, Claude

✱ Clarice has the form of a '50s French favorite, but it dates from the Middle Ages. It was a romantic choice then, used in tales of heraldry. Today the derivative Clarissa is more romantic, and Clarice echoes with the creepy voice of Anthony Hopkins talking to Jodi Foster's FBI agent Clarice in *The Silence of the Lambs*.

Clarissa

1990s: #251

Popularity: #378
Style: Lacy and Lissome, New Classics
Nicknames: Clare
Variants: Clarice
Sisters: Angelica, Carina, Larissa, Miranda, Adrianna
Brothers: Colin, Brandon, Lucas, Emmanuel, Christian

✱ A pretty, prissy name, scented with flowers and the dust of nineteenth-century romantic novels.

Claudia

1940s: #149

Popularity: #243
Style: German/Dutch, Italian, Timeless
Nicknames: Claudie
Sisters: Marina, Antonia, Bettina, Johanna, Lucia
Brothers: Marcus, Lorenzo, Joel, Ruben, Raphael

✱ Claudia has been an English name for centuries, but it still sounds appealingly foreign. Whether in the classical form of a female counterpart to Claudius, or the impeccable form of German model Claudia Schiffer, the name conveys a stately grace.

Clementine

1910s: #520

Popularity: Rare
Style: Ladies and Gentlemen, French
Nicknames: Clemmie, Clem
Sisters: Millicent, Violette, Henrietta, Marguerite, Eloise
Brothers: Bertram, Archibald, Ferdinand, Hugo, Sylvester

✱ One part fusty and one part cute-as-a-button, darling Clementine has tons of potential now that Madeline and friends have paved the way.

Cleo

1910s: #201

Popularity: Rare
Style: Exotic Traditional, Little Darlings, Why Not?
Variants: Clio
Sisters: Zora, Nell, Avis, Ione, Lila
Brothers: Albin, Jasper, Enzo, Emmett, Ike

✱ Chloe is the modern darling, a stylish favorite in English and French. A tiny twist gives you Cleo, which is a little quirkier but every bit as charming . . . and completely undiscovered. The spelling Cleo is short for Cleopatra; Clio was the Greek Muse of history. The name may strike a chord with cartoon fans as the goldfish in *Pinocchio* and a dog in the *Clifford* series.

Colette
1960s: #467

Popularity: Rare
Style: French, Mid-Century, Saints
Sisters: Nanette, Patrice, Roxanna, Therese, Yvette
Brothers: Gerard, Mathias, Reginald, Vincent, Marcel

✶ Coquettish with literary underpinnings, this name could satisfy your serious and girly sides at once. The name was a mid-century hit in both France and the U.S. thanks to the novelist known by the single name Colette (born Sidonie-Gabrielle Colette).

Colleen
1960s: #95

Popularity: #630
Style: Celtic, Mid-Century, Nickname-Proof
Sisters: Sheila, Denise, Brenda, Penny, Maureen
Brothers: Keith, Darrell, Rodney, Danny, Kurt

✶ Colleen is an Irish word for girl, but the name sounds more like an American mom than a Celtic lass. It's a twentieth-century creation seldom used in Ireland or England.

Connie
1950s: #42

Popularity: Rare
Style: Mid-Century, Nicknames
Sisters: Terry, Jackie, Suzanne, Dianne, Lynne
Brothers: Ronnie, Gerry, Chuck, Jerald, Barry

✶ A pure mid-century classic, with squeaky-clean sweetness personified by singing star Connie Francis. Unlike most hits of that period, Connie still has most of the crispness and effervescence that sent it to the top. Instead of old-fashioned, it sounds cheerfully retro. Try it as a nickname for Constance, Cornelia, Consuela, or—like Connie Francis herself—Concetta.

Constance
1940s: #109

Popularity: Rare
Style: Charms and Graces, Solid Citizens
Nicknames: Connie
Sisters: Rosemary, Jeanne, Merry, June, Glenna
Brothers: Franklin, Allen, Ted, Richard, Warren

✶ Virtue names are in full flower today, but dear Constance has been left behind. Unlike cousins Patience and Faith, Constance was extremely popular during the twentieth century, so she lacks the element of surprise. She does, though, have the classic nickname Connie, which gives her a chance to kick up her heels.

Cora
1900s: #80

Popularity: #439
Style: Antique Charm, Ladies and Gentlemen
Nicknames: Corrie
Sisters: Stella, Nora, Alma, Esther, Iva
Brothers: Julius, Leo, Hugh, Ernest, Henry

✶ Cora was one of the trendiest hits of the 1870s–'80s. You picture a Cora sitting, tightly corseted, in a stiff formal portrait. Today she may be ready to cut loose. Also consider the related names Corinna and Corinne.

Coral
1910s: #859

Popularity: Rare
Style: Charms and Graces
Nicknames: Cori
Sisters: Azure, Emerald, Ivory, Fleur, Garnet
Brothers: Moss, Sterling, Elgin, Pierce, Jasper

✶ Coral is one of the rarest names in the gem family, and one of the most modern sounding. Images of sea and sand make this a perfect contemporary nature name.

Cordelia
1900s: #452

Popularity: Rare
Style: English, Ladies and Gentlemen, Shakespearean
Nicknames: Corrie, Delia, Dell
Sisters: Ophelia, Eleanora, Delphia, Beatrice, Almeda
Brothers: Ferdinand, Eldridge, Ambrose, Leopold, Cecil

✶ Cordelia was King Lear's virtuous daughter, a worthy literary exemplar. Yet conniving sister Regan has the hit name of the moment. The naming life can be so unfair. You can help resuscitate this respectable name or just use Delia, a lighter but equally traditional option.

Corinne
1920s: #303

Popularity: #675
Style: French, Timeless
Nicknames: Cory, Cora
Variants: Corinna
Sisters: Clarice, Marcelle, Marion, Celia, Adele
Brothers: Marcel, Sterling, Forrest, Vincent, Clinton

✶ This French standard is a model of decorum. It's feminine without frills or flash and immune to the winds of fashion. The English Corinna is equally classic with a more poetic spirit.

Courtney
Popularity: #104
Style: Androgynous, Last Names First
Nicknames: Court
Variants: Kourtney, Cortney
Sisters: Caitlin, Kelsey, Danielle, Brianne, Lindsay
Brothers: Brandon, Cody, Kyle, Dustin, Derek

1990s: #20

★ Forty years ago, Courtney was a fancy-pants boy's name, derived from a Norman baronial name. (Neville and Aubrey are similar examples.) More recently, it emerged as part of a new group of girls' names that became the sound of the '80s and '90s. Like its companions Brittany and Ashley, Courtney is still widely used but no longer the cusp of fashion.

Crystal
Popularity: #168
Style: '70s–'80s, Charms and Graces, Modern Meanings
Nicknames: Kris, Chrystie
Variants: Kristal, Chrystal, Krystal, Krystle, Cristal
Sisters: Heather, Tiffany, Amber, Brandy, April
Brothers: Dustin, Chad, Brent, Corey, Bryan

1980s: #21

★ Crystal was a staple of the '70s and '80s, a shimmering choice that perfectly fit the sound of the times. Today that shimmer is down to an ember, as the name is feeling dated. The original spelling is holding up better than its creative variants—it has old roots as a gem name from the era of Ruby and Opal.

Cynthia
Popularity: #201
Style: Mid-Century
Nicknames: Cindy, Tia, Cinda, Thea
Sisters: Teresa, Pamela, Deborah, Belinda, Denise
Brothers: Gregory, Randall, Douglas, Darrell, Reginald

1950s: #11

★ This '50s favorite has held up beautifully. The name Cynthia comes from a title for the goddess Artemis and its classical feminity has kept it current. The nickname Cindy has not been as fortunate, but Tia is a fashionable alternative.

Daisy
Popularity: #138
Style: Antique Charm, Charms and Graces, Nickname-Proof
Sisters: Josie, Sophie, Grace, Ruby, Lily
Brothers: Max, Riley, Walker, Ben, Jake

1900s: #102

★ Daisy is the cutest and lightest of the classic flower names. Its innocent, old-fashioned charm is irresistible. The images of Daisy Mae of Dogpatch and Daisy Duke of Hazzard County keep the name homey.

Dale
Popularity: Rare
Style: Brisk and Breezy, Solid Citizens
Sisters: Kay, Janis, Gayle, Gwen, Lynne
Brothers: Garry, Rex, Dwight, Van, Glynn

1950s: #309

★ Dale has been primarily a boy's name for many years, but it's worth reconsidering for girls. It's swift and androgynous in a modern style.

Dalia
Popularity: #753
Style: Jewish, Lacy and Lissome, Nickname-Proof, Why Not?
Variants: Dahlia
Sisters: Iliana, Ariel, Chaya, Paloma, Amira
Brothers: Asher, Jaron, Ari, Nico, Elan

2003: #753

★ This soft, gentle name is a cross-cultural gem, used in languages from Hebrew to Spanish to Arabic. The floral spelling Dahlia is primarily British. For a more old-fashioned spin on the name, consider Delia.

Damaris
Popularity: #834
Style: Biblical, Exotic Traditional, Latino/Latina
Sisters: Athena, Marisol, Noemi, Sapphira, Delilah
Brothers: Orlando, Titus, Marco, Demetrius, Lorenzo

1970s: #491

★ A biblical name with a distinctive Greek rhythm, Damaris is a stylish choice that will never become too trendy. The same formality that draws parents to the name also keeps it a step outside the mainstream.

Dana
1970s: #59
Popularity: #376
Style: Androgynous, Surfer Sixties
Variants: Dayna
1900 Today
Sisters: Gina, Stacy, Heidi, Jodi, Carla
Brothers: Troy, Marc, Brad, Darren, Toby

✦ The name Dana was just for boys a century ago, but the rise of Donna and Diana in the '50s made it a tempting choice for girls. After a peak from the '60s to the '80s, the name has entered a quiet period, neither in nor out of fashion.

Daniela
2003: #109
Popularity: #109
Style: Italian, Lacy and Lissome, Slavic
Nicknames: Dani
1900 Today
Variants: Daniella, Danielle, Danila
Sisters: Gabriela, Adriana, Sara, Alina, Juliana
Brothers: Maxwell, Caleb, Nicolas, Preston, Tristan

✦ This fluid twist on Daniel, common in Southern and Eastern Europe, sounds just perfect to American ears. It has a hint of glamour without veering far from the tried and true. See also: Danielle.

Danielle
1980s: #25
Popularity: #84
Style: French, New Classics
Nicknames: Dani
Variants: Daniela, Daniella
1900 Today
Sisters: Nicole, Erica, Amanda, Rachel, Stephanie
Brothers: Derek, Jeremy, Sean, Travis, Adam

✦ Danielle and Michelle led a solid group of French favorites through the '70s and '80s. Danielle was the most romantic of the bunch, wearing its French form like a designer gown. Today the familiar French names are starting to give way to Italian and Slavic variants. Danielle is still popular, but Daniela is ascendant.

Daphne
2001: #456
Popularity: #599
Style: English, Mythological, Timeless, Why Not?
Variants: Dafne, Dafna
1900 Today
Sisters: Juliet, Sonia, Camille, Phoebe, Hope
Brothers: Graham, Damon, Jude, Quentin, Noel

✦ Daphne is an easy name to fall in love with. It has a soft-focus beauty, as befits a Greek nymph. But soft-headed, Daphne's not: There's a keen intelligence radiating through the gauzy romance.

Darcy
1970s: #457
Popularity: Rare
Style: Androgynous, Last Names First, Surfer Sixties
Variants: Darcie, D'Arcy
1900 Today
Sisters: Aubrey, Deana, Leigh, Trina, Jody
Brothers: Tad, Dexter, Bradford, Dirk, Kraig

✦ This '60s choice hasn't aged a bit. It's still a vivid, British-style alternative to Marcie or Tracy. It's also a more romantic alternative, thanks to Mr. Darcy of *Pride and Prejudice*.

Daria
rarely used
Popularity: Rare
Style: Italian, Saints, Slavic, Why Not?
Sisters: Katia, Renata, Basia, Marina, Hana
1900 Today
Brothers: Marek, Donato, Alban, Lukas, Matteo

✦ Daria is the female form of Darius, and is equally saintly and accessible. It has the smooth European styling of hits like Gabriela and Nadia, and an MTV animated series to its credit. Yet you never meet a real-life Daria . . . isn't it time?

Darlene
1950s: #71
Popularity: Rare
Style: Mid-Century, Nickname-Proof, Solid Citizens
Variants: Darla, Darleen, Darline
1900 Today
Sisters: Charlene, Nancy, Joanne, Suzanne, Glenda
Brothers: Duane, Ronald, Tommy, Wayne, Johnny

✦ The name Darlene was coined as an endearment—the word "darling" shaped into name form. It's a sweet sentiment, but the sound of the name hasn't been fashionable for some time. Cheri is a French-accented take on the same theme.

Dawn
1960s: #37
Popularity: Rare
Style: Charms and Graces, Surfer Sixties
Sisters: Robin, Lori, Melodie, Shawn, Dina
1900 Today
Brothers: Scot, Todd, Dirk, Brad, Darin

✦ The sunrise image of Dawn is tender and lovely. The name was so trendy in the '60s and '70s, though, that it can be hard to hear that ethereal essence. (Especially if you remember Dawn Dolls, the Barbie competitors in minidresses and go-go boots.) For a more exotic twist consider Aurora, the goddess of the dawn.

Deanna — 1970s: #120
Popularity: #427
Style: Lacy and Lissome, New Classics
Nicknames: Dee
Variants: Deana, Deanne
Sisters: Tamara, Laurel, Sonia, Leslie, Melinda
Brothers: Marc, Terrence, Darren, Gregory, Jeffrey
★ Your grandma may think of the golden-age Hollywood star Deanna Durbin. You'll think of . . . what? This name won't be pinned down easily. You can convince yourself it's lacy or simple, creative or old-fashioned. A flexible choice.

Debbie — 1960s: #52
Popularity: Rare
Style: Mid-Century, Nicknames
Nicknames: Deb
Variants: Debby, Debi
Sisters: Cathy, Laurie, Kim, Vickie, Cindy
Brothers: Ricky, Tony, Jeff, Curt, Danny
★ Debbie Reynolds helped form our image of a wholesome 1950s America, and her bubbly stage name (she was born Mary Frances) became a favorite for two decades. Today, the biblical distinction of the full name Deborah is the stronger draw.

Deborah — 1950s: #5
Popularity: #617
Style: Biblical, Mid-Century
Nicknames: Deb, Debbie
Variants: Debra, Devorah
Sisters: Cynthia, Pamela, Diane, Teresa, Carolyn
Brothers: Mark, Douglas, Randall, David, Craig
★ Deborah was ahead of its time. In the '50s, when cheery little names like Nancy, Karen, and Linda were the rage, this graceful Old Testament name elbowed its way to the top of the charts. Deborah tends to be overlooked today because of overfamiliarity, but it's as gracious as ever.

Deirdre — 1960s: #375
Popularity: Rare
Style: Celtic, Surfer Sixties
Nicknames: Dee, DiDi
Variants: Deidre, Diedre
Sisters: Maura, Daphne, Grania, Tamara, Rhiannon
Brothers: Craig, Kelvin, Declan, Rory, Donovan
★ Deirdre was a beautiful heroine of Irish legend. The name enjoyed a brief jump in popularity in the '60s, but never became American enough to undermine its Irish subtlety.

Deja — 2001: #352
Popularity: #505
Style: African-American, Little Darlings
Sisters: Asia, Tyra, Kenia, Skye, Dalia
Brothers: Darian, Nico, Devon, Isai, Tre
★ This is a newly popular name . . . but do you feel like you've heard it before? The name Deja does come from "déjà vu," the uncanny feeling that you've already experienced something in the past. It's an enigmatic remix of the popular name Jade.

Delaney — 2003: #179
Popularity: #179
Style: Last Names First
Nicknames: Laney, Lane
Sisters: Kennedy, Avery, Cassidy, Rylie, Mckenna
Brothers: Cooper, Drake, Donovan, Keegan, Landon
★ Parents first discovered Delaney when actress Kim Delaney was starring on the TV series *NYPD Blue*, but the name is quickly leaving that small-screen origin in the dust. It's smart, polished, and on the way up.

Delia — 1900s: #250
Popularity: 952
Style: Ladies and Gentlemen
Sisters: Flora, Estella, Ione, Adela, Nola
Brothers: Jules, Emmett, Leo, Charley, Willis
★ This sweet old name shouldn't be left waiting in the wings. It has the lyrical grace of the feminine classics with an extra frisky step.

Delilah — 2003: #618
Popularity: #618
Style: Biblical, Exotic Traditional, Namesakes
Nicknames: Del, Lila
Sisters: Salome, Drucilla, Jemima, Lilith, Magdalena
Brothers: Simeon, Alonzo, Magnus, Emanuel, Samson

★ Delilah is one of the few biblical girls' names that sound glamorous and sensual. Unfortunately, it also sounds treacherous. The dirty dealings of Samson's lover Delilah have limited the name's appeal, but recently more parents have been falling for its undeniable charms. The popular radio host Delilah has helped play up the name's softer side.

Della

Popularity: Rare
Style: Guys and Dolls, Why Not?
Nicknames: Dell

1900s: #122
1900 — Today

Sisters: Lottie, Nell, Freda, Mae, Reva
Brothers: Archie, Bert, Otto, Dee, Mack

✴ Like Ella, Della is a sunny jazz-age favorite associated with a popular singer (Della Reese). Unlike the top-100 favorite Ella, the name Della hasn't been heard from in years. It may sound a little dowdy, but so did Ella fifteen years ago. Della also gives you the option of the winning nickname Dell.

Delphine

Popularity: Rare
Style: French, Why Not?
Sisters: Eloise, Celestine, Giselle, Vivienne, Elodie

1920s: #492
1900 — Today

Brothers: Armand, Gaston, Valentin, Gustave, Lucien

✴ A near-forgotten French classic with traffic-stopping good looks. Delphine is coming off a spike of popularity in its native land and should have tons of potential here as well.

Denise

Popularity: #330
Style: French, Mid-Century, Nickname-Proof, Surfer Sixties
Sisters: Renee, Cindy, Teresa, Robin, Michele

1960s: #29
1900 — Today

Brothers: Steven, Darrell, Gregory, Keith, Mark

✴ In the '50s and '60s, this feminine form of Dennis turned into an American perennial. Modern and energetic, it was a perfect choice for the generation that launched the sexual revolution. Today Denise is no longer modern but a reliable, adaptable favorite.

Desiree

Popularity: #216
Style: '70s–'80s, African-American, French, Modern Meanings
Nicknames: Rae, Desi
Variants: Désirée, Desirae

1990s: #137
1900 — Today

Sisters: Monique, Sasha, Dominique, Simone, Raven
Brothers: Damien, Andre, Jarrett, Emmanuel, Marquis

✴ Désirée is French for "desired," indicating a wished-for child. It's an altogether different kind of desire that inflames the name today, though. This may be the most purely sensuous name you can give a girl.

Destiny

Popularity: #37
Style: African-American, Modern Meanings
Nicknames: Dez, Dessie

2001: #22
1900 — Today

Sisters: Jasmine, Autumn, Genesis, Journey, Savannah
Brothers: Chance, Isaiah, Devin, Dakota, Gabriel

✴ Destiny is a blast of inspirational energy packaged in the style of a traditional girl's name. It's one of the most popular of the new meaning names, and thanks to its classic sound, this one has a chance to stick around for the long haul. Especially popular for Latina and African-American girls.

Devin

Popularity: #807
Style: Androgynous, Nickname-Proof, The -ens
Variants: Devyn, Devan, Devon, Deven

1990s: #344
1900 — Today

Sisters: Ashton, Tyler, Darian, Darby, Taryn
Brothers: Keenan, Quinton, Conor, Dalton, Darius

✴ Devin was discovered at the same time for boys and girls. It now appears to be settling in as a popular *boy's* name, with half a dozen common spellings. If you're looking for a gender-bender, no problem . . . but if you're just looking for a fresh invention with no baggage for a girl, keep looking.

Diamond

Popularity: #238
Style: African-American, Charms and Graces, Modern Meanings
Nicknames: Di

2001: #170
1900 — Today

Sisters: Genesis, Jade, Destiny, Sapphire, Sun
Brothers: Justice, Dante, Chance, Marquise, Emmanuel

✴ This name describes itself: glittering, strong, sharp, and flashy. It's a jazzy choice that deserves its newfound popularity, but the glitz isn't for everyone. If your tastes are more modest, there's always Pearl.

Diana
Popularity: #108
Style: Mythological, Shakespearean, Timeless
Nicknames: Di
Variants: Diane

1950s: #57

Sisters: Laurel, Sonia, Jacqueline, Daphne, Rebecca
Brothers: Gregory, Philip, Curtis, Neil, Timothy
★ The exquisite goddess of the moon; the huntress. The image of the Roman goddess Diana still fits this name well. It's strong, lovely, and timeless. The late Princess of Wales is a powerful association but does not dominate the name.

Diane
Popularity: #914
Style: French, Mid-Century
Nicknames: Di
Variants: Dianne, Dyan, Diana

1950s: #17

Sisters: Sharon, Lynne, Gail, Valerie, Denise
Brothers: Barry, Douglas, Stephen, Kenneth, Gary
★ Diane is a '50s-era name that's maturing into a classic. It has a smooth sound and a nice no-nonsense attitude. While Diane is French (a form of the Roman goddess name), it is most common in the English-speaking world. The English version Diana stays closer to the name's mythological essence.

Dimitra
Popularity: Rare
Style: Greek
Nicknames: Demi, Mitra
Variants: Demitra, Demetria

rarely used
1900   Today

Sisters: Despina, Evanthia, Katerina, Irini, Melina
Brothers: Stavros, Alexios, Andreas, Petros, Christos
★ A popular choice in modern Greece, Dimitra has a classic femininity that translates well.

Dina
Popularity: Rare
Style: Italian, Jewish, Surfer Sixties
Nicknames: Dee
Variants: Deena

1960s: #279

Sisters: Jodi, Trina, Janine, Tamra, Lori
Brothers: Daren, Scot, Tad, Vince, Darryl
★ This lively cross-cultural name was most often heard in the '60s and '70s, when similar choices like Tina and Gina were huge. For a twist, you could consider updating the name to the sunny Dia—following the model of Tia and Gia.

Dinah
Popularity: Rare
Style: Biblical
Nicknames: Di
Variants: Dina

1950s: #577

Sisters: Ronna, Jemima, Adah, Merry, Gayla
Brothers: Les, Rubin, Lemuel, Monte, Dell
★ This is a simple, pretty, biblical name, familiar but uncommon. One reason it's stayed uncommon, unfortunately, is that it has held the stigma of a "slave name." That association is finally fading, and the name has started to pop up on stylish TV and movie characters. It should have a brighter future in the decades to come.

Dixie
Popularity: Rare
Style: Country & Western, Guys and Dolls, Nicknames

1930s: #202

Sisters: Patsy, Dolly, Reba, Billie, Jo
Brothers: Buddy, Doyle, Roy, Jimmy, Bubba
★ You'll find Georgias and Carolinas north of the Mason-Dixon Line, but Dixie is one name that's strictly a Southern belle.

Dolly
Popularity: Rare
Style: Country & Western, Guys and Dolls, Namesakes, Nicknames

1920s: #361

Sisters: Reba, Fanny, Rosie, Loretta, Pearl
Brothers: Willie, Dee, Buster, Wiley, Harlan
★ Dolly, a jolly old nickname for Dorothy, was adopted as the name of a cute child's toy. As a result, the name is mighty hard to take seriously. In contemporary use it has become a "one-woman name," referring to country legend Dolly Parton.

Dolores
Popularity: Rare
Style: Latino/Latina, Porch Sitters
Nicknames: Dolly, Lola
Variants: Doloris, Deloris

1930s: #20

Sisters: Norma, Geraldine, Carmela, Inez, Phyllis
Brothers: Eugene, Ramon, Marvin, Norman, Donald
★ This Spanish name was a glamorous favorite in the '30s. More recently it has been rejected for sounding too . . . well, dolorous. It's rather downbeat in both sound and meaning. (Dolores is Spanish for sorrows, as in the Virgin Mary appellation "Mary of the Sorrows.")

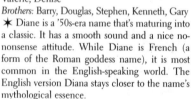

Dominique

Popularity: #446
Style: African-American, Androgynous, French
Sisters: Nicolette, Christiane, Justine, Cassandra, Chantal
Brothers: Marquis, Quentin, Brandon, Antoine, Stefan

1990s: #135 · 1900 – Today

✳ This French classic is a lesson in the right way to sound sexy. Dominique is sultry and seductive, but serious. Unlike Tawny and Misty, she can put on a business suit and demand your respect. After work, of course, she can put on a slinky gown and demand anything she wants.

Donatella

Popularity: Rare
Style: Italian
Sisters: Seraphina, Flavia, Violetta, Maddalena, Miuccia
Brothers: Cosimo, Demitrius, Leandro, Giovanni, Giorgio

rarely used · 1900 – Today

✳ This romantic name is waiting to be swept off its feet by parents who appreciate its womanly beauty. It's lushly traditional, and newly familiar thanks to fashion designer Donatella Versace.

Donna

Popularity: #773
Style: Mid-Century, Nickname-Proof
Variants: Dona

1950s: #10 · 1900 – Today

Sisters: Carol, Diane, Janice, Susan, Karen
Brothers: Douglas, Bruce, Dennis, Gary, Wayne
✳ If you take the time to give Donna some thought, you'll see the charms that kept it near the top of the charts for forty years. It has a trim, all-American sound with hints of both Italy (it's Italian for "lady") and Scotland (a feminine form of Donald). To most parents, though, it's just too familiar to be interesting.

Dora

Popularity: Rare
Style: Ladies and Gentlemen
Sisters: Ada, Leona, Estelle, Vera, Lottie
Brothers: Claude, Archie, Luther, Charley, Bert

1900s: #87 · 1900 – Today

✳ Dora was at its peak in the 1870s, when it was a fashionable offshoot of Theodora, Dorothy, and Isadora. Today the longer versions hold more interest, but Dora still works well as a nickname. For your kids, cartoon heroine Dora the Explorer will be the name's touchstone.

Doris

Popularity: Rare
Style: Mythological, Solid Citizens
Nicknames: Dorrie, Dora

1920s: #8 · 1900 – Today

Sisters: Lois, Rhoda, Phyllis, Wilma, Norma
Brothers: Norman, Lyle, Bill, Wallace, Ray
✳ The -is ending was trendy for girls in the '20s. Names like Doris, Phyllis, Mavis, and Lois stormed into style together, then receded together. Now they're stuck together in generational limbo. If the sound intrigues you, fresher examples include Hollis, Glynis, Iris, Carys, and Dilys.

Dorothea

Popularity: Rare
Style: Ladies and Gentlemen, Why Not?
Nicknames: Dot, Dottie, Dora, Thea

1910s: #189 · 1900 – Today

Variants: Dorothy
Sisters: Estella, Beatrice, Marguerite, Josefa, Eleanora
Brothers: Domenick, Cornelius, Emerson, Augustus, Ellsworth
✳ Dorothea sounds like the responsible older sister of today's carefree antique-revival names. She's just as attractive but more reserved. That's the sort who could be a pleasant surprise for those who take the time to appreciate her charms.

Dorothy

Popularity: #846
Style: Solid Citizens
Nicknames: Dot, Dottie, Dodie, Dolly, Dee

1920s: #2 · 1900 – Today

Variants: Dorothea
Sisters: Frances, Marjorie, Eleanor, Vivian, Ruth
Brothers: Bernard, Raymond, Francis, Lewis, Gordon
✳ Dorothy's popularity has been plummeting ever since Judy Garland's Dorothy followed the yellow brick road. It was a monster hit until then, and its deep-seated sweetness still shines. This name has comeback potential. It may surprise people, but in a nice way.

Drew

Popularity: Rare
Style: Androgynous
Sisters: Shea, Devin, Casey, Blair, Alex

2001: #880 · 1900 – Today

Brothers: Kendall, Ryne, Quinn, Colt, Tevin
✳ Drew is still a boy's name and shows no signs of tipping fully to the girls' side. Actress Drew Barrymore has opened up that possibility, though, with her perfectly crafted image of upbeat, accessible charm.

Ebony

1980s: #159

Popularity: #754
Style: African-American, Charms and Graces, Modern Meanings
Variants: Eboni
Sisters: Amber, Tasha, Crystal, Keisha, Charity
Brothers: Jermaine, Shaun, Derek, Antoine, Donte

✳ Ebony is a nature name, a tropical tree with dark wood prized for rarefied uses like violin fittings. It is a feminine name, with the effortless grace of Emily. But above all it is an African-American name. The suggestion of dark-hued beauty has made it a modern classic for black parents.

Eden

2003: #340

Popularity: #340
Style: Little Darlings, Modern Meanings, The -ens
Sisters: Haven, Sage, Zoey, Jada, Skye
Brothers: Justice, Kai, Liam, Eli, Zion

✳ A glimpse of paradise, demurely. If you feel that names like Heaven and Miracle lay it on a little thick, try this gentle little choice that feels like a classic.

Edith

1900s: #25

Popularity: #683
Style: Ladies and Gentlemen, Saints
Nicknames: Edie
Sisters: Clara, Alice, Alma, Esther, Eleanor
Brothers: Julius, Hugh, Ernest, Harold, Louis

✳ Try to put the image of Edith Bunker from *All in the Family* out of your mind. Instead, focus on the nineteenth-century decorum of novelist Edith Wharton. This name isn't for everybody, but it's ready for a modest comeback. The nickname Edie is a bonus.

Edna

1900s: #17

Popularity: Rare
Style: Porch Sitters
Nicknames: Eddie, Edie
Sisters: Gladys, Ethel, Hilda, Mildred, Agnes
Brothers: Herman, Lester, Edwin, Lloyd, Otis

✳ It's little and arguably cute, but Edna is many years away from a comeback. Its sound is too dense for current fashion. If you want to name a child in honor of an Edna, Eden comes from the same Hebrew root.

Eileen

1920s: #97

Popularity: #679
Style: Celtic, Nickname-Proof, Solid Citizens
Variants: Ilene, Aileen
Sisters: Myra, Jeanne, Glenda, Sheila, Lorraine
Brothers: Glenn, Gordon, Douglas, Lyle, Warren

✳ Most of us identify Eileen as an Irish name, but for many years its popularity crossed all ethnic boundaries. America is full of grown-up Eileens with last names like Cohen and Rodriguez. Now that the name is no longer broadly fashionable, its Gaelic roots are reappearing. It still sounds great with a traditional Irish surname.

Elaine

1940s: #47

Popularity: #614
Style: Solid Citizens
Nicknames: Laney
Sisters: Janice, Patricia, Carol, Lorraine, Judith
Brothers: Lawrence, Dale, Richard, Jerome, Roger

✳ Elaine has a no-nonsense attitude but a romantic core. Despite the name's French sound, its English roots run deep, including the mother of Galahad in Arthurian legend. This name has slipped quietly off the style radar and entered the "pleasant surprise" category. One factor in its decline was *Seinfeld*, perhaps the only TV hit that ever made its characters' names *less* popular.

Eleanor

1910s: #31

Popularity: #309
Style: Antique Charm, Ladies and Gentlemen
Nicknames: Nell, Ellie, Nora, Lana
Variants: Elinor, Eleanora, Leonor
Sisters: Evelyn, Josephine, Clara, Violet, Beatrice
Brothers: Louis, Everett, Willis, Charles, Marshall

✳ Our unscientific survey ranks Eleanor and Lillian as the names men and women disagree on most. Women find them gentle and dignified: elegant ladies with a backbone. Men just think they sound old. How could men be so wrong . . . er, I mean, what an unfortunate difference of opinion. If you can talk him into Eleanor, there's a great selection of nicknames he can pick from.

 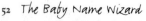

Elena

Popularity: #218 — 2003: #218 — 1900 Today
Style: Italian, Latino/Latina, Slavic, Timeless
Variants: Alaina, Alayna
Sisters: Daniela, Elise, Sofia, Juliana, Leah
Brothers: Eli, Mario, Isaac, Ivan, Simon

✶ Helen's face launched a thousand ships, and her name has launched a thousand variations. The international favorite Elena is the softest and most timeless.

Eleni

Popularity: Rare — rarely used — 1900 Today
Style: Greek
Sisters: Irini, Elisabet, Demitra, Stephania, Anthi
Brothers: Kostas, Nikos, Alexios, Panos, Stavros

✶ An everyday classic in Greece, Eleni is due for a try in America. Pronounce it eh-LAY-nee.

Elise

Popularity: #232 — 2003: #232 — 1900 Today
Style: French, Timeless
Nicknames: Ellie, Lise, Lisa
Variants: Elyse
Sisters: Camille, Elena, Hope, Celeste, Noelle
Brothers: Miles, Graham, Nolan, Quentin, Damien

✶ The name Elise has always been around, but suddenly we're sitting up and taking notice. Its timelessness is soothing, its elegance unforced. A power name of the next generation.

Eliza

Popularity: #334 — 1900s: #240 — 1900 Today
Style: Antique Charm, English
Nicknames: Liza, Liz, Ellie
Sisters: Phoebe, Amelia, Bella, Hallie, Lydia
Brothers: Silas, Simon, Coleman, Jonas, Hugo

✶ This short form of Elizabeth can sound elegant or feisty, like the two incarnations of Eliza Doolittle in *My Fair Lady*. A stylish choice that's not yet too common.

Elizabeth

Popularity: #9 — 1900s: #6 — 1900 Today
Style: Biblical, Timeless
Nicknames: Beth, Bess, Betsy, Betty, Bette, Buffy, Eliza, Elle, Elsie, Elsa, Izzy, Liz, Lisa, Liza, Lizbeth, Lise, Liddy, Libby
Variants: Elisabeth, Elspeth, Elisheba, Isabel
Sisters: Anna, Katherine, Sarah, Julia, Margaret
Brothers: Joseph, William, Samuel, Edward, Charles

✶ Elizabeth is the chameleon name. It changes into a remarkable array of nicknames, letting you tweak the style to fit any personality. This abundance dates back to the days when Elizabeth was such a ubiquitous name in England that many alternatives were needed to tell women apart. You can feel confident that this classic can handle its ongoing modern popularity with ease.

Ella

Popularity: #44 — 1900s: #55 — 1900 Today
Style: Antique Charm, Guys and Dolls
Nicknames: Ellie
Sisters: Lucy, Sophie, Lillie, Grace, Lena
Brothers: Leo, Oliver, Milo, Jack, Archie

✶ Ella has emerged from the pack of soft, cute grandma names to become the height of style. Its secret weapon is jazz legend Ella Fitzgerald, who breathes swinging life into the name. A tisket/A tasket/A green and yellow basket/I found a name so short and sweet/I just could not resist it.

Elle

Popularity: #558 — 2003: #558 — 1900 Today
Style: Brisk and Breezy, Little Darlings, Why Not?
Sisters: Jolie, Brynn, Lia, Eden, Reese
Brothers: Finn, Jair, Ari, Jude, Kai

✶ This is emerging as a more modern, glossy take on Ella, thanks to model Elle McPherson, the fashion magazine *Elle*, and Elle Woods, the heroine of *Legally Blonde*. It's most often pronounced as one syllable.

Ellen

Popularity: #447
Style: Solid Citizens, Why Not?
Nicknames: Ellie, Elle
Sisters: Janet, Sue, Carol, Marian, Ann
Brothers: Lawrence, Allen, Roger, Lewis, Glenn

1900s: #78

★ Ellen is a straight arrow that has flown true for generations. Sure, the name doesn't jump off the page, but that modesty can be an asset. The splashiest names are often the first to sound dated. Despite its drop in popularity, Ellen still sounds timeless.

Ellery

Popularity: Rare
Style: Androgynous, Last Names First, Why Not?
Nicknames: Ellie, Elle
Sisters: Sheridan, Everly, Chandler, Hollis, Hartley
Brothers: Watson, Ryder, Garrison, Barrett, Sawyer

rarely used

★ Fictional detective Ellery Queen was dreamed up in 1929 as a fancified intellectual. A *male* intellectual. But fancy-sounding surnames have jumped the fence, and now sound more natural for girls than boys. Ellery's musical rhythm and girlish nickname make an especially attractive package.

Elodie

Popularity: Rare
Style: Exotic Traditional, French, Saints, Why Not?
Variants: Elodia
Sisters: Esme, Amelie, Sabine, Cecily, Ariane
Brothers: Blaise, Mathias, Florian, Raphael, Emeric

rarely used

★ This downy beauty has been a chart-topper in France for years and is ready for import. The only drawback is confusion with the more familiar American name Melody.

Eloise

Popularity: Rare
Style: French, Ladies and Gentlemen
Variants: Eloisa, Heloise
Sisters: Cecile, Harriet, Leonor, Geneva, Mathilde
Brothers: Rudolph, Clement, Jules, Claude, Edmond

1920s: #177

★ For the past fifty years, Eloise has been a precocious children's book character who lives at the Plaza Hotel. Real-world Eloises are rare, but this sweet heirloom name could follow in the footsteps of fellow kid-lit superstar Madeline.

Elsa

Popularity: #727
Style: German/Dutch, Scandinavian, Timeless, Why Not?
Nicknames: Elsie
Variants: Else
Sisters: Margot, Greta, Celia, Ingrid, Rena
Brothers: Karl, Victor, Werner, Paul, Hugh

1900s: #278

★ Elsa sounds like an antique, but the name has never really gone out of style. This German and Swedish name (a pet form of Elisabeth) has always been quietly used in the U.S. It's a slightly more formal alternative to Ella.

Elsie

Popularity: Rare
Style: Guys and Dolls, Nicknames
Sisters: Bessie, Dovie, Mabel, Lettie, Della
Brothers: Archie, Gus, Charley, Abe, Haskell

1900s: #35

★ While many cutie-pie nicknames have a sassy kick, Elsie has remained a little dowdy. Borden Dairy's "Elsie the Cow" is one major reason. The name is sweet and huggable, though, and ready for rediscovery as a nickname if not a given name.

Elvira

Popularity: Rare
Style: Namesakes, Porch Sitters
Sisters: Velma, Melvina, Leona, Opal, Eldora
Brothers: Roscoe, Grover, Enoch, Verne, Waldo

1900s: #251

★ So you want to name your daughter Elvira. And yes, you know all about the schlock-horror queen by that name. And yes, you can sing the hokey Oak Ridge Boys' chorus ("Oom-Poppa-Oom-Poppa-Mow-Mow") by heart. Ok, at least you're going in with your eyes open.

Emeline

Popularity: Rare
Style: Ladies and Gentlemen
Nicknames: Emma, Mel, Millie
Variants: Emmaline
Sisters: Mathilde, Christabel, Imogene, Harriet, Dulcie
Brothers: Rudolph, Webster, Emory, Rupert, Bertram

rarely used

★ Is there room at the top for yet another form of Emily? If you vote yes, then cast your lot with this demure little lady.

Emerald

2001: #957

Popularity: Rare
Style: Modern Meanings,
Charms and Graces, Why Not?
Nicknames: Emmie
Variants: Esmeralda
Sisters: Jewell, Terra, Meadow, Ivory, Essence
Brothers: Stone, Sterling, Merit, Frost, Price
✱ An uncommon gem name, Emerald has the sparkly style of Diamond without the conceit.

Emily

2003: #1

Popularity: #1
Style: Timeless
Nicknames: Emmy, Millie, Em
Variants: Emilie, Amelie,
Emilee, Amelia
Sisters: Hannah, Lauren, Rachel, Molly, Caroline
Brothers: Jacob, Evan, Alexander, Nicholas, Andrew
✱ You've just got to like Emily. It's bright and friendly, traditional and unpretentious. So sure enough, everybody does like it, making this simple classic the number-one name in the English-speaking world. It tops the charts in England and Australia as well as the U.S. The literary Emilys, from Brontë to Dickinson to Post, lend the name added substance.

Emlyn

Popularity: Rare   rarely used
Style: Celtic, The -ens,
Androgynous
Sisters: Keelin, Wynne, Rhian,
Fallon, Brody
Brothers: Brogan, Tavis, Gareth, Baird, Steffan
✱ Emlyn is a classic Welsh man's name. It's never been familiar in the U.S., and American parents who come across it are starting to hear feminine potential—a natural blend of Emily and Kaitlyn.

Emma

2003: #2

Popularity: #2
Style: Antique Charm,
Nickname-Proof
Sisters: Grace, Lily, Julia, Isabel, Chloe
Brothers: Owen, Noah, Julian, Max, Eli
✱ A breath of gentle simplicity, Emma has returned to the heights of popularity it reached a century ago. It's a smash in Europe, too, one of the top favorites in countries from France to Sweden. You now meet enough young Emmas that the name no longer feels so quaint, but it's still soft and sweet without silliness.

Erica

1980s: #36

Popularity: #164
Style: '70s–'80s, New Classics,
Nickname-Proof
Variants: Erika, Ericka
Sisters: Erin, Danielle, Heather, Tara, Kristen
Brothers: Jeremy, Dustin, Derek, Jared, Aaron
✱ Erica swept in on the coattails of Eric and soon established itself as part of the basic American naming stock. It's clean and energetic, with a girl-next-door familiarity. For extra '80s points, Erica is also Latin for Heather.

Erin

1980s: #28

Popularity: #81
Style: Celtic, New Classics,
Nickname-Proof
Sisters: Megan, Erica, Holly,
Tara, Allison
Brothers: Ryan, Sean, Evan, Jeremy, Kyle
✱ Erin is derived from a poetic name for Ireland. It's not an Irish name per se, but rather a loving nod to your Irish heritage. Thanks to its simplicity, it's been embraced by families of every ethnicity.

Esme

Popularity: Rare   rarely used
Style: Exotic Traditional, Little
Darlings
Variants: Esmé, Esmée
Sisters: Elodie, Clio, Ivy, Noa, Fleur
Brothers: Axel, Noel, Japheth, Mathias, Milo
✱ Name watchers report increased sightings of this rare bird among the literary and artistic elite. It's still genuinely exotic, but so irresistibly trim and chic that it could be winging toward the mainstream soon. Esmé has old French roots but is seldom used in France; it is most common in Scotland and the Netherlands.

Esmeralda

2003: #199

Popularity: #199
Style: Antique Charm,
Latino/Latina
Nicknames: Esme
Sisters: Alejandra, Estefania, Mariana, Angelica, Selena
Brothers: Enrique, Armando, Marco, Javier, Rodrigo
✱ This name, Spanish for emerald, is associated with the sweet Gypsy girl of *The Hunchback of Notre Dame*. It's currently hot, especially in Spanish-speaking families. With the Spanish pronunciation it's lilting and romantic; with an English accent it's an offbeat antique.

Esperanza

2001: #572

Popularity: #671
Style: Charms and Graces,
Latino/Latina
Nicknames: Pelancha

1900   Today

Sisters: Estrella, Catalina, Monserrat, Fernanda,
Annabella
Brothers: Agustin, Santiago, Emiliano, Joaquin,
Cruz
✸ This luminous classic is staging a welcome
comeback. Esperanza is Spanish for hope and
makes a perfect vessel for romantic dreams.

Essence

2003: #757

Popularity: #757
Style: African-American,
Modern Meanings
Sisters: Diamond, Justice,
Allure, Jasmine, Destiny

1900   Today

Brothers: Jett, Dante, Chance, Quinton, Triton
✸ Essence is an upbeat meaning name, spurred
on by the image of *Essence* magazine. This
name looks fabulous on paper and sounds great
in your mind, but be sure to try speaking it out
loud, fast. It's awfully hard to say.

Estella

1900s: #183

Popularity: Rare
Style: Ladies and Gentlemen,
Why Not?
Nicknames: Ella

1900   Today

Variants: Estelle, Stella, Estela
Sisters: Louisa, Clarice, Viola, Harriet, Adela
Brothers: Edmund, Truman, Julius, Emory,
Arthur
✸ An old-fashioned name with the appealing
meaning "star." Most people you ask will tell you
Estella is a lovely choice, a romantic charmer on
the model of Isabella. A few (mostly menfolk)
will say they can't picture the name on anyone
under seventy. The nickname Ella might help
split the difference.

Esther

1900s: #30

Popularity: #297
Style: Biblical, Jewish, Ladies
and Gentlemen
Nicknames: Hettie, Etta, Essie
Variants: Ester

1900   Today

Sisters: Clara, Edith, Alma, Ruth, Miriam
Brothers: Walter, Arthur, Ernest, Julius, Reuben
✸ One of the great biblical heroines, Esther
was also one of the great classic girl's names until
the mid twentieth century. The name dropped
off suddenly and acquired a mildly dowdy
image. It has now begun a quiet comeback and
deserves a spot next to Abigail and Hannah in
the new biblical mainstream.

Ethel

1900s: #12

Popularity: Rare
Style: Porch Sitters
Sisters: Agnes, Edna, Myrtle,
Pearl, Thelma

1900   Today

Brothers: Lester, Cyril, Floyd, Morris, Herman
✸ Ethel is an Old English name element
meaning "noble." Originally, it was combined
with other name pieces to produce winners like
Ethelbert and Etheldreda. Around the 1870s,
that Dark Ages sound surprisingly came into
vogue and Ethel began a fifty-year run as a wildly popular full name for girls. Like the similar
name Hilda, it has now essentially disappeared.

Etta

1900s: #163

Popularity: Rare
Style: Guys and Dolls
Nicknames: Ettie
Sisters: Lula, Essie, Della,
Mable, Nell

1900   Today

Brothers: Mose, Mack, Louie, Dock, Archie
✸ Cute and jazzy, Etta is the kind of old-fashioned name that we think of as a fun-loving
grandma. So far, that's kept it off most parents'
short lists. But as other cuddly classics like Mollie
and Ella rise to the top, Etta is getting closer to a
comeback. It could also work as a nickname for
lacy choices like Violetta or Henrietta.

Eva

1900s: #39

Popularity: #215
Style: Antique Charm
Nicknames: Evie, Evita
Variants: Eve, Aoife

1900   Today

Sisters: Clara, Lucy, Rose,
Esther, Lena
Brothers: Leo, Sam, Julius, Carl, Theo
✸ This Latin form of Eve has always been the
preferred version in the U.S., especially a centu-
ry ago when it reigned alongside Ada and Iva.
That history makes Eva the traditional choice,
while Eve travels in faster circles.

Eve

2001: #534

Popularity: #559
Style: Biblical, Little Darlings,
Timeless
Nicknames: Evie
Variants: Eva

1900   Today

Sisters: Maia, Juliet, Ivy, Daphne, Belle
Brothers: Simon, Jonas, Asher, Eli, Miles
✸ While Adam has settled in comfortably as a
new classic, his old garden mate, Eve, is seldom
heard from. The name's image is complex: simple yet sophisticated, sweet with a dangerous
edge. Its light touch is the standard that names
like Rose and Grace aspire to. See also: Eva.

Evelyn — 1910s: #11
Popularity: #89
Style: Antique Charm
Nicknames: Evie
Variants: Evaline, Evalyn, Evelin
Sisters: Vivian, Rose, Josephine, Marian, Lillian
Brothers: Edward, Oliver, Charlie, Hugh, Raymond
★ That was quick! For years, Evelyn was one of the ladies your grandma played bridge with. Suddenly it's the most stylish name on the block. This sweetheart of a name has the rhythm to win over fans of Kaitlyn and Madison, and the style to charm admirers of Olivia and Eleanor.

Faith — 2003: #52
Popularity: #52
Style: Charms and Graces, Country & Western
Sisters: Lily, Hope, Autumn, Sophie, Ava
Brothers: Mason, Owen, Isaac, Miles, Noah
★ Faith is pure and pretty with an uplifting meaning. It was quietly timeless until the ascent of singer Faith Hill. She has jump-started the name with a country twist.

Fallon — 1980s: #545
Popularity: Rare
Style: Celtic, Nickname-Proof, The -ens
Sisters: Meghan, Siobhan, Shasta, Shannon, Felicia
Brothers: Damian, Jarrett, Brannon, Adrian, Ramsey
★ Fallon was a brief pop-culture-driven phenomenon in the '80s, thanks to a character on the prime-time soap *Dynasty*. (Fellow characters Krystle, Blake, and Alexis had even bigger impacts.) It's an attractive choice with a chance to come into its own today.

Fatima — 2001: #227
Popularity: #242
Style: Muslim
Nicknames: Tima
Sisters: Yasmin, Layla, Samira, Pilar, Loreto
Brothers: Ali, Omar, Amir, Khalid, Cruz
★ A favorite Muslim name (after Mohammed's daughter), Fatima has also been used by Catholics in honor of the famed visitation of Our Lady of Fatima.

Felicia — 1970s: #135
Popularity: #701
Style: '70s–'80s, Lacy and Lissome
Variants: Felisha, Felice
Sisters: Melinda, Monique, Christina, Shawna, Adrienne
Brothers: Derrick, Brent, Dustin, Byron, Lance
★ Felicia is as flamboyantly feminine as you can get, with a sunny boost from its meaning, "lucky." The name is as attractive as ever, though it's no longer the exotic surprise it was in the '60s. Today, demure sister Felicity is the up-and-comer.

Felicity — 2001: #507
Popularity: #625
Style: Charms and Graces, English, Saints
Nicknames: Fliss
Sisters: Willow, Piper, Patience, Meadow, Serenity
Brothers: Sebastian, Rowan, Landen, Graham, Dawson
★ If you can ignore the collegiate TV drama by this name, Felicity is an underappreciated virtue name with a sly British sense of fun.

Fern — 1910s: #176
Popularity: Rare
Style: Charms and Graces
Sisters: Opal, Flora, Jewel, Hazel, Mae
Brothers: Forrest, Buck, August, Willis, Earl
★ Leafy and lacy, a fern is a graceful botanical image for a girl's name. The name also holds a timeless place in children's literature as the main human character in *Charlotte's Web*. In the early 1900s, Fern was especially popular as a middle name, which would be a perfect way to revive it.

Fifi — rarely used
Popularity: Rare
Style: Fanciful, French, Nicknames
Sisters: Gigi, Nanette, Fleur, Coco, Babette
Brothers: Duke, Rémy, Dino, Rex, Pepe
★ Frivolous? Fluffy? Fit for a poodle? Ok, ok . . . but Fifi could be cute for a little girl. It's a French nickname for Josephine, so the practical parent can just choose that venerable classic. Then, if your daughter doesn't seem like a natural Fifi (and how many of us do?), she can simply slip into something a little more comfortable.

Finola

Popularity: Rare   rarely used
Style: Celtic
Nicknames: Nola   1900   Today
Variants: Fionola, Fionnuala
Sisters: Niamh, Grania, Aoife, Sinead, Catriona
Brothers: Fergus, Colm, Donal, Cormac, Eamon
✶ A hard-core Celtic classic, for families that really want Irish heritage and not just a trendy Irish sound. From the Gaelic name Fionnghuala; Finola is the Irish version, Fenella the Scottish.

Fiona

Popularity: #344   2003: #344
Style: Celtic, English, Lacy and Lissome, Why Not?
Nicknames: Fi   1900   Today
Sisters: Dahlia, Maeve, Felicity, Gillian, Camilla
Brothers: Graham, Rowan, Jude, Malcolm, Griffin
✶ It's baffling why this British standby didn't hit the U.S. sooner. But don't question, just enjoy: a romantic knockout with a playful spirit.

Flora

Popularity: Rare   1900s: #110
Style: Charms and Graces, Ladies and Gentlemen, Mythological, Saints
Nicknames: Flo, Flossie   1900   Today
Sisters: Adela, Olive, Rhea, Althea, Viola
Brothers: Rudolph, Jules, Leo, Foster, Albin
✶ When Lily, Rose, and Daisy were at their peaks, so was this name: the Roman goddess of flowers. More than any of the others, Flora keeps its nineteenth-century flavor.

Florence

Popularity: Rare   1900s: #11
Style: Ladies and Gentlemen, Place Names
Nicknames: Flo, Flossie, Florrie   1900   Today
Sisters: Vera, Estelle, Ada, Blanche, Louise
Brothers: Chester, Herman, Walter, Clarence, Herbert
✶ In the nineteenth century, Florence was a hero name. Florence Nightingale was the founder of modern nursing and the most admired woman of her time. She made this formerly obscure old name wildly fashionable. (Nightingale was named Florence after the city where she was born.) Today Florence has returned to obscurity; Flora is a more promising option.

Frances

Popularity: #580   1910s: #9
Style: Ladies and Gentlemen, Solid Citizens
Nicknames: Fran, Francie, Frankie, Fanny   1900   Today
Variants: Francesca
Sisters: Helen, Alice, Pauline, Dorothy, Edith
Brothers: Harold, Louis, Clarence, Leonard, Walter
✶ Like her old pals Helen and Dorothy, Frances is fighting an uphill style battle. But also like those others, this is a name that will come back—maybe sooner than you expect. Frances is today where Eleanor was fifteen years ago, on the cusp of rediscovery. For now, Francesca is the more common source for Fran.

Francesca

Popularity: #420   2001: #394
Style: Italian, Lacy and Lissome
Nicknames: Fran, Frankie
Variants: Frances, Francisca   1900   Today
Sisters: Alessandra, Christiana, Daniella, Paola, Giovanna
Brothers: Lorenzo, Antonio, Demetrius, Marco, Dario
✶ One of the most vividly Italian girls' names, Francesca is sumptuous and womanly. The plainspoken nicknames assure that Francesca's heft won't weigh it down.

Gabriela

Popularity: #87   2003: #87
Style: Lacy and Lissome, Latino/Latina, Slavic
Nicknames: Gaby, Gabi, Gab   1900   Today
Variants: Gabriella, Gabrielle
Sisters: Daniela, Natalia, Angelica, Mariana, Iliana
Brothers: Lukas, Fabian, Maxim, Roman, Emmanuel
✶ This steamy name has three equally traditional forms: the Slavic/Spanish Gabriela, Italian Gabriella, and French Gabrielle. All three have shot up in popularity—expect a Gabi in every schoolyard.

Gabrielle

Popularity: #68
Style: French, New Classics
Nicknames: Gabby, Gabi, Gab
Variants: Gabriella, Gabriela
Sisters: Alexandra, Brooke, Natalie, Noelle, Jocelyn
Brothers: Tristan, Garrett, Nicolas, Colin, Trevor

✱ This old French classic earns high marks on both style and substance. It's a mature, well-built name with plenty of polish. If you like the name's sophistication, though, the lightweight nicknames might give you pause. See also: Gabriela.

Gaia

Popularity: Rare
Style: Little Darlings, Mythological
Sisters: Lyra, Gala, Luna, Juno, Dafne
Brothers: Amon, Joah, Leander, Teo, Orion

✱ The Greek goddess of the Earth, Gaia is an otherworldly name with the magic of legend. It's also a simple, cute name that shouldn't cause any raised eyebrows. That makes it a natural sister for Zoe, which is Greek for "life."

Gail

Popularity: Rare
Style: Mid-Century, Why Not?
Variants: Gale, Gayle
Sisters: Lynne, Kaye, Janis, Gwen, Margo
Brothers: Gary, Bruce, Dennis, Alan, Dale

✱ Most of the mid-century nicknames were dimple-cute: Trudy, Peggy, Vicki. Gail was smooth and mature, with a briskness that plays well today. It's seldom heard, though, and could be a strong choice alone or as a nickname for Abigail.

Gemma

Popularity: Rare
Style: English, Italian, Saints, Why Not?
Nicknames: Gem
Variants: Jemma
Sisters: Gillian, Felicity, Camilla, Violet, Flora
Brothers: Crispin, Alec, Carlo, Albin, Blaine

✱ This Italian name, meaning gem, is a favorite in England that could arrive with fanfare in the U.S. It's cute, tidy, and reflects current trends without following them.

Genesis

Popularity: #181
Style: Modern Meanings
Nicknames: Genny
Sisters: Trinity, Jade, Serenity, Heaven, Journey
Brothers: Justice, Chance, London, Maverick, Honor

✱ Genesis is a splashy combination of meaning name and Bible name—and a perfect sister for Trinity.

Geneva

Popularity: Rare
Style: Ladies and Gentlemen, Place Names, Why Not?
Nicknames: Genie, Jenny, Evie
Sisters: Althea, Virginia, Willa, Verona, Josefa
Brothers: Conrad, Emmett, Jasper, Emory, Richmond

✱ One part refined elegance and one part sauciness, Geneva is ready for a new turn in the spotlight. You can consider it a place name (after the Swiss city) or a form of Genevieve.

Genevieve

Popularity: #388
Style: Exotic Traditional, French, Ladies and Gentlemen, Saints
Nicknames: Ginny, Genny, Gen, Eve
Variants: Geneviève
Sisters: Beatrice, Marguerite, Angeline, Violet, Josephine
Brothers: Domenick, Bertrand, Felix, Benedict, Florian

✱ If your top priority in a name is elegance, look no further. Genevieve is the patron saint of Paris, a fact that perfectly illustrates the name's timeless grace.

Georgia

Popularity: #374
Style: Antique Charm, Country & Western, Place Names
Nicknames: Georgie
Variants: Georgina, Georgiana, Georgette
Sisters: Charlotte, Lucy, Josephine, Virginia, Violet
Brothers: Julius, Roy, Charles, Hardy, Oliver

✱ The southern state gives this name an extra kick. Like Carolina, it has the sound of a proper lady but the style of a red-hot mama. It also has a worldly elegance—the name Georgia is actually more popular in England and Greece than the U.S. It's a strong classic that's likely to continue its upward momentum.

Gertrude
1900s: #22

Popularity: Rare
Style: German/Dutch, Porch Sitters
Nicknames: Gert, Trudy, Gertie
Variants: Gertrud
Sisters: Bertha, Edna, Florence, Mildred, Hester
Brothers: Herman, Lester, Albert, Otto, Horace
✱ There was a craze for Germanic names in the nineteenth century, much like the Irish craze now. Imagine how opulent Gertrude must have sounded. How refined and continental! Can't imagine it? You're not alone, and that craze won't be coming back around for a good long time.

Gia
2002: #741

Popularity: #755
Style: Little Darlings
Sisters: Lia, Macy, Paola, Elle, Anya
Brothers: Luca, Nico, Finn, Aldo, Matteo
✱ This little winner puts an Italian spin on the petite names of the moment. It's a perfectly respectable full name (though not used as one in Italy), and it can also serve as a nickname for ornate imports like Gianna and Giovanna.

Gianna
2003: #146

Popularity: #146
Style: Italian
Nicknames: Gia, Gigi
Sisters: Paola, Gabriella, Bianca, Francesca, Giulia
Brothers: Leonardo, Giovanni, Aldo, Luca, Matteo
✱ A few years ago, Gianna was a foreign name you couldn't even find in an American baby name book. Today it's an across-the-board smash. The name is like the distilled essence of Italy, with all the lushness of names like Francesca and Alessandra concentrated into six smooth letters.

Gillian
2001: #347

Popularity: #467
Style: English
Nicknames: Jill, Gilly
Variants: Jillian
Sisters: Chloe, Regan, Felicity, Gemma, Autumn
Brothers: Tristan, Gavin, Trevor, Sebastian, Colin
✱ This English favorite is an upscale choice we can expect to see more of in the coming years. It's soft and serious, a rare and coveted combination. You can pronounce it with either a hard or soft G. See also: Jillian.

Gina
1960s: #73

Popularity: #462
Style: Italian, Surfer Sixties
Variants: Geena
Sisters: Dana, Tamara, Renee, Carla, Wendy
Brothers: Troy, Darren, Dino, Todd, Randy
✱ This Italian nickname was an all-American favorite alongside Dina and Tina in the '60s. With a bit of distance, it's starting to sound Italian again.

Ginger
1970s: #242

Popularity: Rare
Style: Charms and Graces, Nicknames, Surfer Sixties
Nicknames: Ginny
Sisters: Trina, Melody, Sandy, Dawn, Robyn
Brothers: Tad, Reggie, Dirk, Greg, Rusty
✱ If it weren't for *Gilligan's Island* . . . if it weren't for Ginger Spice . . . wouldn't this be a great name? But as it is, it's a little tough to take seriously. To hedge your bets, try it as a nickname for Virginia.

Giovanna
2001: #628

Popularity: #721
Style: Italian, Lacy and Lissome
Nicknames: Gianna, Gia, Vanni, Vanna
Sisters: Francesca, Alessandra, Luisa, Gabriella, Paola
Brothers: Giancarlo, Matteo, Antonio, Leonardo, Luciano
✱ Giovanna is the sumptuous Italy of our dreams. Long considered "too foreign" to be an American hit, it's now on the rise.

Giselle
2003: #185

Popularity: #185
Style: French, Nickname-Proof, Latino/Latina
Variants: Gisele, Gisela
Sisters: Paola, Camille, Natalia, Celeste, Germaine
Brothers: Tristan, Griffin, Mateo, Fabian, Miles
✱ A sophisticated French classic that's as swift as a gazelle. This knockout has finally found well-deserved popularity in the U.S. Brazilian model Giselle Bundchen has helped fuel that rise—the name is a favorite in South America.

Gladys

1900s: #15

Popularity: Rare
Style: Celtic, Porch Sitters
Sisters: Myrtle, Edna, Agnes, Opal, Pauline
Brothers: Lester, Morris, Floyd, Murray, Cyril
✴ In the late 1800s, the Welsh name Gladys became an international sensation. Back then Gladys sounded like a sensuous, exotic heroine. Try Gwyneth, Carys, or Emlyn for a similar effect today.

Glenda

1940s: #97

Popularity: Rare
Style: Celtic, Mid-Century
Nicknames: Glen
Variants: Glinda
Sisters: Marcia, Gayle, Lynda, Janis, Colleen
Brothers: Roger, Garry, Duane, Dwight, Gerald
✴ Americans aren't the only ones who invent new names. Glenda is a Welsh name, but not a traditional one—it was born in the twentieth century. As a result, it's currently in a no-man's-land of fashion, neither classic nor contemporary. One possible freshener is Glenna, on the model of Brenda/Brenna.

Gloria

1940s: #26

Popularity: #425
Style: Nickname-Proof, Solid Citizens
Variants: Glory
Sisters: Joyce, Barbara, Rosemary, Elaine, Marilyn
Brothers: Gerald, Roger, Donald, Larry, Richard
✴ Gloria (Latin for glory) is a name of the twentieth century. It was born in a George Bernard Shaw play at the dawn of the century, and by the year 2000, the name was fading away. It's easy to see the velvety elegance that enticed generations of parents, but the name is entering grandma territory now. A strong revival possibility a generation or two down the line.

Glynis

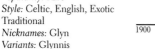

1960s: #978

Popularity: Rare
Style: Celtic, English, Exotic Traditional
Nicknames: Glyn
Variants: Glynnis
Sisters: Bronwyn, Gemma, Lilias, Carys, Bethan
Brothers: Griffith, Vaughn, Wynn, Steffan, Rhys
✴ This Welsh name is an individualist. It's not unfashionable, exactly—it just opts out of the fashion race altogether. Glynis could be a gentle way to stand out from the crowd.

Golda

1900s: #351

Popularity: Rare
Style: Jewish, Ladies and Gentlemen
Nicknames: Goldie
Sisters: Frieda, Dovie, Leona, Bess, Adelia
Brothers: Gus, Julius, Meyer, Otto, Rudolph
✴ Golda may sound old-a, but it has a chance at a second youth now that similar names like Bella and Cora are on the upswing.

Grace

1900s: #18

Popularity: #13
Style: Antique Charm, Charms and Graces
Nicknames: Gracie
Sisters: Daisy, Emma, Julia, Sophie, Amelia
Brothers: Maxwell, Owen, Samuel, Oliver, Simon
✴ This lovely classic is bursting with positive meanings: beauty, refinement, mercy, and blessings. It was neglected for much of the twentieth century, except among Asian Americans. Today it's a full-bore hit—even more than its high rank suggests. Grace is an especial powerhouse as a *middle* name, where its artful simplicity complements more elaborate first names.

Gracie

2003: #126

Popularity: #126
Style: Guys and Dolls, Nicknames
Sisters: Hallie, Josie, Ava, Lilly, Bella
Brothers: Jake, Eli, Max, Joe, Zack
✴ This pet form plays up the cuteness and dizzy-dame fun, but loses some of the grace that is, of course, the very core of Grace.

Graciela

2001: #822

Popularity: #851
Style: Lacy and Lissome, Latino/Latina, Why Not?
Nicknames: Gracie, Chela, Ella
Variants: Graziella
Sisters: Selina, Mariela, Noemi, Marisol, Lisandra
Brothers: Rolando, Emmanuel, Antony, Ruben, Carlos
✴ Graciela is the Spanish equivalent of Gracie, and it is as opulent as Gracie is impish. It's an uncommon choice that sounds like the peak of fashion. A promising alternative to the popular Gabriela.

Greta

1930s: #372

Popularity: #705
Style: German/Dutch, Ladies and Gentlemen, Scandinavian
Sisters: Petra, Elsa, Ingrid, Rheta, Mina
Brothers: Conrad, Lars, Karl, Johan, Bertram

✶ Swedish film star Greta Garbo was the international epitome of sophistication. Her name, originally a pet form of Margareta, is a bit old-fashioned now but still worldly and sophisticated. A good choice for understated elegance.

Gretchen

1970s: #220

Popularity: #760
Style: German/Dutch, Nickname-Proof, Timeless
Sisters: Heidi, Lisbeth, Ingrid, Astrid, Sonya
Brothers: Erich, Stefan, Gunnar, Dirk, Niels

✶ As other Germanic girls' names like Hilda and Gertrude have slipped into oblivion, Gretchen has surprisingly held steady. It does have a certain style-defying confidence, shown off by "Redneck Woman" singer Gretchen Wilson. But the grinding-gear sound of the name has kept it from gaining wider popularity.

Guadalupe

2001: #241

Popularity: #249
Style: Androgynous, Latino/Latina
Nicknames: Lupe, Lupita, Pita
Sisters: Esmeralda, Mercedes, Dulce, Berenice, Lourdes
Brothers: Salvador, Guillermo, Enrique, Octavio, Santiago

✶ Guadalupe is the quintessential Mexican name. It celebrates the sixteenth-century appearance of the Virgin Mary to a poor Indian named Juan Diego. "Our Lady of Guadalupe" grew to become a national symbol of Mexico, representing the fusion of Spanish Catholicism with native Mexican cultures. The name is used for both boys and girls, but is predominantly female in the U.S.

Gwen

1950s: #325

Popularity: Rare
Style: Mid-Century
Sisters: Gail, Janis, Lynn, Betsy, Margo
Brothers: Dale, Garry, Rex, Hal, Gregg

✶ Gwen's appeal is its dispatch. It doesn't put on airs, nor does it try to masquerade as a boy's name. It's up front and female, like it or not. (You'll find that many do like it very much.) For contrast, you can use it as a nickname for the more elaborate Gwendolyn.

Gwendolyn

1950s: #134

Popularity: #598
Style: African-American, Celtic, Solid Citizens
Nicknames: Gwen, Wendy
Variants: Gwendolen
Sisters: Rosemary, Marianne, Muriel, Constance, Glenda
Brothers: Vaughn, Clark, Randolph, Clifford, Stanton

✶ The Welsh classic Gwendolyn bucks fashion. Such a heaping helping of consonants is decidedly old school. While the name's heft will scare some away, it's actually Gwendolyn's biggest asset. This is a substantial name, full of character and impossible to forget.

Hadassah

rarely used

Popularity: Rare
Style: Biblical, Jewish
Sisters: Shoshana, Miriam, Allegra, Margalit, Elisheva
Brothers: Mordecai, Hillel, Doron, Asa, Simeon

✶ Hadassah is the Hebrew form of Esther. Depending on the background of the person you're talking to, it could sound either exotically contemporary or slightly frumpy. It will remind some of the volunteer women's organization Hadassah.

Haley

2001: #35

Popularity: #34
Style: Bell Tones, Last Names First, Nickname-Proof
Variants: Hailey, Hayley, Haylie, Hailee, Haleigh
Sisters: Bailey, Kelsey, Jordan, Sydney, Kayla
Brothers: Connor, Hunter, Kane, Logan, Dalton

✶ This former surname became popular in Britain in the '60s thanks to child actress Hayley Mills. Americans didn't catch on until the '90s, but then took to the name like mad. The spelling Hailey is equally popular, and creative variants abound.

Hallie

2001: #345

Popularity: #413
Style: Guys and Dolls
Variants: Halle
Sisters: Josie, Phoebe, Eliza, Sadie, Lina
Brothers: Max, Charley, Eli, Jake, Owen

✶ Hallie is the antique answer to Haley, an old-fashioned cutie with time-tested tenderness. The similar name Halle, familiar thanks to actress Halle Berry, has separate origins as a Scandinavian name.

Hannah

2001: #3

Popularity: #4
Style: Antique Charm, Biblical, Nickname-Proof
Variants: Hanna, Hana
Sisters: Abigail, Olivia, Chloe, Ava, Emily
Brothers: Caleb, Noah, Austin, Ethan, Jacob

✴ Looking for a warm, old-fashioned biblical name? Male choices abound, but for girls' names, it's slim pickings. Hannah is one that hits the bull's-eye. It's simple and sweet and sounds great with almost any type of surname. Hugely popular, especially in cold-climate states where warmth is always in fashion.

Harley

2003: #313

Popularity: #313
Style: Androgynous, Last Names First
Sisters: Kendall, Skylar, Cassidy, Paris, Presley
Brothers: Hudson, Quinn, Colton, Sawyer, Remington

✴ Harley's been a boy's name for years, but its modern feminine incarnation is all about Harley-Davidson motorcycles. A popular soap opera character jump-started the use of Harley for girls, but even that character was named after the bikes. If you live to hit the open road on your hog, jump on the name. But if you just like the sound of it, consider a similar alternative with a little less horsepower.

Harmony

2003: #592

Popularity: #592
Style: Modern Meanings, Nickname-Proof
Sisters: Cadence, Meadow, Journey, Haven, Serenity
Brothers: Chance, Sterling, Elijah, Merit, Phoenix

✴ It's only fitting that Harmony should have a meaning with two parts that work together. It suggests beautiful music and the even more beautiful image of peace. Just don't use it as a sister for Melody, or Harmony will always feel like she's playing second fiddle.

Harriet

1910s: #113

Popularity: Rare
Style: Ladies and Gentlemen
Nicknames: Hattie, Ettie
Variants: Harriett
Sisters: Eloise, Marion, Mathilda, Vera, Esther
Brothers: Rudolph, Luther, Willis, Hubert, Chester

✴ Let's go out on a limb and call for a Harriet revival. The name has been out of commission for generations, but its whimsical charm could fit adorably on a little girl. The renewal of similar names like Charlotte and Eleanor should help pave the way.

Haven

2003: #595

Popularity: #595
Style: Modern Meanings, The -ens, Why Not?
Sisters: Journey, Eden, Aria, Sky, Meadow
Brothers: Judah, Sage, Jett, Gideon, Ronan

✴ This strong new name is ready to blossom. It has the auspicious meaning and glossy style of favorites like Heaven and Raven, but doesn't sound gaudy. While the other names strut, this one glides.

Hazel

1900s: #20

Popularity: #681
Style: Antique Charm, Charms and Graces, Nickname-Proof
Sisters: Pearl, Violet, Fern, Beryl, Olive
Brothers: Waldo, Hardy, Julius, Theo, Homer

✴ In most places, the idea of naming a little girl Hazel is still unthinkable. But this name is ultrafashionable in certain circles and it could get hotter. The handful of parents who love Hazel today are the same cutting-edge tastemakers who led names like Ruby and Lillian back from the desert in the '90s.

Heather

1970s: #8

Popularity: #208
Style: '70s–'80s, Charms and Graces, Nickname-Proof
Sisters: Shannon, Tara, April, Holly, Melissa
Brothers: Jeremy, Chad, Derrick, Brian, Jason

✴ This flower name is tender and pretty, but America had a national Heather overdose in the '70s and '80s. (Remember the movie *Heathers*, where all the popular girls in school had the same name?) If you love the name's original floral essence, consider Calla, Violet, or Laurel.

Heaven

Popularity: #267
Style: Fanciful, Modern
Meanings, The -ens
Sisters: Miracle, Eden, Bliss,
Nevaeh, Serenity
Brothers: Romeo, Phoenix, Jaxon, Maverick,
Prince

2003: #267

★ This name is a bit fanciful and a lot for any girl to live up to. But Heaven does have a lovely sound for a girl's name, and perhaps your little angel can rise to the challenge. Parental advisory: It's also an extremely popular stage name for strippers and porn stars.

Heidi

Popularity: #316
Style: '70s–'80s,
German/Dutch, Surfer Sixties
Sisters: Sonya, Holly, Christa,
Kelli, Marcie
Brothers: Brian, Brent, Darren, Craig, Brad

1970s: #77

★ A nickname for the ever-popular Adelheid and Heidrun—and, of course, the heroine of a classic children's story. Heidi's heady heyday was in the '60s and '70s, and it may sound too cutesy today. But it may also give you a jolly little alternative to Zoe and Chloe.

Helen

Popularity: #389
Style: Ladies and Gentlemen,
Solid Citizens
Nicknames: Ella, Lena, Ellie
Variants: Helena, Helene, Ellen
Sisters: Ruth, Marie, Alice, Martha, Clara
Brothers: Louis, Hugh, Walter, Henry, Carl

1910s: #2

★ If you like your names both classic and classical, Helen is an impeccable choice. A little boring? Perhaps, but less so every day. Think of it this way: There are now twenty-five Madisons born for every Helen. When your daughter looks around her classroom, which of those names will seem more interesting?

Helena

Popularity: #519
Style: Saints, Shakespearean,
Timeless, Why Not?
Nicknames: Lena
Sisters: Antonia, Celia, Sophia, Violet, Amelia
Brothers: Solomon, Anton, Jasper, Duncan,
Edgar

1900s: #278

★ Helena borrows Helen's understated manner but ties it up in a poetic bow. The name is a standard in Shakespeare's romantic comedies, and that age-old lyricism still serves it well.

Henrietta

Popularity: Rare
Style: English, Ladies and
Gentlemen
Nicknames: Etta, Hettie, Ettie,
Hattie, Hennie, Nettie
Variants: Henriette
Sisters: Winifred, Cordelia, Beatrice, Matilda,
Wilhelmina
Brothers: Rupert, Archibald, Chester,
Theodore, Cornelius

1900s: #133

★ In England, Henrietta is a fearsomely aristocratic name. In America, it's an old-fashioned girl, soft, sweet, and hopelessly out of date. If you're looking for something unexpected but not strange, note how familiar and natural the name sounds, despite the fact that few of us can even name a Henrietta, past or present.

Hermione

Popularity: Rare
Style: Exotic Traditional,
Mythological, Saints,
Shakespearean
Sisters: Olympia, Beatrix, Philomena, Minerva,
Ariadne
Brothers: Horatio, Matthias, Aldric, Benedict,
Linus

rarely used

★ A grand mythological name, glowing with dignity but darned hard to pronounce. (It's her-MY-uh-nee.) Luckily, today's kids have all been schooled in the name via the Harry Potter books. Every ten-year-old on the block will think this is a cool pick.

Hilda

Popularity: Rare
Style: German/Dutch, Porch
Sitters
Nicknames: Hildy
Variants: Hilde
Sisters: Elsa, Sigrid, Ida, Greta, Inga
Brothers: Bertram, Emil, Herman, Otto, Franz

1900s: #91

★ Hilda is in dire straits as a name, a relic of a long-ago Teutonic craze. If you want to resurrect it, you could do well with the Scandinavian spelling Hilde, which roots the name in modern Europe. The nickname Hildy still sounds surprisingly sharp.

Hillary

1980s: #265

Popularity: Rare
Style: Androgynous, Last Names First, Nickname-Proof
Variants: Hilary
Sisters: Lindsay, Mallory, Whitney, Blair, Lacy
Brothers: Kelsey, Ross, Schuyler, Dalton, Jamison

✱ For many people, Hillary simply *is* Hillary Clinton. She's been referred to by first name for years to distinguish her from that other Clinton, Bill. The future of her career may well determine the name's future popularity . . . unless younger Hillarys, like actress Hilary Duff, rise up to share the spotlight.

Hollis

rarely used

Popularity: Rare
Style: Androgynous, Last Names First
Nicknames: Holly
Sisters: Meryl, Glinda, Sybil, Ellery, Corinne
Brothers: Fraser, Newton, Hughes, Dexter, Carleton

✱ One of the few androgynous surnames from an earlier age, Hollis has a long, quiet history as a girl's name. It could sound pleasantly contemporary given the chance.

Holly

1970s: #58

Popularity: #263
Style: Charms and Graces, New Classics, Nickname-Proof
Variants: Hollie, Holli
Sisters: April, Heather, Tara, Robyn, Laurel
Brothers: Lance, Brian, Brett, Heath, Derek

✱ This charming botanical is generations removed from Lily and Daisy, but gives off the same good vibes. A natural for girls born in the Christmas season.

Honor

rarely used

Popularity: Rare
Style: Charms and Graces
Variants: Honorée
Sisters: Verity, Dove, Topaz, Fleur, Mercy
Brothers: August, Forest, Hart, Ulysses, Justus

✱ A virtue name that's more stately than sweet, Honor can be used for either girls or boys.

Hope

2001: #153

Popularity: #177
Style: Charms and Graces, Timeless
Sisters: Faith, Leah, Camille, Summer, Lily
Brothers: Grant, Preston, Miles, Noah, Reid

✱ The name Hope is warmth, pure and simple. It has the positive energy of modern inspiration names like Destiny, but it's also charmingly modest, in keeping with its Puritan origins. Hope is now fashionable in a suitably modest way, climbing slowly and gracefully toward the top.

Ida

1900s: #41

Popularity: Rare
Style: German/Dutch, Ladies and Gentlemen, Saints, Scandinavian
Sisters: Mae, Ada, Stella, Lottie, Iva
Brothers: Gus, Homer, Ike, Leo, Charley

✱ Ida is still out of the picture in the U.S., but in trend-setting pockets of Europe, she's the toast of the town. Throughout Scandinavia, Ida is soaring alongside stylish revivals like Emma and Sofie. And why not? The name is bright and simple with only a little dowdiness to overcome.

Ileana

1970s: #934

Popularity: Rare
Style: Lacy and Lissome
Nicknames: Lea, Ana
Variants: Iliana
Sisters: Corinna, Gisella, Simona, Sabina, Graciela
Brothers: Florin, Antony, Ion, Tobin, Marius

✱ Originally a Romanian form of Helen, this lyrical name has star potential.

Imani

2001: #304

Popularity: #331
Style: African, African-American
Variants: Iman
Sisters: Kenia, Aleah, Nia, Jamila, Kamaria
Brothers: Malik, Femi, Isaiah, Tariq, Jelani

✱ This strong and elegant African name, which means "faith," is shaping up to be an African-American classic. It's a favorite of Ivy League parents and was the name of a pioneering black fashion doll.

1900   Today

India

2001: #298

Popularity: #415
Style: African-American, Lacy and Lissome, Place Names
Sisters: Siena, Talia, Athena, Clio, Geneva
Brothers: Judah, Myles, Rohan, Isaias, Justus

✶ While most of the top place names of the moment have a country-western twang, this one shimmers with silk and spices. India is a sophisticated name that feels timeless, despite its recent burst of popularity.

Ingrid

1970s: #480

Popularity: #696
Style: German/Dutch, Scandinavian, Timeless
Nicknames: Inga
Sisters: Elsa, Gretchen, Johanna, Astrid, Margit
Brothers: Stefan, Lars, Markus, Josef, Anton

✶ Ingrid will never be a top-ten smash, but its simple formality will always win some fans. It's a model of elegant restraint, the essence of Northern Europe.

Ione

1900s: #324

Popularity: Rare
Style: Celtic, Exotic Traditional, Mythological
Nicknames: Nonie
Variants: Iona
Sisters: Avis, Danae, Althea, Lilias, Clio
Brothers: Felix, Finn, Leander, Ivor, Magnus

✶ It's breezy, exotic, and traditional. What more can you ask? How about not one but two trendy origins: Ione's a Celtic name and a sea nymph from Greek mythology. The pronunciation is eye-OH-nee.

Ireland

2001: #908

Popularity: Rare
Style: Place Names
Sisters: Sydney, Kendall, India, Cadence, Meadow
Brothers: Phoenix, London, Finn, Sullivan, Boston

✶ If you want to honor your Irish heritage, there's no more direct way. Ireland has a nice strut to its step, but it's a mouthful and has no natural nickname. Most promising as a middle name choice.

Irene

1910s: #17

Popularity: #581
Style: Greek, Mythological, Solid Citizens
Nicknames: Rene
Variants: Irina, Eirene, Irini
Sisters: Helen, Frances, Ruth, Sylvia, Marie
Brothers: Louis, Albert, Frank, Carl, Walter

✶ Irene is still a sweetheart, but most new parents don't give the name a second thought. It's comfy, warm, and out of fashion. The key is the -een ending, which is becoming an endangered species. You could consider the original pronunciation "eye-REE-nee," the Greek word for peace.

Iris

1930s: #175

Popularity: #380
Style: Charms and Graces, Mythological, Shakespearean, Timeless
Sisters: Georgia, Flora, Ruby, Ione, Violet
Brothers: Jasper, Alvin, Felix, Roy, Davis

✶ As a flower, the iris is a lovely curiosity with delicate, meandering forms that you could never confuse with a lily or rose. As a name, too, this is the classic individualist of the flower family.

Isabel

2003: #82

Popularity: #82
Style: Antique Charm, Latino/Latina
Nicknames: Izzy, Bella, Chavela
Variants: Isabelle, Isobel, Isabella
Sisters: Madeline, Lily, Phoebe, Sophie, Amelia
Brothers: Simon, Max, Owen, Isaac, Samuel

✶ Originally a Spanish form of Elizabeth, Isabel has a regal heritage and nineteenth-century charm that have sent it roaring up the charts. As with similar names like Annabel, different endings convey different images: Isabel is chic, Isabelle is girly, and Isabella trails flowers in its wake. Take all three forms together and you have the number-one choice of Ivy League grads for their daughters.

Isabella
Popularity: #11   2003: #11
Style: Antique Charm, Italian, Lacy and Lissome, Shakespearean
Nicknames: Izzy, Bella
Variants: Isabela, Izabella, Isabel, Isobel, Isabelle
Sisters: Sophia, Arabella, Juliana, Gabriella, Angelina
Brothers: Sebastian, Isaiah, Julian, Adrian, Tristan
✷ Isabella offers a warmly traditional route to a lacy, ultra-feminine name. It's one of the fastest-rising names in years. See also: Isabel.

Isadora
Popularity: Rare   rarely used
Style: Exotic Traditional
Nicknames: Dora, Izzy
Sisters: Phyllida, Artemisia, Esme, Mehitabel, Beatrix
Brothers: Thelonius, Auberon, Horatio, Piers, Atticus
✷ Isadora is a respectable lady's name with an untamed spirit, thanks to flamboyant dancer Isadora Duncan. It could be an adventurous parent's alternative to Isabella.

Isis
Popularity: #576   2001: #529
Style: Exotic Traditional, Fanciful, Mythological, Nickname-Proof
Sisters: Athena, Lyric, Sky, Gaia, Luna
Brothers: Orion, Blaze, Apollo, Ajax, Phoenix
✷ The simplicity of this goddess name reins it in from the realm of the fanciful. An accessible, dynamic fashion statement.

Ivy
Popularity: #407   2001: #354
Style: Antique Charm, Charms and Graces, Little Darlings, Timeless
Sisters: Phoebe, Hope, Iris, Eva, Cleo
Brothers: Eli, Miles, Ezra, Hugo, Jasper
✷ Ivy is as stylish a name as you'll find in America today. Its botanical meaning places it with the turn-of-the-century sweethearts, but unlike demure Lily and Rose, Ivy is vigorous and self-assured. While the name's popularity is rising, it's still rare enough to take people by surprise.

Jacey
Popularity: #847   2002: #811
Style: Bell Tones
Sisters: Laney, Riley, Jada, Quinn, Carly
Brothers: Jaren, Cade, Layton, Rowan, Kole
✷ A peppy little entry that echoes fashionable nicknames (Josie) and surnames (Lacey). Jacey itself, though, is neither—a contemporary creation.

Jacqueline
Popularity: #101   1960s: #51
Style: Timeless, French
Nicknames: Jackie, Jacqui
Variants: Jaclyn, Jacquelyn
Sisters: Diana, Valerie, Adrienne, Cynthia, Julianne
Brothers: Noel, Anthony, Quentin, Terrence, Geoffrey
✷ This French classic bears the lasting stamp of First Lady Jacqueline Kennedy. Luckily, hers is a versatile image: elegant, honorable, pretty, and strong. All of those qualities apply to her name, too.

Jada
Popularity: #80   2001: #75
Style: African-American, Bell Tones, Little Darlings
Variants: Jayda, Jade
Sisters: Maya, Kylie, Nia, Jayla, Ava
Brothers: Liam, Jalen, Cade, Kai, Wyatt
✷ This fun and pretty Spanish variation on Jade got a boost from actress Jada Pinkett Smith. It sounds an awful lot like other trendy names from Jaden to Kayla, but Jada has so much personality that it has carved out its own niche.

Jade
Popularity: #100   2002: #87
Style: Brisk and Breezy, Charms and Graces, Modern Meanings
Variants: Jayde, Jada
Sisters: Diamond, Summer, Sage, Jasmin, Skye
Brothers: Gage, Blake, Stone, Quinn, Jett
✷ A recent addition to Pearl and Ruby's family with a sultry character all her own. Jade has the feminine allure of longer, frilly names, but she's no shrinking violet—she looks you right in the eye. Sexy-tough.

Jaden   2003: #229

Popularity: #229
Style: Androgynous, Bell Tones, The -ens
Nicknames: Jade
1900   Today
Variants: Jayden, Jaiden, Jaidyn
Sisters: Jayla, Addison, Peyton, Rylie, Kaelyn
Brothers: Caden, Jaxon, Camden, Bryson, Keegan
✶ This fast riser is equally new and equally trendy for girls and boys. See the discussion under Jaden in the boys' section.

Jaelyn   2003: #535

Popularity: #535
Style: Bell Tones, The -ens
Variants: Jaylin, Jailyn, Jalynn, Jaylyn, Jalyn, Jaylynn

1900   Today
Sisters: Reagan, Skyla, Jazlyn, Kaelyn, Ryleigh
Brothers: Landen, Kenyon, Jayce, Zander, Rylan
✶ This kind of name is "sneaky popular." It spreads out across so many spellings that you don't realize just how common it is: There are now seven variants in the top 1,000 names. When you add in all the Jadyns, Jaylas, and Kaylins, not to mention male Jalens, any Jaelyn had better brace for a lifetime of confusions and misspellings.

Jamie   1980s: #35

Popularity: #174
Style: '70s–'80s, Androgynous
Variants: Jaime, Jayme, Jaimie, Jami

1900   Today
Sisters: Nikki, Shannon, April, Lindsay, Kari
Brothers: Shawn, Jeremy, Derrick, Corey, Travis
✶ Jamie is a grown-up tomboy, upbeat and capable. Two perfect examples: actress Jamie Lee Curtis, and "Bionic Woman" Jaime Sommers, whose TV heroics turbocharged the name in the '70s.

Jamila   1990s: #976

Popularity: Rare
Style: African-American, Muslim, Why Not?
1900   Today
Sisters: Aisha, Samira, Ayanna, Annika, Shakira
Brothers: Rashad, Khalid, Stefan, Omar, Malik
✶ This name gleams. It comes from the Arabic word for beautiful, and it's worthy of the meaning. Jamila has never really broken through to broad popularity and could be a stylish choice.

Jane   1940s: #40

Popularity: #432
Style: Solid Citizens
Nicknames: Janie, Jenny
1900   Today
Variants: Jayne
Sisters: Ellen, Ann, Janet, Martha, Sue
Brothers: Paul, Ted, Richard, Joe, Thomas
✶ Plain Jane is the gold standard for simplicity, and that's a terrific distinction. The founders of *Jane* magazine banked on the name's directness to cement their image. It's straight-shooting and genuine.

Janet   1940s: #21

Popularity: #508
Style: Mid-Century, Solid Citizens
Nicknames: Jan
1900   Today
Variants: Janette
Sisters: Nancy, Sue, Carolyn, Donna, Judy
Brothers: Roger, Gary, Allen, Richard, Dennis
✶ This is one '50s name that still has legs. Its no-nonsense sound and nimble little nickname make it a twenty-first-century contender.

Janice   1940s: #24

Popularity: #909
Style: Mid-Century, Solid Citizens
Nicknames: Jan
1900   Today
Variants: Janis
Sisters: Joanne, Sharon, Gayle, Diane, Marcia
Brothers: Larry, Gerald, Wayne, Ronald, Bruce
✶ Janice teamed up with Janet to flood the country with little Jans in the '50s. Today, the spelling Janis may be the stronger candidate, thanks to the legendary Ms. Joplin.

Janine   1960s: #268

Popularity: Rare
Style: Surfer Sixties
Nicknames: Jan, Nina

1900   Today
Variants: Jeannine, Janina
Sisters: Denise, Colleen, Marla, Rhonda, Suzette
Brothers: Vince, Darren, Joey, Gregg, Randall
✶ The French Jeannine, slimmed down to Surfer Sixties style. Janine is a traditional variant of the name in France, but it sounds purely American. That's working against the name, since authentically foreign names are more fashionable. Right now Jeannine is the stronger choice.

Jasmine   1990s: #25
Popularity: #27
Style: African-American,
Charms and Graces, Modern
Meanings
Nicknames: Jaz, Minnie
Variants: Jasmin, Jazmin, Jasmyn, Yasmin,
Yasmine
Sisters: Jade, Autumn, Alexa, Destiny, Ariel
Brothers: Jordan, Devon, Isaiah, Xavier, Chance
✴ Jasmine is a fragrant, exotic companion to
Lily and Rose. This name (in the form Yasmin)
has long been popular in the Arab world and
makes a lush new presence in the list of
American standards. Disney deserves an assist
here: *Aladdin's* Princess Jasmine helped boost
the name's profile.

Jayla   2003: #203
Popularity: #203
Style: African-American, Bell
Tones
Sisters: Kyla, Jada, Kamryn,
Aliyah, Kiana
Brothers: Kyler, Braden, Jamari, Davion, Bryson
✴ A lively confection that merges the top hits
Jada and Kayla. Jayla is quickly catching up to
those popular choices.

Jazlyn   2003: #593
Popularity: #593
Style: The -ens
Nicknames: Jaz
Sisters: Ryann, Jaelyn, Teagan,
Jaida, Kenzie
Brothers: Jaxon, Braeden, Jayce, Kolton, Brycen
✴ It was bound to happen: Jasmine meets
Kaitlyn in this new hybrid.

Jean   1920s: #16
Popularity: Rare
Style: Solid Citizens
Nicknames: Jeanie
Variants: Jeanne
Sisters: Rita, Lois, Ann, Eileen, Frances
Brothers: Warren, Ray, Gene, Raymond,
Lawrence
✴ The male John morphs into the female Jean,
Jane, and Joan. Right now Jane sounds the snap-
piest, Joan is the most mature, and Jean the most
flexible. Jean is actually a Scottish form of the
name; the original French spelling Jeanne is a
bit dressier.

Jeanette   1930s: #103
Popularity: #988
Style: French, Solid Citizens
Nicknames: Jean, Jeanie
Variants: Jeannette, Janette,
Jannette
Sisters: Roberta, Loretta, Charlene, Rosemary,
Rita
Brothers: Roland, Gene, Glenn, Lawrence,
Franklin
✴ In the '40s and '50s, the French diminutive
-ette was a favorite choice for the modern girl.
Names like Nanette, Paulette, and Jeanette
sounded so much perkier than old-fashioned
Edna and Florence. Today, endings are smoother
and -ette is seldom heard. Consider Janina,
Gianna, or Janay.

Jemima
Popularity: Rare   rarely used
Style: Biblical, English,
Namesakes
Nicknames: Jem
Sisters: Mahala, Jerusha,
Dahlia, Philippa, Mehitabel
Brothers: Amos, Hosea, Jem, Mahlon, Jethro
✴ Alas, lovely Jemima is still buried under the
image of a kerchiefed "mammy" figure dishing
out pancakes. (The advertising icon Aunt
Jemima actually got a modern makeover years
ago. She now looks more like a bridge partner for
Betty Crocker.) It's a big hurdle, but this biblical
classic is so perfectly lovable in every other way
that it could be well worth taking the plunge.
You'll meet Jemimas in England, where the
name was never as stigmatized.

Jenna   2001: #45
Popularity: #55
Style: Little Darlings, New
Classics
Nicknames: Jen
Variants: Jena
Sisters: Lauren, Brooke, Maya, Chloe, Paige
Brothers: Ian, Cole, Jared, Blake, Drew
✴ The new century's answer to Jenny. Jenna
captures that old favorite's upbeat spirit while
shedding its '70s style.

Jennifer

1970s: #1

Popularity: #31
Style: '70s–'80s
Nicknames: Jen, Jenny
Variants: Jenifer, Guinevere
Sisters: Melissa, Heather, Jessica, Michelle, Amy
Brothers: Jason, Brian, Eric, Christopher, Jeremy
✳ Hi, Jen! Looking up your name? Yep, Jennifer is the most common name for today's expectant mothers. It's actually an old Cornish form of Guinevere, and if you think of it that way, you can imagine how intriguing it sounded to the '50s parents who first started using the name in the U.S. Today, though, it sounds purely American. This is the top name for Latinas, thanks to entertainer Jennifer Lopez.

Jenny

1970s: #133

Popularity: #421
Style: Nicknames
Nicknames: Jen
Variants: Jennie
Sisters: Angie, Carrie, Christy, Bridget, Holly
Brothers: Joel, Toby, Andy, Jamie, Lance
✳ Jenny, like Jennifer, sounds like pure 1970s. The name's real heyday, though, was in the nineteenth century when singer Jenny Lind was an international sensation. (Think of it as the 1850s Britney.) Back then Jenny was a nickname for Jane, but the recent Jennifer glut has numbed us to that possibility.

Jeri

1950s: #321

Popularity: Rare
Style: Nicknames, Surfer Sixties
Variants: Geri, Jerry, Jerri, Jerrie, Gerri, Gerry
Sisters: Joni, Vicki, Teri, Ginger, Jan
Brothers: Curt, Randy, Kris, Donnie, Russ
✳ The girl's name Jeri, in every imaginable spelling, was a staple of the '50s and '60s. As a boy's name (Jerry), it had been a staple of the '30s and '40s. Today the name seems to be reverting quietly to the boys' side.

Jessica

1980s: #1

Popularity: #18
Style: '70s–'80s, New Classics, Shakespearean
Nicknames: Jessie, Jess
Sisters: Nicole, Erica, Jennifer, Vanessa, Amanda
Brothers: Jeremy, Ryan, Brandon, Jonathan, Christopher
✳ Everything parents have always loved about Jessica still applies. It's a delicately feminine name with Shakespearean heritage and a peppy nickname. It's an impeccable choice, but not one that will attract much notice — Jessica's been so popular for so long it gets taken for granted. Less common lacy classics include Marina, Tabitha, and Veronica.

Jessie

1900s: #61

Popularity: #475
Style: Nicknames
Variants: Jessye, Jesse, Jessi
Sisters: Katie, Cassie, Mollie, Jennie, Maggie
Brothers: Ben, Adam, Jake, Will, Alex
✳ We know Jessie as a nickname for Jessica, but the name was a hit on its own back when Jessica was still a Shakespearean oddity. In Scotland, it was a pet form of Jean or Janet; in the U.S., a girlish favorite. Today we can't separate Jessie from the recent swarm of Jessicas, so the name is getting a rest.

Jewel

1920s: #234

Popularity: #738
Style: Antique Charm, Charms and Graces, Modern Meanings
Variants: Jewell
Sisters: Hazel, Violet, Lila, Lucy, Belle
Brothers: Jasper, Justice, Grady, Emmett, Pierce
✳ Jewel flourished in the age of Ruby and Pearl, yet it harmonizes with modern affirmation names like Angel and Destiny. That makes it the most forward-looking of the classic gem and flower names. The singer Jewel has helped bring the name back to parents' attention.

Jill

1960s: #61

Popularity: Rare
Style: Surfer Sixties, Why Not?
Sisters: Beth, Jody, Tina, Robin, Lisa
Brothers: Dean, Jay, Brad, Scott, Mark
✳ Jill could be the 1960s' first revival candidate. The name's directness gives it a kind of grown-up girl power: fun and fearless. Plus the phrase Jack and Jill, dating back 600 years, shows that the image of Jill as a spirited lass is genuinely timeless.

Jillian

2001: #123

Popularity: #137
Style: '70s–'80s, The -ens
Nicknames: Jill, Jilly
Variants: Gillian
Sisters: Jocelyn, Summer, Mallory, Jenna, Allyson
Brothers: Colin, Brendan, Micah, Jarrett, Drew
✴ Jill was a '50s–'60s favorite, beloved but plain. So in the '70s and '80s, parents turned it into the fancier Jillian. The traditional spelling, Gillian, has always been preferred in the U.K., and is gaining steam in the U.S.

Jo

1940s: #62

Popularity: Rare
Style: Mid-Century, Nicknames, Solid Citizens
Nicknames: Joey
Sisters: Judy, Kay, Gail, Nan, Meg
Brothers: Ted, Don, Tommy, Gene, Hal
✴ Since the publication of *Little Women* in 1868, Jo has meant the independent, artistic tomboy Jo March. It was purely a nickname at first, but became a popular given name in the '30s (sometimes as part of a compound name like Jo Anne). Today that fad has passed, but the name is still full of energy. If you're considering Jo as a nickname, see the Nicknames style section for given name ideas.

Joan

1930s: #7

Popularity: Rare
Style: Solid Citizens
Nicknames: Joanie, Jo
Variants: Jeanne, Jean, Joanne
Sisters: Barbara, Joyce, Carol, Rita, Nancy
Brothers: Gene, Donald, Richard, Bill, Jerry
✴ Joan is somewhat plain, but not quite plain enough. Parents who really want to make a back-to-basics style statement choose Jane. Joan, the beloved favorite of the '30s and '40s, is simply perceived as too ordinary to be interesting. It's not the first time that's happened to this boom-or-bust name. There was such a glut of Joans in the Middle Ages that the name acquired a "common" reputation and virtually disappeared for centuries.

Joanna

1980s: #137

Popularity: #255
Style: Biblical, Timeless
Nicknames: Jo, Joey, Jody, Joanie
Variants: Johanna
Sisters: Susanna, Bethany, Andrea, Christina, Rachel
Brothers: Marcus, Matthew, Derek, Aaron, Christopher
✴ While other female forms of John wax and wane, Joanna remains modest and timeless. It was a nineteenth-century favorite, held steady through the Joanne-dominated 1950s, and now fits with soft favorites like Daniela and Adriana.

Joanne

1930s: #56

Popularity: Rare
Style: Mid-Century, Solid Citizens
Nicknames: Jo, Joey, Joanie
Variants: Joann, Jo Anne, Joan
Sisters: Carole, Peggy, Janice, Gayle, Marcia
Brothers: Duane, Allen, Ronald, Gerald, Dale
✴ Joanne comes from an Old French form of Joan, and sounds more like the compound names of the '40s (Ruthann, Maryjo). Joanna, a similar but separate name, has a more timeless appeal.

Jocelyn

2003: #88

Popularity: #88
Style: New Classics, The -ens
Nicknames: Joss, Jo, Josie
Variants: Jocelyne
Sisters: Daniela, Jasmine, Avery, Allison, Jillian
Brothers: Evan, Jonah, Colin, Nicholas, Brendan
✴ The name Jocelyn is the hero that names like Madison want to grow up like. A man's name for centuries, it has turned completely feminine yet kept its style intact. It's a familar, traditional choice in a trendy vein.

Jodi

1970s: #105

Popularity: Rare
Style: '70s–'80s, Nicknames, Surfer Sixties
Variants: Jody, Jodie
Sisters: Lori, Gina, Kris, Jill, Teri
Brothers: Tad, Scotty, Bart, Curt, Gregg
✴ This boyish '60s star still charms us with its good humor. As a nickname, it's pitch-perfect. As a full name, though, it's more limited. Picture actress Jodi Foster as Johanna instead . . . doesn't it suit her dignity better? Other formal options include Judith, Jordan, and Josephine.

Johanna

1900s: #234

Popularity: #517
Style: German/Dutch, Scandinavian, Timeless
Nicknames: Jo, Joey, Jody, Joanie, Hanna
Variants: Johana, Joanna
Sisters: Katherine, Eliza, Amelia, Elsa, Kristina
Brothers: Jesse, Anton, Stefan, Simon, Elliott
✳ This is the Central and Northern European form of Joanna, and a timeless choice in the U.S. A bit more forceful than the gentle Joanna, it's a good match for brawny surnames. In Europe the name is pronounced yo-HAAH-na. Americans can choose between that and jo-HA-na.

Jordan

2002: #46

Popularity: #49
Style: Androgynous, Last Names First, Place Names, The –ens
Nicknames: Jordy, Jody, Jo
Variants: Jordyn, Jordana
Sisters: Morgan, Bailey, Logan, Madison, Taylor
Brothers: Connor, Devin, Trevor, Landon, Austin
✳ You like the punch of an androgynous surname, but you want something familiar enough to not sound pretentious. You've found it. Jordan is now a solid hit for girls.

Josefa

1900s: #389

Popularity: Rare
Style: Ladies and Gentlemen, Slavic, Why Not?
Nicknames: Jo, Josie, Jody, Posy
Variants: Josepha
Sisters: Aurelia, Cecile, Adela, Petra, Rafaela
Brothers: Edmund, Anton, Emory, Alden, Bertram
✳ Josefa is a traditional name in many languages and was once common in the U.S. It's barely familiar today, though—Josephine became the standard feminine form of Joseph. That's left Josefa sounding fresh, more like a discovery than a revival.

Josephine

1910s: #23

Popularity: #260
Style: Antique Charm, Saints
Nicknames: Jo, Josie, Josette, Fifi, Jody, Posy
Variants: Josephina, Josefina
Sisters: Genevieve, Violet, Georgia, Eleanor, Charlotte
Brothers: Julius, Rudolph, Benedict, Louis, Theodore
✳ With Caroline a chart-topper, it's time to look again at opulent Josephine. You just can't beat this name for ladylike grandeur. If you're concerned that it sounds a bit *too* grand, one look at the nickname choices should ease your mind.

Josie

2002: #284

Popularity: #310
Style: Guys and Dolls, Nicknames
Variants: Josey
Sisters: Hallie, Gracie, Clare, Callie, Eliza
Brothers: Jack, Max, Alex, Walker, Zack
✳ Here's a surprise: In the '60s and '70s, when Josie and the Pussycats were first shaking their tails in the pages of *Archie* comic books, the name Josie was at its absolute low point of popularity. This is not a Surfer Sixties name but an 1800s name—a lighter spin on the then wildly popular Josephine. It's back now, and welcome, though the full Josephine is still the more versatile choice.

Journey

2003: #910

Popularity: #910
Style: Modern Meanings, Why Not?
Sisters: Haven, Meadow, Aria, Harmony, Star
Brothers: Sage, Justus, Gideon, Chance, Judah
✳ Journey is a contemporary choice that even a traditionalist could admire. It combines the femininity of a classic virtue name with the punch of a modern meaning name.

Joy

1970s: #145

Popularity: #492
Style: Charms and Graces, Mid-Century, Why Not?
Sisters: Gail, Merry, Iris, Sue, May
Brothers: Kent, Alan, Dwight, Rex, Hal
✳ What could be a more natural name for the soft little bundle in a new parent's arms? Joy is a sweet, loving choice for a baby and matures smoothly into womanhood.

Joyce

1930s: #12

Popularity: #643
Style: Solid Citizens
Sisters: Janet, Elaine, Gloria, Nancy, Carol
Brothers: Gerald, Bobby, Allan, Wayne, Donald

✳ Joyce is incorruptible. She's a pillar of the community, a sympathetic ear, a refuge in hard times. She's also likely to be your grandma's age. This is a classic name currently in a slump. Look for a comeback in your grandchildren's generation.

Judith

1940s: #8

Popularity: #633
Style: Biblical, Mid-Century, Solid Citizens
Nicknames: Judy, Jude
Sisters: Carol, Janet, Deborah, Sharon, Linda
Brothers: Roger, Allen, Gerald, Glenn, Richard

✳ In the '30s and '40s, Old Testament names were at their lowest ebb. Judith bucked the trend to become one of the most stylish hits of the day. Today we tend to group it with dated cohorts like Carol and Barbara, but you'd do well to focus on Judith's biblical style instead. It's a strong and now uncommon alternative to Abigail and Hannah.

Judy

1940s: #17

Popularity: Rare
Style: Mid-Century, Nicknames
Variants: Judie, Judi
Sisters: Lynda, Bonnie, Sandra, Sue, Peggy
Brothers: Jerry, Terry, Dennis, Jimmy, Bruce

✳ This name has been swept up in a generational turnover and virtually disappeared. The Judy Garland–era flock of little Judies may be graying, but the name is still warm and charming. Your best bet today is choosing it as a nickname for the sturdier classic Judith.

Julia

1900s: #45

Popularity: #33
Style: Antique Charm, Shakespearean, Timeless
Nicknames: Julie, Jules, Jill
Variants: Julie, Giulia
Sisters: Grace, Isabel, Emma, Sophia, Caroline
Brothers: Samuel, Max, Simon, Victor, Isaac

✳ This warm and lovely classic was a nineteenth-century standby. By the 1950s, the French form Julie took over, leaving Julia sounding slightly old-fashioned. Today, that very quaintness is part of its appeal. Julia is currently the height of fashion throughout Europe.

Juliana

2003: #158

Popularity: #158
Style: Lacy and Lissome, Saints
Nicknames: Julie, Jules
Variants: Julianna, Julianne
Sisters: Mariana, Elise, Juliet, Liliana, Camilla
Brothers: Jackson, Miles, Jonah, Harrison, Sebastian

✳ Juliana has been quietly used for centuries alongside timeless sister Julia. It's ornamental with a gentle, poetic touch. The name has suddenly caught fire, much like fellow lacy traditionals Isabella and Olivia.

Julianne

2003: #538

Popularity: #538
Style: New Classics
Nicknames: Julie, Jules
Variants: Juliana, Julienne
Sisters: Jacqueline, Diana, Marianne, Laurel, Candace
Brothers: Terrence, Kendall, Quinton, Patrick, Mitchell

✳ Julianne is a twentieth-century creation: the traditional Juliana reimagined in the age of compound names like Rosanne and Maribeth. Its ongoing popularity is a credit to its smooth style and to the classy actress Julianne Moore.

Julie

1960s: #18

Popularity: #240
Style: French, Mid-Century, Surfer Sixties
Nicknames: Jules
Variants: Julia
Sisters: Renee, Lisa, Denise, Wendy, Christine
Brothers: Scott, Jeffrey, Keith, Steven, Timothy

✳ Together, the Latin Julia and the French Julie make up a timeless classic. The stately Julia was the favorite a hundred years ago. Then Julie's cute, nicknamelike sound took over mid-century. Today, stately gentleladies are back in and Julie's handing off the baton.

Juliet

2001: #568

Popularity: #605
Style: Shakespearean, Timeless, Why Not?
Nicknames: Julie, Jules
Variants: Juliette
Sisters: Victoria, Hope, Lilian, Helena, Camille
Brothers: Duncan, Lincoln, Raphael, Graham, Pierce

✳ Juliet is simple, traditional, and drenched in romance. Unlike her star-crossed lover Romeo, Juliet doesn't sound too showy. The name conjures a ravishing image in an understated, thoughtful way.

June

1920s: #46

Popularity: Rare
Style: Charms and Graces, Solid Citizens, Why Not?
Sisters: Sue, Ellen, May, Lila, Kaye
Brothers: Clark, Ellis, Jack, Ray, Ward
✴ Sweet simplicity is in—just ask Rose, Grace, and Faith. But so far parents have skipped over June, which offers the same attractions as either a first or middle name.

Junia

rarely used

Popularity: Rare
Style: Biblical
Sisters: Aquila, Sapphira, Damaris, Tamar, Magdalene
Brothers: Aeneas, Raphael, Jabez, Jude, Matthias
✴ In Romans 16:7, Junia was described as "of note among the apostles." If you don't find her in your Bible, it's because scribes in the Middle Ages thought such a description of a woman must be wrong. They scratched out Junia and came up with the masculine Junias in its place. Translators today are reversing that decision. Call this a traditional name that bucks tradition.

Justice

2002: #403

Popularity: #456
Style: African-American, Androgynous, Modern Meanings, Nickname-Proof
Sisters: Skye, Essence, Genesis, Journey, Liberty
Brothers: Noble, Maverick, Freeman, Truth, Judge
✴ Like Destiny, this name is a power punch of affirmation. But Justice takes a step past self-empowerment to embrace a broader social agenda. It's a message name, for better and worse. A big load for a little girl, but tremendous upside.

Justine

1990s: #238

Popularity: #589
Style: '70s–'80s, French, Nickname-Proof
Variants: Justina
Sisters: Danielle, Chelsea, Mallory, Jaclyn, Adrienne
Brothers: Morgan, Kurtis, Jarrett, Kyle, Bryant
✴ While most similar-sounding names (Janine, Francine) were on the way out by the '80s, Justine was just hitting its stride. The booming popularity of Justin for boys helped, as did the actress Justine Bateman of *Family Ties*. Today, though, Justine is fading back into the pack. The Latin form, Justina, may sound more contemporary.

Kaitlyn

2001: #31

Popularity: #32
Style: Bell Tones, The -ens
Nicknames: Kait, Katie, Kay
Variants: Caitlin, Kaitlin, Caitlyn, Katelyn, Kaitlynne, Katlyn
Sisters: Morgan, Makayla, Kylee, Jordan, Kendall
Brothers: Kyler, Tristan, Kieran, Connor, Devin
✴ Caitlin is Gaelic and traditional, but Kaitlyn is a phenomenon. There's something about the name that has struck a chord with "kreative" namers in the U.S., who have placed a dozen different spellings of it in the top-thousand girls' names. In the years to come, expect to meet countless Kaitlyns, no two spelled the same.

Kara

1980s: #105

Popularity: #246
Style: Little Darlings, New Classics, Nickname-Proof
Variants: Cara
Sisters: Erin, Jena, Holly, Tara, Kendra
Brothers: Erik, Brett, Ryan, Derek, Casey
✴ Spelled Cara, this name means "dear" or "beloved." Spelled Kara, it also means you like cute little names that start with K. Most people you meet will share your opinion. Kara's been a solid favorite for two generations.

Karen

1950s: #8

Popularity: #143
Style: Mid-Century, New Classics, Nickname-Proof
Variants: Karin, Karyn, Carin, Karon, Karren
Sisters: Kathy, Susan, Cynthia, Sharon, Lynn
Brothers: Gregory, Jeffrey, Alan, Kevin, Mark
✴ Every Kaitlyn, Megan, and Devin in the land should tip her hat to Karen. When this Scandinavian form of Katherine took off sixty years ago, it established a whole new sound for the all-American girl.

Karina

1990s: #134

Popularity: #159
Style: Lacy and Lissome, Scandinavian
Nicknames: Kari
Variants: Carina, Karena
Sisters: Tessa, Kira, Serena, Clarissa, Annika
Brothers: Devon, Collin, Micah, Stefan, Kane
✴ The pure happiness of this name is contagious. Karina's easy femininity, a gentle twist on favorites from Karen to Christina, could turn it into an American perennial. The spelling Carina has the deepest roots, from an early Orthodox saint to a constellation in the southern sky.

Kateri

Popularity: Rare

Style: Saints

Sisters: Kinnia, Winema, Savina, Averil, Shadi

Brothers: Sakari, Kohana, Kilian, Vitus, Chayton

✷ An Iroquois form of Katherine, this is a striking, highly individual name with cross-cultural strength. Kateri Tekakwitha, a seventeenth-century Mohawk Christian, was beatified by Pope John Paul II. The original pronunciation was ga-deh-lee; most modern namesakes opt for ka-TER-ee.

rarely used
1900 — Today

Katherine

Popularity: #36

Style: Timeless

Nicknames: Kat, Kate, Kathy, Katie, Kay, Kit, Kitty, Kari, Katia

Variants: Katharine, Catherine, Kathryn, Katerina, Katharina

Sisters: Sarah, Rachel, Christina, Caroline, Elizabeth

Brothers: Andrew, Benjamin, Matthew, Nicholas, Alexander

✷ If you want a name to stay fashionable until your daughter is a grandma, you can't find a better bet than Katherine. This is a name of saints, queens, and empresses, with countless versions and derivatives. Several different spellings are traditional, but Katherine is timeless. See also: Catherine.

1980s: #32
1900 — Today

Kathleen

Popularity: #286

Style: Celtic, Mid-Century

Nicknames: Kathy, Kat

Sisters: Sharon, Maureen, Carolyn, Patricia, Susan

Brothers: Gary, Kenneth, Douglas, Barry, Neal

✷ Kathleen is the Anglicized form of the Gaelic Caitlin. For many years it was a favorite of Irish families in America, but today most parents have redirected their affections to the Gaelic original. The result, surprisingly, is to make Kathleen sound even better. Its retro style now makes it a comfort name, glowing with warmth.

1950s: #15
1900 — Today

Kathy

Popularity: #804

Style: Mid-Century, Nicknames

Nicknames: Kath, Kat

Variants: Cathy, Kathie, Kathi

Sisters: Cindy, Diane, Becky, Karen, Debra

Brothers: Terry, Bruce, Greg, Douglas, Alan

✷ This is a name that's full of heart and free of pretense. As either nickname or full name, Kathy is a worry-free choice made to cherish.

1950s: #22
1900 — Today

Katia

Popularity: Rare

Style: Slavic, Why Not?

Nicknames: Kat, Katie

Variants: Katya

Sisters: Renata, Mira, Nadia, Dasia, Lida

Brothers: Dimitri, Marek, Brice, Lukas, Viktor

✷ Just a single vowel separates Katia and Katie, but it makes a literal world of difference. Katia's heart lies across the globe in Russia, and Katie's right here in the U.S. Both can be used as nicknames of Katherine and its many variants.

2001: #880
1900 — Today

Katie

Popularity: #110

Style: Nicknames, Timeless

Variants: Katy, Kate, Cate

Sisters: Sara, Kristen, Cassie, Rachel, Molly

Brothers: Alex, Andrew, Jesse, Adam, Kyle

✷ Many parents skip right past Katherine and choose this cute, unpretentious nickname. It's a sure way to avoid your daughter being called Kathy or Kat against your wishes, but it forces her to sound girlish—even at times when she might prefer womanly. For a middle path, consider the given name Kate. That's the stylish nom du jour for Hollywood stars.

1980s: #43
1900 — Today

Katrina

Popularity: #277

Style: '70s–'80s, New Classics

Nicknames: Trina, Kat, Katia

Variants: Catrina, Catriona, Katerina, Katrine

Sisters: Tabitha, Kara, Candice, Vanessa, Nicole

Brothers: Brett, Jeremy, Derek, Shannon, Shaun

✷ This lively contraction of Katherine has Scandinavian form and Celtic rhythm. (It's used as an English version of the Gaelic Catriona.) A sunny favorite, classic yet cheerleader-ready. If you like the style but want a more serious sound, go with an extra syllable in Katerina.

1980s: #100
1900 — Today

Kay

Popularity: Rare

Style: Nicknames, Solid Citizens

Variants: Kaye

Sisters: Sue, Tess, Jan, Gail, Jo

Brothers: Don, Ted, Drew, Ty, Alex

✷ Kay is one of the trendiest *nicknames* in America. It's the short form for such hits as Kayla, Kaylee, Kaylin, and Makayla. That completely transforms the perception of this name, a '40s fireball that was once a glamorous pet name for Katherine. *Washington Post* publisher Katherine (Kay) Graham was a legendary example.

1940s: #98
1900 — Today

Kayla 1990s: #12

Popularity: #16
Style: African-American, Bell Tones
Nicknames: Kay
Variants: Kaila, Kaela, Kaylah
Sisters: Jada, Alyssa, Aspen, Janae, Kyra
Brothers: Jordan, Kyler, Austin, Zachary, Dylan
✶ In the class of "Kay" names, Kayla is looking like the valedictorian. Its simple elegance makes it most likely to succeed over the long term. The main danger may be overexposure, as the name is in its second decade of enormous popularity.

Kaylee 2003: #54

Popularity: #54
Style: Bell Tones
Nicknames: Kay
Variants: Kayleigh, Kaylie, Kayley, Kailee, Kailey, Kayleen
Sisters: Kylie, Jaycee, Haleigh, Skylar, Kenzie
Brothers: Jalen, Kyler, Braden, Trace, Parker
✶ This name sits squarely at the center of a trend that has given an entire generation of kids a trademark sound. The sounds Kay and Lee are enormously popular building blocks used in dozens of names, and the name Kaylee itself is found in every spelling you can imagine.

Kaylin 2003: #445

Popularity: #445
Style: Bell Tones, The -ens
Variants: Kailyn, Kaylyn, Kaylynn, Kaelyn, Kalyn
Sisters: Bailey, Katelynn, Kiersten, Makayla, Taylor
Brothers: Keegan, Braden, Kane, Darien, Jalen
✶ Halfway between Kayla and Kaitlyn falls this reasonable compromise. Kaylin keeps Kayla's smooth sound, but shapes it into Kaitlyn's trendy boyish rhythm.

Keisha 1970s: #293

Popularity: Rare
Style: '70s–'80s, African-American, Nickname-Proof
Variants: Kesha, Kisha, Lakeisha, Lakesha, Keshia
Sisters: Tasha, Keri, Shana, Tamika, Krista
Brothers: Jermaine, Courtney, Kelvin, Derrick, Jarrod
✶ The African-American sister to Krista and Trisha, Keisha was a '70s–'80s splash. This energetic name has faded surprisingly fast, perhaps a victim of its own popularity.

Kelly 1970s: #14

Popularity: #125
Style: Androgynous, Celtic, New Classics, Surfer Sixties
Variants: Kelli, Kellie
Sisters: Kimberly, Stacy, Shannon, Kerry, Robin
Brothers: Shawn, Brian, Kevin, Lance, Jeffrey
✶ Kelly is the original androgynous Irish surname. (See Riley, Mackenzie, Ryan.) While it's still popular, this standby is now getting swamped by thousands of little Kaylees, Kylies, and Kelseys. As a result, Kelly now has an image that would have been unimaginable when it first broke out in the '60s: It's the mature, traditional alternative.

Kelsey 1990s: #33

Popularity: #131
Style: Androgynous, Bell Tones, Last Names First, Nickname-Proof
Variants: Kelsie
Sisters: Shelby, Mallory, Peyton, Lindsey, Aubrey
Brothers: Dalton, Taylor, Trevor, Keenan, Dillon
✶ Kelsey was a mild-mannered boy's name (think actor Kelsey Grammer) that suddenly exploded as a girl's name. With its energetic, faintly androgynous style, it pals around comfortably with Courtney and Shelby. One of the hottest names of the '90s, Kelsey already shows signs of cooling off.

Kendall 2003: #157

Popularity: #157
Style: Androgynous, Celtic, Last Names First
Variants: Kendal
Sisters: Logan, Mckenna, Peyton, Kennedy, Addison
Brothers: Brennan, Donovan, Keenan, Griffin, Chandler
✶ An unexpected gender crossover, Kendall has a particularly boyish sound (like a Ken doll, not a Barbie). Also consider Kimball, which has a similar strong surname sound but a more feminine nickname.

Kendra

1990s: #133

Popularity: #261
Style: '70s–'80s, African-American, New Classics, Nickname-Proof

1900 — Today

Sisters: Erika, Krista, Nicole, Jaclyn, Kara
Brothers: Kyle, Jared, Justin, Brett, Derrick

✱ This is a Welsh/Gaelic/Norse/Anglo-Saxon name meaning knowledge/champion/magical/high hill/water baby/royal power. In other words, nobody knows where it came from so don't worry yourself about it. Kendra *sounds* like a modern blend of Kenneth and Sandra, which makes it a solid mainstream choice.

Kennedy

2003: #123

Popularity: #123
Style: Androgynous, Celtic, Last Names First

1900 — Today

Sisters: Riley, Reagan, Kendall, Delaney, Cassidy
Brothers: Brennan, Cameron, Parker, Griffin, Connor

✱ Americans first took up this Irish boy's name in the '60s to honor president John F. Kennedy. Today it's an apolitical hit for girls, but still an unlikely choice for die-hard Republicans (who may opt for Reagan instead).

Kenya

1970s: #366

Popularity: #585
Style: African-American, Place Names
Variants: Kenia

1900 — Today

Sisters: Zaria, Ayanna, Ericka, Nia, India
Brothers: Omari, Kendrick, Mekhi, Zaire, Terrell

✱ The nation of Kenya has a catchy name that's been a natural target for African-American parents seeking to reflect their African roots. The reflection is so direct, though, that it can sound more like a country than a girl. The spelling Kenia is standard in many other languages, and more traditionally namelike in English.

Kerri

1970s: #194

Popularity: Rare
Style: '70s–'80s
Variants: Kerry, Keri

Sisters: Staci, Leigh, Tricia, Kristi, Leann

1900 — Today

Brothers: Shaun, Derrick, Dusty, Brent, Kraig

✱ Remember Kerri Strug, the Olympic gymnast who charmed the country with her courageous performance on an injured leg? That's the classic Kerri: cute, spunky, and born in 1977. Yet Kerri's just a stone's throw from current hits like Kira and Kylie, and could fit in comfortably with any age group.

Kia

1990s: #873

Popularity: Rare
Style: Little Darlings
Sisters: Jena, Kara, Tai, Jesse, Kala

1900 — Today

Brothers: Aric, Chaz, Travis, Ryne, Bo

✱ This miniature name would be irresistible to many parents, except for the association with a low-priced line of cars.

Kiana

2002: #294

Popularity: #321
Style: African-American, Bell Tones, Lacy and Lissome
Variants: Quiana

1900 — Today

Sisters: Ayana, Shayla, Kailey, Malia, Kierra
Brothers: Javon, Braden, Davion, Amari, Keanu

✱ Kiana is an attractive member of a mix-and-match name family that includes Kiara, Tiana, and Tiara. A tropical breeze sets Kiana apart: It is especially popular in Hawaii, where it has the sound of a traditional name.

Kiara

2001: #136

Popularity: #167
Style: African-American, Celtic, Lacy and Lissome, Saints
Variants: Ciara, Kiera, Kira, Chiara, Ceara

1900 — Today

Sisters: Tatiana, Aleah, Caitlyn, Breanna, Alexa
Brothers: Collin, Devon, Darius, Kane, Griffin

✱ Kiara's newfound popularity has come from many directions. Some parents choose it as an Irish Gaelic name, pronounced KEE-ra or KEE-a-ra. Pronounced kee-AH-ra, it can be a Kenyan name, a version of the Italian Chiara, or the cub in Disney's *Lion King II*. That's enough associations that no one really sticks. If you choose the name, choose it because you love the sound.

Kiki

Popularity: Rare
Style: Nicknames, Scandinavian
Sisters: Saga, Britt, Edie, Pella, Romy

rarely used

1900 — Today

Brothers: Zeke, Rune, Teo, Rafer, Niels

✱ It's easy to file this name with the ooh-la-la sisters Fifi and Mimi, but Kiki is made of sterner stuff. It's Scandinavian (a nickname for Kristina) and has artistic associations and an independent spirit. As a nickname, it could free you from the overly common Kristy.

Kim

Popularity: Rare
Style: Mid-Century, Nicknames
Sisters: Kris, Beth, Debbie, Liz, Lynn
Brothers: Greg, Tim, Todd, Keith, Jay

1960s: #44

✴ We usually hear Kim as a nickname for Kimberly, but it used to be given just as often as a full name. In the '50s, it sounded crisp and modern, like *Vertigo* actress Kim Novak. It's still snappy today, though more conventional. Some unconventional uses could be as a nickname for Kimball, Kimberlin, or Kimery.

Kimberly

Popularity: #63
Style: New Classics, Surfer Sixties
Nicknames: Kim, Kimber
Variants: Kimberley, Kimberlee
Sisters: Michelle, Kelly, Angela, Amy, Melissa
Brothers: Jeffrey, Timothy, Brian, Scott, Kevin

1970s: #5

✴ Kimberly's been a favorite for decades thanks to its bright sound, like a tinkling of bells. The name's enormous popularity in the '60s and '70s is now starting to slow it down, as every new parent knows at least a couple of Kims.

Kinsey

Popularity: 984
Style: Last Names First
Nicknames: Kin
Sisters: Kendall, Brody, Larkin, Ripley, Arly
Brothers: Bannon, Ridley, Kane, Ryker, Bridger

2001: #878

✴ You can thank mystery writer Sue Grafton for this name, introduced in her popular series about detective Kinsey Millhone. It's a fresh alternative to the more popular Kelsey. Parental advisory: Keep in mind the Kinsey Reports on sexual behavior.

Kirsten

Popularity: #282
Style: New Classics, Scandinavian, The -ens
Nicknames: Kirsty, Kirstie
Variants: Kerstin, Kirstin, Kiersten
Sisters: Allyson, Kara, Megan, Kaitlyn, Bethany
Brothers: Colin, Drew, Erik, Kendall, Brandon

1990s: #175

✴ Kirsten, the Danish and Norwegian form of Christine, first hit America in the same 1970s wave that brought so many Kristens and Kristas. (It hit Scotland much earlier, thanks to its kinship with the traditional Scottish pet name Chirsty.) The name has held firm over the years and still sounds current.

Krista

Popularity: #444
Style: '70s–'80s
Nicknames: Kris
Variants: Christa
Sisters: Trisha, Kari, Meredith, Alisa, Tara
Brothers: Shaun, Derrick, Brent, Shannon, Lance

1980s: #127

✴ Krista was a card-carrying member of the '70s Kris Brigades. It was a quiet choice at the time, but it turned out to be a trendsetter. Krista helped set the blueprint for current favorites like Tessa and Jenna, and those names in turn have kept Krista contemporary.

Kristen

Popularity: #226
Style: '70s–'80s, The -ens
Nicknames: Kris, Kristie, Krissy
Variants: Kristin, Kristina, Kirsten, Christen
Sisters: Lindsay, Erica, Danielle, Katrina, Heather
Brothers: Derrick, Jeremy, Corey, Justin, Brett

1980s: #38

✴ Every possible form of Christine was a hit in the '70s and '80s. One of the biggest was Kristen, which sounds so much like a Scandinavian girls' classic it's hard to believe it's a modern creation.

Kyla

Popularity: #169
Style: Bell Tones
Sisters: Lexi, Kira, Jada, Kailyn, Anya
Brothers: Cade, Braden, Kyler, Ashton, Koby

2003: #169

✴ This is what name dictionaries like to call "a euphonious invention." Which is a "euphonious" way to say that folks made it up 'cause it sounds nice. As modern as Skylar and as girlish as Kayleigh, Kyla is rising fast.

Kylie

Popularity: #50
Style: Bell Tones
Variants: Kylee, Kiley
Sisters: Kyra, Hailey, Darby, Macy, Jayla
Brothers: Jaden, Kaleb, Bryce, Colby, Hayden

2003: #50

✴ This is an Australian name, but it fits perfectly into current American tastes. So when American parents encountered the name via Aussie entertainer Kylie Minogue, they jumped on it.

Kyra 2001: #210
Popularity: #222
Style: Little Bell Tones, Darlings, Nickname-Proof
Variants: Kira, Keira
Sisters: Macy, Jada, Kiley, Nia, Mara
Brothers: Kane, Jalen, Ian, Brady, Kameron
✴ This springy, attractive name is traditionally pronounced KEE-ra, but you'll also hear KY-ra (like Tyra). If you want to clarify the KEE pronunciation, try the spelling Kira. And just to muddy the waters even more, see also: Kiara.

Lacey 1980s: #148
Popularity: #375
Style: Bell Tones, Last Names First
Nicknames: Lace
Variants: Lacy, Lacie
Sisters: Lindsay, Kelsey, Whitney, Jaclyn, Hillary
Brothers: Brenton, Derek, Beau, Jared, Tyson
✴ The name Merry is merry, Joy is joyous, so shouldn't Lacey be lacy? In fact, this surname is closer to the sleek style of Lindsay and Whitney. It has a patrician element, exemplified by the *Doonesbury* comic strip congresswoman Lacey Davenport.

Lana 1940s: #207
Popularity: #499
Style: Mid-Century, Why Not?
Sisters: Sandra, Gail, Dinah, Lola, Rita
Brothers: Dana, Cary, Douglas, Rod, Kent
✴ It's the purest old Hollywood legend. Young Julia Turner is discovered at a soda fountain and transformed into glamorous star Lana. The name was perfect for Turner's sweater-girl image: youthful in form, sultry in demeanor. The golden Hollywood glow it cast back then still works its magic today.

Laney 2003: #564
Popularity: #564
Style: Bell Tones, Last Names First
Variants: Lainey
Sisters: Kiley, Hailey, Kira, Piper, Jacey
Brothers: Easton, Rylan, Coby, Kian, Landen
✴ Laney is new but tantalizingly familiar. It could be a twist on Lonnie, a nickname for Elaine, or a merger of Lacey and Lindsay. It's a strong, clean sound with power-name potential.

Lara 1970s: #338
Popularity: #685
Style: New Classics, Slavic
Sisters: Lesley, Cara, Katrina, Kelly, Tanya
Brothers: Damon, Lance, Shawn, Andre, Toby
✴ This variation on Laura and Larissa emerged in the '60s when round, full sounds were getting trimmed down to pocket size. It was starting to fade from view until the *Tomb Raider* heroine Lara Croft reenergized the name.

Larissa 1990s: #390
Popularity: #521
Style: African-American, Lacy and Lissome, Slavic
Nicknames: Lara, Rissa
Sisters: Alina, Leanna, Viviana, Kiara, Marissa
Brothers: Dimitri, Jovan, Trent, Desmond, Quinton
✴ If Larissa hadn't existed, it would have been invented in the '80s. It sounds like a natural extension of Melissa, Clarissa, and other frilly classics. In fact, Larissa is a Slavic classic in its own right, as well as an ancient Greek town and a moon of Neptune.

Lark
Popularity: Rare
Style: Brisk and Breezy, Charms and Graces, Modern Meanings rarely used
Sisters: Bay, Tyne, Caprice, Calla, Linden
Brothers: Flint, Hays, Teague, Leif, Birch
✴ Lark has two common meanings in English: a cheery songbird and a spontaneous, lighthearted adventure. Both suit a girl's name to a T. Contemporary and catchy.

Lashonda 1970s: #509
Popularity: Rare
Style: African-American
Nicknames: Shon
Variants: Lashanda, Lashaunda, Lashawn
Sisters: Lakesha, Sharonda, Tamika, Shanika, Latosha
Brothers: Tremayne, Laron, Jamaal, Torrance, Dedrick
✴ The sound of the '70s, African-American style. This name hit the sweet spot with its elaborate construction and sensuous lilt. In fact, its elements were all so popular you can rearrange them to form another hit name of the time, Shalonda.

Latasha 1980s: #195
Popularity: Rare
Style: '70s–'80s, African-
American
Nicknames: Tasha
Variants: Latosha
Sisters: Shantell, Keisha, Chandra, Tanesha, Lakisha
Brothers: Antwan, Courtney, Tremayne, Jamaal, Marques
✳ The "La" prefix that dominated the African-American name scene for years is suddenly passé, leaving favorites like Latasha in the lurch. The new hot sound: "Ja," as in up-and-comers like Jakayla.

LaToya 1980s: #101
Popularity: Rare
Style: African-American
Nicknames: Toya
Sisters: Latasha, Shanika, Sheena, Ebony, Sharonda
Brothers: Jamaal, Courtney, Dejuan, Jermaine, Marlon
✳ This name is generally attributed to entertainer LaToya Jackson, who was born in 1956. Her name hit the spotlight in the '70s when her Jackson 5 brothers became singing sensations. (*American Idol* star LaToya London was among those born at the peak of disco fever.) It was a splashy hit but has now virtually disappeared.

Laura 1960s: #15
Popularity: #122
Style: Timeless
Nicknames: Laurie, Lori, Lolly
Variants: Laurel, Lauren
Sisters: Rebecca, Amy, Christine, Lisa, Teresa
Brothers: Patrick, Stephen, Mark, Timothy, David
✳ One of the steadiest choices around the world. Laura's smooth sound has made it a favorite in song and story for centuries—from Petrarch to *General Hospital*—and it's a hit in almost every European language. This author has spent many happy years with the name, for which she thanks her parents.

Laurel 1950s: #288
Popularity: #662
Style: Charms and Graces, New Classics
Nicknames: Laurie
Sisters: Robin, Melody, Patrice, Diana, Julianne
Brothers: Geoffrey, Brett, Lance, Seth, Colin
✳ This attractive botanical name mirrors the classic softness of Laura but gives that standard an unexpected twist. It's a lovely choice, but keep in mind that there are thirty Laurens (and a dozen Lauras) for every Laurel, so the name will be mis-heard constantly.

Lauren 1990s: #13
Popularity: #15
Style: New Classics, The -ens
Nicknames: Laurie
Variants: Loren
Sisters: Megan, Samantha, Brooke, Jenna, Nicole
Brothers: Brandon, Lucas, Nathan, Zachary, Joshua
✳ This Laura variant first hit the scene in the 1940s in the glamorous form of actress Lauren Bacall. It rode along quietly for many years, then suddenly burst into popularity in the '80s. In this tight-knit name family, Lauren is the modern girl, Laura most traditional, and Laurel most creative.

Lavender
Popularity: Rare — rarely used
Style: Charms and Graces
Sisters: Linden, Cinnamon, Emerald, Juniper, Silver
Brothers: Birch, River, Lysander, Blue, Lennox
✳ This elegant color and botanical name is ready to become a girl's name. It's quirky but not silly, and familiar to the younger set via a character in the Harry Potter books.

Lavinia 1910s: #718
Popularity: Rare
Style: Lacy and Lissome, Ladies and Gentlemen, Mythological, Why Not?
Nicknames: Liv, Vin
Sisters: Rafaela, Althea, Linnea, Ariadne, Allegra
Brothers: Leander, Everett, Benedict, Linus, Domenick
✳ Traditional, feminine, and extremely rare, Lavinia is a choice with spectacular potential. The name has been a favorite in literature from Virgil to Shakespeare to Dickens. Its melodious beauty comes across just as well today.

Lea

1970s: #455

Popularity: #670
Style: French, Little Darlings
Variants: Léa, Leia
Sisters: Cara, Noelle, Tia, Mara, Elisa
Brothers: Ari, Noel, Abel, Quentin, Andre

✶ Léa, the French form of Leah, is one of the hottest names in France. Without the accent, it's a popular Hawaiian name, after a goddess. In either form the name has a smooth, elusive delicacy, like a fine chocolate.

Leah

2003: #83

Popularity: #83
Style: Biblical, Timeless
Nicknames: Lee
Variants: Lea
Sisters: Rachel, Molly, Sarah, Joanna, Katie
Brothers: Joel, Nathan, Seth, Jared, Aaron

✶ One of the simplest and sweetest biblical names for girls. Leah is similar in feeling to Hannah, but its popularity has grown more slowly and quietly.

Leanna

1990s: #506

Popularity: #722
Style: Lacy and Lissome
Nicknames: Lee
Variants: Liana, Leanne
Sisters: Clarissa, Alana, Shayla, Arielle, Daniella
Brothers: Kendall, Jarvis, Shane, Mitchell, Jarrod

✶ Leanna started life as a minor offshoot of Leanne, but it's now the more popular and fashionable choice. The extra syllable softens Leanne's country twang into a more universal femininity.

Leanne

1960s: #372

Popularity: Rare
Style: Country & Western, Surfer Sixties
Nicknames: Lee
Variants: Lianne, Leann, Lee Ann, Leanna
Sisters: Jolene, Bobbi, Annmarie, Deana, Rochelle
Brothers: Rusty, Terrance, Clint, Kraig, Scotty

✶ This combination name, first heard in the '40s, has an infectious cheer but is now a step behind current fashion. It's always been most popular in the South and Southwest, and that association has been reinforced by country singers LeAnn Rimes and Lee Ann Womack.

Lee

1950s: #226

Popularity: Rare
Style: Androgynous
Variants: Leigh
Sisters: Dale, Jan, Anita, Gwen, Lynn
Brothers: Van, Rex, Perry, Cliff, Neal

✶ Lee is simple, direct, and compact. It's ready to take on whatever style your daughter brings to it, from cute to corporate. As a middle name, it turns retro and a little bit country.

Leigh

1970s: #230

Popularity: Rare
Style: '70s–'80s, Androgynous, Brisk and Breezy
Sisters: Kerry, Blair, Hilary, Jodie, Paige
Brothers: Clint, Shannon, Lance, Brent, Derrick

✶ Leigh's time as a full given name is mostly past, but it has been absorbed deep into our naming culture. This spelling now pops up to "personalize" names like Ashleigh, Kayleigh, and Ryleigh.

Leila

2003: #349

Popularity: #349
Style: Lacy and Lissome, Muslim, Timeless
Variants: Layla, Laila
Sisters: Bella, Hallie, Celia, Yasmin, Amina
Brothers: Simon, Carlo, Jonas, Ali, Amir

✶ From an Arabic term for night, Leila is a tender flower petal of a name. The spelling Layla, associated with the iconic Eric Clapton song, is a rising contemporary choice.

Leilani

2003: #345

Popularity: #345
Style: Exotic Traditional
Nicknames: Lani
Sisters: Malia, Kamea, Willow, Kiana, Delilah
Brothers: Keanu, Landon, Malachi, Alonso, Lukas

✶ Leilani is the one Hawaiian name that has been widely embraced in America. It carries a gentle, lavishly feminine island breeze.

Lena
1900s: #60
Popularity: #500
Style: Antique Charm,
German/Dutch, Little Darlings
Nicknames: Leni
Variants: Lina
Sisters: Lucy, Stella, Meta, Rose, Cora
Brothers: Leo, Sam, Oscar, Anton, Charlie
★ Lena is a nice old-fashioned nickname for some nice old-fashioned names (Helena, Magdalena). If it doesn't sound old-fashioned to you, thank the timeless style of singer Lena Horne. This name is experiencing a huge revival in Europe and is worthy of the same in the U.S.

Leona
1900s: #73
Popularity: Rare
Style: Ladies and Gentlemen,
Namesakes
Nicknames: Lee, Leonie
Variants: Leonie
Sisters: Flora, Estelle, Iona, Alberta, Viola
Brothers: Horace, Rudolph, Luther, Hubert, Willis
★ If you love old-fashioned names, here's one that still has its full antique style. Leona is a slow-paced name, not exactly fashionable but warm and handsome. The variation Leonie has been more common in England and France.

Leora
1900s: #389
Popularity: Rare
Style: Jewish, Ladies and
Gentlemen, Why Not?
Sisters: Josefa, Adela, Ione,
Dalia, Cecile
Brothers: Jules, Foster, Asher, Theo, Haskell
★ Leora means "light," and it glowed brightly in the nineteenth century. The name quietly disappeared, though it does pop up occasionally as a modern Hebrew name. For extra grace points, pronounce it lay-OH-ra.

Leslie
1970s: #69
Popularity: #92
Style: Androgynous, Celtic,
New Classics
Variants: Lesley
Sisters: Kelly, Melanie, Bridget,
Darcy, Meredith
Brothers: Bradley, Kevin, Marc, Patrick, Bryan
★ Leslie has had nine lives. Initially a Scottish surname, it crossed over to become a male first name. In the '50s it caught on as a girl's name with other peppy choices like Cindy and Denise. Today, the old Scottish surname roots are driving its popularity once more.

Leticia
1970s: #227
Popularity: #699
Style: African-American, Lacy
and Lissome
Nicknames: Tish, Tisha, Lettie
Variants: Letitia, Latisha, Laetitia, Laticia, Lettice
Sisters: Corinna, Roxanna, Livia, Yolanda, Demetria
Brothers: Cedric, Marcellus, Terrence, Reginald, Cornelius
★ One pronunciation gives you a whole spectrum of names. At one end is Laetitia: archaic, Roman, and white. At the other end, Latisha: modern, American, and black. Nestled in the middle is Leticia, the most common spelling with the broadest appeal.

Liberty
2002: #485
Popularity: #502
Style: Modern Meanings
Nicknames: Libby
Sisters: Journey, Lyric, America, Harmony, Skye
Brothers: Phoenix, Justice, Lincoln, River, Maverick
★ This meaning name was heard occasionally in the flower-child generation, then surfaced in large numbers in the wake of the 9/11 tragedies. Its message speaks with equal power to people at both ends of the political spectrum. The nickname Libby lightens the name perfectly for a baby girl.

Lila
1920s: #193
Popularity: #562
Style: Antique Charm, Little
Darlings, Nickname-Proof, Why Not?
Variants: Lyla
Sisters: Adela, Belle, Willa, Rose, Lena
Brothers: Ellis, Theo, Marshall, Jasper, Murphy
★ Lila is a name you want to say tenderly. It's simple and old-fashioned, yet seductive. A stylish selection.

Liliana
2003: #245
Popularity: #245
Style: Italian, Lacy and
Lissome, Latino/Latina
Nicknames: Lili, Lily
Sisters: Viviana, Natalia, Giselle, Paola, Mariela
Brothers: Marco, Fabian, Lorenzo, Dante, Sergio
★ The original Italian form of Lilian, Liliana has a gracious style that makes it universal.

Lilias

Popularity: Rare
Style: Celtic, Exotic Traditional,
Why Not?
Nicknames: Lily, Lil
Variants: Lileas, Lillias
Sisters: Ione, Elspeth, Davina, Sidony, Aisling
Brothers: Ivor, Alistair, Callum, Evander, Tavish
✦ This Scots Gaelic form of Lilian gives that sweet old name a fresh kick. It's an unknown in the U.S., but composed of familiar and fashionable elements that let it slide right into style.

rarely used

1900	Today

Lillian

Popularity: #77
Style: Antique Charm
Nicknames: Lillie, Lil
Variants: Lilian, Liliana
Sisters: Clara, Josephine, Eva, Violet, Eleanor
Brothers: Julius, Henry, Oliver, George, Everett
✦ A true turn-of-the-century classic. Graceful and dignified, Lillian is the perfect lady—and Lillie gives you a feisty alter ego. If you find that not everyone agrees with this assessment, see the discussion under Eleanor.

1900s: #13

1900	Today

Lily

Popularity: #69
Style: Antique Charm, Charms and Graces
Nicknames: Lil
Variants: Lillie, Lilly, Lilia
Sisters: Sophie, Ava, Isabel, Faith, Ivy
Brothers: Owen, Julian, Liam, Eli, Caleb
✦ Lily has become the darling of upscale parents. It's lively and delicate, with a classic femininity that doesn't feel forced. If you're looking for a quaint, unexpected choice, though, you should know that Lily is now racing to the top of the charts, with Lillian close behind.

2003: #69

1900	Today

Linda

Popularity: #412
Style: Mid-Century
Nicknames: Lynn, Lindy
Variants: Lynda
Sisters: Judith, Sandra, Susan, Carolyn, Diane
Brothers: Dennis, Roger, Gary, Bruce, Jerry
✦ Linda is legendary in baby-naming lore as the first name to pass Mary into the number-one spot. Its heyday is now long past—chances are you're looking up Linda because it's your mom's name rather than a top choice for your baby. But it's still a very pretty name (in fact, it's Spanish for "pretty"), and to your child's generation it will sound sweetly old-fashioned.

1940s: #2

1900	Today

Linden

Popularity: Rare
Style: Charms and Graces, The -ens
Nicknames: Lin, Lindy
Sisters: Larkin, Bay, Senna, Arden, Calla
Brothers: Brogan, Elkan, Birch, Corin, Archer
✦ A linden is a flowering tree. It could be a nature lover's reinterpretation of Linda, just as Laurel is for Laura.

rarely used

1900	Today

Lindsay

Popularity: #262
Style: '70s–'80s, Last Names First
Nicknames: Lin
Variants: Lindsey, Lyndsay, Lynsey, Linsey
Sisters: Whitney, Kristen, Danielle, Lacey, Bethany
Brothers: Derrick, Bradley, Brett, Wesley, Dustin
✦ In the wake of the '70s *Bionic Woman* icon Lindsay Wagner, this surname became a standard overnight. While Lindsay's popularity has plummeted, the name is still fashionable in sound and style. Kinsey, Laney, and Ainsley are among the hot new names walking in Lindsay's footsteps.

1980s: #47

1900	Today

Linnea

Popularity: Rare
Style: Exotic Traditional, Lacy and Lissome, Scandinavian, Why Not?
Nicknames: Lin, Nea
Variants: Linnéa, Linnaea
Sisters: Elsa, Rafaela, Amalia, Thora, Lavinia
Brothers: Simeon, Leif, Magnus, Elias, Nils
✦ This Swedish classic is pretty and serious, an attractive combination that should appeal far beyond its Scandinavian base. It even has both pretty and serious roots: The name is taken from a flower native to Sweden, which in turn was named for the great botanist Carl Linnaeus. The standard pronunciation is lin-AY-uh.

1900s: #819

1900	Today

Lisa

Popularity: #370
Style: Surfer Sixties
Nicknames: Lise
Variants: Liza, Leesa
Sisters: Tina, Denise, Julie, Teresa, Cindy
Brothers: Todd, Randy, Chris, Scott, Craig
✦ Lisa was the number-one girl's name of the 1960s. Unlike girlfriends Lori and Tina, though, it's not trapped in that era. Lisa is a classic with plenty of history: It was one of the top names for girls back in medieval Florence. It's not trendy right now, but clean and faultless.

1960s: #1

1900	Today

Lise 1950s: #994

Popularity: Rare
Style: Brisk and Breezy, French, Scandinavian, Why Not?
Variants: Lisette

Sisters: Kaye, Esme, Britt, Elin, Margot
Brothers: Rune, Brice, Marcel, Rand, Finn
✴ This international form of Lisa is disarmingly simple and uncommon. It gives you a fresh sound with traditional roots. The exact pronunciation is up to you: LEEZE is the most standard, but you'll also hear LEESE, LEESA, and LEEZA.

Liza 1970s: #424

Popularity: Rare
Style: '70–'80s, Guys and Dolls, Nicknames
Sisters: Holly, Tricia, Bess, Reva, Marlena
Brothers: Jamey, Brant, Jed, Lionel, Gabe
✴ Entertainer Liza Minelli single-handedly rescued this Elizabeth variant from the dustbin, and she's done us all a favor. Liza is cute and confident, a terrific combination.

Lizbeth 2002: #136

Popularity: #148
Style: Nicknames
Nicknames: Liz
Variants: Lisbeth
Sisters: Lauryn, Margit, Maribel, Tessa, Lise
Brothers: Brody, Jake, Gunnar, Griffith, Drew
✴ This contraction of Elizabeth is a sudden chart-topper. It cleverly splits the difference between the formality of Elizabeth and the plainness of Liz. The sheer density of sounds makes it a bit of a tongue-twister, though. Consider also the Scottish contraction Elspeth.

Logan 2001: #305

Popularity: #351
Style: Androgynous, Celtic, Last Names First
Sisters: Harley, Kendall, Ashton, Carson, Hunter
Brothers: Quinn, Brennan, Tucker, Lane, Brock
✴ Logan sounds so virile on a boy that it's a surprise that it works well for girls, too. The models are Morgan and Jordan, which set the stage for this whole name style. A character on the soap opera *The Bold and the Beautiful*, referred to by her last name Logan, helped as well.

Lois 1920s: #21

Popularity: Rare
Style: Biblical, Solid Citizens
Sisters: Jean, Marjorie, Lorraine, Mavis, Betty
Brothers: Gordon, Lyle, Raymond, Howard, Roy
✴ It's a long shot, but here's hoping Lois makes a reappearance. Right now the name sounds like a nosy old neighbor kibitzing over a backyard fence. But think about the ageless zest of Lois Lane, tracking down Superman! Better yet, think of Lois as a trim little biblical classic that hasn't been heard in years.

Lola 1900s: #112

Popularity: #623
Style: Guys and Dolls
Sisters: Mae, Carmela, Florida, Roxie, Della
Brothers: Archie, Mack, Major, Theo, Rocco
✴ It's Lolita, all grown up! Lola has that same dangerous sensuality, but she's a strong, mature woman who knows what she wants—and is going to have fun getting it. That's old-fashioned girl power. In song, a Lola is in-your-face feminine: "What Lola wants, Lola gets"; "Her name was Lola, she was a showgirl"; and the Kinks' not-*quite*-feminine "lo-lo-lo-lo Lola."

Lorelei 1950s: #921

Popularity: Rare
Style: Exotic Traditional
Nicknames: Lori
Sisters: Lucinda, Margot, Evangeline, Ione, Salome
Brothers: Florian, Rand, Magnus, Leander, Hansel
✴ In old German legend, Lorelei was a beautiful siren who lured sailors to the rocks on the banks of the Rhine. In *Gentlemen Prefer Blondes*, Lorelei was Marilyn Monroe, and the risky rocks were diamonds. The name is extremely unusual, but its exotic style is instantly familiar.

Loretta 1930s: #88

Popularity: Rare
Style: Solid Citizens
Nicknames: Lori, Etta
Sisters: Rosalie, Roberta, Jeanette, Lorraine, Annetta
Brothers: Gene, Vernon, Roland, Bob, Gilbert
✴ In the '30s, this sounded lush and womanly like actress Loretta Young. Our movie stars are skinny and girlish today, and the name is out of style.

Lori

1960s: #16

Popularity: Rare
Style: Surfer Sixties
Variants: Laurie, Lorri
Sisters: Tammy, Sheri, Dawn, Beth, Tracey
Brothers: Greg, Todd, Chris, Tony, Scott

★ This nickname was a top-twenty smash in the '60s. It is now completely out of the picture, as today's parents are making the root Laura longer (Lauren, Laurel) rather than shorter. Still a fine nickname, though.

Lorraine

1920s: #55

Popularity: Rare
Style: Solid Citizens
Nicknames: Lori, Rain
Sisters: Maxine, Jeanne, Marjorie, Phyllis, Nadine
Brothers: Warren, Gene, Doyle, Gordon, Wendell

★ Lorraine comes from the name of a French province (the one thing it has in common with Brittany). You won't meet many young Lorraines, but the name's still worth a look. When your daughter's an artsy fifteen-year-old, she'll love the chance to adopt the nickname Rain.

Lottie

1900s: #118

Popularity: Rare
Style: Guys and Dolls, Nicknames
Variants: Lotte, Lotty
Sisters: Tillie, Nettie, Nell, Mae, Flossie
Brothers: Archie, Sol, Charley, Mose, Dock

★ This bubbly nickname paints a lovable picture of a young girl. Today it's a bit too cute to stand on its own, but charming as an everyday nickname. The usual full name is Charlotte; you can also consider Lieselotte or simply Lotte, a traditional full name in Scandinavia.

Louisa

1900s: #371

Popularity: Rare
Style: Ladies and Gentlemen, Saints, Why Not?
Nicknames: Lou, Lulu
Variants: Lovisa, Louise, Luisa
Sisters: Adela, Eleanor, Cecile, Maud, Josefa
Brothers: Edmund, Foster, Hugh, Jules, Clement

★ Louisa has always been a quiet shadow of the French Louise. Today, it's the version with all the potential. Louisa's ladylike rhythm lightens its rich sound and sets it up well for the twenty-first century. The impression is of old-fashioned warmth with intelligence, personified by *Little Women* author Louisa May Alcott.

Louise

1910s: #18

Popularity: Rare
Style: French, Ladies and Gentlemen
Nicknames: Lou, Lulu
Variants: Luise, Louisa
Sisters: Marion, Lucille, Beatrice, Harriet, Estelle
Brothers: Claude, Herman, Ernest, Arthur, Walter

★ During the long and dignified life of Louise, the name lost its continental elegance and settled into a cozy matronliness. It still has an old-fashioned charm but would be a retro choice today. See Louisa and Eloise for likelier versions of the name.

Lourdes

1960s: #347

Popularity: Rare
Style: Exotic Traditional, Latino/Latina
Nicknames: Lulu
Sisters: Luz, Pilar, Loreto, Altagracia, Madonna
Brothers: Josue, Rosario, Cruz, Salvador, Modesto

★ Lourdes, France, was the site of a famous apparition of the Virgin Mary. Like many names associated with the Virgin, it has been most popular in Spanish. The unusual rhythm of Lourdes makes it a particularly unconventional choice. It will be familiar to some as the name of Madonna's daughter.

Lucia

2003: #469

Popularity: #469
Style: Italian, Saints, Timeless, Why Not?
Nicknames: Lucy
Sisters: Helena, Paola, Eliza, Lydia, Emilia
Brothers: Roman, Angelo, Carlo, Ivan, Raphael

★ This pitch-perfect choice has a swinging international style and a cute, trendy persona. Two great names for the price of one! In fact, more than two, since you can also choose from several traditional pronunciations: the English LOO-sha, Italian loo-CHEE-a, and Spanish/Germanic loo-SEE-a.

Lucille

Popularity: 954
Style: Country & Western,
French, Ladies and Gentlemen
Nicknames: Lucy
Variants: Lucile, Lucilla, Lucia
Sisters: Estelle, Leonor, Ruby, Pauline, Louise
Brothers: Francis, Earl, Leonard, Roy, Harry

✳ Thanks to comedienne Lucille Ball, we tend to picture this name in the '40s and '50s. In fact, Lucille's day was largely past by that point. The name belongs to the earlier age of Estelle and Eleanor—she's their brassy southern cousin, come to shake things up a little.

1910s: #30
1900   Today

Lucinda

Popularity: Rare
Style: Mid-Century
Nicknames: Lucy, Cindy, Cinda
Variants: Lucia
Sisters: Marietta, Rosalind, Ramona, Suzanne, Louisa
Brothers: Randolph, Dwight, Denver, Frederick, Judson

✳ Lucinda is an old literary offshoot of Lucia, used by Cervantes and Molière. It sounds a little bit heavy today, but lovely Lucy lightens it right up. Singer Lucinda Williams adds a honky-tonk edge.

1950s: #294
1900   Today

Lucy

Popularity: #221
Style: Antique Charm, Guys and Dolls
Variants: Lucie, Lucia
Sisters: Annie, Ruby, Stella, Nora, Gracie
Brothers: Charlie, Leo, Harry, Oliver, Mose

✳ The numbers may look modest, but don't be fooled. Lucy's stealth hit among affluent, trend-setting urbanites who appreciate its sweetness and absolute lack of pretension. It's also a favorite in England and Scotland. Lucille has not risen with it, but Lucinda, Lucia, and Luciana are possibilities.

1900s: #71
1900   Today

Luna

Popularity: 885
Style: Little Darlings, Mythological, Why Not?
Sisters: Rhea, Allegra, Leda, Ione, Flora
Brothers: Bram, Foster, Jasper, Wolf, Carsten

✳ Misty, magical Luna is the goddess of the moon. That's a voluptuous image, yet the name is just four little letters with a gentle sound. A great choice for parents with a poetic heart and a practical head.

2003: #885
1900   Today

Luz

Popularity: #555
Style: Latino/Latina, Little Darlings
Nicknames: Lucha
Sisters: Joy, Milagros, Carmen, Blanca, Lupe
Brothers: Ramon, Gil, Efrain, Rene, Santos

✳ The Spanish word for "light" makes a delicate, airy classic. The only thing holding it back from broader use is that it sounds like the word "loose."

1940s: #186
1900   Today

Lydia

Popularity: #129
Style: Antique Charm, Biblical, Timeless
Nicknames: Liddy, Lida
Variants: Lidia
Sisters: Cecilia, Grace, Nina, Helena, Amelia
Brothers: Simon, Harrison, Lincoln, Victor, Henry

✳ Lydia is an elegant classic with a light touch. It is increasingly fashionable but still a long way from overused. Jump right in!

1900s: #111
1900   Today

Lynn

Popularity: Rare
Style: Brisk and Breezy, Mid-Century, Surfer Sixties
Variants: Lynne
Sisters: Sherry, Beth, Jill, Terry, Jan
Brothers: Kent, Barry, Robin, Jon, Dana

✳ Lynn was a mid-century mainstay, a boyish counterpart to Linda. It's uncommon on its own today but is still part of the sound of the times, thanks to hits like Katelynn and Ashlynn. For a change of pace, Lynn's sound is echoed in the Welsh names Brynn and Wynne.

1950s: #67
1900   Today

Lyra

Popularity: Rare
Style: Little Darlings, Why Not?
Sisters: Luna, Vega, Jael, Calla, Esme
Brothers: Triton, Cael, Luc, Niko, Sirius

✳ The constellation Lyra, the lyre, makes for a light, artistic name. Lyra is also familiar to readers as the heroine of *The Golden Compass* fantasy trilogy.

rarely used
1900   Today

Lyric
2003: #686

Popularity: #686
Style: African-American, Fanciful, Modern Meanings
Sisters: Cadence, Haven, Sky, Journey, Aria
Brothers: Orion, Phoenix, Sage, River, Tyme

✳ Lyric is a bit self-conscious as a name, but its intensity and verve win you over. Unlike most names lifted from the world of music (Melody, Harmony), this name is no marshmallow. It's pretty but tough, and utterly modern. Its exact date of birth as a name is 1994, in the film *Jason's Lyric*.

Mabel
1900s: #27

Popularity: Rare
Style: Guys and Dolls
Nicknames: May, Mabs
Variants: Maybelle, Mable
Sisters: Elsie, Bess, Ida, Madge, Pearl
Brothers: Bert, Archie, Ira, Dewey, Gus

✳ If you're seriously considering Mabel, I don't have to tell you that it hasn't been heard from in half a century. Or that it sounds like a sassy diner waitress from a Technicolor film. If you're considering Mabel, you know all that, and you like it. You're perfectly delighted to fly in the face of convention, and more power to you.

Mackenzie
2001: #41

Popularity: #46
Style: Androgynous, Celtic, Last Names First
Nicknames: Mac, Kenzie
Variants: Mckenzie, Makenzie
Sisters: Kennedy, Riley, Reagan, Mckenna, Madison
Brothers: Logan, Brennan, Mason, Donovan, Hunter

✳ Seventies sitcom star Mackenzie Phillips was named by her rock-star dad, John, in honor of singer Scott McKenzie. It was an unconventional, aggressively androgynous choice at the time. But a generation later, the name is thriving in the mainstream. It's the standard-bearer for a whole crop of elaborate Celtic surnames for girls.

Macy
2003: #219

Popularity: #219
Style: Bell Tones, Last Names First, Little Darlings
Variants: Macey, Macie, Maci
Sisters: Eden, Harley, Mia, Riley, Jada
Brothers: Lane, Bryson, Carson, Reece, Cooper

✳ Macy is the newest member of the girls' surname family that includes Tracy, Lacey, and Stacy. It is by far the most contemporary of the group, with a tough edge that the others can't match. Avid shoppers may consider Macy a department store name (and a perfect sister for Dayton and Hudson?).

Madeline
2001: #55

Popularity: #60
Style: Antique Charm
Nicknames: Maddy
Variants: Madeleine, Madilyn, Maddalena
Sisters: Isabelle, Angelina, Caroline, Lily, Sophia
Brothers: Julian, Pierce, Maxwell, Harrison, Sebastian

✳ Madeline is a classic that still sounds charmingly old-fashioned, even though it's more popular today than ever before. Ludwig Bemelman's beloved children's books have helped fuel the vogue for the name. Note that a little Maddy risks confusion with the many Madisons in the playground.

Madison
2001: #2

Popularity: #3
Style: Last Names First, Place Names, The -ens
Nicknames: Maddie
Variants: Maddison, Madisen, Madisyn, Madyson
Sisters: Sydney, Payton, Mackenzie, Brooklyn, Hailey
Brothers: Jackson, Logan, Dayton, Mason, Hunter

✳ When the mermaid in the 1984 movie *Splash* chose this name from a Manhattan street sign, it was a big joke. But it seems the film's youngest fans weren't laughing—they were taking notes. Two decades later, Madison is one of the top girls' names in the country. It hits a trendy trifecta of place name, surname, and androgyny, all with a traditional girl's nickname.

Mae

Popularity: Rare
Style: Charms and Graces, Guys and Dolls
Sisters: Bessie, Pearl, Lula, Nell, Rae
Brothers: Mose, Archie, Gus, Fritz, Abe

★ Read the entry for May, then crank up the volume a notch for the spirit of Mae West, the brassiest dame of them all. This attractive spelling was the dominant one in the 1800s and could be again today.

1900s: #62
1900　Today

Maeve

Popularity: #658
Style: Antique Charm, Celtic, Why Not?
Sisters: Brynn, Fiona, Niamh, Phoebe, Nola
Brothers: Rowan, Finn, Cael, Duncan, Pierce

★ Here's a strong, classic, and intensely Irish name seldom heard in America. Think of it as the Celtic Claire, with all of that name's gentle seriousness. Maeve is just starting to catch on in elite pockets of the U.S. It's the Ivy League Irish favorite.

2003: #658
1900　Today

Magdalena

Popularity: #915
Style: Biblical, Latino/Latina, Scandinavian, Slavic
Nicknames: Lena, Maggie, Magda
Variants: Magdalene, Maddalena
Sisters: Antonina, Tatiana, Renata, Paulina, Catalina
Brothers: Lorenzo, Antonio, Roman, Constantin, Dimitri

★ This Latinate form of Madeline is a bit of a mouthful, but striking and mysterious. The nicknames Maggie and Lena make it more accessible.

1900s: #485
1900　Today

Maggie

Popularity: #190
Style: Nicknames
Sisters: Josie, Callie, Lizzie, Ella, Mollie
Brothers: Will, Ben, Reuben, Sam, Oliver

★ Maggie's simple sweetness aims straight for your heart. As with Annie and Molly, the nickname's fun-loving style has made it a star, while the traditional source (Margaret) is taking a back seat.

1900s: #104
1900　Today

Magnolia

Popularity: Rare
Style: Charms and Graces, Country & Western
Nicknames: Maggie, Nola, Meg
Sisters: Winona, Violet, Clementine, Shenandoah, Carolina
Brothers: Richmond, Beauregard, Raleigh, Lafayette, Crawford

★ If you're a true son or daughter of the South, this old-fashioned beauty is bound to catch your eye. It's a bit of a showboat, but simple nicknames like Maggie and Nola take some of the pressure off.

1910s: #539
1900　Today

Maia

Popularity: #551
Style: Little Darlings, Mythological
Variants: Maya
Sisters: Zoe, Anya, Thalia, Iris, Phoebe
Brothers: Miles, Eli, Nico, Abel, Noel

★ Maya is the more common spelling, but Maia has a longer history as a name. It was the name of the Roman goddess of Spring and growth.

2002: #535
1900　Today

Maisie

Popularity: Rare
Style: Celtic, Nicknames
Variants: Mazie
Sisters: Effie, Elspeth, Greer, Bess, Nellie
Brothers: Angus, Archie, Hamish, Mose, Ramsey

★ This is a name so cute and impish you just want to pinch its cheeks. Maisie is an old Scottish nickname for Margaret (or the Gaelic form Mairead), and would make a charming alternative to Maggie.

rarely used
1900　Today

Makayla

Popularity: #51
Style: Bell Tones
Nicknames: Kay, Kayla
Variants: Michaela, Makaila, Mikaela, Mikayla, McKayla
Sisters: Katelynn, Madelyn, Brianna, Alexia, Haleigh
Brothers: Braden, Kyler, Jalen, Kaleb, Kameron

★ Makayla is a creative new spelling that has far outpaced the traditional Michaela. It's closer in spirit to surnames like Mckenna and innovations like Kaylee.

2003: #51
1900　Today

Mallory

Popularity: #234
Style: Androgynous, Last Names First, Nickname-Proof
Sisters: Aubrey, Lindsey, Morgan, Meredith, Hayley
Brothers: Jarrett, Brennan, Addison, Brady, Drew

1990s: #181

✱ Mallory was an obscure, mostly male name until the '80s, when its melodious sound and a character on the sitcom *Family Ties* boosted it into the female mainstream. The name's rhythm, mimicking favorites from Valerie to Hillary, makes it sound more common and familiar than it is.

Mara

Popularity: #639
Style: Biblical, Little Darlings, Nickname-Proof
Variants: Marah
Sisters: Lena, Ava, Mariah, Sarai, Dara
Brothers: Abel, Eli, Markus, Ari, Carson

2002: #611

✱ Mara has come into style in sync with Maya and Mia, but its personality is quieter. This biblical name's hallmark is restraint, a quality that makes it sound timeless.

Marcella

Popularity: Rare
Style: Italian, Lacy and Lissome, Saints, Why Not?
Nicknames: Marcie, Markie, Ella, Chela
Variants: Marcela, Marcelle
Sisters: Carmela, Marietta, Angeline, Geneva, Antonia
Brothers: Rocco, Salvatore, Roland, Gilbert, Clifton

1920s: #171

✱ Choose your favorite Marcella: pronounced Mar-CHELL-a, it's lavishly Italian and a particular favorite in Rome. As Mar-SELL-a, it's a soft-spoken old American favorite.

Marcia

Popularity: Rare
Style: Mid-Century
Nicknames: Marcie
Variants: Marsha
Sisters: Glenda, Diane, Janis, Maureen, Gail
Brothers: Allen, Dennis, Roger, Jerry, Garry

1940s: #87

✱ Marcia's soft sound made it a mid-century sweetheart but now sends parents running the other way. It's a pleasant enough name, just swimming against the fashion tide. If you're looking for a trendier way to feminize Mark, try Marcella.

Marcy

Popularity: Rare
Style: Nicknames, Surfer Sixties
Variants: Marci, Marcie
Sisters: Trina, Jodie, Darcy, Karin, Dina
Brothers: Robbie, Curt, Tim, Donny, Darren

1970s: #338

✱ Marcy is one of the youthful '60s names that belongs in an endless summer.

Margaret

Popularity: #130
Style: Timeless
Nicknames: Meg, Peg, Margie, Maggie, Madge, Maisie, Greta, Megan, May, Maj, Meta
Variants: Margarita, Marguerite, Margit, Margot, Margery
Sisters: Catherine, Mary, Cecilia, Miriam, Ruth
Brothers: George, Edward, Henry, James, Charles

1910s: #4

✱ Margaret, Katherine, and Elizabeth are the timeless English trio. They're long but not showy, with bushels of nickname options to allow your personal touch. Yet, unlike her style sisters, Margaret has been slipping out of notice the past forty years. Time to bring on the Maggies! Or Megs, or Gretas, or Maisies . . .

Margarita

Popularity: #828
Style: Latino/Latina, Timeless
Nicknames: Rita, Marita, Marguita
Variants: Margherita, Marguerite, Margaretha
Sisters: Carmen, Rosemary, Gloria, Josefina, Angelita
Brothers: Ramon, Fredrick, Marlin, Alberto, Lorenzo

1930s: #225

✱ Margarita is an old-fashioned classic with a flirtatious style—ingredients that should add up to a smash. But if the ingredients that spring to your mind are tequila and lime, you've hit on the problem. Here's hoping the name's gracious style overcomes its alcoholic associations.

Margo
1950s: #362

Popularity: Rare
Style: Mid-Century, Nickname-Proof, Why Not?
Variants: Margot, Margaux
Sisters: Marianne, Gwen, Janis, Nan, Aurea
Brothers: Hal, Jerome, Stuart, Rex, Stanton
✴ The unusual "o" ending gives Margo character and makes the name virtually trend-proof. It's one classic that will never get lost in the crowd. The European spelling Margot can be pronounced with a silent or spoken "t."

Marguerite
1900s: #82

Popularity: Rare
Style: African-American, French, Ladies and Gentlemen, Saints
Nicknames: Margot
Sisters: Beatrice, Antoinette, Estelle, Cordelia, Genevieve
Brothers: Clement, Bertrand, Julius, Claude, Domenick
✴ The French form of Margaret was once an everyday choice in America. It's been gone long enough to shake off its slumber and reemerge with renewed grace and polish.

Maria
1960s: #32

Popularity: #40
Style: Biblical, Italian, Latino/Latina, Timeless
Nicknames: Ria, Mimi, Mai, Mia, Mari, Masha
Variants: Mariah
Sisters: Angela, Teresa, Sonia, Michele, Diana
Brothers: David, José, Roberto, Stephen, Marcus
✴ Timeless Maria is a classic favorite in languages from Spanish to Swedish, Polish to Portuguese. In the U.S., it is most commonly associated with Spanish and Italian, but it makes a handsome choice for girls of any heritage.

Mariah
1990s: #78

Popularity: #115
Style: Antique Charm, Lacy and Lissome, Nickname-Proof
Variants: Maria
Sisters: Michaela, Emilee, Sierra, Marissa, Carolina
Brothers: Caleb, Alec, Austin, Josiah, Darius
✴ An antique variation on Maria, this name was seldom heard before singer Mariah Carey came on the scene. It is traditional, though, and a pretty choice, whether or not you're a fan of Carey's.

Marian
1920s: #71

Popularity: Rare
Style: Ladies and Gentlemen, Solid Citizens, Why Not?, Nickname-Proof
Variants: Marion
Sisters: Cecile, Willa, June, Margery, Elinor
Brothers: Willis, Edmund, Foster, Hugh, Benedict
✴ Marion was originally a French name, Marian its English version. While the names are pronounced the same and have a similar history of use in the U.S., the effect they make is subtly different. Marian's roots in medieval England, including Robin Hood's Maid Marian, give it an especially soft, romantic cast with great comeback potential.

Mariana
2003: #244

Popularity: #244
Style: Lacy and Lissome, Latino/Latina, Saints, Shakespearean
Nicknames: Mari, Maria
Variants: Marianna
Sisters: Natalia, Valeria, Annika, Adriana, Liliana
Brothers: Rodrigo, Fabian, Diego, Mateo, Lorenzo
✴ A lyrical Latina hit with big potential for girls of all backgrounds. With its familiar "Mari" root, Mariana's like an old friend after a diet and makeover. And if anyone asks how you thought of it, tell them you've been reading Shakespeare — it's a favorite choice in his comedies.

Marianne
1950s: #189

Popularity: Rare
Style: French, Solid Citizens
Nicknames: Mari
Sisters: Therese, Gayle, Rosalind, Jeannine, Janis
Brothers: Gerard, Van, Wendell, Randolph, Laurence
✴ This Frenchified version of Marian has been familiar in English for centuries. Starting in the 1940s, it supplanted Marian as the standard American choice. Parents back then thought it sounded more feminine and sophisticated — exactly how parents feel about the Spanish/Italian Mariana today. All three versions remain solid, attractive choices.

Maribel 1970s: #300

Popularity: #841
Style: Latino/Latina, Why Not?
Sisters: Beatriz, Simone, Marisol, Juliet, Graciela
Brothers: Orlando, Javier, Tobias, Aldo, Judah
✷ This pretty and delicate Spanish name should be high on the list of Isabel and Annabel fans.

Marie 1900s: #8

Popularity: #496
Style: Biblical, French, Solid Citizens
Nicknames: Manon
Variants: Maria, Mary
Sisters: Irene, Eva, Rose, Lucy, Alice
Brothers: Albert, Carl, Louis, Roy, Francis
✷ This cheerful French form of Maria was the source, ages ago, for the English name Mary. Marie itself has been adopted so thoroughly into our language that it no longer sounds especially French. These days the name is most often bumped down a slot and selected as a middle name.

Mariela 2003: #608

Popularity: #608
Style: Lacy and Lissome, Latino/Latina, Why Not?
Variants: Mariella, Mariel
Sisters: Viviana, Thalia, Carina, Natalia, Liliana
Brothers: Rodrigo, Mateo, Fabian, Jaron, Alvaro
✷ Mariela is a Spanish diminutive of Mary. It's a favorite in South America, especially Argentina, but has only recently become familiar in the U.S. This exceptionally graceful name will appeal across cultures, like rising stars Gabriela and Natalia.

Marietta 1920s: #438

Popularity: Rare
Style: Lacy and Lissome, Place Names
Nicknames: Etta, Mara, Mia
Variants: Marieta, Mariette
Sisters: Rafaela, Geneva, Adela, Georgia, Josephina
Brothers: Benedict, Raleigh, Grady, Garland, Fletcher
✷ This pet form of Maria has a delicacy that could bring it back into contention. It's also the name of a Georgia city, a connection that has done wonders for Savannah.

Marilyn 1930s: #16

Popularity: #550
Style: Solid Citizens
Variants: Marilynn, Marylyn
Sisters: Barbara, Joyce, Beverly, Marlene, Gloria
Brothers: Gene, Donald, Franklin, Gerald, Roger
✷ Doesn't Marilyn have a perfectly contemporary sound? It's a smooth hybrid of Madison, Kaitlyn, and Caroline; what could be trendier? Of course, we can't really hear it that way because every Marilyn we know is eligible for AARP membership. As attractive as the name is, most of us are stuck picturing it as an awkward mixture of grandma's canasta partners and Marilyn Monroe in her heyday.

Marina 1990s: #260

Popularity: #399
Style: Italian, Saints, Shakespearean, Timeless
Nicknames: Mari, Mia, Mina, Rina
Sisters: Camille, Tatiana, Juliet, Elena, Miranda
Brothers: Antonio, Adrian, Raphael, Quentin, Ivan
✷ This sophisticated name has near-universal appeal. It gives you classical origins, Shakespearean pedigree, and a romantic association with the sea. Need more? How about international appeal: Marina is used as a Scottish form of Mary, and Saint Marinas have hailed from Spain, Turkey, and Japan. A little Marina will fit in handsomely the world over.

Marisol 1970s: #291

Popularity: #386
Style: Latino/Latina
Nicknames: Mari, Mai, Misa
Sisters: Damaris, Raquel, Graciela, Noemi, Maribel
Brothers: Rolando, Javier, Mario, Armando, Marco
✷ This is a have-it-all name: sexy, serious, and sophisticated, without attitude problems. It's a modern classic for Spanish-speaking families, a creative alternative for others.

Marissa 1990s: #62
Popularity: #98
Style: Lacy and Lissome
Nicknames: Mari, Missy
Variants: Marisa

1900 Today
Sisters: Angelica, Gabriela, Miranda, Alexa, Cassandra
Brothers: Brendan, Spencer, Colin, Tristan, Garrett
★ The new Melissa. Marissa is a lively, lacy favorite born in the twentieth century. The spelling Marisa gives it a Spanish/Italian slant, while the double S version plays up the frills.

Marjorie 1920s: #20
Popularity: Rare
Style: Solid Citizens, Why Not?
Nicknames: Marj, Margie, Jo
Variants: Margery, Marjory
1900 Today
Sisters: Marian, June, Dorothy, Rosemary, Vivian
Brothers: Harris, Lyle, Campbell, Warren, Russell
★ Marjorie boomed, ebbed, then vanished during the twentieth century, yet it doesn't sound old. Instead, it sounds like a creative alternative to Stephanie or Melanie. Especially attractive is the antique spelling Margery (as in the nursery rhyme "See-Saw, Margery Daw"), which lets you choose from Margaret's smorgasbord of nicknames.

Marlene 1930s: #63
Popularity: #512
Style: Mid-Century
Nicknames: Marly, Marlee, Lena
Variants: Marlena
1900 Today
Sisters: Sondra, Joanne, Rosemarie, Elsa, Margot
Brothers: Gerald, Franklin, Wayne, Dwight, Karl
★ Marlene is a German name, a contraction of Maria Magdalene made famous by actress Marlene Dietrich. For Dietrich, it was three syllables, "mar-LAY-na." If you know an American Marlene, though, you most likely know a "mar-LEEN." The pronunciation is key: The American version is fading like Darlene, the German still fashionable like Elena.

Marley 2003: #582
Popularity: #582
Style: Last Names First, Nickname-Proof
Sisters: Madisyn, Ansley, Rylie, Piper, Zaria
1900 Today
Brothers: Easton, Paxton, Reece, Davion, Zion
★ Like Macy, a cheerfully tough surname that grows up handsomely. But most unlike Macy, which conjures up shopping and Thanksgiving parades, Marley conjures up the Rasta and reggae world of music legend Bob Marley.

Marlo 1970s: #620
Popularity: Rare
Style: Nickname-Proof, Surfer Sixties
Nicknames: Marly
1900 Today
Variants: Marlowe
Sisters: Trina, Dionne, Jill, Darcy, Jody
Brothers: Tad, Tobin, Scotty, Lorne, Baron
★ Everyone is familiar with this name, but how many of us have met a Marlo in the flesh? Despite the '60s vogue of "That Girl" Marlo Thomas, Marlo has remained a pleasant rarity. The surname spelling Marlowe gives it a more dramatic literary style.

Martha 1910s: #25
Popularity: #487
Style: Biblical, Ladies and Gentlemen
Nicknames: Marty, Mattie, Patsy
1900 Today
Variants: Marta
Sisters: Alice, Edith, Rosa, Ann, Margaret
Brothers: Frederick, Walter, Roy, Carl, Lawrence
★ Parents who find themselves drawn to George should give Martha a second look. It has that same no-frills appeal that frees you from the shackles of passing fashion. The most prominent Martha of recent times, tastemaker Martha Stewart, suffered a very public demise that could have sunk lesser names. But this stalwart classic will pull through just fine.

Martina 1980s: #679
Popularity: Rare
Style: Timeless
Nicknames: Marty, Tina
Sisters: Renata, Audra, Marcela,
1900 Today
Mariel, Daria
Brothers: Marcus, Carlo, Anton, Jude, Ivan
★ This dignified classic has Latin origins and Renaissance style, all filtered through the strings of a tennis racquet. Center-court legend Martina Navratilova and her namesake Martina Hingis make this a power serve of a name.

Mary

1920s: #1

1900 Today

Popularity: #61
Style: Biblical, Timeless
Nicknames: Molly, Mamie, May, Mitzi, Polly
Variants: Maria, Marie
Sisters: Margaret, Catherine, Martha, Rosa, Anne
Brothers: John, Charles, George, Edward, Paul

✷ The most popular girl's name of the twentieth century. And the nineteenth, and the eighteenth . . . but the Grand Old Name is remarkably uncommon in century twenty-one. Modern parents have shied away from Mary precisely because of its past popularity. Ironically, that now gives you the opportunity to choose the name as a distinctive fashion statement. It is warm, pretty, and the ultimate "back-to-basics" classic.

Matilda

1900s: #177

1900 Today

Popularity: Rare
Style: Ladies and Gentlemen, Saints
Nicknames: Tilda, Tillie, Mattie
Variants: Mathilda, Mathilde
Sisters: Adelaide, Louisa, Aurelia, Maude, Beatrice
Brothers: Leopold, Rudolph, Ambrose, Bertram, Foster

✷ In France and Scandinavia, Matilda/Mathilde is a hot name, a stylish sister for Sophie or Isabel. In the U.S., its image as a dusty antique still lingers. Consider this chance to be ahead of the curve. Matilda's brightest days could still be ahead.

Mattea

rarely used

1900 Today

Popularity: Rare
Style: Lacy and Lissome, Why Not?
Nicknames: Mattie
Sisters: Chiara, Danila, Rafaela, Linnea, Marietta
Brothers: Enzo, Bram, Marius, Maddox, Carlo

✷ An old Italian offshoot of Matthew, Mattea sounds trendy, yet is virtually unknown. A smart, snappy discovery.

Maude

1900s: #103

1900 Today

Popularity: Rare
Style: Ladies and Gentlemen
Nicknames: Maudie
Variants: Maud
Sisters: Olive, Augusta, Viola, Belle, Thora
Brothers: Claude, Jules, Otto, Luther, August

✷ Maude is a dignified classic with two strikes against it. First is its bluntness, which doesn't sound particularly feminine to modern ears. Second is the '70s Bea Arthur sitcom with its stick-in-your-head theme song. ("And then there's Maude . . .") Maude remains regal and distinctive, but it's far from fashionable.

Maura

2001: #678

1900 Today

Popularity: #789
Style: Celtic, Nickname-Proof, Saints
Sisters: Bridget, Nola, Deirdre, Brenna, Dara
Brothers: Kelvin, Rory, Bryan, Murphy, Garret

✷ Maura is a Celtic classic especially favored by Irish-American parents. Its style is gentle and serious, more contemporary than the more familiar Maureen.

Maureen

1950s: #101

1900 Today

Popularity: Rare
Style: Celtic, Mid-Century
Nicknames: Mo, Reenie
Variants: Maurine
Sisters: Glenda, Kathleen, Gail, Suzanne, Roseanne
Brothers: Douglas, Garry, Duane, Kenneth, Roger

✷ In the '40s–'50s heyday of Irish screen beauty Maureen O'Hara, this name was the glamorous favorite of Irish-American families. Its decline was swift—so swift that it's already sounding interesting again. Not trendy, certainly, but spirited, especially paired with a perfect surname like O'Hara. Also consider the svelter Maura.

Maxine

1920s: #82

1900 Today

Popularity: Rare
Style: Solid Citizens
Nicknames: Maxie
Sisters: Rosalie, Margot, Lorraine, Jeanne, Helene
Brothers: Roland, Gordon, Marvin, Doyle, Jerome

✷ Maxine was a glamour name in the '20s, and it's easy to see why. It sounded modern and sassy in a world full of Marthas and Ediths. Today, in a world of Madisons and Savannahs, Maxine is out of step. It should be ready for a fresh look in another generation.

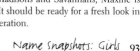

May

Popularity: Rare
Style: Charms and Graces, Why Not?
Sisters: Belle, Iva, Bess, Dove, Violet
Brothers: Theo, Ben, Clyde, Jess, Charley

1900s: #120

★ A wee and lovely turn-of-the-century name that has escaped popular attention. May's sunlit optimism makes a natural alternative (or sister) for Hope. Also, be sure to consider the spelling Mae, which is less rooted to the common word.

Maya

Popularity: #85
Style: Little Darlings, Nickname-Proof
Variants: Maia
Sisters: Zoe, Ava, Jada, Chloe, Nadia
Brothers: Liam, Noah, Ian, Carter, Miles

2003: #85

★ Maya feels familiar and timeless, but in fact it's a fairly new creation that seems to have come out of nowhere. (The best-known Maya, writer Angelou, was christened Marguerite.) With its warm vibes of goddesses and sunshine, expect this name to stick around for a good long time. See also: Maia.

Mckenna

Popularity: #194
Style: Celtic, Last Names First
Nicknames: Kenna
Variants: Makenna
Sisters: Delaney, Cassidy, Kiara, Kendall, Macy
Brothers: Keegan, Donovan, Camden, Kane, Cooper

2002: #180

★ Mckenna is a twin sister to Mackenzie, but not identical. Like most twins, they mirror each other but carve out their own niches of style. Where Mackenzie is playful and boyish, Mckenna is more traditionally feminine on the model of cousin Makayla. The pet form Kenna could stand on its own as a given name, too.

Meadow

Popularity: #769
Style: Charms and Graces, Modern Meanings
Sisters: Lyric, Haven, Harmony, Willow, Lark
Brothers: River, Stone, Shadow, Frost, Heath

2003: #769

★ This nature name is a gentle free spirit. It had a flower-child aura until the TV series *The Sopranos* gave the name a Jersey gangster spin.

Megan

Popularity: #30
Style: Celtic, New Classics, The -ens
Nicknames: Meg
Variants: Meagan, Meghan, Meaghan
Sisters: Lauren, Caitlin, Jenna, Morgan, Allison
Brothers: Ryan, Brandon, Colin, Sean, Kyle

1990s: #10

★ Megan started off in Wales as a pet form of Margaret but has found huge popularity as a U.S. given name. The alternate spelling Meaghan, which gives the name an Irish look, is in fact a modern American creation. Also consider Bethan, a similar Welsh take on Elizabeth.

Mehitabel

Popularity: Rare
Style: Biblical, Exotic Traditional
Nicknames: Bella, Mel, Hettie
Sisters: Hermione, Zilla, Leocadia, Guinevere, Amabel
Brothers: Jedidiah, Barnabas, Algernon, Simeon, Phineas

rarely used

★ This name may be unrealistic for most families. But if you just love Madeline and Isabel and just can't bear the thought of a popular name, this whimsical rarity is an option. Mehitabel is chiefly known—among those who know it at all—as an alley cat who kept company with a literary cockroach named Archy.

Melanie

Popularity: #94
Style: French, New Classics
Nicknames: Mel, Melly
Variants: Melany, Melania
Sisters: Andrea, Leslie, Valerie, Meredith, Cara
Brothers: Bradley, Erik, Marc, Jeremy, Derek

1970s: #56

★ A rare medieval French saint's name. What, that's not your image of Melanie? Then thank *Gone With the Wind*, which brought the name to America's notice—it's been a standard ever since. Thoroughly likable and unaffected.

Melia

Popularity: Rare
Style: Lacy and Lissome, Mythological
Variants: Meliya, Maleia
Sisters: Stefania, Danae, Luna, Despina, Calla
Brothers: Tobin, Aris, Leander, Rider, Rex

rarely used

★ Melia was a nymph in Greek mythology. Feel free to pass that tidbit on to people who think you've just messed up the name Amelia. The two names sound similar, but Melia has a more modern style. If you prefer to pronounce it me-LEE-ya, consider the alternate spellings.

Melina

Popularity: #609
Style: Greek, Lacy and Lissome,
Why Not?
Nicknames: Mel, Lina
Sisters: Thalia, Katerina, Mariela, Alana, Mariana
Brothers: Griffin, Dimitri, Holden, Andreas, Lukas

2001: #494
1900 Today

✴ From the Greek word for "honey," Melina is as smooth and sweet as its meaning suggests. Despite its mainstream sound, this name has never been widely used in the U.S. It is mostly known as the name of two actresses of Greek heritage: Melina Mercouri and Melina Kanakaredes.

Melinda

Popularity: Rare
Style: '70s–'80s, Lacy and Lissome
Nicknames: Mindy, Mel, Lindy
Variants: Malinda
Sisters: Tamara, Melissa, Rochelle, Christy, Deanna
Brothers: Brent, Shannon, Michael, Geoffrey, Derrick

1970s: #90
1900 Today

✴ A mellifluous name created in the 1800s when the "-inda" ending was the height of romance. Melinda's popularity peaked in the 1970s, and the nickname Mindy (à la sitcom *Mork & Mindy*) is still planted firmly in the Me Decade. If you're looking for nickname alternatives, Mel is the rising choice and Lindy a quiet charmer. Also consider the full name Melina, which shares the same Greek root and smooth style.

Melissa

Popularity: #97
Style: '70s–'80s, Lacy and Lissome, New Classics
Nicknames: Missy, Mel, Lissa
Variants: Melisa, Malissa
Sisters: Heather, Amy, Melinda, Jennifer, Christina
Brothers: Brian, Jeremy, Chad, Shawn, Jeffrey

1970s: #3
1900 Today

✴ Melissa was the lacy sound of the '70s. It's still as sweet as ever, and a host of new hits pays homage to the name's delicate rhythm. Together, Carissa, Alyssa, Larissa, and Marissa make up a Melissa tribute band.

Melody

Popularity: #303
Style: Modern Meanings
Nicknames: Mel
Variants: Melodie
Sisters: Kimberly, Laurel, Summer, Melinda, Renee
Brothers: Lance, Marc, Colin, Geoffrey, Brett

1960s: #192
1900 Today

✴ This name waltzed into America's hearts hand in hand with Melanie. The two sound similar enough to be confused, but the musical associations of Melody make it at once frothier and more tender.

Mercedes

Popularity: #333
Style: Latino/Latina
Nicknames: Meche, Mercy, Sadie
Sisters: Guadalupe, Alejandra, Madeleine, Bianca, Valeria
Brothers: Bernardo, Emilio, Salvador, Dominick, Vicente

1990s: #187
1900 Today

✴ This lovely name, meaning "mercies," comes from a title for the Virgin Mary. Of course, you could just as well say, "This lovely car, meaning status, comes from Germany." The automotive association is now so strong that people may consider this a brand name like Lexus or Armani. Other reverent names to consider include Milagros, Altagracia, and Socorro.

Mercy

Popularity: Rare
Style: Charms and Graces, Timeless, Why Not?
Nicknames: Merce, Merry
Variants: Merce
Sisters: Amity, Joy, Ruth, Violet, Calla
Brothers: Forrest, Christian, Gideon, Judah, Merit

rarely used
1900 Today

✴ This Puritan favorite has been mysteriously overlooked by modern parents. Its generous spirit compares well with current favorites Faith and Hope, and its sound is effortlessly contemporary.

Meredith

Popularity: #361
Style: Androgynous, New Classics
Nicknames: Merry, Mere
Sisters: Tabitha, Alison, Bethany, Cara, Mallory
Brothers: Jared, Bryant, Christopher, Brennan, Damon

1980s: #156

★ Here's a good one to consider if you and your partner are deadlocked on names. Looking for a hushed, gentle name to whisper to your sweet baby? Meredith. A modern-sounding choice with an androgynous edge? Meredith. A comfortable old favorite with a cute nickname? You get the idea. A name for all seasons.

Merry

Popularity: Rare
Style: Charms and Graces, Mid-Century
Variants: Meri
Sisters: Bonnie, Cinda, Gale, Constance, Patty
Brothers: Donnie, Roger, Garry, Mickey, Skip

1950s: #558

★ Merry's upbeat meaning charmed parents two generations ago, when jolly names like Cherry and Bonnie were frequently heard. It was especially favored for births in the Christmas season. Joy is another happy Yuletide option.

Meta

Popularity: Rare
Style: German/Dutch, Little Darlings, Nicknames, Scandinavian
Sisters: Mina, Lida, Vita, Elsa, Thora
Brothers: Anton, Fritz, Magnus, Joss, Nils

1900s: #371

★ A German nickname for Margareta, Meta was stylish in the 1890s. It's unfamiliar enough today that it may sound more like a prefix than a name.

Mia

Popularity: #35
Style: Little Darlings, Nickname-Proof
Sisters: Zoe, Jada, Ava, Sofia, Lily
Brothers: Liam, Gavin, Aidan, Eli, Cole

2003: #35

★ This little charmer of a name was quietly stylish until the ascent of soccer star Mia Hamm. Today, forget quiet—picture a raucous playroom full of little Mias. Like Hamm herself, the name suggests a modern All-American girl: the delightful dynamo.

Michaela

Popularity: #237
Style: Antique Charm
Nicknames: Mickey, Kayla, Kaelie, Mica, Mischa, Mike
Variants: Michela, Makayla, Mikayla, Micaela
Sisters: Carolina, Mariah, Alexandra, Daniella, Madeline
Brothers: Alec, Maxwell, Chandler, Caleb, Dalton

1990s: #145

★ This feminine form of Michael was extremely uncommon until the countless Mikes of the mid-century started having daughters. Then TV's Dr. Quinn, Medicine Woman put it over the top. The original spelling Michaela still has an antique flavor, but it's been overtaken by the trendy modern variant Makayla (see separate entry).

Michelle

Popularity: #62
Style: '70s–'80s, French, New Classics
Nicknames: Missy, Chelle, Shelly
Variants: Michele
Sisters: Kimberly, Melissa, Amy, Stephanie, Stacey
Brothers: Brian, Marc, Jeffrey, Eric, Kevin

1970s: #4

★ Michelle is no longer the French "belle" the Beatles sang about in the '60s. It's entering a second generation as an all-American girl. As a feminine form of Michael, Michelle is now rivaled by Michaela. It's still the number-one favorite of Asian Americans, boosted by skater Michelle Kwan and golfer Michelle Wie.

Mildred

Popularity: Rare
Style: Porch Sitters
Nicknames: Millie
Sisters: Gladys, Myrtle, Edna, Bernice, Ethel
Brothers: Wilbur, Irving, Lester, Floyd, Willard

1910s: #6

★ Mildred was once a smash hit, but her day is done. If you love the nickname Millie, try Amelia or Millicent.

Millicent

Popularity: Rare
Style: Ladies and Gentlemen
Nicknames: Millie
Sisters: Dorothea, Harriet, Winifred, Elinor, Eloise
Brothers: Ernest, Sylvester, Clarence, Frederick, Chester

1920s: #484

★ The queen of the old-lady names. It's hard to picture a Millicent in little girl's pigtails instead of white hair . . . but if you manage, it's a surprisingly adorable image. This is a long shot that could pay off handsomely.

Mimi

1960s: #888

Popularity: Rare
Style: Mid-Century, Nicknames
Sisters: Mitzi, Barbie, Debi, Nanette, Kiki
Brothers: Dino, Rod, Monty, Rico, Duke

★ Mimi is a pet form of Maria or Mary, and the heroine of *La Bohème*. Like Fifi and Gigi, this name tends to make Americans giggle a bit. But it still makes a fun, freewheeling nickname.

Mindy

1970s: #192

Popularity: Rare
Style: '70s–'80s, Nicknames
Sisters: Kristy, Tricia, Amy, Marcie, Shana
Brothers: Jamey, Brent, Dusty, Bryan, Shaun

★ Mindy swept through America in the '70s, usually as a nickname but often enough on its own. This kind of spun-sugar name is sweet for a girl but can be insubstantial for a grown woman. The current preference is to stick with Melinda or Miranda on the birth certificate.

Minerva

1900s: #423

Popularity: Rare
Style: Exotic Traditional, Ladies and Gentlemen, Mythological
Nicknames: Mina
Sisters: Althea, Zelda, Evangeline, Avis, Hermione
Brothers: Philo, Cornelius, Linus, Casper, Hermes

★ Minerva doesn't sound like a young girl's name. It has a stern, gray-haired demeanor. Yet the name's mythical, magical style (the Roman goddess of wisdom) helps it shine above other old-lady names. It could be a striking choice for a fantasy aficionado.

Mira

2003: #985

Popularity: #985
Style: Little Darlings, Nickname-Proof, Slavic
Variants: Myra
Sisters: Anya, Jolie, Tisa, Katia, Lyra
Brothers: Joah, Nico, Lev, Jair, Marek

★ Pronounced MEE-ra, Mira's a gentle little beauty with a contemporary style. If you prefer MY-ra, spell it with the "y" to avoid confusion and gain a Scottish flavor.

Miracle

2003: #493

Popularity: #493
Style: Fanciful, Modern Meanings
Sisters: Heaven, Genesis, Harmony, Essence, Destiny
Brothers: Justice, Sage, Shadow, Chance, Phoenix

★ Miracle has only recently been adopted as an English given name. It's a passionate, emotional choice, and some people may be discomfited by its intensity. Unlike the Spanish Milagros, which is a general celebration of divine miracles, the name Miracle tends to focus on the baby girl herself. It's often chosen in cases where the child represents a triumph over adversity, such as infertility or premature birth.

Miranda

1990s: #83

Popularity: #160
Style: Lacy and Lissome, New Classics, Shakespearean
Nicknames: Mandy, Randi, Mindy, Mira, Mimi
Variants: Maranda, Myranda
Sisters: Sabrina, Diana, Ariel, Gabriela, Adriana
Brothers: Colin, Zachary, Lucas, Nathaniel, Spencer

★ Shakespeare conjured up this name to sound beautiful, strong, and all-around admirable. Darned if the guy didn't know what he was doing, too. Four centuries later, that image is still holding strong.

Miriam

1910s: #150

Popularity: #290
Style: Biblical, Jewish, Timeless
Nicknames: Mira, Mimi, Miri
Variants: Miryam, Maryam
Sisters: Naomi, Esther, Leora, Nina, Ruth
Brothers: Reuben, George, Saul, Julius, Henry

★ Miriam has been one of the steadiest biblical names for girls. The name sounds responsible, so it's natural to picture Miriam as a successful professional. But beneath the practicality is the sense of a gentle and intuitive individual. Perfect for a pediatrician, judge, or sociology professor.

Misty

1970s: #78

Popularity: Rare
Style: '70s–'80s, Modern Meanings
Variants: Misti
Sisters: Christal, Sunny, Desiree, Starla, Brandy
Brothers: Clint, Stoney, Chad, Brock, Rod

★ Forgive me, all of you fine, blameless women who were named Misty back in the '70s, but this name has now returned to its rightful realms: horses and strippers.

Molly
Popularity: #102
Style: Antique Charm, Guys and Dolls, Nicknames
Variants: Mollie

1990s: #93

1900   Today

Sisters: Tess, Sadie, Leah, Bridget, Sophie
Brothers: Jake, Spencer, Max, Alex, Cole
✴ Molly was traditionally a nickname for Mary, but it's now riding high on its own. Parents love Molly because it's energetic, unpretentious, and just plain adorable.

Monica
Popularity: #205
Style: New Classics
Nicknames: Mo, Mona
Variants: Monique, Monika

1970s: #45

1900   Today

Sisters: Veronica, Andrea, Stephanie, Erica, Melanie
Brothers: Bradley, Derrick, Andre, Marc, Geoffrey
✴ Blessedly, the details of the Monica Lewinsky affair are already fading from memory. Nonetheless, the months of tawdry headlines were a big blow to this classic name, and Monicas everywhere took a while to recover. The Monica of Friends helped counter the blow, though, and new little Monicas should do just fine.

Monique
Popularity: #460
Style: African-American, French, New Classics
Nicknames: Mique, Nikki, Mo
Variants: Monica

1980s: #132

1900   Today

Sisters: Janelle, Desiree, Felicia, Raquel, Nicole
Brothers: Antoine, Quentin, Jarvis, Derrick, Andre
✴ The French form of Monica, Monique was a huge mid-century hit in France. In the U.S., it became popular in the '60s alongside Monica. It's a smoother, glam version of that favorite.

Montana
Popularity: #827
Style: Androgynous, Country & Western, Place Names

2001: #671
1900   Today

Sisters: Cheyenne, Savannah, Sierra, Scarlett, Carolina
Brothers: Hunter, Colton, Trace, Dakota, Maverick
✴ Parents flirted with Montana as a cowboy-ready boy's name, but it seems to have settled down on the girls' side. It's tough but flouncy, an unusual combination that's not for everyone. Great for a country singer, though.

Morgan
Popularity: #29
Style: Androgynous, Celtic, Nickname-Proof, The –ens
Variants: Morgana

2001: #29

1900   Today

Sisters: Jordan, Mackenzie, Kaitlyn, Cameron, Shelby
Brothers: Brendan, Trevor, Dylan, Gavin, Connor
✴ Whew, that was fast! It seems only yesterday that Morgan was an uncommon Welsh name with a masculine swagger. Now it's tremendously popular—and feminine. Parents love Morgan's androgynous Celtic style, and are quickly adopting similar names like Logan for girls as well.

Muriel
Popularity: Rare
Style: Celtic, Ladies and Gentlemen, Nickname-Proof, Solid Citizens
Variants: Meriel

1920s: #138

1900   Today

Sisters: Marion, Elinor, Enid, Iona, Harriet
Brothers: Wallace, Lyle, Hubert, Kermit, Floyd
✴ Muriel is a distinguished Celtic classic, but it feels mighty old-fashioned. The problem is the "yoo" sound—consider how much more youthful Muriel sounds. You can stick with the name and trust that its virtues will shine through, or consider the traditional variant Meriel, or just Muir, meaning "sea."

Myra
Popularity: #945
Style: Nickname-Proof, Solid Citizens

1940s: #249

1900   Today

Sisters: Rita, Polly, Lorna, Arlene, Glenna
Brothers: Clark, Glenn, Doyle, Wendell, Hal
✴ The tart simplicity of this name has kept it in modest favor for generations. For a similar but trendier sound, consider Mira.

Nadia
Popularity: #209
Style: Lacy and Lissome, Nickname-Proof, Slavic
Variants: Nadya

2003: #209
1900   Today

Sisters: Alina, Tatiana, Dasia, Anya, Natalia
Brothers: Damian, Lukas, Ivan, Alexis, Maxim
✴ In the 1976 Olympics, Romanian gymnast Nadia Comaneci became the world's sweetheart. Her first name (traditionally short for Nadezhda) also vaulted into America's consciousness, and today it still carries her image of petite foreign beauty.

Nancy 1940s: #7

Popularity: #269
Style: Mid-Century, Nicknames, Solid Citizens
Nicknames: Nan
Variants: Nancie
Sisters: Janet, Patricia, Carol, Peggy, Bonnie
Brothers: Larry, Allen, Ronald, Roger, Gary
✱ Nancy's a nickname (for Ann) that still sounds right for the little girl in the *Nancy* comic strip. In real life, though, many Nancys are now sporting gray hair. By their sheer numbers, they've forced their name to grow up with them.

Naomi 1920s: #147

Popularity: #162
Style: Biblical, Nickname-Proof, Timeless
Variants: Noemi
Sisters: Miriam, Nina, Rebekah, Lila, Sophie
Brothers: Simon, Felix, Elliot, Max, Joel
✱ Naomi doesn't sound like anything else. That's its secret weapon. The name is traditional and timeless, but because it can't get lost in a cluster of similar alternatives, it still has the ability to surprise.

Natalia 2003: #136

Popularity: #136
Style: Lacy and Lissome, Latino/Latina, Saints, Slavic
Nicknames: Natasha, Talia
Variants: Natalya, Natalie
Sisters: Tatiana, Anastasia, Mariana, Gabriela, Valentina
Brothers: Fabian, Alexander, Maxim, Lukas, Sebastian
✱ A Russian classic, from which the familiar nickname Natasha springs. It's currently popular as a Spanish take on Natalie. Lush and elegant.

Natalie 2003: #23

Popularity: #23
Style: French, New Classics
Nicknames: Nat, Tali
Variants: Natalia, Nathalie, Nataly
Sisters: Gabrielle, Brooke, Noelle, Jacqueline, Bethany
Brothers: Evan, Zachary, Ian, Lucas, Aaron
✱ This steady favorite is especially popular for Christmas babies, thanks to its meaning "birthday of the Lord." It's taken from the French form of the saint's name Natalia. Natalie sounds more classically American, Natalia more dramatic.

Natasha 1980s: #75

Popularity: #304
Style: '70s–'80s, African-American, Slavic
Nicknames: Tasha
Sisters: Tatiana, Monique, Kendra, Desiree, Katrina
Brothers: Darius, Ivan, Fabian, Desmond, Brandon
✱ Slavic and seductive . . . it's tempting to say it with a cartoon Russian accent. For the most authentically Russian version, try the full name Natalia with Natasha as its nickname.

Nayeli 2001: #164

Popularity: #410
Style: Latino/Latina
Variants: Nayely, Nallely
Sisters: Eliana, Anahi, Ximena, Aracely, Citlali
Brothers: Emiliano, Yadiel, Mateo, Adan, Josue
✱ A red-hot name that's flown into the U.S. on the backs of Latin-American entertainers like singer Nayeli Nesme and actress Nayeli Dainzú. Nayeli is a Latina name, but not a Spanish one; it comes from the Zapotec language of Mexico. Its supple grace translates beautifully.

Nell 1900s: #201

Popularity: Rare
Style: Guys and Dolls, Nicknames, Why Not?
Nicknames: Nellie
Variants: Nelle, Nella
Sisters: Bess, Reba, Evie, Millie, Rhea
Brothers: Charley, Theo, Gus, Jess, Major
✱ Nell is a nickname for Eleanor or Helen, and its pet form Nellie was once a wildy fashionable name in its own right. Today the trim Nell hits the spot, carrying on the sweet essence of Nellie in a more mature form.

Nevaeh 2003: #150

Popularity: #150
Style: African-American, Modern Meanings
Sisters: Serenity, Haven, Genesis, Arcadia, Harmony
Brothers: Malachi, Maximus, Zion, Seraph, Josiah
✱ Here's a unique name phenomenon. Nevaeh is a sudden hit, rising out of the mist to star status. Is it a foreign name? An obscure biblical rediscovery? Nope, it's Heaven backwards. A subtly spiritual choice.

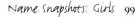

Nia

2001: #311

Popularity: #347
Style: African, Celtic, African-American, Little Darlings, Nickname-Proof
Sisters: Jada, Zoe, Macy, Kira, Asia
Brothers: Kai, Miles, Liam, Ty, Nico

✶ Nia's like a compact SUV or a shot of espresso. A trim little burst of personality, perfectly suited to the moment.

Niamh

Popularity: Rare
Style: Celtic, Mythological
Variants: Neve, Nia
Sisters: Aoife, Finola, Aine, Riona, Caoimhe
Brothers: Dermot, Niall, Eamon, Colm, Cormac

rarely used

1900 — Today

✶ An ancient Celtic goddess name, Niamh is one of the hottest choices in Ireland and Scotland today. It's pronounced "neev," and in the U.S., you'd best be prepared to spell and pronounce it over and over again. Irish folksinger Niamh Parsons is one prominent namesake. (Actress Neve Campbell is not—her name, pronounced "nev," is from her mother's Dutch surname.)

Nicole

1980s: #8

Popularity: #39
Style: French, New Classics
Nicknames: Nikki, Nic
Variants: Nichole, Nicola
Sisters: Danielle, Stephanie, Alison, Megan, Erica
Brothers: Adam, Jeremy, Sean, Derek, Ryan

✶ Michael, Daniel, Nicholas. Michelle, Danielle, Nicole. When the male names became popular, their French feminine forms soon followed. And just as Nicholas continues to be a strong choice for boys, Nicole is still a favorite for its round, crisp sound.

Nina

1900s: #153

Popularity: #241
Style: Little Darlings, Nickname-Proof, Timeless
Sisters: Celia, Anna, Lydia, Naomi, Lila
Brothers: Simon, Edgar, Marshall, Will, Felix

✶ A name that seems to exist outside of the normal constraints of fashion—you just can't pin it down. Nina has origins in languages ranging from Russian to Hebrew to Swahili. It can be a nickname or a full name. It's never trendy, yet never goes out of style. It's sweet and strong and sassy. So what is it, really? Perhaps a refreshingly clean slate for your daughter's own unique personality.

Noelle

2003: #409

Popularity: #409
Style: French, New Classics
Nicknames: Noe
Variants: Noël
Sisters: Simone, Lea, Eden, Giselle, Nathalie
Brothers: Ian, Victor, Miles, Adrian, Spencer

✶ This is the *usual* feminine form of the name Noel, which is *usually* given to babies born around Christmas. But don't let either "usual" hold you back. For spellings, Noelle is soft and classic, but Noël is equally chic. And despite the Yuletide connotations, the name is welcome and stylish any time of year.

Noemi

2001: #553

Popularity: #620
Style: Biblical, Italian, Latino/Latina
Variants: Noemí, Noémie, Naomi
Sisters: Damaris, Graciela, Marisol, Araceli, Beatriz
Brothers: Ruben, Ramiro, Moises, Nestor, Leonel

✶ The Spanish/Italian form of Naomi is one of smoothest, sunniest names on the planet. It's still fairly unfamiliar to English speakers but thoroughly appealing. In Spanish, the final "i" is usually accented; Noémie is the French version.

Nora

1900s: #95

Popularity: #368
Style: Antique Charm, Celtic
Variants: Norah
Sisters: Lena, Celia, Mina, Lillie, Eva
Brothers: Murphy, Charlie, Oliver, Sam, Reuben

✶ In origin, Nora is a nickname for Eleanora, Leonora, or Honora. In the U.S., though, simple Nora has always been more popular than those three stately sisters put together. The name hit its peak in the 1880s and spent the twentieth century in gentle decline. Recently it's begun to reemerge as a stylish, upscale choice for families of Irish descent.

Norma

1930s: #28

Popularity: Rare
Style: Nickname-Proof, Solid Citizens
Sisters: Arlene, Doris, Gloria, Rita, Joyce
Brothers: Marvin, Eugene, Gordon, Leonard, Ralph

✴ Norma Shearer was one of Hollywood's biggest stars of the '30s, a buoyant modern woman with a wardrobe to die for. Today she's overlooked and largely forgotten. The same fate has befallen her name, which has gone from the top of the heap to the waste bin. Its doughy style just doesn't appeal to today's parents.

Nyla

2002: #455

Popularity: #477
Style: African-American, Little Darlings
Sisters: Maia, Zoie, Anya, Maci, Lyra
Brothers: Kai, Luca, Rylan, Jovani, Jair

✴ This lithe little name is building a following. It's simple and sultry, with echoes of hits like Tyra and Nia.

Olga

1910s: #136

Popularity: Rare
Style: Slavic
Nicknames: Olya
Sisters: Ludmila, Vera, Lida, Irina, Berta
Brothers: Boris, Emil, Vladimir, Igor, Pavel

✴ Olga is a cultured classic with an elegant lilt . . . in Russian. The Russian pronunciation centers on a "soft l," a velvety sound that's hard to reproduce in English. The American pronunciation mires the name in leaden Soviet style.

Olive

1900s: #106

Popularity: Rare
Style: Charms and Graces, Ladies and Gentlemen
Nicknames: Ollie, Liv
Variants: Olivia
Sisters: Pearl, Opal, Myrtle, Maude, Beryl
Brothers: Luther, Claude, Earnest, Horace, Chester

✴ Olivia sounds like a nineteenth-century revival, but it was staid sister Olive who really won hearts back in Victorian days. The name is virtually forgotten today except as Popeye's sweetheart Olive Oyl. A choice with similar charms but more current potential is Hazel.

Olivia

2003: #5

Popularity: #5
Style: Antique Charm, Lacy and Lissome, Shakespearean
Nicknames: Liv, Livvy
Variants: Livia, Olive
Sisters: Isabella, Abigail, Hannah, Sophia, Victoria
Brothers: Caleb, Isaiah, Maxwell, Sebastian, Ethan

✴ Starting in the '90s, thousands of parents simultaneously discovered the lovely and underused name Olivia. It is a faultless choice, with its antique charm and hip nickname. In pockets of the country, including upscale neighborhoods of New England and the upper Midwest, the name's popularity is now reaching epidemic proportions.

Olympia

Popularity: Rare
Style: Exotic Traditional

rarely used

Sisters: Hermione, Artemisia, Averil, Minerva, Araminta
Brothers: Lazarus, Cassius, Maximilian, Lucian, Horatio

✴ Perhaps you came across this entry while browsing for Olivia? If so, linger a moment and consider the name's womanly charms. Olympia is more imposing than Olivia but just as classic and warm. You'll need a bit of creativity to work up a nickname, though.

Orly

Popularity: Rare
Style: Jewish, Little Darlings

rarely used

Sisters: Tova, Shira, Ariel, Talia, Anya
Brothers: Avi, Jaco, Noam, Raz, Asher

✴ This sunny sprite of a name means "my light" in Hebrew. You can think of it as a contemporary remix of Leora (though others may think of it as a Paris airport).

Paige

2003: #47

Popularity: #47
Style: Brisk and Breezy
Variants: Page
Sisters: Brooke, Jordan, Sage, Gabrielle, Shea
Brothers: Blake, Devin, Chase, Lucas, Cole

✴ Cheerfully preppy, Paige is a sunlit alternative to Brooke and Brett. It's especially popular as a middle name.

Paloma 2003: #855

Popularity: #855
Style: Exotic Traditional, Why Not?
Sisters: Fabiola, Yazmin, Scarlett, Reina, Dove
Brothers: Dimitri, Xavier, Gideon, Justus, Giovanni
✳ Lush and romantic, Paloma (Spanish for "dove") is also a sign of peace.

Pamela 1950s: #13

Popularity: #434
Style: Mid-Century
Nicknames: Pam
Variants: Pamella, Pamala
Sisters: Brenda, Cynthia, Cheryl, Karen, Deborah
Brothers: Randall, Terry, Douglas, Bruce, Darrell
✳ Think of the Breck Girl, the advertising icon with the flowing locks. For forty years, she was the timeless, glamorous American beauty. Then one day she disappeared and became a retro sweetheart looked back on with fondness. The name Pamela has followed her along that same path.

Paola 2001: #194

Popularity: #230
Style: Italian, Nickname-Proof
Variants: Paula
Sisters: Gianna, Francesca, Nicola, Donatella, Bianca
Brothers: Sergio, Giovanni, Matteo, Luciano, Orlando
✳ Simple men's classics like John, Frank, and Paul are slipping from the charts, but they're not forgotten. We see them resurrected in their Italian feminine forms: Gianna, Francesca, and Paola are fresh new hits.

Paris 2003: #275

Popularity: #275
Style: Androgynous, Nickname-Proof, Place Names
Sisters: Venice, Alexis, Sydney, Darby, India
Brothers: London, Justus, Tate, Kingston, River
✳ The ultimate place name, Paris risks the "pretentious" label but gets by thanks to its simple sound. It's self-assured, but not arrogant—though socialite Paris Hilton has tilted the name toward the flashy side.

Parker 2001: #762

Popularity: #809
Style: Androgynous, Last Names First
Sisters: Ashtyn, Rylie, Payton, Marley, Piper
Brothers: Paxton, Easton, Sawyer, Hudson, Keegan
✳ Parker is still solidly male, but magnetic actress Parker Posey has lured the name toward the girls' side. If you want a more feminine name in the same genre, Piper is one possibility.

Patience 2003: #881

Popularity: #881
Style: Antique Charm, Charms and Graces
Nicknames: Pat, Patty
Sisters: Mercy, Jewel, Willow, Abigail, Charity
Brothers: Levi, Tobias, Honor, Pierce, Abraham
✳ The fashion for virtues has brought back this quintessential Puritan name. It's endearing, but the irony during the patience-free toddler years might just make you rue the choice.

Patrice 1950s: #277

Popularity: Rare
Style: French, Mid-Century
Nicknames: Pat, Patti, Tricia
Variants: Patricia
Sisters: Colette, Yvonne, Terese, Marta, Valerie
Brothers: Robin, Philip, Cary, Michel, Dean
✳ This French alternative to Patricia is seldom heard today, but could sound snappy for a little girl. In French-speaking areas, including parts of Africa, it is typically a male name.

Patricia 1940s: #4

Popularity: #289
Style: Mid-Century, Solid Citizens
Nicknames: Pat, Patty, Patsy, Trish, Tricia, Tia
Variants: Tricia, Patrice
Sisters: Janet, Barbara, Judith, Carolyn, Beverly
Brothers: Richard, Roger, Dennis, Gerald, Allen
✳ Patricia is one of the true mid-century classics. The name's dignity sets it apart from its cutesier comrades—but Patty is pure 1950s, like actress Patty Duke. Get creative with nicknames, or stick with the full Patricia, and you have a gem.

Paula

1960s: #53

Popularity: #655
Style: Mid-Century, Nickname-Proof
Variants: Paola
Sisters: Donna, Susan, Annette, Sheila, Pamela
Brothers: Bruce, Rodney, Douglas, Barry, Dean
★ It's hard to find fault with this name, which is a straightforward feminine form of the equally straightforward Paul. It's just not especially exciting and thus out of fashion. Of all the Paul offshoots—Paulette, Pauline, etc.—only Paulina is a real player today.

Paulina

2002: #361

Popularity: #408
Style: Latino/Latina, Shakespearean, Slavic
Variants: Pauline
Sisters: Daniella, Perla, Mariana, Mariam, Alina
Brothers: Lukas, Santiago, Fabian, Brody, Rodrigo
★ This unlikely comeback queen has acquired a sensuous sheen. The reasons: Mexican pop star Paulina Rubio and Czech model Paulina Porizkova.

Pauline

1910s: #33

Popularity: Rare
Style: French, Porch Sitters
Variants: Paulina
Sisters: Lucille, Bernice, Alberta, Helene, Jeannette
Brothers: Herbert, Roland, Stanley, Leonard, Franklin
★ Back around the First World War, Pauline was a huge hit—bigger than now-beloved old-timers like Emma, Clara, and Julia. By the end of the Roaring Twenties, the name had started a nosedive that took it completely out of the running. Now consigned to the sidelines, Pauline must sit and watch as sidekick Paulina takes center stage.

Payton

2001: #166

Popularity: #207
Style: Androgynous, Last Names First, Nickname-Proof, The -ens
Variants: Peyton
Sisters: Skylar, Addison, Parker, Carson, Kendall
Brothers: Dawson, Ashton, Cooper, Dalton, Brady
★ This contempory favorite is used equally for boys and girls. The image is the same for both sexes: prosperous and soap-opera slick.

Pearl

1900s: #36

Popularity: Rare
Style: Charms and Graces
Sisters: Mae, Olive, Madge, Fern, Nellie
Brothers: Homer, Otto, Lester, Dock, Cecil
★ Once upon a time, Pearl sounded as light as Lily, as romantic as Rose, and as radiant as Ruby. Yet today's parents seem to feel that it's as old as Olive. Pearl still has great charm; it just takes a little daring to use. That makes it a particularly appealing middle-name choice.

Peggy

1930s: #36

Popularity: Rare
Style: Mid-Century, Nicknames
Nicknames: Peg
Variants: Peggie
Sisters: Sue, Bonnie, Judy, Jo, Nancy
Brothers: Jimmy, Jerry, Bob, Ted, Billy
★ Thanks to Buddy Holly's "Peggy Sue," this name gives off the sunny glow of a mythical, clean-scrubbed 1950s. (Compare to the more serious style of the full name Margaret.) Despite the cute nickname style, Peggy sounds like a grown-up, and a smart, likable one at that. The slimmed-down Peg sounds even smarter.

Penelope

1940s: #288

Popularity: #709
Style: Mythological, Timeless, Why Not?
Nicknames: Penny, Nellie, Nell, Pip
Sisters: Rosemary, Patricia, Marjorie, Gwendolyn, Daphne
Brothers: Graham, Laurence, Randolph, Benedict, Vaughn
★ Penelope is ravishing and dignified, an individualistic classic. Its galloping Greek pronunciation (pe-NELL-uh-pee) makes it memorable, yet keeps it from becoming too popular. Nickname Penny was once a big hit on its own, and Pip is a fun choice heard in England and Australia.

Penny

1960s: #105

Popularity: Rare
Style: English, Mid-Century, Nicknames
Nicknames: Pen
Sisters: Becky, Dee, Patty, Sherry, Connie
Brothers: Mitch, Rick, Skip, Curt, Chuck
★ Penny, a nickname for Penelope, is best known and loved as a coin. "Bright as a penny." "Pennies from Heaven." "Pick it up, all the day you'll have good luck." The thought of a shiny penny brings a smile to your face, and that gives this name a fairy-tale charm that transcends its '50s style.

Petra

Popularity: Rare
Style: German/Dutch, Ladies and Gentlemen
Sisters: Willa, Josefa, Adela, Beryl, Flora
Brothers: Emory, Elden, Bertram, Jules, Rudolph

1910s: #361
1900 Today

✴ This name won't be for everyone. It's stately rather than spry. But it has a quiet sweetness that should win a few hearts.

Philomena

Popularity: Rare
Style: Exotic Traditional, Ladies and Gentlemen, Saints
Nicknames: Mena, Phil
Variants: Filomena
Sisters: Aurelia, Winifred, Theodora, Zora, Magdalene
Brothers: Constantin, Bertrand, Casimir, Sylvan, Adolphus

1910s: #399
1900 Today

✴ Quite common a hundred years ago, the name Philomena has virtually disappeared from our culture. It may seem a curiosity today, but it's a handsome one. The Italian spelling Filomena tilts the style from antique to exotic.

Phoebe

Popularity: #437
Style: Antique Charm, Little Darlings, Nickname-Proof, Shakespearean
Variants: Phebe
Sisters: Lily, Emma, Eliza, Daphne, Zoe
Brothers: Owen, Walker, Miles, Pierce, Simon

2001: #388
1900 Today

✴ An absolute sweetheart of a name, Phoebe carries its girlish sound with graceful maturity. The sophisticated spelling is the key—a Feebie wouldn't have a chance.

Phyllis

Popularity: Rare
Style: Mythological, Solid Citizens
Nicknames: Phyl
Sisters: Doris, Marilyn, Jean, Rosalie, Beverly
Brothers: Raymond, Norman, Eugene, Gordon, Franklin

1930s: #27
1900 Today

✴ Phyllis has appealing ingredients: mythological roots and a contemporary rhythm. But the name just can't shake its "grandma" aura. Its mythological spirit is better captured now by names like Avis, Luna, and Danae.

Piper

Popularity: #343
Style: Last Names First, Nickname-Proof
Sisters: Laney, Kennedy, Willow, Zoe, Eden
Brothers: Reece, Carter, Finn, Walker, Riley

2003: #343
1900 Today

✴ With the ascension of Parker and Hunter, the moment is right for Piper: a bit more spirited and a bit less self-important.

Pippa

Popularity: Rare
Style: English, Little Darlings
Sisters: Gemma, Dulcie, Penny, Esme, Dahlia
Brothers: Corin, Alec, Davy, Robin, Clive

rarely used
1900 Today

✴ This little Brit nickname is as lively as they come, a kicky Carnaby Street creation. The full version, Philippa, is every bit as British, but stiffly formal.

Polly

Popularity: Rare
Style: Nicknames, Solid Citizens
Sisters: Kitty, Glenna, Patty, Sue, Rosie
Brothers: Teddy, Hal, Doyle, Ned, Rex

1930s: #325
1900 Today

✴ Polly is cozy, sunny, and jolly. Like Molly, it was once a common nickname for Mary, but unlike Molly, it has slipped into obscurity. It's old-fashioned and endearing.

Portia

Popularity: Rare
Style: Exotic Traditional, Nickname-Proof, Shakespearean
Sisters: Camilla, Hermione, Linnea, Astrid, Phyllida
Brothers: Piers, Horatio, Antony, Tristram, Corin

1980s: #839
1900 Today

✴ This Shakespearean standard has a regal elegance few names can match. Parents who love its literary style, though, will be dismayed by constant confusions with the sports car Porsche.

Precious

2001: #393

Popularity: #526
Style: Fanciful, Modern Meanings
Sisters: Diamond, Princess, Honey, Star, Miracle
Brothers: Marquis, Peerless, Adonis, Sincere, Blaze

1900   Today

★ This name is a sweet sentiment to show a new daughter how much she is loved. Unfortunately, the name does not grow up well. Picturing a corporate executive with the name Precious is like picturing her walking into a meeting holding a fluffy teddy bear. For a similar expression in a name that will be taken more seriously, try Joy.

Presley

2003: #664

Popularity: #664
Style: Androgynous, Last Names First
Sisters: Harley, Everly, Cassidy, Scarlett, Marley
Brothers: Jagger, Colt, Buddy, Sawyer, Bo

1900   Today

★ If it's a boy, we'll call him Jagger. And if it's a girl . . . ah, of course! If Peyton and Ainsley are too tame for your taste, Presley is a surname that cranks up the volume.

Priscilla

1940s: #146

Popularity: #287
Style: Biblical, Timeless
Nicknames: Cilla, Prissy, CeCe
Variants: Prisca

1900   Today

Sisters: Jacqueline, Patricia, Claudia, Susana, Penelope
Brothers: Mitchell, Raymond, Curtis, Calvin, Ronald

★ Priscilla has a prim reputation, thanks to the pet form Prissy and a storied history as a Puritan name. Today, the name is smart but exceedingly formal. If you can scare up a good nickname, it could be a stylish choice. (Ironically, Priscilla itself started off life as a pet form of Prisca. The biblical Priscilla is referred to by both names.)

Rachel

1990s: #15

Popularity: #28
Style: Biblical, Nickname-Proof, Timeless
Variants: Rachael, Rochelle, Raquel

1900   Today

Sisters: Sarah, Leah, Emily, Megan, Rebecca
Brothers: Aaron, Benjamin, Nicholas, Matthew, Adam

★ Rachel is a biblical classic that reemerged as a hit after decades of hibernation. It doesn't sound like a quaint heirloom, though — it's thoroughly contemporary. The name hit its modern peak with the *Friends* character Rachel and her eponymous hairstyle. This is one of the most flexible and risk-free names you can choose.

Rae

1900s: #349

Popularity: Rare
Style: Guys and Dolls
Variants: Ray
Sisters: Roxie, Faye, Reba, Mae, Della

1900   Today

Brothers: Dee, Wiley, Mack, Dewey, Gus

★ Rae has always been a flexible name, used equally as a nickname, middle name, and compound element (Rae Ann, Raelyn). It makes an airy little first name, too.

Ramona

1930s: #161

Popularity: Rare
Style: Mid-Century
Nicknames: Rae, Mona
Sisters: Wanda, Jeannine, Roberta, Loretta, Dolores

1900   Today

Brothers: Wendell, Gerald, Barton, Duane, Marlin

★ Ramona was a romantic choice for many years, thanks to a popular novel in the 1880s and a popular song in the 1920s. Then, in 1968, Beverly Cleary published the children's classic *Ramona the Pest*, and this dignified name was saddled with a teasing tagline that has been hard to shake.

Randi

1980s: #258

Popularity: Rare
Style: Nicknames, Surfer Sixties
Variants: Randy
Sisters: Jaimie, Rikki, Tasha, Lacy, Bobbi

1900   Today

Brothers: Dusty, Brandt, Tory, Jarrod, Kurtis

★ Like Toni and Jerri, Randi was an attempt to make a male name feminine with a wave of the magic "i." It was a hot trend in the '60s, and you see its descendants in new feminized "y" creations like Ryleigh, Jordyn, and Sydnie.

Raquel

1970s: #260

Popularity: #393
Style: Latino/Latina
Nicknames: Rocky, Raqui, Kelly
Variants: Raquelle
Sisters: Alicia, Janelle, Marisol, Selena, Tia
Brothers: Antonio, Quincy, Julio, Omar, Damon
★ The Spanish form of Rachel, this name has a sensuous vibe in the U.S. thanks to the voluptuous star Raquel Welch. It's also simple and classic, and plays well to both Spanish- and English-speaking audiences.

Raven
1990s: #161

Popularity: #233
Style: African-American, Charms and Graces, Modern Meanings, The -ens
Nicknames: Rae
Sisters: Jasmin, Asia, Jade, Summer, Eden
Brothers: Chance, Devon, Storm, Talon, Ryder
★ How do you like your romantic heroines, lacy and proper or glossy and bold? If bold is your style, Raven has a dramatic flair that begs for the spotlight. It's strong and supremely confident.

Reagan
2003: #202

Popularity: #202
Style: Androgynous, Last Names First, Namesakes
Nicknames: Rea
Sisters: Addison, Peyton, Skylar, Parker, Kennedy
Brothers: Cooper, Carter, Landon, Hudson, Drake
★ From Jefferson and Madison to Carter and Reagan, presidential surnames are hotter than ever. In most cases parents are focusing more on style than politics (though Watergate has ruled out the otherwise pitch-perfect name Nixon). For girls, Reagan is gaining on front-runner Madison.

Reba

1910s: #239

Popularity: Rare
Style: Country & Western, Guys and Dolls, Nicknames
Variants: Reva
Sisters: Dolly, Nell, Evie, Rosie, Della
Brothers: Archie, Mack, Gus, Wiley, Hal
★ A charming 1900s flirt, Reba could tempt the same parents who are drawn to Ruby and Lily. The name also has a country style thanks to singer Reba McEntire.

Rebecca

1970s: #13

Popularity: #64
Style: Biblical, Timeless
Nicknames: Becky, Becca, Reba
Variants: Rebekah, Rebekka
Sisters: Christina, Rachel, Veronica, Laura, Andrea
Brothers: Daniel, Patrick, Joel, Michael, Stephen
★ Tender and graceful, Rebecca has long been a literary favorite. Recently, biblical "rediscoveries" like Abigail and Hannah have been more popular, but Rebecca remains an unquestioned classic.

Reese
2003: #312

Popularity: #312
Style: Androgynous, Brisk and Breezy
Sisters: Sage, Quinn, Rylie, Brynn, Addison
Brothers: Kade, Rylan, Carter, Finn, Greyson
★ This was a preppy boy's name until actress Reese Witherspoon hit the movie screen with 100 watts of charm. Witherspoon (whose given name is Laura) is a perfect Reese: trim, attractive, and tough.

Regan

2001: #390

Popularity: #452
Style: Nickname-Proof, Shakespearean, The -ens
Sisters: Kaylin, Eden, Aspen, Piper, Jillian
Brothers: Corbin, Griffin, Duncan, Brennan, Cade
★ A Shakespearean name that has found a new audience because of its Celtic flavor. It's a worthy alternative to Megan, but parents considering this name should take a quick look at its origins in the play *King Lear*. An ungrateful daughter who double-crosses her dad . . . hmm, maybe Megan isn't so bad after all? Reagan is a popular variation that shifts the emphasis from literature to politics.

Regina

1960s: #84

Popularity: #637
Style: African-American, Mid-Century, Saints
Nicknames: Gina, Reggie
Sisters: Anita, Colette, Yolanda, Paula, Yvonne
Brothers: Rodney, Gerard, Darrell, Dean, Lyndon
★ Regina is Latin for "queen," and it's a tasteful way to anoint your daughter with regal majesty. That's assuming you pronounce it re-JEE-na . . . as re-JY-na, it's far, far too close to a part of the female anatomy.

Reina
Popularity: #894
Style: Latino/Latina
Variants: Reyna
Sisters: Roxana, Mariela, Rocío, Chaya, Alina
Brothers: Alvaro, Jovan, Jairo, Adan, Rey

2001: #826

★ Reina is Spanish for "queen," but it nonetheless feels more sweet than grandiose. This old-fashioned favorite is climbing back into fashion, especially in the spelling Reyna.

Renata
Popularity: Rare
Style: Italian, Slavic, Why Not?
Variants: Renate
Sisters: Daria, Mariel, Linnea, Marina, Audra
Brothers: Carlo, Tomas, Ivan, Anton, Bram

1980s: #954

★ The original Latin form of Renée, Renata has classic gravity and poise that travels well. It's been quietly used in many languages, including Czech, Italian, German, and Polish.

Renee
Popularity: #457
Style: French, Surfer Sixties
Variants: Renée
Sisters: Julie, Carla, Michele, Robin, Christine
Brothers: Craig, Keith, Jeffery, Timothy, Troy

1960s: #74

★ This French name means "reborn." Various forms of the name have been used since the time of the early Christians, for whom it signified a spiritual rebirth. Renee's airy sound sent it soaring in the '60s, and it became so common that both its French origins and religious meaning took a back seat. Today you'll meet Renees of every background and persuasion.

Reva
Popularity: Rare
Style: Guys and Dolls, Why Not?
Sisters: Nola, Willa, Fay, Iva, Roma
Brothers: Harris, Ward, Mack, Truman, Hardy

1920s: #385

★ Like Reba, this is an old-time country gal name. The one-letter switch, though, makes it sharp enough for any setting. Reva's always been a stand-alone name (created when Vera and Iva were the height of fashion), but you could also try it as a nickname for Rebecca.

Rhea
Popularity: Rare
Style: Ladies and Gentlemen, Little Darlings, Mythological, Why Not?
Sisters: Flora, Cleo, Althea, Willa, Lena
Brothers: Jules, Milo, Ellis, Alden, Royce

1900s: #485

★ Rhea grafts the old-time warmth of names like Bella and Lucy onto the breeziness of new favorites Mia and Zoe. A compromise that should satisfy many tastes.

Rhiannon
Popularity: #584
Style: Celtic, Mythological
Variants: Rhian
Sisters: Guinevere, Siobhan, Aeron, Scarlett, Bronwyn
Brothers: Rowan, Donovan, Evander, Griffin, Emmanuel

2001: #508

★ Rhiannon was a goddess in Welsh mythology. Her name (hree-AN-un) generally wasn't used by humans until the past century, which contributes to its romantic essence. The Fleetwood Mac song about a shadowy, elusive Rhiannon reinforces the image.

Rhoda
Popularity: Rare
Style: Biblical, Nickname-Proof, Solid Citizens
Sisters: Willa, Sybil, Clarice, Reba, Nola
Brothers: Alton, Murray, Harris, Emory, Burton

1920s: #291

★ The '70s sitcom *Rhoda* is most Americans' touchstone for this name. If you can suppress that image, you might find that Rhoda surprises you. It's a quiet name from the New Testament that reached its peak in the nineteenth century alongside Willa, Petra, and Zelda.

Rhonda
Popularity: Rare
Style: African-American, Surfer Sixties
Nicknames: Ronnie
Variants: Ronda
Sisters: Sherry, Yvette, Gina, Laurie, Carla
Brothers: Darryl, Rodney, Todd, Kerry, Gregg

1960s: #46

★ The year: 1965. The song: "Help Me, Rhonda" by the Beach Boys. At that moment, the name was a cool, contemporary invention riding a wave of popularity. That wave quickly crested and the name is now beached. Nonetheless, its grown-up sound makes it a stronger choice than other, more lightweight '60s hits.

Riley

Popularity: #72
Style: Androgynous, Celtic, Last Names First
Variants: Rylee, Reilly, Rylie, Ryleigh
Sisters: Kennedy, Logan, Bailey, Darby, Skylar
Brothers: Rowan, Carson, Connor, Donovan, Parker

 2003: #72 / 1900 Today

★ This classic Irish boy's name is a hot up-and-comer for girls. In the feminine version, the boyishness dominates and Riley's Celtic style slips to the background. This is a case where alternate spellings really change the nature of the name: Ryleigh is closer in spirit to Kayleigh than Riley.

Rita

Popularity: Rare
Style: Italian, Solid Citizens
Sisters: June, Iris, Glenna, Maxine, Rosa
Brothers: Warren, Bill, Gene, Norman, Gerald

 1920s: #48 / 1900 Today

★ There's an eternal appeal to punchy, pint-sized girls' names. Kira and Mia fill the bill today, just as Rita did back in the '20s. Like many of these miniature hits, Rita has nickname roots—it's short for Margarita. Rita now has a vintage style, but there's still plenty of life to it.

Roberta

Popularity: Rare
Style: Italian, Solid Citizens
Nicknames: Bobbi, Robbie
Sisters: Donna, Loretta, Carole, Rita, Paula
Brothers: Gene, Franklin, Donald, Dale, Richard

 1930s: #94 / 1900 Today

★ Time was, to make a feminine form of a name you had to add a vowel at the end. Nowadays you can just switch around the vowels inside, and . . . voilà! Ryley and Camaryn are girls. That could be one reason that Roberta has come to sound so dated. (Just say no to Robyrt, though. Stick with Robyn.)

Robin

Popularity: #943
Style: Androgynous, Charms and Graces, Nickname-Proof, Surfer Sixties
Variants: Robyn
Sisters: Denise, Cindy, Beth, Michele, Tina
Brothers: Craig, Jeff, Randall, Timothy, Todd

1960s: #36 / 1900 Today

★ Robin is an old boy's nickname, but the image of robins in springtime enlivens the girl's version. That sweetness keeps it fresher than other '60s favorites. It could fit in with old-timers like May and Hope, or upstarts like Eden and Lark.

Romy

Popularity: Rare
Style: Nicknames, Why Not?
Sisters: Reba, Sylvie, Nelly, Mina, Evie
Brothers: Nat, Eamon, Zack, Baz, Hal

rarely used / 1900 Today

★ Romy is an old nickname for Rosemary with a sound that's youthful and new. It's nestled right in that style sweet spot, unusual yet not a bit strange.

Rosa

Popularity: #396
Style: Italian, Ladies and Gentlemen
Nicknames: Rosie
Variants: Rose, Rosita
Sisters: Sylvia, Ruth, Cora, Lucia, Alma
Brothers: Carl, Angelo, Leo, Luther, Joe

 1900s: #88 / 1900 Today

★ The Spanish and Italian form of Rose, Rosa has a floral sweetness all its own. It's a bit less dainty and more womanly than the English version. It also gives you an appealing hero in civil rights pioneer Rosa Parks.

Rosalind

Popularity: Rare
Style: Shakespearean, Solid Citizens
Nicknames: Rosie, Rosa, Lindy, Sal
Variants: Rosalyn, Rosalinda, Rosaline
Sisters: Bernadette, Constance, Myra, Roseanne, Maribeth
Brothers: Randolph, Clifford, Laurence, Cornell, Benedict

 1940s: #357 / 1900 Today

★ Rosalind was the essence of romance in the sixteenth century, a heroine of Shakespeare and Spenser. In the twentieth century, actress Rosalind Russell added a brassy edge. And for the twenty-first century? Rosalind's heavy sound scares parents away, but its romantic strength could lure them back.

Rosanna

Popularity: Rare
Style: Italian, Lacy and Lissome, Why Not?
Nicknames: Rosie
Variants: Roseanna, Rosanne, Roxanna
Sisters: Audra, Melinda, Marianne, Leanna, Felicia
Brothers: Barrett, Leif, Orlando, Ross, Garrick

1980s: #591 / 1900 Today

★ Try to separate Rosanna from Roseanne in your mind. Roseanne is currently stuck in the '50s, and the image of "domestic goddess" comedienne Roseanne Barr didn't help. Rosanna, though, is a nineteenth-century literary beauty. It should be considered alongside Juliana and Daniela.

Rose

Popularity: #358
Style: Antique Charm, Charms and Graces
Nicknames: Rosie
Variants: Rosa
Sisters: Violet, Grace, Ruby, Eva, Flora
Brothers: Henry, Julius, Sam, George, Leo

1900s: #14

✳ Rose is an eternal symbol of beauty, as a flower or a name. It was the queen of the flower names that blossomed for a generation starting in the 1880s. That Victorian flavor adds an heirloom quality to the name's inherent charms. It's not especially common as a first name today, but huge as a middle name.

Rosemary

Popularity: #672
Style: Charms and Graces, Solid Citizens, Why Not?
Nicknames: Romy, Rosie, Rose, Roxie
Variants: Rosemarie
Sisters: Constance, Marjorie, June, Penelope, Beverley
Brothers: Jerome, Calvin, Lawrence, Roland, Stanton

1940s: #91

✳ After decades on the outs, this name's day is due. It has an old-fashioned femininity and an exceptional nickname assortment. Rosie lures you with sweetness, Roxie with sauciness, and Romy sounds snappy and contemporary.

Roxanne

Popularity: Rare
Style: Surfer Sixties
Nicknames: Roxie
Variants: Roxana, Roxanna
Sisters: Belinda, Patrice, Rochelle, Maribeth, Janine
Brothers: Steven, Terence, Timothy, Randall, Curt

1950s: #196

✳ Roxanne has a long and storied history, going back to the wife of Alexander the Great. Unfortunately, that heritage is currently buried by the name's outmoded '60s image. The Latin version Roxana feels more up to date. Also see Roxie for a brassy twist on the name.

Roxie

Popularity: Rare
Style: Guys and Dolls
Sisters: Mamie, Goldie, Lula, Kitty, Tessie
Brothers: Wiley, Gus, Roscoe, Ike, Fritz

1900s: #292

✳ Roxie Hart, the fame-seeking missile from the musical *Chicago*, is a great mascot for this name's jazz-age sass. If you're looking for an interesting formal version, try Roxana, Rosalind, or Rosemary.

Ruby

Popularity: #197
Style: Charms and Graces, Guys and Dolls
Sisters: Sadie, Mae, Lillie, Hazel, Rosie
Brothers: Mose, Harry, Leo, Max, Roy

1910s: #24

✳ While Violet and Pearl were blushing in the parlor, Ruby was kicking up her heels at the music hall. She's the spitfire of this old-fashioned name family.

Ruth

Popularity: #350
Style: Biblical, Solid Citizens
Nicknames: Ruthie
Sisters: Helen, Rose, Esther, Alice, Marion
Brothers: Frank, Carl, Albert, Louis, Charlie

1910s: #5

✳ Yoo-hoo! Over here! An underused biblical classic, yours for the taking! Ruth has the hushed dignity of Hannah, yet remains uncommon and gently surprising.

Ryan

Popularity: #485
Style: Androgynous, Celtic, The -ens
Variants: Ryann, Rianna
Sisters: Kasey, Taryn, Shea, Devin, Kendall
Brothers: Keenan, Tyson, Brennan, Beau, Garrett

1980s: #385

✳ Starting in the '80s, parents took a run at turning this top boys' favorite into a girl's name. It has a clean, modern appeal, but remains primarily masculine. The up-and-coming idea today is the melodious variant Rianna; see also Rhiannon.

Sabrina

Popularity: #139
Style: New Classics
Nicknames: Bree
Sisters: Miranda, Angelica, Bethany, Vanessa, Marisa
Brothers: Colin, Jared, Brett, Spencer, Brendan

1990s: #89

✳ This is an old name out of Celtic legend, but rendered eternally youthful by Sabrina, the Teenage Witch. Positively sparkly.

Sade 1990s: #668

Popularity: Rare
Style: African-American, Namesakes
Sisters: Simone, Aja, Chantal, Iman, Shante
Brothers: Stephon, Omari, Jamal, Tariq, Jovan
✴ Not common, but a quiet favorite thanks to the classy "Smooth Operator" singer (whose given name was Helen). It's pronounced shar-DAY . . . *not* like the Marquis de Sade.

Sadie 1900s: #93

Popularity: #195
Style: Antique Charm, Guys and Dolls, Jewish, Nicknames
Sisters: Allie, Sophie, Stella, Mollie, Lucy
Brothers: Sam, Harry, Max, Solomon, Ben
✴ Sadie is a nickname for Sarah, and it once held a place in the roster of nickname classics alongside Betsy, Molly, and Maggie. Then it vanished. So now it's old-fashioned and utterly charming to a new generation of parents. Folks old enough to remember the last round of Sadies may still consider it exclusively an old-lady name.

Sage 2003: #405

Popularity: #405
Style: Brisk and Breezy, Charms and Graces, Modern Meanings
Sisters: Skye, Haven, Serenity, Brynn, Willow
Brothers: Chance, Cael, Jude, Blaine, Lukas
✴ Sage is a fragrant herb, which gives the name softness. It means wise, which gives it depth. And it's a swift single syllable, which gives it snap.

Sally 1930s: #70

Popularity: Rare
Style: Nicknames, Solid Citizens
Nicknames: Sal
Sisters: Sue, Nancy, Polly, Joyce, Janie
Brothers: Eddie, Gene, Dale, Tommy, Bobby
✴ Sally was Charlie Brown's sister in *Peanuts*. The name fits the retro sweetness of that comic strip's eternal childhood. Sally has fallen far out of style, but with Lucy staging a comeback, this name looks like a good bet. It's also a nickname for the stylish classic Sarah.

Samantha 1990s: #5

Popularity: #10
Style: New Classics
Nicknames: Sam, Sammy
Sisters: Miranda, Lauren, Allison, Alexandra, Megan
Brothers: Zachary, Brandon, Ryan, Jared, Trevor
✴ Through the magic of reruns, generations of girls have grown up *Bewitched* by TV's suburban sorceress Samantha Stevens. The television show sparked the initial popularity of the name, and it continues to reflect our impression of Sam: clever, attractive, and fun. A more recent TV model was Kim Cattrall's Samantha on *Sex and the City*.

Samira 2003: #770

Popularity: #770
Style: Lacy and Lissome, Muslim
Nicknames: Sammie, Mira
Sisters: Amina, Fatima, Leila, Maryam, Shakira
Brothers: Amir, Bilal, Hassan, Ahmed, Khalid
✴ The lyrical beauty of this Islamic name should win it fans from all cultures.

Sandra 1940s: #6

Popularity: #266
Style: Italian, Mid-Century
Nicknames: Sandy
Variants: Saundra
Sisters: Sharon, Linda, Kathleen, Connie, Diane
Brothers: Dennis, Stephen, Douglas, Patrick, Ronald
✴ Sandra was a stylish hit from the '40s to '60s, with the wholesome image of actress Sandra Dee. Of course, that was just Miss Dee's stage name . . . she jettisoned a long, clunky ethnic name that simply wouldn't do. Her original name? Alexandra, which is now all the rage while Sandra is taking a lower profile.

Sandy 1960s: #166

Popularity: #839
Style: Nicknames, Surfer Sixties
Variants: Sandi
Sisters: Laurie, Robin, Becky, Gina, Liz
Brothers: Curt, Kelly, Ron, Marty, Bart
✴ Sandy makes sunny Sandra even sunnier. Also consider it as a traditional but unexpected nickname for Alexandra, standing out in the sea of Alexes.

Sarah

1980s: #5

Popularity: #12
Style: Biblical, Timeless
Nicknames: Sally, Sadie, Sal
Variants: Sara
Sisters: Rachel, Katherine, Jessica, Leah, Emily
Brothers: Andrew, Benjamin, Daniel, Samuel, Matthew

✳ Sarah has been steadily popular for decades now—really, for millennia. But the name is such a simple, pure classic that it will never wear out its welcome. For a change of pace, the nicknames Sally and Sadie are both worth a look.

Sarai

2003: #464

Popularity: #464
Style: Biblical, Exotic Traditional, Nickname-Proof
Sisters: Atara, Danae, Mara, Micah, Vashti
Brothers: Simeon, Jabez, Axel, Rohan, Joah

✳ In the Bible, Abram and Sarai were the original names of the couple whom God blessed and renamed Abraham and Sarah. Abram has a familiar sound in English, but Sarai has always been rare and exotic. In the past few years, that has begun to change. It is still uncommon, but increasingly fashionable.

Sasha

1980s: #265

Popularity: #367
Style: '70s–'80s, Slavic
Sisters: Nadia, Larissa, Alina, Lana, Natasha
Brothers: Lukas, Fabian, Brice, Roman, Stefan

✳ Sasha is Russia's version of Alex, a hugely popular unisex nickname for Alexander and Alexandra. In English, it's decidedly feminine. Alex tones down the steamy side of Alexandra; Sasha heats it up.

Savannah

2001: #43

Popularity: #42
Style: Country & Western, Place Names
Nicknames: Savvy, Vanna
Variants: Savanna
Sisters: Sierra, Cheyenne, Madison, Sydney, Shenandoah
Brothers: Dakota, Austin, Cameron, Bryce, Hunter

✳ The name Savannah took off after the book *Midnight in the Garden of Good and Evil* made Savannah, Georgia, a hot spot. The city's quirky Southern charm, coupled with the name's velvety, sassy sound, make Savannah a major hit.

Scarlett

2003: #764

Popularity: #764
Style: Country & Western, Exotic Traditional, Modern Meanings, Namesakes
Sisters: Ivy, Aurora, Lark, Savannah, Jewell
Brothers: Lane, Wyatt, Gunnar, Stone, Rhett

✳ A sassy spitfire, thanks to Scarlett O'Hara (and Miss Scarlett from the board game Clue). This name packs a wallop, and for a girl with a red-hot personality, it can be a smashing success.

Selena

2001: #218

Popularity: #274
Style: Lacy and Lissome, Latino/Latina, Mythological
Variants: Selina
Sisters: Thalia, Marisa, Liliana, Amaya, Shakira
Brothers: Marco, Omar, Mateo, Lorenzo, Sergio

✳ The late Tejano music star Selena made this name her own. Before she came on the scene, it was a quiet international name with a literary style.

Serena

2002: #246

Popularity: #259
Style: Lacy and Lissome, Saints
Variants: Serina, Sarina
Sisters: Mariana, Noelle, Alana, India, Natalia
Brothers: Darius, Fabian, Isaiah, Adrian, Marcos

✳ Serena means "calm," and was the name of an early saint. Serena also sounds lavish, and is the name of a charismatic tennis star. You can have it both ways with this snazzy classic.

Serenity

2003: #235

Popularity: #235
Style: Charms and Graces, Modern Meanings
Sisters: Harmony, Meadow, Journey, Patience, Verity
Brothers: Storm, Phoenix, Tristan, River, Endymion

✳ Serenity's meaning and rhythm combine for an image of gentle grace. It's deceptively long, though, and you'll have to be creative with nicknames. The anime series *Sailor Moon* launched the name into popular use.

Shakira

Popularity: #739
Style: Latino/Latina, Muslim
Nicknames: Kira
Sisters: Fabiola, Yasmine, Paulina, Layla, Thalia
Brothers: Ezequiel, Adan, Khalid, Jairo, Tariq

2002: #514

✸ Ready for a global ride? The Latin diva Shakira is Colombian, but her heritage is Lebanese and her name Arabic. (The singer's publicists translate it as "woman full of grace"; the more standard translation is "thankful.") In the U.S., the name has been used occasionally by Arab- and African-Americans and is now a hot choice for Latinas.

Shana

Popularity: Rare
Style: '70s–'80s, Nickname-Proof
Variants: Shauna, Shawna, Shanna, Shayna, Shaina
Sisters: Tasha, Jayme, Terra, Misty, Shayla
Brothers: Dusty, Brannon, Brant, Cory, Darrick

1970s: #250

✸ With six popular variations, Shana rose out of nowhere to become one of the top names of the '70s. The "SHAH-na" variants disappeared just as quickly, but "SHAY-na" is still going strong. (Shayna is also the Yiddish word for pretty.) It's not hard to see the appeal of the name, which is like a whispered midnight endearment, but there were too many Shanas too soon.

Shania

Popularity: #329
Style: Country & Western, Namesakes, Nickname-Proof
Sisters: Savanna, Winona, Aspen, Cheyenne, Scarlett
Brothers: Colton, Trace, Rhett, Sage, Garth

2003: #329

✸ Just as Shania Twain brought a sexy pop style to country music, she has also introduced a new breed of sexy pop/country name. Another possibility in this vein is Sedona, after the scenic Arizona city.

Shannon

Popularity: #227
Style: '70s–'80s, Androgynous, Celtic, Nickname-Proof
Sisters: Heather, April, Tara, Rhiannon, Kelly
Brothers: Brian, Heath, Brendan, Trevor, Shane

1970s: #21

✸ Shannon is a soft, smooth spitfire of a name. Like Erin, it's an homage to Ireland rather than a traditional Irish name. (The River Shannon forms a spine through the country.) The name is now in decline from its '70s to '80s glory days, but no worse for wear.

Sharon

Popularity: #523
Style: Mid-Century
Nicknames: Shari
Variants: Sharen, Sharyn, Sharron
Sisters: Diane, Sandra, Kathleen, Donna, Janice
Brothers: Dennis, Bruce, Alan, Douglas, Gary

1940s: #9

✸ Here's an inspiring example for parents torn between creativity and tradition: a twentieth-century Bible name. Sharon is a place name in the Bible, and wasn't adopted as a personal name until the 1920s. It then became a staple for fifty years. Today it's entered a period of relative neglect, but it's too well-liked a name to disappear completely.

Shawn

Popularity: Rare
Style: Androgynous, Celtic, Surfer Sixties
Variants: Shawna, Shaun, Sian
Sisters: Kerry, Shari, Leigh, Robyn, Trina
Brothers: Scott, Darren, Stoney, Tod, Kraig

1970s: #223

✸ Given the current rush to convert boys' names to girls', it's worth looking at this '60s-era example. The masculine Sean became the feminine Shawn on the model of names like Dawn and Fawn. If you like the result at a few decades' distance, then you can proceed happily to Jordyn and Skyler.

Shayla

Popularity: #314
Style: Bell Tones, Lacy and Lissome
Nicknames: Shay
Variants: Shyla
Sisters: Kira, Alana, Selena, Hayley, Alysha
Brothers: Kyler, Weston, Tucker, Myles, Brock

2001: #307

✸ Shayla's a name so smooth and slinky it almost purrs. It's not overtly sexy, though, and on a little girl sounds like a sweet term of endearment.

Shea

Popularity: #783
Style: Androgynous, Brisk and Breezy, Celtic, Why Not?
Variants: Shay
Sisters: Brynn, Logan, Riley, Neve, Sage
Brothers: Kane, Donovan, Reid, Colt, Garret

2001: #745

✸ Why weigh yourself down with a big, clunky name? Shea hits all the Celtic surname highlights in a single, whisper-soft syllable.

Sheila

1960s: #59

Popularity: #798
Style: Celtic, Mid-Century, Nickname-Proof
Variants: Sile

Sisters: Brenda, Colleen, Kathy, Paula, Sherry
Brothers: Glenn, Douglas, Steve, Bruce, Keith
✴ Sheila was once a quintessential Irish name, but it became so broadly popular that it lost its Celtic connections. (A glimpse into Caitlin's future?) In Australia, it's even a generic slang term for a girl. Celia, another form of the same name, now sounds more distinctive.

Shelby

1990s: #39

Popularity: #96
Style: Androgynous, Last Names First
Nicknames: Shell
Variants: Shelbi, Shelbie
Sisters: Kelsey, Jordan, Bailey, Hunter, Aubrey
Brothers: Tanner, Dalton, Shane, Trevor, Garrett
✴ This soft surname follows in the tradition of favorites like Ashley and Lindsay. It sounds thoroughly modern but has been used for girls since the '30s, when its trendsetter was Shirley.

Shenandoah

Popularity: Rare
Style: Country & Western, Place Names
Nicknames: Shena, Doe

rarely used

Sisters: Savannah, Cheyenne, Winema, Sedona, Magnolia
Brothers: Dakota, Stetson, Montana, Richmond, Tecumseh
✴ The Shenandoah River valley of Virginia is the subject of song and story. The name, according to legend, is a Native American one meaning "daughter of the stars." It could be a poetic choice for a baby girl.

Sherry

1960s: #55

Popularity: Rare
Style: Mid-Century, Surfer Sixties
Variants: Sherri, Sherrie, Sheri, Cheri, Shari
Sisters: Connie, Sheryl, Darla, Cindy, Jeri
Brothers: Jon, Randy, Barry, Dana, Jay
✴ Sherry's girlish style comes at you from many directions. It's a cute nickname for Shirley or Sheryl. It sounds like an endearment, similar to the French *chérie*. And it's sweet like a Spanish Sherry wine. The name faded from view in the '80s; in its place came Shelby, which is similarly sweet with a surname twist.

Shirley

1930s: #4

Popularity: #766
Style: Solid Citizens
Variants: Shirlee
Sisters: Marilyn, Arlene,

Beverly, Norma, Phyllis
Brothers: Donald, Billy, Marvin, Duane, Gordon
✴ This is a name we can no longer judge on its own merits. There are so many Shirleys pushing seventy right now (thanks to 1930s kiddie superstar Shirley Temple) that it's hard to picture the name any other way. It will take another generation or two before we can appreciate the name's sweetness anew.

Shoshana

Popularity: Rare
Style: Jewish, Lacy and Lissome
Nicknames: Sue, Shosh, Shoshi

rarely used

Variants: Shoshanna, Susanna
Sisters: Elisheva, Hadassah, Ilana, Aviva, Margalit
Brothers: Noam, Asher, Shimon, Doron, Jaron
✴ Shoshana is Hebrew for "lily," and the source of the English Susanna. This is a gentle old name, like leaves rustling in the wind. It's quaint in Israel but exotic and sophisticated in the U.S.

Sienna

2003: #650

Popularity: #650
Style: Charms and Graces, Lacy and Lissome, Nickname-Proof
Variants: Siena
Sisters: Aspen, Willow, Calista, Thalia, Jetta
Brothers: Stone, Easton, Canyon, Damian, Judah
✴ The popularity of the name Sierra has attracted attention to this lovely neighbor. Sienna is a clay used in pigments. Treated with fire it becomes burnt sienna, a lush reddish-brown tint familiar to every child with a sixty-four pack of Crayolas. Coincidence or not, it started to be heard as a name right after the introduction of the Toyota Sienna minivan.

Sierra

2001: #56

Popularity: #73
Style: Country & Western, Nickname-Proof, Place Names
Variants: Cierra

Sisters: Mariah, Savannah, Autumn, Cassidy, Alexa
Brothers: Bryce, Dillon, Sawyer, Cole, Shane
✴ The name Sierra is taken from the word for a jagged ridge of mountains. It suggests a bond with nature's rugged beauty. The effect is subtle, though, since the name sounds traditionally feminine. It's a natural, with the makings of a classic.

Simone
1990s: #430

Popularity: #548
Style: African-American, French, Nickname-Proof, Why Not?

1900   Today
Variants: Simonne
Sisters: Celine, Camille, Juliet, Maribel, Noelle
Brothers: Brice, Graham, Quentin, Nathanael, Andre
✷ Silky but serious, Simone is a fine example of mature elegance.

Siobhan
1980s: #775

Popularity: Rare
Style: Celtic, Exotic Traditional
Nicknames: Vannie
Variants: Siobhán, Shevaun, Chevonne
1900   Today
Sisters: Deirdre, Sinead, Niamh, Grainne, Catriona
Brothers: Tiernan, Cormac, Eamon, Kieran, Declan
✷ Here's an opportunity to vex every relative who has to write your child a birthday card. Siobhan has a soft, easy sound (shi-VON), but it's devilish to spell. To pacify those who find the name baffling, just explain that it's Irish for Joan.

Skye
2003: #417

Popularity: #417
Style: Brisk and Breezy, Modern Meanings
Variants: Sky
1900   Today
Sisters: Eden, Sage, Haven, Lark, Summer
Brothers: Trace, Jett, Stone, Holden, Tate
✷ This attractive creation has a fresh-faced femininity and, naturally, a sunny demeanor. It's still a creative choice for a full name, but you'll meet quite a few Skylars who go by Sky. The spelling Skye is taken from the name of a Scottish island. It is one of several isle names (Iona, Isla) currently stylish for girls in Scotland.

Skylar
2002: #144

Popularity: #147
Style: Androgynous, Last Names First
Nicknames: Sky
Variants: Skyler
1900   Today
Sisters: Rylie, Payton, Sydney, Addison, Parker
Brothers: Cooper, Kolby, Dawson, Landon, Tucker
✷ America met this girl's name in 1997 in two very differerent incarnations. On TV, Skylar was the name of a new *Baywatch* babe. In the movies, she was the cerebral Harvard student in *Good Will Hunting*. Amazingly, the name fits both images equally well—perfect for the brainy cheerleader. This is a very trendy name for both boys and girls.

Sonia
1970s: #164

Popularity: #545
Style: Nickname-Proof, Slavic, Timeless
Variants: Sonya, Sonja

1900   Today
Sisters: Tamara, Jana, Daphne, Ingrid, Laura
Brothers: Joel, Ivan, Marcus, Byron, Adrian
✷ Sonia is brandy by the fire on a wintry night. It's luxurious, simple, and classic, a power combination. The spelling Sonia is the most timeless; Sonya's more Slavic but more '60s, too.

Sophia
2003: #20

Popularity: #20
Style: Antique Charm
Nicknames: Sophie, Sonya
Variants: Sofia, Sophie
1900   Today
Sisters: Chloe, Olivia, Madeline, Lilian, Faith
Brothers: Isaac, Sebastian, Julian, Luke, Elias
✷ The ultimate in Sophi-stication. This name is currently prized by upscale parents. It sounds serious, mature, and intelligent, but it's also pretty: a feminine power name. See also: Sophie.

Sophie
1910s: #109

Popularity: #151
Style: Antique Charm, French, German/Dutch, Guys and Dolls

1900   Today
Variants: Sophia, Sofie
Sisters: Isabelle, Rose, Eliza, Grace, Charlotte
Brothers: Max, Oliver, Henry, Jasper, Leo
✷ Sophie has a nickname style, but it's perfectly traditional as a given name. It's the French and German form of Sophia, and a century ago it was the more standard American version, too. Back then, the name bridged the gap between immigrant names like Sigrid and dance-hall sweethearts like Lillie. Today Sophie and Sophia are equally chic.

Stacy

Popularity: #653
Style: '70s–'80s, Androgynous, Surfer Sixties
Variants: Stacey, Stacie
Sisters: Kerry, Tanya, Shannon, Tracy, Leigh
Brothers: Brent, Chad, Toby, Jeremy, Darren
✳ Stacy and Tracy were the original sparkly surnames for girls. Their sunny demeanor still shines, but parents are now looking for fresher choices with the same spirit. Macy and Riley are two top contenders.

Stefania

Popularity: Rare
Style: Italian, Lacy and Lissome, Slavic, Why Not?
Nicknames: Stevie
Variants: Estefania, Stephania
Sisters: Viviana, Renata, Damiana, Liliana, Rafaela
Brothers: Carlo, Gideon, Graham, Marco, Dario
✳ This Italian form puts a new shine on Stephanie, just as Daniela has done for Danielle. Note that it's ste-FAHN-ya, not Ste-fa-NI-a.

Stella 1900s: #66

Popularity: #379
Style: Antique Charm, Guys and Dolls
Sisters: Lucy, Clara, Celia, Belle, Nora
Brothers: Harry, Clifford, Leo, Louis, Sam
✳ Stella is a 'tweener. On one side, you have Ella: trim, jazzy, and ultra-fashionable. On the other side, Estella: stately, graceful, and antique. Stella takes some from each, which results in a modest, charming compromise.

Stephanie 1980s: #6

Popularity: #48
Style: New Classics
Nicknames: Steph, Stevie, Steffi
Variants: Stefanie, Stephany, Estefania, Stephania
Sisters: Michelle, Christina, Danielle, Erica, Amanda
Brothers: Jeremy, Eric, Adam, Sean, Christopher
✳ Stephanie has joined its male counterpart Steven as an American classic. They are handsome choices that even the nitpickingest relative can't find fault with. The spelling Stefani, common during the name's '80s heyday, now reads like an Italian surname thanks to singer Gwen Stefani.

Sue

Popularity: Rare
Style: Nicknames, Solid Citizens, Why Not?
Sisters: Jo, Peggy, Judy, Kay, Bonnie
Brothers: Ted, Gene, Allen, Jim, Don
✳ Sweet Sue has been missing from the scene for decades. It's still heard occasionally as a nickname, but its cute, plain-Jane style has nixed it as a stand-alone first name. Now that deft little names like Lily and Hope have surged back into fashion, Sue may find new life.

Summer 2001: #147

Popularity: #154
Style: Charms and Graces, Modern Meanings, Nickname-Proof
Sisters: Sierra, Raven, Autumn, Jasmine, Hope
Brothers: Damian, Chance, Brady, Trevor, Micah
✳ A sunny name, in both meaning and personality. Parents choose a name like Summer as a big warm hug for their new daughter. It's sweet but not silly, and can sound adult and sophisticated when required. Read more under Autumn.

Susan 1950s: #4

Popularity: #514
Style: Mid-Century
Nicknames: Sue, Susie, Sukie, Suze
Variants: Susanna, Suzanne, Suzan
Sisters: Diane, Sharon, Kathleen, Ellen, Linda
Brothers: Gary, Douglas, Peter, Dennis, Alan
✳ Picture a woman named Susan. Don't you just want to like her? This is a name that positively screams "nice." It does not, however, scream "interesting," and in an era of creative naming, that has left nice, likable Susan spiraling out of style.

Susana 1990s: #554

Popularity: #869
Style: Biblical, Timeless, Why Not?
Nicknames: Sue, Susie, Suze
Variants: Suzanne, Susannah, Shoshana
Sisters: Joanna, Bethany, Leah, Priscilla, Marina
Brothers: Nathanael, Marcus, Graham, Elliot, Spencer
✳ Susana is as familiar and traditional as Susan but has the graceful flow of trendier names like Juliana. That makes Susana the most fashionable form of the classic name. The spelling Susannah shows off its antique roots.

Suzanne 1960s: #65

1900   Today

Popularity: Rare
Style: Mid-Century
Nicknames: Suzie, Sue
Variants: Suzann, Susannah, Susana
Sisters: Cheryl, Annette, Maureen, Rosanne, Connie
Brothers: Barry, Douglas, Randall, Jay, Curtis
✱ The name Susan, in all its many forms, is at its lowest popularity in generations. The worst off is this French variant, which is rooted so firmly in the '50s and '60s that it won't be coming back soon. Susannah may be a more promising candidate.

Sydney 2001: #25

1900   Today

Popularity: #25
Style: Androgynous, Last Names First, Place Names
Nicknames: Syd
Variants: Sidney, Sydnee
Sisters: Mackenzie, Bailey, Aubrey, Jordan, Shelby
Brothers: Hunter, Logan, Parker, Connor, Dalton
✱ Creative names tend to drift over time from male to female, and Sydney's a dramatic example. A hundred years ago, parents came up with Sidney as an aristocratic-sounding choice for their sons. Today it's passé as a boy's name but red-hot for girls. The Australian city helps make the spelling Sydney the most contemporary.

Sylvia 1910s: #73

1900   Today

Popularity: #561
Style: Ladies and Gentlemen, Solid Citizens
Nicknames: Syl, Sylvie
Variants: Silvia, Sylvie
Sisters: Vivian, Martha, Geneva, Irene, Loretta
Brothers: Raymond, Leon, Howard, Bernard, Francis
✱ Concentrate hard on this one. Put aside your preconceptions, close your eyes, and really listen to the name. Lovely, isn't it? To encourage others to drop their preconceptions, too, you might choose the original Italian spelling, Silvia. Or try the French Sylvie, which makes a great alternative to Sophie.

Tabitha 1980s: #154

1900   Today

Popularity: #404
Style: Biblical, New Classics
Nicknames: Tabby, Tab
Sisters: Katrina, Bethany, Meredith, Cara, Sabrina
Brothers: Drew, Casey, Geoffrey, Terrance, Derek
✱ The creators of the '60s sitcom *Bewitched* had a genius for unearthing names that captured the spirits of their characters. Tabitha is a biblical name, but it wasn't until it appeared as an adorable, otherworldly TV toddler that the name took its current shape. It's classically pretty with an impish streak. In England, Tabitha has been a favorite cat name—note the nickname Tabby.

Talia 2003: #357

1900   Today

Popularity: #357
Style: Jewish, Lacy and Lissome
Nicknames: Tally, Tal
Variants: Talya
Sisters: India, Malia, Daniela, Chaya, Annika
Brothers: Jaron, Lukas, Quinn, Asher, Conor
✱ Whether you call it a modern Hebrew name, a short form of Natalia, or just a contemporary creation, Talia is a winner. Its smart, smooth sound has cross-cultural strength.

Tamara 1970s: #86

1900   Today

Popularity: #495
Style: Biblical, Lacy and Lissome, Surfer Sixties
Nicknames: Tammy, Mara
Variants: Tamar
Sisters: Deana, Rochelle, Belinda, Heidi, Roxanna
Brothers: Darren, Joel, Bradley, Timothy, Craig
✱ This serene biblical name emerged in the sixties as a source for the super-popular nickname Tammy. Tammy is now on the outs, but Tamara remains an attractive possibility. Try Mara for the short form.

Tamika 1970s: #228

1900   Today

Popularity: Rare
Style: African-American
Nicknames: Tami, Mika, Mimi
Variants: Tameka, Tomika, Tanika, Tomiko
Sisters: Nakia, Shanta, Catrina, Latasha, Keisha
Brothers: Jermaine, Darrick, Dameon, Cedrick, Torrance
✱ For a time, Tamika was a reigning queen of African-American names. It seems to have come and gone in the blink of an eye. One heir to the throne is the slimmed-down version Tamia.

Tammy   1960s: #14
Popularity: Rare
Style: Nicknames, Surfer Sixties
Variants: Tammie, Tammy
Sisters: Lori, Dawn, Tracy, Tina,
Sherri
Brothers: Todd, Robbie, Greg, Scottie, Troy
✳ Short of Gidget, no name sits more squarely
in the square '60s. Debbie Reynolds's sunny
country gal in the movie *Tammy* made this nick-
name a symbol of wholesome sweetness.

Tamsin
Popularity: Rare
Style: English, The -ens, Why   rarely used
Not?
Nicknames: Tam, Tams, Tammy
Variants: Tamsyn
Sisters: Keelin, Fiona, Dulcie, Larkin, Emlyn
Brothers: Crispin, Tiernan, Griffith, Corin,
Dunstan
✳ This feminine form of Thomas has been well
used throughout Britain but never crossed over
to the U.S. Its sound is now perfectly current,
and the name is ripe for discovery.

Tanya   1970s: #66
Popularity: #600
Style: '70s–'80s, Nickname-
Proof, Slavic
Variants: Tania, Tonya
Sisters: Stacy, Tricia, Shawna,
Kerry, Larissa
Brothers: Shannon, Marc, Derrick, Troy, Kurtis
✳ Tanya is a Russian nickname for Tatiana that
sounds energetically American. (The similar
name Tonya comes from Antonina.) The name
hit a huge peak in the '70s but is far from fin-
ished. The spelling Tania is currently the most
fashionable form.

Tara   1970s: #43
Popularity: #336
Style: '70s–'80s, Little Darlings,
Nickname-Proof
Sisters: April, Cara, Jena, Holly,
Erin
Brothers: Jeremy, Dustin, Ryan, Casey, Brett
✳ For such a quiet little name, Tara arrived
with quite a splash in the '70s. Believe it or not,
in that decade more girls were named Tara than
Kristen and Krista combined. Today, it fits in
seamlessly with the new crop of swift little names
like Mia and Jada.

Tasha   1980s: #170
Popularity: Rare
Style: '70s–'80s, African-
American, Nicknames
Variants: Tosha
Sisters: Keisha, Mandy, Nikki, Trisha, Shanna
Brothers: Derrick, Courtney, Bryan, Terrance,
Jamey
✳ A nickname for a nickname (see Natalia),
Tasha became the center of a mini-style of its
own in the '70s. The core sound still appeals, but
the swirl of Tashas, Natashas, and Latashas got to
be too much. Sasha, the Russian nickname for
Alexandra, is a more stylish option today.

Tatiana   2001: #242
Popularity: #272
Style: Lacy and Lissome, Saints,
Slavic
Nicknames: Tanya, Tati, Tiana
Variants: Tatyana
Sisters: Anastasia, Natalia, Mariana, Gabriela,
Serena
Brothers: Darius, Fabian, Lukas, Maxim, Dimitri
✳ Tatiana's a perfect choice for residents of
enchanted forests and faerie palaces. Certainly,
this is a serious name—in fact, intensely digni-
fied. It's a classic from the early days of
Christianity, popular in Russia for hundreds of
years. Its sound, though, is the stuff of daydreams.

Tatum   2003: #391
Popularity: #391
Style: Last Names First
Sisters: Quinn, Ainsley, Rylie,
Reese, Teagan
Brothers: Rowan, Gideon, Brody, Hudson, Zane
✳ This old English surname made a direct leap
to girl's first name thanks to the example of
actress Tatum O'Neal. Its sound is quite boy-
ish, but since it never was a boy's name, the effect is
more merry than masculine. Still uncommon,
but poised to rise fast.

Tayla
Popularity: Rare
Style: Bell Tones   rarely used
Variants: Taylah
Sisters: Sheyla, Kylie, Janay,
Bria, Jalisa
Brothers: Cale, Darrien, Kylan, Ridge, Tevin
✳ Never met a Tayla? Wait a few years. This
name is one of the hottest hits in Australia and
fits current American fashions to a T. Expect to
see it hit our shores soon.

Taylor   1990s: #9

Popularity: #19
Style: Androgynous, Last Names
First
Nicknames: Tay
Sisters: Jordan, Bailey, Ashton, Kelsey, Hunter
Brothers: Tanner, Austin, Keaton, Trevor, Dalton

★ Taylor is the name that opened the floodgates to tradesman names for girls. It surged in the '90s after its use on the soap opera *The Bold and the Beautiful*. (The actress who played that Taylor, Hunter Tylo, gets a double nod for popularizing her own first name as well.) Ironically, Taylor is now so popular for girls that the boyish image that drew parents to it is quickly fading.

Terra   1970s: #446

Popularity: Rare
Style: Little Darlings, Modern
Meanings, Why Not?
Variants: Tierra
Sisters: Raven, Siena, Mara, Lark, Skye
Brothers: Storm, Jude, Heath, Garrick, Bryce

★ Terra first appeared with '70s cuties like Tara and Tasha, but its meaning—Latin for "earth"—sets it apart. This can be a contemporary choice for nature lovers and a match for creative names from Lyric to Meadow.

Terry   1950s: #97

Popularity: Rare
Style: Androgynous, Mid-
Century, Nicknames
Variants: Terri, Teri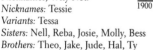
Sisters: Jackie, Lynn, Sheryl, Connie, Trudy
Brothers: Rick, Garry, Danny, Steve, Bruce

★ Terry was the queen—and king—of the androgynous nicknames of the '50s and '60s. It was a tremendous hit for both sexes but has lost its edge in recent years. Today Terry works best as a nickname, either for the traditional Theresa or a new creation like Terra or Terrian.

Tess   2003: #567

Popularity: #567
Style: Guys and Dolls,
Nicknames, Why Not?
Nicknames: Tessie
Variants: Tessa
Sisters: Nell, Reba, Josie, Molly, Bess
Brothers: Theo, Jake, Jude, Hal, Ty

★ This nickname (from Teresa) makes a stylish statement on its own: trim, buoyant, and confident.

Tessa   2003: #283

Popularity: #283
Style: Little Darlings,
Nicknames
Nicknames: Tess, Tessie
Sisters: Jenna, Alexa, Tia, Callie, Talia
Brothers: Drew, Ian, Brody, Colin, Reese

★ Originally a pet form of Theresa, Tessa has begun to outpace its mother name. It wraps up the cute, compact style of the 1900s hit Tessie in a more sophisticated form. This name is popping up in Europe and has the makings of an international hit.

Thalia   2003: #603

Popularity: #603
Style: Lacy and Lissome,
Latino/Latina, Mythological,
Nickname-Proof
Sisters: Selena, Mireya, Reyna, Athena, Maya
Brothers: Dimitri, Jairo, Darian, Rodrigo, Alvaro

★ The Greek Muse of comedy, Thalia is starting to find an audience in the U.S. largely due to a Mexican singing star. A creative choice with classical pedigree to back it up.

Thea   1960s: #978

Popularity: Rare
Style: Ladies and Gentlemen,
Why Not?
Sisters: Luna, Rhea, Cecile,
Estella, Iva
Brothers: Jules, Milo, Reuben, Hal, Casper

★ This subtle, pretty name is seldom heard, which is a shame. Originally a short form of Dorothea and Theadora, Thea is simple but serious enough to stand on its own.

Theda   1910s: #485

Popularity: Rare
Style: Ladies and Gentlemen,
Nickname-Proof
Sisters: Geneva, Alma, Petra,
Neoma, Larue
Brothers: Armand, Milo, Rudolph, Carlyle, Odell

★ Those who are familiar with silent film star Theda Bara, the original "vamp," will admire this name for its discreet seductiveness. Those who've never heard of her may find the name a bit dowdy.

Thelma
Popularity: Rare
Style: Porch Sitters
Sisters: Louise, Opal, Fern, Gladys, Ruby
Brothers: Earl, Herbert, Virgil, Lester, Lloyd

1910s: #28

✶ The sort of soft, squishy name that's currently off the fashion map. Thelma's actually a rather nice example of the style, but it's still a tough sell.

Theodora
Popularity: Rare
Style: Greek, Ladies and Gentlemen
Nicknames: Thea, Dora
Sisters: Rafaela, Aurelia, Eleanora, Delphine, Evanthia
Brothers: Rudolph, Benedict, Domenick, Leander, Everett

1900s: #582

✶ A grand old name, but a mouthful. For a similar but lighter touch, try reversing the elements to yield Dorothea ("gift of God" vs. "God's gift").

Theresa
Popularity: #566
Style: Mid-Century, Timeless
Nicknames: Terry, Tess, Tessa, Tressa, Tracy
Variants: Teresa, Therese
Sisters: Anita, Pamela, Denise, Susan, Cynthia
Brothers: Peter, Curtis, Russell, Douglas, Paul

1960s: #43

✶ Theresa always seemed like a first-ballot timeless classic, but in the past few years it has plummeted out of style. Mysterious, given that the sound of the name is still impeccably fashionable. Is the '50s-style nickname Terry the problem? Switch to Tess and you're back in business.

Therese
Popularity: Rare
Style: French, Saints, Solid Citizens, Why Not?
Nicknames: Terry, Tess, Reese
Variants: Terese
Sisters: Marianne, Rosalind, Ramona, Jeanne, Colette
Brothers: Gerard, Stanton, Randolph, Jerome, Stewart

1950s: #302

✶ An intriguing name wth two different pronunciations. "Teh-REZZ" is authentically French and elegant, but a bit downbeat. "Teh-REESE" is brighter but less exotic. Both are uncommon and handsome.

Thomasina
Popularity: Rare
Style: Exotic Traditional
Nicknames: Tommie, Tamsin
Sisters: Genevieve, Araminta, Violetta, Josepha, Evangeline
Brothers: Benedict, Thaddeus, Tristram, Ivor, Bartholomew

rarely used

✶ Thomasina is a genuine antique that was past its heyday by the year 1700. It's a bit heavy but has a romantic rhythm and a cute tomboy nickname. And given its three centuries of slumber, it is completely free of preconceptions.

Tia
Popularity: #481
Style: Little Darlings, Nicknames
Sisters: Cara, Lea, Tess, Kira, Abby
Brothers: Chaz, Ian, Stefan, Noel, Ari

1990s: #290

✶ Tia used to be a nickname for elaborate Latin creations like Laetitia, but there's no reason not to choose it straight up. It's a little pocketful of cheer.

Tiara
Popularity: #612
Style: Modern Meanings
Nicknames: Tia, Tee
Sisters: Diamond, Raven, Karissa, Desiree, Cierra
Brothers: Marquis, Quinton, Storm, Jovan, Trey

1990s: #240

✶ This is the subtlest of the fantasy princess names. It sounds like a mainstream girl's name but glitters like a diamond tiara.

Tierra
Popularity: #906
Style: Charms and Graces, Modern Meanings
Sisters: Carina, Aspen, Summer, Kelsey, Bria
Brothers: Keenan, Stone, River, Markus, Dillon

1990s: #351

✶ Tierra is the Spanish word for "earth." It has a trendy sound for a girl's name and is sometimes chosen as a symbol of kinship with nature. In sound, origin, and associations, very close to Sierra.

Tiffany

1980s: #11

Popularity: #149
Style: '70s–'80s
Nicknames: Tif
Variants: Tiffani
Sisters: Crystal, Amber, Natasha, Whitney, Brittany
Brothers: Travis, Corey, Chad, Marquis, Wesley
✶ The spiritual grandma of all the brand-name names. Tiffany is actually a religious name from the Middle Ages, but its modern use is all about the New York jewelry emporium. Unfortunately, this has given the name a "downwardly mobile" reputation. The assumption is that people who actually shop at Tiffany's don't name their kids after the store.

Tilda

Popularity: Rare
Style: Ladies and Gentlemen, Scandinavian
Sisters: Thora, Dulcie, Allegra, Willa, Petra
Brothers: Emory, Willis, Lonzo, Elden, Merritt
✶ A short form of Matilda that lightens and modernizes that name.

rarely used

Tina

1960s: #30

Popularity: #697
Style: Surfer Sixties
Sisters: Tracy, Lisa, Dawn, Julie, Tamara
Brothers: Todd, Scott, Tony, Craig, Keith
✶ This model nickname was propelled to full-name status in the '60s, like Gina and Lori. That style has largely passed, but as a nickname Tina still has classic appeal. If you're at a loss for a full version, consider Bettina, Christina, Martina, Santina, or Valentina.

Toni

1960s: #154

Popularity: #732
Style: Nicknames, Surfer Sixties
Sisters: Teri, Sandy, Carla, Jody, Liz
Brothers: Brad, Joey, Randy, Kurt, Chris
✶ The nickname Toni broke free from Antonia generations ago. Despite the model of author Toni Morrison, the name sounds more bubbly than scholarly.

Topaz

Popularity: Rare
Style: Charms and Graces
Sisters: Azure, Juniper, Lark, Opal, Hazel
Brothers: Birch, Forest, Cyrus, Sterling, Theo
✶ The next step past Ruby and Pearl. Topaz was occasionally heard in the heyday of gem names and would be a high-style choice for adventurous parents today.

rarely used

Tori

1990s: #201

Popularity: #299
Style: Nicknames
Variants: Tory
Sisters: Carli, Tia, Abby, Paige, Kyra
Brothers: Drew, Trey, Conor, Cody, Tucker
✶ Tori used to be just a minor nickname for Victoria, but it's well established now as a given name. It's as cute and lightweight as '50s counterpart Vicki, with a '90s spin thanks to singer Tori Amos and *Beverly Hills, 90210* star Tori Spelling.

Tova

Popularity: Rare
Style: Jewish, Little Darlings, Nickname-Proof, Scandinavian
Variants: Tove
Sisters: Noa, Meta, Orly, Aviva, Pella
Brothers: Avi, Noam, Rune, Niels, Tal
✶ Fashionably swift and petite, Tova also has a gentle graciousness. You can picture a Tova zipping masterfully down a ski slope, then baking brownies afterward. The name has both Norse and Hebrew origins for a global sound.

rarely used

Tracy

1970s: #25

Popularity: #819
Style: Androgynous, Last Names First, Surfer Sixties
Variants: Traci, Tracey, Tracie, Tracee
Sisters: Stacey, Kelly, Robin, Tina, Sonya
Brothers: Todd, Brad, Jeffrey, Darren, Randy
✶ In the film *The Philadelphia Story*, Katharine Hepburn played glamorous socialite Tracy Lord. That sparkling image sent the name soaring for decades. Tracy's high-society image gradually mellowed, and today it's more often heard on moms than babies.

Tricia

Popularity: Rare
Style: '70s–'80s, Nicknames
Nicknames: Trish
Variants: Trisha

1970s: #150
1900 Today

Sisters: Trina, Christie, Nicola, Kerry, Ami
Brothers: Jamie, Brett, Clint, Toby, Torrance
✷ A tale of two Patricias: The name Tricia took off just as Patty disappeared from view. Tricia is just as breezy but far less cutesy. Think of the independent spirit of country singer Trisha Yearwood, as opposed to the brokenhearted sweetness of predecessor Patsy Cline.

Trina

Popularity: Rare
Style: '70s–'80s, African-American, Nicknames, Surfer Sixties

1970s: #229
1900 Today

Sisters: Tamara, Deana, Marcy, Jodie, Kara
Brothers: Kris, Brad, Timothy, Lance, Tobin
✷ Trina comes from the recent past when the style was to trim down to the bare essentials, like a miniskirt or a Volkswagen Beetle. It's a charming, sunny name that could still be stylish as a nickname for Katrina or Trinity.

Trinity

Popularity: #57
Style: Modern Meanings
Nicknames: Trini, Trina
Sisters: Serenity, Jade, Destiny, Sierra, Genesis

2003: #57
1900 Today

Brothers: Maximus, Orion, Tristan, Josiah, Bryce
✷ Enter *The Matrix.* . . . That massively popular sci-fi franchise launched the name Trinity, but it's thriving on its own merits. A powerhouse.

Trista

Popularity: #503
Style: '70s–'80s
Sisters: Jaclyn, Tasha, Kristal, Kendra, Nikki

2003: #503
1900 Today

Brothers: Kory, Brenton, Shaun, Kiel, Casey
✷ Trista made a brief appearance in the '80s, a glossy hybrid of Tricia and Krista. More recently, the name's profile was raised by television's "real-life" bachelorette Trista Rehn.

Trudy

Popularity: Rare
Style: Mid-Century, Nicknames
Nicknames: Tru
Variants: Trudie, Trudi

1950s: #310
1900 Today

Sisters: Connie, Vicki, Dee, Penny, Margo
Brothers: Garry, Ron, Donnie, Ken, Dana
✷ Is any nickname farther removed from the full name that gave it life? Trudy is cute, perky, and all-American. It's happily rooted in the 1950s and a jolly (if uncommon) choice today. But if you're tempted to use it as a nickname, you have to face the fact that it's short for Gertrude. Or Ermintrude, if that's any help.

Tyler

Popularity: #606
Style: Androgynous, Last Names First
Nicknames: Ty
Sisters: Hunter, Ashton, Logan, Darby, Chandler

1990s: #340
1900 Today

Brothers: Weston, Keaton, Jarrett, Dillon, Tucker
✷ Tyler and Taylor were both on androgynous turf in the '90s, but they've recently agreed to split up the territory. Tyler is now firmly established as a top choice for boys, Taylor for girls. Tyler still makes a catchy girl's name, but be aware that you'll be courting confusion on two fronts: She'll be called Taylor half the time, and mistaken for a boy the other half.

Tyra

Popularity: #706
Style: African-American, Bell Tones, Little Darlings
Sisters: Mara, Deja, Ayla, Jena, Taryn

2001: #578
1900 Today

Brothers: Darian, Tate, Tristan, Brice, Abel
✷ Most of us find one social niche where we feel comfortable: the jocks, the geeks, the glamour girls. But then there are those enviable few who can move smoothly among groups, fitting in and getting along wherever they go. That's Tyra, a simple but seductive, new but familar name with cross-racial appeal.

Valencia 1960s: #711
Popularity: Rare
Style: Lacy and Lissome, Place Names
Nicknames: Val
Variants: Valentia
Sisters: Angelia, Venetia, Galilea, Alexandria, Graciela
Brothers: Orlando, Roderick, Ramiro, Phoenix, Paris
✱ Valencia is most familiar as a name of cities and oranges, but it's also an ornate, pretty first name. If you prefer a classical rather than citrus flavor, go with Valentia.

Valentina 2003: #454
Popularity: #454
Style: Exotic Traditional, Saints, Slavic
Nicknames: Val, Tina
Variants: Valentine
Sisters: Anastasia, Tatiana, Angelina, Mirabella, Natalia
Brothers: Maximilian, Dominik, Blaise, Demetrius, Isaias
✱ This form of Valentine, used in Eastern Europe, has the intriguing effect of making the name more feminine yet less girly. Valentina is ravishing but drop-dead serious. It's one of the few names you can picture equally on an executive door and a lingerie label. Great potential.

Valentine 1900s: #884
Popularity: Rare
Style: Exotic Traditional, Fanciful
Nicknames: Val
Variants: Valentina
Sisters: Salome, Evangeline, Tempest, Magdalene, Violette
Brothers: Florian, Constantin, Romeo, Peregrine, Magnus
✱ Valentine is traditionally a man's name, as in the St. Valentine whose feast day we celebrate with hearts and candy. Its romantic connotations, though, make it a lavish choice for a girl. The simple nickname Val is a nice antidote to the name's excesses; Valentina is an increasingly popular import.

Valeria 2003: #171
Popularity: #171
Style: Italian, Lacy and Lissome, Latino/Latina, Shakespearean
Nicknames: Val, Ria, Valya
Variants: Valerie
Sisters: Mariana, Natalia, Juliana, Alondra, Viviana
Brothers: Lorenzo, Armando, Xavier, Francisco, Andres
✱ The French form Valerie is more familiar in the U.S., but Valeria is a graceful international favorite. It's especially popular in Argentina and Brazil and a rising choice for American Latinas.

Valerie 1960s: #70
Popularity: #172
Style: French, Mid-Century
Nicknames: Val
Variants: Valarie, Valérie, Valery, Valeria
Sisters: Melanie, Denise, Cynthia, Jacqueline, Diane
Brothers: Gregory, Dean, Randall, Patrick, Marc
✱ Valerie is an old and elegant French name that rolls off your tongue. A '60s–'70s smash in France, the name has a steadier history and a more mature image. To some, "mature" can mean boring, but that doesn't have to be. The name was never overly common, and Val is a smart little nickname.

Vanessa 1980s: #46
Popularity: #70
Style: African-American, Lacy and Lissome, New Classics
Nicknames: Nessa
Sisters: Cassandra, Miranda, Bethany, Angelica, Sabrina
Brothers: Brandon, Garrett, Antonio, Bradley, Marcus
✱ The name equivalent of an evening gown, Vanessa is timeless, lacy luxury.

Vashti rarely used
Popularity: Rare
Style: Biblical
Sisters: Avital, Zilla, Tamar, Lilith, Elisheva
Brothers: Azriel, Boaz, Joachim, Phineas, Jabez
✱ In the Bible, Vashti was a disobedient queen who met an ugly fate. But before you lump the name with Jezebel and Delilah, consider her crime: She refused the King's order to parade around and show off her hot bod to his drinking buddies. To which many modern parents would say, "You go, girl!"

Venice

Popularity: Rare
Style: Place Names
Sisters: Geneva, Danae, Verity, Milan, Allegra

rarely used

1900 Today

Brothers: Tarquin, Rider, Dublin, Garrick, Boston

✷ A romantic, immortal European city—and a more creative name choice than Paris.

Venus

1970s: #755

Popularity: Rare
Style: Fanciful, Mythological
Sisters: Electra, Tempest, Athena, Dove, Isis

1900 Today

Brothers: Baron, Thor, Adonis, Jupiter, Cassius

✷ You would expect tennis star Venus Williams to be seeing legions of young girls bearing her magnetic name by now. It's a classical alternative to lofty names like Heaven, Princess, and Tiara. Yet so far there have been few takers. The name sounds too sexy to some, and it's easy pickings for teasing rhymes.

Vera

1900s: #64

Popularity: Rare
Style: Ladies and Gentlemen, Nickname-Proof, Slavic
Sisters: Alma, Viola, Marion, Ada, Cora

1900 Today

Brothers: Clarence, Luther, Willis, Ernest, Alfred

✷ Vera is a Slavic name meaning "faith," and it coincides with the Latin word for "true." That's a lot of positive energy, and the name's direct, womanly sound carries the message well. Unfortunately, Americans overindulged in this name a few generations back and there's still a lingering hangover. Give it a few more years.

Verity

Popularity: Rare
Style: Charms and Graces, English, Why Not?
Sisters: Calla, Mercy, Serenity, Evening, Gemma

rarely used

1900 Today

Brothers: Crispin, Royce, Justice, Corin, Bishop

✷ An uplifting, thoroughly unusual meaning name. Usually that spells flamboyant, yet Verity is modest and ladylike.

Veronica

1980s: #68

Popularity: #175
Style: Saints, Timeless
Nicknames: Ronnie, Vera
Variants: Veronika

1900 Today

Sisters: Christina, Adrienne, Felicia, Victoria, Amanda

Brothers: Marcus, Geoffrey, Nicholas, Lance, Bradley

✷ Many timeless names are demure and understated, but Veronica is sizzling. Certainly, it's a respectable classic, with Latin and saintly roots. It's just respectably, classically seductive. *Archie* comics got this name just right with their raven-haired dreamgirl—compare to Betty.

Vickie

1950s: #80

Popularity: Rare
Style: Mid-Century, Nicknames
Variants: Vicky, Vicki, Vikki
Sisters: Patti, Cathy, Jan, Terry, Lynn

1900 Today

Brothers: Rick, Dana, Randy, Butch, Gregg

✷ Vickie is an adorable nickname that serves a woman well throughout her lifetime. So go ahead and call your daughter Vickie . . . but name her Victoria. During the '50s and '60s, thousands of parents chose the nickname straight, which is simply a waste. Victoria is one of the great combinations of dignified name and cute nickname. Why mess with it?

Victoria

1990s: #21

Popularity: #22
Style: Antique Charm, English, Timeless
Nicknames: Vicky, Tori, Vivi

1900 Today

Sisters: Emily, Caroline, Alexandra, Veronica, Abigail

Brothers: Alexander, Nicholas, Benjamin, Spencer, Nathaniel

✷ Victoria is more popular today than ever before, but there's no chance of it sounding faddish. The image of Queen Victoria remains too strong to permit such an undignified fate. Thoroughly proper and elegant.

Violet

1910s: #74

Popularity: #597
Style: Antique Charm, Charms and Graces
Nicknames: Vi

1900 Today

Variants: Violette, Violetta
Sisters: Jewell, Stella, Ruby, Georgia, Josephine
Brothers: Julius, Everett, Jasper, Theo, Oliver

✷ This proper lady could make a splash . . . a demure, respectable splash. Richer than Lily but lighter than Hazel, Violet strikes a lovely balance.

Virginia

1920s: #7

Popularity: #411
Style: Country & Western, Ladies and Gentlemen, Place Names
Nicknames: Ginny, Ginger
Sisters: Georgia, Charlotte, Eleanor, Geneva, Josephine
Brothers: Marshall, Everett, Vernon, Roy, Theodore
✸ A grand old dame with a flirtatious side, Virginia is bubbling over with personality. Yet it's less common than ever, even as neighbors Georgia and Carolina climb the charts. Why? Well, there is that pesky "virgin" problem. Just accept that during the self-conscious adolescent years, your daughter may insist on Ginny.

Vivian

1920s: #73

Popularity: #223
Style: Saints, Solid Citizens
Nicknames: Viv, Vi, Vivi
Variants: Vivienne, Viviana
Sisters: Marian, Eleanor, Clarice, Violet, Evelyn
Brothers: Hugh, Gilbert, Stuart, Lyle, Willis
✸ This polished old favorite is ready to shine again. The full name Vivian has a no-nonsense elegance, while the nickname Viv is impish and contemporary.

Viviana

2003: #397

Popularity: #397
Style: Italian, Lacy and Lissome, Latino/Latina
Nicknames: Vivi, Viv
Sisters: Mariela, Liliana, Natalia, Adriana, Valeria
Brothers: Marco, Lorenzo, Brennan, Jarrett, Giovanni
✸ What a difference an "a" makes. Vivian is stylish but sober; Viviana ardently romantic.

Wanda

1930s: #51

Popularity: Rare
Style: African-American, Mid-Century, Nickname-Proof, Slavic
Sisters: Ramona, Joanne, Paula, Yvonne, Gwen
Brothers: Wayne, Roger, Glenn, Jerome, Gene
✸ The softly nasal sound of Wanda has sent it to the back of the pack. If you actually met a Wanda, though, you'd be pleased. Give the name time and it grows on you.

Wendy

1970s: #37

Popularity: #288
Style: Surfer Sixties
Variants: Wendi
Sisters: Julie, Tina, Jill, Cindy, Heidi
Brothers: Keith, Troy, Jeffrey, Brad, Chris
✸ Wendy first appeared as the eldest of the Darling children in *Peter Pan*. That image—a girl on the verge of growing up—still suits the name well. It's youthful but responsible. For a more adventurous take on the name, try it as a nickname for Gwendolyn.

Whitney

1980s: #66

Popularity: #448
Style: '70s–'80s, Last Names First, Nickname-Proof
Sisters: Lindsay, Jaclyn, Desiree, Lacey, Chelsea
Brothers: Dustin, Wesley, Jarrett, Kurtis, Brandon
✸ This tony surname has risen and fallen with the career arc of singer Whitney Houston. It started out as a swank-sounding boy's name back when the Whitneys, Morgans, and Vanderbilts were gilded-age kingpins. Like most names of this style, it gets friendlier and more approachable with age.

Wilhelmina

1900s: #299

Popularity: Rare
Style: German/Dutch, Ladies and Gentlemen
Nicknames: Willie, Willa, Mina, Minnie, Wilma, Willow
Sisters: Henrietta, Hester, Philomena, Magdalene, Petra
Brothers: Ferdinand, Emil, Leopold, Constantin, Sigmund
✸ If we went by sound alone, Wilhelmina would be in the running. It's expressive and romantic, with plenty of prime nicknames. But written down, all those dense consonants seem like a heavy load.

Willa

1930s: #291

Popularity: Rare
Style: Antique Charm, Ladies and Gentlemen, Little Darlings, Why Not?
Sisters: Rhea, Gracie, Lena, Belle, Lila
Brothers: Silas, Alden, Cael, Jasper, Pierce
✸ Willa sounds like a natural hit, combining the jazzy sweetness of revivals like Lily and Ella with the airy swiftness of Mia and Skye. Oddly enough, though, Willa is not a hit: The name has hardly been heard for generations. It could be a stylish surprise.

Willow 2002: #510

Popularity: #530
Style: Charms and Graces, Nickname-Proof
Sisters: Meadow, Sienna, Felicity, Jasmine, Bay
Brothers: Landen, River, Tate, Carter, Birch
✱ This name is plain and simple but nonetheless wildly romantic. Choose it to indulge your girly side without drowning in frills. Not yet common, but coming on strong.

Winifred 1910s: #157

Popularity: Rare
Style: English, Ladies and Gentlemen, Saints
Nicknames: Winnie, Freddie
Sisters: Adelaide, Philomena, Beatrice, Matilda, Millicent
Brothers: Casper, Benedict, Godfrey, Sylvester, Giles
✱ This Welsh/English old-timer takes you deep into the territory of maiden great-aunts. So deep, in fact, that it may have a chance as a quirky surprise. Winifred's rhythm is delicate and literary, and nickname Winnie is a cute little sprite.

Winona 1920s: #444
Popularity: Rare
Style: Country & Western
Nicknames: Winnie, Nona
Variants: Wenona, Wynonna
Sisters: Mahala, Tallulah, Magnolia, Virginia, Shenandoah
Brothers: Chayton, Dakota, Seattle, Lafayette, Shane
✱ If this name only conjures up actress Winona Ryder and singer Wynonna Judd, here's a new perspective. Winona is a classic American Indian name, that of a legendary princess. Among the Dakota Sioux, it was the traditional name for a firstborn daughter. Doesn't it sound better already?

Yesenia 1990s: #184
Popularity: #302
Style: Latino/Latina
Nicknames: Yesi
Variants: Yessenia
Sisters: Marisa, Selena, Angelica, Liliana, Alejandra
Brothers: Sergio, Gerardo, Gustavo, Omar, Josue
✱ The name Yesenia has bloomed thanks to a pair of popular telenovelas. Actress Adela Noriega's portrayal of a passionate gypsy cemented the name's romantic image, but its sound is dreamy all on its own.

Yolanda 1970s: #111

Popularity: Rare
Style: African-American, Latino/Latina, Mid-Century
Nicknames: Lani, Yoli
Variants: Yolande
Sisters: Regina, Annette, Ivette, Ladonna, Sonia
Brothers: Roderick, Darrell, Reginald, Shannon, Alfonzo
✱ In the '30s and '40s, Yolanda was a romantic exotic, steeped in its French and Hungarian heritage. Later it became an African-American favorite. And all along, it's been used by Spanish-speaking families. Today, it's still silky-smooth, but slinking out of style.

Yvette 1960s: #173

Popularity: #784
Style: African-American, French, Surfer Sixties
Nicknames: Yvie
Sisters: Sonya, Brigitte, Renee, Suzette, Cherie
Brothers: Gerard, Vince, Duane, Andre, Derek
✱ This French diminutive purrs like a kitten but shows some restraint.

Yvonne 1930s: #123

Popularity: Rare
Style: African-American, French, Mid-Century
Nicknames: Vonnie, Yvie
Sisters: Therese, Annette, Sondra, Marianne, Gayle
Brothers: Gerard, Stuart, Maurice, Glen, Jerome
✱ The French classic Yvonne doesn't fit any of the hot current trends, so chances are you haven't even considered the name. But if you take the time, you might find it a pleasant surprise. Yvonne is simple, elegant, and uncommon, and that's a nice combination. The unusual spelling makes it look especially distinguished in print.

Zaria 2001: #525
Popularity: #647
Style: African-American, Place Names
Variants: Zahra
Sisters: Tamia, Nyla, Amari, Samara, Kenia
Brothers: Mekhi, Zander, Orion, Luca, Jayce
✱ Zaria comes from an Arabic word for "flower" and is best known as the name of a Nigerian city. (The variation Zahra is more traditional as a given name.) In the U.S., Zaria is a rising star that nods to African heritage but sounds creative and classy for girls of any background.

Zelda

1910s: #416

Popularity: Rare
Style: Exotic Traditional, Ladies and Gentlemen, Nickname-Proof
Sisters: Theda, Petra, Ione, Evangeline, Zola
Brothers: Foster, Wiley, Ulysses, Ferdinand, Felix

★ Zelda falls into the special category of literary exotics. If you're considering the name, chances are you and all your friends know all about Zelda Fitzgerald. (Or you've spent way too many nights up late playing the Legend of Zelda games.) That can make the name feel a little forced, but it does have a cool sound in its own right.

Zilla

Popularity: Rare

rarely used

Style: Biblical, Exotic Traditional, Little Darlings
Variants: Zillah
Sisters: Tamar, Iole, Esme, Tova, Avis
Brothers: Axel, Zeb, Jabez, Noam, Magnus

★ A zippy girl's name starting with Z! And it's straight out of the Old Testament! This is great! Yes, it truly is. But it's my duty to point out the potential Godzilla problem. Whether you care is up to you.

Zoe

2003: #58

Popularity: #58
Style: Greek, Little Darlings, Nickname-Proof
Variants: Zoë, Zoey, Zoie
Sisters: Maya, Chloe, Nia, Ava, Piper
Brothers: Ian, Noah, Liam, Eli, Wyatt

★ If you want to know how surprising the popularity of Zoe is, just look at *Sesame Street*. They like to keep their Muppet names far from the mainstream: Kermit, Grover, Elmo. When the character Zoe was created, it seemed a safe bet. But the vitality of this name was bound to catch on eventually, and it has in a hurry. A lovably quirky hit.

Zora

1900s: #448

Popularity: Rare
Style: African-American, Exotic Traditional, Why Not?
Variants: Zorah
Sisters: Cleo, Augusta, Viva, Aurelia, Belle
Brothers: Palmer, Alonzo, Mose, Lucius, Sargent

★ This jazzy little name gets an extra artistic kick from novelist Zora Neale Hurston. Simple yet distinctive.

Name Snapshots: Boys

Aaron

1980s: #32

Popularity: #49
Style: Biblical, New Classics, Nickname-Proof
Sisters: Rachel, Jessica, Megan, Leah, Nicole
Brothers: Jared, Adam, Brian, Seth, Joshua

✱ Along with Nathan and Joshua, this is one of the new biblical classics. It fits in smoothly with both traditional and contemporary names, and only an Aaliyah will keep Aaron from being first in every elementary school lineup.

Abel

2002: #344

Popularity: #359
Style: Biblical, Little Darlings
Nicknames: Abe
Sisters: Mara, Eden, Leah, Anya, Tia
Brothers: Noah, Axel, Eli, Micah, Levi

✱ The sad fate of the biblical Abel has always limited the popularity of this name. Stylewise, it has it all: Old Testament style in a bright, boyish sound. Lately parents have decided they can put the fratricide aside, and Abel is looking like a surprise hit.

Abraham

1900s: #135

Popularity: #196
Style: Antique Charm, Biblical
Nicknames: Abe, Bram
Variants: Abram, Avraham
Sisters: Amelia, Hester, Violet, Sadie, Cecilia
Brothers: Solomon, Ezra, Lincoln, Cornelius, Jonas

✱ Abraham is a relatively uncommon choice, even in the midst of an Old Testament craze. The name seems to be having trouble shaking its white-beard image. But with its perfect nicknames and presidential pedigree, this dignified selection is bound to find more takers soon.

Adam

1980s: #22

Popularity: #60
Style: Biblical, New Classics, Nickname-Proof
Sisters: Alison, Rachel, Sara, Erin, Leah
Brothers: Jared, Evan, Aaron, Seth, Ryan

✱ Adam, a "new" classic? Yes, the name of the first man wasn't much heard until the '60s, when it suddenly joined the roster of English standards. As a consequence, it's now an unusual example of a popular Old Testament name that doesn't feel like a polished antique. Adam sounds fresh and modern, despite its obviously ancient origins.

Addison

2003: #539

Popularity: #539
Style: Androgynous, Last Names First
Sisters: Haleigh, Aubrey, Kendall, Kiley, Jocelyn
Brothers: Preston, Coleman, Riley, Avery, Jamison

✱ Addison is the sort of surname that used to sound like a stuffy banker. After a long absence, it has reemerged sounding trendier and more contemporary—for both boys and girls. Also consider the less common Edison, which gains you a hero namesake and the option of Eddie if the full name turns out to be too much of a mouthful.

Adonis

2003: #829

Popularity: #829
Style: Fanciful, Mythological
Nicknames: Don
Sisters: Venus, Electra, Artemis, Oceana, Isis
Brothers: Apollo, Achilles, Morpheus, Orion, Caesar

✱ Adonis sounds as cool as can be, but it's a gamble. If he's anything but a perfect physical specimen, this name, symbolic of male beauty, could be a burden.

Adrian

2003: #68

Popularity: #68
Style: Antique Charm, Nickname-Proof, Saints, Shakespearean
Variants: Adrien
Sisters: Olivia, Sophia, Mariah, Alexis, Ava
Brothers: Damian, Dominic, Trevor, Julian, Miles
✻ An old and dignified name, borne by popes and emperors. Adrian has always been well used in Britain but less so in the U.S., where it used to be confused with the girl's name Adrienne. Today, though, the name is both popular and reliably masculine.

Aidan

2003: #39

Popularity: #39
Style: Celtic, The -ens, Nickname-Proof, Saints
Variants: Aiden, Aden, Ayden
Sisters: Chloe, Avery, Caitlin, Brenna, Sydney
Brothers: Liam, Gavin, Connor, Dylan, Riley
✻ It's a fair bet that few of the parents now choosing this name have ever met an adult Aidan. As recently as the late 1980s, it was an obscure Irish saint's name. Today, Aidan's sublimely clean sound is the sound of a generation. In fact, with its authentic Celtic roots, Aidan is now the traditional alternative to names like Brayden, Kaden, and Jaiden.

Aidric

Popularity: Rare
Style: Exotic Traditional, Saints
Variants: Aidrick

rarely used

Sisters: Averil, Flavia, Beatrix, Amabel, Savina
Brothers: Tavis, Alistair, Cormac, Matthias, Tarquin
✻ A bona fide exotic, Aidric is not merely uncommon but genuinely unfamiliar. It's a medieval saint's name that still sounds lost in the mists of time. Twenty years ago, that would have made the name weird. Today, it makes it irresistible. Fellow saint names like Aidan and Dominic are star revivals, and Aidric could hit the same fashion bull's-eye.

Ajax

Popularity: Rare
Style: Fanciful, Mythological
Nicknames: Jax
Sisters: Electra, Ione, Cleopatra, Isis, Echo

rarely used

Brothers: Thor, Jupiter, Orion, Atom, Lex
✻ There's powerful potential in this classical warrior name. The only thing stopping it is the image of the cleanser. If you're confident that your little boy will wash all thoughts of scrubbing bubbles from people's minds, you might have a winner in Ajax.

Alan

1950s: #45

Popularity: #131
Style: The -ens, Mid-Century, Timeless
Nicknames: Al
Variants: Allen, Allan, Alun
Sisters: Diana, Karen, Cynthia, Valerie, Susan
Brothers: Mark, Gary, Dennis, Stephen, Jay
✻ A fine, reliable fellow, that Alan. Sure, he hit his peak in the middle of the last century, but he's kept his youthful good looks. The name has been used in the British Isles since the time of William the Conquerer and should keep going strong. Alternate spellings like Allen, once equally popular in the U.S., are now showing more age.

Alban

Popularity: Rare
Style: Saints, The -ens, Why Not?
Nicknames: Albie, Al
Variants: Albin

rarely used

Sisters: Cecily, Adela, Aurea, Linden, Danae
Brothers: Eamon, Egan, Alistair, Colman, Tobin
✻ A nifty old saint's name, Alban has a modern sound and plenty of history. It has been virtually unknown in the U.S., except for Harry Truman's Vice President Alben Barkley.

Albert

1900s: #16

Popularity: #311
Style: Ladies and Gentlemen
Nicknames: Al, Bert, Albie
Variants: Alberto

Sisters: Ruth, Irene, Frances, Helen, Esther
Brothers: Louis, Raymond, Frank, Arthur, Harold
✻ Albert is teetering on the edge right now. A nudge one way, and he's a gracious chap from the old school. A prod the other way, and he's a hopeless dweeb. The bet here is that the wind will blow in Albert's favor and his gentlemanly essence will prevail. A toddler named Albert is cute as a button, too.

Alden

Popularity: #730
Style: The -ens, Last Names
First, Why Not?
Sisters: Camilla, Annabel,
Hallie, Mercy, Willa
Brothers: Ellis, Porter, Grady, Edison, Lawson
 1900s: #464
✷ If you like the prep school aura of surnames, you can't do better than this Mayflower original. It's a gentler, less trendy alternative to Peyton and Chandler.

Aldo

2002: #407

Popularity: #576
Style: Italian, Latino/Latina
Sisters: Dulce, Ava, Gianna,
Leora, Perla
Brothers: Marco, Sergio, Milo, Ezra, Emilio
✷ Parents are heading up to the attic and shaking the dust off this old-timer. It has a continental playboy style softened by a whiff of geekiness.

Alec

1990s: #137

Popularity: #225
Style: Celtic, English,
Nickname-Proof
Variants: Alick
Sisters: Claire, Abby, Chloe,
Lise, Ava
Brothers: Trevor, Brendan, Reid, Liam, Conor
✷ A debonair variant on Alex. The romance of this name was fixed in many girls' minds at an early age thanks to the hero of *The Black Stallion*.

Alejandro

2001: #85

Popularity: #97
Style: Latino/Latina
Nicknames: Ale, Alex
Variants: Alessandro
Sisters: Esmeralda, Angelica,
Alondra, Guadalupe, Valeria
Brothers: Andres, Nicolas, Miguel, Francisco,
Antonio
✷ Like every form of Alexander, this one's racing up the charts. An elegant and trendy Spanish choice.

Alex

2002: #62

Popularity: #62
Style: Nicknames, Timeless
Variants: Alec
Sisters: Abby, Emily, Molly,
Tess, Kate
Brothers: Jake, Cole, Evan, Drew, Luke

✷ Long a nickname for Alexander, Alex is increasingly standing on its own. Parents choose it for simplicity, and to emphasize the "x" sound. The result is a casual, breezy, and confident name.

Alexander

2002: #15

Popularity: #16
Style: Timeless
Nicknames: Alex, Sandy, Sasha,
Xander, Zander, Sander, Lex
Variants: Alexandre, Alistair, Alejandro,
Alexandros
Sisters: Emily, Victoria, Hannah, Gabrielle,
Caroline
Brothers: Nathaniel, Jacob, Nicholas, Christian,
Benjamin
✷ Alexander has been a classic for thousands of years. It's lordly, cultured, and valiant. It's also wildly fashionable, and on the girls' side you'll find Alexandra, Alexis, Alexa, Alexandria . . . that, of course, makes for an awful lot of Alexes. Zander, or the Dutch version Sander, are alternatives.

Alfred

1900s: #33

Popularity: #683
Style: Ladies and Gentlemen
Nicknames: Alf, Fred, Al
Variants: Alfredo, Avery
Sisters: Edith, Frances, Ida, Cora, Alice
Brothers: Ernest, Arthur, Clarence, Harold,
Ralph
✷ If you know a young Alfred, chances are he was named after a relative. Parents today just aren't choosing this burly old Saxon name on its own merits. The medieval variation Avery is far trendier.

Alistair

Popularity: Rare
Style: Celtic, English, Exotic
Traditional, Why Not?
Nicknames: Alec, Alick
Variants: Alastair, Alister, Alasdair
Sisters: Elspeth, Beatrix, Cecily, Finola, Tamsin
Brothers: Magnus, Hamish, Evander, Gareth,
Brannock
rarely used
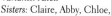
✷ This Scottish form of Alexander is ready to bring its dashing style to the U.S. It pairs especially well with a Scottish surname.

Alonzo

1900s: #257

Popularity: #535
Style: African-Amerian, Exotic Traditional, Shakespearean
Nicknames: Lon, Al, Zo
Variants: Alonso
Sisters: Zora, Emilia, Carmela, Adelaide, Clara
Brothers: Oscar, Augustus, Luther, Mariano, Solomon

✻ This Latin lover crosses many boundaries. In the nineteenth century, it was a stately name for a rural gentleman. More recently, it's become a charismatic African-American favorite. Never common in any guise, Alonzo is an intriguing choice to consider alongside quirky gent names like Felix and Julius.

Alvin

1920s: #71

Popularity: #512
Style: Solid Citizens
Nicknames: Al
Sisters: Vivian, Marie, Irene, Fay, Dorothy
Brothers: Leon, Lewis, Ray, Clifford, Ellis

✻ This is a sweetheart of a name for a little boy, but it carries some baggage. The squeaky-voiced Alvin and the Chipmunks add to a cloud of geekiness that surrounds the name. But with the growing popularity of Gavin, Devin, and even Calvin, Alvin has another chance to shine.

Ambrose

1900s: #338

Popularity: Rare
Style: English, Ladies and Gentlemen, Saints
Nicknames: Broz
Sisters: Augusta, Philomena, Aurelia, Delphia, Eugenie
Brothers: Rupert, Oswald, Aloysius, Leopold, Armand

✻ Ambrose is like a handlebar mustache, so cheerfully outdated and overblown that it's actually a lot of fun. A revival candidate for parents who live on the edge.

Amos

1900s: #202

Popularity: Rare
Style: Biblical, Namesakes, Porch Sitters
Sisters: Hester, Beulah, Elvira, Opal, Ada
Brothers: Homer, Enoch, Grover, Rufus, Horace

✻ The *Amos 'n' Andy Show* casts a long, uncomfortable shadow over this name. That really is too bad, because such unpretentious biblical names are in short supply. A bold parent might try to resurrect it.

Anderson

2003: #613

Popularity: #613
Style: Last Names First, Timeless
Nicknames: Andy
Sisters: Hollis, Emilia, Aubrey, Eliza, Hadley
Brothers: Jefferson, Sterling, Nicholson, Bennett, Lawson

✻ A classic surname, sedate but handsome. Anderson sounds like the bright, diligent type who'll rise quickly up the corporate ladder. Note that this is one surname that still sounds resolutely like a last name, so tread carefully . . . an Anderson Henry or even Anderson Tyler ends up sounding backwards.

Andre

1970s: #139

Popularity: #210
Style: African-American, French, New Classics
Nicknames: Dre
Variants: Andrei, Andrés, Andreas, Andrew
Sisters: Adrienne, Lea, Simone, Noelle, Tania
Brothers: Antoine, Lance, Dion, Marcus, Damien

✻ Andre has retained the continental flair of its French roots while becoming comfortably American. It's a stylish twist on Andrew, swank but not ostentatious. The Spanish Andrés is equally popular, and the Greek/biblical Andreas another sophisticated option.

Andrew

1980s: #13

Popularity: #5
Style: Biblical, Timeless
Nicknames: Andy, Drew
Variants: Andre, Andreas, Andrés
Sisters: Emily, Katherine, Rachel, Sarah, Elisabeth
Brothers: Matthew, Nicholas, Benjamin, Anthony, Daniel

✻ This classic Scottish-tinged name escapes the stodgy air of most British standards, and parents have noticed. While Charles, George, and Edward are sounding old-fashioned, Andrew remains a steady contemporary favorite. For nicknames, Drew is rising in place of Andy.

Angel

2003: #43

Popularity: #43
Style: Androgynous, Latino/Latina
Sisters: Alondra, Valeria, Dulce, Esmeralda, Amaya
Brothers: Jesús, Alejandro, Andres, Xander, Diego

★ Like Jesús, Angel is a Spanish hit that's been virtually taboo for boys in English. The pronunciation is key: Said the Spanish way (AHN-hel), it's fashionably suave. With an English pronunciation, it's still chiefly for girls and vampires.

Angelo

1910s: #159

Popularity: #271
Style: Italian, Nickname-Proof, Shakespearean
Sisters: Carmela, Emilia, Marcella, Lucia, Caterina
Brothers: Silvio, Donato, Leonardo, Romeo, Gaetano

★ This classic has remained quietly fashionable year after year without losing its grand Italian style.

Angus

1900s: #560

Popularity: Rare
Style: Celtic, Shakespearean
Nicknames: Gus
Sisters: Maisie, Fiona, Elspeth, Muriel, Davina
Brothers: Magnus, Finlay, Lachlan, Rory, Fraser

★ Ready to go *really* Celtic? Angus is pure Scottish, undiluted and unmistakable. It also has a classic nickname that makes the other Celtic-come-lately names green with envy. Many will think of the Angus breed of beef cattle, which originated around Angus County, Scotland. It's an odd but pleasantly brawny association.

Anthony

1990s: #18

Popularity: #10
Style: Timeless
Nicknames: Tony, Tonio
Variants: Antony, Antonio, Anton, Antoine
Sisters: Rachel, Andrea, Rebecca, Veronica, Stephanie
Brothers: Andrew, Daniel, Matthew, Patrick, Benjamin

★ Robust, timeless—and Italian. Despite generations of steady use across all ethnicities, Tony remains the classic Italian-American name in our cultural imagination. That may account for its continuing freshness in an age where most of the English men's classics are losing steam. In fact, you were probably surprised to learn Anthony is as popular as it is, since it does not feel overused.

Antoine

1980s: #314

Popularity: #636
Style: African-American, French
Nicknames: Twan
Variants: Antwan, Antwon, Antwain
Sisters: Monique, Desiree, Chantal, Natasha, Joelle
Brothers: Germaine, Andre, Cedric, Dante, Dion

★ Antoine was one of several French classics embraced by African-American parents starting in the '70s. Many kept the name's sound but cast aside its French roots with spellings like Antwan. All of these variants are now on the wane. For a new look, consider the Russian Anton, Spanish Antonio, or even classical Antonius.

Anton

1900s: #173

Popularity: #726
Style: German/Dutch, Slavic, Why Not?
Nicknames: Tony
Variants: Antony, Antonin
Sisters: Helena, Belle, Cleo, Leora, Margit
Brothers: Tomas, Theo, Florian, Reuben, August

★ Anton's the handsome, exotic stranger on the train . . . mysterious and just a little bit dangerous. It's also a simple and familiar name that won't make your relatives roll their eyes. A delectable combination.

Antonio

2002: #86

Popularity: #94
Style: Italian, Latino/Latina, Shakespearean, Timeless
Nicknames: Tonio, Tony
Variants: Anthony, Anton
Sisters: Elena, Mariana, Adriana, Valeria, Camille
Brothers: Lorenzo, Adrian, Marco, Nicolas, Orlando

★ This was Shakespeare's favorite name for characters in exotic, romantic plays. If you're Latino or Italian, Antonio is a handsome classic. If not, it's a flourishy yet familiar possibility.

Apollo

Popularity: Rare
Style: Fanciful, Mythological, Saints
Sisters: Venus, Eternity, Cleopatra, Avalon, Isis
Brothers: Achilles, Mars, Ajax, Orion, Jupiter

rarely used

1900   Today

★ The ultimate in hubris: Forget flying too close to the sun; with Apollo you *are* the sun. Fictional boxer Apollo Creed from the *Rocky* films exemplifies this name's gaudy, magnetic style.

Archer

Popularity: Rare
Style: Last Names First, Why Not?
Nicknames: Archie, Arch
Sisters: Lila, Belle, Adela, Rhea, Violet
Brothers: Rider, Flynn, Campbell, Alden, Foster

rarely used

1900 — Today

✱ This overlooked name has a light touch befitting a skilled bowman. Too many of the popular "profession" names have a counterfeit feeling, a forced heartiness. Archer—with amiable nickname Archie—is far more comfortable in its own skin. It's waiting patiently for a chance to hit the bull's-eye.

Ari

2003: #671

Popularity: #671
Style: Jewish, Little Darlings, Nickname-Proof, Scandinavian, Why Not?

1900 — Today

Variants: Arieh, Are
Sisters: Hava, Eden, Daphne, Nia, Tove
Brothers: Nico, Asher, Avi, Kai, Finn

✱ Ari's light touch is unusual for a male name, but there's muscle behind it. Think Greek shipping magnates and Israeli fighter pilots. (The name is Hebrew for "lion," Old Norse for "eagle," and short for Aristotle.) An underappreciated gem that doesn't take itself too seriously.

Arlo

1910s: #678

Popularity: Rare
Style: Guys and Dolls, Nickname-Proof
Sisters: Maxie, Nell, Lula, Etta, Mazie
Brothers: Buck, Dock, Lonzo, Mose, Gus

1900 — Today

✱ This unassuming old-timer will remind many people of folk singer Arlo Guthrie. Nonetheless, you can picture an Arlo being any age from one to 100. He looks easygoing, trustworthy, and lovable.

Armand

1900s: #348

Popularity: Rare
Style: French, Ladies and Gentlemen, Nickname-Proof
Variants: Armando
Sisters: Cecile, Eloise, Zelda, Josefa, Delphine
Brothers: Claude, Edmond, Frederic, Jules, Ambrose

1900 — Today

✱ This French variant of Herman is impressively genteel but desperately in need of a decent nickname.

Arnold

1910s: #96

Popularity: #820
Style: Solid Citizens
Nicknames: Arnie
Variants: Arnaldo, Arno, Arnaud, Arne
Sisters: Verna, Eunice, Lorene, Erma, Bernadine
Brothers: Norman, Milton, Herbert, Vernon, Leonard

1900 — Today

✱ Even Arnold Schwarzenegger's muscles weren't enough to keep this venerable name from sagging sadly out of fashion. The German name Arno and the Scandinavian Arne are possibilities to lighten it up.

Arthur

1900s: #14

Popularity: #353
Style: Ladies and Gentlemen
Nicknames: Art, Artie
Variants: Artur, Arturo
Sisters: Alice, Martha, Helen, Rose, Clara
Brothers: Walter, Louis, Albert, Theodore, Henry

1900 — Today

✱ My father, as a young boy growing up in the Depression, wished his name were Arthur. It was regal, valiant, and romantic. Today, the name's slightly doughy sound and animated-aardvark associations keep it out of vogue. If you conjure up the noble image, though, the classic might ride again. And how many names have their own adjective, like Arthurian?

Asher

2003: #416

Popularity: #416
Style: Biblical, Jewish, Why Not?
Nicknames: Ash
Sisters: Ariel, Dalia, Piper, Darcy, Allegra
Brothers: Judah, Ari, Gideon, Lincoln, Rider

1900 — Today

✱ Asher is a one-of-a-kind meeting point for two opposite name trends: It's a biblical classic that sounds like a trendy modern surname. That should help solve naming arguments in plenty of households.

Ashton

2003: #101

Popularity: #101
Style: Androgynous, The -ens, Last Names First
Nicknames: Ash
Sisters: Aubrey, Jordyn, Jasmin, Alexia, Macy
Brothers: Parker, Colby, Trenton, Landon, Drake

1900 — Today

✱ It's safe to call a boy Ash again, as Ashton has taken up the mantle of the dear departed male Ashley. Actor Ashton Kutcher has made the name a familiar choice for boys. But watch out, there are female Ashtons around the corner, too.

Atticus

Popularity: Rare

rarely used

Style: Exotic Traditional, Namesakes, Nickname-Proof

Sisters: Beatrix, Artemisia, Athena, Paloma, Anaïs

1900　Today

Brothers: Phineas, Alistair, Lincoln, Augustus, Galen

✷ This classical name has long been associated with intellect and learning, which suits its exalted sound. The best-known example today is noble Atticus Finch of *To Kill a Mockingbird.*

August

1900s: #129

Popularity: #657

Style: Charms and Graces, Ladies and Gentlemen

Nicknames: Gus, Augie

1900　Today

Variants: Augustus

Sisters: Jewel, Alma, Helena, Honoré, Viola

Brothers: Julius, Everett, Leopold, Forest, Theodore

✷ Parents who love names like Max and Sam are increasingly drawn to the less common Gus. The full name Augustus is a stretch, though . . . but what about August? Simple enough, with a formal, gentlemanly style that's ready to be dusted off.

Austin

1990s: #23

Popularity: #33

Style: The –ens, Last Names First, Nickname-Proof, Place Names

1900　Today

Variants: Austen, Austyn, Osten

Sisters: Taylor, Alexis, Emma, Shelby, Paige

Brothers: Dylan, Chandler, Riley, Trevor, Carson

✷ A hundred years ago, Austin (a form of Augustine) was a prim, starch-collared name. But it echoes Justin's youthful sound, and when you throw in the Western twang of the capital of Texas and the cheeky Brit style of Austin Powers, you get a name that's cooking on all burners.

Avery

2003: #222

Popularity: #222

Style: Androgynous, Last Names First, Nickname-Proof

Sisters: Juliana, Aubrey, Giselle, Sophia, Haley

1900　Today

Brothers: Donovan, Riley, Miles, Chandler, Adrian

✷ This traditional male name is at an all-time popularity peak for baby boys—and is even more common for girls. Once a name starts to turn feminine, parents of boys usually run in the other direction. But lately, favorites like Jordan and Hunter have been bucking the trend. Cross your fingers that elegant Avery sticks around.

Axel

2001: #247

Popularity: #333

Style: Exotic Traditional, Little Darlings, Scandinavian

Sisters: Zoe, Eden, Elle, Astrid, Cleo

1900　Today

Brothers: Eli, Cael, Maxim, Ezra, Kai

✷ A pocket-size powerhouse, Axel is one of the jazziest traditional names going. It was originally Scandinavian, a form of Absalom.

Bailey

2001: #266

Popularity: #360

Style: Androgynous, Bell Tones, Last Names First

Sisters: Lauryn, Sidney, Hayley, Logan, Gillian

1900　Today

Brothers: Chandler, Parker, Avery, Tanner, Brennan

✷ Bailey is perfectly traditional as a boy's name. It's an old surname with a cheerfully preppy outlook that was heard most often in the 1800s. But that was before it got a starring role on the '90s TV show *Party of Five.* That male example catapulted the name into the limelight for both boys and girls. By now, female Baileys (and Baylees) are in the majority.

Barnaby

Popularity: Rare

rarely used

Style: Biblical, English, Exotic Traditional

Nicknames: Barney

1900　Today

Variants: Barnabas

Sisters: Cordelia, Beatrice, Portia, Sidony, Amabel

Brothers: Horatio, Lambert, Benedict, Bartholomew, Leopold

✷ Barnaby is fancified but fun, a playful alternative to serious names like Dominic and Sebastian. It's also exceptionally rare given how comfortable and familiar the name sounds. If you prefer a dark, brooding style, try the biblical version Barnabas.

Barney

1900s: #253

Popularity: Rare

Style: Guys and Dolls, Namesakes, Nicknames

Sisters: Winnie, Bess, Lorna, Irma, Madge

1900　Today

Brothers: Bert, Roscoe, Gus, Murray, Archie

✷ Barney has vintage charm, much like current darlings Gus and Charley. You might even be able to cope with Bedrock's Barney Rubble. But the singing purple dinosaur is too much to look past. If you're tempted nonetheless, consider it as a nickname for Barnaby.

Baron

Popularity: Rare
Style: The –ens, Fanciful
Variants: Barron
Sisters: Melody, Dawn, Belinda, Cheri, Tamra
Brothers: Thad, Cliff, Major, Tobin, Price

1970s: #961

★ This name risks grandiosity but gets by on its classically namelike sound. It's a handsome heir to earlier grandiose names like Noble and King.

Barrett

Popularity: #843
Style: Last Names First, Why Not?
Nicknames: Barry
Sisters: Eliza, Kate, Autumn, Ivy, Haley
Brothers: Jamison, Harris, Brenton, Pierce, Foster

2003: #843

★ This strong surname was popular during the nineteenth century. It has made a quiet comeback as an elaboration on Barry.

Barry

Popularity: #881
Style: Mid-Century
Nicknames: Baz
Variants: Berry
Sisters: Diane, Sheila, Paula, Lynne, Donna
Brothers: Bruce, Terry, Kent, Steve, Randy

1950s: #75

★ The name Barry is a familiar friend, but it has largely been abandoned as a mid-century relic. The Australian nickname Baz (most familiar from film director Baz Luhrmann) gives it some new pizzazz.

Bart

Popularity: Rare
Style: Nicknames, Surfer Sixties
Sisters: Laurie, Beth, Liz, Candy, Lisa
Brothers: Curt, Vince, Dino, Kip, Rod

1960s: #337

★ Bart may be short for Bartholomew, but it's a world apart from that paragon of gentility. Bart can be a brash pirate or a star quarterback, or even a bratty cartoon character. But genteel it ain't.

Bartholomew

Popularity: Rare
Style: Biblical, Exotic Traditional, Saints
Nicknames: Bart, Bartley, Batt
Sisters: Augusta, Philomena, Drucilla, Adelaide, Hermione
Brothers: Benedict, Thaddeus, Maximilian, Justus, Ferdinand

1900s: #976

★ Sure, it's a mouthful, but you won't find a better combination of classic refinement and quirky cool. The nickname Bart gives you a dramatic change of pace.

Beau

Popularity: #423
Style: Brisk and Breezy, Country & Western
Variants: Bo
Sisters: Jenna, Shea, Joss, Carissa, Trista
Brothers: Colt, Shane, Heath, Brice, Casey

1980s: #297

★ They may sound alike, but Bo and Beau do not travel in the same circles. Bo is pure simplicity, and Beau is pure romance. The name is French for handsome, for heaven's sake. It's associated with the Regency dandy Beau Brummel and pulpy Foreign Legion hero Beau Geste. But it sounds so simple that you can get away with it.

Beckett

Popularity: Rare
Style: Last Names First, Namesakes, Why Not?
Nicknames: Beck
Sisters: Harper, Flannery, Sheridan, Brody, Carson
Brothers: Maddox, Burke, Baldwin, Faulkner, Eliot

rarely used

★ Irish playwright Samuel Beckett is an icon of modernism, and his name has a stylish snap. This is a literary name with a rock-star spirit.

Benedict

Popularity: Rare
Style: Exotic Traditional, Saints, Shakespearean
Nicknames: Ben
Variants: Bennett
Sisters: Beatrice, Louisa, Evangeline, Rafaela, Marian
Brothers: Edmund, Thaddeus, Barnaby, Constantin, Domenick

1910s: #548

★ Frustrated that Dominic and Sebastian are too common? Have I got a name for you. Benedict is saintly, literary, sophisticated, and extremely rare. Plus the sturdy nickname Ben makes this one exotic choice that's virtually risk free (unless you still hold a grudge against Benedict Arnold).

Benjamin

Popularity: #25
Style: Biblical, Timeless
Nicknames: Ben, Benno, Benji
Sisters: Rachel, Sarah, Victoria, Leah, Emily
Brothers: Nicholas, Samuel, Jonathan, Adam, Alexander

 2001: #27 · 1900 · Today

✷ Benjamin is a name of perfect balance. It's popular, but not trendy. It's biblical, but not conspicuously antique. It's manly, but not heavy or blunt. The full Benjamin is handsome, Benji is cute, and Ben's an all-around good guy. You're all set.

Bennett

Popularity: #431
Style: Last Names First, Timeless
Nicknames: Ben
Variants: Bennet
Sisters: Juliana, Lesley, Piper, Sophia, Avery
Brothers: Davis, Harrison, Duncan, Reid, Walker

 2003: #431 · 1900 · Today

✷ An exceptionally flexible name, Bennett plays well to many audiences. As a crisp surname, it's finding favor in this age of Paytons and Carters. The nickname Ben appeals to no-frills traditionalists. And as the medieval form of Benedict (and surname of *Pride and Prejudice* heroine Elizabeth Bennet), it wins over the literary romantics.

Bernard

Popularity: #791
Style: Ladies and Gentlemen, Saints, Solid Citizens
Nicknames: Bernie
Sisters: Vivian, Martha, Eleanor, Sylvia, Dorothy
Brothers: Francis, Vernon, Leonard, Gilbert, Roland

 1920s: #47 · 1900 · Today

✷ Bernard is a proud old Germanic name that has mellowed over time. The burly St. Bernard dog helps make the name warmer and cuddlier than most (and a perfect playmate for Clifford), and the fun nickname Bernie reinforces that softer side.

Bertram

Popularity: Rare
Style: German/Dutch, Ladies and Gentlemen, Shakespearean
Nicknames: Bert
Variants: Bertrand
Sisters: Cordelia, Petra, Marion, Eleanora, Eloise
Brothers: Rupert, Clement, Florian, Herman, Rudolph

 1900s: #432 · 1900 · Today

✷ Bertram is uncommon and likely to stay that way. It was never popular enough to be a revival candidate, nor quirky enough to be a glamorous exotic. It's a stately, serious name that charts its own path.

Bishop

Popularity: Rare
Style: Fanciful
Sisters: Golden, Evening, Easter, Silver, Bliss
Brothers: Major, Parrish, Judge, Regis, Price

 1900s: #925 · 1900 · Today

✷ Bishop was occasionally heard a century ago during a fad for titles as first names. It sounds like a jaunty surname today.

Blaine

Popularity: #486
Style: Brisk and Breezy, Saints, Timeless
Variants: Blane
Sisters: Brynn, Reese, Elle, Juliet, Blair
Brothers: Reid, Baird, Graham, Elliot, Keir

2001: #408 · 1900 · Today

✷ Blaine sounds sharp in all senses of the word: piercing, intelligent, and stylish. It sounds trendy today, but has been used in the U.S. for generations.

Blaise

Popularity: #810
Style: Brisk and Breezy, French, Saints
Variants: Blaze
Sisters: Brynn, Giselle, Anaïs, Elle, Delphine
Brothers: Jude, Xavier, Pierce, Cael, Maxim

 2003: #810 · 1900 · Today

✷ A few cutting-edge parents are catching on to this intriguing entry. It was the name of a French saint, and the renowned philosopher-mathematician Blaise Pascal. What could be more respectable? Yet it also sounds like a blaze of glory. A refined way to indulge your need for speed.

Blake

Popularity: #80
Style: Brisk and Breezy
Sisters: Paige, Brynn, Jenna,
Jade, Sierra
Brothers: Chase, Bryce, Drew, Devin, Cole

★ One of the breeziest names for boys. Blake is debonair and jet-setting, and possibly a bit of a rascal. If you're looking for a name with cross-racial appeal, Blake has an unusual pair of origins: It arises from the Old English words for both black and white.

Bond

Popularity: Rare
Style: Brisk and Breezy, Saints
Sisters: Tyne, Lise, Honor, Britt,
Sloane
Brothers: Beck, Gage, Piers, Burke, Holt

rarely used

★ "The name is Bond . . . yes, just Bond." Bond is indeed a legitimate first name, borne by a seventh-century French saint. It makes a fabulous impact in English, with secret agent–style bravado.

Boris

1900s: #976

Popularity: Rare
Style: Slavic
Nicknames: Borya
Sisters: Vera, Maude, Helga,
Olga, Natasha
Brothers: Anton, Eugene, Claude, Fritz, Basil

★ Boris is a name that comes across far better in Russian (bah-REESE). The English pronunciation conjures up horror king Boris Karloff as well as Rocky and Bullwinkle's nemesis Boris Badenov. That nefarious image could actually work to the name's advantage, though, making it devilish rather than merely drab.

Brad

1970s: #127

Popularity: #811
Style: Nicknames, Surfer Sixties
Sisters: Robyn, Toni, Sonya,
Dana, Stacey
Brothers: Kirk, Darin, Kurt,
Marc, Tad

★ Brad is pure surfer cuteness. It's direct and masculine, with a breezy, undemanding style. At its best, that translates to Brad Pitt. At its worst, think of the Brad from the *Rocky Horror Picture Show*. As a nickname, Brad beefs up and remains very popular.

Braden

2003: #171

Popularity: #171
Style: Bell Tones, The -ens
Nicknames: Brad, Brade
Variants: Brayden, Braeden,
Braiden, Bradyn, Braydon
Sisters: Ashlyn, Kylee, Brooklyn, Jayla, Payton
Brothers: Jalen, Caden, Landon, Cooper, Bryson

★ One of the trendiest boy's names in years, Braden has a whole library of popular spellings. Its best feature is an infectiously confident style. It's easy to picture an Braden as an upbeat, self-assured boy. There's a risk, though, that this will be a name with a "freshness date" that quickly passes.

Bradley

1980s: #54

Popularity: #166
Style: Last Names First, New Classics
Nicknames: Brad
Variants: Bradford
Sisters: Monica, Bridget, Andrea, Holly, Alison
Brothers: Derek, Sean, Geoffrey, Brett, Travis

★ This old surname is a longtime American favorite. Its first surge came in honor of WWII General Omar Bradley, but it really took off as a formal version of the hit name Brad. Bradley adds a little preppy dignity to that '60s cutie.

Brady

2003: #146

Popularity: #146
Style: Bell Tones, Last Names First, Nickname-Proof
Sisters: Avery, Payton, Macy,
Brenna, Madelyn
Brothers: Parker, Riley, Carter, Bryson, Drake

★ Brady's been used quietly for many years, but it was swept into the limelight with the surname style explosion. A preppy counterpart to Cody.

Bram

Popularity: Rare
Style: Exotic Traditional,
German/Dutch, Nicknames,
Why Not?
Sisters: Sanne, Nell, Elke,
Fleur, Luna
Brothers: Gregor, Wolf, Carsten, Evert, Till

rarely used

★ This Dutch version of Abraham is a smart and coolly tough possibility. *Dracula* author Bram Stoker is the best-known bearer, giving the name a dark and stormy undercurrent.

136   *The Baby Name Wizard*

Brandon 1990s: #12

Popularity: #21
Style: The -ens, New Classics
Nicknames: Bran
Variants: Branden
Sisters: Lauren, Megan, Samantha, Brooke, Vanessa
Brothers: Ryan, Justin, Travis, Damon, Shane

✱ Brandon sounds dashing, so it's no surprise it swept onto the scene as a popular soap opera name. It also sounds classically masculine, which has given it staying power. The name is still in the very mainstream of fashion, but with so many Brandons arriving through the '80s and '90s, this dashing hero could be coming due for a well-earned rest.

Brannock

Popularity: Rare
Style: Celtic, Saints
Nicknames: Bran
Sisters: Kennera, Bronwyn, Catriona, Finola, Averil
Brothers: Kilian, Broderick, Lorcan, Brogan, Cormac

rarely used

✱ This old Celtic saint's name could earn oohs and aahs as an alternative to Brandon.

Braxton 2003: #305

Popularity: #305
Style: Last Names First
Sisters: Baylee, Makenna, Cassidy, Madison, Haleigh
Brothers: Grayson, Brody, Drake, Lennox, Paxton

✱ This brawny surname is brand new as a given name, but thoroughly familiar to expectant couples who've been reading up on Braxton Hicks contractions.

Brendan 2001: #115

Popularity: #145
Style: Celtic, The -ens, New Classics, Nickname-Proof
Sisters: Caitlin, Jocelyn, Briana, Kiara, Regan
Brothers: Colin, Trevor, Alec, Garrett, Duncan

✱ This Irish classic is finally catching up in popularity with the more soap opera–styled Brandon. With an Irish last name, it has echoes of literary icon Brendan Behan and the old country.

Brennan 2002: #277

Popularity: #279
Style: Celtic, The -ens, Last Names First, Nickname-Proof
Sisters: Kendall, Logan, Baylee, Mckenna, Aubrey
Brothers: Quinn, Keegan, Donovan, Chandler, Griffin

✱ Brennan is this close to Brendan and Brandon, but its smooth surname style is a new twist.

Brent 1970s: #85

Popularity: #384
Style: Brisk and Breezy, '70s–'80s
Variants: Brant
Sisters: Leigh, April, Felicia, Tanya, Stacey
Brothers: Clint, Derrick, Brian, Kirk, Heath

✱ The '60s and '70s saw a raft of these "blunt instrument" names: Clint, Dirk, Curt. They pack a pile of sounds into a single manly syllable. The names still have their fans, but they're losing momentum to a lighter, swifter generation: Kane, Jace, Trey.

Brett 1980s: #67

Popularity: #219
Style: Brisk and Breezy, New Classics
Variants: Bret
Sisters: Cara, Bethany, Alison, Megan, Kelly
Brothers: Eric, Lance, Travis, Drew, Shane

✱ Brett splits the difference between the rock-hard '60s studs like Kirk and Brent and their breezy descendants Tate and Cade. It's clean, modern, and solid.

Brian 1970s: #8

Popularity: #58
Style: Celtic, New Classics, Nickname-Proof, '70s–'80s
Variants: Bryan
Sisters: Kelly, Michelle, Shannon, Bridget, Amy
Brothers: Kevin, Sean, Mark, Eric, Jeffery

✱ Brian has been an Irish favorite for centuries and an American one since the '50s. It is one of the "can't miss" names, reliable and teaseproof. Lately Brian's been dividing the territory with the rhyming fellow Irishman Ryan. If you're choosing between the two, Brian is warmer, Ryan more boyish.

Brock 2003: #244

Popularity: #244
Style: Last Names First
Sisters: Kiley, Alana, Raven, Blair, Macy
Brothers: Drake, Trent, Jarrett, Burke, Tyson
★ It's always a surprise to encounter a Brock in real life. Shouldn't he be busy saving a soap opera heroine from a burning building, his sculpted muscles glistening in the night? Happily, Brock's growing popularity is starting to humanize the name. It's still ultra-studly, but no longer so showy.

Brody 2003: #235

Popularity: #235
Style: Last Names First, Nicknames
Sisters: Kiley, Macy, Skyler, Lexi, Makenna
Brothers: Reece, Colby, Keaton, Bailey, Tucker
★ This trendy new name has a double appeal: It takes the boyish style of Corey and packages it up as a surname. Punk diva Brody Dalle hints at a possible crop of female Brodies in the future.

Brooks 2003: #709

Popularity: #709
Style: Brisk and Breezy, Timeless
Sisters: Lindsay, Tyne, Kate, Victoria, Blair
Brothers: Graham, Elliot, Reid, Brice, Quentin
★ You choose Brooks because you want your son to look good in pinstripes. (That's a pinstripe *suit*, not Yankee pinstripes, Brooks Robinson fans.) It's an old-money name that doesn't get its hands dirty.

Bruce 1950s: #32

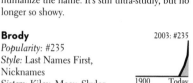

Popularity: #493
Style: Mid-Century
Sisters: Donna, Diane, Susan, Paula, Janet
Brothers: Wayne, Barry, Dennis, Todd, Gary
★ The world is full of macho guys named Bruce. Think Bruce Lee, Bruce Willis, Bruce Smith, Bruce Springsteen. Their combined muscle and swagger help to offset the name's softness.

Bruno 1910s: #271

Popularity: #778
Style: German/Dutch, Guys and Dolls, Italian, Saints
Sisters: Ida, Carmela, Marcella, Lola, Hilda
Brothers: Otto, Milo, Buster, Carmine, Rocco
★ A brawny name you can only picture on a barrel-chested man. While the first image that springs to mind may be a bodyguard, the name also has a cuddly teddy bear side. If you come from a family of football linemen, this could be a winner.

Bryant 1990s: #278

Popularity: #301
Style: Last Names First, Nickname-Proof
Sisters: Kasey, Alyson, Brenna, Mallory, Clarissa
Brothers: Brock, Jarett, Tyson, Kendrick, Brent
★ Bryant is a genteel surname, but it's far tougher than most of its ilk. This is one elegant lad who won't get pushed around.

Bryce 2001: #93

Popularity: #103
Style: Brisk and Breezy, Celtic, Country & Western, Place Names
Variants: Brice
Sisters: Paige, Alexa, Jade, Bailey, Shea
Brothers: Chase, Blake, Cole, Drake, Quinn
★ A snappy Celtic updating of Bruce, with echoes of Western landmark Bryce Canyon. The spelling Brice is a French classic. Extremely trendy.

Bryson 2003: #216

Popularity: #216
Style: The -ens, Last Names First
Nicknames: Bryce
Variants: Brycen
Sisters: Baylee, Brooklyn, Aubrey, Makenna, Harley
Brothers: Grayson, Keegan, Payton, Braxton, Brody
★ Bryson seems created by central casting to fit the zeitgeist. A surname with a style that's half prep school and half cowboy, it's roping in tons of parents.

Byron

Popularity: #483
Style: The -ens, Nickname-Proof, Timeless
Sisters: Regina, Sonia, Renee, Adrienne, Tamara
Brothers: Curtis, Roderick, Russell, Vance, Eliot

1960s: #233

★ Byron first joined the name pool in tribute to the poet Lord Byron. It has held up exceptionally well for almost two centuries, even as the literary association has faded. It's a pleasantly traditional cousin to contemporary favorites like Bryson and Landon.

Cade

Popularity: #221
Style: Brisk and Breezy
Variants: Kade
Sisters: Kyla, Jada, Sage, Reese, Camryn
Brothers: Gage, Braden, Kai, Jace, Drake

2001: #202

★ Quarterback Cade McKnown was drafted by the Chicago Bears in 1999. He made an immediate impact . . . in America's nurseries. The name Cade just struck a nerve. It's tough and cute and contemporary, and it's been gathering attention ever since. Like many other familiar names, Cade has roots as a character in *Gone With the Wind*.

Caden

Popularity: #114
Style: Bell Tones, The -ens
Nicknames: Cade
Variants: Cayden, Caiden, Kadin, Kaiden, Kayden
Sisters: Jayla, Avery, Peyton, Ashlyn, Kyla
Brothers: Jaden, Camden, Colby, Bryson, Rylan

2003: #114

★ A very catchy name, but an entire classroom of rhyming boys is a real risk here. Caden, meet Hayden, Aidan, Jadon, and Braeden. . . . Each name has several spellings in the top-1,000 list.

Cale

Popularity: #755
Style: Brisk and Breezy
Variants: Cael, Kale, Kaile
Sisters: Keely, Bay, Kira, Tai, Saige
Brothers: Kane, Rhett, Coby, Brice, Quinn

2003: #755

★ This speedy little name sounds equally at home on a stock-car driver or a banker. The spelling Cael is a hot up-and-comer with heartthrob potential. Kale is a variety of cabbage.

Caleb

Popularity: #34
Style: Antique Charm, Biblical
Nicknames: Cale, Cal
Variants: Kaleb
Sisters: Abigail, Chloe, Hannah, Sophie, Isabel
Brothers: Gabriel, Cole, Connor, Elijah, Noah

2002: #35

★ A terrific biblical rediscovery, Caleb is equal parts Puritan antique and soap-opera chic. Until recently, this name seemed like a fresh alternative to the super-popular Jacob, but today it's a super hit in its own right.

Callum

Popularity: Rare
Style: Celtic, Why Not?
Nicknames: Cal
Variants: Calum, Colm
Sisters: Maeve, Ione, Nola, Fiona, Ciara
Brothers: Murphy, Fergus, Donal, Rory, Finn

rarely used

★ This Scots Gaelic name has recently soared in popularity throughout the U.K. and Australia. It's now ready for its U.S. debut. Callum can also be used as a nickname for Malcolm; Colm is the Irish equivalent.

Calvin

Popularity: #223
Style: Timeless
Nicknames: Cal
Sisters: Elaine, Lydia, Mercy, Susana, Audrey
Brothers: Curtis, Simon, Grant, Neil, Duncan

1920s: #82

★ It used to be that the first Calvin who came to mind was Calvin Coolidge, one of the least exciting men in American history. Now, the top Calvins are fashion designer Calvin Klein and the young hero of the comic strip *Calvin and Hobbes*. The name is gathering youthful momentum that Coolidge could scarcely have imagined.

Camden

Popularity: #255
Style: Celtic, The -ens, Place Names
Nicknames: Cam
Sisters: Brenna, Logan, Quinn, Regan, Sydnee
Brothers: Keegan, Corbin, Dayton, Rohan, Landen

2003: #255

★ Camden has been most familiar as a city in New Jersey, but it is an old Scottish boy's name. It has recently attracted attention as a succinct alternative to Cameron.

Cameron 2001: #35
Popularity: #40
Style: Androgynous, Celtic
Nicknames: Cam
Variants: Kameron
Sisters: Caitlin, Mckenna, Kiara, Rhiannon, Abigail
Brothers: Logan, Connor, Dylan, Donovan, Griffin
✳ Cameron is one of the great Scottish clan names. To most parents, the name sounds exotic, since it was rare when we were growing up. Today, though, it's firmly mainstream. It's also heard for girls, but nine out of ten Camerons are still male.

Campbell 2003: #984
Popularity: 984
Style: Last Names First, Why Not?
Nicknames: Cam
Sisters: Sheridan, Nola, Camilla, Piper, Margery
Brothers: Archer, Richmond, Dennison, Newell, Beckett
✳ Campbell sounds like a familiar classic, despite the fact that nobody ever uses it. That makes a smashing opportunity for a unique name that will have no trouble fitting in.

Carl 1900s: #20
Popularity: #357
Style: Solid Citizens
Variants: Karl
Sisters: Marie, Ruth, Irene, Rose, Alice
Brothers: Roy, Louis, Albert, Clark, Martin
✳ Carl is the kind of quiet, sturdy name that many of us take for granted. It may not reach out and grab you, but if you give it your full consideration, you'll be pleasantly surprised. It's strong, masculine, and one of the sharpest old-timers around.

Carlos 2001: #55
Popularity: #64
Style: Latino/Latina
Nicknames: Carlitos, Carlito
Variants: Carlo
Sisters: Marisa, Raquel, Ana, Andrea, Marisol
Brothers: Luis, Miguel, Ricardo, Antonio, Marcos
✳ This Spanish version of Charles is a long-time Latino hit with major crossover potential. It's starting to pop up among non-Latinos looking for a cool and creative classic. The Italian version Carlo is equally stylish.

Carlton 1920s: #245
Popularity: Rare
Style: Last Names First
Nicknames: Carl
Variants: Carleton
Sisters: Marcella, Therese, Glenna, Althea, Corrine
Brothers: Clifton, Stewart, Clark, Sanford, Gilbert
✳ This steady surname may not have the bounce of new hits like Keaton and Bryson, but its grounded style has a lasting appeal, like model trains in the age of air travel. The spelling Carleton is characteristically English.

Carmelo 1930s: #351
Popularity: Rare
Style: Italian
Sisters: Felicita, Marcella, Serafina, Concetta, Sabina
Brothers: Gregorio, Domingo, Pasquale, Anton, Mariano
✳ This was a barely familiar Sicilian name until basketball star Carmelo Anthony brought it to America's attention. He shows off the name's smooth magnetism to excellent effect.

Carson 2003: #90
Popularity: #90
Style: Celtic, The -ens, Last Names First, Nickname-Proof
Sisters: Regan, Piper, Maya, Morgan, Kelsey
Brothers: Riley, Carter, Owen, Holden, Jackson
✳ Carson has it all: It's a surname, a Celtic name, and a cowboy name (for Kit Carson). It's even an MTV name, thanks to *TRL* host Carson Daly. That's a natural winning combo, and it makes for a very popular and likable choice.

Carsten
Popularity: Rare
Style: The -ens, German/Dutch, Nickname-Proof, Why Not?
Variants: Karsten
Sisters: Anja, Larkin, Sabine, Elke, Arden
Brothers: Stefan, Tristan, Gunnar, Evert, Soren
✳ Germanic form of Christian. Carsten is rarely used in English, but is straightforward and catchy. Tons of potential.

Carter

2003: #102

Popularity: #102
Style: Last Names First, Nickname-Proof
Sisters: Avery, Faith, Peyton, Chloe, Lily
Brothers: Riley, Carson, Nolan, Cooper, Jackson

✳ This smart surname feels sturdier and less trendy than most examples of the style. Playful and brainy, it's a fun name that's not afraid to grow up.

Cary

1960s: #305

Popularity: Rare
Style: Mid-Century
Sisters: Cathleen, Margo, Trudy, Yvette, Rita
Brothers: Dana, Monty, Tracy, Von, Robin

✳ On paper, Cary still has much of the breezy, debonair character it inherited from actor Cary Grant. Spoken aloud, though, it becomes a confusing match for the girl's name Carrie.

Casey

1980s: #84

Popularity: #264
Style: Celtic, Country & Western, New Classics
Nicknames: Case
Variants: Kasey
Sisters: Kara, Megan, Bethany, Kendra, Alison
Brothers: Shane, Cody, Ryan, Derek, Wesley

✳ Casey's just as cute as Cody and Corey, but twice as tough. This Irish/Western favorite has a rugged disposition closer in spirit to Jack than Corey. You should know, though, that the name is used equally for boys and girls today. No matter how manly the name, a -y ending is an invitation to androgyny.

Casper

1900s: #585

Popularity: Rare
Style: Ladies and Gentlemen, Namesakes, Saints
Nicknames: Cap
Variants: Caspar, Kasper, Gaspar, Jasper
Sisters: Matilda, Sibyl, Cordelia, Louisa, Eugenie
Brothers: Rudolph, Albin, Leopold, Julius, Rupert

✳ It should take more than one little Friendly Ghost to scare parents off of this name. Casper is one of the few boys' names with the same light, nostalgic charm that has made names like Lily and Sophie such favorites for girls. Granted, Casper is quirkier than those hits. If you're on the fence, Jasper is another stylish form of the same name without the ghost trouble.

Cassius

Popularity: Rare
Style: Exotic Traditional
Nicknames: Cass

rarely used

Sisters: Portia, Isadora, Maxima, Beatrix, Artemisia
Brothers: Atticus, Lazarus, Aldric, Marcellus, Leander

✳ A classical contender, very memorable if a bit too lean and hungry. The best-known modern Cassius was boxer Cassius Clay, who became Muhammad Ali.

Cecil

1900s: #68

Popularity: Rare
Style: English, Ladies and Gentlemen, Nickname-Proof
Sisters: Leona, Beatrice, Ada, Henrietta, Olive

Brothers: Basil, Claude, Virgil, Clement, Percy

✳ Boys continued to be named Cecil in the generations after Cecil B. DeMille produced his Hollywood epics, but the name remains frozen in time. Even with names like August and Cyrus inching toward comebacks, Cecil is still determinedly of a time gone by.

Cedric

1970s: #261

Popularity: #541
Style: African-American, Exotic Traditional
Nicknames: Rick
Variants: Cedrick

Sisters: Leticia, Damaris, Maribel, Angelique, Simone
Brothers: Desmond, Quincy, Orlando, Andre, Demetrius

✳ A name with Welsh forebears, dashing Cedric was introduced by Sir Walter Scott in his novel *Ivanhoe*. In the U.S., it has been primarily an African-American name. With the growing popularity of names like Alec and Dominic, Cedric's now a candidate for broader use.

Cesar

2002: #161

Popularity: #168
Style: Latino/Latina
Variants: Cezar, Caesar
Sisters: Alejandra, Bianca, Reyna, Dulce, Perla

Brothers: Sergio, Marco, Omar, Josue, Javier

✳ Spanish speakers are lucky with this one. As an English name, Caesar is charismatic but too flamboyant for comfort. The Spanish Cesar takes the charisma mainstream. Handsome and trendy.

Chad
1970s: #30

Popularity: #338
Style: '70s–'80s
Sisters: Tara, Christy, Aimee, Heather, Mandy
Brothers: Shawn, Jeremy, Brent, Jamie, Cory
✶ Chad is a preppy chieftain, captain of the racquetball team. Constant talk of "hanging chads" in the 2000 presidential election helped hasten the name's decline.

Chaim
2003: #922

Popularity: #922
Style: Jewish
Variants: Haim, Jaim, Hyam, Hyman
Sisters: Chaya, Dalia, Ariel, Yaffa, Dafna
Brothers: Yosef, Asher, Jaron, Elisha, Dov
✶ A burst of positive energy, Jewish style. Chaim means "life," as in the traditional toast *l'chaim*, or "to life!" (It's also the preferred way to honor an ancestor with the luckless name Hyman.) A common name among religious Jews, it is seldom heard in secular and non-Jewish communities.

Chance
2001: #230

Popularity: #246
Style: Brisk and Breezy, Modern Meanings
Sisters: Raven, Summer, Aubrey, Jade, Hayley
Brothers: Trent, Drake, Colby, Ty, Chandler
✶ Like Maverick, Chance is a lone gunman, following the wind and seeking adventure on his own terms. Unlike Maverick, Chance also has a softer side, a reflection of prep school names like Chauncey and Trey. That unlikely combination is a winner, making Chance the top Modern Meaning name for boys.

Chandler
2001: #207

Popularity: #263
Style: Last Names First
Sisters: Cassidy, Hayley, Skylar, Logan, Phoebe
Brothers: Bailey, Dawson, Spencer, Garrison, Drake
✶ Chandler has an offhand elegance that fits the spirit of the times. It probably would have been a popular choice even if it weren't featured on *Friends*, the most popular sitcom of the last decade. Probably. If you like the style but balk at the television association, look at Palmer and Archer.

Charles
1930s: #6

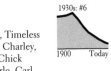

Popularity: #59
Style: Solid Citizens, Timeless
Nicknames: Charlie, Charley, Chuck, Chaz, Cal, Chick
Variants: Carlos, Carlo, Carl
Sisters: Mary, Margaret, Dorothy, Sylvia, Frances
Brothers: William, Richard, George, Edward, James
✶ Charles is stately and dignified, and Charlie is warm and friendly. That sounds like a killer combo, yet Charles has dropped significantly in popularity for seven decades in a row. That should change, as Charlie offers an attractive alternative to such popular nice-guy names as Sam.

Charlie
1900s: #59

Popularity: #372
Style: Nicknames, Solid Citizens
Variants: Charley
Sisters: Lucy, Alice, Nora, Susie, Nell
Brothers: Ray, Archie, Joe, Hal, Harry
✶ Forget the downtrodden everyman Charlie Brown. Today Charlie is chosen by chic parents as a fashionably fusty revival, simple and lovable. (Chuck, however, is still a nonstarter.)

Chase
2001: #80

Popularity: #87
Style: Brisk and Breezy
Sisters: Paige, Brooke, Sierra, Alexa, Haley
Brothers: Blake, Bryce, Cole, Grant, Devin
✶ A breezily wealthy name. Chase doesn't just sound like a banker, it sounds like the bank. Of course, that kind of association with moneyed brand names can end up sending a name downscale; just ask Tiffany. But Chase's swift simplicity should keep the name smoothly on track.

Chayton

Popularity: Rare
Style: The -ens
Nicknames: Chay
Sisters: Arden, Kateri, Shadi, Linden, Shenandoah
Brothers: Larson, Sakari, Quinlan, Tarian, Branson
✶ Chayton sounds like one more preppy cousin to Payton and Clayton. In fact, it's a Sioux Indian name meaning "falcon," a heritage that gives Chayton a little extra loft.

rarely used

Chester

1910s: #54

1900 — Today

Popularity: Rare
Style: Ladies and Gentlemen
Nicknames: Chet
Sisters: Leona, Harriet, Estelle, Ada, Louise
Brothers: Hubert, Wallace, Bertram, Luther, Cecil

✴ Chester is a relic today, feeble but oddly fetching. It's full of personality in the offbeat style of a picture-book character.

Christian

2001: #24

1900 — Today

Popularity: #24
Style: The -ens, New Classics
Nicknames: Chris
Variants: Kristian
Sisters: Kaitlyn, Alexis, Abigail, Taylor, Victoria
Brothers: Dylan, Alexander, Austin, Caleb, Gabriel

✴ This fast-rising name is bidding to supplant Christopher as the dominant "Chris" name. Parents like the modern two-syllable sound of Christian and the forthright declaration of faith that it represents. Beware alternate spellings that feminize the name.

Christopher

1980s: #2

1900 — Today

Popularity: #9
Style: New Classics
Nicknames: Chris, Kit, Kip, Topher
Variants: Kristofer, Christophe, Cristobal
Sisters: Jessica, Stephanie, Amanda, Lauren, Rebecca
Brothers: Jonathan, Matthew, Nicholas, Adam, Justin

✴ Christopher epitomizes the "new man" image—masculine but sensitive. After decades at the top, it's still completely fashionable. The nickname Chris, though, has vaulted into overuse as Christophers share the space with Christians, Christinas, and Crystals. The British nicknames Kip and Kit offer possible escape.

Clarence

1900s: #18

1900 — Today

Popularity: #717
Style: Ladies and Gentlemen, Nickname-Proof
Sisters: Alma, Beatrice, Esther, Cornelia, Louise
Brothers: Ernest, Clifford, Francis, Gilbert, Rudolph

✴ Clarence sounds like a kindly gentleman, old-fashioned and reliable. It's not a rugged name, but a friendly one—the guardian angel in *It's a Wonderful Life* is a fine model. The name's Achilles' heel is a total lack of nicknames.

Clark

1900s: #277

1900 — Today

Popularity: #802
Style: Solid Citizens, Why Not?
Sisters: Ellen, Ann, Polly, Martha, Libby
Brothers: Guy, Ward, Carlton, Lewis, Gordon

✴ Simple, straightforward, and as manly as actor Clark Gable. Perhaps more people think of Superman's alter ego Clark Kent, but is that really such a bad image? A mild-mannered exterior with surprising inner strength.

Claude

1900s: #71

1900 — Today

Popularity: Rare
Style: French, Ladies and Gentlemen
Variants: Claud, Claudio
Sisters: Cecile, Marion, Louise, Leora, Estelle
Brothers: Jules, Clement, Horace, Luther, Edmund

✴ The perfect French gentleman, Claude has been dragged down a bit by the clodlike English pronunciation of the name. It's still a distinguished choice, but not a popular one.

Clay

2002: #425

1900 — Today

Popularity: #487
Style: Brisk and Breezy, Timeless
Sisters: Mara, Lea, Hope, Abby, Paige
Brothers: Reid, Blaine, Ty, Davis, Lane

✴ You're most likely to find Clay as a nickname for Clayton these days. On its own, it's friendly and confident, and less likely to get lost in the surname pack. Singer Clay Aiken has livened the name up, so teenage girls will approve this choice.

Clayton

2001: #164

1900 — Today

Popularity: #187
Style: Last Names First, The -ens, Timeless
Nicknames: Clay
Sisters: Audrey, Caroline, Avery, Jillian, Mallory
Brothers: Harrison, Preston, Davis, Nolan, Spencer

✴ Perhaps the most timeless of the trendy surnames, Clayton is polished, substantial, and ready for grown-up responsibility. It's not a bucket of laughs . . . but that's where carefree nickname Clay comes in.

Clifford
1910s: #58

Popularity: #942
Style: Ladies and Gentlemen, Namesakes, Solid Citizens
Nicknames: Cliff
Sisters: Dorothy, Frances, Cora, Harriet, Clarice
Brothers: Bernard, Sherman, Lewis, Gilbert, Vernon
★ Clifford the Big Red Dog has given this name a shaggy image among kids. Once a young Clifford makes it past elementary school, he'll be fine, though. If you're drawn to the attractive nickname Cliff, Clifton is another strong alternative. (Not Heathcliff, which just turns the cartoon dog problem into a cartoon cat problem.)

Clifton
1910s: #155

Popularity: #955
Style: Last Names First, Solid Citizens
Nicknames: Cliff
Sisters: Cecilia, Corrine, Marian, Vivian, Dorothea
Brothers: Carlton, Ellis, Everett, Burton, Russell
★ Clifton is a hunk, but a standoffish one. He has a cool, remote demeanor that draws you to him yet doesn't let you get too close. Ah, but nickname Cliff is a big gruff teddy bear, so no worries.

Clint
1970s: #256

Popularity: Rare
Style: Brisk and Breezy, Country & Western
Sisters: Leigh, Holly, Christa, Brooke, Trisha
Brothers: Brant, Shane, Casey, Brett, Garrick
★ The essence of this name comes straight from the flinty stare of Clint Eastwood. His image gives Clint ageless grit.

Clinton
1980s: #156

Popularity: #737
Style: The -ens, Last Names First, Timeless
Nicknames: Clint
Sisters: Carrie, Joanna, Adrienne, Tracy, Christine
Brothers: Ross, Garrick, Nelson, Clayton, Ramsey
★ This name was calmly timeless until Bill Clinton took office. Seeking to avoid a political statement, parents shied away. With a few years' distance, though, this handsome classic should come back strong. Just look at Carter, a popular choice for Democrats and Republicans alike.

Clive
rarely used

Popularity: Rare
Style: Brisk and Breezy, English
Variants: Cliff
Sisters: Dulcie, Camilla, Glynis, Pippa, Gemma
Brothers: Piers, Niles, Crispin, Hugh, Graeme
★ This smooth, urbane old British name comes from the same root as gruff old buddy Cliff. So far, Americans have left the sleeker cousin on the other side of the Atlantic. It's sounding more promising today, though, as other sleek Brits like Trevor and Sebastian have settled in stateside.

Clyde
1900s: #58

Popularity: Rare
Style: Solid Citizens
Sisters: Velma, Leona, Helene, Rhoda, Mae
Brothers: Luther, Ervin, Ward, Leon, Claude
★ Between *Bonnie and Clyde* and Walt "Clyde" Frazier, this name acquired a cocky swagger in the late '60s. It's quite a contrast with the name's natural country-gentleman restraint. The result is an odd but intriguing chimera, part gent and part jive.

Cody
1990s: #26

Popularity: #79
Style: Country & Western, Last Names First, Nickname-Proof
Variants: Kody
Sisters: Taylor, Kasey, Kayla, Cassidy, Shelby
Brothers: Tyler, Cory, Dillon, Colt, Trevor
★ A classic "new cowboy" name, calling up the image of showman Buffalo Bill Cody and the Wyoming city that bears his name. A potential drawback is its eternal boyishness. Like Toby or Corey, Cody is a name that just doesn't want to grow up. Wyatt is one rising Western alternative.

Colby
2001: #99

Popularity: #184
Style: Bell Tones, Last Names First
Nicknames: Cole
Variants: Kolby
Sisters: Aubrey, Regan, Daniela, Kiley, Alexa
Brothers: Brody, Landon, Carson, Brock, Skyler
★ Colby is the leader of the popular pack of boyish surnames. It's currently exclusively male, but a likely candidate to follow Bailey into the girls' ranks.

Cole

2002: #69

Popularity: #70
Style: Brisk and Breezy, Nicknames
Variants: Nicholas
Sisters: Brooke, Caroline, Paige, Faith, Abby
Brothers: Grant, Luke, Chase, Spencer, Lane
★ Cole is a politician's dream—a name that pleases every constituency. It has the bluntness of a cowboy name, the briskness of a preppy name, and the sophistication of a Cole Porter tune. A showstopper.

Coleman

2002: #565

Popularity: #593
Style: Last Names First
Nicknames: Cole
Variants: Colman
Sisters: Hallie, Shelby, Clare, Isabelle, Blake
Brothers: Bennett, Lawson, Walker, Cooper, Harrison
★ This lively surname is anchored by the strong nickname Cole. It's a colorful, rugged antique. Also consider the Irish saint's name Colman for a Celtic kick.

Colin

2003: #89

Popularity: #89
Style: Celtic, English, The -ens, New Classics
Variants: Collin
Sisters: Jenna, Caitlin, Jocelyn, Chloe, Audrey
Brothers: Brendan, Alec, Ian, Trevor, Lucas
★ This Celtic favorite is a balanced choice, contemporary but familiar. You can also choose it as an old-fashioned nickname for Nicholas, akin to Robin for Robert.

Colton

2001: #120

Popularity: #135
Style: Country & Western, The -ens, Last Names First
Nicknames: Colt
Sisters: Cassidy, Sierra, Devyn, Jasmin, Cheyenne
Brothers: Dillon, Wyatt, Cash, Tanner, Landon
★ Colt has a clear image: young, tough, and feisty. The extended-play version Colton dresses the young cowboy up in his Sunday best.

Conan

Popularity: Rare
rarely used
Style: Celtic, The -ens, Saints
Sisters: Kennera, Arden, Riona, Tamsin, Larkin
Brothers: Colman, Egan, Lorcan, Brannock, Tiernan
★ If you pronounce it like Conan the Barbarian (Co-NANN), this one is right out. If you pronounce it CO-nyn, like the Irish saint (or late-night host Conan O'Brien), it has potential.

Connor

2003: #44

Popularity: #44
Style: Celtic
Nicknames: Con, Connie
Variants: Conor, Conner
Sisters: Morgan, Kaitlyn, Maura, Chloe, Paige
Brothers: Logan, Cameron, Riley, Gavin, Trevor
★ A bold and likable Irish standard that has become a favorite of Americans of every heritage. Connor has some of the flavor of surnames, like Tanner, but is a classic first name that has always been well used in Ireland. The spellings Connor and Conor are both traditional; Conner adds an unnecessary image of con men.

Conrad

1930s: #247

Popularity: #713
Style: Ladies and Gentlemen, Shakespearean
Nicknames: Con, Connie
Variants: Konrad
Sisters: Frances, Amalia, Josefa, Ardith, Antonia
Brothers: Gilbert, Roland, Bertram, Emmitt, Lowell
★ You'll meet plenty of little boys answering to "Con," almost all of them Connors. Conrad is a heavier name but a powerful one. An authority figure named Conrad is a force to be reckoned with.

Cooper

2003: #170

Popularity: #170
Style: Last Names First
Nicknames: Coop
Sisters: Macy, Peyton, Avery, Piper, Tatum
Brothers: Carter, Brody, Addison, Walker, Davis
★ Cooper is one tradesman name that makes even skeptical traditionalists smile. Its infectious good humor helps it overcome its trendiness.

Corbin

2003: #281

Popularity: #281
Style: The -ens
Nicknames: Cory
Variants: Korbin
Sisters: Kendall, Logan, Kiley, Brenna, Regan
Brothers: Keegan, Payton, Tucker, Kenyon, Brennan

✷ Corbin is boyishly attractive, a modern hit in the mold of Celtic classics. Its emergence in the '80s was part zeitgeist and part the influence of *L.A. Law* star Corbin Bernsen.

Corey

1980s: #65

Popularity: #200
Style: Bell Tones, Nickname-Proof, '70s–'80s
Variants: Cory, Korey, Kory
Sisters: Nikki, Amber, Jamie, Ashlee, Krista
Brothers: Dustin, Jeremy, Casey, Brett, Chad

✷ This was *the* cute boy's name for years, epitomized by Lisa Simpson's mooning over *Corey!* magazine. Surprisingly, the name has shown real staying power. It started out with '70s pals like Chad and Dusty, but fits in with newcomers Brody and Kolby. With the first batch of Coreys now in their thirties, it's growing up in a hurry.

Cormac

Popularity: Rare
Style: Celtic, Saints, Why Not?
Nicknames: Mac, Corey
Sisters: Riona, Aine, Kinnia, Averil, Finola
Brothers: Finian, Dermot, Conan, Gregor, Callum

rarely used

✷ It's remarkable that the success of writer Cormac McCarthy (*All the Pretty Horses*) hasn't brought this Irish favorite to America's attention. A potential winner.

Cornelius

1900s: #196

Popularity: #794
Style: Exotic Traditonal, Ladies and Gentlemen, Shakespearean
Nicknames: Con, Corny, Neil
Variants: Cornell, Cornelis
Sisters: Cordelia, Nola, Philomena, Viola, Maude
Brothers: Ferdinand, August, Archibald, Conrad, Marcellus

✷ Cornelius is a name straight out of ancient Rome. If you're tempted to pronounce it with an Irish accent, though, you're not alone. The name was popular in Ireland as a variant on the Gaelic Conchobar (much like contemporary favorite Connor). Choose a strong nickname like Con or Neil to counteract the "corny" sound.

Cosmo

Popularity: Rare
Style: Exotic Traditional, Italian
Variants: Cosimo
Sisters: Carmela, Luisa, Cleo, Flavia, Gia
Brothers: Rocco, Enzo, Felix, Arlo, Vito

rarely used

✷ This quirky classic acts as a "personality multiplier." It makes a cool guy seem cooler, a stylish guy snappier, a leader more dynamic. For a geeky or pudgy kid, though, it just adds to the burden.

Craig

1960s: #45

Popularity: #428
Style: Celtic, Surfer Sixties
Sisters: Julie, Christine, Michele, Tina, Beth
Brothers: Keith, Jeffrey, Curt, Scott, Gregg

✷ Craig came on like gangbusters in the '50s and '60s, but there's no need for it to fade as quickly. Its craggy Scottish sound meshes with current favorites from Brett to Donovan.

Crispin

Popularity: Rare
Style: English, The -ens, Saints, Why Not?
Nicknames: Cris
Sisters: Tamsin, Gemma, Beatrix, Savina, Larkin
Brothers: Dunstan, Colman, Albin, Tiernan, Barnaby

rarely used

✷ In the past, American parents found Crispin a little too cute for comfort. But now that we have little Devins and Kaydens on every block, Crispin's medieval saintly flavor shines through. This high-impact name will make other parents say, "Ooh, good one!"

Curtis

1960s: #78

Popularity: #327
Style: Shakespearean, Timeless
Nicknames: Curt
Sisters: Theresa, Annette, Diana, Paula, Cynthia
Brothers: Neil, Douglas, Dwight, Peter, Stuart

✷ Curtis is a quiet, solid man's name that deserves a place alongside the core classics. The nickname Curt gives it toughness, while the full name reflects its origin in the word "courteous."

Cyrus

2002: #470

Popularity: #491
Style: Biblical, Ladies and Gentlemen
Nicknames: Cy
Sisters: Augusta, Maude, Viola, Eugenie, Iva
Brothers: Ezra, Hugo, Leopold, Cornelius, Silas

✶ Cyrus is a genuine surprise. For generations, the name nestled in the dustbin with historical curiosities like Hiram and Cyril. Yet it's nudging its way toward a comeback, and once you stop to pay attention, the name does show off some creaky magnetism. Hiram, you're up next!

Dakota

1990s: #81

Popularity: #130
Style: Androgynous, Country & Western, Place Names
Nicknames: Koty, Dak
Variants: Dakotah
Sisters: Sierra, Cheyenne, Savanna, Mariah, Cassidy
Brothers: Marshal, Tanner, Chayton, Montana, Dillon

✶ This popular choice evokes the wide-open Western skies. It jumps right out at you because it doesn't sound like a traditional boy's name. That kind of distinctive style can backfire, though, when a name becomes too common. You can meet a dozen Toms and think nothing of it, but meet a few Dakotas and the name starts to sound mighty faddish.

Dale

1950s: #51

Popularity: #562
Style: Androgynous, Solid Citizens
Sisters: Janet, Anita, Jo, Elaine, Gwen
Brothers: Roger, Hale, Allen, Glenn, Bill

✶ Dale, the simple, urbane hit of the '30s and '40s, now has a rebellious side. It's linked to "The Intimidator," legendary NASCAR driver Dale Earnhardt.

Dallas

1990s: #294

Popularity: #391
Style: Country & Western, Nickname-Proof, Place Names
Sisters: Carolina, Sydney, Kasey, Daniella, Savanna
Brothers: Dillon, Hayden, Denver, Colton, Beau

✶ Dallas was originally a Scottish place name and surname, but today it locates you deep in the heart of Texas. Unlike other Western place names, though, Dallas isn't a cowboy throwback. It's a name of the new, urban West.

Dalton

2001: #98

Popularity: #147
Style: The -ens, Last Names First, Nickname-Proof
Sisters: Shelby, Karina, Jordyn, Aubrey, Regan
Brothers: Parker, Landon, Weston, Trevor, Bryson

✶ Dalton's one of the old-time surnames, part of the staid, pipe-smoking world of Palmer, Truman, and Winston. But while the others are still out puffing in the parlor, Dalton's come out of nowhere to become a smash hit.

Damian

2003: #164

Popularity: #164
Style: Exotic Traditional, Nickname-Proof, Saints
Variants: Damien
Sisters: Athena, Nadia, Giselle, Jasmin, Anastasia
Brothers: Sebastian, Dominic, Elias, Xavier, Emmanuel

✶ Several decades of steady use haven't robbed this name of its exotic flair. Damian is handsome, elegant, and decidedly devilish. The '70s horror flick The Omen played off Damian's demonlike sound in naming its hell child—and oddly enough, the name's popularity has soared ever since.

Damon

1970s: #144

Popularity: #299
Style: The -ens, Mythological, New Classics, Nickname-Proof
Sisters: Tania, Alana, Jocelyn, Angel, Daniella
Brothers: Andre, Dorian, Corbin, Brock, Quinn

✶ This age-old name has a bold modern sound that has made it a favorite of American parents. For extra positive vibes, the classical Greek tale of Damon and Pythias celebrates friendship and loyalty.

Dana

1950s: #183

Popularity: Rare
Style: Androgynous, Mid-Century
Sisters: Marla, Vicky, Sheryl, Teri, Patrice
Brothers: Gregg, Robin, Cary, Kent, Russ

✶ A blithe, upscale boy's name, done in by gender confusion. Try Dane for a contemporary, boys-only successor.

Dane

Popularity: #445
Style: Brisk and Breezy
Variants: Dana, Dean
Sisters: Cara, Lise, Lindsay, Jena, Elle
Brothers: Brice, Drew, Derrick, Colt, Cale

✳ As Dana has lost ground on the boys' side, this simple variant has taken hold in its place. Previously a British name, Dane is still on the preppy side but has picked up some of the cowboy aura of similar names Shane and Zane.

Daniel

Popularity: #8
Style: Biblical, Timeless
Nicknames: Dan, Danny
Variants: Danyel
Sisters: Rebecca, Rachel, Joanna, Andrea, Sarah
Brothers: Matthew, Michael, David, Joel, Benjamin

✳ Daniel is one of the few Old Testament names to be rock-solid American classics. It was a top hit even back when Jacob and Joshua were considered ancient relics. As a result, Daniel sounds less tied to its biblical roots and more grounded in the modern world. It's friendly, handsome, and universally liked.

Dante

Popularity: #253
Style: African-American, Italian
Variants: Donte, Dontae, Deonte, Durante
Sisters: Kiana, Gianna, Camille, Angel, Paola
Brothers: Marco, Quinn, Javon, Dario, Giovanni

✳ This name was originally bestowed in honor of *Inferno* poet Dante Alighieri, an association that gave the name arty pizzazz. That pizzazz has stuck around even as the name has become more popular and less exotic. If you're really in the market for the unusual, consider that Dante was a pet form of the poet's given name, Durante.

Darian

Popularity: #527
Style: African-American, The -ens, Nickname-Proof
Variants: Darien, Darrian, Darrien, Darrion
Sisters: Tiana, Ashton, Kenia, Taryn, Jazmin
Brothers: Quinton, Devon, Alexis, Trevon, Keenan

✳ An attractive collage, Darian is part Damian, part Dorian, part the ultra-preppy Connecticut suburb Darien. For bonus points, it's even an anagram of another top name. (Got it yet? Adrian.)

Darius

Popularity: #258
Style: African-American, Nickname-Proof, Saints
Variants: Dario
Sisters: Tatiana, Celeste, Ava, Chantal, Marina
Brothers: Quentin, Damian, Marco, Ivan, Elias

✳ This name still sounds exotic, but its rare combination of graces is propelling it into the mainstream. Antique and creative, serious and sexy, Darius is a thinking girl's hunk.

Darrell

Popularity: #566
Style: African-American, Mid-Century, Nickname-Proof, Surfer Sixties
Variants: Darryl, Daryl, Darrel, Daryle, Derrell
Sisters: Sheila, Denise, Yolanda, Rhonda, Suzanne
Brothers: Randall, Dwayne, Rodney, Bruce, Dean

✳ Darrell is a Norman baronial surname that parents flocked to in the middle of the last century. By now its aristocratic aura has worn off, but the name continues along amiably. The '60s variant Darryl is aging faster than the original.

Darren

Popularity: #304
Style: New Classics, Nickname-Proof, Surfer Sixties
Variants: Darin, Darrin, Daren, Daron, Darron
Sisters: Gina, Kelly, Deanna, Renee, Traci
Brothers: Troy, Brad, Kelvin, Derrick, Brent

✳ The "Mack the Knife" singer was Bobby *Darin*. The *Bewitched* husband was *Darrin* Stephens. And every spelling of this name you can dream up hit the charts simultaneously in the '60s. The name has survived that tumultuous childhood and is now a smooth, steady choice for a grown man.

Darwin

Popularity: #845
Style: Last Names First, Namesakes
Sisters: Edwina, Arlene, Doretha, Beverley, Lorna
Brothers: Linwood, Barton, Weldon, Lowell, Newton

✳ This name is powerfully linked to Darwin's theory of evolution. Perhaps you don't care a whit about Charles Darwin's studies in the Galapagos Islands, but others do—making this either a hero name or a guilt-by-association name depending on personal convictions.

Dashiell

Popularity: Rare
Style: Exotic Traditional
Nicknames: Dash
Sisters: Zella, Salome, Isadora, Beatrix, Olympia
Brothers: Thelonius, Lazar, Marlowe, Bartholomew, Cassius

rarely used

1900 — Today

✳ Can a name be too cool? With the imprint of Sam Spade creator Dashiell Hammett and the nickname Dash, this one is a veritable dry martini. If you think your kid can pull it off, go for it.

David

Popularity: #14
Style: Biblical, Timeless
Nicknames: Dave, Davy
Sisters: Karen, Deborah, Diana, Susan, Kathy
Brothers: Michael, Stephen, Alan, Mark, Daniel

1960s: #2

1900 — Today

✳ The classic boys' names always have snappy good-guy nicknames: Mike, Matt, Jim, Jake . . . and Dave. But you can get too much of a good-guy thing. The generation raised in the '70s and '80s was surrounded by Daves and is starting to shy away from the name. Of course, that could mean an opportunity for your little Dave to be the only one in his class.

Davis

Popularity: #381
Style: Last Names First, Timeless
Nicknames: Dave, Davey
Sisters: Clare, Macy, Hope, Kate, Caroline
Brothers: Reid, Avery, Preston, Miles, Harrison

2001: #370

1900 — Today

✳ This handsome name is pleasantly familiar, even though you've probably never met a Davis in person. It's distinctive in a quiet way that appeals across generations.

Dawson

Popularity: #204
Style: The -ens, Last Names First, Nickname-Proof
Sisters: Skylar, Camryn, Delaney, Mckenna, Felicity
Brothers: Parker, Dalton, Nash, Chandler, Grayson

2001: #188

1900 — Today

✳ The TV series *Dawson's Creek* spawned this name. (What, you thought it was from Richard Dawson of *Family Feud*?) The name's muscular surname sound has helped it outlive the TV show.

Dayton

Popularity: #505
Style: The -ens, Last Names First, Nickname-Proof, Place Names
Sisters: Sydney, Kailyn, Hallie, Aubrey, Madelyn
Brothers: Walker, Easton, Keaton, Sawyer, Hudson

2003: #505

1900 — Today

✳ Like Trenton and Camden—and unlike Paris—this city name is usually chosen for its sound, not its geography. But the rust belt is surprisingly fertile ground for contemporary names. (How about Flint while we're at it?)

Dean

Popularity: #385
Style: Brisk and Breezy, Last Names First, Mid-Century, Surfer Sixties
Variants: Deane, Dane
Sisters: Tina, Dawn, Christine, Teresa, Lynn
Brothers: Keith, Kent, Tad, Ross, Troy

1960s: #88

1900 — Today

✳ Dean is an old favorite with a clean sound. It's square in the best way, like a letterman sweater or a formal dinner date.

Declan

Popularity: #425
Style: Celtic, Saints
Nicknames: Dec, Dex
Sisters: Ciara, Maeve, Brynn, Dara, Siobhan
Brothers: Ronan, Kieran, Blaine, Seamus, Griffin

2003: #425

1900 — Today

✳ Declan was an exclusively Irish name until the '90s. Its handsome, saintly style is now widely in demand, and the name is popping up in the U.S. For now, though, it's still exotic enough that you'll have to tutor friends on the pronunciation (DECK-lon.)

Demetrius

Popularity: #462
Style: African-American, Exotic Traditional, Saints, Shakespearean
Variants: Dimitrios, Demetrio, Dimitri
Sisters: Angelique, Serena, Damaris, Anastasia, Genevieve
Brothers: Darius, Orlando, Zachariah, Isaias, Emmanuel

1990s: #322

1900 — Today

✳ Classical names have a natural gravity that lets them get away with pushing the style envelope. Case in point: Demetrius, an ornate name that sounds dignified rather than fancified. (Sounds pretty studly, too.)

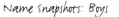

Dennis 1940s: #20

Popularity: #280
Style: Mid-Century
Nicknames: Denny
Variants: Dennison
Sisters: Kathleen, Sandra, Sharon, Diane, Janice
Brothers: Roger, Gary, Kenneth, Allen, Randall
★ It's time to forget about Dennis the Menace. Dennis isn't a little ruffian anymore. He's a stand-up guy, the good-natured, honorable sort you always want on your side. Yet as grown-up as the name sounds, it's still cheery enough for a young boy.

Denver 1910s: #482

Popularity: Rare
Style: Country & Western, Place Names
Sisters: Marietta, Roma, Shelby, Delta, Aspen
Brothers: Hardy, Thurman, Walton, Dallas, Miller
★ This mile-high place name has an old-fashioned feel but fits in with newcomers like Aspen and Savannah.

Denzel 1990s: #397

Popularity: #772
Style: African-American, Namesakes
Variants: Denzil
Sisters: Dania, Amani, Nia, Shanice, Kenia
Brothers: Omari, Kai, Savion, Quinn, Nico
★ A quirky old Cornish surname, now overwhelmingly associated with actor Denzel Washington. As we start to meet more little Denzels, the connection will loosen, but for the time being the name will be taken as an homage to the star.

Derek 1980s: #53

Popularity: #143
Style: New Classics, Nickname-Proof
Variants: Derrick, Deric, Dietrich, Dirk
Sisters: Alicia, Erin, Holly, Lindsey, Megan
Brothers: Brett, Jared, Bradley, Shane, Marcus
★ To your grandparents, Derek was a name like Nigel or Clive—slick and exclusively British. The name has now discarded its British image but kept a grown-up elegance that distinguishes it from other more boyish '80s favorites. The popular alternate spelling Derrick is completely American and conjures up oil rigs.

Desmond 1990s: #340

Popularity: #460
Style: African-American, Celtic, Exotic Traditional
Nicknames: Des, Dez
Sisters: Larissa, Roxanna, Simone, Mallory, Kiara
Brothers: Quinton, Demitrius, Kendall, Garret, Quincy
★ This still uncommon name is a find: Gaelic and sophisticated with a cool nickname. It can also be chosen to honor Nobel Laureate Bishop Desmond Tutu.

Devin 2001: #71

Popularity: #74
Style: Androgynous, The -ens, Nickname-Proof
Variants: Devon, Deven
Sisters: Morgan, Caitlin, Paige, Brooke, Jenna
Brothers: Colin, Trevor, Adrian, Blake, Logan
★ Arguably a Celtic name, Devin owes its growing use more to its coltish sound, like a devilish Kevin. Like many light, contemporary choices, it shows up as a girl's name as well. See also: Devon.

Devon 1990s: #128

Popularity: #161
Style: African-American, The -ens, Place Names
Nicknames: Dev, Von
Variants: Devin, Deven, Devonta, Devonte
Sisters: Jasmin, Tiana, Katlyn, Jocelyn, Ariel
Brothers: Jaron, Colin, Malik, Dante, Quinton
★ Devon is actually two names in one. As an alternate spelling of Devin, it harkens back to County Devon in England. But pronounce it de-VON and you have an African-American favorite akin to names like Javon and Devonte.

Dexter 1960s: #345

Popularity: #852
Style: English, Last Names First, Timeless
Nicknames: Dex
Sisters: Avis, Maribel, Lacy, Iris, Daphne
Brothers: Quincy, Elliot, Baxter, Terence, Barrett
★ It's cool. It's geeky. It's geeky-cool? That's really not a bad niche. If you want to push Dexter firmly into cool territory, the nickname Dex does the trick.

Diego 2003: #76
Popularity: #76
Style: Latino/Latina, Saints
Variants: Diogo
Sisters: Dulce, Mariana, 1900 Today
Jimena, Fabiola, Esmeralda
Brothers: Mateo, Rodrigo, Josue, Andres, Marco
✱ Diego is a name familiar to every American, thanks to the city of San Diego and famous Diegos from painters Rivera and Velázquez to *futbol* star Maradona. In practice, though, the name has been rare and rather old-fashioned. That's all changed now: Diego is suddenly one of the hottest Spanish names around, one you're as likely to encounter in a schoolyard as on an atlas.

Dillon 1990s: #115
Popularity: #190
Style: Country & Western, The -ens, Last Names First
Variants: Dylan 1900 Today
Sisters: Jordan, Paige, Aspen, Shelby, Logan
Brothers: Colton, Austin, Tanner, Devon, Zane
✱ An intriguing twist on a familiar name. While the spelling Dylan is all Welsh, *Gunsmoke*'s Marshal Dillon lends this version a decidedly Western air. See also: Dylan.

Dimitri 2001: #751
Popularity: #824
Style: Exotic Traditional, Greek, Slavic
Nicknames: Dima 1900 Today
Variants: Dmitri, Dimitrios, Demetrius
Sisters: Katerina, Larissa, Athena, Anastasia, Paloma
Brothers: Andreas, Ivan, Dominic, Thaddeus, Maxim
✱ Dimitri is foreign in the best way, mysterious enough to pique our interest but familiar enough to get cozy with. You expect a Dimitri to be intelligent, sophisticated, and easy on the eyes.

Dion 1970s: #418
Popularity: #854
Style: African-American, Shakespearean
Variants: Deon, Deion 1900 Today
Sisters: Simone, Lara, Selina, Tyra, Angelique
Brothers: Orlando, Cedric, Quincy, Andre, Darian
✱ Americans first met Dion in the form of "Runaround Sue" singer Dion Dimucci. It has a French sound but is actually an English adaptation of the Greek Dionysios. The name particularly struck a chord with African-American parents, who have embraced it in a variety of spellings (à la sports star Deion Sanders.)

Dirk 1960s: #471
Popularity: Rare
Style: German/Dutch, Surfer Sixties
Sisters: Mari, Deena, Cheri, 1900 Today
Renee, Dawn
Brothers: Rod, Kirk, Scott, Dino, Kent
✱ Dirk has an exaggerated masculinity, like porn star Dirk Diggler in the film *Boogie Nights*. It was originally a Dutch form of Derek, but is more often associated with a Scottish term for a dagger.

Dominic 2003: #82
Popularity: #82
Style: Antique Charm, Saints
Nicknames: Dom
Variants: Dominick, Domenic, 1900 Today
Dominique, Domingo, Domenico
Sisters: Natalia, Ava, Alexis, Gabriella, Sabina
Brothers: Xavier, Sebastian, Ivan, Tristan, Julian
✱ An old religious name, Dominic has always had a romantic, mysterious image in the U.S.— a curious blend of suave ladies' man and cloistered monk. Today, Dominic is as cool and sophisticated as ever, but no longer so exotic. It's one of the new elegant standards.

Donald 1930s: #7
Popularity: #257
Style: Solid Citizens
Nicknames: Don, Donnie
Variants: Donal 1900 Today
Sisters: Shirley, Arlene, Betty, Phyllis, Gloria
Brothers: Jerome, Richard, Franklin, Gene, Gerald
✱ Donald has slipped slowly out of style, while its nickname is still going strong. (Picture TV star Don Johnson as Donald Johnson—suddenly he looks his age.) If you choose Donald for your son, you'll certainly get no objections. But if it's Don you're after, Donovan is now the more popular choice.

Donovan 2003: #180
Popularity: #180
Style: Celtic, Last Names First
Nicknames: Don, Donny, Van
Variants: Donavan 1900 Today
Sisters: Logan, Avery, Rhiannon, Ciara, Shea
Brothers: Brennan, Riley, Connor, Cameron, Garrett
✱ Mmm, mmm . . . that's smooooooth. Namesakes like the '60s "Mellow Yellow" singer Donovan and football star Donovan McNabb reinforce this name's image as a sleek man about town. Donovan has trendy Irish surname roots but has been heard as a first name for a century, making for a modern-sounding classic.

Dorian 2001: #417
Popularity: #449
Style: The -ens, Nickname-
Proof
Sisters: Taryn, Noelle, Marina, 1900 Today
Regan, Serena
Brothers: Tristan, Corbin, Quentin, Blaine,
Damian
✶ This name made its debut as the decadent
title character in Oscar Wilde's *The Picture of
Dorian Gray*. That's not the most attractive ori-
gin, but feel free to ignore the character's short-
comings and enjoy Wilde's perfect ear for
names. Dorian is still unusual and sounds like a
timeless classic.

Douglas 1950s: #28
Popularity: #309
Style: Celtic, Mid-Century
Nicknames: Doug
Variants: Douglass 1900 Today
Sisters: Kathleen, Teresa, Pamela, Susan,
Patricia
Brothers: Bruce, Kenneth, Rodney, Kent, Dwight
✶ Douglas is a classic surname borne by one of
the great families of Scotland. In America, it
acquired a swashbuckling image thanks to the
screen heroics of Douglas Fairbanks Jr. and Sr.
and the real-world heroics of General Douglas
MacArthur. That heroic image has softened over
the past generation. Douglas is still handsome,
but now more respectable than adventurous.

Drake 2001: #264
Popularity: #276
Style: Brisk and Breezy, Last
Names First
Sisters: Macy, Logan, Delaney, 1900 Today
Sidney, Kyra
Brothers: Lane, Reece, Donovan, Brody, Keane
✶ Parents choose Drake for its lordly sound,
which projects a timeless strength. The name is
not really timeless, of course, but a rising star
taken from the familiar surname. Explorer Sir
Francis Drake is a dashing model for the name.

Drew 1990s: #178
Popularity: #224
Style: Androgynous, Brisk and
Breezy, New Classics,
Nicknames 1900 Today
Sisters: Kara, Brooke, Carly, Shea, Allison
Brothers: Erik, Alex, Evan, Brett, Trent
✶ As a nickname for Andrew, Drew adds a
Scottish punch and modern sound. As a given
name, it's a preppy jock, akin to Chad but with-
out the '80s aura.

Duane 1930s: #118
Popularity: Rare
Style: Celtic, Mid-Century,
Solid Citizens
Variants: Dwayne, Dwain, 1900 Today
Dwane
Sisters: Patty, Darlene, Joyce, Gwen, Jeanette
Brothers: Glenn, Lonnie, Eddie, Wayne,
Dwight
✶ Duane was an American standard for fifty
years. It started out sounding like a slick young
Irish dude and gradually mellowed into a plain-
spoken fatherly type (as slick young dudes so
often do). It has now mellowed so far it has fall-
en out of fashion altogether. See also: Dwayne.

Dudley 1900s: #389
Popularity: Rare
Style: English, Porch Sitters
Sisters: Enid, Hester, Eunice,
Dolly, Wilma 1900 Today
Brothers: Cecil, Godfrey, Sylvester, Chester,
Waldo
✶ A perfectly reasonable name in England,
Dudley has been a dud in the U.S. It used to
remind us of Dudley Do-Right, the cartoon
Mountie, who at least lent it a prim kind of
respectability. But thanks to Harry Potter's oafish
cousin Dudley Dursley, it is now virtually off-
limits.

Duke 1950s: #806
Popularity: Rare
Style: Guys and Dolls, Mid-
Century, Nicknames
Sisters: Kitty, Fay, Maxie, 1900 Today
Queenie, Jo
Brothers: Ike, Major, Doc, Mack, Spike
✶ We're naming kids Princess and Diamond
now, so why is Duke such a hard sell? Granted,
even the classic American Dukes—Ellington,
Snider, and John Wayne—were christened by
other names (Edward, Edwin, and Marion,
respectively). You can follow the same path, using
Duke as a nickname for any name you please.

Duncan 2001: #479
Popularity: #548
Style: Celtic, The -ens,
Shakespearean, Timeless,
Why Not? 1900 Today
Sisters: Marina, Regan, Juliet, Eva, Gillian
Brothers: Griffin, Reid, Colin, Graham,
Quentin
✶ A handsome and dashing Scot, this timeless
name is bristling with potential. In some parts of
the country, the occasional nickname "Dunkin'
Donuts" may be inevitable.

Dunstan

Popularity: Rare
Style: English, The -ens,
Nickname-Proof, Saints
Sisters: Gemma, Linden,
Dahlia, Arden, Fiona
Brothers: Crispin, Colman, Dermot, Rupert,
Tiernan

rarely used

1900   Today

★ This fine old saint's name has been ignored, even as similar choices from Dustin to Austin have soared. It's an uncommon choice that should have no trouble fitting in, except for the occasional "dunce" joke.

Dustin

Popularity: #209
Style: The -ens, '70s–'80s
Nicknames: Dusty
Sisters: Erica, Lindsay,
Danielle, Kristen, Kendra

1980s: #45

1900   Today

Brothers: Corey, Travis, Derek, Jeremy, Brett
★ Justin's little brother, who tagged along with him to the top of the charts in the '80s. Unlike big bro, Dustin also gives you a perfect little-boy/cowboy nickname in Dusty.

Dwayne

Popularity: #617
Style: African-American, Surfer
Sixties
Variants: Duane, Duwayne,
Dwain, Dwane

1960s: #130

1900   Today

Sisters: Shelly, Gina, Suzette, Rhonda, Wendy
Brothers: Darryl, Lorne, Scotty, Donnell, Randy
★ It may seem like splitting hairs, dividing up Duane and Dwayne. But the two spellings have different histories and associations: Irish or American, white or black, '40s or '60s. Take your pick which best fits your family. See also: Duane.

Dwight

Popularity: #928
Style: Mid-Century, Timeless
Nicknames: Dewey
Sisters: Gayle, Anita, Diane,
Janice, Marcia

1950s: #152

1900   Today

Brothers: Stuart, Neal, Kent, Thomas, Allen
★ Dwight's never been a common name, yet you always seem to find Dwights in positions of prominence. From politicians to athletes to musicians, they somehow rise to the top. Not a fashionable name, but a strong one.

Dylan

Popularity: #19
Style: Celtic, The -ens
Nicknames: Dyll
Variants: Dillon

2001: #21

1900   Today

Sisters: Morgan, Kaitlyn, Kiara, Alexis, Regan
Brothers: Logan, Colin, Reese, Connor, Gavin
★ Bob Dylan named himself after Welsh poet Dylan Thomas, and now those two Dylans together give the name breadth. A sensitive Celtic with a rock-and-roll heart. And yes, in the past decade, Dylan has gone electric. Thank the generation that grew up gazing at Luke Perry's Dylan on *Beverly Hills, 90210.* See also: Dillon.

Eamon

Popularity: Rare
Style: Celtic, The -ens,
Nickname-Proof, Why Not?
Variants: Éamon, Éamonn

rarely used

1900   Today

Sisters: Bryn, Riona, Aisling, Davina, Lilias
Brothers: Egan, Colm, Gareth, Ivor, Brogan
★ This is a soulful Irish hit in waiting. The Gaelic form of Edmund, Eamon has the kind of artful simplicity that has made Aidan a smash. (The pronunciation is similar, too: AY-mon.)

Earl

Popularity: #882
Style: African-American,
Country & Western, Solid
Citizens
Variants: Earle

1900s: #27

1900   Today

Sisters: Irene, Rita, Mae, Ruth, Doris
Brothers: Roy, Vernon, Ellis, Duke, Ralph
★ This is a name distinctive to America. Only the land without aristocracy uses aristocratic titles as names. Within that genre, Earl is the most enduring choice. It was a solid hit a century ago, but more recently has become Hollywood's choice for slow-witted hicks and corrupt, beer-bellied sheriffs.

Edgar

Popularity: #167
Style: Antique Charm, English,
Saints, Shakespearean
Nicknames: Ed
Variants: Edgardo

1900s: #75

1900   Today

Sisters: Amelia, Lilian, Helena, Clara, Edith
Brothers: Oscar, Julius, Abraham, Edmund,
Hugh
★ One of the chunky Old English classics, Edgar comes across as sophisticated but self-effacing, like a gentleman with a charming stammer. It owes a good part of its continuing popularity to Latino parents who have adopted this name in large numbers.

Edison   1910s: #688
Popularity: Rare
Style: Last Names First, Why
Not?
Nicknames: Ed, Eddie
Sisters: Adela, Marian, Marley, Clara, Bell
Brothers: Truman, Foster, Willis, Hamilton,
Richmond
✴ Edison is a handsome, traditional surname
that has yet to be rediscovered. Its sound is per-
fectly current, it has classic nicknames, and it
even gives you a historical hero in inventor
Thomas Edison. So what's stopping you?

Edmund   1900s: #144
Popularity: Rare
Style: English, Ladies and
Gentlemen, Saints, Why Not?
Nicknames: Ed, Ned, Ted,
Eddie
Variants: Edmond, Eamon
Sisters: Louisa, Marian, Adela, Matilda,
Beatrice
Brothers: Hugh, Foster, Rupert, Carleton,
Everett
✴ Edmund has been lumped in with fusty gen-
tlemen like Chester and Herman. It's time for
the name to step out on its own. Edmund has
extra refinement, a courtliness closer in spirit to
elegant hits like Julian. Yet it's blessedly unpre-
tentious, especially with nicknames like Ed and
Ned to choose from.

Edward   1910s: #8
Popularity: #128
Style: Timeless
Nicknames: Ed, Eddie, Ned,
Ted
Variants: Eduardo
Sisters: Margaret, Catherine, Evelyn, Martha,
Anne
Brothers: George, Charles, William, Paul,
Henry
✴ Edward has always been kingly and sophisti-
cated, a fine choice of fine gentlemen. Its sound,
though, is no longer current. In an age of breezy
names, Edward can seem a little slow. None-
theless, this is too pure a classic to be discarded.
The nickname Ned is a particularly stylish
throwback.

Edwin   1910s: #53
Popularity: #172
Style: Ladies and Gentlemen
Nicknames: Ed
Sisters: Edith, Leona, Alma,
Frances, Cora
Brothers: Arthur, Ernest, Bernard, Willis,
Herman
✴ This Old English name has a thoroughly
outdated sound but has held on admirably.
You'll still meet Edwins of all ages and all races.
It's the gentlest of gentleman names.

Egan
Popularity: Rare   rarely used
Style: Celtic, The -ens, Why
Not?
Variants: Eoghan
Sisters: Fallon, Emlyn, Rory, Nola, Arden
Brothers: Brogan, Doran, Cormac, Keir,
Riordan
✴ Irish and voguish, Egan may be unfamiliar
but people will like it when they hear it. The
standard pronuciation is EE-gan.

Eli   2003: #192
Popularity: #192
Style: Antique Charm, Biblical,
Little Darlings, Nickname-Proof
Sisters: Ivy, Lily, Hannah, Eden,
Zoe
Brothers: Levi, Noah, Axel, Jake, Caleb
✴ As a rule, to get a gruff, old-time manly
sound you reach for the hard-edged letters. You
want names with a high Scrabble value: Jake,
Levi, Max. But Eli gives you the same style in a
softer form. No good for Scrabble, but high scor-
ing in the real world.

Elias   2003: #211
Popularity: #211
Style: Antique Charm, Exotic
Traditional, Greek, Saints
Nicknames: Eli
Variants: Ellis, Elijah
Sisters: Ava, Sofia, Ivy, Astrid, Paloma
Brothers: Julian, Dominick, Roman, Phineas,
Ezra
✴ Elias is the rarefied Greek form of Elijah. It
may sound like a time traveler from the eigh-
teenth century, but this elegant name has made
a sudden leap into contemporary style.

Elijah

1900   Today

Popularity: #37
Style: African-American, Antique Charm, Biblical
Nicknames: Eli
Variants: Eliahu, Elias
Sisters: Abigail, Aliyah, Grace, Hannah, Mara
Brothers: Isaiah, Malachi, Tobias, Ezra, Josiah
★ One of the most resoundingly biblical of the popular Old Testament names. Elijah still sounds like a prophet, and that lends it an uplifting spirit. The name has been particularly popular among African-Americans, especially Muslims, but is now a favorite of all groups.

Elisha

2003: #612

1900   Today

Popularity: #612
Style: African-American, Androgynous, Biblical, Jewish
Sisters: Chaya, Lydia, Hallie, Zilla, Sarai
Brothers: Asa, Ezekiel, Judah, Gideon, Malachi
★ The biblical prophet Elisha was Elijah's successor, and his name is pronounced similarly (ee-LYE-shuh). The name was a no-show in America for generations, used occasionally for girls as eh-LEE-sha. Elisha remained in use for boys chiefly among religious Jews, and in Africa and the Caribbean. The rising interest in unusual Bible names has nudged it back toward broader use in the U.S.

Elliott

1990s: #445

Popularity: #513
Style: Nickname-Proof, Timeless
Sisters: Celia, Camille, Daphne, Theresa, Corinne
Brothers: Graham, Duncan, Reid, Miles, Spencer
★ Elliott's a charmer, in the intellectual rather than brawny vein. Guaranteed to melt girls' hearts in cafés and college classrooms.

Ellis

1900s: #176

Popularity: #831
Style: Last Names First, Nickname-Proof, Solid Citizens, Why Not?
Sisters: Nell, Lila, Dorothea, Adele, Cleo
Brothers: Grady, Forrest, Everett, Hugh, Clifton
★ Ellis is the kind of name that nobody ever thinks of but almost everybody likes. Its surname roots make it an attractive match for contemporary favorites like Parker and Jackson.

Elmer

1900s: #35

1900   Today

Popularity: #654
Style: Namesakes, Porch Sitters
Variants: Elmo
Sisters: Agnes, Ida, Myrtle, Bertha, Opal
Brothers: Earl, Homer, Ervin, Grover, Lloyd
★ Elmer is buried by the image of cartoon rube Elmer Fudd. If the name's ultra-retro style grabs you, your best bet is the closely related name Elmo. Yes, it just trades in a Looney Toon for a Muppet, but the -o ending shifts the style from pure fuddy-duddy to potential geek-chic.

Elvis

2002: #612

1900   Today

Popularity: #679
Style: Namesakes
Sisters: Janis, Presley, Delilah, Scarlett, Viva
Brothers: Rhett, Jagger, Arlis, Jude, Holden
★ This is an American creation of obscure origins that sounded fancy to parents a hundred years ago. Elvis is a rare survivor among that style, with similar names like Clovis long since . . . pardon me, what was that? Oh, THAT Elvis! Yes, forget everything else, the King rules this name absolutely. If your kid is the cool and confident type, he'll probably revel in the image.

Emerson

1900s: #384

Popularity: #714
Style: Ladies and Gentlemen, Last Names First, Nickname-Proof
Sisters: Florence, Jewel, Avery, Lina, Estella
Brothers: Newton, Freeman, Edison, Porter, Merritt
★ If you want a creative but serious-sounding name for your child, a strong historical namesake is a perfect solution. Ralph Waldo Emerson exhorted young people to "hitch your wagon to a star" and "always do what you are afraid to do." Those could be inspiring messages to grow up with.

Emil

1900s: #109

1900   Today

Popularity: Rare
Style: German/Dutch, Ladies and Gentlemen, Scandinavian
Variants: Emile, Emilio
Sisters: Thora, Inez, Avis, Olive, Maude
Brothers: Cecil, Bertram, Otto, Claude, Basil
★ Emil sounds more foreign and exotic today than it used to, even as the feminine forms of the name—Emily, Amelia, and their kin—sound ever more American. In much of Europe, the male version is equally trendy.

Emmanuel

2003: #183

Popularity: #183
Style: Biblical, Exotic Traditional
Nicknames: Manny
Variants: Emanuel, Manuel, Immanuel
Sisters: Angelica, Jasmine, Gabriela, Bianca, Damaris
Brothers: Damian, Nathanael, Giovanni, Xavier, Darius
✹ A classic in other languages, Emmanuel (the name of the Messiah) was long considered immodest as an English name. In recent decades, though, it has gained new acceptance. Like other elaborate biblical names, Emmanuel caught on first with African-Americans and is now more broadly used.

Emmett

1900s: #155

Popularity: #684
Style: Ladies and Gentlemen, Nickname-Proof, Timeless, Why Not?
Variants: Emmitt, Emmet, Emmit
Sisters: Clara, Adela, Lillie, Celia, Esther
Brothers: Reuben, Everett, Leo, Jasper, Ellis
✹ The perfect little gentleman to accompany your little lady. Lily, Isabel, Olivia, and friends have conquered the playground with their genteel femininity, but male counterparts have been harder to find. If you want the same sweetness in a neatly masculine form, Emmett is your man.

Enzo

2003: #864

Popularity: #864
Style: Italian, Little Darlings
Sisters: Chiara, Flavia, Nicola, Paola, Renata
Brothers: Aldo, Luca, Cosmo, Nico, Carlo
✹ This Italian name is an old-timer with a swagger. Enzo Ferrari, the legendary founder of the sports car company, perfectly captures the name's combination of jet-set and old-country styles. Still rare in the U.S., Enzo has become a fashionable favorite in France.

Eric

1970s: #14

Popularity: #57
Style: New Classics, Scandinavian, '70s–'80s
Nicknames: Ric
Variants: Erik, Erick, Aric
Sisters: Stephanie, Andrea, Erin, Michelle, Alison
Brothers: Adam, Sean, Brian, Kevin, Justin
✹ Eric is a rare example of an Old Norse name among the English standards. It was a huge hit in the '70s and '80s and it is aging well. Its crisp -c ending is more stylish than ever, echoed in such up-and-coming hits as Alec and Dominic. For a more purely Norse image, try the spelling Erik.

Ernest

1900s: #26

Popularity: #599
Style: Ladies and Gentlemen
Nicknames: Ernie
Variants: Earnest, Ernesto, Ernst
Sisters: Edith, Alma, Clara, Martha, Lucille
Brothers: Alfred, Francis, Clarence, Everett, Walter
✹ Ernest comes across as a slow-moving old-timer. He's still reliable, just not as spry as he used to be. On a young boy, the name will surprise people, but they'll warm to it quickly.

Ethan

2002: #5

Popularity: #7
Style: Biblical, The -ens
Nicknames: Than
Sisters: Abigail, Regan, Chloe, Hannah, Lauren
Brothers: Caleb, Isaac, Dylan, Jonah, Mason
✹ This lovely biblical classic used to be primarily a Jewish name, but today the colonial Ethan Allen associations take the fore. One of the most broadly fashionable names in America.

Eugene

1920s: #25

Popularity: #578
Style: Ladies and Gentlemen, Solid Citizens
Nicknames: Gene
Variants: Yevgeni
Sisters: Frances, Muriel, Doris, Arlene, Louise
Brothers: Harold, Norman, Gilbert, Francis, Roland
✹ A distinguished classic it may be, but today Eugene has charisma problems. For Russian families looking to translate Yevgeni, perhaps Evan or Egan can stand in.

Evan

2003: #45

Popularity: #45
Style: Celtic, The -ens, New Classics, Nickname-Proof
Variants: Ifan
Sisters: Megan, Jocelyn, Erin, Jenna, Brooke
Brothers: Colin, Ian, Kyle, Brendan, Gavin
✷ Sean (Irish), Ian (Scottish), and Evan (Welsh) are all Celtic forms of John that are on their way to becoming American classics. Evan is particularly upbeat and youthful.

Evander

Popularity: Rare   rarely used
Style: Celtic, Exotic Traditional, Why Not?
Nicknames: Van, Andy, Vander
Sisters: Beatrix, Artemas, Lilias, Ione, Finola
Brothers: Alistair, Magnus, Kilian, Colman, Leander
✷ This romantic name is out of classical legend, filtered through the Scottish Highlands. It's elegant and colorful, with an extra knockout punch thanks to heavyweight Evander Holyfield.

Everett

1900s: #82

Popularity: #575
Style: Antique Charm, Ladies and Gentlemen, Last Names First, Why Not?
Sisters: Genevieve, Cora, Adele, Estella, Antonia
Brothers: Foster, Emmett, Grady, Willis, August
✷ Many of the stately gentleman names seem a bit sluggish. This one snaps to attention. Everett is courtly but crisp and full of life, an unbeatable combination.

Ewan

Popularity: Rare   rarely used
Style: Celtic, The -ens, Nickname-Proof
Variants: Euan, Ewen, Eoghan
Sisters: Kinnia, Fallon, Aoife, Riona, Aisling
Brothers: Eamon, Tiernan, Wynn, Egan, Niall
✷ A Scottish favorite, much in vogue in its homeland in the spelling Euan. In the U.S., it is primarily known through actor Ewan McGregor. Pronounce it YOO-in.

Ezekiel

2003: #325

Popularity: #325
Style: Antique Charm, Biblical, Exotic Traditional
Nicknames: Zeke
Sisters: Keziah, Sarai, Jemima, Drusilla, Patience
Brothers: Elijah, Levi, Zachariah, Ezra, Malachi
✷ One of the unlikeliest beneficiaries of the Old Testament revival. The name Ezekiel was dead during the middle of the twentieth century, a biblical relic akin to Ebenezer. But the ultra-hip nickname Zeke has helped carry this quirky antique back into contention.

Ezra

2003: #402

Popularity: #402
Style: Antique Charm, Biblical, Exotic Traditional, Nickname-Proof
Sisters: Ivy, Astrid, Aviva, Phoebe, Sarai
Brothers: Hugo, Eli, Jonas, Axel, Levi
✷ After long years lumped with losers like Enoch and Hiram, Ezra's finally coming up in the world. Creative parents are warming to the name's unconventional appeal and pocket-size punch. It's confident with an eccentric edge.

Fabian

2002: #260

Popularity: #260
Style: German/Dutch, Nickname-Proof, Saints, Shakespearean
Sisters: Nadia, Adriana, Anastasia, Natalia, Paola
Brothers: Dimitri, Justus, Xavier, Antony, Damian
✷ For a certain generation, Fabian will forever mean a teen heartthrob. Yet the '60s icon didn't inspire many namesakes in his day. The name Fabian is only now entering the mainstream, following in the footsteps of hits like Damian and Sebastian.

Felix

1900s: #140

Popularity: #354
Style: Exotic Traditional, Nickname-Proof, Saints, Timeless
Sisters: Cleo, Genevieve, Zella, Nina, Avis
Brothers: Leo, Oliver, Julius, Rudolph, Benedict
✷ Tired of Alex? Here's an uncommon classic with that elusive -x ending and an idiosyncratic panache. The '20s cartoon character Felix the Cat and *The Odd Couple*'s Felix Unger scared parents off Felix for generations, but those connotations are fading. The name's brio should overcome its baggage.

Ferdinand

1900s: #279

Popularity: Rare
Style: Exotic Traditional, Ladies and Gentlemen, Shakespearean
Nicknames: Ferdie, Ferd, Nando
Variants: Fernando
Sisters: Philomena, Magdalene, Hester, Cornelia, Agatha
Brothers: Leopold, Archibald, Sylvester, Bertram, Basil
★ If you want a traditional name that you're guaranteed not to hear on every corner, consider Ferdinand. Be prepared, though, for howls from friends and relatives who consider the name over the top. Many people will also think of the beloved children's story of Ferdinand, the gentle bull.

Finian

Popularity: Rare
Style: Celtic, Saints
Nicknames: Fin
Sisters: Maura, Siobhan, Riona, Kennera, Finola
Brothers: Dermot, Lorcan, Brannock, Kilian, Malachy

rarely used

★ Finian is 100 percent Irish, as green as a shamrock, and remarkably contemporary. A few people may be reminded of the creaky leprechaun musical *Finian's Rainbow*, but most will consider this name fresh and interesting. It also trims down to the nifty nickname Fin, which gives it a leg up on the similar choice Kilian.

Finley

1910s: #899

Popularity: Rare
Style: Celtic, Last Names First, Why Not?
Nicknames: Fin
Variants: Finlay
Sisters: Nola, Maida, Lillias, Maeve, Elinor
Brothers: Leamon, Murphy, Foster, Kermit, Darby
★ This Scottish favorite is a rare choice—for now. But it's so catchy that all the parents of Baileys and Rileys will wish they'd thought of it first. For the fullest Scots flavor, go with the spelling Finlay.

Finn

2003: #659

Popularity: #659
Style: Brisk and Breezy, Celtic, Scandinavian, Why Not?
Sisters: Maeve, Maia, Shea, Britt, Tova
Brothers: Cale, Rowan, Keane, Ean, Leif
★ Finn is a welcome burst of Irish (or Scandinavian) energy. It gives you the light touch of a new, creative name, yet sidesteps the common traps: it doesn't sound forced or fussy or made up. The unfussy American icon Huck Finn helps the cause.

Fletcher

1900s: #429

Popularity: #992
Style: Last Names First, Why Not?
Nicknames: Fletch
Sisters: Willa, Reva, Ione, Clementine, May
Brothers: Truman, Archer, Newton, Murphy, Foster
★ If you could buy stock in a name, I'd be putting my money on Fletcher. The ingratiating cheer of this tradesman name (for a maker of arrows) would make it a pleasure to have around the house.

Floyd

1900s: #49

Popularity: Rare
Style: Porch Sitters
Sisters: Velma, Eunice, Florine, Irma, Bernice
Brothers: Homer, Lloyd, Lester, Odell, Otis
★ A pure dose of the least trendy sounds of the moment. It's a tough time to be a Floyd, and the tide isn't likely to turn any time soon. The name began as a valiant attempt to convey the true Welsh pronunciation of Lloyd. (Try the authentic "Ll" yourself by placing your tongue in position to say "L," then hissing air.)

Flynn

Popularity: Rare
Style: Brisk and Breezy, Last Names First, Why Not?
Sisters: Sloane, Hollis, Bryn, Kiara, Ellery
Brothers: Keane, Hayes, Fife, Archer, Wynn

rarely used

★ This energetic Irish surname is used as a given name in Australia, and would make a strong choice for an American boy. It sounds like a natural leader on the playground.

Forrest

1900s: #164

Popularity: #888
Style: Charms and Graces, Last Names First, Timeless, Why Not?
Variants: Forest, Forrester
Sisters: Violet, Cecelia, Estella, Fern, Miriam
Brothers: Emmett, Aubrey, Palmer, Marshall, Clifton

✱ Nature names for boys are scarce, and sometimes scary. (Thorn, anyone?) Forrest is a happy exception. It's old-fashioned, understated, and durable. As the image of Forrest Gump recedes, this name should reemerge.

Foster

1900s: #373

Popularity: Rare
Style: Ladies and Gentlemen, Last Names First, Nickname-Proof, Why Not?
Sisters: Alma, Lila, Clarice, Louisa, Harriet
Brothers: Palmer, Truman, Dewitt, Fraser, Harmon

✱ Look backward and forward at the same time with this promising selection. Its courteous, old-school ways pair nicely with Lily or Eleanor, while its surname style makes it a natural for the age of Parker and Tanner.

Francis

1910s: #34

Popularity: #509
Style: Ladies and Gentlemen, Solid Citizens
Nicknames: Frank, Fran
Variants: Francisco
Sisters: Eleanor, Edith, Clara, Helen, Dorothy
Brothers: Louis, Alfred, Eugene, Bernard, Theodore

✱ Francis is a classic name of saints and gentlemen. You expect a Francis to hold doors for ladies and become the leader of his local Elks Lodge. The women's name Frances has complicated the male version, though. It's now the one gentlemanly standard that sounds androgynous.

Frank

1900s: #8

Popularity: #228
Style: Nicknames, Solid Citizens
Nicknames: Frankie
Sisters: Ruth, Helen, Marie, Elsie, Margaret
Brothers: Fred, Albert, Ralph, Lewis, Henry

✱ A name that neatly defines itself. Open, straightforward, and a little bit blunt.

Franklin

1930s: #75

Popularity: #470
Style: Solid Citizens
Nicknames: Frank
Sisters: Arlene, Rosemary, Marilyn, Joyce, Eileen
Brothers: Donald, Lawrence, Gordon, Charles, Alvin

✱ Franklin is a clean-cut, hardworking name with a fundamentally American character. Think of Benjamin Franklin and Franklin Delano Roosevelt, the latter of whom sparked a wave of young Franklins in the 1930s.

Fred

1900s: #19

Popularity: Rare
Style: Nicknames, Solid Citizens
Nicknames: Freddy
Sisters: Elsie, Irene, Annie, Susie, Alice
Brothers: Earl, Frank, Charlie, Bert, Harry

✱ Frederick has the antique sound, but it's Fred that's the real old-fashioned name. A hundred years ago, baby Freds outnumbered Fredericks three to one. Today those numbers are reversed, and Fred sounds rather plain by itself.

Frederick

1910s: #56

Popularity: #430
Style: Ladies and Gentlemen, Shakespearean, Timeless
Nicknames: Fred, Fritz, Rick
Variants: Frederic, Federico, Friedrich, Frederik, Fredrick
Sisters: Martha, Sylvia, Charlotte, Marian, Rosa
Brothers: Theodore, Laurence, Arthur, Francis, Walter

✱ This German classic has been in a long, steady decline, but the old boy still has some life in him. Like a three-piece suit and wing-tip shoes, Frederick carries a timeless air of authority that cuts through fashion. If the nickname Fred seems too plain, you could give Fritz a try.

Fritz

1900s: #370

Popularity: Rare
Style: German/Dutch, Guys and Dolls
Sisters: Meta, Helga, Dovie, Golda, Belle
Brothers: Ernst, Franz, Otto, Dock, Mose

✱ Fritz has its work cut out for it. There's the phrase "on the fritz," and there's the pornographic '60s cartoon *Fritz the Cat*. More important, there's a fashion trend away from German names. But this name is so playful and good-humored that it should find a few takers—especially as a snappy nickname for Frederick.

Gabriel
Popularity: #30
Style: Antique Charm, Biblical
Nicknames: Gabe
Sisters: Abigail, Hannah, Olivia, Juliana, Alexis
Brothers: Noah, Elijiah, Caleb, Dominic, Julian

2003: #30
1900　Today

✱ This lyrical name is one of the most buoyant biblical choices for boys. It is currently riding a wave of popularity that takes some of the edge off its impact. That's good news if you're worried that the name's too exotic, bad if you're in search of the unusual.

Gage
Popularity: #136
Style: Brisk and Breezy
Sisters: Maya, Jade, Genesis, Macy, Skye
Brothers: Grant, Zane, Cade, Landon, Tate

2003: #136
1900　Today

✱ Like Stone or Chance, this is a name that doesn't quite sound real. It belongs to an impossibly virile hero trapped in the pages of a romance novel. But this style of name is coming on strong, and Gage is a particularly likable example. Soon it may be hard to picture the name on anyone but a rambunctious toddler.

Galen
Popularity: Rare
Style: The -ens, Exotic Traditional
Sisters: Aurea, Cleo, Carmen, Ione, Althea
Brothers: Royce, Lucian, Rex, Gerard, Albin

1940s: #475
1900　Today

✱ Galen sounds modern, a happy meeting of Jalen and Gavin. It's also classical, the name of an ancient Greek physician whose writings have taught us much of what we know of ancient medicine. A natural choice for a doctor's child.

Gannon
Popularity: #694
Style: The -ens, Last Names First
Sisters: Marley, Madisyn, Hadley, Parker, Aubrie
Brothers: Landen, Dawson, Ryker, Garrick, Brady

2003: #694
1900　Today

✱ The name Gannon started popping up in large numbers when quarterback Rich Gannon was leading the Oakland Raiders to glory (or close enough). It has a macho sound, like the tough big brother of surnames like Brennan and Landon. For an even tougher twist, try Cannon.

Gareth
Popularity: Rare
Style: Celtic, English, Why Not?
Nicknames: Gary
Sisters: Rhian, Gemma, Gwyneth, Tamsin, Emlyn
Brothers: Griffith, Rhys, Graeme, Ellis, Callum

rarely used
1900　Today

✱ Gareth is a Welsh and English classic that Americans have missed out on. It has a familiar, comfortable sound—Gary meets Kenneth—but a refined attitude that makes it a stylish choice.

Garrett
Popularity: #108
Style: Celtic, English
Nicknames: Garry
Variants: Garret, Garett
Sisters: Gillian, Ciara, Brooke, Miranda, Paige
Brothers: Trevor, Alec, Colin, Graham, Spencer

2001: #81
1900　Today

✱ Equal parts rugged and sophisticated, Garrett is a solid hit. Also a nice choice to honor a grandpa named Gary.

Garth
Popularity: Rare
Style: Country & Western, Exotic Traditional, Namesakes
Sisters: Aida, Glynis, Winona, Avis, Shasta
Brothers: Theron, Judd, Gaylon, Regis, Leif

1960s: #555

1900　Today

✱ This used to be a quirky, uncommon name with a style that was hard to pin down. You could convince yourself it was exotic, or upper-crusty, or plodding. But these days it's easy to pin down: pure country, thanks to the big shadow of music star Garth Brooks.

Gary
Popularity: #326
Style: Mid-Century
Sisters: Sharon, Diane, Sandra, Linda, Judy
Brothers: Dennis, Barry, Bruce, Alan, Wayne

1950s: #12
1900　Today

✱ Most names that end in -y end up either boyish or androgynous. Gary is an exception, easygoing but reassuringly grown up. Think Corey with a cardigan and some pipe tobacco. Gary has surname roots, and was jump-started as a first name by actor Gary Cooper.

Gavin 2003: #51
Popularity: #51
Style: Celtic, The -ens,
Nickname-Proof
Variants: Gawain
Sisters: Chloe, Morgan, Gabriella, Zoe, Ava
Brothers: Aidan, Owen, Riley, Garrett, Liam
★ Gavin has a sophisticated flair that's gallant rather than showy. And for tradition, you can't beat a Knight of the Round Table. (If the name doesn't sound Arthurian to you, the alternate version Gawain might ring a bell.)

Gene 1930s: #67
Popularity: Rare
Style: Nicknames, Solid
Citizens
Sisters: Roberta, Betty, Pat, Arlene, Joann
Brothers: Bill, Gerald, Donald, Bob, Franklin
★ Gene was once an American mainstay, borne by icons like singing cowboy Gene Autry and dancing star Gene Kelly. It disappeared hand in hand with the full name Eugene, and few parents today give the name a second thought. It's suffering not rejection so much as neglect.

Geoffrey 1970s: #211
Popularity: #763
Style: New Classics
Nicknames: Geoff
Variants: Jeffrey, Joffrey
Sisters: Candace, Holly, Meredith, Adrienne, Katrina
Brothers: Terrance, Bradley, Cedric, Brent, Timothy
★ The traditional form of Jeffrey, Geoffrey was one of the stylish hits of the Middle Ages. It's perfectly familiar today, but its arcane spelling still romantically echoes the days of Geoffrey Chaucer.

George 1900s: #4
Popularity: #137
Style: Ladies and Gentlemen,
Timeless
Variants: Jorge
Sisters: Alice, Margaret, Evelyn, Ruth, Helen
Brothers: Edward, Henry, Charles, Walter, Frederick
★ Of all the classic kingly names, none has fallen farther than George. In fact, it has fallen far enough to lend it some cachet among upscale, contrarian parents. Rather than going out on a limb with an exotic name, why not surprise people with a classic?

Gerald 1930s: #21
Popularity: #471
Style: Mid-Century, Solid
Citizens
Nicknames: Gerry, Jerry
Variants: Jerald, Jerold, Jerrold, Gerold, Geraldo
Sisters: Gloria, Joyce, Elaine, Marilyn, Nancy
Brothers: Donald, Jerome, Marvin, Allen, Richard
★ A stately old name with a happy-go-lucky nickname, Gerald struck the perfect balance for generations of men. It's a quieter choice today, manly but mellow.

Gerard 1950s: #202
Popularity: Rare
Style: English, French, Saints,
Solid Citizens
Nicknames: Gerry
Sisters: Therese, Anita, Yvonne, Myra, Elaine
Brothers: Stuart, Laurence, Jerome, Frederic, Randolph
★ Unlike all-American Gerald, Gerard still sounds like the medieval classic it is. This is by far the more romantic choice of the two.

Gianni 2003: #653
Popularity: #653
Style: Italian
Sisters: Eliana, Paola, Chiara, Valentina, Lia
Brothers: Matteo, Luca, Alessandro, Dario, Dante
★ This Italian version of Johnny can be pronounced the same but has a much flashier style. Seldom used in English before the emergence of fashion designer Gianni Versace.

Gideon 2003: #688
Popularity: #688
Style: Biblical, Exotic
Traditional, Why Not?
Sisters: Thalia, Adina, Tamar, Paloma, Isadora
Brothers: Judah, Raphael, Simeon, Asher, Josiah
★ Ladies and gentlemen, may I present a handsome, familiar biblical name that is still unusual! Right now Gideon calls to mind hotel-room Bibles, but soon it may sound like the most stylish boy in town. The lack of a solid nickname is the only thing holding it back.

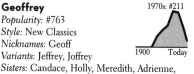
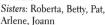
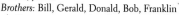

Gilbert

1930s: #105
1900 — Today

Popularity: #592
Style: Ladies and Gentlemen, Saints, Solid Citizens
Nicknames: Gib, Gil
Variants: Gilberto
Sisters: Frances, Vivian, Rosalie, Mavis, Edith
Brothers: Clifford, Roland, Lewis, Alvin, Clifton
✱ There's nothing trendy about Gilbert, and its close resemblance to cartoon antihero Dilbert threatens to send it over the edge to geekdom. This old name still has some life to it, though. It offers the same kind of charmingly stuffy dignity as August and Julius in a more modest form.

Giles

1900s: #758
1900 — Today

Popularity: Rare
Style: English, Saints
Nicknames: Gil
Variants: Gilles, Gil
Sisters: Beryl, Viola, Enid, Eugenia, Rowena
Brothers: Basil, Lucius, Cecil, Chauncey, Ewell
✱ Giles (pronounced "Jiles") is an exceptionally refined name. It's smoothed out to the point where it may be too slick for comfort. If you love the sound, Miles is a handsome, reliable alternative.

Giovanni

2003: #178
1900 — Today

Popularity: #178
Style: Italian
Nicknames: Gianni, Gio
Variants: Jovanni, Jovany
Sisters: Paola, Gianna, Alessandra, Bianca, Francesca
Brothers: Sergio, Leonardo, Dante, Giancarlo, Lorenzo
✱ Traditionally, Giovanni has been an exclusively Italian name. In the past generation it has caught on with Spanish speakers, and it's now a solid cross-cultural hit. Giovanni's spirit, though, is still solidly Italiano.

Glenn

1950s: #68
1900 — Today

Popularity: #664
Style: Celtic, Mid-Century, Solid Citizens
Variants: Glen
Sisters: Janet, Ellen, Gail, Bonnie, Anita
Brothers: Allen, Dale, Russell, Paul, Lawrence
✱ Glenn may be Scottish in origin, but it's celebrating a century as the all-American man. Trendy in the days of bandleader Glenn Miller and actor Glenn Ford, it has aged nicely into a reliable friend.

Glyn

rarely used
1900 — Today

Popularity: Rare
Style: Brisk and Breezy, Celtic
Variants: Glynn
Sisters: Gwen, Glenda, Bryn, Aurea, Lise
Brothers: Vaughn, Keir, Wynn, Baird, Rand
✱ This swift Welsh name is a close relative of Glenn, but takes you a step off the beaten track.

Gordon

1930s: #79
1900 — Today

Popularity: #758
Style: Solid Citizens
Nicknames: Gordie
Sisters: Jeanette, Eileen, Rita, Dorothy, Frances
Brothers: Warren, Arnold, Gilbert, Alvin, Lewis
✱ Gordon feels a little doughy, as if those full, round sounds have gone straight to its waistline. The name has actually held on better than most of its compatriots from the '20s. It sounds manlier than Norman or Howard, just a little outmoded. Gordons still abound in Canada, where the name has remained a steady classic.

Grady

1910s: #212
1900 — Today

Popularity: #597
Style: Last Names First, Why Not?
Sisters: Nell, Reva, Lillie, Della, Annie
Brothers: Ellis, Alden, Dewey, Edison, Hardy
✱ This name, which sounds like one of the trendy new surname hits, was actually most popular a hundred years ago. Grady can hold his own with young preppies like Brody and Colby, but he's just as happy hanging out on the back porch, swapping fish tales with the boys.

Graham

2003: #397
1900 — Today

Popularity: #397
Style: Celtic, English, Timeless
Variants: Graeme
Sisters: Juliet, Fiona, Maeve, Camille, Gillian
Brothers: Duncan, Miles, Reid, Garrett, Alec
✱ This English and Scottish standard has never fully taken hold in the U.S. Why is a mystery. It's handsome as all get-out, sexy but with impeccable manners. Even the graham cracker association really shouldn't hurt: slim, sweet, and snappy. Graham is the fellow all the girls want to meet and the guys have to respect.

Grant

2002: #127

Popularity: #140
Style: Brisk and Breezy, Last Names First, Timeless
Sisters: Paige, Hope, Elena, Victoria, Claire
Brothers: Reid, Miles, Bond, Spencer, Preston

✱ Ooh . . . that's one fine-looking man! Maybe it's because of Cary Grant, or because it sounds so Grand. Most folks will agree that Grant is one of the most tall, dark, and handsome names around.

Grayson

2003: #298

Popularity: #298
Style: The -ens, Last Names First
Nicknames: Gray
Variants: Greyson
Sisters: Madison, Cassidy, Ashlyn, Gillian, Haleigh
Brothers: Easton, Keaton, Brennan, Dawson, Brody

✱ This hot newcomer has a popular rhythm and an attractive preppy nickname. It does seem to be trying awfully hard to sound elegant, which is a warning sign. That's the path that led names like Milton and Sidney toward oblivion.

Gregory

1960s: #23

Popularity: #186
Style: New Classics
Nicknames: Greg
Variants: Gregor, Grigori
Sisters: Cynthia, Valerie, Deborah, Teresa, Michele
Brothers: Timothy, Jeffrey, Douglas, Philip, Stephen

✱ Popes, saints, and Gregory Peck! Can a name get any more distinguished? Except you know he'll go by Greg, which may conjure up Greg Brady's bell-bottoms instead. Nonetheless, a can't-miss classic that's not too common.

Griffin

2003: #227

Popularity: #227
Style: Celtic, The -ens
Nicknames: Griff
Variants: Griffith
Sisters: Gillian, Kyra, Macy, Bethan, Jocelyn
Brothers: Duncan, Gavin, Jonah, Carson, Conor

✱ The griffin (or gryphon) is a majestic creature of legend, part eagle and part lion. As a name, Griffin is a form of the Welsh Griffith. It's spirited, traditional, and just plain cute.

Gunnar

2002: #559

Popularity: #588
Style: German/Dutch, Scandinavian
Variants: Gunner
Sisters: Lisbeth, Annika, Meta, Avery, Sofia
Brothers: Stefan, Axel, Walker, Markus, Anton

✱ Americans used to shy away from this Northern European classic because of its warlike sound. These days, that's exactly what draws them to it. (The proof? The spelling Gunner is equally popular.) It's handsome and rugged and makes a fine comrade for Hunter and Rider.

Gus

1900s: #223

Popularity: Rare
Style: Guys and Dolls, Nicknames
Sisters: Millie, Nell, Madge, Reba, Lottie
Brothers: Abe, Ned, Charley, Ike, Archie

✱ Gus has a "shabby chic" appeal that's catching the attention of the Max and Gracie crowd. Parents swoon over the name, but don't actually pull the trigger. It's just not serious enough for a birth certificate. So what can you use for a formal version? How about August, Augustus, Gustave, and Angus?

Guy

1900s: #117

Popularity: #935
Style: Saints, Solid Citizens
Variants: Guido
Sisters: Rena, Marie, Flora, Susie, Rosa
Brothers: Hugh, Clark, Clifton, Ward, Carl

✱ The obvious problem here is lowercase "guy," the everyday term for a man. "Hey, Guy," you say, and nobody thinks you're using his name. If you can cope with that, the name is utterly charming, a handsome shot of retro chic.

Hal

1950s: #343

Popularity: Rare
Style: Nicknames, Solid Citizens, Why Not?
Sisters: Kathryn, Polly, Nita, June, Nan
Brothers: Rex, Stewart, Glen, Ted, Clark

✱ Simple but steeped in tradition, Hal should fit in handsomely with the new crop of Charlies and Leos. It can be a strong nickname (or namesake) for Harry, Henry, or Harold.

Hamilton

1910s: #659

Popularity: Rare
Style: Last Names First
Nicknames: Ham
Sisters: Eleanor, Harriet, Cecilia, Belle, Louisa
Brothers: Watson, Crawford, Edison, Nicholson, Jennings

✷ Presidential surnames from Jefferson to Carter are popular choices right now. Hamilton is not technically a presidential surname, but the next best thing (a Founding Father). This could be a hit if you manage to work around the nickname Ham.

Hamish

Popularity: Rare
Style: Celtic

rarely used

Sisters: Iona, Mhairi, Lilias, Muriel, Maisie
Brothers: Magnus, Alistair, Tavish, Finlay, Gregor

✷ A Scottish form of Seamus (which is a Gaelic form of James), Hamish is thoroughly charming but inevitably mispronounced. Use a long A sound: HAY-mish. The name is seldom heard outside of Australia, where Scottish name traditions run deep.

Hardy

1900s: #593

Popularity: Rare
Style: Country & Western, Last Names First
Sisters: Della, Rhea, Bettie, Nell, Lucille
Brothers: Palmer, Grady, Ellis, Harmon, Dewey

✷ Despite its boyish sound, Hardy has a battle-ready toughness. It's a name that people feel equally comfortable cuddling up to and saluting.

Harlan

1930s: #281

Popularity: Rare
Style: Last Names First, Nickname-Proof
Variants: Harland
Sisters: Lenore, Rosetta, Reva, Melba, Faye
Brothers: Burton, Hollis, Leland, Haywood, Lowell

✷ Harlan is a bygone name that needn't be forgotten. Its southern lilt and easy confidence are a slower-paced answer to the slew of zippy new cowboy names.

Harold

1920s: #14

Popularity: #595
Style: Ladies and Gentlemen
Nicknames: Harry, Hal
Variants: Harald
Sisters: Frances, Irene, Evelyn, Helen, Edith
Brothers: Ralph, Leonard, Albert, Bernard, Walter

✷ This noble old Anglo-Saxon name has fallen sadly from grace. It could be cute for a little boy and solid for a grown man, but runs into nerd trouble in adolescence. The renewed luster of the nickname Harry could help smooth those bumps.

Harris

1910s: #380

Popularity: Rare
Style: Last Names First, Solid Citizens, Why Not?
Nicknames: Harry
Sisters: Marian, Helene, Rhoda, Althea, Nell
Brothers: Truman, Foster, Ellis, Murphy, Edison

✷ Harris tweed is the perfect emblem for this name's button-down style. Harris is a great choice to dress up Harry, or mellow down Harrison.

Harrison

2002: #199

Popularity: #213
Style: Last Names First, Timeless
Nicknames: Harry
Sisters: Caroline, Hanna, Kiley, Juliana, Madeline
Brothers: Preston, Davis, Clayton, Dennison, Spencer

✷ Harrison is a timeless gentleman's name that is on the upswing. It's on the dignified end of the surname spectrum, a contrast with the jauntier tradesman names. If all that dignity seems a bit frosty, have no fear: The nickname Harry will warm you right up.

Harry

1900s: #13

Popularity: #517
Style: Guys and Dolls
Nicknames: Hal
Sisters: Annie, Lucy, Stella, Marie, Hazel
Brothers: Ben, Walter, Leo, Charley, Roy

✷ Young wizard Harry Potter has pulled off another dazzling trick: He's made the most unassuming name in English remarkable. Harry is aggressively ordinary, which is a big source of its charm. It's like your favorite, coziest old sweater that you curl up with at the end of the day. If that's not quite enough, it can also be a nickname for Henry, Harold, Harris, or Harrison, or a young Prince of Wales.

Hart

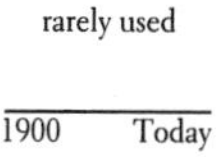
rarely used
1900
Today

Popularity: Rare
Style: Brisk and Breezy, Charms and Graces
Sisters: Bay, Calla, Dove, Honor, Lark
Brothers: Leif, Stone, Beck, Rand, Frost
✶ A hart is a male deer. The similar terms stag and buck suggest masculinity run wild, but a Hart sounds calm and self-possessed—and has the biggest antlers in the herd.

Harvey

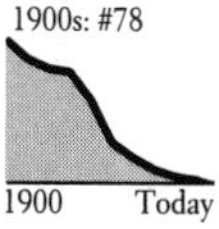
1900s: #78
1900
Today

Popularity: Rare
Style: Guys and Dolls
Nicknames: Harve
Sisters: Rosie, Harriet, Della, Pearl, Freda
Brothers: Archie, Haskell, Bernie, Sidney, Mack
✶ Harvey sounds like a burly, honest, hard-working guy circa 1940. That's a far cry from its origins as an elegant surname for boys, much like androgynous favorites Ashley and Sidney. Don't expect Harvey to follow them to the girls' side any time soon.

Haskell

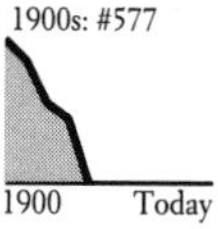
1900s: #577
1900
Today

Popularity: Rare
Style: Guys and Dolls, Jewish, Last Names First, Nickname-Proof
Variants: Haskel
Sisters: Leora, Hazel, Sadie, Freda, Viola
Brothers: Elkan, Merritt, Hillel, Freeman, Hirsch
✶ Haskell is a Yiddish version of Ezekiel, as well as an English surname. That's an unusual mix with a likable result. Haskell sounds like a fun-loving guy.

Hayden

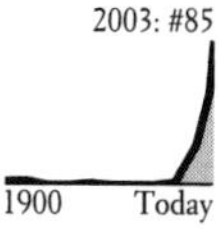
2003: #85
1900
Today

Popularity: #85
Style: Bell Tones, The -ens, Last Names First
Variants: Haden
Sisters: Hailey, Riley, Regan, Skylar, Madison
Brothers: Carson, Harlan, Carter, Parker, Peyton
✶ To your parents, this name sounds like a tough old football coach. They'll be shocked to hear that Hayden is now used for girls, too. Today's parents hear this surname as a pal to Brayden and Cayden, not a grizzled lord of the gridiron.

Heath

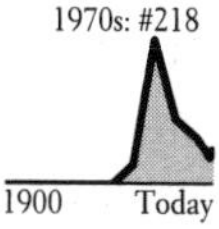
1970s: #218
1900
Today

Popularity: #724
Style: Brisk and Breezy, Charms and Graces, '70s–'80s
Sisters: April, Leigh, Autumn, Holly, Sage
Brothers: Lance, Shannon, Rhett, Clint, Birch
✶ Heath was a modest hit in the '70s and '80s, never common enough to be too trendy. Now a few of those early Heaths, like actor Heath Ledger, are finding adult fame, and their name sounds completely contemporary. It's a nice balance between preppy and tree-hugging.

Hector

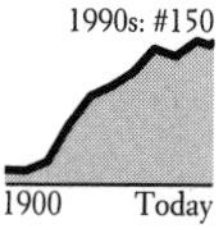
1990s: #150
1900
Today

Popularity: #176
Style: Latino/Latina, Mythological, Nickname-Proof
Sisters: Hester, Inez, Violet, Manuela, Serena
Brothers: Oscar, Ruben, Victor, Hugo, Edgar
✶ Like many top names from classical literature, Hector has taken a nosedive as an English first name. Among Spanish speakers, though, the name is still going strong as a classic, stylish name for boys. Other parents would do well to follow their lead and rediscover Hector's quirky macho charm.

Henry

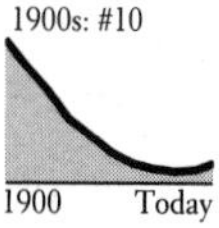
1900s: #10
1900
Today

Popularity: #116
Style: Ladies and Gentlemen, Timeless
Nicknames: Harry, Hank, Hal
Variants: Henri, Henrik, Enrico, Enrique
Sisters: Alice, Margaret, Catherine, Eleanor, Clara
Brothers: Louis, George, Edward, Arthur, Frederick
✶ A name of warmth and respectability. Good old Henry felt a little sluggish in the second half of the twentieth century, when lighter boys' names dominated. But parents are starting to come back to the fold, and Henry is now positively trendy in upscale neighborhoods. Check out the "similar boys" list for some other good bets that have not yet made the full comeback.

Herbert

1900s: #32

Popularity: Rare
Style: Ladies and Gentlemen
Nicknames: Herb, Bert
Sisters: Pauline, Frances, Harriet, Alma, Thelma
Brothers: Alfred, Francis, Bernard, Howard, Vernon

★ Starting in the 1800s, Herbert had a century-long run of popularity. It's unlikely to happen again soon. Like many names descended from Old German, it sounded regal and valiant, circa 1850, but seems simply old-fashioned today.

Herman

1900s: #44

Popularity: Rare
Style: German/Dutch, Ladies and Gentlemen
Nicknames: Herm, Manny
Variants: Hermann, Armand, Armando, Armin
Sisters: Bertha, Harriet, Louise, Vera, Esther
Brothers: Luther, Horace, Alfred, Claude, Walter

★ One of the hearty German favorites of the 1900s, Herman is a big ole lunk of a name, too heavy to be fashionable today. What it does offer is dignity, a precious commodity that keeps it safe from the depths of the dustheap. Also consider the related name Armin, a touch lighter but still serious.

Hirsch

rarely used

Popularity: Rare
Style: Jewish
Variants: Hirsh, Hersch, Herschel, Heshel

Sisters: Yaffa, Leora, Tova, Resha, Dalia
Brothers: Avi, Haskell, Dov, Asher, Noam

★ Hirsch is best known as a surname in the U.S., but it's a traditional first name (the Yiddish word for "deer"). The diminutive Herschel is more familiar and a smidgen nerdier; Zvi is a modern Hebrew counterpart.

Holden

2002: #415

Popularity: #421
Style: The -ens, Last Names First, Namesakes, Nickname-Proof

Sisters: Macy, Hallie, Eden, Daniela, Harper
Brothers: Walker, Dalton, Carter, Lukas, Weston

★ Holden Caulfield, the brooding young protagonist of *The Catcher in the Rye*, makes this name a bit edgier than the many other surname choices. The book has been popular for over fifty years, but current trends are making the name Holden a hit for the first time.

Homer

1900s: #87

Popularity: Rare
Style: Namesakes, Porch Sitters
Sisters: Velma, Opal, Fannie, Hilda, Leona
Brothers: Amos, Horace, Grover, Roscoe, Earl

★ D'oh! In a world without Homer Simpson, this name would be a player. It has the simplicity, roots, literary clout, and surprise factor that avant-garde parents love. But who would want to live in a world without Homer Simpson, anyway?

Horace

1900s: #125

Popularity: Rare
Style: Ladies and Gentlemen, Nickname-Proof
Variants: Horatio
Sisters: Hester, Elvira, Flora, Estelle, Harriet
Brothers: Virgil, Luther, Hubert, Roscoe, Homer

★ The classical literary icons Horace, Virgil, and Homer share a sad fate in modern namehood. They're hopelessly outmoded, and typically portrayed as hicks. Of the three, though, Horace may be the most intriguing possibility. It's closer to the world of cigar-smoking bankers and farther from the Beverly Hillbillies. Also consider the more adventurous Horatio.

Horatio

rarely used

Popularity: Rare
Style: Exotic Traditional, Shakespearean
Nicknames: Ray
Variants: Horace
Sisters: Portia, Hermione, Isadora, Lilias, Cordelia
Brothers: Philo, Lazarus, Japheth, Atticus, Barnabas

★ Thanks to real-life naval hero Admiral Horatio Nelson and fictional counterpart Horatio Hornblower, this name sounds ready to take to the high seas. It's madly outdated, but so vigorous it seems not to have noticed. An eccentric stud name.

Howard

1910s: #26

Popularity: #721
Style: Solid Citizens
Nicknames: Howie

Sisters: Frances, Irene, Doris, Martha, Muriel
Brothers: Earl, Harold, Milton, Leonard, Vernon

★ Howard was a standard for generations, but it's gradually sinking out of sight. The name's slow, gentle sound is out of fashion, and the lack of a zippy nickname seals its fate.

Hudson

Popularity: #396
Style: Last Names First, Place Names
Nicknames: Hud

1900 Today

Sisters: Aubrey, Marley, Piper, Hayley, Willow
Brothers: Landen, Hayden, Reece, Sawyer, Cooper

✶ Hudson has an old-fashioned heft that keeps it from disappearing in the current flood of perky surnames. It conjures up the long curves of old Hudson automobiles and the steady flow of the Hudson River. Gruff and reliable.

Hugh

1900s: #101

Popularity: #865
Style: English, Ladies and Gentlemen, Saints, Solid Citizens

1900 Today

Sisters: Antonia, Rosa, Vivian, Clara, Marian
Brothers: Louis, Guy, Clifford, Ellis, Everett

✶ Hugh is a simple classic with a big surprise factor. It sounds like a standard, but has never ranked among the top-100 boys' names. That makes for a nice opportunity to choose a name that's both familiar and distinctive.

Hugo

2003: #366

Popularity: #366
Style: French, Ladies and Gentlemen, Latino/Latina
Nicknames: Huey

1900 Today

Sisters: Ivy, Eliza, Astrid, Phoebe, Lucia
Brothers: Ezra, Cyrus, Milo, Edgar, Oscar

✶ Hugo is an unexpected revival. Once relegated to the dustheap with Amos and Buford, it has reemerged as a funky classic. (In its native France, the long-neglected name is skyrocketing.) It's especially adorable for a stocky little toddler.

Hunter

2001: #36

Popularity: #41
Style: Androgynous, Last Names First
Nicknames: Hunter

1900 Today

Sisters: Madison, Haley, Peyton, Abigail, Macy
Brothers: Logan, Parker, Carter, Dylan, Mason

✶ The primal power of the hunt mixed with the fearless gonzo style of writer Hunter S. Thompson make this a name with machismo to burn. Yet the understated sound of the name keeps it in check. That's turning out to be a killer combination for today's parents.

Ian

Popularity: #66
Style: Celtic, Little Darlings, New Classics, Nickname-Proof
Variants: Iain, Ean

1900 Today

Sisters: Jenna, Chloe, Mia, Megan, Cara
Brothers: Colin, Evan, Liam, Trevor, Alec

✶ Light and swift, Ian makes a great match for long Scottish surnames. While no longer the exotic choice it was a generation ago, it remains energetic and decidedly Celtic.

Ike

1910s: #531

Popularity: Rare
Style: Guys and Dolls, Nicknames
Sisters: Evie, Goldie, Nell, Mazie, Mae

1900 Today

Brothers: Abe, Mose, Lonzo, Dock, Gus

✶ Ike is traditionally a nickname for Isaac, and occasionally for other strong I names like Ivan or Isaiah. (Or, in the case of I-Like-Ike Eisenhower, for Dwight.) It's tough and playful, like Spike without the silliness. If you want to make absolutely certain your son goes by Ike, it's not out of bounds to choose it as a full name.

Irving

1900s: #105

Popularity: #759
Style: Guys and Dolls, Porch Sitters
Nicknames: Irv
Variants: Irvine

1900 Today

Sisters: Gladys, Frieda, Ethel, Goldie, Ida
Brothers: Sidney, Milton, Harvey, Morris, Edwin

✶ Irving is straight out of the immigrant 1890s. New Americans chose this Scottish surname because it sounded dashing and highbrow. Case in point: Irving Berlin, born in Russia as Israel Baline. Ironically, these fancy "aspirational names" now sound antiquated while the old-fashioned ethnic names they replaced (Mose, Molly, Sadie) are back in bloom.

Isaac

2003: #48

Popularity: #48
Style: Biblical, Timeless
Nicknames: Ike, Zak
Variants: Isaak

1900 Today

Sisters: Leah, Sophia, Abigail, Hope, Claire
Brothers: Caleb, Samuel, Noah, Nathaniel, Seth

✶ Like Noah, Isaac used to sound forbiddingly ancient. Today, parents are noticing the name's long-neglected charms. It is simple, familiar, and handsome. It has strapping nicknames. And with broader use, Isaac's archaic image has softened to become glowingly distinguished.

Isaiah   2002: #45

Popularity: #50
Style: African-American,
Antique Charm, Biblical
Nicknames: Izzy, Ike
Sisters: Sophia, Isabella, Jasmine, Ariana,
Michaela
Brothers: Elijah, Gabriel, Levi, Tobias, Jeremiah
★ The new popularity of Old Testament names
like Ethan and Noah has opened the doors to
more exotic examples. They're great ways to
indulge your taste for elaborate names without fear
that your son will sound flowery or silly. Like the
similar Elijah, Isaiah first caught on with African-
Americans and is now across-the-board popular.

Ivan   2003: #125

Popularity: #125
Style: Saints, Slavic, Timeless
Nicknames: Vanya
Sisters: Marina, Hana, Ava,
Claire, Gabriela
Brothers: Julian, Roman, Dominick, Isaac, Lukas
★ Russian men's names tend to be intriguing
but inaccessible. Ivan's a notable exception—
simple, strong, and pleasantly mysterious. The
English pronunciation EYE-vin and the Russian/
Spanish ee-VAHN are equally strong.

Ivor

Popularity: Rare   rarely used
Style: Celtic, English, Exotic
Traditional
Variants: Ifor
Sisters: Ione, Alys, Sidony, Averil, Glynis
Brothers: Piers, Gareth, Glyn, Torquil, Tavis
★ Craving the unusual? Drawn to the traditional?
Take a look at Ivor. This simple, distinctive name
has Norse roots and became popular in Scotland
and Wales. It was once modestly common in
England, but in the U.S., it's delightfully fresh.

Jabez

Popularity: Rare   rarely used
Style: Biblical, Exotic
Traditional
Sisters: Salome, Atara, Keziah,
Avital, Jael
Brothers: Lazar, Boaz, Barak, Japheth, Azriel
★ Now that Ezra and Zachariah have found
their way into our preschools, the path is clear
for serious biblical rarities. Jabez certainly fits
the bill. It's barely familiar but short and sweet
with a snazzy Z ending. The biblical Jabez was
an honorable man who had his prayers
answered, and "the prayer of Jabez" has recently
attracted a devoted following.

Jace   2003: #250

Popularity: #250
Style: Brisk and Breezy
Variants: Jayce, Jase
Sisters: Sage, Bay, Eden, Lexi,
Kira
Brothers: Kade, Drake, Zane, Ty, Jair
★ This is the new, leaner, meaner version of
Jason. Jace is slick and tough, ready to roll as a
race-car driver or teen idol.

Jack   1920s: #17

Popularity: #46
Style: Guys and Dolls,
Nicknames, Timeless
Variants: John, Jake
Sisters: Molly, Julia, Caroline, Katie, Tess
Brothers: Joe, Henry, Max, Cole, Samuel
★ This traditional nickname for John turns the
classic upside down. John is the strong silent
type, whereas Jack is a tough but fun-loving
bloke. It's an irresistible image to parents, who
are flocking to Jack as a given name while John
slips out of fashion. Leonardo DiCaprio's heart-
throb Jack in the film *Titanic* helped the cause.
The number-one name in England and Ireland.

Jackson   2003: #52

Popularity: #52
Style: The -ens, Last Names
First
Nicknames: Jack, Jax
Variants: Jaxon
Sisters: Juliana, Faith, Hailey, Chloe, Mckenna
Brothers: Carter, Mason, Bennett, Connor,
Preston
★ Jackson has history, and a spot-on stylish sound.
As a firmly masculine surname, it makes a good
sibling match for androgynous girls' names like
Bailey and Taylor. Painter Jackson Pollock lends
the name an extra creative-power panache.

Jacob   2001: #1

Popularity: #1
Style: Biblical, Timeless
Nicknames: Jake, Jay, Jaco, Cub
Variants: Jakob, Yakov

Sisters: Emily, Hannah, Victoria, Abigail, Sarah
Brothers: Isaac, Zachary, Caleb, Nathan,
Alexander
★ This is the name that unseated Michael from
its longtime perch as America's favorite boy's
name. Jacob has it all: Old Testament origins,
turn-of-the-century style, the popular j, ay, and k
sounds, and strong nicknames. The playgrounds
are now crammed with Jakes, but the name
should be enough of a classic to weather the
popularity storm.

Jaden

2003: #83

Popularity: #83
Style: Androgynous, Bell Tones, The -ens
Nicknames: Jay, Jade
Variants: Jayden, Jadon, Jaiden
Sisters: Kylie, Camryn, Aylin, Jacey, Riley
Brothers: Camden, Ashton, Jalen, Kaleb, Landen

✳ There is a minor Jadon in the Old Testament, but this is no biblical revival. Cross Jacob with Aidan, and voilà: the sound of the times. The name's popularity shot up starting in 1998, when celebrity parents Will Smith and Jada Pinkett chose this male twist on Mom's name.

Jagger

2002: #658

Popularity: #777
Style: Last Names First, Namesakes
Nicknames: Jag
Sisters: Tatum, Presley, Sky, Cadence, Marley
Brothers: Gunnar, Cash, Ryker, Maddox, Jett

✳ Jagger was an old Yorkshire term for a peddler, but you're excused if the only occupation that comes to mind is rock star. Mick Jagger makes this name the cockiest of all the tradesmen names.

Jake

2003: #98

Popularity: #98
Style: Guys and Dolls, Nicknames
Sisters: Molly, Tess, Jenna, Abby, Bailey
Brothers: Alex, Cole, Jonah, Luke, Max

✳ Like Jack, this is a brash nickname that parents are choosing on its own, bypassing the more reserved formal version. But be prepared to say over and over again, "No, not Jacob, it's just Jake."

Jalen

2001: #127

Popularity: #156
Style: African-American, Bell Tones, The -ens
Nicknames: Jay
Variants: Jaylen, Jaylin, Jaylon
Sisters: Mikayla, Ashlyn, Jordyn, Jada, Skylar
Brothers: Caden, Landon, Devon, Parker, Kaleb

✳ This contemporary name first became familiar via basketball star Jalen Rose. Today it's a hit chosen widely for babies of all races and both sexes.

Jamal

1990s: #262

Popularity: #399
Style: African-American, Muslim, Nickname-Proof
Variants: Jamaal, Jamil
Sisters: Aisha, Jamila, Amani, Yasmin, Shakira
Brothers: Rashad, Kareem, Tariq, Ahmad, Malik

✳ From the Arabic word for beauty, Jamal is a modern African-American standard. It has plenty of company, with such similar-styled names as Jamar and Jajuan, but Jamal is the real deal. Its meaning and roots will keep it around for the long term.

James

1940s: #1

Popularity: #18
Style: Biblical, Timeless
Nicknames: Jim, Jamie, Jem, Jaime, Jimmy
Sisters: Mary, Elizabeth, Anne, Camilla, Charlotte
Brothers: Robert, William, Thomas, Philip, John

✳ James is one of the strongest of all names, an elegant, slashing verbal sword. Jim, on the other hand, is a laid-back sort of guy. And this is a name where you have to pick sides—if a guy is called Jim, he's always, only Jim. If you want just an occasional nickname, try Jamie, or go the initial route à la James "JT" Taylor, or James "JC" Penney.

Jameson

2003: #567

Popularity: #567
Style: Last Names First
Nicknames: Jamie
Variants: Jamison
Sisters: Haleigh, Cassidy, Kasey, Susana, Aubrey
Brothers: Bryant, Dennison, Preston, Brody, Garrison

✳ Jameson is part of a small, thriving genre of names: first names made out of surnames that were made out of first names. Watch it in action: the old favorite Jack yielded Jackson (Jack's son). Elegant Jackson is now a trendy given name . . . with the nickname Jack. Same story for Jameson, which exchanges the regal style of James for a contemporary rhythm.

Japheth

Popularity: Rare

Style: Biblical, Exotic Traditional, Why Not?

rarely used

1900   Today

Nicknames: Japh, Jay

Sisters: Tamar, Zilla, Avital, Dinah, Vashti

Brothers: Boaz, Simeon, Phineas, Jabez, Gideon

✱ Parents are willing to dig deep for biblical names right now—just look at the popularity of Ezekiel and Zechariah. How, then, to explain the neglect of this attractive example? Japheth was the eldest son of Noah, and his name is rare but accessible. JAY-feth is the usual pronunciation, with JA-feth running a close second.

Jared

2001: #67

Popularity: #107

Style: Biblical, New Classics, Nickname-Proof

Variants: Jarrod, Jarod, Jered, Jerrod, Jarred

1900   Today

Sisters: Allison, Jenna, Bethany, Erin, Leah

Brothers: Aaron, Seth, Ian, Justin, Kyle

✱ A modern biblical favorite, Jared is unfussy and comfortably straddles the line between boyish and manly. The popular variation Jarrod transforms the name from biblical to surname. Another surprisingly popular spelling, Jarred, transforms the name into a jar of preserves.

Jaron

2001: #447

Popularity: #627

Style: African-American, The -ens, Jewish, Nickname-Proof

Sisters: Amira, Ariel, Jada, Talia, Aviva

1900   Today

Brothers: Jaden, Asher, Ari, Elkan, Devon

✱ With the stress on the first syllable, Jaron is a modern Hebrew name with an appealing meaning (to call out or sing) and a contemporary sound. Place the stress on the second syllable and you have an equally contemporary African-American name.

Jarrett

2001: #337

Popularity: #419

Style: Last Names First, Nickname-Proof, '70s–'80s

Variants: Jarred, Jarret

1900   Today

Sisters: Ashton, Julissa, Brenna, Shayla, Kendall

Brothers: Brock, Keaton, Kendrick, Braxton, Drake

✱ Some parents wanted to put their own personal spin on Jared. Others wanted a strong-sounding surname. Still others were fans of NASCAR driver Dale Jarrett. Together, they've given birth to a new name with some staying power.

Jarvis

1980s: #376

Popularity: #900

Style: Country & Western, Nickname-Proof, '70s–'80s

Variants: Gervase

1900   Today

Sisters: Leann, Janelle, Marlena, Lacy, Jamie

Brothers: Lamar, Casey, Clinton, Dustin, Kurtis

✱ Jarvis is either a Texas rabble-rouser or a proper English butler. Can't reconcile the two? That might be why this memorable name has never quite found its footing.

Jason

1970s: #3

Popularity: #42

Style: Mythological, New Classics, '70s–'80s

Nicknames: Jay, Jase

1900   Today

Variants: Jayson

Sisters: Jennifer, Amy, Michelle, Melissa, Heather

Brothers: Brian, Jeremy, Christopher, Chad, Eric

✱ To your kids' generation, Jason is going to be the quintessential Dad name. It was everywhere in the '70s and '80s, part of the sound of its time. Yet that certainly doesn't rule it out for today. In fact, similar new hits like Jaden and Mason are tributes to Jason's continuing appeal. It's settling into comfortable middle age as a familiar and lasting favorite.

Jasper

1910s: #260

Popularity: #518

Style: Antique Charm, Charms and Graces, Exotic Traditional, Why Not?

1900   Today

Nicknames: Jaz

Variants: Casper

Sisters: Violet, Lila, Sophie, Hazel, Celia

Brothers: Emmett, Grady, Reuben, Theo, Benedict

✱ Jasper is a old-time favorite that hums with potential. It's not classically macho, but has the kind of mischievous charm that makes all the girls swoon.

Javier

2001: #143

Popularity: #154

Style: Latino/Latina

Nicknames: Javi

Variants: Xavier

1900   Today

Sisters: Bianca, Marisa, Yesenia, Raquel, Selena

Brothers: Omar, Sergio, Cesar, Jorge, Marco

✱ This sophisticated Spanish and Portuguese classic is an up-and-coming hit. So far, it's remained an exclusively Latino name. Families of other backgrounds are jumping on the more "x-otic" version Xavier.

Jaxon

Popularity: #289
Style: The -ens
Nicknames: Jax
Variants: Jackson

2003: #289

1900 Today

Sisters: Madisyn, Ansley, Haven, Alivia, Jazlyn
Brothers: Ayden, Xzavier, Camron, Izaiah, Jett
✷ Two trends collide. . . . X is the hottest letter around right now, and surnames like Jackson are all the rage. So around the country, hundreds of parents simultaneously thought up this new creation.

Jay

Popularity: #350
Style: Nicknames, Timeless
Sisters: Beth, Kim, Christine, Jill, Kathy

1960s: #90

1900 Today

Brothers: Jon, Dean, Tony, Chris, Mark
✷ This Jay is a rare bird: a timeless nickname. With its light, sunny style and effortless masculinity, it's a name that can carry you anywhere. You'd trust the big game to a quarterback named Jay, and your life to a surgeon named Jay. A baby named Jay is mighty cuddly, too. Take it straight or as a nickname for any name with a strong "jay" sound, like Jacob or Jaden.

Jed

Popularity: Rare
Style: Country & Western, Nicknames
Variants: Jedidiah

1970s: #642

1900 Today

Sisters: Annie, Liza, Nell, Ginger, Sallie
Brothers: Nat, Hank, Cal, Ty, Buck
✷ Jed is as plain as Ed and Ted, but feistier. It's a dandy little cowboy of a name.

Jedidiah

Popularity: Rare
Style: Biblical, Exotic Traditional
Nicknames: Jed

1990s: #941

1900 Today

Sisters: Susannah, Mehitabel, Jerusha, Mariah, Damaris
Brothers: Zachariah, Gideon, Eliezer, Judah, Jeremiah
✷ An Old Testament name with full-fledged Puritan flavor. It may be a bit much for some families, but the cool little moniker Jed will win many over.

Jefferson

Popularity: #735
Style: Last Names First, Timeless
Nicknames: Jeff

1900s: #484

1900 Today

Sisters: Helena, Caroline, Juliet, Eliza, Johanna
Brothers: Lincoln, Turner, Bennett, Harrison, Sterling
✷ Jefferson brings Jeffrey into the twenty-first century, while summoning images of the eighteenth. This remains the most presidential of the president surnames.

Jeffrey

Popularity: #142
Style: New Classics, Surfer Sixties
Nicknames: Jeff
Variants: Geoffrey, Jeffery

1960s: #10

1900 Today

Sisters: Kimberley, Julie, Michele, Renee, Jill
Brothers: Timothy, Steven, Gregory, Jason, Craig
✷ This reliable favorite is one of the stalwarts of the past fifty years. For most of us, it's been a basic feature of our naming landscape: Every group of friends has a Jeff. The first generation of Jeffreys is now approaching retirement, but the name remains youthful. See also: Geoffrey.

Jeremiah

Popularity: #91
Style: African-American, Biblical
Nicknames: Jerry, Jem
Variants: Jeremy

2003: #91

1900 Today

Sisters: Rebekah, Gabriela, Lydia, Leah, Julianna
Brothers: Isaiah, Sebastian, Nathaniel, Gabriel, Josiah
✷ The older brother of Jeremy—much, much older. Jeremiah's antique style is currently at the height of fashion.

Jeremy

Popularity: #104
Style: Biblical, New Classics, '70s–'80s
Nicknames: Jem, Jerry
Variants: Jeremiah

1980s: #28

1900 Today

Sisters: Jessica, Stephanie, Erica, Heather, Amanda
Brothers: Joshua, Adam, Dustin, Jared, Christopher
✷ A '70s blockbuster, Jeremy has long-term staying power. Its biblical roots are one reason, but the real secret is the name's unusual sound. Unlike Brad and Chad, Eric and Derek, Brian and Ryan, Jeremy has no close competitors. In fact, this name's biggest competition is its own biblical source: see Jeremiah.

Jermaine 1970s: #191
Popularity: #440
Style: African-American
Variants: Germain, Jermayne
Sisters: Keisha, Janelle, 1900 Today
Monique, Tamika, Latoya
Brothers: Antoine, Marlon, Derrick, Terrell, Cedric
✴ A popular African-American name, created as a remix of the French classic Germaine. (Antwan and D'Andre are similar examples.) Singer Jermaine Jackson gave this one legs in the '70s, and it held on to become a standard.

Jerome 1930s: #100
Popularity: #549
Style: African-American, French, Saints, Solid Citizens
Nicknames: Jerry 1900 Today
Variants: Geronimo
Sisters: Elaine, Therese, Regina, Annette, Gloria
Brothers: Gerard, Franklin, Gilbert, Roland, Bernard
✴ Jerome is a stout-hearted teddy bear of a name. It's smooth and easy—lovable, if not exactly cool. The name's been scarce lately, but it has the robustness of a classic. If you love Jerome, go ahead and use it with confidence. It should weather its current drought just fine.

Jerry 1940s: #19
Popularity: #287
Style: Mid-Century, Nicknames
Variants: Gerry
Sisters: Nancy, Janet, Sandra, 1900 Today
Donna, Judy
Brothers: Larry, Jimmy, Roger, Ronald, Tommy
✴ Jerry is a handshake and a smile. The name isn't especially macho or sophisticated, and it doesn't try to be. What it tries to be is happy. From Jerry Mathers ("as the Beaver") to Jerry Garcia, this is a feel-good name.

Jesse 1980s: #49
Popularity: #96
Style: Biblical, Timeless
Nicknames: Jess
Variants: Jess, Jessie 1900 Today
Sisters: Sarah, Katie, Leah, Joanna, Rachel
Brothers: Benjamin, Aaron, Jared, Casey, Joshua
✴ Like many Old Testament favorites, Jesse carries echoes of an earlier America, a land of farms and frontier. But while Jeremiah and Joshua were splitting rails and tilling soil, Jesse was robbing stagecoaches. Timelessy, lawlessly cool.

Jesús 2001: #63
Popularity: #67
Style: Biblical, Latino/Latina
Nicknames: Chuy, Chucho 1900 Today
Variants: Jesus
Sisters: Guadalupe, Maria, Dulce, Ana, Mercedes
Brothers: Angel, Juan, Lucas, Josue, Miguel
✴ In English, the name Jesus has traditionally been considered an immodest choice. In Spanish, though (pronounced hay-SOOSE), it's a classic, a heartfelt religious statement, and an established U.S. hit.

Jethro
Popularity: Rare rarely used
Style: Biblical, Porch Sitters
Sisters: Dorcas, Elvira, Jerusha, 1900 Today
Hester, Eula
Brothers: Enos, Abner, Roscoe, Clem, Hosea
✴ In the Bible, Jethro was the father of Zipporah, wife of Moses. On TV, he was the nephew of Jed Clampett, Beverly Hillbilly. Guess which association has won out? The sitcom image of slow-witted Jethro Bodine has helped keep this name a funky relic. But if the next generation can lay off the late-night reruns, it could make a comeback.

Jett 2002: #609
Popularity: #621
Style: Brisk and Breezy, Charms and Graces, Modern Meanings
Variants: Jet 1900 Today
Sisters: Journey, Haven, Aria, Sky, Jade
Brothers: Blaze, Watt, Maverick, Jaxon, Nash
✴ A swaggering rock-and-roll power name. The spelling Jet is also a deep black mineral and a magazine—a natural counterpart to Ebony.

Joaquin 2003: #443
Popularity: #443
Style: Latino/Latina
Nicknames: Quino
Variants: Joachim, Joaquim 1900 Today
Sisters: Jimena, Valeria, Dulce, Liliana, Mariam
Brothers: Esteban, Jairo, Santiago, Vicente, Leonel
✴ Joaquin's a Spanish classic that English speakers used to avoid because its pronunciation (hwa-KEEN) seemed tricky. Now that actor Joaquin Phoenix has made the name more familiar, its audience is growing.

Joe

1930s: #27

Popularity: #321
Style: Guys and Dolls, Nicknames
Variants: Joseph
Sisters: Annie, Jane, Nan, Molly, Sue
Brothers: Ray, Eddie, Jack, Carl, Pete

✷ Over the years, a remarkably large number of men have been named just plain Joe. What's wrong with Joseph? Everyone will be happy to call him Joe anyway. So just go ahead and give him the more formal option to use on special occasions.

Joel

1980s: #69

Popularity: #123
Style: Biblical, Timeless
Sisters: Leah, Julie, Leslie, Rachel, Lara
Brothers: Jared, Adam, Marc, Aaron, Nathan

✷ Joel's not flashy. It has been steadily popular for many years, but not in the top 100. It's biblical, but unlike the Isaiahs and Ezekiels of the world, doesn't shout the fact from the rooftops. It's quiet, warm, and big-hearted, and you'll never tire of it.

John

1900s: #1

Popularity: #17
Style: Biblical, Timeless
Nicknames: Jack, Johnny
Variants: Jon, Johann, Juan, Jean, Sean, Ian, Jan
Sisters: Mary, Margaret, Elizabeth, Catherine, Anne
Brothers: William, Paul, Charles, Thomas, James

✷ John is strength in simplicity. The name's popularity falls further each year, but it's actually a good match for current tastes. Parents tempted by the vigorous burst of names like Trace and Colt might want to reconsider the classic, which achieves the same force without trying so hard. And parents lured by the stylish Jack can go the traditional route, conferring John with the nickname Jack, à la JFK.

Jonah

2003: #165

Popularity: #165
Style: Biblical
Variants: Jonas
Sisters: Hanna, Faith, Chloe, Maya, Abigail
Brothers: Micah, Caleb, Noah, Asher, Eli

✷ Jonah has cute, teen-heartthrob style, but finds strength and gravity in its biblical roots. While the biblical Jonah had his ups and downs (most notably down into the belly of a fish), he is a symbol of personal growth and divine mercy. Combine that with a light, boyish sound and you have a name on the rise. See also: Jonas.

Jonas

2002: #446

Popularity: #465
Style: Antique Charm, Biblical
Variants: Jonah
Sisters: Ivy, Halle, Naomi, Lucia, Eliza
Brothers: Ezra, Isaac, Tobias, Judah, Silas

✷ Jonah is the form of this name that you'll hear most today, but the Greek Jonas has historically been the preferred English version. That gives Jonas a double punch: It's less common and has a throwback, pioneer style.

Jonathan

1980s: #17

Popularity: #22
Style: Biblical, New Classics
Nicknames: Jon, Than, Jonty
Variants: Jonathon
Sisters: Samantha, Jessica, Rachel, Christina, Stephanie
Brothers: Joshua, Justin, Aaron, Benjamin, Nicholas

✷ The number of young Johns has been shrinking for generations, but few have noticed because Jons kept multiplying to keep pace. Jonathan is the warmer, gentler choice. Its rolling antique rhythm is still perfectly current.

Jordan

1990s: #28

Popularity: #38
Style: African-American, Androgynous, The -ens, Last Names First
Nicknames: Jordie, Judd, Jody
Sisters: Taylor, Kayla, Lauryn, Kaitlin, Jasmine
Brothers: Logan, Tyler, Austin, Hunter, Morgan

✷ The number of female Jordans has been rising, but the popularity of basketball legend Michael Jordan has helped keep this name high on the boys' charts as well. It's traditional with a modern sound and should have the legs to keep going, even though Michael's playing days are over.

José

Popularity: #28
Style: Biblical, Latino/Latina, Timeless
Nicknames: Joe, Pepe, Chepo, Zé
Variants: Joseph
Sisters: Ana, Alicia, Elena, Isabel, Maria
Brothers: Juan, Luis, Carlos, Jesús, Antonio

2002: #27

✴ This biblical classic is overwhelmingly popular in the Spanish-speaking world, as John once was among English speakers. In fact, in areas with a large Latino population, like Texas, José now tops the overall popularity charts. It is equally popular in Portuguese—the Portuguese pronunciation is zho-ZAY, the Spanish ho-SAY.

Joseph

Popularity: #6
Style: Biblical, Timeless
Nicknames: Joe, Joey, Jody, Jo Jo, Joss
Variants: Josef, José
Sisters: Elizabeth, Anna, Mary, Catherine, Margaret
Brothers: William, Charles, John, Samuel, Alexander

1910s: #5

✴ The quintessential man's name—a Joe even means an ordinary guy. While others falter, Joseph carries on generation after generation with its dignified, old-world masculinity firmly intact. As rock-solid a choice as ever.

Joshua

Popularity: #3
Style: Biblical, New Classics
Nicknames: Josh
Variants: Joshuah, Josue
Sisters: Jessica, Rachel, Lauren, Sarah, Samantha
Brothers: Aaron, Jeremy, Zachary, Seth, Jonathan

1980s: #4

✴ Joshua joins Jacob at the head of the pack of wildly popular Old Testament names. The full name is quaintly rough-hewn, suggesting horse-drawn plows and logs ready for splitting, while the nickname Josh is full of fun. Sensitive/manly, fit for any occasion.

Josiah

Popularity: #152
Style: African-American, Antique Charm, Biblical
Nicknames: Jo, Josey, Joss
Variants: Josias
Sisters: Mariah, Naomi, Journey, Delilah, Patience
Brothers: Eli, Isaiah, Tobias, Judah, Levi

2003: #152

✴ Great biblical/cowboy flavor and flair. Josiah is eye-catching but classic, and makes a creative way to name a boy after good old Uncle Joe.

Joss

Popularity: Rare
Style: Brisk and Breezy, Country & Western, Why Not?
Sisters: Britt, Tyne, Reba, Liza, Bay
Brothers: Cal, Hayes, Wynn, Jem, Clint

rarely used

✴ Joss is simple as can be, with the mellow Western style of a real cowboy. Either on its own or as a nickname for Joseph or Josiah, this one grows on you.

Juan

Popularity: #55
Style: Biblical, Latino/Latina
Variants: John
Sisters: Ana, Elena, Lea, Maria, Raquel
Brothers: Luis, Jesús, José, Carlos, Miguel

2002: #52

✴ Like its English counterpart John, Juan is classic, strong, and reliable—but ordinary. So ordinary, in fact, that in major U.S. cities, Juan Rodriguezes now easily outnumber John Smiths. It's a solid choice for traditionalists, especially if you have an uncommon surname to set you apart.

Judah

Popularity: #665
Style: Biblical, Why Not?
Nicknames: Jude, Judd
Variants: Judas, Jude, Yehuda
Sisters: Adah, Delilah, Mara, Eliza, Naomi
Brothers: Levi, Gideon, Josiah, Micah, Jed

2002: #652

✴ This name has been out of fashion for so long that you picture Judahs living in black and white. There's nothing fragile about this antique, though. Judah sounds like a warrior, and the nickname Jude may be even tougher. Different versions of the name point to the three major biblical Judahs: Judah typically means the son of Jacob; Jude is the apostle St. Judas Thaddeus; Judas is the traitor Judas Iscariot.

Judd

1970s: #806

Popularity: Rare
Style: Country & Western
Sisters: Reba, Tricia, Bess, Liza, Chrissy
Brothers: Joss, Ike, Nate, Clint, Gabe

1900   Today

★ Judd's not light or melodic, but it is strong, timeless, and 100 percent masculine. It was originally a nickname for the much softer Jordan.

Jude

2003: #446

Popularity: #446
Style: Biblical, Brisk and Breezy, Saints, Why Not?
Sisters: Ava, Tess, Susana, Sophie, Maeve
Brothers: Cole, Levi, Luke, Caleb, Pierce

1900   Today

★ This name has a pioneer style and a strong religious heritage that give it impressive gravity. It also has a zippy sound that keeps it unpretentious. The one other choice with that same style combo is Luke, a soaring hit name. Jude is an uncommon alternative with breakout potential. In England, the native land of actor Jude Law, the name is already rising. See also: Judah.

Jules

1900s: #414

Popularity: Rare
Style: French, Ladies and Gentlemen, Why Not?
Variants: Julius

1900   Today

Sisters: Cecile, Beatrice, Alma, Josefa, Adele
Brothers: Edmund, Giles, Armand, Merritt, Hugh

★ Jules is a dapper gent with a French accent and a fast punch. The name is polished to a high sheen, but there's no mistaking the steel it's made of. This is a smart, sleek choice that's hot in Paris today.

Julian

2003: #78

Popularity: #78
Style: Antique Charm, English, Saints, Timeless
Nicknames: Jules
Variants: Julien, Julius

1900   Today

Sisters: Sophia, Olivia, Ava, Claire, Victoria
Brothers: Adrian, Ivan, Dominic, Isaac, Sebastian

★ In the middle of the twentieth century, when Julie was hugely popular for girls, parents shied away from Julian. The top boys' names then were scraggy, like Scott and Keith. Today, smooth and elegant is in, and Julian is back with all its connotations of saints, emperors, and gentlemen.

Julius

1900s: #98

Popularity: #393
Style: Antique Charm, Ladies and Gentlemen, Saints
Nicknames: Jules

1900   Today

Variants: Julian, Jules
Sisters: Clara, Eleanor, Evelyn, Josephine, Violet
Brothers: Oliver, Leo, Everett, Felix, Theodore

★ From Julius Caesar to Julius Erving, this is a name that rings with grand achievements. It treads softly, though, with a mild manner that suits an accountant as comfortably as a conqueror. Out of vogue since the '20s, Julius is making a suitably mild-mannered comeback. Julian is a sleeker variant.

Jupiter

rarely used

Popularity: Rare
Style: Fanciful, Mythological
Sisters: Venus, Electra, Isis, Tempest, Avalon

1900   Today

Brothers: Apollo, Orion, Thor, Cassius, Marvel

★ Jupiter is certainly formidable: the king of the Roman pantheon, the largest planet in the solar system. Yet despite all the trappings, this name comes across as fun and cute. It also has American roots in poet Jupiter Hammon, the first published African-American writer.

Justin

1980s: #12

Popularity: #26
Style: The -ens, New Classics, Nickname-Proof, Saints
Variants: Justen, Justyn

1900   Today

Sisters: Megan, Jessica, Lauren, Ashley, Samantha
Brothers: Ryan, Derek, Brandon, Kyle, Jared

★ Justin is the name for the really nice, cute boy all the girls in the seventh-grade English class have secret crushes on. The amazing part is that it has managed to retain that image for over thirty years. (For the prototypical Justin, see the dashing young rat hero in the 1971 children's classic *Mrs. Frisby and the Rats of NIMH.*) Perennially youthful, but not frivolous.

Justus

2002: #648

Popularity: #792
Style: Biblical, Exotic Traditional, Saints
Variants: Justice
Sisters: Paris, Valentina, Athena, Paloma, Haven
Brothers: Samson, Jude, Blaise, Isaias, Maximilian
✶ An arresting variation on Justin that highlights its Latin roots and powerful meaning. In its traditional spelling, Justus has a historic force and a saintly pedigree. Spelled Justice, it's a Modern Meaning name increasingly chosen for girls.

Kai

2003: #265

Popularity: #265
Style: Androgynous, Brisk and Breezy, Little Darlings, Scandinavian
Sisters: Nia, Lark, Kira, Sky, Eden
Brothers: Tate, Jace, Cael, Shay, Quinn
✶ A popular name in Northern Europe, also used in Hawaii. You can sense both styles in Kai, giving it a particularly refreshing feel: a ski trip and beach vacation all in one.

Kane

2001: #610

Popularity: #705
Style: Brisk and Breezy, Celtic, Last Names First
Sisters: Kiley, Logan, Kaylin, Macy, Sloane
Brothers: Quinn, Reid, Donovan, Dane, Tate
✶ This is the kind of strong, swift name that you expect to see on the hero of a romance novel. Kane is an Anglicized Irish name, and was exclusively a surname in the U.S. until recently. Not to be paired with a brother named Abel.

Kareem

2001: #608

Popularity: #670
Style: African-American, Muslim
Variants: Karim
Sisters: Aisha, Yasmin, Kenya, Jamila, Tiana
Brothers: Rashad, Jamaal, Hassan, Khalid, Tariq
✶ This Muslim name has been particularly favored by African-Americans since basketball star Lew Alcindor changed his name to Kareem Abdul-Jabbar in 1971. For Muslims of other heritage, Karim is the more common spelling. (This spelling pattern also holds for other names such as Raheem/Rahim, Shareef/Sharif.)

Keane

Popularity: Rare   rarely used
Style: Brisk and Breezy, Celtic, Last Names First, Why Not?
Variants: Kean, Cian
Sisters: Bryn, Keelin, Sloane, Aisling, Keyna
Brothers: Teague, Wynn, Killian, Egan, Blaine
✶ A traditional English take on the Gaelic Cian, Keane is a handsome addition to the growing roster of breezy favorites.

Keaton

2003: #368

Popularity: #368
Style: Bell Tones, The -ens, Last Names First
Sisters: Ashton, Baylee, Kaylin, Harley, Mckayla
Brothers: Grayson, Weston, Keegan, Tucker, Braxton
✶ Hey, look at all the Buster Keaton fans! No? OK, more likely it's the snappy sound that has brought this name to the fore—a perfect masculine counterpart to Kaitlyn. And its sudden appearance after the introduction of the Keaton family on the sitcom *Family Ties* is surely no coincidence.

Keegan

2002: #256

Popularity: #261
Style: Celtic, The -ens, Last Names First, Nickname-Proof
Sisters: Carson, Makenna, Emilee, Kiley, Kennedy
Brothers: Brennan, Kieran, Logan, Tucker, Keaton
✶ Keegan's a common Irish surname, rarely a first name—until now. This is a completely contemporary name that would have been hard to imagine as recently as the '70s. In style, it's like the "X Games," young and adventurous with no patience for convention.

Keenan

1990s: #385

Popularity: #582
Style: African-American, Celtic, The -ens
Variants: Keenen
Sisters: Devin, Kaitlyn, Shayna, Ciera, Camryn
Brothers: Kieran, Kendall, Darian, Brennan, Brice
✶ Familiar as a surname, Keenan doesn't miss a beat as a first name. It's sharp and swift with a Celtic style—a Kevin for the new millennium. The best-known Keenans to date have been African Americans like actor Keenen Ivory Wayans and football player Keenan McCardell.

Keith

1960s: #34

Popularity: #254
Style: Celtic, Surfer Sixties
Sisters: Julie, Christine, Teresa, Denise, Carla
Brothers: Craig, Bruce, Timothy, Steven, Scott
✶ This Scottish import has kept a youthful spirit for generations. There are more Keiths at retirement age than school age today, but the name still sounds boyish—a perennial younger brother to Kenneth.

Kelly

1960s: #126

Popularity: Rare
Style: Androgynous, Celtic
Sisters: Sheri, Deirdre, Stacy, Colleen, Beth
Brothers: Jody, Shannon, Kip, Rory, Kerry
✶ Over the course of two generations, girls have taken command of this name. Kelly's Irish-surname style is still attractive, but if the girl–boy ratio worries you, consider choices like Riley and Casey, which have maintained a more even gender balance.

Kelvin

1960s: #232

Popularity: #367
Style: African-American, Celtic, New Classics, Nickname-Proof
Sisters: Bridget, Karla, Ericka, Kendra, Tania
Brothers: Kendall, Darren, Cedric, Derrick, Terrance
✶ Kelvin has quietly become a classic by appealing to many audiences. It has been an African-American name, a Celtic name, and a way to customize the perennially popular Kevin. It's even a choice if you're looking to raise a young scientist, like the Lord Kelvin who gave his name to a temperature scale.

Kendall

1990s: #344

Popularity: #500
Style: Celtic, Last Names First
Nicknames: Ken
Variants: Kendal
Sisters: Kelsie, Maura, Logan, Selina, Karissa
Brothers: Garret, Keenan, Kendrick, Bryant, Brennan
✶ This Ken never achieved the heights of popularity of Kenneth. As a result, it feels a little livelier and more modern, and has even been taken up recently as a girl's name.

Kendrick

1990s: #407

Popularity: #472
Style: African-American, Celtic, Last Names First, New Classics
Nicknames: Ken, Rick
Variants: Kendric
Sisters: Ericka, Larissa, Kasey, Whitney, Janelle
Brothers: Quincy, Jarrett, Desmond, Kendall, Jamison
✶ This Welsh/Scottish surname made a natural leap to first-name status. Its familar rhythm recalls favorites from Kenneth to Cedric and yields simple, popular nicknames.

Kenneth

1940s: #16

Popularity: #109
Style: Celtic, Timeless
Nicknames: Ken, Kenny
Variants: Kent, Kennith
Sisters: Kathleen, Nancy, Janet, Patricia, Carolyn
Brothers: Richard, Neil, Allan, Keith, Douglas
✶ After a century as a leading man, this handsome Scot is still on the A-list. Kenneth may be showing a bit of silver around the temples, but that simply adds character. Would that we could all age so gracefully.

Kent

1960s: #169

Popularity: #889
Style: Mid-Century, Surfer Sixties
Sisters: Lynn, Sandy, Teri, Gwen, Sheryl
Brothers: Kurt, Gregg, Todd, Dean, Barry
✶ Kent's prime time was the '50s, but the name feels more modern than that. Its crisp sound fits in with current styles and could make it a strong choice. Be careful matching with last names, though. The final T likes to graft onto whatever comes after, turning a name like "Kent Oliver" into "Ken Tolliver."

Kermit

1910s: #250

Popularity: Rare
Style: Celtic, Namesakes
Variants: Dermot
Sisters: Wilma, Effie, Ione, Zelda, Prairie
Brothers: Grover, Boyd, Linus, Finlay, Casper
✶ Kermit comes from the same Gaelic source as Dermot but has an extra *hop* that keeps it ever *green*. Nonetheless, the name has essentially *croaked* in the U.S., sinking into a *bog* of disuse. OK, enough frog jokes . . . but that is what most people will think of. At least the association is a positive one, and the name is awfully cute.

Kevin
1960s: #14
Popularity: #31
Style: Celtic, New Classics, Nickname-Proof
Sisters: Karen, Kelly, Alison, Leslie, Michelle
Brothers: Brian, Sean, Eric, Kyle, Justin
✴ The decades flow by, but Kevin keeps finding some key style point that keeps it fashionable. In the '60s, it was fresh and breezy like Keith. In the '80s, it was cute and sensitive like Justin. Today, it's Irish with the rhythm of new favorites like Kieran and Aidan. A longtime Asian-American favorite, too.

Kieran
2003: #536
Popularity: #536
Style: Bell Tones, Celtic, The -ens, Saints
Variants: Ciaran
Sisters: Caitlin, Kamryn, Maeve, Kennedy, Ainsley
Brothers: Declan, Kane, Rowan, Keegan, Brennan
✴ This snappy Irish saint's name hits all of today's fashion highlights. It's also increasingly familiar, thanks to actor Kieran Culkin.

Kilian
Popularity: Rare
rarely used
Style: Celtic, Saints, Why Not?
Variants: Killian
Sisters: Keelin, Finola, Averil, Kennera, Aisling
Brothers: Cormac, Finian, Tiernan, Brannock, Eamon
✴ Kilian blooms with Irish charm. In the States, it's best known as a beer, "Killian's Irish Red," which is actually a domestic Coors product. This storied old saint's name deserves a more suitable namesake.

Kip
1960s: #488
Popularity: Rare
Style: English, Surfer Sixties
Sisters: Penny, Meg, Kim, Joni, Liz
Brothers: Tad, Wes, Robin, Kent, Toby
✴ This good-humored name would be fun to call out across the playground to a little boy. If you worry that it's not enough name for an adult, it can also be a nickname for Christopher.

Kirk
1960s: #153
Popularity: Rare
Style: Surfer Sixties
Sisters: Teri, Belinda, Joni, Robin, Sheri
Brothers: Scot, Kent, Tad, Craig, Dirk
✴ Kirk is an action hero's name. It's emphatically masculine in a way that goes beyond reality, like *Star Trek*'s Captain Kirk. In the '60s, Kirk was the epitome of this style; Drake is a contemporary equivalent.

Kobe
2001: #225
Popularity: #268
Style: African-American, Little Darlings
Variants: Koby, Coby
Sisters: Nyla, Macy, Skye, Halle, Kya
Brothers: Kai, Mekhi, Luca, Jair, Nico
✴ Kobe Bryant's catchy name and flashy basketball moves inspired thousands of little namesakes. For what it's worth, Bryant's parents reportedly chose the name from a dinner menu: Kobe is a top-quality Japanese beef.

Kurt
1960s: #128
Popularity: #744
Style: German/Dutch, Surfer Sixties
Variants: Curt
Sisters: Tina, Lynn, Jill, Karla, Cindy
Brothers: Craig, Brad, Kent, Dirk, Mark
✴ Kurt/Curt is name and description wrapped up in one. It's brusque, virile, and all business. If you'd like to give the name a softer side, use it as a nickname for Curtis.

Kyle
1990s: #22
Popularity: #53
Style: New Classics, Nickname-Proof
Sisters: Megan, Erin, Kelly, Kara, Morgan
Brothers: Ryan, Kevin, Sean, Brandon, Trevor
✴ This old Scottish surname was a hit ahead of its time. Back when the trendy boys' names were curt and brusque (Scott, Kirk), Kyle was bright and smooth—a glimpse of a generation of names to come. The name has grown into a top modern classic reflected in spin-offs like Kyler and Kylie.

Kyler

Popularity: #290
Style: Last Names First
Nicknames: Ky
Sisters: Haylee, Katelynn, Mikayla, Lauryn, Janae
Brothers: Brody, Keegan, Kolby, Tucker, Bryson

2002: #278

✹ Crafty parents have merged the modern classic Kyle with the trendy hit Skyler, producing a soundalike for the powerhouse Tyler. The result is a name that strikes all the right notes but may blend in *too* well with its surroundings.

Lachlan

Popularity: Rare
Style: Celtic
Nicknames: Lachie, Lockie
Sisters: Finola, Elspeth, Lilias, Iona, Davina
Brothers: Gregor, Angus, Callum, Alistair, Lorcan

rarely used
1900   Today

✹ This name fairly shouts its Scottish roots. But if you meet a Lachlan today, chances are he'll hail not from Scotland but Australia. Lachlan's a classic hit down under, thanks to Scottish forebears like Governor Lachlan Macquarie, "The Father of Australia."

Lamar

Popularity: #783
Style: Country & Western, Nickname-Proof, Timeless
Variants: Lamarr
Sisters: Lucille, Winona, Corinne, Lacy, Larue
Brothers: Harlan, Jarvis, Lamont, Dorsey, Leland

1980s: #328
1900   Today

✹ Lamar is a courtly classic of the American South. It's a natural for hardy gentlemen like football coaches and oil barons.

Lance

Popularity: #272
Style: Brisk and Breezy, New Classics
Sisters: April, Katrina, Lara, Leigh, Amber
Brothers: Brett, Heath, Grant, Leif, Brock

1970s: #140
1900   Today

✹ Lance is a name for dashing heroes. Sir Lancelot was a perfect Lance; cycling champion Lance Armstrong's not half bad either. Among everyday folks, the name sounds light and windswept, just right for a surfer.

Landon

Popularity: #99
Style: The -ens, Last Names First
Nicknames: Lan, Land
Variants: Landen
Sisters: Payton, Kennedy, Marley, Hadley, Ashton
Brothers: Dawson, Easton, Colby, Parker, Brennan

2003: #99

✹ With a flick of the wrist, Brandon is softened to a perfect little modern surname. Landon's natural, relaxed sound appeals across generations. Television star Michael Landon's three decades on the air helped make it familiar.

Lane

Popularity: #277
Style: Brisk and Breezy, Country & Western, Last Names First
Variants: Layne
Sisters: Logan, Macy, Cassidy, Sloane, Carly
Brothers: Reece, Cole, Reid, Blake, Trey

2003: #277

✹ This quiet mid-century favorite has recently come roaring to life alongside Dane, Kane, Shane, and Zane. Lane sounds like the refined and responsible one of the bunch, but plenty tough. Bull rider Lane Frost was a rodeo legend.

Larry

Popularity: #314
Style: Mid-Century, Nicknames, Solid Citizens
Variants: Lawrence, Lars
Sisters: Nancy, Linda, Judy, Marcia, Connie
Brothers: Jerry, Ronald, Garry, Tommy, Roger

1940s: #11
1900   Today

✹ You don't really picture this as a baby name—a Larry ought to emerge in instant middle age. But if you are considering Larry for a new generation, the good news is it's an affable, easygoing name that's ready to make friends.

Lawrence

Popularity: #344
Style: Solid Citizens, Timeless
Nicknames: Larry, Lon, Lorne, Laz, Loz
Variants: Laurence, Lorenzo, Lorenz
Sisters: Ellen, Jane, Margot, Kathryn, Vivian
Brothers: Russell, Frederick, Raymond, Charles, Marshall

1940s: #29

✹ Classic, elegant Lawrence belongs to the category of nickname victims. Larry fell out of fashion and took Lawrence with it. Imagine Lon or Laz for your nickname and the whole picture changes. This name sounds far stronger than its plummeting popularity would suggest.

Lawson
Popularity: #826
Style: The -ens, Last Names First
Nicknames: Law, Laz

2003: #826

Sisters: Laney, Annabel, Clare, Hadley, Joslyn
Brothers: Turner, Landon, Paxton, Porter, Dayton
★ This surname has an easy drawl to it. It could sound like an old-money gent or a rough-and-tumble cowboy.

Lazarus
Popularity: Rare
Style: Biblical, Exotic Traditional, Saints
Nicknames: Laz

rarely used

Variants: Lazar, Lazaro, Eleazar
Sisters: Artemas, Junia, Damaris, Sapphira, Salome
Brothers: Matthias, Lucius, Bartholomew, Tarquin, Nicodemus
★ Lazarus has a fabulously stylish sound and a perfect nickname. It also has two strong and separate biblical associations. There's the Lazarus whom Jesus raised from the dead, and then there's a sore-covered beggar. This last unfortunate fellow caused the name to become a term for lepers in the Middle Ages. It's time to get past that and raise Lazarus up from the ashes once more.

Leander
Popularity: Rare
Style: Exotic Traditional, Mythological, Saints
Nicknames: Lee, Andy, Ander

1900s: #667

Variants: Leandro
Sisters: Sabina, Ione, Lavinia, Camilla, Genevieve
Brothers: Thaddeus, Evander, Benedict, Damon, Florian
★ This great, tragic lover out of Greek myth is an imaginative and romantic choice with solid, down-to-earth nicknames.

LeBron
Popularity: Rare
Style: African-American

rarely used

Sisters: Nakia, Danelle, Laquita, Jalisa, Shanice
Brothers: Deion, Juwan, Ladarius, Tremayne, Jomar
★ Thanks to basketball star LeBron James, this name is ready to follow Shaquille from the arena to the nursery.

Lee
Popularity: #559
Style: Androgynous, Brisk and Breezy, Solid Citizens
Variants: Leigh

1900s: #72

Sisters: Ellen, Rosa, Rena, Fay, Nan
Brothers: Ray, Dale, Leon, Van, Carl
★ For such a simple name, Lee carries a lot of nuance. It has a southern "good ole boy" angle, thanks to namesakes of Robert E. Lee, but it's also been a favorite of Jewish families. Lee even has managed to hold on against an onslaught of female Lee-annes and Lee-ahs. It's now the most laid-back option in the high-energy zippy category.

Leif
Popularity: Rare
Style: Brisk and Breezy, Exotic Traditional, Scandinavian, Why Not?

1980s: #769

Sisters: Britt, Lise, Dania, Signe, Audra
Brothers: Aric, Lance, Garrick, Bret, Magnus
★ Leif's brisk Nordic style should earn plenty of admiring nods. The name made a brief appearance in the U.S. during the reign of '70s heartthrob Leif Garrett, but it remains a neglected gem. Leif's sound is creative and contemporary, and its Viking heritage makes it an unquestioned classic.

Leland
Popularity: Rare
Style: Last Names First
Nicknames: Lee
Sisters: Leonor, Clarice, Sybil, Lorine, Nola

1920s: #192

Brothers: Weldon, Dorsey, Garland, Lowell, Rowland
★ This soft surname now sounds best as a caption on an old portrait of a company founder. (Or a college founder, as in Leland Stanford Junior University, otherwise known as Stanford.) Landen is a trendy modern alternative.

Lemuel
Popularity: Rare
Style: Biblical
Nicknames: Lem
Sisters: Adah, Esther, Bethel, Beryl, Adelia

1900s: #518

Brothers: Rubin, Mahlon, Truman, Hosea, Hiram
★ With Samuels on every corner, this lesser-known biblical name may be ready to step up. Lem still sounds centuries older than Sam, but it's a pleasantly archaic surprise.

Lennox

Popularity: Rare
Style: Last Names First,
Shakespearean
Nicknames: Len
Variants: Lenox
Sisters: Tierney, Larkin, Kinsey, Sheridan,
Everly
Brothers: Cabot, Larson, Beckett, Maddox,
Brigham
✱ This natty surname could catch on in an
instant. It's powerful but elegant, like British-
born boxer Lennox Lewis.

rarely used

1900 — Today

Leo

Popularity: #288
Style: Antique Charm, Guys
and Dolls, Saints
Sisters: Lucy, Clara, Ruby,
Lillie, Eva
Brothers: Julius, Milo, Felix, Sam, Theo
✱ Could "o" be the next "x"? X is the hottest
letter in town, lending its offbeat style to powerhouses like Max and Alex. But an "o" at the end
of a name brings you plenty of quirky cool and a
less crowded playing field. And Leo's a perfect
pal for Max.

1900s: #43
1900 — Today

Leon

Popularity: #498
Style: African-American, Solid
Citizens
Sisters: Vivian, Rosa, Ruth,
Irene, Loretta
Brothers: Lewis, Alvin, Ray, Vernon, Earl
✱ This proud name, meaning lion, has a
wealth of colorful namesakes, from boxer Spinks
to jazzman Redbone to Bolshevik Trotsky. Leon
is a favorite around the world, but in America,
the name has been losing its luster.

1920s: #76
1900 — Today

Leonard

Popularity: #571
Style: Solid Citizens
Nicknames: Len, Leo, Lon,
Lenny
Variants: Lenard, Leonardo, Lennart
Sisters: Frances, Martha, Bernice, Doris,
Loretta
Brothers: Stanley, Milton, Francis, Harold,
Alvin
✱ This mighty lion isn't roaring as loud as
he used to. The -nard sound places Leonard
squarely in the last century. Today Leo, Leon,
and Leonardo are all more fashionable forms of
the name.

1920s: #39
1900 — Today

Leonardo

Popularity: #212
Style: Italian, Shakespearean
Nicknames: Leo, Nardo
Sisters: Mariana, Bianca,
Viviana, Alessandra, Francesca
Brothers: Orlando, Lorenzo, Dante,
Emmanuel, Marco
✱ You can't ask for a finer prototype for a name
than Leonardo da Vinci, one of the most creative
individuals in history. The Leonardo who did the
most for the name, though, was actor Leonardo
DiCaprio, who sent this name skyward in the
late '90s. All DiCaprio really did was remind
America of a magnetic classic that was due for
another renaissance.

2003: #212
1900 — Today

Leopold

Popularity: Rare
Style: Ladies and Gentlemen
Nicknames: Leo
Sisters: Augusta, Eugenie,
Cordelia, Rosamond, Wilhelmina
Brothers: Rudolf, Archibald, Casper, Godfrey,
Theodore
✱ Smashingly distinctive and brimming with
confidence, Leopold fairly leaps off the page. To
some folks, though, it will sound like a leap off
the deep end. Here's a simple test: If you're sur-
rounded by little boys named Julius and Oliver,
Leopold is a strong, imaginative choice. If your
neighborhood is full of Kylers and Braydens, best
look elsewhere.

1900s: #524
1900 — Today

Leroy

Popularity: #813
Style: African-American, Solid
Citizens
Nicknames: Roy, Lee
Variants: Leeroy, LeRoi
Sisters: Doris, Lucille, Norma, Wilma, Laverne
Brothers: Leon, Vernon, Clyde, Virgil, Earl
✱ Taken from the French for "the king," Leroy
became an American standard. For African-
Americans, in particular, its popularity helped
define a generation of names with French
accents. You won't meet many young Leroys
anymore, though. The king has stepped down
from his throne and now sounds more like a
country boy.

1920s: #52
1900 — Today

Levi   2002: #171

Popularity: #174
Style: Antique Charm, Biblical,
Country & Western
Nicknames: Lee
Sisters: Leah, Carolina, Ivy, Adah, Tess
Brothers: Eli, Saul, Caleb, Micah, Ezra
✴ Levi used to be a primarily Jewish name, but no more. It's finding a new audience thanks to its snappy sound and rustic Levi Strauss image. The biblical Levi was a son of Jacob whose descendants, the Levites, included Moses.

Liam   2003: #115

Popularity: #115
Style: Celtic, Little Darlings,
Nickname-Proof
Sisters: Chloe, Ava, Lily, Riley,
Mia
Brothers: Gavin, Riley, Aidan, Carson, Conor
✴ This Gaelic form of William has only recently made it past the shores of Ireland. (Actor Liam Neeson led the ocean crossing.) It's now embraced by parents looking for an up-to-date flourish but a trim, simple sound.

Lincoln   2003: #553

Popularity: #553
Style: Last Names First,
Namesakes, Timeless, Why
Not?
Nicknames: Linc
Sisters: Lilian, Juliet, Annabel, Lila, Harriet
Brothers: Jefferson, Turner, Bennett, Pierce, Coleman
✴ With the enormous popularity of surnames like Jackson and zippy little names like Linc, how can Lincoln still be so rare? This name surely seems to have it all, with an impeccable historical hero for good measure.

Linus

Popularity: Rare
Style: Mythological,
Namesakes, Saints,
Scandinavian
     rarely used
Sisters: Flora, Esme, Aurora,
Britta, Astrid
Brothers: Philo, Casper, Felix, Matthais, Niels
✴ The specter of a blanket-toting cartoon character has hung over Linus for decades, but the name deserves a fresh chance. It's a stylishly quirky Greek classic and a Scandinavian favorite. Linus has recently gotten more attention thanks to computer programmer Linus Torvalds and his namesake Linux operating system.

Lionel   1910s: #324

Popularity: Rare
Style: African-American, Solid
Citizens
Nicknames: Leo
Sisters: Rhoda, Corrine, Faye, Margot, Loretta
Brothers: Stewart, Earl, Harris, Lewis, Roland
✴ This is a square name but not old or creaky. Lionel train sets help keep it youthful, with their timeless image of masculinity in training. And when your young Lionel's ready to grow up, the name is ready, too. Sophisticated examples abound, from actor Barrymore to jazz legend Hampton.

Lloyd   1910s: #57

Popularity: Rare
Style: Porch Sitters
Variants: Loyd
Sisters: Velma, Eunice, Doris,
Mabel, Arline
Brothers: Lester, Willard, Merle, Vern, Clyde
✴ This once-classic Welsh name has sunk to the style cellar. One warning sign: It was the name of Jim Carrey's character in *Dumb and Dumber*. Owen, Evan, and Dylan are now the standard-bearers for Welsh-American names. See also: Floyd.

Logan   2003: #29

Popularity: #29
Style: Celtic, The -ens, Last
Names First, Nickname-Proof
Sisters: Madison, Mackenzie,
Regan, Kiley, Avery
Brothers: Connor, Hunter, Dylan, Devin, Riley
✴ Logan is one of the hottest names in America. It's Scottish, rakish, and creative without sounding "made up." The name is starting to take off for girls, too, but its deep roots keep it masculine . . . for now.

Lon   1950s: #531

Popularity: Rare
Style: Nicknames, Solid
Citizens
Nicknames: Lonnie
Sisters: Nita, Polly, Lee, Kay,
Gwen
Brothers: Hal, Van, Clark, Gene, Rex
✴ Lon is a breezy name of an earlier era, calmer than today's breezy cowboys like Colt and Beau. As a nickname, it gives a fresh face to old friends Lawrence, Leonard, or (as in the case of actor Lon Chaney) Alonzo.

London 2003: #892

Popularity: #892
Style: The -ens, Place Names
Nicknames: Don, Lon
Sisters: Brooklyn, Ireland,
Jasmin, Paris, Aspen
Brothers: Easton, Trenton, Gannon, Lane,
Boston
✱ This place name has a trendy, playful sound that's just a bit glitzy. It should be a perfect male counterpart to Paris . . . but be aware that female Londons are popping up too.

Loren 1930s: #235

Popularity: Rare
Style: Androgynous, Solid
Citizens
Sisters: Glenna, Corrine,
Rosetta, Mavis, Margot
Brothers: Carroll, Lyle, Eldon, Gale, Marlin
✱ This was a quiet, steady men's classic until the girl's name Lauren took hold. Today, with Lauren soaring, Loren simply sounds too feminine.

Lorenzo 2002: #297

Popularity: #310
Style: Italian, Latino/Latina,
Shakespearean, Timeless
Nicknames: Enzo, Lencho
Sisters: Mariana, Liliana,
Celeste, Dulce, Lucia
Brothers: Antonio, Marcos, Quentin, Armando,
Orlando
✱ Need a damsel rescued? A fresco painted? A swash buckled? This Italian and Spanish standby has a heroic, artistic style for the ages.

Lorne 1960s: #662

Popularity: Rare
Style: Mid-Century
Sisters: Rhonda, Yvette, Gwen,
Regina, Mona
Brothers: Vince, Pernell, Curt, Gordon, Garth
✱ This plainspoken name is chiefly a Canadian import. The best-known U.S. Lornes, actor Greene and TV producer Michaels, are both from north of the border.

Louis 1900s: #21

Popularity: #278
Style: Ladies and Gentlemen
Nicknames: Lou, Louie
Variants: Lewis, Luis
Sisters: Helen, Clara, Sylvia, Rose, Marie
Brothers: Arthur, Francis, Carl, Walter, Henry
✱ Here's a grandly stylish name. Yes, I'm really talking about Louis. The name has gathered dust in recent years, but it polishes up nicely to reveal a name of kingly strength. In France, where the name's kingly tradition is strongest, Louis is already making a comeback.

Lucas 2003: #71

Popularity: #71
Style: Biblical, New Classics
Nicknames: Luke
Variants: Lukas, Luke
Sisters: Jenna, Bethany, Miranda, Brooke,
Gabrielle
Brothers: Colin, Zachary, Ian, Nathaniel, Jared
✱ Lucas is the Latin form of Luke, and both names are soaring up the charts. Lucas sounds more formal and old-fashioned and gives you the option of Luke as a nickname. Very popular with Ivy League grads as both a first and middle name.

Lucius 1900s: #560

Popularity: Rare
Style: Biblical, Exotic
Traditional, Saints
Nicknames: Lou
Variants: Lucio, Luciano
Sisters: Aurelia, Zella, Magdalene, Ione, Sabina
Brothers: Florian, Domenick, Magnus, Theron,
Albin
✱ Devilishly exotic with a splash of saintly style, this could be an unexpected alternative to the popular name Damian. Just remember, it's LOO-shuss, not luscious.

Luis 2001: #44

Popularity: #54
Style: Latino/Latina
Nicknames: Lucho, Güicho,
Lou
Variants: Louis, Luís
Sisters: Marisa, Selena, Jasmine, Alejandra,
Raquel
Brothers: Juan, José, Carlos, Miguel, Jesús
✱ The Spanish Luis is a classic favorite that's still perfectly contemporary. It has risen steadily even as the French Louis and English Lewis declined.

Luke

Popularity: #47
Style: Biblical, Brisk and
Breezy, Country & Western
Variants: Lucas, Lukas

Sisters: Faith, Paige, Rachel, Maya, Olivia
Brothers: Cole, Gabriel, Jude, Isaac, Jake

✷ This New Testament name is bold and tough, and was surprisingly uncommon through much of the twentieth century. The current generation of parents raised on Luke Skywalker, *General Hospital's* Luke and Laura, and *90210's* Luke Perry is changing all that. Luke is now one of the most popular men's classics. For a less common alternative, consider Jude. See also: Lucas.

Luther

1900s: #100

Popularity: Rare
Style: African-American, Ladies
and Gentlemen
Nicknames: Lou

Sisters: Leona, Estelle, Alberta, Louise, Marion
Brothers: Horace, Malcolm, Lionel, Maurice, Claude

✷ Luther is an old-timer. The name has stayed marginally more current among African-American families, partially in honor of Martin Luther King, Jr., but parents of any color should brace for some raised eyebrows if they choose this classic. Unlike contemporaries Hubert and Chester, though, Luther has a subtle sexy groove. The name is a reach, but a potentially stylish one.

Lyle

1920s: #165

Popularity: Rare
Style: Celtic, Solid Citizens
Sisters: Nola, Eileen, Roma,
Faye, Myra

Brothers: Ray, Willis, Doyle, Hugh, Carl

✷ Lyle is one of the most fluid names for boys. It dropped out of sight back when names like Kirk and Todd were the flinty pinnacle of fashion, but it could make a comeback among the new smoother favorites.

Mack

1900s: #198

Popularity: Rare
Style: Country & Western, Guys
and Dolls
Variants: Mac

Sisters: Reba, Fay, Millie, Nell, Etta
Brothers: Buck, Gus, Judge, Dock, Wiley

✷ Too many Jacks on your block? Do them one better with Mack, the ultimate smiling tough-guy name. It can work on its own or as a nickname for Macaulay, Cormac, or any Mac- surname.

Maddox

2003: #586

Popularity: #586
Style: Last Names First
Variants: Madoc
Sisters: Larkin, Marley, Quinn,
Skye, Brody
Brothers: Jagger, Lennox, Burke, Gannon,
Ryker

✷ Most new names created from surnames sound like they're ready to lounge around at prep school. This one's too busy skinning bears and catching bullets with its teeth. The name was unheard of before actress Angelina Jolie chose it for her son, but hundreds of parents quickly jumped on the idea. Macho, yet surprisingly elegant.

Magnus

1900s: #881

Popularity: Rare
Style: Celtic, Exotic Traditional,
Saints, Scandinavian
Sisters: Linnea, Glynis, Thora,
Sigrid, Ione

Brothers: Mathias, Florian, Aldric, Nils, Angus

✷ You can't ask for a grander name than Magnus, a Latin epithet meaning "great." It's a regal classic in Scandinavia and an old favorite in Scotland, too.

Mahlon

1920s: #640

Popularity: Rare
Style: African-American,
Biblical, The -ens
Sisters: Bethel, Adah, Carmel,
Dinah, Zilla

Brothers: Rubin, Lemuel, Hosea, Ephraim,
Hiram

✷ This forgotten biblical name has a modern sound (MAY-lun), reminiscent of new inventions, like Jaylen. It was once a popular African-American name, with bearers like nineteenth-century diplomat Rev. Mahlon Van Horn and Negro League ballplayer Mahlon Duckett.

Malachi

2003: #195

Popularity: #195
Style: African-American,
Biblical, Exotic Traditional
Nicknames: Kai, Mal
Variants: Malakai, Malachy
Sisters: Delilah, Atara, Charity, Athena, Vashti
Brothers: Josiah, Ezekiel, Gideon, Elijah,
Nehemiah

✷ Malachi, a biblical prophet, is a strong new alternative to Elijah and Isaiah. The standard pronunciation is MA-la-kai. This name is often confused with Malachy, an Irish saint's name, pronounced MA-la-kee.

Malcolm

1990s: #289

Popularity: #494
Style: African-American, Celtic, Timeless
Nicknames: Callum
Sisters: Nola, Gwendolyn, Fiona, Adrienne, Cleo
Brothers: Desmond, Jasper, Marshall, Duncan, Luther
✴ Malcolm is a Scottish perennial bursting with offbeat charisma. For African-Americans, it has also been a political statement. Considering the name's familiarity and broad appeal, it has remained surprisingly uncommon.

Malik

2001: #198

Popularity: #230
Style: African-American, Muslim
Sisters: Kiana, Imani, Deja, Yasmine, Shakira
Brothers: Tariq, Khalid, Devon, Ahmad, Marquise
✴ This Arabic name is heard throughout the Islamic world. Its trim, powerful sound (mah-LEEK) is attracting non-Muslim parents in droves; it has struck a special chord with African-Americans.

Manuel

1920s: #94

Popularity: #173
Style: Latino/Latina, Saints
Nicknames: Manny, Manolo, Méme
Variants: Manoel, Emmanuel
Sisters: Cecilia, Mariana, Luisa, Margarita, Carmen
Brothers: Ramon, Alfonso, Pedro, Victor, Oscar
✴ Manuel is such a reliable Spanish classic that it actually sounds more familiar in America than the English Emmanuel. Manny, the world's friendliest nickname, is the icing on the cake.

Marcel

1990s: #625

Popularity: #769
Style: French, Nickname-Proof, Saints, Timeless
Variants: Marcellus
Sisters: Simone, Elise, Chantal, Delphine, Germaine
Brothers: Quentin, Luc, Vincent, Blaise, Noel
✴ For fans of French names, Marcel's gentle-manly reserve makes it a handsome choice. In France, it's an old standard, akin to our Warren or Raymond.

Marco

2001: #178

Popularity: #191
Style: Italian, Latino/Latina
Nicknames: Marc
Variants: Marcos, Marc, Marcus
Sisters: Bianca, Paola, Marisa, Selena, Francesca
Brothers: Sergio, Carlo, Antonio, Roberto, Dante
✴ A spirited makeover of Marc. Images of Marco Polo spring to mind, lending the name an adventurous style and plenty of cross-cultural potential. Marco is one of the most popular names in Milan, Italy's fashion capital.

Marcus

1980s: #68

Popularity: #119
Style: African-American, Timeless
Nicknames: Marc
Variants: Markus, Mark
Sisters: Susana, Leah, Veronica, Tabitha, Camille
Brothers: Matthew, Joel, Antonio, Nathan, Andre
✴ Marcus is the original Latin form of Mark. Like Lucas vs. Luke, this form of the name is more elegant but a bit less vigorous. It gains strength from the imperial style of Marcus Aurelius and the determination of Marcus Garvey.

Marek

rarely used

Popularity: Rare
Style: Saints, Slavic
Sisters: Daria, Katia, Savina, Danika, Basia
Brothers: Roman, Pavel, Milan, Jerzy, Viktor
✴ Marek is the Polish form of Mark. It puts a foreign spin on a familiar favorite in a strong, unfussy manner.

Mario

1980s: #111

Popularity: #169
Style: Italian, Latino/Latina, Timeless
Variants: Marius
Sisters: Lucia, Bianca, Marisa, Carmela, Francesca
Brothers: Antonio, Marco, Roberto, Angelo, Carlo
✴ Americans tend to think of Mario as an Italian name. It is indeed a classic in Italy, as well as for Italian-Americans such as Governor Mario Cuomo and *Godfather* author Mario Puzo. (Not to mention Nintendo's pseudo-Italian Mario Brothers.) But Mario is actually used in several different languages and has become a steady favorite of Latino Americans. It's a charismatic, macho choice.

Marius

Popularity: Rare
Style: Exotic Traditional, German/Dutch, Nickname-Proof

rarely used

1900 — Today

Variants: Mario
Sisters: Linnea, Signe, Elsa, Margit, Mina
Brothers: Rainer, Mathias, Johann, Bernhard, Magnus
✳ This ancient Roman name is a favorite in northern Europe. It's a sophisticated choice that pairs well with simple surnames.

Mark

1960s: #6

Popularity: #106
Style: Biblical, Mid-Century, Timeless
Variants: Marc, Marcus, Markus, Marek

1900 — Today

Sisters: Karen, Julie, Teresa, Susan, Laura
Brothers: Steven, Timothy, Keith, Paul, Michael
✳ Mark was a '50s and '60s blockbuster and has inevitably declined from that peak, but it's unlikely ever to go out of style. It's plain, sturdy, and enduringly appealing. The Latin version Marcus is now equally popular.

Marquis

1990s: #294

Popularity: #480
Style: African-American, Fanciful
Nicknames: Marc
Variants: Marques, Marquise

1900 — Today

Sisters: Tierra, Cristal, Soleil, Asia, Essence
Brothers: Quinton, Desmond, Tyrell, Regis, Kendrick
✳ An aristocratic-themed riff on Marcus that causes some pronunciation woes. You'll hear MAR-kis, MAR-kwiss, and mar-KEEZE in addition to the French mar-KEE. The variant Marquise actually means the *wife* of a marquis, but is popular thanks to marquise-cut diamonds.

Marshall

1910s: #170

Popularity: #351
Style: Last Names First, Timeless
Nicknames: Marsh, Marty
Variants: Marshal

1900 — Today

Sisters: Audrey, Ellen, Lesley, Susana, Meredith
Brothers: Forrest, Ellis, Nelson, Mitchell, Clayton
✳ Marshall is timeless, with the kind of steady decency you can't manufacture overnight. The name's rugged history of army generals and Western lawmen stands in contrast to its gentle style.

Martin

1900s: #64

Popularity: #199
Style: African-American, Solid Citizens
Nicknames: Marty

1900 — Today

Sisters: Ellen, Anne, Rose, Catherine, Theresa
Brothers: Paul, Karl, Philip, Lawrence, Allen
✳ Martin's the sort of name parents tend to ignore, but it has plenty to offer. Never overused, gently old-fashioned, and warmly masculine. Squint and you can convince yourself it's kin to the trendier Austin and Mason. Also a possible hero name to honor Martin Luther King, Jr.

Marvin

1930s: #48

Popularity: #337
Style: African-American, Solid Citizens
Nicknames: Marv

1900 — Today

Sisters: Sylvia, Norma, Anita, Laverne, Wanda
Brothers: Leonard, Vernon, Franklin, Bernard, Melvin
✳ There's no way around it: The impact of this name depends on the color of your skin. Marvin has remained a perfectly normal, strong name for black men, whereas white Marvins are out of luck.

Mason

2002: #55

Popularity: #56
Style: The -ens, Last Names First, Nickname-Proof
Sisters: Hailey, Madison, Mackenzie, Sydney, Avery

1900 — Today

Brothers: Spencer, Logan, Riley, Parker, Carson
✳ Here's a rare find: a handsome tradesman name that doesn't end in -er. That makes Mason a perfect brother for Cooper, Tucker, or Spencer. It's similar in feeling but not sound, to avoid the "butcher, baker, candlestick maker" syndrome.

Mateo

2003: #335

Popularity: #335
Style: Latino/Latina
Nicknames: Teo
Variants: Matteo, Matthew

1900 — Today

Sisters: Eliana, Aniya, Salma, Brisa, Dulce
Brothers: Aldo, Emiliano, Rodrigo, Luca, Adan
✳ Mateo is one of the fastest-rising Spanish names. Its clean, sophisticated sound makes it a handsome choice that can cut across cultures. Mateo is the Italian version.

Matthew

1980s: #3

Popularity: #4
Style: Biblical, Timeless
Nicknames: Matt
Variants: Mathieu, Mathew, Matthias, Mateo, Mads
Sisters: Rachel, Sarah, Amanda, Stephanie, Joanna
Brothers: Andrew, Daniel, Anthony, Benjamin, Nicholas

✴ Matthew comes through for parents as a new classic that feels like an old classic. It mingles just as comfortably with John and William as Justin and Brandon. Try bouncing it off your parents, grandparents, nieces, and nephews: Nobody has a complaint about the name Matt.

Matthias

Popularity: Rare
Style: Biblical, Exotic Traditional, German/Dutch, Saints

rarely used

Nicknames: Matt
Variants: Mathias, Matthew
Sisters: Beatrix, Margit, Mariel, Damaris, Linnea
Brothers: Marius, Florian, Andreas, Niels, Stefan

✴ Matthew is a globally fashionable classic. Whether it's Matteo in Italy, Mads in Denmark, or Mathieu in Quebec, the name is uniformly hot. The form Matthias is heard in Germany and in English Bibles. It's mysteriously rare for American boys and could be a real prize.

Maurice

1900s: #99

Popularity: #362
Style: African-American, French
Nicknames: Maury
Variants: Morris
Sisters: Pauline, Georgia, Laverne, Clarice, Lauretta
Brothers: Leon, Claude, Arthur, Bernard, Luther

✴ Maurice comes from the Latin Mauritius, and has a long history in England with the pronunciation "Morris." In the U.S., it's generally considered a French name pronounced "more-EESE," thanks in part to *Gigi* star Maurice Chevalier, the ultimate Frenchman. It's been a steady favorite of African Americans since the '50s.

Maverick

2003: #732

Popularity: #732
Style: Country & Western, Fanciful, Modern Meanings
Nicknames: Rick, Mav
Sisters: Sky, Lyric, Journey, Isis, Meadow
Brothers: Phoenix, Blaze, Gannon, Ranger, Chance

✴ Word names can be vessels for parents' own dreams. From "Princess" to "Rocky," we see glimmers of reflected fantasies. Maverick is the cowboy, the rebel, the daring jet pilot—or, nowadays, the upstart entrepreneur. Just be prepared that when you give a boy the name Maverick, you're tacitly approving his decision twenty years later to drop out of college and take his band on the road.

Max

1900s: #83

Popularity: #162
Style: Antique Charm, Brisk and Breezy, Guys and Dolls, Nicknames
Variants: Maxim, Maximus, Maximo
Sisters: Sophie, Ella, Lily, Lucy, Nell
Brothers: Leo, Oliver, Felix, Theo, Sam

✴ The young hero of Maurice Sendak's *Where the Wild Things Are* was named absolutely perfectly. Max is a name that makes you smile, with tons of mischievous life packed into three little letters. It's one of the top choices for Ivy Leaguers and upscale urbanites. Let the wild rumpus start!

Maxim

2003: #832

Popularity: #832
Style: Exotic Traditional, Slavic, Saints
Nicknames: Max
Variants: Maxime
Sisters: Valentina, Tatiana, Anya, Maia, Aurora
Brothers: Roman, Dominic, Justus, Ivan, Dimitri

✴ This Russian classic is the trim and chic choice for a formal version of Max. It's a hot name in France, spelled Maxime. It is also, for better or worse, associated with a flashy men's magazine.

Maximilian

Popularity: #334
Style: Exotic Traditional, Saints
Nicknames: Max
Variants: Maximillian
Sisters: Valentina, Mariana, Ariadne, Anastasia, Tatiana
Brothers: Leonardo, Sebastian, Xavier, Isaias, Emmanuel

2002: #322

✶ This is a showy name with the class and breeding to carry it off. Unlike modern pretenders, Maximilian is exactly what it sounds like: a sophisticated classic with centuries of regal heritage.

Maximus

Popularity: #375
Style: Fanciful, Saints
Nicknames: Max
Variants: Maxim
Sisters: Journey, Trinity, Lyric, Cleopatra, Diamond
Brothers: Adonis, Justus, Jett, Morpheus, Apollo

2002: #315

✶ For now, everyone will think you're naming your son after Russell Crowe's character in *Gladiator*. But as long as you think that's cool, Maximus is a particularly grand elaboration on Max. It will maintain that grandeur long after the movie's impact fades. Magnus is a more restrained name in the same vein.

Maxwell

Popularity: #132
Style: Antique Charm, Last Names First
Nicknames: Max
Sisters: Avery, Caroline, Bailey, Mallory, Madelyn
Brothers: Carter, Owen, Harrison, Julian, Bennett

2001: #126

✶ Maxwell is a popular name, but the real driving force is the nickname: energetic, lovable Max. Most parents feel that it needs a longer formal version . . . Maximilian? A mouthful. Maxim? A magazine. Maximus? Get serious. Thus Maxwell. It's a fine name, but if you really just love plain old Max, you hereby have permission to let it stand on its own.

Mckinley

Popularity: Rare
Style: Last Names First
Nicknames: Mick, Kin
Sisters: Emelia, Kennedy, Meredith, Cady, Logan
Brothers: Roosevelt, Walker, Taft, Murphy, McGuire

1900s: #532

✶ A craggy Scottish spin on presidential surnames. Yes, President McKinley was assassinated, but that hasn't hurt the popularity of names Lincoln or Kennedy. And Mount McKinley stands tall as a rugged symbol of wilderness.

Melvin

Popularity: #383
Style: African-American, Solid Citizens
Nicknames: Mel
Variants: Melvyn
Sisters: Maxine, Lorraine, Gwendolyn, Joyce, Wanda
Brothers: Vernon, Leon, Eugene, Marvin, Bernard

1930s: #54

✶ Melvin has been a familiar name since the 1800s, comfortable kin to the fancy surname Melville and Welsh import Mervyn. It has been most popular with African-American families over the past several decades. In fact, if you meet a man who calls himself Melvin, odds are he's black. White Melvins have typically gone by the nickname Mel, like comedian Mel Brooks and singer Mel Torme.

Merle

Popularity: Rare
Style: Country & Western, Porch Sitters
Variants: Merl
Sisters: Lucille, Dolly, Fay, Leola, Magnolia
Brothers: Mack, Harlan, Roscoe, Hardy, Lloyd

1910s: #198

✶ Several Grand Ole Opry types, led by the legend Merle Haggard, make Merle pure country. In England, it has been generally considered a female name.

Merlin

Popularity: Rare
Style: Fanciful, Namesakes
Nicknames: Merl
Sisters: Rowena, Ardith, Minerva, Zelda, Lenore
Brothers: Newton, Eldon, Sanford, Edison, Albus

1920s: #314

✶ The sound is a bit squishy for current tastes, but the legendary wizard makes an enchanting progenitor.

Micah

Popularity: #175
Style: Biblical
Nicknames: Mike
Sisters: Mara, Hanna, Resha, Sophie, Ariel
Brothers: Jonah, Levi, Ethan, Josiah, Abel

2003: #175

✳ Micah is a biblical name with a light, creative touch. It's one of the most youthful and contemporary of the Old Testament revivals, and it comes with the time-tested nickname Mike. A natural way to honor a relative named Michael.

Michael

Popularity: #2
Style: Biblical, Timeless
Nicknames: Mike, Mickey, Mick, Mitch
Variants: Micheal, Mikel, Miguel
Sisters: Rebecca, Diana, Christine, Rachel, Laura
Brothers: David, Steven, Matthew, Daniel, Patrick

1970s: #1

✳ The dominant name of the late twentieth century, Michael reigned as America's top choice from the '50s until Jacob finally stole the crown in 1999. Its hallmark is versatility: It's Old Testament! It's New Testament! It's black! It's white! It's Mike, it's Mickey, it's Mitch! And Michael's immense popularity has only contributed to its standing as a name without boundaries or preconceptions.

Miguel

Popularity: #93
Style: Latino/Latina
Variants: Michael
Sisters: Mariela, Selena, Esmeralda, Elena, Reyna
Brothers: Antonio, Carlos, Alejandro, Marco, Andres

2002: #83

✳ Michael was a huge hit in the middle of the twentieth century, but its familiar Spanish counterpart didn't surge along with it. Miguel is just as strong but only now hitting star status.

Miles

Popularity: #231
Style: Nickname-Proof, Timeless
Variants: Myles, Milo
Sisters: Phoebe, Helena, Sophie, Lydia, Clare
Brothers: Simon, Malcolm, Davis, Julian, Graham

2003: #231

✳ Miles is a terrific choice if you're drawn to "elegant gentleman" names. It sounds strong, smooth, and unflappable. In fact, this name has been quietly cool for a thousand years, never too common but never disappearing. In the U.S., the name is associated with the *Mayflower* pilgram Miles Standish, which adds a fashionably antique flavor.

Milo

Popularity: #799
Style: Exotic Traditional, Ladies and Gentlemen, Nickname-Proof
Variants: Miles
Sisters: Willa, Leora, Ione, Rhea, Avis
Brothers: Emmett, Mose, Theo, Arlo, Casper

1900s: #394

✳ Milo is cutting-edge cool right now, an offbeat name that takes a pinch of guts to use. In the Middle Ages, it was the formal Latin form of Miles, but today it's by far the more casual version.

Milton

Popularity: #733
Style: Porch Sitters, Solid Citizens
Nicknames: Milt
Sisters: Irene, Frances, Sylvia, Lois, Helene
Brothers: Leonard, Sidney, Stanley, Monroe, Howard

1910s: #75

✳ Milton is a cautionary tale for surnames. It's not a bad name by any means, but it's not what the parents who chose it originally intended. Like Grayson or Dalton today, Milton was supposed to sound high-class and elegant. It ended up the king of the borscht belt, a world apart from the aristocracy it aspired to join.

Mitchell

1990s: #89

Popularity: #197
Style: Last Names First, Timeless
Nicknames: Mitch
Variants: Mitchel
Sisters: Molly, Susana, Mallory, Katie, Leah
Brothers: Spencer, Marcus, Bryant, Dexter, Preston

✶ Here's a surname with some heft. Mitchell can dress up spiffy with swells like Preston and Chandler, but when it's time to take the gloves off, good old Mitch will rule the day. In origin, Mitchell is a version of Michael—the two names even share the nickname Mitch.

Moe

1900s: #827

Popularity: Rare
Style: Guys and Dolls
Variants: Mo
Sisters: Dell, Ettie, Bess, Flo, Sadie
Brothers: Ike, Nat, Mose, Sol, Gus

✶ The next step past Sam and Gus for parents who like the "corner barber" style of names.

Mohammed

2001: #482

Popularity: #605
Style: Muslim
Variants: Mohammad, Muhammad, Mohamed
Sisters: Fatima, Yasmin, Aisha, Maryam, Samira
Brothers: Ahmed, Ibrahim, Abdullah, Jamal, Mustafa

✶ The name of the Prophet of Islam, Mohammed is the most popular name on the planet. In English, this classic has a tremendous array of spellings that puts even Kaitlyn to shame. Variations beginning with "Mo" are most often favored in the U.S., "Mu" in the United Kingdom.

Montgomery

1960s: #947

Popularity: Rare
Style: Exotic Traditional, Last Names First
Nicknames: Monty, Monte
Sisters: Evangeline, Violetta, Cordelia, Blanche, Georgiana
Brothers: Ellsworth, Jennings, Sheridan, Carlyle, Stanford

✶ The elegance of this name could sound dreamy—think actor Montgomery Clift—or fusty—think Montgomery Burns from *The Simpsons*. Montague is a similar choice that also yields the nickname Monty.

Morgan

1990s: #273

Popularity: #364
Style: Androgynous, Celtic, The -ens, Nickname-Proof
Sisters: Megan, Justine, Taryn, Kelsey, Brenna
Brothers: Owen, Duncan, Logan, Jordan, Trevor

✶ Morgan is a strapping old Welsh name. Parents should be aware, though, that it has exploded in popularity as a girl's name. Nine out of ten new Morgans today are female.

Morris

1900s: #85

Popularity: Rare
Style: Last Names First
Nicknames: Mo, Morrie
Variants: Maurice
Sisters: Velma, Gladys, Irma, Ethel, Mable
Brothers: Lester, Virgil, Harvey, Willard, Monroe

✶ This alternate spelling of Maurice was hot in the 1800s when its surname look was elegant and trendy. It was also a common choice of Jewish parents as an English version of Moshe. Like similar choices Milton and Sidney, it's now completely out of fashion.

Mose

1900s: #407

Popularity: Rare
Style: Guys and Dolls, Nicknames
Variants: Moss
Sisters: Mae, Bess, Cleo, Nell, Mazie
Brothers: Arch, Dock, Sol, Ike, Clem

✶ This nickname takes Moses downtown. It's a smoky, bluesy throwback with just a hint of hayseed thrown in. Stylish and unusual.

Moses

1900s: #278

Popularity: #503
Style: Biblical, Timeless
Nicknames: Mo, Mose
Sisters: Miriam, Ruth, Leora, Helena, Esther
Brothers: Solomon, Ezra, Judah, Rueben, Levi

✶ With due respect to Abraham and Noah, Moses is the ultimate biblical name. It's also one of the few to resist the recent Old Testament craze—your best bet to meet a Moses is still in the pages of Exodus, not the neighborhood playground. The ingredients are all there, though: It's simple, old-fashioned, and heartily masculine.

Murphy

Popularity: Rare
Style: Celtic, Last Names First,
Why Not?
Sisters: Nola, Ainsley, Iona,
Marian, Connolly
Brothers: Finley, Miller, Edison, Palmer,
Carleton

1920s: #704

1900 — Today

✶ Murphy is the number-one surname in
Ireland. It was once a steady given-name choice
in the U.S. and is ready to step back in without
missing a beat. Unpretentious and enormously
likable.

Napoleon

Popularity: Rare
Style: Exotic Traditional,
Namesakes
Nicknames: Nap, Leo
Sisters: Evangeline, Zola, Avis,
Cordelia, Magdalene
Brothers: Ferdinand, Luther, Augustus,
Lafayette, Constantin

1900s: #506

1900 — Today

✶ First the baggage: Napoleon is highfalutin,
imperialist, and popularly associated with insan-
ity. Still reading on? If so, consider that this historical throwback can hold its own with the gentlemanly revivals like Dominic, make mischief
with pals Gus and Max, or strut with newcomers
like Maximus and Destiny. Risky but stylish.

Nathan

Popularity: #27
Style: Biblical, The -ens,
Timeless
Nicknames: Nat, Nate
Sisters: Rachel, Leah, Lauren,
Natalie, Emily
Brothers: Benjamin, Isaac, Simon, Samuel,
Nolan

2003: #27

1900 — Today

✶ Nathan was one of the first Old Testament
revivals to strike a chord with American parents.
While similar choices like Ethan didn't rise until
the '90s, Nathan's been a favorite for thirty years
now. That familiarity adds to the name's quiet
strength.

Nathaniel

Popularity: #65
Style: Biblical, Shakespearean,
Timeless
Nicknames: Nate, Nat, Than,
Nathan
Variants: Nathanael
Sisters: Emily, Caroline, Abigail, Hope, Elizabeth
Brothers: Alexander, Luke, Gabriel, Benjamin,
Nicholas

2002: #65

1900 — Today

✶ Nathaniel is the perfect understated antique.
It's like that elegant sideboard that's been in the
family for generations. Yes, the name's biblical
style is the height of fashion, but it doesn't make a
fuss about it. It's handsome, confident, and modest—an American classic. The alternate spelling
Nathanael is standard in the New Testament.

Ned

Popularity: Rare
Style: Guys and Dolls,
Nicknames
Sisters: Nell, Reva, Nan, Rae,
Rosie
Brothers: Archie, Ted, Roy, Arlo, Hal

1910s: #340

1900 — Today

✶ A merry little nickname that adds zest to
Edward or Edmund. Best, though, to keep Ned
a pet form and put the full name on the birth
certificate.

Neil

Popularity: #579
Style: Celtic, Timeless
Variants: Neal, Niall
Sisters: Kathleen, Donna,
Lynne, Joy, Susan
Brothers: Dean, Douglas, Keith, Alan, Glenn

1950s: #170

1900 — Today

✶ Scottish, sturdy, and swift, Neil should be at
the top of many parents' lists. America seems
to have developed a blind spot for the name,
though. It's familar enough to be taken for granted. If you're after a more eye-catching style, you
can try the Gaelic spelling Niall, which pairs up
well with trendy hits like Declan and Liam.

Nelson

Popularity: #394
Style: Last Names First,
Timeless
Sisters: Ellen, Jeanette, Rosa,
Kathryn, Vivian
Brothers: Marshall, Carlton, Lawrence, Warren,
Russell

1930s: #190

1900 — Today

✶ Nelson was first adopted as a given name in the
1800s in honor of British Admiral Horatio Nelson.
Today, Nelson Mandela is a more likely honoree.
In between, the name was a modest, all-American
workhorse.

Nicholas

1990s: #8

Popularity: #13
Style: Greek, Saints, Timeless
Nicknames: Nick, Cole, Nico, Niels, Nikos, Colin, Klaus
Variants: Nicolas, Nickolas, Nikolas, Nicholaus, Nils
Sisters: Emily, Sarah, Victoria, Caroline, Natalie
Brothers: Benjamin, Alexander, Christian, Nathaniel, Timothy

★ Nicholas made its big leap in popularity back in the '70s, but it hasn't lost any of its zing. Its crackling rhythm, unique among classic English boys' names, still rings with its Greek origins. International forms of the name like Nils and Nico are worth considering as nicknames.

Nicholson

Popularity: Rare — rarely used
Style: Last Names First, Why Not?
Nicknames: Nick, Cole, Nico, Nikos, Colin
Sisters: Sheridan, Hollis, Lacey, Ellery, Maribel
Brothers: Richmond, Campbell, Dennison, Broderick, Robinson

★ A surname twist on the ever-popular Nicholas. Nicholson is less common—even surprising—but keeps the terrific range of Nicholas nicknames to choose from.

Nico

2002: #713

Popularity: #757
Style: Italian, Little Darlings
Variants: Niko
Sisters: Gia, Halle, Anika, Ivy, Elle
Brothers: Luca, Kai, Dario, Axel, Matteo

★ An Italian nickname for Nicholas (or Nicola), Nico is suave but cute, with no ego problems.

Nigel

1990s: #500

Popularity: #716
Style: English, Nickname-Proof
Sisters: Anthea, Felicity, Dulcie, Phillipa, Daphne
Brothers: Niles, Clive, Rupert, Terence, St. John

★ To Americans, this is the British name to end all British names. Nigel sounds like the perfect Englishman, despite the fact that the name has been out of favor in England for generations. It's actually starting to creep into use in the States today; get ready for little Nigels with Brooklyn and Texas accents.

Niles

1940s: #932

Popularity: Rare
Style: English
Sisters: Portia, Dulcie, Glynis, Pippa, Sidony
Brothers: Clive, Giles, Nigel, Corin, Gareth

★ This name is elegant and refined, but perhaps too much so. The *Frasier* TV character has tilted Niles's image into primness.

Nils

1900s: #667

Popularity: Rare
Style: Scandinavian
Variants: Niels, Nicholas
Sisters: Else, Meta, Signe, Linnea, Inga
Brothers: Sven, Magnus, Olaf, Finn, Lars

★ Nils is thoroughly Scandinavian yet easy to picture on a little American boy. It's ready for import—pronounce it like "kneels." The Danish version Niels makes that pronunciation clearer.

Noah

2001: #28

Popularity: #32
Style: Biblical, Little Darlings, Nickname-Proof
Sisters: Hanna, Maya, Chloe, Ivy, Abigail
Brothers: Jonah, Ethan, Caleb, Owen, Eli

★ Not long ago, the biblical patriarch herding animals to his ark dominated our image of Noah. Today, this former white-beard name is the toast of the cradle and diaper set. It's a lovely rediscovery, and the bevy of young Noahs have lightened up the name so that it's positively cute.

Noam

Popularity: Rare — rarely used
Style: Jewish, Little Darlings
Sisters: Tova, Dafna, Aviva, Orly, Yael
Brothers: Elan, Avi, Jaco, Lev, Zvi

★ An unconventional pleaser, Noam is a modern Hebrew name from the same root as Naomi. It appropriately means "pleasant." You'll hear it pronounced as one syllable ("nome") or two ("NO-um"). It is often associated with the linguist and political theorist Noam Chomsky.

Noel

1970s: #296

Popularity: #476
Style: French, Little Darlings, Timeless
Variants: Noël
Sisters: Camille, Hope, Lea, Elise, Jenna
Brothers: Quentin, Graham, Reid, Vaughn, Elliot

✴ Noel is perpetually chic. Its guiding spirit was the British actor and dramatist Noel Coward, whose urbane image shaped the name's modern image. Noel comes from the word for Christmas but is generally pronounced closer to one syllable, rhyming with Lowell.

Nolan

2002: #174

Popularity: #177
Style: The -ens, Nickname-Proof, Timeless
Sisters: Katie, Elise, Claire, Kelsey, Audrey
Brothers: Mason, Spencer, Nathan, Davis, Clayton

✴ Nolan is a descendant of an old Gaelic name, but it has sounded like a mild-mannered American for generations. Recently, parents have started to notice the name's modern sound and Irish roots. It makes for a nice compromise if she wants Aidan and he wants Tom.

Norman

1930s: #41

Popularity: #784
Style: Solid Citizens
Nicknames: Norm
Sisters: Doris, Wilma, Geraldine, Sylvia, Martha
Brothers: Arnold, Leonard, Marvin, Gordon, Stanley

✴ Norman is off the beaten track of fashion, a slow, steady name of an earlier generation. The sitcom barfly Norm of *Cheers* typifies the name's image as an ordinary guy.

Oliver

1900s: #127

Popularity: #243
Style: Antique Charm, English, Saints, Shakespearean
Nicknames: Ollie
Sisters: Helena, Cecilia, Lucy, Sophie, Violet
Brothers: Julius, Leo, Edgar, Felix, Solomon

✴ Oliver seemed a little eccentric a generation ago, but fashion has come around to its charms. The name's offbeat style now sounds handsome and rakish. Oliver is already in full fashion flower in the U.K., where they've always appreciated unconventional heartthrobs.

Omar

2001: #145

Popularity: #151
Style: African-American, Biblical, Latino/Latina, Muslim
Sisters: Aisha, Mara, Shakira, Sarai, Nadia
Brothers: Marco, Cesar, Jamal, Levi, Ahmad

✴ Omar is well known as a name of Arabic origin, thanks to poet Omar Khayyam and actor Omar Sharif. It's also a biblical name, a Latino and African-American favorite, and the name of WWII General Omar Bradley. What do all those associations add up to? A name that's completely familiar but uncommonly striking.

Omarion

2003: #537

Popularity: #537
Style: African-American
Variants: Omari
Sisters: Shaniya, Iyanna, Kaliyah, Zaria, Ashanti
Brothers: Keshawn, Savion, Jamari, Mekhi, Shamar

✴ This splashy newcomer owes its existence to a star of singing group B2K. That original Omarion was christened with the African name Omari, but it's his stage name that's hitting the big time. It has become the prototype for a family of names including Damarion and Jamarion.

Orion

2001: #539

Popularity: #572
Style: Fanciful, Mythological
Sisters: Vega, Maia, Journey, Lyra, Aquila
Brothers: Adonis, Shadow, Griffin, Triton, Sirius

✴ The mythical hunter Orion, immortalized in a constellation, is a new entry into our name pantheon. Its celestial style works as a nature name as well as a mythological name. A young Orion will feel a special connection with the night sky.

Orlando

1970s: #250

Popularity: #361
Style: Exotic Traditional, Italian, Latino/Latina, Shakespearean
Variants: Rolando
Sisters: Bianca, Noemi, Silvia, Mariana, Angelica
Brothers: Lorenzo, Antonio, Demitrius, Leonardo, Antony

✴ This Italian version of Roland has always given off a romantic, artistic image in English. It has a regal literary lineage from Shakespeare to Virginia Woolf. Actor Orlando Bloom is now giving the name teen-dream style, just as Leonardo DiCaprio did for his romantic moniker.

Orville

1910s: #130

Popularity: Rare
Style: Porch Sitters
Variants: Orval
Sisters: Eula, Ora, Verna, Luella, Inez
Brothers: Wilfred, Virgil, Wilbur, Homer, Lloyd
✱ A highflier back when Orville Wright and his brother Wilbur were building planes, but firmly grounded today.

Oscar

1900s: #56

Popularity: #121
Style: Antique Charm, Latino/Latina, Nickname-Proof, Scandinavian
Variants: Oskar
Sisters: Lucy, Amelia, Maeve, Lydia, Sadie
Brothers: Julius, Max, Edgar, Magnus, Victor
✱ This name has so many powerful associations that they cancel one another out. Yes, your son would be called Oscar the Grouch and Oscar Meyer on occasion. And yes, Academy Award season could be a little disconcerting. But if you love this cool, quirky name, stick with it—you won't be sorry.

Otis

1900s: #138

Popularity: Rare
Style: African-American, Porch Sitters
Variants: Ottis
Sisters: Irma, Eunice, Opal, Etta, Leola
Brothers: Horace, Amos, Clyde, Virgil, Roscoe
✱ Otis is light, cute, and desperately out of fashion. Prominent bearers like singer Otis Redding helped the name hang on with African-American parents for a time, but it's now settling into nostalgia territory.

Otto

1900s: #92

Popularity: Rare
Style: German/Dutch, Guys and Dolls, Nickname-Proof
Sisters: Hilda, Mamie, Tillie, Freda, Lotte
Brothers: Fritz, Dock, Ernst, Mose, Bruno
✱ Otto disappeared in the U.S. during World War I along with other assertively German favorites. Today it's a fun, fresh choice but a bit cartoonish. (Sgt. Snorkel's dog in the comic strip *Beetle Bailey* is, alas, a perfect example.) Nonetheless, stylish parents are starting to tiptoe back toward this name. It's the playful side of the avant-garde.

Owen

2003: #72

Popularity: #72
Style: Antique Charm, Celtic, The -ens, Nickname-Proof
Sisters: Ava, Lily, Isabel, Maya, Emma
Brothers: Gavin, Carter, Eli, Mason, Julian
✱ The O makes it sound old-fashioned, the -en keeps it up to date. That elegant compromise makes this Welshman one of the most fashionable names of the moment.

Palmer

1900s: #480

Popularity: Rare
Style: Last Names First, Nickname-Proof
Sisters: Estella, Belle, Rhea, Cecile, Willa
Brothers: Truman, Garner, Harmon, Merritt, Foster
✱ Two at one blow: Palmer is both a gentlemanly turn-of-the-century name and a tradesman-style surname. It's a distinguished cousin to young rascals like Tucker and Cooper.

Parker

2001: #124

Popularity: #127
Style: Androgynous, Last Names First, Nickname-Proof
Sisters: Avery, Maya, Aubrey, Payton, Cassidy
Brothers: Riley, Dalton, Payton, Skyler, Brady
✱ Parker was one of the quiet, preppy surnames for generations, but it has suddenly exploded in popularity—for boys and girls alike. If you love the style but feel crushed by the swarm of new Parkers, try Porter, Walker, or Turner.

Patrick

1980s: #38

Popularity: #92
Style: Celtic, Timeless
Nicknames: Pat, Patsy, Paddy, Rick
Variants: Padraig
Sisters: Rebecca, Leslie, Andrea, Bridget, Christina
Brothers: Michael, Timothy, Brian, Andrew, Stephen
✱ Lest you forget that this name represents the patron saint of Ireland, you'll get a convenient reminder every March 17. It's the definitive Irish name, timeless and handsome. Yet parents looking to show off their Irish roots are increasingly turning to more exotic choices. The Gaelic version Padraig (pronounced PAWD-rig or POH-ric) could pull the old favorite toward exotic territory.

Paul

1960s: #19

Popularity: #124
Style: Biblical, Solid Citizens, Timeless
Variants: Pavel, Pablo, Paolo
Sisters: Ellen, Ann, Mary, Catherine, Theresa
Brothers: Martin, Carl, Peter, Glenn, John
✷ Paul is as stalwart as John, but not as stiff. It's a warm, old-fashioned, manly name that will never steer you wrong.

Pedro

1930s: #141

Popularity: #215
Style: Latino/Latina, Shakespearean
Nicknames: Pete, Perico, Pedrinho
Variants: Pietro
Sisters: Ana, Elena, Mercedes, Julia, Guadalupe
Brothers: Francisco, Julio, Pablo, Alfonso, Manuel
✷ Spanish Pedro is much like his English counterpart Peter: a classic that doesn't care much about trends and fashions.

Percy

1900s: #146

Popularity: Rare
Style: Ladies and Gentlemen
Variants: Percival
Sisters: Beryl, Pansy, Winifred, Blanche, Maude
Brothers: Cecil, Emory, Willis, Chauncey, Luther
✷ Percy is a surname transfer, or occasionally a nickname for Percival. A few generations back, it was also the generic name for the prissy kid most likely to get roughed up in the schoolyard. That connotation has faded in recent years, and Percy may now be salvageable—though it's just as likely to start showing up as a girl's name.

Perry

1950s: #179

Popularity: #857
Style: Mid-Century
Sisters: Polly, Kathryn, Lee, Janie, Faye
Brothers: Lonnie, Guy, Vance, Tommy, Allen
✷ Perry was the precursor to names like Corey—boyish nicknamelike constructions that were designed to stand alone. (Actually, Perry can be a nickname for Peregrine. No matter.) The beauty of Perry is that over the years, folks like Perry Mason and Perry Como have given the youthful name a grown-up style. It still sounds light, but it's not a lightweight.

Peter

1950s: #39

Popularity: #148
Style: Biblical, Timeless
Nicknames: Pete
Variants: Pedro, Pierre, Piet
Sisters: Theresa, Mary, Kathryn, Susan, Laura
Brothers: Philip, Stephen, Paul, Thomas, Martin
✷ There will always be Peters, but for now the momentum is moving away from this biblical classic. Pete just sounds a bit out of sync with current tastes—a white-bread name in a low-carb world. Take comfort, though, that nobody actually dislikes the name. Its day will come again.

Peyton

2001: #180

Popularity: #207
Style: Androgynous, The –ens, Last Names First, Nickname-Proof
Variants: Payton
Sisters: Kennedy, Riley, Cameron, Ashlyn, Skylar
Brothers: Jaden, Parker, Bryson, Cooper, Carson
✷ Cross melodrama *Peyton Place* with quarterback Peyton Manning and what do you get? How about a formerly preppy, delicate name that's gained some jock cred.

Philip

1940s: #60

Popularity: #292
Style: Timeless
Nicknames: Phil, Pip, Flip
Variants: Phillip
Sisters: Theresa, Anne, Ellen, Diana, Kathryn
Brothers: Lawrence, Paul, Stuart, James, Martin
✷ Philip is the handsome, enduring choice for a modern gentleman. So why is the name becoming an endangered species? Let's lay the blame on nickname Phil, which has acquired a middle-aged-talk-show-host vibe. Just focus on the full name; it's a winner.

Phineas

rarely used

Popularity: Rare
Style: Biblical, Exotic Traditional
Nicknames: Fin
Variants: Phinehas, Pinchas
Sisters: Beatrix, Octavia, Ariadne, Elisheva, Damaris
Brothers: Gideon, Japheth, Eliezer, Evander, Tobias
✷ This rare biblical name sounds distinctly old-fashioned, yet the overall effect is smart and jazzy. It's a creative sleeper that could pick up the trail of recent hits like Elias and Julian.

Phoenix

2003: #574

Popularity: #574
Style: Charm and Graces, Country & Western, Fanciful, Place Names
Sisters: Aspen, Lyric, Willow, Sienna, Isis
Brothers: Maverick, River, Blaze, Dakota, Jett
★ The mythical bird the phoenix was a symbol of immortality. Consumed by fire every 500 years, it would rise up reborn from the ashes. The word is also used to mean a paragon of beauty or quality. Such fabulous imagery is uncommon for a boy's name, but the capital of Arizona does ground Phoenix in the real world.

Pierce

2003: #485

Popularity: #485
Style: Antique Charm, Brisk and Breezy, Why Not?
Variants: Piers
Sisters: Maeve, Lilian, Fiona, Elle, Felicity
Brothers: Walker, Reese, Alec, Grant, Reid
★ Zippy and preppy, but strong as steel. (Like Pierce Brosnan's James Bond—or Remington Steele.) Pierce makes newer zippy names like Bryce and Chance look like lightweights.

Porter

2003: #649

Popularity: #649
Style: Antique Charm, Last Names First, Why Not?
Sisters: Belle, Lila, Clare, Hadley, Laney
Brothers: Turner, Coleman, Foster, Grady, Lincoln
★ Porter pulls off a nice sleight of hand, persuading you it's a stately old gentleman's name one moment, a trendy new workman name the next. That kind of versatility can take you far in life.

Preston

2003: #155

Popularity: #155
Style: Last Names First, Timeless
Nicknames: Pres
Sisters: Daniela, Leah, Cassidy, Natalie, Caroline
Brothers: Harrison, Spencer, Clayton, Porter, Grant
★ Preston is a fashionable surname with an old-time courtly quality. It's exceedingly formal yet doesn't seem stiff—that bow tie and cummerbund fit comfortably.

Prince

2003: #874

Popularity: #874
Style: African-American, Fanciful, Modern Meanings
Sisters: Heaven, Liberty, Marvel, Journey, Diamond
Brothers: Romeo, Royal, Jett, Baron, Sargent
★ This name is currently associated with the enigmatic one-named musician, but it's been used in the U.S. for many generations. Prince is flamboyant, yet more grounded than its Disney-styled counterpart Princess.

Quentin

2003: #343

Popularity: #343
Style: The -ens, French, Saints, Timeless
Sisters: Camille, Marina, Gillian, Noelle, Tatiana
Brothers: Graham, Raphael, Blaine, Elliot, Tristan
★ Timeless elegance with a splash of creativity. The Q is this name's calling card and sets it apart, gracefully. In fact, most Quentins you meet will answer to "Q," the snappiest one-letter nickname around.

Quincy

2002: #426

Popularity: #466
Style: African-American, Last Names First
Nicknames: Quin
Sisters: Noelle, Kendra, Marisol, Tyra, Cassandra
Brothers: Jamison, Kendrick, Andre, Quentin, Bryant
★ This name has a prim colonial style, but it swings nonetheless. The feeling is more Quincy Jones than John Quincy Adams.

Quinn

2003: #293

Popularity: #293
Style: Androgynous, Brisk and Breezy, Celtic, Last Names First
Sisters: Logan, Maeve, India, Kiley, Annika
Brothers: Reece, Griffin, Brice, Reid, Donovan
★ Quinn is one of the meatiest one-syllable names around. Equally familiar as a first name and an Irish surname, it's a dynamic choice that stands up well to power names of every description.

Quinton

1990s: #336

Popularity: #410
Style: African-American,
The -ens, Exotic Traditional
Nicknames: Quint, Quin
Variants: Quinten, Quintin
Sisters: Alexa, Giselle, Jocelyn, Dominique,
Larissa
Brothers: Damian, Xavier, Darius, Adrian,
Tristan
✶ Assertively classy, Quinton is a name that
demands your attention. It's not quite the refined
classic that Quentin is, but it has the advantage
of stronger nicknames. The spelling Quintin is
traditionally used for the fifth son in a family.

Ralph

1910s: #21

Popularity: #660
Style: Solid Citizens
Variants: Rolf
Sisters: Edith, Rhoda, Lois,
Thelma, Pauline
Brothers: Roy, Earl, Leonard, Arnold, Fred
✶ A dignified classic for generations, Ralph has
fallen on hard times. From Ralph Malph of
Happy Days to Ralph Wiggum of *The Simpsons*,
the name has been relegated to comic relief.
Looking for a twist that might help? You can try
pronouncing it "Rafe," like actor Ralph Fiennes,
but be prepared for some blank stares.

Ramon

1930s: #131

Popularity: #341
Style: Latino/Latina, Timeless
Nicknames: Ray
Variants: Ramón
Sisters: Carmen, Margarita,
Raquel, Delores, Anita
Brothers: Raul, Hector, Ruben, Alfredo, Mario
✶ Like its English counterpart Raymond,
Ramon is a timeless workhorse of a name. It's
sturdy, dignified, and couldn't care less about the
vagaries of fashion.

Ramsey

1980s: #934

Popularity: Rare
Style: Last Names First
Nicknames: Ram
Sisters: Audra, Lacy, Ripley,
Sheridan, Darcy
Brothers: Garrick, Finley, Rider, Ridley,
Campbell
✶ This underused surname gives you dinner-
party elegance, with the tough-guy nickname
Ram standing by for less domesticated moments.

Randall

1950s: #61

Popularity: #529
Style: Mid-Century
Nicknames: Randy
Variants: Randal
Sisters: Pamela, Cynthia, Sheryl, Donna,
Denise
Brothers: Dennis, Gary, Kent, Darrell, Phillip
✶ Randall is a name that has lost favor without
really going out of style. It has simply been ne-
glected as parents move on to the next new trend.
A new Randall today will surely be the only one
in his class, yet the name will fit right in and
everyone will accept it without batting an eyelash.

Randolph

1950s: #197

Popularity: Rare
Style: Ladies and Gentlemen,
Solid Citizens
Nicknames: Randy, Dolph,
Rand
Sisters: Marianne, Rosalind, Roberta,
Gwendolyn, Susanne
Brothers: Gerard, Stewart, Douglas, Cornell,
Dwight
✶ Even when Randy and Randall were atop the
charts, Randolph was left behind. It was perhaps
too gentlemanly, a bit heavy-handed for a mod-
ern little boy. That could change today, what
with names like Cyrus and Porter at the cutting
edge of fashion. Try Rand as a nickname instead
of Randy for a contemporary twist.

Randy

1950s: #33

Popularity: #318
Style: Mid-Century,
Nicknames, Surfer Sixties
Sisters: Cindy, Denise, Laurie,
Kathy, Robin
Brothers: Ricky, Keith, Terry, Chris, Gregg
✶ A top-forty name on the 1950s hit parade,
Randy is approaching golden oldie status today
but has kept his boyish demeanor. In the U.K.,
that boyishness has a naughtier spin, as the
libidinous meaning of "randy" is more standard.

Ranger

rarely used

Popularity: Rare
Style: Country & Western,
Fanciful, Last Names First
Sisters: Tempest, Cassidy, Star,
Electra, Sedona
Brothers: Hardy, Marshal, Gunner, Jarret, River
✶ Ranger sounds perilously close to a cartoon,
until you think of all the boys named Hunter
and Maverick. In that light, the name starts to
show star potential. Boyish and tough, fun and
cocky, Ranger may be ready for the limelight.

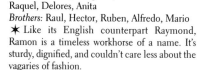

Raphael

Popularity: #710
Style: Biblical, Exotic Traditional, Saints, Timeless
Nicknames: Raffi, Rafe, Rafer, Raph, Rafa
Variants: Rafael
Sisters: Marina, Catalina, Susannah, Giselle, Aurora
Brothers: Roman, Gideon, Emmanuel, Gabriel, Isaiah

2002: #678

1900 — Today

✹ Consider three archangels: Michael was the most popular name in America for half a century. Gabriel is a fast-rising favorite. And Raphael? Still lurking quietly in the shadows. Elegant and mildly exotic, Raphael is a promising choice for adventurous traditionalists.

Raul

Popularity: #232
Style: Latino/Latina, Timeless
Variants: Raoul
Sisters: Ana, Raquel, Noemi, Blanca, Marisol
Brothers: Ruben, Julio, Rafael, Marco, Hector

2001: #230

1900 — Today

✹ Raul is timeless and familiar, yet its one-of-a-kind style still leaps out at you. No other name comes close to its syrupy-rich sound, masculine and mysterious. It's technically a form of Ralph, but a world removed from that name.

Ray

Popularity: #611
Style: Nicknames, Solid Citizens
Variants: Rey
Sisters: Rosie, Ann, Ruth, Jane, Ellen
Brothers: Lee, Charlie, Joe, Guy, Carl

1930s: #64

1900 — Today

✹ Without the added weight of the full name Raymond, Ray is spry but a little unsettled. It has no clearly defined image. It could be a Ray of sunshine, or a sting Ray, or a Sugar Ray. It's a Teflon name that will accommodate any image, but not stick to it.

Raymond

Popularity: #188
Style: Solid Citizens, Timeless
Nicknames: Ray
Variants: Ramon, Raimondo, Raymundo, Reamann, Redmond
Sisters: Frances, Margaret, Ruth, Evelyn, Helen
Brothers: Lawrence, Edward, George, Russell, Albert

1930s: #64

1900 — Today

✹ If you were asked to compile a top-forty countdown of the most popular baby names of the last century, would Raymond even cross your mind? This name has been a steady soldier, strong but so modest that its decades of popularity went virtually unnoticed. It's now slipping just as modestly out of fashion.

Reese

Popularity: #374
Style: Androgynous, Brisk and Breezy
Variants: Reece, Rhys
Sisters: Kiley, Sage, Piper, Logan, Tatum
Brothers: Tate, Pierce, Drake, Quinn, Brody

2003: #374

1900 — Today

✹ This old-time preppy classic is enjoying a burst of popularity. Actress Reese Witherspoon has inspired a small crop of female Reeses, but it's still a solid boy's choice. For extra masculine panache, consider the traditional Welsh version Rhys.

Reginald

Popularity: #478
Style: African-American, Timeless
Nicknames: Reggie, Reg
Sisters: Yolanda, Valerie, Patrice, Roxanne, Yvette
Brothers: Roderick, Terrence, Bradford, Tyrone, Rodney

1960s: #134

1900 — Today

✹ Reginald is formal and a bit of a dandy. As Reg or Reggie, though, it's bubbling over with good-humored energy. The name was common in Britain early in the twentieth century, then was taken up by African-Americans a generation later.

Regis

Popularity: Rare
Style: Exotic Traditional, French
Sisters: Rheta, Leonor, Stasia, Twyla, Avis
Brothers: Artis, Rex, Benedict, Galen, Royce

1930s: #652

1900 — Today

✹ This is an Anglicized version of an old French name with saintly and regal associations. It's elegant, but a bit fussy. For the moment, the name is primarily linked with TV host Regis Philbin.

Reid

2002: #449

Popularity: #469
Style: Brisk and Breezy, Celtic, Last Names First, Timeless
Varians: Reed
Sisters: Claire, Audrey, Paige, Cara, Macy
Brothers: Grant, Davis, Ross, Graham, Lane
✱ Reid somehow manages to make preppiness sexy, which is a good recipe for success in life.

Rene

1970s: #260

Popularity: #442
Style: French, Latino/Latina
Variants: René
Sisters: Maribel, Yvette, Patrice, Blanca, Rocío
Brothers: Pierre, Noel, Rolando, Jaime, Dion
✱ The French male name René was nearly killed off in the U.S. by its female counterpart Renée. As befits its meaning, "rebirth," René is slowly reemerging as a Spanish name.

Reuben

1900s: #199

Popularity: #800
Style: Biblical, Jewish, Timeless, Why Not?
Nicknames: Rube
Variants: Ruben
Sisters: Celia, Miriam, Nina, Esther, Leora
Brothers: Anton, Moses, Emmett, Solomon, Theo
✱ Reuben is perfectly biblical, perfectly familiar, and perfectly charming. Yet it's perfectly unpopular, with a mellower style than the trendy Old Testament frontiersmen like Eli and Jeremiah. It also summons up mouthwatering images of corned beef on rye. The Spanish Ruben is currently more fashionable.

Rex

1950s: #216

Popularity: #915
Style: Brisk and Breezy, Why Not?
Sisters: Della, Luna, Belle, May, Twila
Brothers: Royce, Van, Lon, Major, Clark
✱ Parents have let Rex go to the dogs, which is a crying shame. It's time to rediscover this name as a splashy alternative to Max.

Rhett

2002: #675

Popularity: #697
Style: Brisk and Breezy, Country & Western, Namesakes
Sisters: Aspen, Cheyenne, Lark, India, Scarlett
Brothers: Shane, Colt, Beau, Quinn, Trey
✱ *Gone With the Wind*'s Rhett Butler makes and breaks this name. You can't beat him for roguish charm and grand romance, but the strong association turns many parents off.

Richard

1940s: #5

Popularity: #86
Style: Solid Citizens, Timeless
Nicknames: Dick, Rich, Rick, Richie, Ricky, Rico
Variants: Ricardo
Sisters: Patricia, Barbara, Nancy, Elaine, Joyce
Brothers: Robert, Kenneth, Thomas, Paul, Allan
✱ The top names of the '30s and '40s are the names today's parents just breeze right past. Richard is fading fast, for no real reason except the cyclical hunt for something new. It's still a solid choice, manly and reliable.

Richmond

1900s: #846

Popularity: Rare
Style: Last Names First, Place Names, Why Not?
Nicknames: Rich, Rick
Sisters: Delta, Violette, Eleanora, Annabell, Delphia
Brothers: Webster, Lee, Rowland, Judson, Harlan
✱ A traditional place name and surname, Richmond used to sound a bit stuffy. Today, it sounds like a contemporary and potentially trendy updating of Richard.

Rider

rarely used

Popularity: Rare
Style: Last Names First, Why Not?
Variants: Ryder
Sisters: Larkin, Amity, Abby, Lacey, Leigh
Brothers: Archer, Carter, Ridley, Ranger, Garrick
✱ This swashbuckling surname sounds custom made for a sports hero, but its muscular frame would look pretty spiffy in a suit and tie, too. The international Ryder Cup is an added draw for golf fans—the spelling Ryder is now the most popular.

Riley

2003: #105

Popularity: #105
Style: Androgynous, Celtic, Last Names First, Nickname-Proof
Variants: Rylee, Reilly
Sisters: Kelsey, Mckenna, Ava, Delaney, Kendall
Brothers: Parker, Reid, Logan, Brady, Donovan
✶ This surname transfer has been a favorite since the nineteenth century, and that heritage warms and strengthens the name. Though Riley is catching on for girls, it's still a dandy boy's name—just stick to the standard surname spellings.

River

2003: #580

Popularity: #580
Style: Charms and Graces, Fanciful
Sisters: Sienna, Willow, Dalia, Lyric, Meadow
Brothers: Ryder, Sage, Sawyer, Talon, Holden
✶ The late actor River Phoenix left behind both his first and last names as new options for boys. River is a pure nature name that can sound as rugged as white water or as gentle as a shady brook.

Robert

1930s: #1

Popularity: #35
Style: Timeless
Nicknames: Bob, Rob, Robin, Robbie, Bobby, Rab, Dobbin
Variants: Roberto
Sisters: Elaine, Mary, Jane, Rosemary, Ann
Brothers: James, Thomas, Charles, Richard, Donald
✶ Robert seems to remind many parents of their own fathers and grandfathers. That's a natural result of the name's overwhelming popularity from the '20s to '60s. But like similar classics William, Charles, and Richard, Robert is finding some new life in a shift of nicknames. The softer Will, Charlie, Rich, and Rob are supplanting Bill, Chuck, Dick, and Bob.

Roberto

1990s: #156

Popularity: #194
Style: Italian, Latino/Latina, Timeless
Nicknames: Rob, Robbie, Beto, Bert, Bob
Sisters: Alicia, Marina, Cristina, Elena, Marisa
Brothers: Mario, Ruben, Marco, Ricardo, Antonio
✶ This is a grown-up name in the best sense of the word. It has an attractively mature, responsible image. Always popular as an Italian name, Roberto has been climbing steadily as a Spanish favorite as well.

Robin

1950s: #191

Popularity: Rare
Style: Androgynous, English, Mid-Century, Nicknames
Sisters: Penny, Margo, Kim, Cindy, Deb
Brothers: Dana, Kerry, Stuart, Terence, Tad
✶ Robin was originally a nickname for Robert—think Robin Hood to get in the swing of its merry English style. A flock of female Robins limited the popularity of the boy's name for years, but that fad has now mostly flown past.

Robinson

Popularity: Rare
Style: Last Names First

rarely used

Nicknames: Rob, Robin
Sisters: Larkin, Hollis, Sheridan, Darcy, Margery
Brothers: Campbell, Nicholson, Rowland, Burke, Forester
✶ This uncommon name contracts neatly into familiar nicknames. Robinson's cultural roots run deep, from castaway Robinson Crusoe to baseball trailblazer Jackie Robinson. A fine choice to honor a grandpa Robert.

Rocco

1910s: #321

Popularity: #675
Style: Guys and Dolls, Italian, Saints
Nicknames: Rock, Rocky
Sisters: Carmela, Roxie, Mamie, Marcella, Luisa
Brothers: Bruno, Vito, Buster, Dock, Carmine
✶ After a long dry spell, Italian names are making a comeback. The suave classics are the favorites: Giovanni, Dante, Leonardo. Rocco, in comparison, is a street fighter, rough and tough with a twinkle of good humor. Think of it as the Italian counterpart to Jack.

Roderick

1970s: #250

Popularity: #748
Style: African-American, English, Saints, Timeless
Nicknames: Rod, Rory, Rick, Roddy
Variants: Roderic, Rodrigo
Sisters: Roxanna, Adrienne, Regina, Penelope, Cecily
Brothers: Reginald, Dexter, Terrence, Orlando, Geoffrey
✶ Parents looking for colorful panache tend to turn to boys' names from foreign languages. Here's a chance to get that same impact from an English classic. Roderick is elegant, easy to pronounce, and chock-full of nicknames.

Rodney

Popularity: #378

Style: African-American, Mid-Century

Nicknames: Rod

1960s: #52

Sisters: Sheila, Rhonda, Shelley, Brenda, Annette

Brothers: Reginald, Darryl, Kelvin, Curtis, Dwayne

✴ Only a few decades ago, Rodney was in the full height of fashion. It remained a solid favorite of African-American parents, but white families largely abandoned the name. (Perhaps the sad-sack image of comic Rodney Dangerfield began to rub off.) If you like the nickname Rod, Roderick is another route to it.

Roger

Popularity: #398

Style: Mid-Century, Saints, Solid Citizens

Nicknames: Rodge

Variants: Rodger

1940s: #25

Sisters: Janet, Nancy, Carolyn, Judith, Marcia

Brothers: Larry, Ronald, Dale, Allen, Glenn

✴ Roger is an old and noble name that was a great hit in the twelfth century. There's nothing medieval about its style, though—Roger sounds like a regular American guy. The name is so disarmingly plain and simple that it could be considered alongside back-to-basics hits like Lucy and Sam.

Rohan

Popularity: #504

Style: African-American, Celtic, The -ens

Variants: Rowan

2003: #504

Sisters: Regan, Maeve, Riley, Ainsley, Kiara

Brothers: Kieran, Rylan, Gavin, Declan, Kane

✴ The name Rohan is many things to many people. It's an alternate spelling of the Irish Rowan, a longtime Jamaican favorite, and a place name from *The Lord of the Rings*. The name is also heard in India, where it means "ascending." Pronunciations naturally vary, too—if you want an Irish style, say "Rowan," otherwise pronounce a hard "h."

Roland

Popularity: #734

Style: French, Solid Citizens

Nicknames: Rollie, Land

Variants: Rolando, Rowland, Orlando

1920s: #113

Sisters: Jeanette, Helene, Margot, Loretta, Vivian

Brothers: Vernon, Gilbert, Jerome, Ellis, Bernard

✴ This venerable, heroic old name is on the cusp of disappearing. It's elegant but slow. Roland's bound to make a comeback someday, but while you're waiting, consider two variants that Shakespeare favored: Rowland, which adds a surname flavor, and Orlando, which adds romance.

Roman

Popularity: #295

Style: Exotic Traditional, Saints, Slavic, Timeless

Sisters: Lucia, Ivy, Marina, Talia, Nadia

2002: #287

Brothers: Ivan, Raphael, Maxim, Dominic, Lukas

✴ Roman is finally poised for the popularity that has always eluded it. The name has an antique, eccentric personality, but a modern rhythm, a combo that should perk up the ears of cutting-edge parents.

Romare

Popularity: Rare

Style: African-American

Sisters: Demetria, Zora, Augusta, Rhea, Otelia

rarely used

Brothers: Croix, Sargent, Patrice, Mahlon, Asante

✴ This smooth, unusual name is associated with African-American artist Romare Bearden. A heritage name with flourish.

Romeo

Popularity: #635

Style: Exotic Traditional, Italian, Namesakes, Shakespearean

2001: #512

Sisters: Scarlett, Isis, Donatella, Dulce, Giovanna

Brothers: Gianni, Matteo, Adonis, Dominik, Leonardo

✴ This loverboy name, inseparable from Shakespeare's tragic young hero, is a bold choice. On a charismatic, outgoing kid, it will blossom into the coolest name on the block. On a shy bookworm, it could be trouble.

Ronald
Popularity: #241
Style: Solid Citizens
Nicknames: Ron, Ronnie
Variants: Ronaldo
Sisters: Nancy, Carol, Gloria, Barbara, Joanne
Brothers: Larry, Roger, Richard, Dale, Gerald
✱ Ronald came in and went out with the twentieth century. It was a dashing Scottish name through the '20s, an upstanding guy from the '30s through the '60s, and has been fading into fuddy-duddiness since the '70s. The nickname Ron, though, remains timeless. Ronan is one alternate route to it.

Ronan
Popularity: #785
Style: Celtic, The -ens, Nickname-Proof, Saints
Sisters: Kiara, Maura, Taya, Aylin, Fallon
Brothers: Finn, Declan, Kian, Jude, Conan
✱ This Celtic saint's name has an assertive style. It's just a small side step from the mainstream of fashion, and that's a classic recipe for high style.

Roosevelt
Popularity: Rare
Style: Last Names First, Namesakes
Nicknames: Rosie
Sisters: Florence, Eleanor, Clara, Josephine, Hariett
Brothers: Carleton, Mckinley, Lincoln, Lafayette, Freeman
✱ The White House is a huge source of names now, with everyone from Jefferson to Kennedy to Carter well represented in the nursery. Yet Roosevelt, one of the classics of the genre, is out of the picture. If you like the style but want something simpler, consider Hayes or Truman.

Rory
Popularity: #651
Style: Androgynous, Celtic, Country & Western
Sisters: Bridget, Dara, Leann, Jana, Deidre
Brothers: Morgan, Casey, Bret, Kelly, Rusty
✱ This roaring Gaelic favorite has the kind of rascally charm that melts hearts. Handsome Western star Rory Calhoun was a fine example. The name is occasionally used for girls, such as filmmaker Rory Kennedy, daughter of Robert and Ethel.

Roscoe
Popularity: Rare
Style: Nickname-Proof, Porch Sitters
Sisters: Elvira, Selma, Mabel, Eula, Opal
Brothers: Rufus, Horace, Amos, Monroe, Otis
✱ Roscoe is one of the ultimate country-rube names, but unlike most of its kin, it has potential. There's a playful, macho energy to the name that could capture the imagination of adventurous parents.

Ross
Popularity: #587
Style: Brisk and Breezy, Last Names First, Timeless
Sisters: Katharine, Lindsay, Cara, Corinne, Elise
Brothers: Davis, Mitchell, Reid, Elliot, Grant
✱ It's cute and brisk and modern, and yet it also sounds like it could be your best friend's dad. A timeless, mature incarnation of the breezy name style.

Rowan
Popularity: #626
Style: Celtic, Last Names First, Why Not?
Variants: Rohan
Sisters: Maeve, Kiara, Brynn, Neve, Ainsley
Brothers: Declan, Finn, Keenan, Brody, Reid
✱ This nifty Celtic name has a merrier bent than most. Thanks go in part to comedian Rowan Atkinson, of *Mr. Bean* and *Blackadder* fame.

Roy
Popularity: #433
Style: Country & Western, Solid Citizens
Sisters: Dolly, Ruby, Annie, June, Fay
Brothers: Lee, Carl, Clyde, Earl, Guy
✱ Roy's a good ole boy, a category of names that has been in steady decline for fifty years. But while buddies Earl and Hoyt languish, Roy is a darkhorse candidate for a comeback. It's short and snappy, with the same playful good humor that has brought Max and Gus back to the limelight.

Royce

1930s: #330

Popularity: Rare
Style: Brisk and Breezy, Solid Citizens, Why Not?
Sisters: Dale, Marlys, Twila, Lorna, Greer
Brothers: Rex, Glynn, Lionel, Van, Stanton

✷ This swank surname, used since the 1800s, makes a decorous alternative to brash newcomers like Trace and Zayne. Royce carries the image of old-fashioned luxury: Its peak was in the '20s and '30s, when Rolls Royce motor cars became synonymous with the high life. The name Lexus is enjoying a similar surge today.

Rudolph

1900s: #121

Popularity: Rare
Style: Ladies and Gentlemen, Namesakes
Nicknames: Rudy, Dolph
Variants: Rudolf, Rodolfo, Rolf
Sisters: Matilda, Harriet, Ada, Marguerite, Flora
Brothers: Edmund, Clement, Sylvester, Bertram, Casper

✷ To think that a single well-meaning red-nosed reindeer could bring a classic name to its knees! Rudolph is a stylish old-timer, elegant (à la Rudolph Valentino) but with a sense of humor. Among the grade school set, though, it's all about the reindeer. If your little Rudolph can make it through those early Christmas seasons, he'll do fine as an adult.

Rupert

1900s: #524

Popularity: Rare
Style: English, Ladies and Gentlemen, Saints
Nicknames: Rip, Rupe
Sisters: Augusta, Henrietta, Beatrice, Winifred, Louisa
Brothers: Leopold, Casper, Edmund, August, Clement

✷ For generations, Rupert has sounded like a British gent with a stiff upper lip and even stiffer dance moves. At long last, actors Rupert Everett and Rupert Graves may be helping to update their name's image. It's a whimsical, memorable choice, as is the nickname Rip.

Russell

1910s: #49

Popularity: #347
Style: Solid Citizens, Timeless
Nicknames: Russ, Rusty
Sisters: Ellen, Margaret, Theresa, Vivian, Jeanette
Brothers: Warren, Lawrence, Lee, Raymond, Marshall

✷ This reliable old favorite is aging gracefully. The full name sounds a little slower and gentler than it used to, but nickname Russ is as fun-loving as ever. Actor Russell Crowe has given the name a new injection of energy.

Rusty

1960s: #382

Popularity: Rare
Style: Country & Western, Nicknames, Surfer Sixties
Sisters: Leanne, Ginger, Jo, Dee, Liza
Brothers: Jed, Randy, Rocky, Dusty, Butch

✷ Traditionally, Rusty was a nickname that would attach to a kid in childhood thanks to his red hair. Starting in the '60s, it had a run as a given name: a fresh-faced young cowboy.

Ryan

1980s: #14

Popularity: #12
Style: Celtic, The -ens, New Classics, Nickname-Proof
Sisters: Megan, Lauren, Kara, Nicole, Erica
Brothers: Justin, Sean, Brandon, Kyle, Colin

✷ Ryan has supplanted Brian as America's top choice to reflect an Irish heritage, just as Brian succeeded Patrick a generation before. It is far more popular in the U.S. than in Ireland, where Ryan is best known as a top-ten *last* name.

Samson

2002: #903

Popularity: Rare
Style: Biblical, Exotic Traditional, Saints
Nicknames: Sam
Variants: Sampson
Sisters: Zena, Paris, Athena, Tamar, Scarlett
Brothers: Justus, Axel, Jude, Magnus, Simeon

✷ The nickname Sam is a rugged classic. Some parents who are drawn to Sam for its brawn find the full Samuel too tame for their tastes. The solution for those few is Samson, a full name that outmuscles the nickname.

Samuel

2001: #26

Popularity: #23
Style: Biblical, Timeless
Nicknames: Sam
Sisters: Hannah, Abigail, Caroline, Emily, Sarah
Brothers: Benjamin, Jacob, Simon, Nathaniel, Alexander

★ Samuel is a trendy hit today, but the name has always been around and always will be. It's biblical, literary, and rustic, appealing to many tastes. And most important, it has that pure classic nickname. Lovable Sam is the true engine behind Samuel's popularity.

Saul

2001: #277

Popularity: #291
Style: Biblical, Jewish, Timeless
Sisters: Ruth, Leora, Sadie, Esther, Sophie
Brothers: Leo, Reuben, Asa, Levi, Seth

★ This is a steady name, never in the limelight but always quietly present. It is now just as quietly stylish. Back in your parents' and grandparents' time, it was primarily a Jewish name, which has left an odd aftereffect: A Saul with a Jewish last name currently sounds older than a non-Jewish Saul.

Sawyer

2003: #452

Popularity: #452
Style: Last Names First, Nickname-Proof
Sisters: Macy, Eden, Serena, Skye, Rylie
Brothers: Tucker, Holden, Archer, Finn, Tate

★ In form, Sawyer fits with preppy surnames like Parker and Spencer, but its spirit is freer. The immortal Tom Sawyer lends the name a warm heart and an eye for mischief.

Scott

1960s: #15

Popularity: #208
Style: Surfer Sixties
Nicknames: Scotty
Variants: Scot
Sisters: Kimberley, Tina, Julie, Angela, Renee
Brothers: Keith, Jeffrey, Craig, Todd, Steven

★ Scott was the granite-jawed man of the '60s. Today, Scott shines as a middle name, where its clipped sound adds a perfect punch to longer, softer first names.

Seamus

2003: #742

Popularity: #742
Style: Celtic, Nickname-Proof
Nicknames: Shem, Shay
Variants: Shamus, Hamish
Sisters: Maeve, Aisling, Fiona, Aoife, Grania
Brothers: Declan, Fergus, Rory, Colm, Ronan

★ A Gaelic form of James, Seamus is a hardcore Irish charmer. It's pronounced SHAY-mus, but resist the impulse to spell the name phonetically. Its Irish quirkiness is the heart of its charm. Hamish is a close Scottish relative.

Sean

1980s: #42

Popularity: #61
Style: Celtic, New Classics
Variants: Shaun, Shawn
Sisters: Erin, Nicole, Megan, Alison, Kara
Brothers: Ryan, Eric, Kevin, Lance, Adam

★ This Irish Gaelic form of John is now a classic throughout the English-speaking world. It's just as clean and simple as John, but softer. The standard spelling Sean looks most Irish. Alternate spellings, especially Shawn, are also used as girls' names.

Sebastian

2002: #74

Popularity: #88
Style: English, Saints, Shakespearean
Nicknames: Seb, Bastien
Variants: Sebastien
Sisters: Sophia, Gillian, Natalia, Ava, Isabella
Brothers: Dominic, Maximilian, Adrian, Nathaniel, Julian

★ Sebastian is a refined name that was always a little too elegant for comfort in the U.S. Your parents may even call it prissy. You can toss all that away now, because elegance has gone mainstream. This paragon of sophistication is now a global hit, and pals like Adrian and Julian will admire Sebastian's classic style.

Sergio

2002: #187

Popularity: #189
Style: Italian, Latino/Latina
Nicknames: Checo
Variants: Serge, Sergei, Sergius
Sisters: Bianca, Liliana, Selena, Viviana, Paola
Brothers: Marco, Arturo, Cesar, Mario, Lorenzo

★ So slick, so suave! This name has a Casanova-style seductiveness, but don't dismiss it as a fly-by-night Romeo. Sergio's intensity also sets it up for a spot in a corporate boardroom. It's a sophisticated classic in both Spanish and Italian.

Seth

Seth 2001: #70

Popularity: #81
Style: Biblical, New Classics
Sisters: Hannah, Sophie, Leah, Lily, Hope
Brothers: Caleb, Eli, Jake, Owen, Lucas

✳ Names like Abraham and Ezekiel are marvelously evocative. They're both patriarchs and pioneers: part Genesis, part Homestead Act. But they're also long and cumbersome. Seth is a plain, soft-spoken alternative that's easy to love.

Shane 1970s: #64

Popularity: #150
Style: Brisk and Breezy, Celtic, Country & Western, New Classics
Variants: Shayne, Sean
Sisters: Brooke, Kasey, Holly, Caitlin, Megan
Brothers: Casey, Beau, Colt, Heath, Travis

✳ This lone gunslinger has been riding the range for decades now. Shane is an anglicized form of Sean, but it's primarily linked to the classic cowboy movie. You can hear Shane's echoes in new Western hits like Trace, and the original is still sitting tall in the saddle.

Shannon 1970s: #106

Popularity: #858
Style: Androgynous, Celtic, Nickname-Proof, '70s–'80s
Sisters: Kerry, Fallon, Shauna, Bridget, Stacy
Brothers: Shawn, Torrey, Bryan, Derrick, Damon

✳ This name is a survivor, hanging on through a storm of female Shannons that swept through a generation back. (See the girls' entry for more background.) Unlike Courtney and Leslie, which have thrown in the towel, Shannon can still sound strong and masculine on the shoulders of a handsome young man.

Shaquille 1990s: #442

Popularity: Rare
Style: African-American, Namesakes
Nicknames: Shaq
Sisters: Chamique, Jamila, Tamika, Chantal, Jessenia
Brothers: Devonte, Dominique, Latrell, Raheem, Marquise

✳ This is all about *the* Shaquille: Mr. O'Neal, the towering master of the hardwood. It's a heck of a name, but in O'Neal's case takes its punch from the perfect pairing with his last name. For a similar effect, you might be better off creating a new perfect pairing of your own.

Sheldon 1930s: #284

Popularity: #773
Style: Solid Citizens
Nicknames: Shel, Shelly
Sisters: Darlene, Myra, Beverley, Gwen, Lorna
Brothers: Wendell, Gilbert, Sherman, Eugene, Milton

✳ Sheldons everywhere curse the movie *When Harry Met Sally*, where Billy Crystal's character argues that it's impossible to have great sex with a guy named Sheldon. Despite generations of steady use, that's the kind of perception the name is up against.

Sherman 1900s: #230

Popularity: Rare
Style: Last Names First, Solid Citizens
Nicknames: Sherm
Sisters: Rhoda, Muriel, Glenna, Dora, Lorraine
Brothers: Clifton, Merrill, Milton, Lyle, Burton

✳ Sherman is a tradesman surname. It originally referred to someone who sheared woolen cloth (a "shear-man"). If etymology were king, that would make it a near neighbor to Tucker and Walker, which are also names for cloth workers. But in style terms, mild-mannered Sherman is worlds apart from those trendy choices.

Silas 2002: #437

Popularity: #457
Style: Antique Charm, Biblical
Sisters: Eliza, Phoebe, Lila, Mercy, Lydia
Brothers: Solomon, Ezra, Pierce, Elias, Jonas

✳ Silas sounds handsome and devilish, like a dapper villain in a silent film. The name eases up, though, when you transport it to the modern world. A Silas today looks comfortable in jeans and is usually seen with a laptop and Starbucks cup.

Simeon 2003: #837

Popularity: #837
Style: Biblical, Exotic Traditional, Nickname-Proof
Variants: Simon
Sisters: Tamar, Aurora, Zilla, Mara, Damaris
Brothers: Gideon, Judah, Raphael, Phineas, Ruben

✳ The Old Testament version of Simon, Simeon has an antique flavor that should go over well today. So far, though, the name hasn't caught on. One reason may be the word simian, meaning "monkeylike." That's an unfortunate association but an obscure one, and shouldn't rule the name out.

Simon

2002: #243

Popularity: #240
Style: Biblical, English, Timeless
Nicknames: Si
Variants: Simeon, Shimon
Sisters: Amelia, Elise, Leah, Lydia, Ivy
Brothers: Julian, Miles, Nolan, Isaac, Graham

✳ The familiar classic Simon has always been well-used in England. In America, it's been heard most in nursery rhymes and children's games. The name is finally getting its due attention in the U.S., and its British aura adds an extra level of handsome charm. Simon stands to be a stylish prize for years to come.

Skyler

2002: #226

Popularity: #234
Style: Androgynous, Last Names First
Nicknames: Sky
Variants: Schuyler, Skylar
Sisters: Baylee, Sidney, Kendall, Peyton, Kassidy
Brothers: Ashton, Parker, Austyn, Addison, Sawyer

✳ This name used to be Schuyler, a quirky-cool surname close in spirit to Dexter. As Skyler, it is androgynous and aggressively modern.

Solomon

1900s: #275

Popularity: #506
Style: Antique Charm, Biblical
Nicknames: Sol, Solly
Variants: Zalman, Shlomo
Sisters: Esther, Amelia, Miriam, Cora, Ruth
Brothers: Abraham, Ezra, Julius, Reuben, Gideon

✳ With the name Solomon, you're telling your son to value wisdom. It's a fine message and a handsome name, but a weighty one. Solomon is at its best on the printed page, where it glows with dignity.

Spencer

2001: #102

Popularity: #141
Style: Last Names First, Timeless
Nicknames: Spence
Variants: Spenser
Sisters: Caroline, Piper, Christina, Hillary, Audrey
Brothers: Grant, Preston, Sawyer, Bennett, Nolan

✳ Spencer straddled the geeky-cool line for years, but the verdict has come in solidly for cool. The full Spencer now sounds respectably grown up (à la actor Spencer Tracy) with Spence its lively alter ego. The *Spenser: For Hire* TV series helped launch the name toward a slicker style.

Stanley

1910s: #36

Popularity: #570
Style: Solid Citizens
Nicknames: Stan
Sisters: Frances, Sylvia, Irene, Martha, Helen
Brothers: Leonard, Raymond, Alvin, Howard, Ralph

✳ Over the years, Stanley has evolved from an elegant surname to a tough-luck everyman name. *A Streetcar Named Desire's* Stanley Kowalski signaled the shift; the hero of the kids' book and movie *Holes*, Stanley Yelnats, is a gentler example.

Stanton

1900s: #881

Popularity: Rare
Style: Last Names First, Solid Citizens, Why Not?
Nicknames: Stan
Sisters: Glenna, Constance, Roslyn, Nila, Beverly
Brothers: Carleton, Richmond, Stanford, Stewart, Newton

✳ The name Stanton was heard occasionally when Stanley (with shared nickname Stan) was at its peak. While Stanley has softened over time, Stanton has kept its elegant surname flavor.

Stefan

1990s: #422

Popularity: #706
Style: Biblical, German/Dutch, Scandinavian
Nicknames: Steve, Steff
Variants: Stephan, Stephon, Steffen, Stefanos
Sisters: Annika, Sofia, Kiersten, Ingrid, Johanna
Brothers: Markus, Andreas, Johan, Lukas, Gunnar

✳ A tweaking of Stephen that leaves the basic name intact but soups up its style. This is the German and Scandinavian form of the name, familiar in America but just foreign enough to attract extra notice. The spelling Stephon is an African-American favorite.

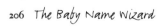

Stephen
1950s: #20

Popularity: #129
Style: Biblical, Timeless
Nicknames: Steve
Variants: Steven, Stephan,
Stefan, Esteban, Istvan

Sisters: Diana, Cynthia, Julie, Laura, Susan
Brothers: Mark, Gregory, Patrick, Alan, Kenneth
✸ Stephen is the classic spelling of an old favorite. This version of the name stays closest to its biblical and nineteenth-century roots, making it a little heartier and less boyish than Steven. See the entry under Steven for more information.

Sterling
1990s: #464

Popularity: #639
Style: Nickname-Proof,
Timeless, Charms and Graces
Sisters: Jewel, Blanche,
Genevieve, Annabel, Daphne
Brothers: August, Maximilian, Emerson, Forest, Merit
✸ Sterling's a little flashy but leans toward real luxury rather than mere glitter. It's like setting out the sterling silver flatware at dinnertime. Sure, stainless is more practical, but there's something to be said for indulgence.

Stetson
1990s: #986

Popularity: Rare
Style: Country & Western,
The -ens
Sisters: Dallas, Aspen,
Cheyenne, Shania, Cassidy
Brothers: Dillon, Montana, Dakotah, Coty, Colton
✸ Stetson may be the most aggressive of all the neo-cowboy names. It has a swaggering sound, but like a Stetson hat, it looks a little out of place once you get too far from rodeo country.

Steven
1950s: #11

Popularity: #69
Style: New Classics
Nicknames: Steve
Variants: Stephen, Stephan,
Stefan, Esteban
Sisters: Karen, Rebecca, Melissa, Christine, Andrea
Brothers: Jeffrey, Eric, Timothy, Michael, David
✸ Steven is one of the safest names you can give a boy. It is universally popular and carries no unpleasant baggage. This spelling, influenced by the nickname Steve, has been the most common since the '50s. Many parents consider the unambiguous pronunciation a plus. See also: Stephen.

Stuart
1960s: #185

Popularity: #959
Style: English, Timeless
Nicknames: Stu
Variants: Stewart

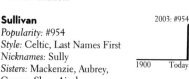

Sisters: Gail, Anita, Therese, Diane, Janet
Brothers: Douglas, Clark, Curtis, Dwight, Roger
✸ Stuart is a playful dash of Scotland, underappreciated in the U.S. The name has had a slightly nerdy image here, especially through its nickname Stu, but today you'll find that most people consider it cool and creative. Stewart is a fine traditional variation.

Sullivan
2003: #954

Popularity: #954
Style: Celtic, Last Names First
Nicknames: Sully
Sisters: Mackenzie, Aubrey,
Carson, Shea, Ainsley
Brothers: Murphy, Kennedy, Dennison, Broderick, Paxton
✸ With Coopers and Baileys on every corner, the line between first names and surnames is blurring. If you're looking for a name that still gives off a full, classic surname feel, consider Sullivan.

Sylvester
1900s: #163

Popularity: Rare
Style: Ladies and Gentlemen,
Saints
Nicknames: Sly, Vet, Syl, Sy
Sisters: Eugenia, Winifred,
Philomena, Adelaide, Cornelia
Brothers: Bertram, Ferdinand, Earnest, Theodore, Maynard
✸ This name manages to sound pompous and nerdy at the same time. So why even bother considering it? Because against all odds, Sylvester also has a cool streak a mile wide. (Sylvester Stallone's nickname Sly helps.) It's a high-stakes gamble, but if the name fits your son, he'll have a colorful calling card for life.

Tanner
2001: #101

Popularity: #120
Style: Last Names First
Sisters: Bailey, Jordan, Cassidy,
Taylor, Shelby
Brothers: Dalton, Hunter, Cooper, Tucker, Keaton
✸ The upbeat sound of this tradesman name has made it a fast-rising hit. Tanner is one name that's *not* chosen for its meaning—tanning hides was always a harsh profession.

Tarquin

Popularity: Rare
Style: English, Exotic
Traditional, Shakespeare
Sisters: Sidony, Amabel,
Phyllida, Anthea, Danae
Brothers: Tristram, Alistair, Auberon, Crispin,
Torquil

rarely used

1900 — Today

✳ Literary and elegant, Tarquin is also a well-proportioned little name sized to modern tastes. It has the stuff to win the hearts of everyone from creative namers to fantasy aficionados to classics buffs. It's worth noting, though, that the classical and literary associations are not pleasant ones, including the legendary villain chronicled in Shakespeare's *The Rape of Lucrece*.

Tate

Popularity: #406
Style: Brisk and Breezy, Last
Names First
Variants: Tait
Sisters: Sage, Tyne, Bailey, Jade, Tatum
Brothers: Kane, Trey, Reece, Lane, Cole

2003: #406

1900 — Today

✳ Tate is utterly modern (the Norse name Tait notwithstanding), yet you can convince yourself it's a traditional prep-school standard. It should stand the test of time nicely.

Taylor

Popularity: #201
Style: Androgynous, Last Names
First
Nicknames: Tay
Variants: Tayler
Sisters: Kelsey, Shelby, Ashton, Jordan, Mariah
Brothers: Dillon, Skyler, Jordan, Tanner,
Dalton

1990s: #62

1900 — Today

✳ Hugely popular just a few years ago, this boy's name has fallen off sharply. The likely culprits: little girl Taylors on every block. Tyler has taken over as the preferred choice for boys.

Ted

Popularity: Rare
Style: Nicknames, Solid
Citizens
Nicknames: Teddy
Sisters: Sue, Polly, Kay, Jo, Sally
Brothers: Hal, Ned, Lyle, Rex, Lon

1930s: #154

1900 — Today

✳ Ted is a classic nickname for Edward, Theodore, or Edmund. The formality of those names is worlds away from Ted's sweet bluntness, so many parents have chosen the nickname straight up. It's a natural impulse and a lovable name, but the "nicknamehood" is part of the charm. For other formal versions, consider Thaddeus and Edison.

Terrance

Popularity: #458
Style: African-American,
English, New Classics
Nicknames: Terry, Teo
Variants: Terence, Terrence
Sisters: Adrienne, Candace, Rochelle, Tonya,
Daphne
Brothers: Geoffrey, Roderick, Dexter, Kelvin,
Lance

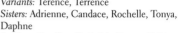

1970s: #205

1900 — Today

✳ A name with an unusual pair of images: British (typically spelled Terence) and African-American (typically Terrance). Either way, a likable name with a rolling masculine rhythm.

Terrell

Popularity: #482
Style: African-American, Last
Names First
Nicknames: Terry
Variants: Tyrell
Sisters: Kendra, Janelle, Alyson, Alisha, Ericka
Brothers: Darnell, Kendrick, Jarrod, Bryant,
Kelvin

1990s: #335

1900 — Today

✳ This handsome surname followed in the footsteps of Darrell and Terrence. Like those similar choices, it's especially popular with African-American families. The pronunciations TERR-uhll and tuh-RELL are equally common.

Terry

Popularity: #400
Style: Androgynous, Mid-
Century, Nicknames
Sisters: Connie, Vicky, Donna,
Cheryl, Brenda
Brothers: Randy, Dana, Danny, Kerry, Bruce

1950s: #29

1900 — Today

✳ In the '50s and '60s, Terry was a ubiquitous name for boys and girls alike. It now seems to have outlived its androgynous period and may be returning to the masculine camp. If you'd like a more formal alternative, Terry is a nickname for either Terrance or Theodore.

Thaddeus

Popularity: #925
Style: Biblical, Exotic
Traditional
Nicknames: Tad, Thad, Ted
Sisters: Catalina, Aurora, Avis, Valentina,
Damaris
Brothers: Atticus, Demetrius, Constantin,
Leander, Matthias

1910s: #359

1900 — Today

✳ Exotic but viable. Thaddeus sounds like a flight of fancy, but it keeps one toe grounded, thanks in part to solid nicknames like Tad and Thad. A good choice if your tastes are fanciful but you don't want your son to resent you for it.

Thelonius

Popularity: Rare
Style: Exotic Traditional
Nicknames: Till, Lon
Variants: Thelonious

rarely used

1900 Today

Sisters: Isadora, Olympia, Pandora, Artemisia, Valentine
Brothers: Algernon, Phineas, Hannibal, Cassius, Dashiell

✷ An arcane variant of the name of St. Tillo, Thelonius would be a mere obscurity except for jazz great Thelonious Monk. Monk (who spelled the name with an extra "o," like an adjective) makes it an artsy choice ready to pair with Isadora.

Theo

1900s: #429

1900 Today

Popularity: Rare
Style: Antique Charm, Nickname-Proof, Nicknames, Why Not?
Sisters: Clara, Lettie, Zella, Eva, Belle
Brothers: Milo, Casper, Anton, Mose, Charlie

✷ Theo has been missing in action since the '30s. Not even a role in the hugely popular *Cosby Show* in the '80s could give the name a boost. But what's not to like? Theo's not as ponderous as Theodore, yet boasts authentic turn-of-the-century cool. A good match for the trendier Max and Sam.

Theodore

1900s: #41

1900 Today

Popularity: #313
Style: Ladies and Gentlemen
Nicknames: Ted, Theo, Terry, Teo
Sisters: Beatrice, Eleanor, Alma, Antonia, Josephine
Brothers: Julius, Frederick, Everett, August, Conrad

✷ A nifty name, bristling with gentlemanly vigor and surprisingly undiscovered in the recent turn-of-the-century revival. Two fine nickname options complete the package: down-to-earth Ted and artistic Theo.

Thomas

1940s: #8

1900 Today

Popularity: #36
Style: Biblical, Timeless
Nicknames: Tom, Tommy
Variants: Tomas
Sisters: Patricia, Mary, Linda, Theresa, Kathryn
Brothers: Richard, Peter, James, Robert, Paul

✷ Thomas was a monster hit in the '30s and '40s, yet unlike other favorites of that time, it doesn't sound the slightest bit stodgy. It continues to be one of the strongest, purest classic choices for boys.

Tiernan

Popularity: Rare
Style: Celtic, The -ens,
Nickname-Proof, Why Not?
Variants: Tiarnan, Tierney

rarely used

1900 Today

Sisters: Aisling, Riona, Larkin, Alannah, Keelin
Brothers: Riordan, Brogan, Teague, Niall, Finian

✷ Tiernan's an authentic, lively Irish boy's name that has yet to be discovered in the U.S. Catch it while you can!

Till

Popularity: Rare
Style: Brisk and Breezy, German/Dutch
Sisters: Elke, Tyne, Bay, Britt, Lise

rarely used

1900 Today

Brothers: Lars, Holt, Bram, Leif, Joss

✷ This quick and catchy German name crosses over comfortably to English. Tillman is a possible extension.

Timothy

1960s: #13

1900 Today

Popularity: #77
Style: Biblical, New Classics, Surfer Sixties
Nicknames: Tim, Timmy
Sisters: Kimberly, Michelle, Valerie, Tamara, Kelly
Brothers: Jeffrey, Steven, Michael, Kevin, Gregory

✷ Timothy has a lyrical sound and is a firmly masculine classic. That's a much-sought-after combination today, so it's surprising to see Timothy's popularity dropping. If you love Nicholas and Zachary, Timothy's a strong alternative to consider.

Tobias

2003: #501

1900 Today

Popularity: #501
Style: Antique Charm, Biblical
Nicknames: Toby
Variants: Tobiah, Tobin
Sisters: Carolina, Lydia, Felicity, Amabel, Patience
Brothers: Jude, Josiah, Caleb, Eli, Jonas

✷ If you're looking for a rustic aura, Tobias is an absolute winner. It's less of a mouthful than Ezekiel or Jedidiah, and the nickname Toby is adorable for a bouncing baby boy.

Tobin

Popularity: Rare
Style: The -ens, Last Names
First, Why Not?
Nicknames: Toby
Sisters: Devyn, Rory, Marlo, Darcie, Lea
Brothers: Brogan, Trevin, Leif, Galen, Corbin

1970s: #840

✳ This is an offbeat choice yet plays well to current fashions. It's an Irish surname as well as a variant of Tobias, and has a young and playful sound.

Toby

Popularity: #439
Style: Nicknames,
Shakespearean, Surfer Sixties
Variants: Tobey
Sisters: Angie, Trina, Jodi, Amy,
Lara
Brothers: Jamie, Brad, Heath, Jody, Tad

1970s: #231

✳ This was one of the '60s to '70s "cute boy" names. It was ready to fade away until *Spiderman* star Tobey Maguire nudged it back into the spotlight. Toby was originally a nickname for Tobias, and with the renewed popularity of biblical classics, that's currently the most stylish way to use the name.

Todd

Popularity: #519
Style: Surfer Sixties
Variants: Tod
Sisters: Tracy, Dana, Dawn,
Jodi, Renee
Brothers: Scott, Troy, Kurt, Craig, Brad

1960s: #31

✳ Todd was a sturdy favorite for a generation, masculine but not heavy-handed. It ran with a gang of similar young colts like Scott and Kurt. All are still solid choices, but their sharp crunch is giving way to new smooth-edged names like Reese and Lane.

Tony

Popularity: #303
Style: Mid-Century, Nicknames
Sisters: Laurie, Cindy, Carla,
Tina, Becky
Brothers: Greg, Marty, Dino,
Ricky, Rod

1960s: #50

✳ For generations, scores of parents have left Anthony, Antonio, and friends by the wayside and written Tony right on the birth certificate. The name's rough-and-ready cheer is timelessly appealing. If you picture the name on a corporate résumé, though, Anthony still reads better.

Trace

Popularity: #499
Style: Brisk and Breezy,
Country & Western
Sisters: Brynn, Aspen, Shea,
Cheyenne, Tess
Brothers: Beau, Ty, Cash, Shane, Rhett

2003: #499

✳ Reclaim the masculinity of Tracy with this clever creation. Country music star Trace Adkins was one of the many boys to be named Tracy in the '60s, only to be swamped by the avalanche of girls with that name. His moniker Trace neatly clips the name into a completely male form.

Travis

Popularity: #160
Style: Country & Western,
Nickname-Proof
Sisters: Amanda, Holly, Bridget,
Vanessa, Tabitha
Brothers: Derek, Casey, Shane, Dustin, Brett

1980s: #44

✳ Travis is an old surname that once had a fancy-pants sound. It has toughened up so thoroughly that it now sounds like a rowdy cowboy. The name hit its peak in the '80s but still has plenty of strength.

Trent

Popularity: #248
Style: Brisk and Breezy
Sisters: Logan, Tessa, Macy,
Paige, Alana
Brothers: Brock, Landon, Drake, Reid, Trevor

2001: #209

✳ Trent is the blunt weapon of the zippy names. Let Chase and Cole toss off bon mots at cocktail parties. Trent has no time for that frippery. A good name for a man of action, but tough to cuddle up to.

Trenton

Popularity: #181
Style: The -ens, Place Names
Nicknames: Trent
Sisters: Jazmin, Brooklyn,
Ashlyn, Skylar, Savanna
Brothers: Landon, Colton, Lane, Devon,
Grayson

2003: #181

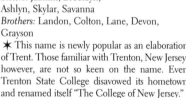

✳ This name is newly popular as an elaboration of Trent. Those familiar with Trenton, New Jersey, however, are not so keen on the name. Even Trenton State College disavowed its hometown and renamed itself "The College of New Jersey."

Trevor 1990s: #65

Popularity: #100
Style: Celtic, English, Nickname-Proof
Variants: Trever
Sisters: Morgan, Paige, Alexandra, Jenna, Chloe
Brothers: Alec, Connor, Garrett, Tristan, Colin
✳ This name has a British upper-crusty ring to it, yet it's not a bit stuffy. On a young boy, in fact, it sounds playful and rough-and-tumble. That side of the name is coming to the forefront with a flock of new little Trevors.

Trey 2002: #217

Popularity: #229
Style: African-American, Brisk and Breezy
Sisters: Kyra, Shea, Reese, Macy, Jade
Brothers: Ty, Lane, Quint, Jalen, Drew
✳ This name, formed from the word *three*, is a traditional nickname for a "third": John Smith III, whose dad and grandpa have already claimed the nicknames Johnny and Jack. It can also be applied to a third child or third son in a family. As a given name, it's still zippy but less preppy.

Tristan 2002: #104

Popularity: #113
Style: English, The -ens, French
Nicknames: Tris
Variants: Tristram, Tristen
Sisters: Chloe, Gillian, Elise, Fiona, Claire
Brothers: Colin, Trevor, Brice, Gavin, Sebastian
✳ Until recently, this French/English classic was one Americans chose to view from afar. Elegant Tristan was most likely to be spotted gamboling through a golden field in a Merchant-Ivory production. Elegance is in vogue now, and Tristan has become a U.S. favorite while keeping its literary style intact.

Troy 1960s: #57

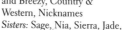

Popularity: #259
Style: Surfer Sixties
Sisters: Tina, Robin, Dana, Heidi, Dawn
Brothers: Darren, Todd, Scott, Kip, Brad
✳ In the late '50s, a studio executive suggested that handsome young actor Merle Johnson change his name to Troy Donahue. A heartthrob was born, and so was a glossy hit name. The name is no longer young, but it still has a golden-boy style. *The Simpsons'* "actor Troy McClure" poked fun at that very image.

Truman 1910s: #371

Popularity: Rare
Style: Last Names First, Why Not?
Sisters: Adele, Nola, Nell, Marion, Bess
Brothers: Edison, Foster, Harris, Newton, Fletcher
✳ Unlike his presidential predecessor Franklin Roosevelt, Harry Truman didn't inspire many namesakes. In fact, the name Truman virtually disappeared after he took office. It's an appealingly genuine name and is worth a fresh look today. As for Harry himself, he's not a bad sort to be linked to: a regular bloke who rose to the occasion and surpassed the world's expectations.

Tucker 2001: #289

Popularity: #297
Style: Last Names First
Nicknames: Tuck
Sisters: Kiley, Logan, Darby, Tessa, Bailey
Brothers: Sawyer, Corbin, Parker, Tanner, Hudson
✳ This tradesman name (it means a cloth finisher) is especially cheerful. Its sound suggests pluck and luck. Of course, it also suggests other -uck words, as the kids in the playground will surely point out.

Turner 2001: #840

Popularity: Rare
Style: Last Names First
Sisters: Marley, Lillie, Hadley, Laney, Clare
Brothers: Porter, Lawson, Coleman, Walker, Lincoln
✳ Turner is just beginning to make its mark as a first name. It has a sly toughness that should keep it climbing. No good nickname, though: Picture shouting "Turn!" in a crowded room.

Ty 2003: #193

Popularity: #193
Style: African-American, Brisk and Breezy, Country & Western, Nicknames
Sisters: Sage, Nia, Sierra, Jade, Lexi
Brothers: Zane, Trey, Cole, Trace, Rhett
✳ The nickname Ty can come from any number of sources. Just scan the list: Tyler, Tyson, Tyrone, and Tyree are only a few of the popular options. All of them have different images and different baggage. Many parents are just skipping the choice altogether and leaping straight to merry, rambunctious Ty.

Tyler 1990s: #9
Popularity: #15
Style: Androgynous, Last Names First
Nicknames: Ty
Variants: Tylor
Sisters: Haley, Taylor, Kayla, Bailey, Ashton
Brothers: Devin, Hunter, Trevor, Cody, Logan
★ Tyler is one of the defining names of its generation. It led a charge of fashionable "tradesman" names and is still their reigning king. It's also tops among the fifteen popular presidential surnames. Names that rise as far and fast as this can fall just as quickly. But for now, you can rest assured that Tyler is solidly beloved, mainstream, and tease-proof.

Tyree 2001: #527
Popularity: #556
Style: African-American
Nicknames: Ty
Sisters: Tiana, Aleah, Kenia, Tatyana, Asia
Brothers: Jovan, Deshawn, Tyrell, Donte, Jamar
★ You can't just mention this name casually. It's a blast of energy that demands to be the focus of any sentence. And it's on the rise, with a boost from popular novelist Omar Tyree.

Tyrell 1990s: #408
Popularity: #554
Style: African-American
Nicknames: Ty
Variants: Tyrel, Terrell
Sisters: Larissa, Kayla, Tyra, Janelle, Alisha
Brothers: Stephon, Trevon, Quinton, Desmond, Kendrick
★ Tyrell combines the surname style of Tyler with the strong ending of Darnell and Latrell. It also shares the popular nickname Ty with a host of new names such as Tyrese and Tyshawn. With all those likenesses, this is a name that blends in seamlessly with its surroundings.

Tyrone 1970s: #150
Popularity: #551
Style: African-American, Celtic
Nicknames: Ty
Sisters: Regina, Adrienne, Yolanda, Tanya, Rochelle
Brothers: Cedric, Terrance, Roderick, Lamont, Reginald
★ Tyrone, a county in Ireland, became a popular name thanks to actors Tyrone Power, Sr., and Jr. It originally had a slick Celtic panache, which around 1960 evolved into a slick African-American panache. The name's enduring charisma has spawned a flock of similar "Ty" names.

Tyson 2003: #296
Popularity: #296
Style: The -ens, Last Names First
Nicknames: Ty
Sisters: Taryn, Alissa, Kiley, Jazmin, Kiara
Brothers: Bryant, Weston, Bryson, Tucker, Devon
★ This name is a perfect strike at the heart of current trends. It gives you a crisp surname with the hot nickname Ty. And for pure fashion credentials, you can't beat a pair of top male models (Tyson Beckford and Tyson Ballou). All of those positives are finally outweighing the name's less attractive associations, like infamous boxer Mike Tyson and Tyson packaged chicken parts.

Ulysses 1900s: #399
Popularity: Rare
Style: Exotic Traditional, Mythological, Nickname-Proof
Sisters: Athena, Evangeline, Salome
Aurora, Genevieve, Salome
Brothers: Augustus, Leopold, Constantin, Magnus, Napoleon
★ I can already hear the grandparents howling in dismay. "Ulysses? You're naming MY grandson Ulysses?!!" It's a bold stroke all right, and not even softened by an easy nickname. But if you're looking for classical panache, you've absolutely found it.

Van 1940s: #323
Popularity: Rare
Style: Brisk and Breezy, Solid Citizens
Sisters: Dale, Nita, Nan, Aurea, Kay
Brothers: Lon, Rex, Clark, Glyn, Royce
★ Parents who are drawn to hot new creations like Jair and Cael might want to take a look back at this oldie but goodie.

Vance 1960s: #401
Popularity: #743
Style: Brisk and Breezy, Timeless
Sisters: Anita, Laney, Margo, Lana, Gwen
Brothers: Dean, Byron, Blaine, Clay, Vaughn
★ An uncommon name with generations of tradition behind it. Originally a surname, Vance is as brash as newcomers like Bryce and Chance but less faddish. It sounds tough enough for a rodeo and posh enough for a dinner jacket and martini.

Vaughn

1940s: #460

Popularity: #809
Style: Brisk and Breezy, Celtic, Last Names First, Timeless
Variants: Vaughan, Von
Sisters: Glenda, Rosalind, Alys, Gwen, Margot
Brothers: Glynn, Rex, Gerard, Ivor, Vance

✻ This Welsh surname is an elegant choice, just uncommon enough for an element of surprise. It's smooth and mellow in a gentlemanly style.

Vernon

1920s: #67

Popularity: #976
Style: African-American, Solid Citizens
Nicknames: Vern, Verne
Sisters: Maxine, Dorothy, Loretta, Frances, Jeanette
Brothers: Roland, Bernard, Leon, Eugene, Gordon

✻ This fine old surname has slowly slipped into the ranks of the fusty. Its full version is still elegant, but nickname Vern emphasizes the same nasal sound that sent names like Merle and Ernie out of fashion.

Victor

2003: #95

Popularity: #95
Style: Latino/Latina, Timeless
Nicknames: Vic
Variants: Viktor
Sisters: Isabel, Amelia, Cecilia, Elena, Julia
Brothers: Vincent, Samuel, Edgar, Simon, Ivan

✻ Truly timeless, never trendy, Victor is the perfect gentleman. The name deserves more attention for its winning combination of worldly sophistication and a good old-fashioned nickname. Like Hector, Victor is currently most popular with Latino parents.

Vincent

1910s: #73

Popularity: #117
Style: French, Saints, Timeless
Nicknames: Vince, Vinnie, Vin, Chente
Variants: Vincente, Vicente, Vincenzo
Sisters: Julia, Marina, Catherine, Antonia, Claire
Brothers: Victor, Martin, Miles, Ivan, Julian

✻ One of the classic gentlemanly names, with a devilish elegance that sets it apart. (Vincent Price was a sterling example.) Vince and Vinnie are familiar nicknames, but action star Vin Diesel helps make Vin the most contemporary choice.

Virgil

1910s: #99

Popularity: Rare
Style: Ladies and Gentlemen, Porch Sitters
Variants: Vergil
Sisters: Eunice, Verna, Eula, Hester, Opal
Brothers: Wilbur, Horace, Enoch, Clyde, Otis

✻ In the nineteenth century, the names Virgil and Horace were bestowed as sophisticated homages to the classics. They held their footing for a while—longest with African-American families—but now they're virtually extinct. The virgin-like sound is an extra hurdle for Virgil.

Wade

1960s: #217

Popularity: #563
Style: Brisk and Breezy, Timeless
Sisters: Dina, Leigh, Shelly, Angela, Wendy
Brothers: Vance, Curt, Byron, Darryl, Todd

✻ The bad news is that Wade is not in fashion. The good news is that it has *never* been in fashion. This is a name that doesn't follow trends but just takes its own quiet path. It's an understated alternative to Cade, Trace, and Gage.

Walden

rarely used

Popularity: Rare
Style: Last Names First, Place Names
Nicknames: Wally
Sisters: Acadia, Linden, Willa, Mercy, Amabel
Brothers: Whitman, Lennox, Birch, Merrick, Soren

✻ Line up, nature and literature lovers: Here's a creative choice that makes a statement, gently. The nod to Thoreau's idyll is clear, but Walden sounds so natural as a boy's name that it's not too big a stretch.

Walker

2001: #406

Popularity: #417
Style: Antique Charm, Last Names First, Nickname-Proof
Sisters: Piper, Regan, Mercy, Phoebe, Lilian
Brothers: Bennett, Davis, Harrison, Colman, Pierce

✻ Walker offers the surname flair of popular choices like Parker and Tanner without the bandwagon trendiness. Its secret is its long history as an American first name, with forebears like photographer Walker Evans lending depth. And in a name style that tends toward androgyny, Walker is still reliably masculine.

Wallace 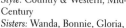1920s: #96

Popularity: Rare
Style: Ladies and Gentlemen
Nicknames: Wally
Sisters: Harriet, Marian, Sybil, Willa, Muriel
Brothers: Chester, Bertram, Gilbert, Emory, Earnest

✱ Wallace is a kindly gentleman in an age of breezy rascals. The name still sounds handsome, just a little behind the times.

Walter 1900s: #11

Popularity: #356
Style: Ladies and Gentlemen
Nicknames: Walt, Wally
Sisters: Alice, Helen, Esther, Frances, Edith
Brothers: Arthur, Louis, Ernest, Henry, Albert

✱ On one hand, Walter is clearly out of style. You expect a Walter to be enjoying his well-earned retirement. On the other hand, if you met a boy named Walt, you would think that was pretty darned cool. If you want a Walt but aren't ready to revive Walter, consider Walton.

Walton 1920s: #549

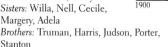

Popularity: Rare
Style: Last Names First
Nicknames: Walt, Wally
Sisters: Willa, Nell, Cecile, Margery, Adela
Brothers: Truman, Harris, Judson, Porter, Stanton

✱ Reconfigure Walter to get this attractive sur-name. It's a trendier sound, but gives you the same friendly nickname Walt.

Warren 1920s: #51

Popularity: #497
Style: Nickname-Proof, Solid Citizens, Timeless
Sisters: Vivian, Eileen, Rita, Marian, Marjorie
Brothers: Gordon, Leonard, Alvin, Raymond, Russell

✱ Warren skyrocketed when Warren G. Harding was elected president in 1920. That's not the brightest star to hitch your wagon to, but Warren had the broad-based appeal to hang on and become an American classic. Today, the name is slowly fading into grandpa status, but is still a solid, conservative choice.

Wayne 1940s: #33

Popularity: #589
Style: Country & Western, Mid-Century
Sisters: Wanda, Bonnie, Gloria, Jo, Sally
Brothers: Gerald, Bruce, Larry, Ronald, Darryl

✱ Simple and swift, Wayne is a zippy grandpa name. Its glory days were from the '30s to the '50s, when western star John Wayne was riding tall. The name is slowing down today, but as a cowboy homage it can still work.

Wesley 1980s: #101

Popularity: #185
Style: Last Names First, Timeless
Nicknames: Wes
Sisters: Lindsay, Whitney, Kristen, Courtney, Lacy
Brothers: Marcus, Jesse, Bryant, Clayton, Bradley

✱ Wesley was originally used to honor Methodist Church founder John Wesley, but it's now well established as a secular name with a preppy style. Action movie star Wesley Snipes has lent it some much-needed toughness, and the nickname Wes helps tone down the preppiness.

Weston 2002: #385

Popularity: #408
Style: The -ens, Last Names First
Nicknames: Wes
Sisters: Kiley, Ashton, Tyler, Aubrey, Mallory
Brothers: Dalton, Darien, Schuyler, Lane, Grayson

✱ This name is like a dream of aristocracy. Unlike the similar choice Austin, Weston's air of privilege isn't tempered by a Texas twang. Easton takes the pampering a step further.

Wilbur 1910s: #95

Popularity: Rare
Style: Porch Sitters
Nicknames: Willie
Variants: Wilber
Sisters: Eunice, Velma, Bernice, Florine, Eula
Brothers: Virgil, Morris, Orville, Elbert, Buford

✱ The combination of the pig in *Charlotte's Web* and the image of Mr. Ed neighing "Willllburrr" makes this arguably the twerpiest name in America.

William

1920s: #4

1900   Today

Popularity: #11
Style: Timeless
Nicknames: Bill, Billy, Will, Willy
Variants: Willem, Wilhelm, Liam
Sisters: Mary, Margaret, Cecelia, Anna, Catherine
Brothers: James, Joseph, Edward, Robert, Charles

✷ Dominant a century ago, William has remained a robust, adaptable classic. It's distinguished but not a bit stuffy. The nickname Bill was among the essential twentieth-century names, while the smoother Will looks like a twenty-first-century winner. Among such trend-setting groups as Ivy Leaguers and uptown New Yorkers, the name is soaring.

Willis

1910s: #136

1900   Today

Popularity: Rare
Style: Ladies and Gentlemen, Last Names First, Solid Citizens
Nicknames: Will
Sisters: Adela, Muriel, Cecile, Rhea, Marian
Brothers: Foster, Harris, Truman, Edison, Murphy

✷ Like Wallace, Willis can come across as a well-mannered fellow who's a generation behind the times. But unlike Wallace, Willis has a fashionable nickname (Will vs. Wally) that helps bring it up to date. Other strong choices in this vein include Ellis and Harris.

Wilson

1910s: #154

Popularity: #507
Style: Last Names First, Timeless
Nicknames: Will

1900   Today

Sisters: Kathryn, Leslie, Ruth, Aubrey, Kate
Brothers: Marshall, Ellis, Clifton, Miller, Watson

✷ Wilson has been a slow but steady American classic. (Its only spike came during Woodrow Wilson's tenure in the White House.) Despite generations of use, it still sounds primarily like a last name.

Winston

1940s: #370

1900   Today

Popularity: #880
Style: Last Names First
Nicknames: Win, Winnie
Sisters: Penny, Charlotte, Delta, Margery, Dahlia
Brothers: Barclay, Branson, Talmadge, Grady, Truman

✷ The top associations for this name are a British prime minister, a pack of cigarettes, and stock-car racing. The result is a name with a split personality, part prep school boy and part good ole boy.

Wolf

Popularity: Rare
Style: Exotic Traditional, German/Dutch
Variants: Wolfe, Vulf, Velvel

rarely used

1900   Today

Sisters: Elke, Lark, Elsbeth, Astrid, Anja
Brothers: Bram, Ivor, Aldric, Till, Lazar

✷ Charisma is not the problem here: This name is loaded with animal magnetism. It's traditional, too, and distinguished, in a ferocious sort of way. You just have to decide if you want your son's name to stick out so prominently from the pack.

Wyatt

2003: #111

Popularity: #111
Style: Country & Western, Nickname-Proof
Sisters: Faith, Carolina, Scarlett, Sierra, Mariah

1900   Today

Brothers: Zane, Colton, Bryce, Jonah, Caleb

✷ Wyatt is rawhide tough, but polished enough for the big city. One of the strongest and most versatile of the retro-cowboy names.

Wynn

Popularity: Rare
Style: Brisk and Breezy, Celtic
Variants: Wynne, Wyn

rarely used

1900   Today

Sisters: Bryn, Carys, Tyne, Alys, Rhian
Brothers: Keir, Emlyn, Steffan, Rhys, Teague

✷ This Welsh favorite can be used for boys and girls alike. It should have smooth sailing as an American name.

Xander

2003: #237

Popularity: #237
Style: Nicknames
Variants: Zander
Sisters: Sienna, Willow, Lexi, Reese, Lizbeth
Brothers: Jaxon, Zane, Kobe, Griffin, Jace

✱ Start with the surging popularity of the name Alexander. Add a national love affair with the letter X. Then throw in a seductive TV vampire. The result is a charismatic overnight name sensation—cool and modern to many ears, but forced and silly to others. Choosing Alexander with the nickname Xander avoids that.

Xavier

2003: #84

Popularity: #84
Style: African-American, French, Saints
Nicknames: Xavy
Variants: Javier, Zavier, Xzavier
Sisters: Paloma, Ivy, Fabiola, Ione, Athena
Brothers: Sebastian, Dominic, Elias, Fabian, Maximilian

✱ You love the eye-catching panache of this X name. But you're stunned to discover it is one of the fastest-rising hit names in America! It's even spawning spin-offs, like Alexavier and Xzavier. Yes, Xavier is not as distinctive as it once was, but it's still plenty cooler than the pack. The traditional English pronunciation is "ZAY-vee-uhr," the religious and X-*men* version ex-AY-vyer.

Zachariah

1990s: #322

Popularity: #390
Style: Biblical, Exotic Traditional
Nicknames: Zach, Zack, Zak
Variants: Zechariah, Zacharias, Zachary
Sisters: Annabella, Rebekah, Clarissa, Patience, Michaela
Brothers: Ezekiel, Demetrius, Nathanael, Levi, Jedediah

✱ This form of Zachary leaves no doubts about the name's biblical roots. Like Jeremiah vs. Jeremy, Zachariah sounds more antique than Zachary, and a whisker trendier.

Zachary

1990s: #16

Popularity: #20
Style: Biblical, New Classics
Nicknames: Zach, Zack, Zak
Variants: Zachery, Zackary, Zakary, Zachariah
Sisters: Samantha, Miranda, Abigail, Rachel, Alexandra
Brothers: Nicholas, Joshua, Alexander, Gabriel, Nathaniel

✱ It's almost hard to believe that in the first half of the twentieth century, no one was being named Zachary. Zack has made an astonishingly quick leap from relic to classic in the U.S. It's now the epitome of biblical cool.

Zane

2003: #220

Popularity: #220
Style: Brisk and Breezy, Country & Western
Variants: Zayne, Zane
Sisters: Sage, Skye, Alexa, Kyra, Zoey
Brothers: Bryce, Trey, Gage, Griffin, Ty

✱ Wandering the plains in search of Z's, parents have recently crossed paths with this charming cowboy. It's only surprising that it didn't happen sooner.

Zeb

Popularity: Rare

rarely used

Style: Biblical, Nicknames
Variants: Zebedee, Zebediah, Zebulon
Sisters: Zilla, Lyra, Edie, Pru, Arlie
Brothers: Zeke, Jem, Baz, Jed, Lev

✱ Trim yet audacious, Zeb takes a step past Zach and Zeke into the land of the truly unusual. If you want to take a step even farther, use the full name Zebedee.

Zion

2001: #325

Popularity: #336
Style: Modern Meanings
Sisters: Selah, Isis, Lyric, Serenity, Star
Brothers: Phoenix, Tyme, Maximus, Orion, Justice

✱ Zion is a biblical term for the promised land. For Rastafarians, it means a utopia or heaven on earth, and it is also widely associated with the drive for a Jewish homeland. Zion wasn't often considered as a name until musicians Lauryn Hill and Rohan Marley (son of Rasta legend Bob Marley) chose it for their son. Scores of parents are now following their example.

Style Families

African

This is an ethnically and linguistically diverse category of names, reflecting the cultures of an entire continent. The origins of specific African names can be challenging to track, with multiple meanings or spellings in different communities. Even the boy/girl division below isn't set in stone, as many of the names are used androgynously in Africa or America. What you *can* count on is that the names below have genuine African origins as first names, and are attractive and easy to pronounce in English. (One pronunciation note: The names beginning with Th- are typically pronounced with a hard T sound, and could be spelled that way for clarity.) In some cases the name featured is a popular short form of longer names, such as Emeka for Nnaemeka and Chukwuemeka.

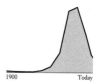

If you're interested in English names with an African connection, consider that Old Testament names such as Elisha and Moses and virtue names such as Charity, Gracious, and Rejoice are popular among Christian Africans. For names of Islamic origin that are common in Africa, see the Muslim name section.

AFRICAN GIRLS

Aaliyah	Ashanti	Kamaria	Nakia	Tanisha
Ajani	Ayanda	Kenyatta	Nia	Thandeka
Akilah	Ayanna	Maisha	Safiya	Thandi
Amani	Dineo	Malaika	Shani	
Amari	Imani	Masika	Sindi	

AFRICAN BOYS

Achebe	Amari	Bakari	Dumisani	Jabari
Ade	Asante	Baraka	Emeka	Jali
Amachi	Ayo	Chima	Femi	Jelani

Kabelo	Kofi	Odion	Shola	Thulani
Kani	Kwame	Omari	Tayo	
Kijana	Neo	Sabelo	Thabo	

African-American

Pop quiz: Which is the African-American name?
A. Devonte
B. Imani
C. Antoine
D. Michael
E. All of the above

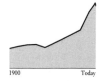

1900   Today

The answer, of course is E: All of the above. Devonte is a modern, uniquely African-American creation. Imani is a Swahili name that many American parents have chosen to reflect their African heritage. Antoine is distinctly French, but an African-American favorite as well. And Michael? That cross-cultural classic has no particular ethnic association at all—but it's the number-one name for African-Americans over the past fifty years.

African-American names are an integral part of America's name tapestry, with styles and traditions that weave in and out of the broader trends around them. Common themes include:

African and Muslim Names. A natural choice to honor a child's African ancestry. Favorites include Imani, Kareem, and Aisha, and African place names such as Kenya.

French and Italian Names. Names from romance languages have flourished, often with creative spellings. Top choices: Antoine/Antwan, Monique, Dante/Donte, Germaine/Jermaine.

Hero Names. Names from African-American history are popular choices to encourage children to take pride in their heritage. Booker (T. Washington) and Marcus (Garvey) were common in earlier generations; Malcolm (X) and Zora (Neale Hurston) are more recent selections.

Combination Names. Blending two names to create one has been an African-American tradition. Basketball player Brevin Knight's name, for instance, is taken from his parents Brenda and Melvin. Other prominent examples include Joycelyn (Elders) and Steveland (Morris, better known as Stevie Wonder).

Biblical Names. Especially popular for boys. Lyrical favorites include Elijah and Emmanuel.

Meaning Names. Uplifting words are chosen to inspire (Justice, Journey) or to sparkle (Diamond, Miracle).

Created Names. New inventions abound, often echoing the rhythms of popular African or European names. Name elements tend to sweep in and out of style, creating trademark generational sounds. (Remember all the La- names of the '70s?) Recent favorites include Trevon, Jakayla, and Tyrese.

Such creative, distinctly African-American names have been staples since the rise of the Black Power movement in the late '60s. The names are popular, but they're also controversial. On the positive side, many parents consider inventions like Shanika and Jojuan a joyful form of creative expression. Fans of these names describe them as part of the African-American improvisational tradition, in line with jazz and hip-hop. A created name can also be a special gift from parent to child, a loving statement about the child's uniqueness.

However, others in the African-American community have criticized invented names as rootless and even frivolous. Beyond the issue of style, many worry that such complex and unusual names will be a barrier to success for children who already face obstacles based on the color of their skin. Will a Devonte get the same opportunities as a David? A recent study dramatically illustrated the reality of "name discrimination." Researchers sent out 5,000 résumés, half with names that were judged to sound black, half that sounded white. The "white" resumes received 50 percent more calls for interviews.*

This kind of name-based prejudice is hardly new. Throughout history, names have been scrutinized as markers of race, class, religion, and social standing. Back in the Middle Ages, the name Joan became so popular that it was considered coarse and "common," and well-to-do families turned to Jane instead. In America a century ago, Irish classics like Bridget were shunned as servant names, while Jewish immigrants gave their sons fancy British surnames like Seymour and Milton hoping they'd be accepted by the Anglo upper classes.

Snap judgments based on names continue today. What's changed is that we're also taking pride in our diverse identities. Parents want their children to find success and acceptance, but they don't want to bury their heritage to achieve it. The latest generation of African-American names includes many that hit both targets. You'll find names with

---

* Marianne Bertrand and Sendhil Mullainathan, "Are Emily and Greg More Employable than Lakisha and Jamal? A Field Experiment on Labor Market Discrimination," MIT Department of Economics Working Paper Series No. 03–22 (May 2003).

African and Muslim origins, such as Nia and Jasmine, that are sliding smoothly into the cross-cultural realm of power names. And Americans as a whole are naming more creatively. Black parents have been the trendsetters for some of America's hottest name styles, notably biblical rediscoveries like Isaiah and affirmation names like Destiny.

The names below have all found favor among African-American parents in the past forty years. For more ideas in particular style areas, refer also to the chapters on Islamic names, African names, meaning names, and biblical names.

GIRLS

Aaliyah	Damita	Justice	Nevaeh	Tamia
Adrienne	Deja	Kaliyah	Nia	Tamika
Aisha	Demetria	Kamilah	Nyla	Tanisha
Aja	Desiree	Kayla	Raven	Taniya
Alisha	Destiny	Keisha	Regina	Tasha
Alondra	Diamond	Kendra	Renae	Tatyana
Amani	Dominique	Kenya	Renita	Tawana
Amari	Ebony	Kiana	Rhonda	Tiana
Angel	Ericka	Kiara	Rochelle	Tonya
Anita	Essence	Kizzy	Rolanda	Toya
Aniyah	Imani	Ladonna	Sade	Trina
Antoinette	India	Lakeisha	Shalonda	Tyra
Aretha	Iyana	Larissa	Shameka	Vanessa
Ariana	Jacquelyn	Lashonda	Shani	Venetia
Ashanti	Jada	Latasha	Shanice	Wanda
Asia	Jakayla	Latonya	Shaniya	Yolanda
Ayanna	Jalisa	Latoya	Shante	Yvette
Beyonce	Jaliyah	Latrice	Shantel	Yvonne
Brandi	Jamila	Laverne	Sharonda	Zaria
Brianna	Jamya	Leticia	Sheree	Zina
Chantal	Janay	Lyric	Shonda	Zora
Charisse	Janelle	Marguerite	Simone	
Charlene	Janiya	Monique	Sojourner	
Corrine	Jasmine	Nakia	Taliyah	
Daisha	Jayla	Natasha	Tamela	

BOYS

Ahmad	Alonzo	Andre	Antwan	Cortez
Akeem	Amari	Antoine	Cedric	Courtney

Croix	Dominique	Jerome	Marcus	Rohan
Dante	Donnell	Jordan	Marlon	Romare
Darian	Dwayne	Josiah	Marquis	Savion
Darius	Earl	Jovan	Martin	Shamar
Darnell	Elijah	Kadeem	Marvin	Shaquille
Darryl	Elisha	Kareem	Maurice	Sharif
Davion	Ervin	Keenan	Mekhi	Stephon
Davon	Freeman	Kelvin	Melvin	Tariq
Deandre	Hakeem	Kendrick	Nakia	Terrance
Deangelo	Irvin	Kenyatta	Omar	Terrell
Dedrick	Isaiah	Keyshawn	Omari	Torrance
Dejuan	Jabari	Khalid	Omarion	Trae
Demarcus	Jaheim	Kobe	Otis	Tremayne
Demetrius	Jalen	Kwame	Patrice	Trevon
Denzel	Jamal	Latrell	Prince	Ty
Deon	Jamar	LeBron	Quincy	Tyree
Derrick	Jamari	Leon	Quinton	Tyrell
Deshawn	Jaquan	Leroy	Raheem	Tyrese
Desmond	Jaquez	Lionel	Rashad	Tyron
Devon	Jaron	Luther	Rasheed	Tyrone
Devonte	Javon	Mahlon	Reggie	Vernon
Dewayne	Jayden	Malachi	Reginald	Xavier
Diamond	Jeremiah	Malcolm	Roderick	Zaire
Dion	Jermaine	Malik	Rodney	

Androgynous

Parents seek out androgynous names—names used for both sexes—for practical, philosophical, and aesthetic reasons. On the practical end, there are expectant parents who choose just one name and plan to use it regardless of the sex of the baby. Others like the practical idea of a name that, on a document like a résumé, will raise no preconceptions about the person's sex. As a philosophical matter, choosing an androgynous name can be a statement of your belief in gender equality. And as a matter of fashion, these names attract parents with their contemporary flair.

The idea of a one-size-fits-all name, though, has come around before. Back in the '20s and '30s, a little Frankie, Tommie, or Bennie was as likely to be a girl as a boy. For their parents, there was no philosophical debate required—boyish names just sounded modern and fun.

But notice that even back then, wanting an androgynous name meant wanting a *boyish* name. Androgyny may sound like a move toward equality, but in reality it's usually a move toward the masculine. Historically, male names have been adapted or adopted for girls: Georgia and Josephine, Carla and Stephanie, Jamie and Shawn. The reverse is virtually unheard of. (Even Mario, which looks like a male counterpart of Maria, actually comes from the Latin Marius.)

The blunt truth is that a cross-gender association is perceived as "strong" for girls, "weak" for boys. As soon as a name starts to tip to the female side, parents of boys abandon it.

For parents seeking equal opportunity for their daughters, choosing a masculine name may send a mixed message. It could point to a world without boundaries or stereotypes, but it could also reinforce the idea that strength has to mean masculinity. Think of the strongest women you've known . . . what were their names? Surely a Margaret or Diana sounds at least as formidable as a Jaime or Peyton.

Below is a menu of androgynous name possibilities, new and old. When you choose one, regardless of practical or philosophical concerns, choose it because you love it. A name that stirs a parent's soul is a great start in life for any child, boy or girl.

Addison	Billie	Dakota	Gene	Jordan
Alex	Bobbie	Dale	Germaine	Joss
Alexis	Britt	Dallas	Gerry	Joyce
Angel	Brody	Dana	Guadalupe	June
Arden	Cameron	Darby	Harley	Justice
Arley	Carmen	Darcy	Hayden	Kai
Ariel	Carroll	Daryl	Hillary	Kelly
Arlis	Carson	Devin	Hollis	Kelsey
Ashley	Casey	Diamond	Hunter	Kendall
Ashton	Chandler	Dominique	Jackie	Kennedy
Aubrey	Charlie	Drew	Jaden	Kerry
Augustine	Clancy	Elisha	Jaime	Kim
Avery	Cody	Ellery	Jalen	Kolby
Bailey	Connie	Emlyn	Jessie	Kristian
Berkeley	Corey	Emory	Jewel	Larkin
Beryl	Courtney	Fay	Jody	Lavin
Blair	Cruz	Gale	Joey	Lee

Leslie	Micah	Ray	Rylee	Stevie
Logan	Mickey	Reagan	Sage	Sydney
London	Montana	Reese	Sammie	Taylor
Loren	Morgan	Ricki	Sandy	Terry
Lupe	Nakia	Riley	Shannon	Tory
Lyn	Paris	Ripley	Shawn	Tracy
Mackenzie	Parker	Robin	Shea	Tyler
Madison	Pat	Ronnie	Shelby	Valentine
Mallory	Peyton	Rory	Sheridan	Vivian
Meredith	Presley	Rosario	Skyler	Whitney
Merle	Quinn	Ryan	Stacy	

Antique Charm

What do names like Sophie, Elias, and Amelia have in common? They're old-fashioned. They're fashionable. And they're fashionable *because* they're old-fashioned.

Alongside the thousands of young Jaydens and Aaliyahs in America, you'll meet many youngsters with names straight out of a nineteenth-century nursery. In part, that reflects a natural generational cycle. Our parents' names sound boring, our grandparents' names sound old. But with our *great*-grandparents' names, things start to get interesting. We view them from enough distance that we can appreciate them anew.

Of course, our great-grandparents' generation of names was every bit as diverse as today's. The names we're reviving are a select group, loaded with sweet, lilting girls' names (Lily yes, Gertrude no) and elegant but lively choices for boys (Oliver yes, Elbert definitely not). The effect is like old tintype portraits in which the past comes to life dressed exclusively in its Sunday best.

Choosing an antique name is choosing to honor the best parts of the past. The sweet names are sweeter, the dignified names more dignified, because they're steeped in generations of meaning. The first place to look is in your own family tree. Reviving a great- or great-great-ancestor's name personalizes the connection to the past. For more ideas (or if you happen to come from a long line of Elberts and Gertrudes), here is the *Wizard* list of antiques that are polished and ready for the twenty-first century.

GIRLS

Abigail	Carolina	Emma	Julia	Molly
Adeline	Caroline	Esmeralda	Katharina	Nora
Amelia	Catalina	Eva	Lena	Olivia
Angelina	Cecily	Evelyn	Lila	Patience
Anna	Charity	Georgia	Lilla	Phoebe
Annabella	Charlotte	Grace	Lillian	Rose
Annabel	Chloe	Hannah	Lily	Sadie
Annalise	Clara	Hazel	Lucy	Sophia
Annie	Cora	Isabel	Lydia	Sophie
Astrid	Daisy	Isabella	Madeline	Stella
Ava	Eleanor	Ivy	Maeve	Victoria
Bella	Eliza	Jewel	Mariah	Violet
Belle	Ella	Josephine	Michaela	Willa

BOYS

Abraham	Elijah	Jonas	Maxwell	Solomon
Adrian	Everett	Josiah	Oliver	Theo
Caleb	Ezekiel	Julian	Oscar	Tobias
Dominic	Ezra	Julius	Owen	Walker
Edgar	Gabriel	Leo	Pierce	
Eli	Isaiah	Levi	Porter	
Elias	Jasper	Max	Silas	

Bell Tones

Listen to parents calling out names at your local playground and it may sound like bells chiming. The sharp clang of a consonant launches clear, bright long vowels: Bay-lee! Cay-den! Ja-cey! It's the distinctive chorus of our time.

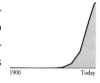

The Bell Tone names aim for freshness with a clean, light touch. They're 180 degrees removed from the Orvilles and Velmas of the "Porch Sitter" era. While a few traditional names like Bailey and Hayden fit the new fashion, many parents are striking out on their own to custom-build names for their children.

The handful of most desirable sounds have become like Lego bricks, a few simple pieces configured into an endless variety of new forms. More than thirty currently popular girls' names start with the sound "Kay" alone, and the hundreds of common Bell names *end* with just three different sounds: -ah (Jayla, Kiana), -ee (Kasey, Haylee), and -n (Jaden, Katelyn). The similarity of all the sounds is balanced by a tremendous diversity of spellings. You're equally likely to meet a young Jalen, Jalon, Jailyn, Jalynn, Jaylin, Jaylyn, Jaylon, or Jaelyn. And that child is equally likely to be a boy or a girl.

You'll find plenty of admirers for these names, regardless of spelling. But with such a small set of sounds being shaped and reshaped into so many names, they're starting to blur together. Jakayla sounds like a whole generation of kids rolled into one. For the Bell Tone names, though, the rule of thumb is "if it feels good, do it." Take the list of common versions below as a starting point.

GIRLS

Ainsley	Haylee	Kaiya	Kiana	Makayla
Ashlyn	Jacey	Kaliyah	Kierra	Mayra
Ayla	Jada	Katlyn	Kiley	Shayla
Aylin	Jaden	Kaya	Kiya	Shayna
Bailey	Jakayla	Kayla	Kyla	Skyla
Caitlin	Jalyn	Kaylee	Kylie	Tayla
Caleigh	Janae	Kaylin	Kyra	Tyra
Camryn	Jayla	Keely	Lacey	
Haley	Kacie	Kelsey	Laney	
Hayden	Kaitlyn	Kenzie	Macy	

BOYS

Ayden	Caden	Jaden	Kelby	Layton
Bailey	Colby	Jalen	Kian	Payton
Braden	Corey	Javen	Kieran	
Brady	Daly	Kadin	Koby	
Brayden	Hayden	Keaton	Kylan	

Biblical

Biblical roots are so fundamental to our name culture that this may hardly seem like a style at all. Of the ten most popular names in America today, seven are straight out of the Bible. When you look at the top

names of the century, it's six out of ten. But those are
not the *same* top names, and that's where the tale of
biblical style turns interesting.

The Bible has two main sections, known to
Christians as the Old and New Testaments. (The
Christian Old Testament corresponds to the Jewish Hebrew Bible, or
Tanakh.) A handful of New Testament names were dominant favorites
in the English-speaking world for centuries. In England, the popularity
of a few core names once reached epidemic proportions. During the
1700s, John and Mary alone accounted for a quarter of English babies.
Those two names led America's 100-year hit list as well.

Now take a look at the top biblical names today: Jacob, Michael, and
Joshua. Michael appears in both Testaments, while Jacob and Joshua
trumpet their Old Testament origins. John and Mary, meanwhile, are
out of the top ten altogether. Today, what's Old is new.

The rising popularity of Old Testament names has dramatically
changed their image. Just a generation ago, brothers named Josh and
Ethan sounded solidly Jewish—and brothers named Josiah and Caleb
sounded positively ancient. Today both pairs sound simply contemporary, with no specific religious association.

What's the secret to these names' broadened appeal? The Old
Testament names are familiar and traditional but were mostly ignored in
our parents' generation. Thus they sound antique (Jonas) or unconventional (Ezra) rather than just plain old. Even among New Testament
names, the hottest choices are those that were most neglected early in
the twentieth century. Matthew and Luke are rapidly overtaking Mark
and John.

If you love biblical names, you can now feel free to dig deep into
your concordance. Names that once sounded clunky or even shocking
are finding a whole new life. With Ezekiel and Delilah soaring, almost
anything goes.

OLD TESTAMENT GIRLS

Abigail	Bethel	Elisheva	Jemima	Mehitabel
Adah	Beulah	Esther	Jerusha	Miriam
Adina	Carmel	Eve	Jezebel	Naomi
Amana	Deborah	Hadassah	Judith	Noemi
Atara	Delilah	Hannah	Keziah	Rachel
Avital	Dinah	Havilah	Leah	Rebecca
Bathsheba	Elisha	Jael	Mara	Rebekah

Rochelle	Sarai	Tamara	Zilla
Ruth	Shifra	Vashti	Zipporah
Sarah	Tamar	Yael	

OLD TESTAMENT BOYS

Aaron	Daniel	Hiram	Jonas	Omar
Abdiel	David	Hosea	Jonathan	Phineas
Abel	Ebenezer	Isaac	Joseph	Raphael
Abner	Ehud	Isaiah	Joshua	Reuben
Abraham	Eli	Ishmael	Josiah	Samson
Abram	Eliezer	Israel	Judah	Samuel
Absalom	Elijah	Jabez	Kenan	Saul
Adam	Elisha	Jacob	Laban	Seth
Adlai	Elon	Jamin	Lemuel	Simeon
Ahijah	Enoch	Japheth	Levi	Simon
Amos	Enos	Jared	Mahlon	Solomon
Asa	Ephraim	Jedidiah	Malachi	Tobias
Asher	Ephron	Jemuel	Micah	Uriah
Azarel	Ethan	Jeremiah	Michael	Uriel
Azriel	Ezekiel	Jeremy	Mordecai	Zachariah
Barak	Ezra	Jeriah	Moses	Zachary
Baruch	Gabriel	Jesse	Naphtali	Zeb
Benjamin	Gershon	Jethro	Nathan	
Boaz	Gideon	Joah	Nathaniel	
Caleb	Hezekiah	Joel	Nehemiah	
Cyrus	Hillel	Jonah	Noah	

NEW TESTAMENT GIRLS

Anna	Dorcas	Junia	Martha	Susana
Aquila	Drusilla	Lois	Mary	Tabitha
Berenice	Elisheva	Lydia	Priscilla	
Bernice	Elizabeth	Magdalena	Rhoda	
Bethany	Eunice	Maria	Salome	
Damaris	Joanna	Marie	Sapphira	

NEW TESTAMENT BOYS

Aeneas	Barnabas	Emmanuel	Jesus	Juan
Andrew	Barnaby	Erastus	John	Jude
Artemas	Bartholomew	Gabriel	José	Justus
Balthazar	Crispus	James	Joseph	Lazarus

Lucas	Matthias	Paul	Thaddeus	Zachary
Lucius	Michael	Peter	Theophilus	Zebedee
Luke	Nathanael	Silas	Thomas	
Mark	Nathaniel	Simon	Timothy	
Matthew	Nicodemus	Stephen	Titus	

Brisk and Breezy

Swift, light, one-syllable names give off an aura of well-being. Many sound rich and preppy (Blair), while others are windswept cowboys (Shane), but all share a healthy glow along with their brisk sound.

The prototypical Brisk and Breezy name, in fact, sounds like the word "brisk." Start with the burst of a hard consonant, then settle into a gentle landing. The effect is a name that's vigorous but doesn't overexert itself. You know the type: the straight-A student who never cracks a book, the quarterback who doesn't break a sweat as the game clock winds down. These cool customers make success look easy.

This category has a contemporary feeling, but its blithe image has held steady for generations. Think of Western stars Dale and Roy riding the range, or Cole Porter's effortless elegance. Nonetheless, some parents find the names a little lightweight. A popular solution is to create a longer formal version, like Coleman for Cole or Brycen for Bryce. Also consider these one-syllable wonders for middle names, where they can lighten up the whole package.

GIRLS

Bay	Dale	Lark	Quinn	Tyne
Blair	Elle	Leigh	Reese	Wynne
Bree	Greer	Lise	Sage	
Britt	Jade	Lynn	Shea	
Brooke	Joss	Neve	Skye	
Brynn	Kaye	Paige	Sloane	

BOYS

Baird	Beck	Blaise	Brant	Brice
Baz	Blaine	Blake	Brent	Brooks
Beau	Blair	Bond	Brett	Bryce

Burke	Dex	Joss	Quinn	Tate
Cade	Drake	Jude	Rand	Teague
Cal	Drew	Kai	Reese	Thane
Cale	Finn	Kane	Reid	Till
Cash	Flynn	Keane	Rex	Trace
Chance	Gage	Keir	Rhett	Trent
Chase	Glyn	Lance	Rhys	Trey
Chaz	Graeme	Lane	Ross	Ty
Clay	Grant	Lee	Royce	Van
Clint	Hale	Leif	Rune	Vance
Clive	Hart	Luke	Ryne	Vaughn
Cole	Hayes	Mace	Sage	Von
Colt	Heath	Max	Shane	Wade
Dane	Jace	Nash	Shay	Watt
Dax	Jair	Pierce	Spence	Wynn
Dean	Jett	Piers	Taft	Zane

Celtic

In the 1990 U.S. Census, the number of Americans reporting to be of Irish ancestry exceeded the total population of Ireland. The key to that remarkable statistic is *reporting*. Most American families today have a mixed ethnic background. If half or even a quarter of that background is Irish (or Scottish or Welsh), chances are that's how people will describe themselves. Americans want to sound Celtic, because today Celtic is cool.

Just what a Celtic name is, though, is up to debate. The ancient Celts gave rise to a whole family of languages and peoples, most prominently the Irish and Scots (who spoke Gaelic) and the Welsh. Many of the names we think of as Celtic, like Patrick and Kathleen, are Anglicized descendants of Celtic originals. In the U.S., longtime favorite Kathleen has now yielded to the old Gaelic version Caitlin, which in Gaelic is pronounced more like . . . Kathleen. And other favorites are Celtic words or surnames that only became given names in America.

In today's Ireland, long-absent Gaelic names have roared back into fashion and share the stage with English standards. The number-one name in Ireland and Scotland is Jack, just as in England. But Sian,

Darragh, and Oisin are also trendy for Irish boys, and Aoife, Niamh, and Caoimhe for girls. (If those spellings give you pause, call them Sean, Dara, Osheen; Eva, Neeve, Kiva.) In Scotland, Callum and Liam are popular boys' choices, while the top names for girls all mirror American favorites. Top Welsh names include Dylan and Rhys for boys, Megan and Ffion (FEE-on) for girls.

The list below includes Gaelic revivals, familiar standards, and Celtic surnames that have been pressed into service as first names. If you're looking for a little Celtic flavor, you're bound to find something to your liking.

GIRLS

Aine	Casey	Glenda	Logan	Rhiannon
Ainsley	Catriona	Glynis	Mackenzie	Riley
Aisling	Ciara	Grainne	Maeve	Riona
Alannah	Cliona	Grania	Maisie	Roisin
Alys	Colleen	Gwendolyn	Maura	Ryan
Anwen	Dara	Iona	Maureen	Shannon
Aoife	Deirdre	Isla	Mckenna	Shawn
Bethan	Dilys	Kathleen	Megan	Shea
Brenda	Eileen	Keelin	Maire	Sheila
Brenna	Eleri	Kelly	Mhairi	Sinead
Bridget	Emlyn	Kendall	Moira	Siobhan
Bronwyn	Erin	Kennedy	Morgan	Tamsin
Brynn	Fallon	Kerensa	Muriel	Una
Caitlin	Ffion	Kerry	Nia	Wynne
Cameron	Finola	Kiara	Niamh	
Caoimhe	Fiona	Leslie	Nora	
Carys	Gladys	Lilias	Rhian	

BOYS

Aidan	Brian	Clancy	Darby	Dougal
Alec	Broderick	Colin	Darragh	Douglas
Alistair	Brogan	Colm	Daveth	Duane
Angus	Bryce	Colman	Declan	Duncan
Archibald	Callum	Conan	Denzil	Dylan
Baird	Camden	Connor	Dermot	Eamon
Brannock	Cameron	Conor	Desmond	Egan
Brendan	Carson	Cormac	Donal	Emlyn
Brennan	Casey	Craig	Donovan	Evander

Ewan	Griffith	Kevin	Neil	Sean
Fergus	Hamish	Kian	Niall	Shane
Fife	Ian	Kieran	Oisin	Shannon
Finbar	Ivor	Kilian	Owen	Sian
Finian	Kane	Lachlan	Patrick	Steffan
Finlay	Keane	Liam	Quinlan	Sullivan
Finn	Keegan	Llewellyn	Quinn	Tam
Forbes	Keenan	Logan	Reid	Tavis
Gareth	Keir	Lorcan	Rhodri	Tavish
Garrett	Keith	Lyle	Rhys	Teague
Gavin	Kelly	Macaulay	Riley	Tiernan
Gawain	Kelvin	Mackenzie	Riordan	Torquil
Glenn	Kendall	Magnus	Rohan	Trevor
Glyn	Kendrick	Malachy	Ronan	Tyrone
Graeme	Kennedy	Malcolm	Rory	Vaughn
Graham	Kenneth	Mervyn	Rowan	Wynn
Gregor	Kermit	Morgan	Ryan	
Griffin	Kerry	Murphy	Seamus	

Charms and Graces

The traditional feminine ideals of grace, beauty, and propriety have found natural reflections in girls' names. Propriety was the focus for the Puritans, who favored virtue names like Patience and Chastity. In the late-Victorian era, the craze was to celebrate tender beauty with names like Lily, Grace, and May.

The Charms and Graces names slid to the background in the mid–twentieth century as a cuter, more girlish femininity was in vogue. Today the names are back, in two distinct flavors. The downy Victorian favorites are part of an antique revival, chosen alongside sweet old-timers like Sophie and Annabel. Meanwhile, a new crop of word-based beauties is showing off a bold modern version of the feminine ideal that the Puritans could scarcely imagine. Instead of Pearl and Dove, we have Diamond and Raven. That bolder style inches toward a unisex vision—you'll see a growing crop of nature names for boys as well. For more on contemporary word-names, see the Modern Meanings style.

GIRLS

Acacia	Dawn	Honor	Mae	Rose
Amber	Diamond	Honoré	Magnolia	Rosemary
Amity	Dove	Hope	Mahogany	Ruby
April	Ebony	Iris	Marigold	Sage
Autumn	Emerald	Ivory	May	Senna
Azure	Esperanza	Ivy	Meadow	Serenity
Bay	Faith	Jade	Melodie	Sienna
Bonnie	Felicity	Jasmine	Mercy	Silver
Calla	Fern	Jewel	Merry	Spring
Cassia	Fleur	Joy	Myrtle	Summer
Charity	Flora	June	Olive	Tierra
Chastity	Garnet	Juniper	Opal	Topaz
Clover	Ginger	Lark	Pansy	Tuesday
Constance	Golden	Laurel	Patience	Verity
Coral	Grace	Lavender	Pearl	Violet
Crystal	Hazel	Lily	Prudence	Willow
Dahlia	Heather	Linden	Raven	Zinnia
Daisy	Holly	Lotus	Robin	

BOYS

August	Earnest	Garnet	Jet	Stone
Birch	Flint	Hart	Phoenix	Storm
Canyon	Forest	Heath	River	Talon
Diamond	Frost	Jasper	Sterling	

Country & Western

Welcome cowpokes, gunslingers, and braves! Home-
steaders, madams, forty-niners, come on in and put your
boots up. There's room for all at the Naming Saloon.

The American West is more than a place: It's a
dream. We close our eyes and imagine wide-open skies,
endless prairie, and men who can mount a horse from a third-story win-
dow. We also picture a world more wild than our own, closer to nature,
where you build your home and your livelihood with your own two
hands. That combination of hard work and personal freedom makes for
a uniquely American mythology. The Country & Western names are as

varied a bunch as Shania Twain, Ma Ingalls, and Jesse James, but they're all rooted in our shared American dreams.

The most popular country names today are Wild West throwbacks like Wyatt and geographical names like Aspen. They're the strongest links to the romance of the frontier and the ideal of boundless opportunity. The Nashville-style names may sound less bold, but their down-home hospitality is always welcome.

WILD WEST: GIRLS

Casey	Cassidy	Oakley

WILD WEST: BOYS

Beau	Cody	Lane	Rusty	Wiley
Bo	Colt	Levi	Shane	Woody
Buck	Colton	Luke	Stetson	Wyatt
Casey	Dillon	Mack	Tex	Zane
Cash	Jed	Maverick	Trace	
Cassidy	Joss	Ranger	Ty	
Clint	Judd	Rory	Wayne	

THE LAND: GIRLS

Abilene	Cheyenne	Montana	Shasta	Virginia
Aspen	Georgia	Savannah	Shenandoah	
Carolina	Laramie	Sedona	Sierra	

THE LAND: BOYS

Branson	Canyon	Dallas	Phoenix
Bridger	Coty	Denver	Reno
Bryce	Dakota	Houston	Ridge

NASHVILLE: GIRLS

Delta	Faith	Lucille	Scarlett
Dixie	Larue	Magnolia	Shania
Dolly	Leanne	Reba	Winona

NASHVILLE: BOYS

Bubba	Gaylon	Jarvis	Rhett	Waylon
Earl	Hardy	Lamar	Roy	
Garth	Hoyt	Merle	Travis	

English

Proud sons and daughters of England, prepare to cringe. When I speak of English names, I'm not referring to origins in the Old English language or prominence in English history or culture. I'm not even thinking of names commonly used in England, since those overlap so broadly with American favorites. What is meant here by an English name is a name that by style, tradition, or stereotype sounds English to American ears. This is not the England of geographical reality; it is the England of our imagination.

For the record, the most popular names in the *real* England today include sturdy old-fashioned boys' names like Jack, Samuel, and Thomas, and sweet throwbacks like Chloe, Emily, and Sophie for girls. But what fun is that?

The England of our imagination is a literary place, full of drawing-room mysteries and perfectly proper romances. Historically it cuts across periods from Jane Austen to J. K. Rowling, but its epicenter is a 1920s and '30s world of gentility in decline. (Think Evelyn Waugh meets Agatha Christie.) The men are a mixture of upstanding gentlemen, cads, and aesthetes, but all are dapper. The ladies are, above all, ladylike. Servants scuttle in the background in a mood of muffled discontent.

It may be more *Masterpiece Theatre* than England, but it's a potent cultural image with a set of names to match. Some of the names benefit from the association. Sebastian and Graham, for instance, float on a cloud of refinement. Others, like Percival and Dudley, get the short end of the stick as ineffectual milquetoasts. For girls, the choice is typically sweet (Charlotte) or forbidding (Agatha). Sit back to read and enjoy, with some biscuits and clotted cream.

GIRLS

Agatha	Cecily	Eliza	Henrietta	Sidony
Amabel	Charlotte	Enid	Jemima	Tamsin
Amelia	Chloe	Felicity	Lettice	Venetia
Anthea	Christabel	Fiona	Nicola	Verity
Araminta	Cordelia	Flavia	Penny	Victoria
Beatrice	Dahlia	Gemma	Philippa	Winifred
Beatrix	Daphne	Gillian	Phyllida	
Camilla	Dulcie	Glynis	Pippa	

Alec	Clive	Gareth	Neville	Simon
Alfie	Colin	Garrett	Nigel	St. John
Alistair	Corin	Gerard	Niles	Stuart
Alwyn	Crispin	Giles	Oliver	Tad
Ambrose	Davy	Godfrey	Percival	Tarquin
Auberon	Dexter	Graham	Piers	Terence
Barnaby	Dudley	Hugh	Robin	Trevor
Basil	Dunstan	Ivor	Roderick	Tristan
Carleton	Edgar	Jonty	Rupert	Tristram
Cecil	Edmund	Julian	Sebastian	

The -ens

This group of names earned its own category by sheer brute force. If you want to know how mild-mannered Ethan muscled its way to the top of the charts, how Laurens came to outnumber Lauras four to one, or why there are now *seven* spellings of Braden among the 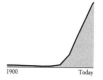 top-1,000 boys' names, look to the power of the -en. (Still reeling over the Bradens? It's Braden, Bradyn, Braeden, Braedon, Braiden, Brayden, and Braydon, if you're keeping score at home.)

America is in love with two-syllable names ending in "n." Beyond the seven Bradens, there are over twenty variations of Aidan, Caden, Hayden, and Jaden, enough to fill a whole rhyming classroom. We haven't seen this kind of dominant naming sound since Ida, Ada, Ora, Iva, Ola, and a dozen others took the 1900s by storm.

The love affair with N cuts across styles, from old-timers like Nathan to new inventions like Brycen. It cuts across races and sexes. We love the -en names because they are compact, upbeat, and accessible. And they are everywhere. If the style speaks to you, you should find your little piece of Heaven, or Eden, below.

GIRLS

Arden	Aylin	Carson	Fallon	Jaden
Ashlyn	Brooklyn	Devin	Golden	Jaelyn
Ashton	Caitlin	Eden	Haven	Jaidyn
Aspen	Camryn	Emlyn	Heaven	Jaylin

Jazlyn	Kaitlyn	Kirsten	Madilyn	Regan
Jazmin	Kathlyn	Kristen	Madison	Ryan
Jillian	Katlyn	Larkin	Megan	Tamsin
Jocelyn	Kaylin	Lauren	Morgan	Taryn
Jordan	Keelin	Linden	Payton	Teagan
Joslyn	Kiersten	London	Raven	

BOYS

Aidan	Camron	Dillon	Jalen	Morgan
Alan	Canton	Dorian	Jaron	Nathan
Alban	Carson	Draven	Javen	Nolan
Alden	Carsten	Duncan	Jaxon	Owen
Alton	Cason	Dunstan	Jordan	Paxton
Alwyn	Chayton	Dustin	Justin	Peyton
Arden	Christian	Dylan	Keaton	Quentin
Ashton	Clayton	Eamon	Keegan	Quinlan
Austin	Clinton	Easton	Keenan	Quinton
Balin	Colin	Egan	Kellen	Riordan
Bannon	Colman	Elden	Kelton	Rohan
Baron	Colton	Elkan	Kenton	Ronan
Bevan	Conan	Elton	Kenyon	Ryan
Boston	Corbin	Emlyn	Kian	Rylan
Braden	Corin	Ethan	Kieran	Soren
Brandon	Crispin	Evan	Kingston	Stetson
Brannon	Cullen	Ewan	Kylan	Talon
Branson	Dallin	Faron	Landon	Tarian
Brendan	Dalton	Galen	Larson	Tevin
Brennan	Damon	Gannon	Lavin	Tiernan
Brenton	Darian	Gavin	Lawson	Timon
Britton	Davin	Glendon	Layton	Tobin
Brogan	Dawson	Grayson	Logan	Trenton
Bronson	Dayton	Griffin	London	Trevin
Bryson	Deon	Hayden	Lorcan	Tristan
Byron	Devin	Holden	Mahlon	Tyson
Caden	Devon	Jackson	Marlon	Weston
Camden	Dillion	Jaden	Mason	

Exotic Traditionals

Ordinary is not for you. You want a name that stands out from the pack, that people will associate with your child alone. Yet you roll your eyes at new inventions with wild spellings—you want a name with roots and resonance. Where to turn?

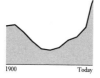

1900   Today

The "Exotic Traditionals" strike a familiar chord yet have the ability to raise a few eyebrows. Some have artistic or literary pedigrees. Others are foreign names ready for import, or ancients awaiting resurrection. A few are popular, a few downright eccentric, but not a one is merely ordinary.

GIRLS

Aida	Charis	Hermione	Monserrate	Tamar
Amabel	Christabel	Iolanthe	Octavia	Thomasina
Anaïs	Cleo	Iole	Olympia	Valentina
Angelique	Damaris	Ione	Paloma	Valentine
Apollonia	Danae	Isadora	Philomena	Violetta
Araminta	Delilah	Isis	Phyllida	Viva
Ariadne	Domicela	Leilani	Portia	Xanthe
Artemisia	Drusilla	Leocadia	Salome	Xanthia
Astrid	Elodie	Lilias	Sapphira	Zelda
Athena	Esme	Linnea	Sarai	Zena
Aurora	Evangeline	Lorelei	Scarlett	Zenobia
Averil	Flavia	Lourdes	Severina	Zilla
Beatrix	Genevieve	Lucretia	Sidony	Zola
Bronwyn	Glynis	Mehitabel	Siobhan	Zora
Catalina	Guinevere	Minerva	Tallulah	

BOYS

Absalom	Alonzo	Axel	Cedric	Dominick
Adelard	Aloysius	Barnabas	Constantin	Elias
Adolphus	Alphonso	Barnaby	Cornelius	Eliezer
Aeneas	Andreas	Bartholomew	Cosmo	Emmanuel
Aidric	Antony	Beauregard	Damian	Ephraim
Alaric	Artemas	Benedict	Dashiell	Erasmus
Aldric	Atticus	Bram	Demetrius	Erastus
Algernon	Auberon	Casimir	Desmond	Evander
Alistair	Augustus	Cassius	Dimitri	Ezekiel

Ezra	Ishmael	Magnus	Peregrine	Thaddeus
Fabio	Ivor	Malachi	Philo	Thelonius
Falco	Jabez	Marcellus	Phineas	Theophilus
Felix	Japheth	Marius	Piers	Theron
Ferdinand	Jasper	Matthias	Quinton	Titus
Florian	Jedidiah	Maxim	Raphael	Torquil
Galen	Joachim	Maximilian	Regis	Tristram
Garth	Justus	Milo	Roman	Ulysses
Gawain	Lafayette	Montague	Romeo	Wolf
Gervase	Lazar	Montgomery	Samson	Zachariah
Gideon	Lazarus	Napoleon	Severin	Zebedee
Hannibal	Leander	Nicodemus	Simeon	
Horatio	Leif	Niels	Stanislaus	
Ignatius	Lucian	Orlando	Tarquin	
Isaias	Lucius	Pascal	Tavish	

Fanciful

Are the Exotic Traditionals not exotic enough for you?
Take a step beyond into the realm of the whimsical and
spectacular with the names below. They come in a
variety of breeds: the heroic (Apollo), the flattering
(Charisma), the trademarked (Lexus), and the just
plain "out there" (Atom). All take a pinch of chutzpah to use, all make
a bold statement, and none will be easily forgotten.

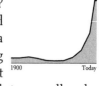

1900   Today

GIRLS

Aeron	Bliss	Electra	Lyric	Queen
Allure	Blossom	Eternity	Madonna	Rainbow
Andromeda	Breeze	Fantasia	Marvel	Riviera
Apple	Chanel	Fifi	Miracle	Saffron
Armani	Chardonnay	Gidget	Moon	Silver
Artemis	Charisma	Heart	Nautica	Star
Aura	Cinderella	Heaven	Nova	Sunday
Avalon	Cinnamon	Honey	Oceana	Sunrise
Bambi	Cleopatra	Isis	Odyssey	Taffeta
Bathsheba	Coco	Lexus	Precious	Tempest
Bijou	Echo	Lotus	Princess	Unique

| Valentine | Velvet | Whisper |
| Vega | Venus | Xena |

BOYS

Achilles	Caspian	Lando	Orion	Shadow
Adonis	Champion	Lex	Orpheus	Sherlock
Ajax	Cicero	Loyal	Peerless	Sinbad
Aladdin	Columbus	Mace	Peregrine	Sincere
Albus	Everest	Magic	Phoenix	Sirius
Altair	Fox	Major	Pilot	Spike
Apollo	General	Marquis	Prince	Tarzan
Aramis	Geronimo	Mars	Prospero	Thor
Aristotle	Gulliver	Marvel	Ranger	Triton
Atom	Halston	Maverick	Ransom	Truth
Baron	Heathcliff	Maximus	Rio	Tyme
Bishop	Hermes	Mercury	River	Valentine
Blaze	Indigo	Merlin	Rock	Wisdom
Blue	Judge	Michelangelo	Royal	Zenith
Caesar	Jupiter	Neo	Saber	Zodiac
Canyon	Lancelot	Noble	Sargent	

French

For Americans, France has always spelled sophistication. Fashions change, but in each age we find French names to capture the moment's ideal of high style. In the early 1900s, that meant stately gentlefolk like Jules and Cecile. In the middle of the century, we created bubbly girls' names by using cute French endings. Voilà, Janine and Suzette, bright and cheery. A generation later, the favorite feminine forms had a slinkier elegance: Danielle, Monique, Nicole.

What's up next? The most intriguing French names in America are either antique or completely new to our shores. For parents with a traditional streak, the turn-of-the-century heirlooms are full of charm. Jules and Cecile are still rare names, but they're coming up on the fashion horizon. For parents on the hunt for something new, the hot choices are French names that sound exclusively French—the less familiar the better. Names like Giselle and Anaïs are climbing.

If your goal is to be in fashion on the streets of Paris today, a good rule of thumb is to go short and light. Forget Antoinette and Marguerite. Names like Léa and Lucas are trendy hits in France and throughout Europe.

GIRLS

Adele	Chantal	Gigi	Lucille	Patrice
Adrienne	Christine	Giselle	Madeleine	Paulette
Aimee	Claire	Helene	Maelle	Pauline
Amelie	Clementine	Heloise	Manon	Renée
Anaëlle	Colette	Honorée	Marcelle	Rosalie
Anaïs	Coralie	Isabelle	Margot	Sabine
Angelique	Corinne	Jacqueline	Marguerite	Salome
Annette	Danielle	Jeanne	Marianne	Sandrine
Anouk	Delphine	Jeannette	Marie	Simone
Antoinette	Denise	Jeannine	Marine	Sophie
Aurore	Desiree	Joelle	Marion	Suzette
Avril	Dominique	Julie	Mathilde	Sylvie
Axelle	Elise	Julienne	Melanie	Therese
Beatrice	Elodie	Juliette	Michele	Valerie
Bernadette	Eloise	Justine	Monique	Violette
Blanche	Estelle	Lea	Nadine	Vivienne
Brigitte	Eugenie	Léonie	Nathalie	Yvette
Camille	Fifi	Leontine	Nicole	Yvonne
Cecile	Fleur	Lise	Nicolette	
Celeste	Gabrielle	Lisette	Noelle	
Celestine	Genevieve	Louise	Noémie	
Celine	Germaine	Lucienne	Océane	

BOYS

Adrien	Blaise	Fabien	Gustave	Luc
Alain	Brice	Fabrice	Henri	Lucien
Alexandre	Christophe	Fernand	Hugo	Marcel
Alphonse	Claude	Florian	Jacques	Mathieu
Andre	Clement	François	Jean	Maurice
Antoine	Damien	Frederic	Jerome	Nicolas
Armand	Denis	Gaston	Jules	Noe
Bastien	Didier	Georges	Julien	Noel
Benoit	Dominique	Gerard	Laurent	Olivier
Bertrand	Emile	Guillaume	Loïc	Pascal

Patrice	Raoul	Roland	Thibaut	Xavier
Phillipe	Regis	Romain	Tristan	Yann
Pierre	Rémy	Sébastien	Valentin	Yannick
Quentin	Rene	Sylvain	Vincent	

German/Dutch

A century ago, stout German classics like Bertha and Herman were the height of fashion in America. Today, they're not even fashionable in Germany.

Throughout Europe, there is a rising trend toward names in the "international" style: smooth classics without any strong ethnic association. Think of them as the name equivalents of the euro. Nowhere is that trend stronger than in Germany, where *none* of the top baby names are distinctively German. The chart-toppers include Alexander, Paul, and David for boys, Julia, Laura, and Sarah for girls. If a name trendy in Germany does have an ethnic style, it's more likely Italian or French than German. You'll find the same development to a large extent in Austria and Switzerland. The Netherlands is something of an exception, with Dutch names like Daan, Bram, Sanne, and Femke still top choices, but international favorites are climbing.

The heaviest Germanic classics are unlikely choices in the United States today, but some of the lighter names, unheard in the heyday of Bertha and Herman, make attractive and imaginative selections. In fact, the more the rest of the world loads up on French and Italian names, the fresher names like Anneliese, Elke, and Bram will sound.

GIRLS

Alina	Christiane	Gisela	Inge	Manuela
Anja	Claudia	Greta	Ingrid	Margit
Anke	Dagmar	Gretchen	Johanna	Margot
Anneliese	Elke	Hannelore	Karin	Mariel
Astrid	Elsa	Heidi	Lena	Meta
Bertha	Elsbeth	Helga	Liselotte	Mina
Bettina	Femke	Hilde	Lisbeth	Petra
Brigitta	Franziska	Hildegard	Lotte	Renate
Christa	Gertrude	Ida	Magdalena	Sabine

Sanne	Sophie	Verena		
Sigrid	Ursula	Wilhelmina		

BOYS

Andreas	Dieter	Georg	Josef	Sigmund
Anton	Dietrich	Gerhard	Jurgen	Soeren
Armin	Dirk	Gregor	Karl	Stefan
Arno	Egon	Gunnar	Klaus	Till
Artur	Emil	Günther	Kurt	Ulrich
Benno	Erich	Hannes	Lars	Volker
Bernhard	Ernst	Hans	Lorenz	Werner
Berthold	Evert	Heinz	Marius	Wilhelm
Bertram	Fabian	Henrik	Markus	Wolf
Bram	Florian	Hermann	Matthias	Wolfgang
Bruno	Franz	Horst	Niels	
Carsten	Friedrich	Jan	Otto	
Detlef	Fritz	Johann	Rainer	

Greek

Greece remains a land of traditional names. The cus-
toms of the Greek Orthodox Church combined with a
formal tradition of family namesakes keep the classic
Greek names on birth certificates generation after generation. Fashions and fads show up fastest in nick-

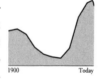

names, which can be especially important in families where a single
given name appears as a grandma, aunt, and cousin.

The current nickname trends in Greece are foreign and exotic. A
Greek Anastasia, for instance, may go by the Russian nickname Natasha.
Yet the Greek names that sound most exotic to Americans, the names of
the major ancient deities, are actually a bit dowdy back in the homeland.
Athena is the Greek equivalent of Martha.

With lyrical, literary names in fashion in America, Greece is a blos-
soming source of ideas. Anastasia and Dimitri already make an impeccable pair of siblings, and Evanthia and Andreas could be right around
the corner.

Anastasia	Despina	Irene	Rania	Zoe
Anthi	Dimitra	Irini	Sofia	
Athanasia	Ekaterini	Kalliopi	Sotiria	
Athena	Eleni	Katerina	Theodora	
Danae	Evanthia	Melina	Xristina	

BOYS

Achilles	Athanasios	Evangelos	Nicholas	Stefanos
Alexandros	Christos	Georgios	Nikos	Thanassis
Alexios	Constantinos	Ilias	Panos	Vassilis
Anastasios	Dimitri	Ioannis	Pavlos	
Andreas	Dimitrios	Kostas	Petros	
Antonios	Dimos	Leonidas	Spiros	
Aris	Elias	Marios	Stavros	

Guys and Dolls

Dizzy dames! Stand-up guys! Jazz babies! Gin runners! The Guys and Dolls names remind us there was a lot more to our great-grandparents' time than just ladies and gentlemen sipping tea in their parlors. Names like Lulu, Roxie, Mack, and Rocco paint a portrait of the saucy side of the early twentieth century. They win our hearts with their sheer brio. If you love old-time names but your style is more cheeky than courtly, these are the guys and dolls for you.

1900   Today

GIRLS

Addie	Dell	Emmy	Gilda	Libby
Allie	Della	Etta	Goldie	Lillie
Annie	Delta	Evie	Gracie	Liza
Arlie	Dixie	Fae	Gussie	Lola
Bess	Dolly	Fanny	Hallie	Lottie
Bessie	Dovie	Florida	Hattie	Lucy
Billie	Effie	Flossie	Jonnie	Lula
Birdie	Ella	Freda	Josie	Lulu
Blossom	Ellie	Georgie	Larue	Mabel
Callie	Elsie	Gertie	Lettie	Madge

Mae	Melba	Queenie	Ruby	Susie
Mamie	Millie	Rae	Ruthie	Tess
Margie	Minnie	Reba	Sadie	Tillie
Mattie	Molly	Reva	Sallie	Tommie
Maxie	Nell	Rilla	Sammie	Trixie
Maybelle	Patsy	Rosie	Sophie	Winnie
Mazie	Pearlie	Roxie	Stella	

BOYS

Abe	Buck	Harry	King	Otto
Alf	Bud	Harvey	Leo	Rocco
Arch	Buster	Haskell	Louie	Rocky
Archie	Carmine	Huey	Mack	Sal
Arlo	Charley	Ike	Major	Sammie
Barney	Dewey	Ira	Max	Si
Benno	Dock	Irving	Meyer	Sol
Benny	Duke	Jack	Moe	Vito
Bernie	Eddie	Jake	Mose	Wiley
Bert	Fritz	Jimmie	Nat	Willie
Bruno	Gus	Joe	Ned	

Italian

Italy may be the world's most fashionable name source. Parents around the world are embracing traditional Italian names, thanks to their smooth elegance and boundary-crossing style. Today, a little Enzo is likely to be from Paris, Giovanni from Santo Domingo, and 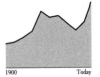 Francesca from Berlin. In the United States, too, baby Leonardos out-number Leonards, and Gianna is a hot new favorite.

Just as with Italian cuisine, Italian names can have distinctive regional flavors. While a Lorenzo or Luisa could hail from any part of Italy, Gennaro is favored overwhelmingly in Naples and Ambrogio is sure to hail from Milan. Owing partly to historical immigration patterns, many names of Italy's South sound old-fashioned in the United States. Characteristic Southern and Sicilian names like Nunzio, Vito, and Concetta have a grandparent style, while Northern names like Giancarlo, Bianca, and Donatella have a contemporary touch that's more glossy than homey.

GIRLS

Alessandra	Daniela	Giovanna	Marcella	Roberta
Alessia	Daria	Gisella	Margherita	Rosa
Antonia	Domenica	Graziella	Maria	Rosanna
Antonina	Donatella	Grazia	Marina	Sandra
Arianna	Elena	Isabella	Marisa	Silvia
Bianca	Emilia	Lia	Michela	Simona
Carla	Felicita	Lidia	Mirella	Stefania
Carmela	Francesca	Liliana	Noemi	Teresa
Caterina	Gabriella	Lucia	Paola	Valeria
Chiara	Gemma	Luciana	Raffaella	Vincenza
Claudia	Gianna	Luisa	Renata	Vittoria
Concetta	Gina	Maddalena	Rita	Viviana

BOYS

Alberto	Cosmo	Gennaro	Luigi	Primo
Aldo	Dante	Giacomo	Marco	Renato
Alessandro	Dario	Giancarlo	Mariano	Rico
Alfredo	Dino	Gianni	Mario	Roberto
Andrea	Donato	Gino	Matteo	Rocco
Angelo	Elio	Giovanni	Mauro	Romeo
Antonio	Emilio	Giuseppe	Michelangelo	Salvatore
Armando	Enrico	Gregorio	Nico	Sergio
Bruno	Enzo	Guido	Nicola	Silvio
Camillo	Ernesto	Guiseppe	Nunzio	Stefano
Carlo	Fabio	Leonardo	Orlando	Tommaso
Carmelo	Fabrizio	Lorenzo	Paolo	Vincenzo
Claudio	Francesco	Luca	Pasquale	Vito
Cosimo	Gaetano	Luciano	Pietro	Vittorio

Jewish

When we talk about a name being "Jewish," the meaning isn't always clear. Compare Irving, a Scottish surname enthusiastically adopted by American Jews, with Ariel, a biblical Hebrew name that most Americans think of as a Disney mermaid. Which one's the Jewish name? And why does it matter?

That back-and-forth between cultural and religious influences carries through many facets of the Jewish naming process. In fact, Jews commonly have two different names, the secular *kinnui* and the religious *shem hakodesh* (or "Hebrew name"). Already, that leaves you with twice as many names to pick out. But for an added wrinkle, many families like to choose religious and secular names that are related, to help link the two sides of life and represent a unified identity. Some will simply choose a single Hebrew name to be used in all contexts. Others choose a translation, a shared meaning, or a similar sound—a process that once turned little Moshe into Morris and today might transform a Shlomo into a Shane.

Beyond the meanings and derivations, there is the day-to-day reality of names that are culturally associated with Jews. Even among biblical names, only a select few—150 names—were traditionally considered suitable models for a Jewish child. That's why Miriam sounds characteristically Jewish, while Vashti does not.

You may be seeking a Jewish-sounding name as a proud cultural calling card for your child. Or you may be avoiding one, fearing discrimination. (For more on "name discrimination," see the section on African-American names.) In either case, you're likely weighing the fate of names like Yitzhak and Freydl in a world full of Daytons and Makaylas.

So where do you find names that satisfy both your American style and your Jewish spirit? The list below is a collection of modern Hebrew names, attractive heirlooms from Jewish heritage, and a few names without religious origins that have been favored by Jewish families. (Consult the biblical section for a list of Hebrew Bible names.) Stylistically, this group runs the gamut. If you're drawn to surnames like Tanner and Haley, check out Asher and Orly. If the old-time names warm your heart, try Hirsch and Leora. And if you're looking for an artistic splash, Raz and Aviva await.

GIRLS

Adi	Chava	Golda	Miriam	Shifra
Adina	Chaya	Hadassah	Nava	Shira
Aliza	Dafna	Haia	Noa	Shoshana
Allegra	Dalia	Ilana	Orly	Talia
Amira	Dina	Keren	Resha	Tova
Ariel	Elisha	Leora	Ronit	Yael
Aviva	Elisheva	Malka	Sadie	Yaffa
Beth	Esther	Margalit	Shani	Ziva

Akiva	Doron	Jaco	Pinchas	Yair
Amir	Dov	Jaron	Raz	Yehuda
Ari	Elan	Lazar	Reuben	Yosef
Ariel	Elisha	Leib	Ronen	Yuval
Asa	Elkan	Mordecai	Saul	Zev
Asher	Gil	Moshe	Shimon	Zvi
Avi	Haskell	Moss	Tal	
Boaz	Hillel	Noam	Tamir	
Chaim	Hirsch	Oz	Uri	

Lacy and Lissome

Femininity takes many forms. It can be sweet or sultry, mature or youthful, bold or demure. And on a really good day, it can be all of them at once.

The "Lacy and Lissome" names capture a particular melodious slice of the feminine spectrum. Even the modern creations among them have an age-old romantic style that could never be mistaken for a male name. These names also, on balance, sound grown up. No "Kitty" or "Buffy" here.

They're old and new, exotic and American-born, but all are clearly and proudly feminine.

Aaliyah	Alina	Annika	Brianna	Eliana
Acadia	Alisa	Antonina	Calista	Elina
Adela	Allegra	Anya	Carissa	Elisha
Adina	Alyssa	Aquila	Cassandra	Felicia
Adriana	Amanda	Arabella	Cassia	Fiona
Alana	Amara	Araminta	Christiana	Francesca
Alejandra	Amaya	Aretha	Clarissa	Gabriela
Alessandra	Amira	Aria	Corinna	Galilea
Alessia	Anastasia	Ariana	Dalia	Giovanna
Alexa	Andrea	Artemisia	Damiana	Graciela
Alexandra	Angelia	Aurea	Dania	Ileana
Alexandria	Angelica	Aviva	Daniela	India
Alexia	Angelina	Ayanna	Davina	Isabella
Alicia	Annabella	Belinda	Deanna	Janessa

..ya	Lilia	Marietta	Rafaela	Sienna
Josefina	Liliana	Marisa	Rianna	Stefania
Juliana	Linnea	Marissa	Rosanna	Talia
Karina	Lisandra	Mattea	Roxanna	Tamara
Katharina	Maddalena	Melia	Sabina	Tatiana
Kiana	Maira	Melina	Samira	Thalia
Kiara	Malia	Melinda	Savanna	Tiana
Larissa	Marcella	Melissa	Selena	Valencia
Lavinia	Mariah	Miranda	Serena	Valeria
Leanna	Mariana	Nadia	Shayla	Vanessa
Leila	Maricela	Natalia	Shayna	Viviana
Leticia	Mariela	Olivia	Shoshana	

Ladies and Gentlemen

The wealthy industrialist. The stern great-aunt. Here are the paragons of stuffy propriety, of heavy gowns and muttonchop whiskers. You may never have met them in person, but they occupy a clear place in your imagination: They are Ladies and Gentlemen, and you could hardly dream of using one of their names on a sweet little baby. Or could you?

Look through the list below, and you may discover that you don't actually *dislike* these names. The worst that can be said is that they're a bit heavy—baked puddings in an age of sorbet. We've already revived the lightest of the turn-of-the-century names, the Lilies and Isabellas, Sams and Maxes. But when everything on the menu is light and refreshing, it's the warm and soothing items that start to stand out. And that's the upside of the stout, slow names: Warmth. Reassurance. Dignity.

Roll them around in your mind for a while. You might find yourself warming to the idea of raising a true little Lady or Gentleman.

GIRLS

Ada	Agatha	Amalia	Aurelia	Cecile
Adela	Alice	Angeline	Avis	Celestine
Adelaide	Allegra	Antoinette	Beatrice	Christabel
Adele	Alma	Audra	Beryl	Clara
Adeline	Althea	Augusta	Blanche	Claribel

Clarice	Eudora	Imogene	Marion	Rowena
Clementine	Eugenia	Inez	Martha	Sybil
Cora	Evangeline	Iona	Matilda	Sylvia
Cordelia	Flora	Iva	Maude	Thea
Cornelia	Florence	Josefa	Millicent	Theda
Delia	Frances	Lavinia	Minerva	Theodora
Delphia	Frieda	Lenora	Muriel	Thora
Dora	Geneva	Leona	Nola	Tilda
Dorothea	Genevieve	Leonor	Olive	Vera
Edith	Golda	Leontine	Ophelia	Viola
Eleanor	Greta	Leora	Petra	Violette
Eleanora	Harriet	Louisa	Philomena	Virginia
Eloise	Helen	Louise	Rafaela	Wilhelmina
Emeline	Heloise	Lucille	Rena	Willa
Estella	Henrietta	Magdalene	Rhea	Winifred
Estelle	Hester	Maida	Rosa	Zelda
Esther	Ida	Marguerite	Rosamond	

BOYS

Albert	Chester	Emmett	Henry	Milo
Alfred	Clarence	Emory	Herbert	Percy
Ambrose	Claude	Ernest	Herman	Philo
Ansel	Clement	Eugene	Hiram	Randolph
Archibald	Clifford	Everett	Horace	Rudolph
Armand	Conrad	Ferdinand	Hubert	Rupert
Arthur	Cornelius	Forest	Hugh	Sylvester
August	Cyrus	Foster	Hugo	Theodore
Augustus	Edmund	Francis	Jules	Virgil
Basil	Edwin	Frederick	Julius	Wallace
Bernard	Elden	George	Leopold	Walter
Bertram	Elgin	Gilbert	Louis	Willis
Casper	Emerson	Godfrey	Luther	
Cecil	Emil	Harold	Merritt	

Last Names First

Conventional surnames have arrived with a splash as first names. They appeal to creative namers with their freshness, while their familiarity and

heritage keep them down-to-earth. Creative-rustic: the
perfect new-millennium combo. No wonder they're
just catching on now . . . right?

Actually, what we're seeing today is only the latest
wave of last-name crossovers. Starting at the turn of the
last century, American parents flocked to classic surnames of English literature and aristocracy. Those parents, including many poor immigrants, had grand dreams for their sons. They wanted to send them into
the world with sophisticated names ready to take their places in high
society. Thus they turned to such historical icons as (John) Milton and
(Sir Philip) Sidney. Unfortunately for poor Milt and Sid, the actual aris-
tocrats continued to give their sons names like John and Philip, and the
elegant image of their surnames quickly faded.

So how are the newly popular surnames different? The new favorites
still lean on their British Isles heritage to conjure up a lifestyle, but that
style is a far cry from the Oxbridge world of Milton and Sidney. Instead
of nobility, we're seeing hardy tradesmen: Coopers, Tanners, and
Masons. And parents have turned away from England to focus on Irish
and Scottish traditions: Riley, Mackenzie, Brennan. These new names
are rugged and rakish—and they're used for boys *and* girls.

Parents of boys delight in a new field of names with classically masculine features. The trade names in particular are brisk, direct, and
stocked with hard consonants. For parents of girls, surnames present an
opportunity to start afresh with lively names that carry no gender baggage.

So will these names escape the fate of Sid and Milt? Certainly, some
portion of the new names will hold their ground over time to join the
ranks of the perennials. Russell, for example, is an old surname that we
now accept as a classic first name. Yet with any surgingly popular name
group comes the risk of a "freshness date" that soon passes. To avoid a
trendy name with a short shelf life, consider some of the similar but less
popular alternatives below. Better yet, search your own family tree for
surnames that might be revived. When a name's significance is personal, it has roots that shifting fashions can't sweep away.

TRADE NAMES

Archer	Bowman
Bailey	Bailiff, county officer
Barker	Tanner or shepherd
Baxter	Baker
Bridger	Builder of bridges

Carter	Transporter of goods
Carver	Carver of wood or stone
Chancellor	Administrative officer
Chandler	Candle maker
Chapman	Merchant or peddler
Cooper	Barrel maker
Coster	Fruit seller or grower
Currier	Leather finisher
Cutler	Knife maker
Dexter	Dyer
Draper	Maker or seller of cloth
Farrier	Ironworker
Faulkner	Falconer
Fletcher	Arrow maker
Forester	Forest warden
Foster	Shearer
Gardner	Gardener
Garner	Keeper of the granary
Glover	Maker or seller of gloves
Gunner	Artillery operator
Harper	Harp player
Hooper	One who fits hoops on barrels
Hunter	Hunter
Jagger	Peddler
Keeler	Boat builder or pilot
Marshall	Tender of horses/military officer
Mason	Stonemason
Mercer	Fabric merchant
Miller	Miller of grain
Packer	Wool packer
Parker	Gamekeeper
Piper	Piper
Porter	Gatekeeper or load carrier
Potter	Pot maker
Ranger	Game warden
Ryder	Mounted soldier or messenger
Sadler	Saddle maker
Sailor	Sailor
Sawyer	One who saws wood
Slater	Slate roof maker

Smith	Metalworker
Spencer	Pantry servant
Sumner	Court summoner
Tanner	Preparer of hides for leather
Taylor	Tailor
Thane	Freeman or feudal baron
Thatcher	Straw roof maker
Tillman	Farmer
Tucker	Dresser of cloth
Turner	Lathe operator
Tyler	Tile maker
Walker	Dresser of cloth
Weaver	Weaver
Webster	Weaver
Wheeler	Wheel maker
Wright	Builder or machinist

BRITISH ISLES SURNAMES

Addison	Bradford	Carson	Delaney	Gannon
Ainsley	Bradley	Cassidy	Dennison	Garrick
Alden	Brady	Chauncey	Dillon	Garrison
Alton	Brannon	Clancy	Dixon	Gibson
Anderson	Branson	Clifton	Donovan	Grady
Arden	Braxton	Clinton	Doyle	Grant
Arley	Brennan	Cody	Drake	Grayson
Ashton	Brigham	Colby	Easton	Greer
Aubrey	Brock	Coleman	Edgerton	Griffith
Austin	Broderick	Colton	Edison	Hadley
Avery	Brody	Connolly	Ellis	Hailey
Baldwin	Brogan	Courtney	Elton	Hamilton
Bannon	Bryant	Dalton	Emerson	Hardy
Barclay	Bryson	Daly	Everett	Harlan
Barrett	Buckley	Darby	Everly	Harley
Barron	Burke	Darcy	Finley	Harmon
Barton	Cabot	Darnell	Flynn	Harris
Beck	Callahan	Darwin	Ford	Harrison
Beckett	Campbell	Davis	Forrest	Hartley
Bennett	Carey	Dawson	Fraser	Haskell
Berkeley	Carlton	Dayton	Freeman	Hayden

Hayes	Kennedy	Maddox	Preston	Stanford
Hillary	Kenton	Madison	Quincy	Stanton
Hilton	Kiley	Maguire	Quinlan	Sullivan
Hogan	Kinsey	Mallory	Quinn	Tate
Holden	Kyler	Marley	Ramsay	Tatum
Hollis	Lacey	Maxwell	Reagan	Terrell
Holt	Landon	McKay	Reid	Thurman
Houston	Lane	Mckenna	Remington	Tierney
Hudson	Laney	Mckinley	Richmond	Tobin
Hughes	Langston	Merrick	Ridley	Tracy
Jackson	Larkin	Merritt	Riley	Truman
Jameson	Larson	Mitchell	Robinson	Tyson
Jarrett	Lawson	Montague	Roosevelt	Vaughn
Jarrod	Leland	Montgomery	Ross	Walden
Jefferson	Lennox	Murphy	Rowan	Walton
Jordan	Lindsay	Neilson	Rowland	Watson
Judson	Logan	Nelson	Schuyler	Watt
Kane	Loudon	Newton	Shea	Waverly
Keane	Lowell	Nicholson	Shelby	Wesley
Keaton	Lyman	Oakley	Sheridan	Weston
Keegan	Mackenzie	Parrish	Sherman	Whitney
Kelsey	Mackinney	Paxton	Sidney	Willis
Kendall	Maclean	Payton	Simpson	Wilson
Kendrick	Macy	Presley	Spencer	Winston

Latino/Latina

Luis. Juan. Jesus. Just look through the top-100 boys' names in America, and you'll see it plainly: Spanish names *are* American names, and they're more popular than ever before.

When we talk about Latino names, of course, it's not just a matter of Spanish. Families of Caribbean descent may have different tastes from Mexican-Americans or South Americans. Brazilians add Portuguese variations to the mix. Names of reverence, such as titles of the Virgin Mary (Guadalupe, Dolores), are popular choices. And pop culture trends bring whole new surprises. Just look at Shakira, an Arabic name that became a Latina sensation thanks to the Arab-Colombian singer by that name.

The picture gets even more complicated when you consider boys and girls. Notice that all the popular examples we began with were male names. If you looked just at boys, you'd come away convinced that Latino-American parents are very traditional namers. Of the top five current Spanish boys' names in the United States—José, Luis, Juan, Angel, and Carlos—all but Angel were also in the top ten a century ago. But here's the kicker: All five are more popular than the top classic girl's name, Maria, despite that name's broad cross-cultural appeal.

So what *are* parents choosing for girls? In many cases, names that were unknown here a few decades ago and that remain unfamiliar outside of Latino communities. Choices like Itzel, Nayeli, and Citlalli are soaring, and celebrities are a huge influence. Current name fashions in Latin America move quickly to the United States thanks to Spanish-language television. And the number-one most popular name for little Latinas is Jennifer, courtesy of superstar entertainer Jennifer Lopez.

The field is wide open for Latino parents, with names old and new, Spanish, Portuguese, English, and beyond. One special consideration for kids who will be growing up in a bilingual environment is choosing names that are attractive and easy to pronounce in both languages. Just try pronouncing Meadow in Spanish, for instance. And Itzel loses a lot of its charm with the English pronunciation IHT-zul.

The list below includes perennials, rising stars, and a scattering of names that are off the beaten track today. This is a mixed Spanish and Portuguese list, so speakers of either language may find some unfamiliar or unexpected choices.

GIRLS

Abril	Aniya	Catalina	Esmeralda	Giselle
Adriana	Araceli	Catarina	Esperanza	Graciela
Alejandra	Arely	Cielo	Estefania	Guadalupe
Alicia	Beatriz	Citlali	Estela	Iliana
Alondra	Belen	Consuelo	Estrella	Ines
Amaya	Berenice	Damaris	Fabiola	Isabel
Ana	Bianca	Dolores	Fernanda	Itzel
Anahi	Blanca	Dulce	Francisca	Ivette
Angelica	Brisa	Elena	Galilea	Jimena
Anita	Carmen	Eliana	Genoveva	Juana

Juanita	Marcela	Mercedes	Raquel	Viviana
Julissa	Margarita	Milagros	Reyna	Yadira
Liliana	Maria	Mireya	Rocío	Yareli
Lisandra	Mariam	Monserrat	Rosario	Yazmin
Litzy	Mariana	Natalia	Roxana	Yesenia
Lorena	Maribel	Nayeli	Salma	Yolanda
Lourdes	Maricela	Noelia	Selena	Yoselin
Lucero	Mariela	Noemi	Shakira	Yuliana
Luisa	Marisela	Odalys	Silvia	
Lupe	Marisol	Paulina	Soledad	
Luz	Maritza	Perla	Thalia	
Magdalena	Mayra	Pilar	Valeria	

BOYS

Abdiel	Cruz	Hector	Luis	Ramon
Adan	Diego	Henrique	Manuel	Raul
Adolfo	Edgardo	Heriberto	Marcelo	Raymundo
Agustin	Eduardo	Hernan	Marco	Rene
Alberto	Efrain	Hugo	Marcos	Rey
Aldo	Efren	Humberto	Mariano	Reynaldo
Alejandro	Elian	Ignacio	Mario	Ricardo
Alfonso	Emiliano	Isidro	Mateo	Roberto
Alfredo	Emilio	Jaime	Mauricio	Rodolfo
Álvaro	Enrique	Jairo	Maximo	Rodrigo
Andres	Ernesto	Javier	Miguel	Rogelio
Angel	Esteban	Jesus	Moises	Rolando
Antonio	Ezequiel	João	Nestor	Ruben
Ariel	Federico	Joaquim	Nicolas	Salvador
Armando	Felipe	Joaquin	Nuno	Santiago
Arturo	Fernando	Jorge	Octavio	Santos
Aurelio	Fidel	José	Omar	Sergio
Benito	Francisco	Josue	Orlando	Tiago
Bernardo	Gerardo	Juan	Oscar	Ulises
Braulio	Gilberto	Julio	Osvaldo	Vicente
Caetano	Gonzalo	Lazaro	Pablo	Victor
Carlos	Guadalupe	Leonel	Pedro	Wilfredo
Cesar	Guillermo	Lisandro	Rafael	Xavier
Cristobal	Gustavo	Lorenzo	Ramiro	Yadiel

Little Darlings

Extremes always make an impact. When you meet a Maximilian or Anastasia, the name's extraordinary length makes it memorable. But you can make your mark at the other extreme, too: not super-size, but pocket-size.

Think of those tiny "power mints" that astonish you with their strength. Names like Mia, Ian, and Zoe are perfect, potent miniatures that pack all their style into compact bursts. As strong as they are, these names are never harsh or heavy. And as cute as they are, they don't sound childish because they're not pet forms but full, self-contained names. These Little Darlings are youthful names that will have no problem growing up.

GIRLS

Ada	Esme	Kira	Meta	Roma
Adi	Eve	Kyra	Mia	Tai
Anya	Fae	Lea	Mira	Tara
Ava	Gaia	Lena	Nava	Terra
Avis	Gia	Lia	Nia	Tessa
Britta	Io	Lida	Nina	Tia
Calla	Ivy	Lila	Noa	Tova
Cara	Jada	Luna	Nyla	Tyra
Chloe	Jael	Luz	Orly	Willa
Cleo	Janna	Lyra	Peta	Zilla
Deja	Jenna	Macy	Phoebe	Ziva
Eden	Kara	Maia	Rhea	Zoe
Elke	Kenna	Mara	Ría	
Elle	Kia	Maya	Rilla	

BOYS

Abel	Eli	Kai	Nico	Teo
Ari	Ian	Kian	Noah	Zvi
Avi	Jair	Kobe	Noam	
Axel	Jere	Liam	Noel	
Cael	Joah	Luca	Rio	

Long Gone

These are the old-timers that have disappeared from the naming pool, possibly for good. In some cases, such as Ingeborg and Candido, they hearken back to an age of immigrants. In other cases (Ozella, Norval), they just remind us of how fickle fashion really is. Chances are you've never even met anyone with these names, so you won't miss them. But all were, at some point in the twentieth century, among the 1,000 most popular choices in America.

For name thrill seekers, I've included a special section of some of the unlikeliest names ever to hit the charts . . . including a few (marked by *) that are finding takers today.

GIRLS

Albina	Fleta	Hulda	Mozell	Providenci
Alverta	Floy	Ingeborg	Myrl	Tennie
Armida	Fonda	Izetta	Myrtis	Velva
Arvilla	Gaynell	Izora	Nova	Verda
Bridie	Gudrun	Lavada	Ocie	Versie
Carma	Hassie	Linnie	Odie	Vesta
Clotilde	Hedwig	Loma	Ollie	Wava
Creola	Herminia	Louvenia	Onie	Wilda
Delma	Herta	Lovie	Orpha	Yetta
Delois	Hertha	Loyce	Otha	Zelma
Ethelyn	Hildred	Ludie	Ottilie	Zoila
Eulalia	Hilma	Mertie	Ouida	Zona
Exie	Hortencia	Mittie	Ozella	

BOYS

Adelbert	Darold	Estel	Hilbert	Oral
Alois	Delmas	Ezell	Isom	Orlo
Americo	Durwood	Finis	Junious	Otho
Arvil	Early	Foy	Loy	Rolla
Berry	Eloy	Garold	Margarito	Urban
Boyce	Elza	Gust	Narciso	Vester
Burdette	Epifanio	Heber	Norval	Waino
Candido	Erasmo	Helmer	Omer	Zigmund

AND WHO KNEW . . . ? GIRLS

Dimple	Jettie	Mossie	Pinkie
Electa	Mammie	Nannie	Shelva
Fairy	Marvel	Novella	Unique*
Icie	Missouri	Ova	Windy

AND WHO KNEW . . . ? BOYS

Alpha	Cloyd	Laddie	Primitivo	Toy
Aryan*	Dorman	Loyal	Ransom	Xzavier*
Brown	Hurley	Okey	Sim	
Burley	Jammie	Pink	Sincere*	

Mid-Century

When you read about the baby boom generation today, it's usually in the context of long-term health care plans or the future of Social Security. Their names, though, reflect the spirit of the days when the boomers really were babies.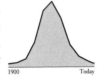

The names that surged after World War Two tend to be a modest, friendly bunch. They don't try to sound fancy or exotic—compare two of the trendiest boys' names of the time, Larry and Roger, to today's hits like Sebastian and Xavier. The biggest foreign influence you'll see is French endings for familiar girls' names, like Suzanne and Annette.

So what were the parents of the '50s aiming for with their name choices? If you scan down the list, the most common theme is that these names sound *happy*. Not breezy and carefree, like the surfer names that followed in the '60s, but happy and relaxed. If the names we give our children represent our hopes for the future, names like Kathie and Jerry, Darlene and Butch are dreams of contentment. A comfortable home, good friends, and kids playing in the yard. That's still a dream plenty of us share.

Of course, the generation bestowed with those contented names ended up far from content. The little Kathies and Jerries born in 1950 grew up to be the protesters, free-lovers, and Woodstock attendees of 1969. Their very discontent revolutionized American society.

The '50s names, though, don't care about the politics. They just want to be happy—and happiness never goes out of style.

GIRLS

Annette	Debra	Joanie	Marsha	Rosanne
Barbra	Dee	Joanne	Maryanne	Sandra
Becky	Denise	Joy	Marybeth	Sharon
Betsy	Diane	Judith	Maureen	Sheila
Bonita	Donna	Judy	Merry	Shelley
Bonnie	Doreen	Julie	Mimi	Sherry
Brenda	Francine	Karen	Mitzi	Suellen
Carol	Gail	Kathleen	Nancy	Susan
Carolyn	Gay	Kathy	Nanette	Suzanne
Charlene	Ginny	Kaye	Pamela	Terry
Cheryl	Glenda	Kim	Patrice	Theresa
Cindy	Glinda	Lana	Patricia	Trudy
Colette	Gwen	Linda	Patti	Valerie
Colleen	Jackie	Lucinda	Paula	Vicki
Connie	Janet	Lynette	Paulette	Wanda
Cynthia	Janette	Lynn	Peggy	Yolanda
Darla	Janice	Marcia	Penny	Yvonne
Darlene	Jayne	Margo	Ramona	
Deanne	Jeannine	Maribeth	Regina	
Debbie	Jerri	Marla	Ronna	
Deborah	Jo	Marlene	Rosalyn	

BOYS

Alan	Del	Jerry	Marty	Robin
Barry	Dennis	Jim	Mel	Rock
Bruce	Dino	Johnny	Mickey	Rod
Butch	Donnie	Jon	Mike	Rodney
Cary	Douglas	Kenny	Mitch	Roger
Chip	Duane	Kent	Monte	Ron
Chuck	Duke	Kerry	Perry	Sandy
Cliff	Dwight	Kim	Phillip	Skip
Dana	Frankie	Larry	Randall	Steve
Danny	Gary	Len	Randy	Terry
Darrell	Gerald	Les	Reggie	Tony
Davey	Glenn	Lorne	Rich	Wally
Dean	Hank	Mark	Ricky	Wayne

Modern Meanings

Most names have literal meanings attached to them, if you dig deeply enough. Cameron comes from a Gaelic phrase meaning "crooked nose." Melissa is Greek for "bee." When you hear Cameron and Melissa, though, you simply hear names. Their derivations are historical curiosities that don't have much of an influence on their style.

For some names, though, meaning is everything. These are names whose origins aren't lost in the mist but come through loud and clear to modern English speakers. For names like Destiny and Maverick, meaning *is* style.

Meaning names are on the rise, with bold, self-affirming words leading the pack. Familiar word-names of generations past were typically gentle souls, like flowers and virtues (see the Charms and Graces style). The Modern Meanings, in comparison, are bursting with confidence. With names like Heaven and Justice, you're making it clear that you expect your children to take on the world, with aplomb.

GIRLS

America	Diamond	Haven	Miracle	Serenity
Angel	Ebony	Heaven	Misty	Skye
Arcadia	Eden	Jade	Nevaeh	Star
Aria	Emerald	Jasmine	(heaven	Summer
Autumn	Essence	Jewel	backward)	Sun
Cadence	Eternity	Journey	Odyssey	Sunshine
Caprice	Evening	Justice	Precious	Tempest
Charisma	Gala	Lark	Princess	Terra
Cherish	Genesis	Liberty	Raven	Tiara
Crystal	Glory	Lyric	Saga	Tierra
Desiree	Golden	Meadow	Sage	Trinity
Destiny	Harmony	Melody	Scarlett	Whisper

BOYS

August	Justice	Noble	Shadow	Winter
Chance	King	Price	Sincere	Wisdom
Diamond	Marshal	Prince	Storm	Worth
Flint	Maverick	Royal	Truth	Zion
Jett	Merit	Sage	Tyme	

Muslim

Names in the Arab and Muslim worlds are typically formed from common Arabic phrases with felicitous meanings. Many popular names represent the values most esteemed in Islam, such as praise (Hamid), purity (Tahira), and service to Allah (Abdullah). Names of the Prophet Mohammed's close associates, such as his daughter Fatima, are also prevalent. And the name Mohammed itself, in many different spellings, is the most common name on the planet.

As with all names, though, the literal origin doesn't tell the full story of the name's popularity. Jamil, for instance, comes from the Arabic word for beautiful, but it is also popular in non-Arabic-speaking regions of Africa that have Muslim traditions. Many non-Muslim African-Americans, in turn, have adopted the name to reflect their African ancestry.

Arabic and Muslim names are increasingly familiar and popular in the United States, with dozens among America's top-1,000 names. For American-born parents, including Black Muslims, names with a strong "ee" sound like Kareem and Malik have been particular favorites. (Double-"e" spellings like Kareem are characteristically American, while "i" spellings, like Karim, are more common internationally.) The selections below include traditional names with a sound and style attractive to American parents.

GIRLS

Aisha	Asma	Jamila	Naima	Shakira
Amani	Aziza	Khadijah	Rania	Tahira
Amina	Basma	Layla	Razia	Yasmin
Amira	Fatima	Leila	Safiya	Zahra
Anisa	Halima	Maryam	Samira	

BOYS

Abdullah	Basim	Hassan	Jamil	Malik
Ahmad	Bilal	Ibrahim	Kamil	Mohammed
Ahmed	Farid	Ismael	Kareem	Muhammad
Ali	Hakeem	Jafar	Khalid	Mustafa
Amir	Hamid	Jaleel	Khalil	Nasir
Bashir	Hamza	Jamal	Latif	Omar

Rasheed	Salim	Syed	Yusuf
Reza	Samir	Tariq	

Mythological

Mythology is a mixture of literature and religion, history and fantasy. Mythological names, in turn, are at once traditional and imaginative. A handful of these names, like Diana and Jason, are familiar enough that their modern associations outweigh their classical origins. Others, like Apollo and Thor, still sound fantastical enough to rule the heavens.

The greatest naming potential may lie with the less familiar deities. Names like Thalia and Clio (Greek Muses) echo their fabulous past gently and gracefully. They could be elegant ways to invoke a bit of magic for your child.

The names below include figures from the Celtic, Norse, Egyptian, and (primarily) Greco-Roman traditions.

GIRLS

Aeron	Danae	Gaia	Lavinia	Selena
Aine	Daphne	Halia	Leda	Silvia
Althea	Diana	Hermione	Luna	Sybil
Aoife	Doris	Hestia	Maia	Thalia
Ariadne	Echo	Ianthe	Melia	Venus
Artemis	Electra	Io	Minerva	Vesta
Athena	Eris	Ione	Niamh	Xanthe
Aurora	Eudora	Irene	Penelope	
Cassandra	Evadne	Iris	Phyllis	
Clio	Flora	Isis	Rhea	
Dafne	Freya	Juno	Rhiannon	

BOYS

Achilles	Damon	Leander	Odin	Ulysses
Adonis	Hector	Linus	Orion	
Ajax	Hermes	Mars	Orpheus	
Amon	Jason	Mercury	Theseus	
Apollo	Jupiter	Morpheus	Thor	

Namesakes

Ever meet a kid named Kermit? It's a quirky Irish classic with a contemporary sound. Shouldn't that make for a hit? Of course, it's also a Muppet frog, and hard to think of any other way. Thus the name, for all its appeal, has disappeared.

Certain characters, real and fictional, simply claim possession of their first names. Elvis *is* Elvis Presley just as Kermit *is* a frog. At least those are positive associations. A young Kermit may be in for a little kidding, but the name remains charming. The situation becomes more serious when a name's associations are sinister. (Adolph is the ultimate example.)

Each of the names on this list is culturally linked to an individual image. Some links are stronger than others, and some work to the name's advantage. But in each case, the association is something you must make peace with before choosing the name for your child.

Alanis (Morissette)
Amos ('n' Andy)
Anaïs (Nin)
Aretha (Franklin)
Ariel (Disney Mermaid)
Atticus (Finch)
Barney (singing dinosaur)
Beckett (Samuel)
Benito (Mussolini)
Booker (T. Washington)
Britney (Spears)
Buffy (Vampire Slayer)
Casper (Friendly Ghost)
Clifford (Big Red Dog)
Darwin (Charles)
Delilah (Biblical villain)
Denzel (Washington)
Dilbert (Comic strip)
Dolly (Parton)
Ebenezer (Scrooge)
Edsel (Ford)

Elmer (Fudd)
Elmo (Muppet)
Elvira (Mistress of the Dark)
Elvis (Presley)
Farrah (Fawcett)
Fidel (Castro)
Garth (Brooks)
Grover (Muppet)
Hannibal (Lecter)
Hester (Prynne)
Holden (Caulfield)
Homer (Simpson)
Iago (Othello)
Imelda (Marcos)
Jagger (Mick)
Jemima (Aunt)
Jezebel (Biblical villain)
Keanu (Reeves)
Kermit (Frog)
Langston (Hughes)
LeBron (James)

Lincoln (Abraham)
Linus (Peanuts)
Lolita (Nabokov's nymphet)
Madonna (Entertainer)
Malcolm (X)
Merlin (Wizard)
Napoleon (Bonaparte)
Oprah (Winfrey)
Presley (Elvis)
Reagan (Ronald)
Romeo (and Juliet)
Roosevelt (Franklin, Theodore)

Rudolph (Red-Nosed Reindeer)
Sade (Singer)
Satchel (Paige)
Scarlett (O'Hara)
Shania (Twain)
Shaquille (O'Neal)
Sojourner (Truth)
Tallulah (Bankhead)
Uma (Thurman)
Waldo (Where's)
Whitman (Walt)

New Classics

Welcome to the "new reliables." These are the names you know best, the ones no one will ever second-guess. When you name a child Eric or Allison, you can breathe easy. Trend-proof and tease-proof, they're the classics of our age.

1900   Today

"Classic" is often a polite way to say old-fashioned, but that's not the case here. Few of us have a Grandpa Eric or a Granny Allison. The New Classics may have old roots, but it's only in the past two generations that they've established themselves as American standards. Without a dusty, sepia-toned legacy behind them, they feel light and unselfconscious. Pair that lightness with year-in, year-out consistency and you have a group of names as approachable and dependable as a childhood friend.

GIRLS

Alexandra	Brooke	Gabrielle	Kelly	Megan
Alicia	Candace	Holly	Kendra	Melanie
Alisa	Cara	Jenna	Kimberly	Melissa
Allison	Cassandra	Jessica	Kirsten	Meredith
Amanda	Clarissa	Jocelyn	Lara	Michelle
Andrea	Danielle	Julianne	Laurel	Miranda
Ariel	Deanna	Kara	Lauren	Monica
Bethany	Erica	Karen	Leslie	Monique
Bridget	Erin	Katrina	Marisa	Natalie

Nicole	Sabrina	Stephanie	Vanessa
Noelle	Samantha	Tabitha	

BOYS

Aaron	Christian	Geoffrey	Justin	Sean
Adam	Christopher	Gregory	Kelvin	Seth
Andre	Colin	Ian	Kendrick	Shane
Bradley	Damon	Jared	Kevin	Steven
Brandon	Darren	Jason	Kyle	Terrance
Brendan	Derek	Jeffrey	Lance	Timothy
Brett	Drew	Jeremy	Lucas	Zachary
Brian	Eric	Jonathan	Marc	
Casey	Evan	Joshua	Ryan	

Nickname-Proof

The title of this style is false advertising. No name is 100 percent nick-name-proof. There's always the first-initial approach, such as "T" for Tiernan, or the descriptive nickname, like Red for a redhead. Or just the total happenstance, like the toddler called Bear because he loves to growl. If it's really meant to be, that nickname will find its way to your child.

More and more, though, full names are fighting back. It's common today to meet a little Daniel or James who doesn't answer to Danny or Jim. The full names sound more fashionable, and parents are insisting on them. If your dream is raising a little Katherine-not-Kathy, your chances of success are better than ever. But for the best possible odds of keeping nicknames at bay, here is a collection of multisyllable names with no common pet forms.

GIRLS

Adrienne	Athena	Brenda	Colleen	Eileen
Aida	Aubrey	Brenna	Daisy	Emma
Alma	Audrey	Charity	Dalia	Erica
Amber	Autumn	Chelsea	Darlene	Erin
Amy	Ava	Chloe	Denise	Fallon
April	Avery	Clara	Devin	Farrah
Asia	Avis	Clarice	Donna	Felicity

Giselle	Keisha	Mia	Piper	Summer
Gloria	Kelsey	Mira	Portia	Tanya
Gretchen	Kendra	Morgan	Rachel	Tara
Haley	Kyra	Muriel	Regan	Thalia
Hannah	Lila	Myra	Rhoda	Theda
Harmony	Mallory	Nadia	Robin	Tova
Hazel	Mara	Naomi	Sarai	Vera
Heather	Margo	Nia	Shana	Wanda
Hillary	Mariah	Nina	Shania	Whitney
Holly	Marian	Norma	Shannon	Willow
Isis	Marion	Paola	Sheila	Zelda
Justice	Marley	Paris	Sienna	Zoe
Justine	Marlo	Paula	Sierra	
Kara	Maura	Payton	Simone	
Karen	Maya	Phoebe	Sonia	

BOYS

Aaron	Cecil	Ellis	Jarvis	Palmer
Adam	Clarence	Emerson	Justin	Parker
Adrian	Cody	Emmett	Keegan	Peyton
Aidan	Corey	Evan	Kelvin	Riley
Alec	Dallas	Everett	Kevin	Ronan
Angelo	Dalton	Ewan	Kyle	Roscoe
Ari	Damian	Ezra	Lamar	Ryan
Arlo	Damon	Fabian	Liam	Sawyer
Armand	Darian	Felix	Logan	Seamus
Atticus	Darius	Foster	Marcel	Shannon
Austin	Darrell	Gavin	Marius	Simeon
Avery	Darren	Harlan	Mason	Sterling
Brady	Dawson	Haskell	Miles	Theo
Brendan	Dayton	Hector	Milo	Tiernan
Brennan	Derek	Holden	Morgan	Travis
Brian	Devin	Horace	Nigel	Trevor
Bryant	Dorian	Ian	Noah	Ulysses
Byron	Dunstan	Jamal	Nolan	Walker
Carson	Eamon	Jared	Oscar	Warren
Carsten	Eli	Jaron	Otto	Wyatt
Carter	Elliott	Jarrett	Owen	

Nicknames

You love the nickname Annie, but Ann seems too plain. You want to name your son after Grandpa Ron . . . but Ronald? No way. You're not alone. Plenty of parents start with a nickname they like and work backward from there. A strong nickname can be the real power behind a full name. Zeke, for instance, has fueled the resurrection of Ezekiel, and Tess gives Theresa a fresh kick.

Some parents even go a step further, ditching the traditional full name and bestowing the nickname straight up. A pure nickname gives parents more control: If you really love Betsy, why choose Elizabeth and risk your daughter ending up a Liz? It's especially tempting when a cool nickname derives from a dud full name. But the downside is a loss of flexibility. Just plain Matt may find himself yearning for the more formal Matthew on serious occasions. Betsy might seem more like an Elizabeth after all. And the occasional use of a longer name can be a sweet term of endearment . . . or a good way to signal that your child darned well better come down to dinner by the count of three, or else!

Below you'll find many familiar short forms of names. If you're a nickname lover, you can just take them straight. But if you're open to full names, this Nickname Wizard includes a variety of formal starting points for each name. You might just find a way to honor that beloved, name-impaired relative after all.

GIRLS

Nickname	Full names
Addie	Adelaide, Adela, Addison, Adelia, Adeline
Alex	Alexandra, Alexa, Alexis, Alexandria
Allie, Ali	Allison, Alice, Alexandra, Alexandria, Alana, Aliyah, Alyssa, Alize, Alisa, Allegra
Angie	Angela, Angel, Angelica, Angelina, Angelique, Angelia
Annie	Ann, Anne, Anna, Annabelle, Annalise, Annika, Annette, Antonia, Roxanne
Becky	Rebecca, Bianca
Beth, Bess	Elizabeth, Bethany, Lisbeth, Maribeth, Elsbeth
Betsy, Betty	Elizabeth, Bettina
Billie	Wilhelmina, Willa, Sybil

Bobbie	Barbara, Roberta, Robin
Bree	Bridget, Brianna, Brittany, Bria, Gabrielle, Sabrina, Brisa
Candy	Candace, Candida
Carly	Carla, Carlotta, Carlene
Carrie	Caroline, Carolyn, Carissa, Carol, Carmen, Carmela, Carolina
Cassie	Cassandra, Cassia, Cassidy, Catherine
Ceil	Cecilia, Cecile, Celine, Celeste, Celia
Chrissy, Chris	Christine, Christina, Christa, Christiane, Christal
Cindy	Cynthia, Lucinda, Cinderella, Cinda, Sinead
Connie	Constance, Concetta, Consuelo, Cornelia
Corrie	Cora, Coralie, Corazon, Cordelia, Corinna, Corliss, Coral
Debbie	Deborah, Debra
Dell	Adelaide, Della, Adele, Delphine, Delta, Delilah, Delaney
Dolly	Dorothy, Dolores, Dorothea
Dottie	Dorothy, Dorothea
Edie	Edith, Edna, Eden
Ellie, Elle	Ellen, Eleanor, Elizabeth, Helen, Ella, Eloise, Electra, Elena, Eleni
Elsie	Elizabeth, Alice, Elsa, Elspeth, Elise
Emmie	Emily, Emmaline, Emma, Emelia, Emerald
Evie	Eve, Eva, Evelyn, Evangeline, Genevieve
Flo	Florence, Flora, Florida, Flossie
Fran	Frances, Francesca, Francisca, Francine
Gigi	Georgine, Virginia, Giovanna, Ginger, Giselle, Regina, Gina
Ginny	Virginia, Ginger, Genevieve
Gracie	Grace, Graciela, Altagracia
Hattie	Harriet, Henrietta
Hetty	Harriet, Henrietta, Ester, Hester, Mehitabel
Jan	Janet, Janice, Janine, Jeanette, Jana, Janelle, Janessa
Jenny	Jennifer, Jane, Jean, Jenna
Jeri, Gerri	Geraldine, Germaine, Jerilyn, Jerrica
Jessie	Jessica, Jane, Jean, Janet, Jessalyn, Jessame, Jessamyn
Jo, Joey	Josphine, Josefa, Joanne, Joan, Johanna, Joelle, Jocelyn, Journey, Marjorie
Jodi	Johanna, Joanna, Judith, Josephine
Josie	Josephine, Josefa, Joselyn

Julie	Julia, Juliana, Juliet, Julissa
Kari	Karen, Karina, Katrina, Karissa
Kate, Katie	Katherine, Kaitlyn, Kathleen, Katia, Katarina, Kateri, Katrina
Kathy	Katherine, Kathleen, Kathlyn
Kay	Katherine, Kayla, Kaylee, Kasey, Kaylin, Kaitlyn
Kiki	Kristina
Kim	Kimberly, Kimball, Kimberlin
Kris, Kristi	Kristina, Kristin, Krista, Kristal, Kristian
Liv	Olivia, Lavinia, Olive, Livia
Laurie, Lori	Laura, Lauren, Laurel, Loretta, Lorraine, Lorelei, Lorna
Liza	Elizabeth, Louise, Eliza, Lizbeth, Lieselotte, Lizette
Lottie	Charlotte, Lieselotte
Lucy	Lucille, Lucinda, Lucia, Luciana, Lucretia
Maddie	Madeline, Madison, Maddalena, Madonna
Maggie, Margie	Margaret, Magdalena, Magnolia, Magda, Margery
Mandy	Amanda, Amandine, Manuela, Miranda
Marci	Marcia, Marcelle, Marcella
Mattie	Matilda, Martha
Meg	Margaret, Megan, Marguerite
Mel	Melanie, Melinda, Melissa, Melody, Amelia, Carmel, Melba, Melina, Pamela
Millie	Millicent, Mildred, Amelia, Emily, Melissa, Camille, Emeline
Mimi	Maria, Michelle, Miriam, Miranda
Mindy	Melinda, Miranda
Minnie	Wilhelmina, Minerva, Amina, Jasmine, Yasmin
Molly	Mary, Margaret, Mahalia, Amalia
Nan	Nancy, Anne, Susannah, Nanette, Hannah, Fernanda
Nell	Eleanor, Helen, Lenora, Cornelia, Janelle, Penelope
Nikki	Nicole, Nicola, Veronica, Nicolette
Pat, Patsy	Patricia, Martha, Patrice, Patience, Cleopatra
Peggy	Margaret, Margery
Penny	Penelope, Aspen
Polly	Mary, Paula, Paulina
Randi	Miranda
Reba	Rebecca
Ricki	Erica, Patricia, America
Romy	Rosemary, Roma, Ramona
Ronnie	Veronica, Rhonda, Rona, Sharon

Rosie	Rose, Rosemary, Rosa, Rosalie, Rosalind, Rosanna, Rosario, Rosetta, Rosita, Roselyn
Sadie	Sarah, Sarai
Sally, Sal	Sarah, Salina, Salma, Salome
Sammie	Samantha, Samara, Samira
Sandy	Alexandra, Sandra, Alessandra, Cassandra, Lisandra
Stevie	Stephanie, Stefania
Sue, Susie	Susan, Suzanne, Susannah, Suzette, Summer
Tammy	Tamara, Tamar, Tamika, Tamia, Tamiko, Tamsin
Tasha	Natasha, Natalia, Latasha
Terry	Teresa, Therese, Terra, Kateri
Tess, Tessa	Teresa, Therese, Tessa, Santesa
Tia	Cynthia, Letitia, Lucretia, Tatiana, Tiana, Tiara
Tillie	Matilda, Clotilde, Tilda
Toni	Antonia, Antoinette, Antonina, Tonya, Payton
Tori	Victoria
Tricia, Trish	Patricia, Patrice, Beatrice, Leatrice, Latricia
Trina	Katrina, Trinity, Trinidad
Trudy	Gertrude, Ermintrude
Val	Valerie, Valeria, Valencia, Valentine, Valentina, Avalon
Vicky	Victoria, Vicenta

BOYS

Nickname	*Full names*
Abe	Abraham, Abram, Abel, Abdiel
Al	Albert, Alfred, Alan, Alaric, Albin, Alistair, Alphonse, Aldrich, Alexander
Alex	Alexander, Alexi, Alistair
Alf	Alfred, Alfredo, Alfonzo
Andy	Andrew, Anderson, Andre, Andreas, Leander
Archie	Archibald, Archer
Art	Arthur, Artis, Arturo
Barney	Barnabas, Barnaby, Bernard
Bart	Barton, Bartholemew, Bertram
Baz	Barry, Barton, Barron
Ben	Benjamin, Benedict, Bennett, Benno, Benton
Bert	Albert, Bertram, Bertrand, Gilbert, Hubert, Robert, Lambert
Bill	William, Willis, Willem
Brad	Bradley, Bradford, Braden, Brady

Bram	Abraham, Abram, Bertram
Brody	Broderick, Broder
Cal	Calvin, Caleb, Callum, Charles, Pascal
Cam	Cameron, Campbell, Camden
Charlie, Chuck	Charles, Charlton, Charleston
Chaz	Charles, Chester
Chet	Chester, Chesley, Charleston
Chris	Christian, Christopher, Crispin
Clem	Clement, Clemens
Cliff	Clifford, Clifton, Heathcliff
Cole	Nicholas, Colby, Colman, Colin
Con, Connie	Conrad, Connor, Cornelius, Cornell, Constantin, Conan
Curt	Curtis, Courtney
Dan	Daniel, Dante
Dave	David, Davis, Davion
Del	Cordell, Delano, Delton, Delmar, Wardell, Adelard, Adelbert
Denny	Dennis, Denver, Denzel, Dennison
Dex, Des	Dexter, Desmond, Desiderio, Destin
Don	Donald, Donovan, Donal, Donato, Donnell, London
Drew	Andrew, Woodrow
Ed	Edward, Edmund, Edgar, Edison, Eduardo
Ernie	Ernest, Ernesto, Ernst
Frank	Francis, Franklin, Francisco
Fred	Frederick, Alfred, Alfredo
Gabe	Gabriel
Gene	Eugene, Genaro
Gil	Gilbert, Giles
Greg	Gregory, Gregor, Gregorio
Gus	August, Augustus, Gustave, Gustavo, Angus
Hal	Henry, Harry, Harold
Hank	Henry, Hannibal, Hans
Ike	Isaac, Isaiah
Jack	John, Jackson
Jake	Jacob, John
Jamie, Jim	James, Jeremy, Jamison, Jamal, Benjamin
Jay	Jacob, Jason, Jaden, Jaylen, James, Japheth
Jed	Jedidiah, Jared
Jeff	Jeffrey, Jefferson

Jem	James, Jeremy, Jeremiah
Jerry	Gerald, Jerome, Jeremy, Jered
Joe	Joseph, Jonah, Jonas, Jovani
Ken	Kenneth, Kendall, Kendrick, Kennedy, Kenton, Kenyatta, Kenyon
Larry	Lawrence, Lars, Larson
Len	Leonard, Lennox
Leo	Leonard, Leonardo, Leopold, Leonidas, Lionel
Les	Lester, Lesley
Lon	Alonzo, Leonard, Lawrence, London, Waylon, Thelonius
Lou, Lew	Louis, Lewis, Llewellyn
Mac	Mackenzie, Macauley, McArthur, McKay, McKinley
Matt	Matthew, Matthais, Matteo
Max	Maxwell, Maximilian, Maxim, Maximus, Maximo
Mel	Melvin, Melton, Melville, Carmelo, Melbourne, Jamel
Mike, Mickey	Michael, Micah, Michelangelo
Mitch	Mitchell, Michael
Monty	Montague, Montgomery, Lamont, Montana
Mort	Morton, Mortimer, Mordecai
Moss	Moses, Morris, Maurice
Nate, Nat	Nathaniel, Nathan, Donato, Ignatius
Ned	Edward, Edmund
Nick	Nicholas, Nicholson, Dominick, Nicodemus
Pat	Patrick, Payton, Paxton, Pasquale
Pete	Peter, Pierre, Petro
Phil	Philip, Theophilus
Ray	Raymond, Rayner, Rayburn, Rayford, Rafer, Raymundo, Raynard, Rayshawn
Randy	Randall, Randolph, Rand, Bertrand
Reggie	Reginald, Regis
Rich	Richard, Richmond
Rick	Richard, Richmond, Ricardo, Frederick, Cedric, Maverick, Patrick, Aldric, Roderick, Derrick, Garrick, Broderick
Rico	Ricardo, Enrico, Richard
Rob, Bob	Robert, Roberto, Robin, Robinson
Robin	Robert, Robinson
Rod	Rodney, Roderick, Roddick, Rodger, Rodolfo, Jarod
Ron	Ronald, Ronan, Tyron, Ronaldo, Aaron

Sal	Salvatore, Salvador, Absalom
Sam	Samuel, Samson, Samir
Sandy	Alexander, Sanford, Santiago, Lisandro, Alessandro
Si	Silas, Seymour, Simon, Sylvester, Simeon, Sinbad
Stan	Stanley, Stanford, Stanton, Dunstan
Steve	Stephen, Steven, Esteban
Ted	Edward, Theodore, Edmund
Teo	Teodoro, Mateo, Theodore, Terrance
Terry	Terrance, Terrell, Theodore
Than	Ethan, Nathan, Nathaniel, Jonathan, Thanassis
Theo	Theodore, Theophilus, Thelonius
Tim	Timothy
Toby	Tobias, Tobin
Tom	Thomas
Tony	Anthony, Antonio, Tonio, Anton
Ty	Tyler, Tyrone, Tyson, Tyrese, Tyrell, Tyree
Vin, Vince	Vincent, Calvin, Devin, Gavin, Vincenzo, Vinson
Wally	Walter, Wallace, Walden, Waldo, Walker, Walton
Wes	Wesley, Westley, Weston
Will	William, Willis, Wilson, Wilbur, Wilfred, Wilhelm, Willard, Wilton
Xander	Alexander
Zack	Zachary, Zachariah, Isaac
Zeke	Ezekiel, Isaac, Hezekiah, Zechariah
Zeb	Zebediah, Zebedee, Zebulun

Place Names

These days, if you say you've visited Paris and Dakota, there's no telling whether you traveled the world or just dropped in on friends. The boundary between place names and personal names is disappearing, and the range of geographic choices grows every day.

A place name connects a child with the world. When you name a child Paris, you tap into generations of artistic dreams. With Dakota, you summon the independence of the American West. Even if you've never known anyone by these names, they're familiar and evocative and require no explanation. That makes place names tempting targets for creative parents: brand-new baby names with built-in meanings.

As a place name becomes popular, though, its geographic ties loosen. Just look at Brittany, which no longer reminds anybody of the French coast (try Normandy instead). Some of the less common choices, of course, may be less common for a reason—Paris is a lot catchier than Grenoble. For a name that strikes the right balance, scan a map of your favorite part of the world or try the global list below.

GIRLS

Acadia	Catalina	India	Normandy	Trinidad
Albany	Chelsea	Ireland	Odessa	Valencia
Alexandria	Cheyenne	Jordan	Paris	Venice
America	China	Kenya	Sahara	Verona
Asia	Dakota	Laramie	Savannah	Vienna
Asmara	Dallas	London	Shasta	Virginia
Aspen	Denali	Madison	Shenandoah	Zaria
Atlanta	Florence	Marietta	Siena	
Brittany	Florida	Marseille	Sierra	
Brooklyn	Geneva	Milan	Sonoma	
Carolina	Georgia	Montana	Sydney	

BOYS

Austin	Coty	Houston	Milan	Trenton
Boston	Dakota	Hudson	Montana	Walden
Brighton	Dallas	Kingston	Phoenix	Zaire
Bryce	Dayton	Lexington	Raleigh	
Camden	Denver	London	Reno	
Canton	Dublin	Macon	Richmond	
Charleston	Everest	Melbourne	Stratton	

Porch Sitters

With due apologies to Gladys and Elmer, this group of names has settled in for a long snooze on the front porch and isn't waking up any time soon. On television, names from this list signal that a character is strictly comic relief: Floyd and Wilbur never get the girl. Their overwhelming image is rural, outmoded, and ploddingly slow.

You may find a name or two on the list that you take exception to. "But my Grandma Velma was a saint!" you say. I understand; my Grandma Ethel was an absolute peach—but her name wasn't the reason.

Take heart that as they rock in their rocking chairs, the Porch Sitters can dream back to the day when they were in high style. These names do have a distinct style, favored for its continental elegance a century ago. Note the round, smooth tones that roll around on your tongue, with velvety consonants l, m, r, and th and full vowels o and u. And then note how those sounds are out of step in the age of Caden and Kaitlyn. Of course, there are now dozens of Cadens and Kaitlyns in every town. If a name on the Porch Sitter list captures your imagination, it will be a bold and individual choice. For most of us, though, these will remain names looked back on with a smile. So good night, Gladys and Elmer—and sweet dreams.

GIRLS

Agnes	Claudine	Eunice	Luetta	Selma
Ardell	Dolores	Geraldine	Lurline	Shirlene
Bernice	Dorcas	Gertrude	Mildred	Thelma
Bertha	Earline	Gladys	Myrtle	Velma
Beulah	Elvira	Helga	Nadine	Verna
Brunilda	Enid	Hester	Noreen	Vernell
Edna	Erma	Hilda	Opal	Vernice
Edwina	Ernestine	Irma	Pauline	Wilma
Florine	Ethel	Laverne	Pearline	

BOYS

Abner	Dillard	Homer	Morris	Rufus
Amos	Dudley	Hoyt	Mortimer	Seymour
Buford	Elbert	Irving	Murray	Wilbur
Burl	Elmer	Jethro	Myron	Wilfred
Burnell	Elmo	Lester	Norbert	Willard
Floyd	Elroy	Lloyd	Norris	Verl
Clem	Elwin	Maynard	Odell	Verne
Cleon	Enoch	Merle	Odie	Virgil
Cletus	Enos	Mervin	Orville	Waldo
Cyril	Erwin	Millard	Otis	
Delbert	Grover	Milton	Pervis	
Delmer	Merl	Monroe	Roscoe	

Saints

Certain names, such as Francis and Mary, come immediately to mind as saintly. Indeed, there are over fifty different saints with those names. If you're looking for a religious or historical role model but your fashion sense is further from the beaten track, try this list of less common names from the roster of Catholic saints.

The list is not intended to be comprehensive, but is selective based on style. In fact, no definitive roster of saints exists. The Church had no formal canonization process until the tenth century, so early saints were anointed by public acclaim, local lore, and tradition. (Some other denominations, such as the Eastern Orthodox Church, have their own rosters of saints; see the International section for more ideas.)

It is customary, though not required, for Roman Catholic parents to choose saints' names for their children. Other Christian parents may also appreciate saintly names for their deep roots in the faith, and almost any parent could be intrigued by some of these striking names that span the globe and 2,000 years of history. Whether you're Catholic or not, the list below is likely to leave you with the realization that saints' names are a lot cooler than you thought.

GIRLS

Ada	Beatrix	Flavia	Leocadia	Rosalia
Adela	Belina	Flora	Louisa	Sabina
Adelaide	Britta	Gemma	Lucia	Savina
Alexis	Camilla	Genevieve	Lucilla	Seraphina
Amalia	Cecilia	Germaine	Marcella	Serena
Amata	Cecily	Helena	Marguerite	Tatiana
Anastasia	Chantal	Hermione	Mariana	Therese
Anatolia	Cleopatra	Ida	Marina	Valentina
Antonia	Colette	Josepha	Matilda	Veronica
Antonina	Daria	Josephine	Maura	Vivian
Apollonia	Demetria	Juliana	Maxima	Winifred
Ariadne	Edith	Justina	Melania	Zita
Augusta	Elodie	Kateri	Natalia	
Aurea	Eugenia	Kennera	Philomena	
Aurelia	Fabiola	Kiara	Raphaela	
Averil	Felicity	Kinnia	Regina	

Adrian	Clement	Evan	Kieran	Rocco
Aidan	Colman	Fabian	Kilian	Roderick
Aidric	Conan	Falco	Lazarus	Roger
Alban	Cormac	Felix	Leander	Roman
Aldric	Crispin	Finian	Leo	Ronan
Alexis	Damian	Florian	Linus	Rowan
Ambrose	Dario	Gennaro	Lucian	Rupert
Antony	Darius	Gerard	Lucius	Samson
Apollo	Declan	Gilbert	Magnus	Sebastian
Balin	Demetrius	Giles	Malachy	Severin
Barnard	Dermot	Guy	Manuel	Severus
Bartholomew	Diego	Hermes	Marcel	Stanislaus
Benedict	Dominic	Hugh	Marcellus	Sylvan
Bernard	Donato	Isaias	Marek	Sylvester
Bertrand	Dunstan	Ivan	Matthias	Tarkin
Blaine	Edgar	Jerome	Maxim	Vincent
Blaise	Edmund	Jude	Maximilian	Vitus
Bond	Egon	Julian	Maximus	Xavier
Brannock	Elgar	Julius	Nicholas	
Brice	Elias	Justin	Oliver	
Bruno	Emeric	Justus	Quentin	
Casper	Erasmus	Kenan	Raphael	

Scandinavian

The names in this category are common in present-day Scandinavia and still carry a Nordic air in America. The style we associate with the region is light and crisp, like a breath of wintry air.

1900   Today

Of course, calling Scandinavian a single style glosses over the region's naming diversity. While traditions overlap, you're most likely to meet a Pelle in Sweden, a Mogens in Denmark, and a Terje in Norway. Finland is a step farther apart, with Eetu and Juho top picks for boys and Viivi and Aino for girls.

If you travel through Sweden, Denmark, or Norway today, though, you'll find that many of the children you meet have names straight out of the "Antique Charm" section of this book. Hot choices for girls include international hits like Emma, Caroline, Julia, Sofie, and Isabella. For boys, you'll hear a lot of Oliver, Jonas, Max, Elias, and Sebastian. In fact, Scandinavia seems to be a few years ahead of the United States on the "antique revival" curve. If you're on the antique trail, you might want to check out some Scandinavian trends that haven't yet caught on in America. For girls, Matilda/Mathilde and Ida are hugely popular. Boys' names ending with a Grecian "s" are all the rage: Mathias, Marius, Jonas, and Tobias are hits. For a more exotic twist, the ultimate Nordic name is quietly climbing in Sweden: Viking.

GIRLS

Annika	Frida	Kiki	Magdalena	Sigrid
Astrid	Greta	Kirsten	Maja	Sofia
Britt	Ida	Kristina	Matilde	Sonja
Britta	Inge	Lempi	Meta	Thora
Dagmar	Ingrid	Linnea	Runa	Tilda
Dagny	Johanna	Lise	Saga	Tove
Elsa	Karina	Lovisa	Signe	

BOYS

Anders	Finn	Johan	Nils	Soren
Arne	Gunnar	Johannes	Olaf	Stefan
Arvid	Gustav	Kai	Ole	Sven
Axel	Hans	Lars	Oscar	Thor
Bjorn	Hannes	Leif	Per	Torsten
Einar	Harald	Linus	Rasmus	Valdemar
Emanuel	Henrik	Mads	Rolf	Viggo
Emil	Jan	Magnus	Rune	
Erik	Jesper	Niels	Sakari	

'70s-'80s

Ah, thanks for stopping by! It gets mighty lonely in this section of the book. You don't meet many parents seeking names to bring back memories of *Charlie's Angels* or the *A-Team*. Not that there's anything remotely objectionable about the baby names of the '70s and '80s . . . but that itself is part of the problem.

1900   Today

For most new parents today, these are the names you barely notice. You meet a couple named Brian and Jennifer and you don't even pause to think about their names, because they just seem *normal*. Fifty years ago, these names would have been creative, but today they seem like defaults: If you don't choose a name for your daughter, she'll end up Jennifer.

Of course, for our children's generation, Kaitlyn will be the default. So what will they think of the '70s–'80s hits? If you choose the right names from that group, you'll be tapping into a classic in the making. Your child will have a proven, admired name with cross-generational appeal. But choose unwisely, and the poor kid might sound like—gulp—somebody's *mom*! As a rule of thumb, names with a distinctive sound and rhythm (e.g., Jeremy, Amanda) generally age better than those that travel in a generational pack (Krista-Trista-Christy-Krystal).

GIRLS

Amanda	Christina	Jodi	Mandy	Shonda
Amber	Christine	Justine	Marcie	Stacy
Amy	Christy	Kami	Marlena	Stevie
April	Crystal	Kari	Melinda	Tanya
Ashley	Desiree	Katrina	Melissa	Tara
Audra	Erica	Keisha	Michelle	Tasha
Brandy	Farrah	Kendra	Mindy	Tawny
Brittany	Felicia	Kerri	Misty	Tiffany
Carrie	Heather	Krista	Natasha	Tonya
Casey	Heidi	Kristen	Nikki	Tricia
Chandra	Jaclyn	Kristi	Rochelle	Trina
Chanel	Jamie	Latasha	Sasha	Trista
Chelsea	Jennifer	Leigh	Shana	Whitney
Cherise	Jessica	Lindsay	Shannon	
Chrissy	Jillian	Liza	Sheena	

BOYS

Brent	Derrick	Heath	Jason	Shannon
Brian	Dustin	Jamey	Jeremy	Shawn
Chad	Dusty	Jarrett	Kristopher	
Corey	Eric	Jarvis	Levar	

Shakespearean

What's in a name? that which we call a rose
By any other name would smell as sweet;
So Romeo would, were he not Romeo call'd,
Retain that dear perfection which he owes
Without that title.

1900   Today

Don't believe it for a second.

Say what he may, the immortal bard was fully attuned to the power of names and the meanings they convey. This is a guy who gave his romantic heroes names like Romeo and Orlando and his fools names like Dogberry and Elbow. In some cases, he went so far as to invent a name to perfectly capture the essence of a character. A famous example is Miranda, a classic conjured up for *The Tempest* from a Latin root meaning "fit to be admired."

The evocative names in Shakespeare's plays still resonate centuries later, with a distinctive style that merits them their own category. This abbreviated list takes some liberties, including spellings and variants that differ from those in the plays. (Benedict, for instance, is a more realistic possibility today than Benedick.) It concentrates on names with a literary flourish and timeless appeal. If you're looking for Falstaff or Fortinbras, get thee to a library.

GIRLS

Adriana	Diana	Jessica	Miranda	Rosaline
Amelia	Emilia	Julia	Olivia	Silvia
Ariel	Francisca	Juliet	Ophelia	Titania
Beatrice	Helena	Juno	Paulina	Ursula
Bianca	Hermia	Katharina	Phoebe	Valeria
Celia	Hermione	Katharine	Portia	Viola
Cordelia	Iris	Mariana	Regan	
Desdemona	Isabella	Marina	Rosalind	

BOYS

Adrian	Antonio	Bertram	Claudio	Curtis
Alonso	Antony	Camillo	Claudius	Demetrius
Alonzo	Balthazar	Cassio	Conrad	Dion
Angelo	Benedict	Cato	Corin	Duncan
Angus	Bernardo	Cicero	Cornelius	Edgar

Fabian	Lennox	Nestor	Prospero	Theseus
Ferdinand	Leonardo	Oliver	Reynaldo	Timon
Francisco	Leonato	Olivier	Rodrigo	Titus
Frederick	Lorenzo	Orlando	Romeo	Toby
Gonzalo	Lysander	Paris	Sebastian	Valentine
Horatio	Marcellus	Pedro	Stefano	
Laurence	Nathaniel	Philo	Tarquin	

Slavic

The Slavic language family includes a dozen languages of Central and Eastern Europe, each with naming traditions that reflect local culture, history, and religion. Slavic names are as diverse as the communities they come from, but together they do make up a distinctive style. Common threads can be seen in regional name choices such as Stanislav and Vladimir, and in typical versions of international names, such as Pavel for Paul. In the United States, the most popular Slavic names today tend to be girls' names, including diminutives like Anya, Katia, and Natasha.

Russian is the most widely spoken Slavic language and has had the biggest impact on American names. The list below focuses on the most common variants of each name, with a selection of local and regional favorites.

GIRLS

Alexandra	Gabriela	Lida	Olga	Stefania
Alina	Galina	Ludmila	Paulina	Svetlana
Anastasia	Halina	Magdalena	Petrina	Tanya
Antonina	Hana	Marcela	Raisa	Tatiana
Anya	Irina	Masha	Raya	Valentina
Basia	Ivana	Michalina	Renata	Valia
Danica	Jana	Mira	Sasha	Vera
Daniela	Josefa	Nadezhda	Severina	Verica
Daria	Katerina	Nadia	Shura	Veronika
Dasia	Katia	Natalia	Simona	Wanda
Denisa	Lara	Natasha	Sonia	
Elena	Larissa	Oksana	Stanislava	

BOYS

Alexi	Casimir	Jiri	Milan	Tomas
Anatoly	Constantin	Jovan	Milos	Vadim
Andrei	Dimitri	Leonid	Oleg	Valentin
Anton	Gennadi	Lev	Pavel	Viktor
Antonin	Goran	Lukas	Roman	Vladimir
Arkady	Igor	Marek	Sergei	
Artur	Ivan	Markian	Stanislav	
Boris	Jerzy	Maxim	Taras	

Solid Citizens

Here are the grown-up names of the *Father Knows Best* world. These are the button-down dads, the demure moms in aprons and pearls. Their kids didn't have full names at all, just nicknames: Bud, Kitten, Beaver.

Ok, that's all a *Nick at Nite* illusion, but it's a strong one. After all, we parents of the twenty-first century weren't there to see the *real* young Vernons and Bettys laugh and bicker and love. But sitcoms are forever, so the Solid Citizens have been firmly established as the squarest names on the block.

Don't turn the page yet, though, because these square standards offer something that the avant-garde can't. The Solid Citizens are comfort names, and like comfort foods they enchant us with their cozy reliability. Everything's okay when you're eating baked macaroni with June and Ward. That warmth is a quality the crisper new hits are lacking. It's also a quality that grows up well, and the world still needs grown-ups. If you find a Solid Citizen name that strikes your fancy, it will make a quiet, understated style statement today with tons of potential for the future.

GIRLS

Anita	Carol	Elaine	Helene	Jo
Ann	Constance	Ellen	Irene	Joan
Arlene	Dale	Faye	Jane	Joanne
Barbara	Darlene	Frances	Janet	Joyce
Bernadette	Doris	Gloria	Janice	Judith
Betty	Dorothy	Gwendolyn	Jean	June
Beverly	Eileen	Helen	Jeanette	Kay

Lois	Marie	Myrna	Rita	Sally
Loretta	Marilyn	Nancy	Roberta	Shirley
Lorna	Marion	Norma	Roma	Sue
Lorraine	Marjorie	Patricia	Rosalie	Sylvia
Margery	Marlys	Phyllis	Rosalind	Therese
Margot	Maxine	Polly	Rosemary	Twila
Marian	Muriel	Rena	Roslyn	Vivian
Marianne	Myra	Rhoda	Ruth	

BOYS

Allen	Duane	Hal	Lyle	Royce
Alvin	Earl	Hale	Martin	Russell
Arnold	Ellis	Harris	Marvin	Sheldon
Bernard	Eugene	Howard	Melvin	Sherman
Bill	Francis	Hugh	Milton	Stanley
Bob	Frank	Jerome	Norman	Stanton
Carl	Franklin	Larry	Paul	Stewart
Charles	Fred	Lawrence	Ralph	Ted
Charlie	Gene	Lee	Randolph	Tom
Clark	Gerald	Leon	Ray	Van
Clifford	Gerard	Leonard	Raymond	Vernon
Clifton	Gilbert	Leroy	Richard	Ward
Clyde	Glendon	Lewis	Roger	Warren
Dale	Glenn	Lionel	Roland	Wendell
Donald	Gordon	Lon	Ronald	Willis
Doyle	Guy	Loren	Roy	

Surfer Sixties

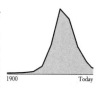

Every era has its sound, in names as well as music. For the new wave of names that hit the beach in the '60s, the sound was brisk, sunny, and windswept. Classic boys' names suddenly felt heavy and old-fashioned, and classic girls' names too elaborate. Welcome Gary and Todd, Lori and Tina.

With the benefit of a few decades' distance, the breeziness of this generation of names is a bit surprising. Their era was fraught with social and political upheaval, but the names are resolutely, even aggressively, carefree. Perhaps they are the personification of the "don't trust anyone over thirty" mentality: names that break with the past and don't look back. Or perhaps they just remind us that the real '60s were as much about Gidget as Woodstock.

The names below surged in the '60s and held on into the '70s, but most have now lost their steam. They have entered generational limbo because today's parents grew up surrounded by them. "Jill? No way, I know a million Jills!" Yes, you do . . . but your daughter won't, because Jill has fallen off the popularity charts. So for now, you may not be able to picture yourself raising a little Tracie or Scottie. But in your grand-children's generation, don't be surprised to see the break-with-the-past '60s names come full circle as old favorites awaiting revival.

GIRLS

Amy	Dawn	Jeannie	Lori	Shelley
Angie	Deena	Jeri	Lynn	Sherry
Aretha	Deirdre	Jill	Marcy	Sonya
Belinda	Denise	Jodi	Marlo	Stacy
Beth	Dina	Jolene	Michele	Starla
Bobbi	Dionne	Joni	Randi	Suzette
Candy	Dori	Julie	Renee	Tamara
Carla	Gidget	Kelly	Rhonda	Tammy
Cherie	Gina	Kerry	Robin	Teri
Chris	Ginger	Kimberly	Rochelle	Tina
Christine	Heidi	Kris	Roxanne	Toni
Cindy	Jan	Laurie	Sandy	Tracy
Dana	Janelle	Leanne	Shari	Trina
Dara	Janette	Lisa	Sharla	Wendy
Darcy	Janine	Liz	Shawn	Yvette

BOYS

Bart	Donnell	Kent	Reggie	Tad
Brad	Dwayne	Kerry	Rob	Terence
Chris	Gregg	Kip	Russ	Thad
Craig	Jeffrey	Kirby	Rusty	Tim
Darrell	Jody	Kirk	Scott	Timothy
Darren	Joey	Kurt	Scotty	Toby
Darryl	Jon	Marty	Stacy	Todd
Dean	Keith	Matt	Steven	Troy
Dirk	Kenny	Randy	Stoney	Vince

Timeless

Meet two couples: Gertrude and Herman, Krista and Cory. Form images of them in your mind. Chances are you've imagined a vast generation gap. Now meet Sarah and Tom. How old are they? If you can't hazard a guess, then you've just encountered the Timeless name style.

1900 Today

Timelessness is a rare quality in a name, subtler than "classic" or "standard." Many timeless names are indeed popular classics, but others have never cracked a top-100 list. What they all share is a steadiness from decade to decade that puts them out of the reach of passing trends.

When you hear a Timeless name, you have no inkling whether the person is aged one, twenty, fifty, or one hundred. The name holds its own in every generation, alongside names from Lester to Logan, Bertha to Baylee. That makes the timeless group the most predictable names in this unpredictable world. It's a good bet that Sarah and Tom, Johanna and Vincent will come across the same way twenty-five years from now as they do today. They may not win points for creativity, but they'll shelter you from the cruel winds of fashion. These are the names built to last a lifetime.

GIRLS

Adrienne	Celia	Elsa	Katherine	Miriam
Angela	Christina	Emily	Kathryn	Naomi
Anna	Claire	Eve	Kate	Nina
Anne	Clare	Gretchen	Laura	Penelope
Antonia	Claudia	Helena	Leah	Priscilla
Audrey	Corinne	Hope	Leila	Rachel
Aurora	Cristina	Ingrid	Lucia	Rebecca
Camilla	Daphne	Iris	Lydia	Sarah
Camille	Diana	Ivy	Margaret	Sonia
Carmen	Elena	Jacqueline	Margarita	Susana
Caroline	Elisa	Joanna	Maria	Theresa
Catherine	Elisabeth	Johanna	Marina	Veronica
Cecilia	Elise	Julia	Mary	Victoria
Celeste	Elizabeth	Juliet	Mercy	

Alan	Dexter	John	Neil	Ruben
Alex	Duncan	José	Nelson	Russell
Alexander	Dwight	Joseph	Nicholas	Samuel
Alfonso	Edward	Julian	Noel	Saul
Anderson	Eliot	Julio	Nolan	Simon
Andrew	Elliott	Karl	Patrick	Spencer
Anthony	Emmett	Kenneth	Paul	Stephen
Antonio	Felix	Lamar	Peter	Sterling
Benjamin	Forrest	Lawrence	Philip	Stuart
Bennett	Frederick	Lincoln	Preston	Thomas
Blaine	George	Lorenzo	Quentin	Tomas
Brooks	Graham	Malcolm	Ramon	Vance
Byron	Grant	Marcel	Raphael	Vaughn
Calvin	Harrison	Marcus	Raul	Victor
Carlo	Henry	Mario	Raymond	Vincent
Charles	Isaac	Mark	Reginald	Wade
Clay	Ivan	Marshall	Reid	Warren
Clayton	Jack	Matthew	Reuben	Wesley
Clinton	Jacob	Michael	Richard	William
Curtis	James	Miles	Robert	Wilson
Daniel	Jay	Mitchell	Roberto	
David	Jefferson	Moses	Roderick	
Davis	Jesse	Nathan	Roman	
Dean	Joel	Nathaniel	Ross	

Why Not?

The names below are a hodgepodge of different sounds and styles, with only two things in common: They're perfectly good, and hardly anybody uses them.

Fashion is fickle, picking out certain names for a ride to the top of the charts and leaving other worthy choices behind. Sure, Orval and Hortense died natural deaths, and Kermit and Grover were Muppeted out of contention. But why are there forty times as many Olivias as Antonias? Why is Max hot and Rex ice cold?

Here, for your consideration, are names seldom heard over the past two decades that have the ingredients to become fashionable. You may quibble over some of the choices ("Rex? Rex is a dog's name!"), but you may also find a neglected gem just waiting to shine.

GIRLS

Adela	Christabel	Helena	Maeve	Romy
Althea	Cleo	Jamila	Marcella	Rosanna
Amalia	Dalia	Janis	Margery	Rosemary
Amity	Daphne	Jill	Margo	Shea
Anthea	Daria	Josefa	Marian	Simone
Antonia	Della	Journey	Maribel	Stasia
Arabella	Delphine	Joy	Mariela	Stefania
Atlanta	Dorothea	Juliet	Marjorie	Sue
Aurea	Elle	June	Mattea	Susannah
Aurelia	Ellen	Katia	May	Sylvie
Aviva	Ellery	Lana	Melina	Tamsin
Beatrix	Elodie	Lavinia	Mercy	Terra
Belle	Elsa	Leora	Mirabelle	Tess
Calla	Emerald	Lila	Nell	Thea
Camilla	Estella	Lilias	Nola	Therese
Cecile	Gail	Linnea	Paloma	Verity
Cecily	Gemma	Lise	Penelope	Willa
Celia	Geneva	Louisa	Rafaela	Zora
Charis	Glenna	Lucia	Renata	
Charity	Graciela	Luna	Reva	
Chiara	Haven	Lyra	Rhea	

BOYS

Alban	Cael	Eamon	Fletcher	Harris
Alden	Callum	Edison	Flynn	Japheth
Alistair	Campbell	Edmund	Forrest	Joah
Anton	Carlo	Egan	Foster	Joss
Archer	Carsten	Ellis	Gareth	Judah
Ari	Clark	Emmett	Garrick	Jude
Asher	Cormac	Evander	Gideon	Jules
Barrett	Crispin	Everett	Grady	Kilian
Bram	Dennison	Finley	Griffith	Leif
Broderick	Duncan	Finn	Hal	Lincoln

Merritt	Porter	Rider	Theo
Murphy	Reuben	Rowan	Tiernan
Nicholson	Rex	Royce	Tobin
Pierce	Richmond	Stanton	Truman

Resource List

Major resources on name meanings, origins, and popularity.

MEANINGS AND ORIGINS

Dunkling, Leslie and William Gosling. *The New American Dictionary of Baby Names*. New York, N.Y.: Penguin Books, 1985.

Hanks, Patrick and Flavia Hodges. *A Dictionary of First Names*. New York: Oxford University Press, 1990.

————. *A Dictionary of Surnames*. New York: Oxford University Press, 1988.

Reaney, Percy, and Richard Wilson. *A Dictionary of English Surnames*, 3rd ed. New York: Oxford University Press, 1997.

Room, Adrian. *Cassell's Dictionary of First Names*. New York: Sterling, 2002.

Withycombe, Elizabeth. *The Oxford Dictionary of English Christian Names*. New York: Oxford University Press, 1947.

POPULARITY

Australia: Office of Consumer & Business Affairs
http://www.ocba.sa.gov.au/bdm/02_babynames.html

Belgium: Nationaal Instituut voor de Statistiek: Voornamen
http://statbel.fgov.be/figures/download_nl.asp

Denmark: Danmarks Statistik
http://www.dst.dk/Statistik/Navne/bestemt_aar.aspx

England and Wales: National Statistics
http://www.statistics.gov.uk/cci/nugget.asp?id=184

France: Prenoms.com
http://www.prenoms.com/

Ireland: Central Statistics Office
http://www.cso.ie/principalstats/princstats.html

Italy: Elenco Telefonico Ricerca Omonimie
http://elenco.libero.it/elencotel/public/RicercaOmonimie.jsp

Norway: Statistics Norway

http://www.ssb.no/navn_en/

Quebec: Banque de prénoms
http://www.rrq.gouv.qc.ca/Interactif/PR2I121_Prenoms/PR2I121_Prenoms/
PR2SPrenoms.aspx?langue=en

Scotland: General Registry Office
http://www.gro-scotland.gov.uk/grosweb/grosweb.nsf/pages/geninfo

Spain (Andalucia): Instituto de Estadística
http://www.juntadeandalucia.es/institutodeestadistica/bd/nombresBD

Spain (Catalunya): Institut d'Estadística de Catalunya
http://www.idescat.es/scripts/onomastica.dll?TC=111

Sweden: Statistics Sweden
http://www.scb.se/templates/Product____30895.asp

United States: Census Bureau
http://www.census.gov/genealogy/names/

United States: Social Security Administration
http://www.ssa.gov/OACT/babynames/index.html

Index

Names and page numbers for full "snapshot" descriptions appear in boldface.

Aaliyah, 14, **21**, 30, 217, 220, 247

Aaron, 27, 55, 71, 81, 99, 105, **127**, 170, 173, 174, 227, 265, 266, 272

Abbie, 38

Abby, 21, 39, 119, 120, 129, 143, 145, 169, 199

Abdiel, 227, 255, 270

Abdullah, 190, 261

Abe, 54, 88, 127, 163, 167, 244, 270

Abel, 81, 88, 89, 121, **127**, 189, 227, 256, 270

Abigail, 14, 18, **21**, 63, 101, 102, 123, 139, 140, 143, 155, 156, 160, 167, 168, 173, 191, 192, 204, 216, 224, 226

Abigale, 21

Abilene, 233

Abner, 172, 227, 275

Abraham, 102, **127**, 153, 206, 224, 227, 270, 271

Abram, 127, 227, 270, 271

Abril, 254

Absalom, 227, 237, 273

Acacia, 40, 232

Acadia, 247, 274

Achebe, 217

Achilles, 29, 127, 131, 239, 243, 262

Ada, **21**, 51, 58, 65, 123, 130, 141, 143, 203, 248, 256, 276

Adah, 21, 50, 174, 180, 182, 184, 226

Adam, 26, 43, 47, 70, 75, 100, 105, 115, **127**, 135, 143, 156, 171, 173, 204, 227, 265, 266

Adan, 26, 99, 107, 112, 186, 255

Addie, 21, 22, 243, 267

Addison, 15, **21**, 38, 68, 76, 89, 103, 106, 114, **127**, 145, 206, 222, 252, 267

Ade, 217

Adela, **21**, 32, 48, 56, 58, 72, 82, 85, 91, 104, 128, 132, 154, 156, 214, 215, 247, 248, 267, 276, 287

Adelaide, **21**, 22, 33, 93, 125, 130, 134, 207, 248, 267, 268, 276

Adelard, 237, 271

Adelbert, 257, 271

Adele, 21, 44, 45, 155, 157, 175, 211, 240, 248, 268

Adelia, 61, 180, 267

Adeline, **22**, 28, 224, 248, 267

Aden, 128

Adi, 246, 256

Adina, **22**, 161, 226, 246, 247

Adira, 33

Adlai, 227

Adolf, 263

Adolfo, 255

Adolphus, 104, 237

Adonis, 105, 123, **127**, 188, 193, 201, 239, 262

Adrian, **22**, 23, 24, 57, 91, 100, 111, 114, **128**, 131, 133, 150, 175, 197, 204, 224, 266, 277, 280

Adriana, **22**, 27, 47, 90, 97, 124, 131, 157, 254, 280

Adrianna, 22, 44

Adrianne, 22

Adriel, 23

Adrien, 41, 128, 240

Adrienne, **22**, 38, 43, 57, 67, 74, 123, 130, 139, 144, 161, 185, 200, 208, 212, 220, 240, 265, 285

Aeneas, 74, 227, 237

Aeron, **22**, 238, 262

Agatha, **22**, 158, 234, 248

Aggie, 22

Agnes, **22**, 34, 52, 56, 61, 155, 275

Agustin, 56, 255

Ahijah, 227

Ahmad, 33, 169, 185, 193, 220, 261

Ahmed, 110, 190, 261

Aida, **22**, 160, 237, 265

Aidan, 14, 96, **128**, 161, 182, 230, 235, 236, 266, 277

Aiden, 128

Aidric, **128**, 237, 277

Aidrick, 128

Aileen, 52

Aimee/Aimée, 26, 36, 142, 240

Aine/Áine, 22, **23**, 100, 146, 230, 262

Ainslee, 23

Ainsley, **23**, 117, 178, 191, 201, 202, 207, 225, 230, 252

Aisha, **23**, 68, 169, 176, 190, 193, 218, 220, 261

Aisling, 83, 153, 157, 176, 178, 204, 209, 230

Aiyana, 33

Aja, 110, 220

Ajani, 217

Ajax, 67, 128, 131, 239, 262

Akeem, 220

Akilah, 15, 217

Akiva, 247

Al, 128, 129, 130, 270

Aladdin, 239

Alain, 240

Alaina, 53

Alan, 39, 59, 72, 74, 75, 112, 115, **128**, 149, 160, 191, 207, 236, 259, 270, 286

Alana, 22, **23**, 27, 81, 95, 111, 112, 138, 147, 210, 267

Alandra, 25

Alanis, **23**, 263

Alanna, 23

Alannah, 23, 209, 230

Alaric, 237, 270

Alasdair, 129

Alastair, 129

Alayna, 24, 53

Alban, 47, **128**, 236, 277, 287

Albany, 274

Albert, 60, 66, 91, 109, **128**, 132, 140, 159, 164, 198, 214, 249, 270

Alberta, 82, 184

Alberto, 89, 128, 245, 255

Albie, 128

Albin, 21, 41, 44, 58, 59, 128, 141, 146, 160, 183, 270

Albina, 257

Albus, 188, 239

Alden, 33, 72, 107, 124, **129**, 132, 162, 236, 252, 287

Aldo, 60, 91, **129**, 156, 186, 245, 255

Aldric, 64, 141, 184, 215, 237, 272, 277

Aldrich, 270

Ale, 129

Aleah, 21, 31, 33, 65, 77, 212

Alec, 30, 31, 59, 90, 96, 104, **129**, 137, 145, 160, 162, 196, 211, 230, 235, 266

Alecia, 24

Alegra, 25

Alejandra, 35, 55, 95, 125, 141, 183, 247, 254

Alejandro, **129**, 131, 189, 255

Alesha, 24

Alessandra, **23**, 27, 58, 60, 162, 181, 245, 247, 270

Alessia, 24, 245, 247

Alex, 23, 24, 25, 38, 39, 51, 70, 72, 75, 98, **129**, 152, 169, 222, 267, 270, 286

Alexa, **23**, 29, 30, 69, 77, 92, 113, 118, 138, 142, 144, 197, 216, 247, 267

Alexander, 18, 55, 75, 99, 123, **129**, 135, 143, 168, 174, 191, 192, 204, 216, 241, 270, 273, 286

Alexandra, **23**, 43, 59, 96, 110, 123, 211, 216, 247, 264, 267, 270, 281

Alexandre, 129, 240

Alexandrea, 24

Alexandria, **24**, 122, 247, 267, 274

Alexandros, 129, 161, 245, 273

Alexea, 23

Alexi, 270, 282

Alexia, **24**, 88, 132, 247

Alexios, 50, 53, 243

Alexis, 18, **24**, 43, 98, 102, 128, 133, 143, 148, 151, 153, 160, 222, 267, 276, 277

Alexus, 24

Alexys, 24

Alf, 129, 244, 270

Alfie, 235

Alfonso, 32, 41, 185, 195, 255, 286

Alfonzo, 125, 270

Alfred, 123, **129**, 156, 159, 166, 249, 270, 271

Alfredo, 129, 197, 245, 255, 270
Algernon, 94, 209, 237
Ali, 23, 24, 25, 57, 81, 261, 267
Alice, 24, 52, 58, 64, 91, 92, 109, 129, 132, 140, 142, 159, 161, 165, 214, 248, 267, 268
Alicia, 24, 106, 150, 174, 200, 247, 254, 264
Alick, 129
Alina, 23, 24, 29, 47, 79, 98, 103, 107, 111, 241, 247, 281
Alisa, 24, 78, 247, 264, 267
Alisha, 24, 208, 212, 220
Alison, 24, 25, 36, 96, 100, 127, 136, 137, 141, 156, 178, 204
Alissa, 23, 25, 212
Alistair, 33, 41, 83, 128, 129, 133, 157, 164, 179, 208, 230, 235, 237, 270, 287
Alister, 129
Alivia, 171
Alix, 24
Aliya, 21
Aliyah, 21, 26, 69, 155, 267
Aliza, 246
Alize, 267
Allan, 73, 128, 177, 199
Allegra, 25, 33, 37, 62, 80, 86, 120, 123, 132, 246, 247, 248, 267
Allen, 36, 54, 68, 71, 73, 89, 99, 102, 115, 128, 147, 150, 153, 161, 162, 186, 195, 201, 283
Allie, 23, 24, 25, 38, 110, 243, 267
Allison, 25, 37, 55, 71, 94, 110, 152, 170, 264, 267

Allure, 56, 238
Ally, 25
Allyson, 25, 71
Alma, 21, 25, 45, 52, 56, 108, 118, 123, 133, 143, 154, 156, 159, 166, 175, 209, 248, 265
Almeda, 45
Alois, 257
Alondra, 25, 29, 122, 129, 131, 220, 254
Alonso, 81, 130, 280
Alonzo, 22, 48, 126, 130, 220, 237, 255, 272, 280
Aloysius, 130, 237
Alpha, 258
Alphonse, 240, 270
Alphonso, 237
Altagracia, 85, 268
Altair, 239
Althea, 21, 24, 25, 32, 58, 59, 66, 80, 97, 107, 140, 160, 164, 248, 262, 287
Alton, 21, 107, 236, 252
Alun, 128
Alvaro/Álvaro, 91, 107, 118, 255
Alverta, 257
Alvin, 66, 130, 159, 162, 162, 181, 206, 214, 283
Alwyn, 235, 236
Aly, 25
Alyce, 24
Alycia, 24
Alys, 24, 168, 213, 215, 230
Alysha, 112
Alyson, 25, 138, 208
Alyssa, 18, 25, 36, 76, 247, 267
Amabel, 94, 128, 133, 208, 209, 234, 237
Amachi, 217

Amalia, 21, 26, 32, 41, 83, 145, 248, 269, 276, 287
Amana, 226
Amanda, 24, 25, 27, 30, 43, 47, 70, 115, 123, 143, 171, 187, 210, 247, 264, 269, 279
Amandine, 269
Amani, 15, 21, 26, 33, 150, 169, 217, 220, 261
Amara, 247
Amari, 30, 77, 125, 217, 217, 220
Amata, 276
Amaya, 24, 25, 26, 111, 131, 247, 254
Amber, 26, 30, 37, 46, 52, 120, 146, 179, 232, 265, 279
Ambrogio, 244
Ambrose, 32, 45, 93, 130, 132, 235, 249, 277
Amelia, 26, 41, 42, 53, 55, 61, 64, 66, 72, 86, 127, 153, 194, 206, 213, 223, 224, 234, 269, 280
Amelie/Amélie, 26, 54, 55, 240
America, 26, 82, 260, 269, 274
Americo, 257
Ami, 26, 121
Amie, 26
Amina, 81, 110, 261, 269
Amir, 26, 57, 81, 110, 247, 261
Amira, 23, 26, 46, 170, 246, 247, 261
Amity, 16, 26, 33, 38, 95, 199, 232, 287
Amon, 59, 262
Amos, 69, 130, 166, 194, 202, 227, 263, 275

Amy, **26**, 29, 40, 70, 78, 80, 96, 97, 137, 170, 210, 265, 279, 284

Amya, 26, 29

Ana, 27, 28, 65, 140, 172, 174, 195, 198, 254

Anaëlle, 240

Anahi, 26, 99, 254

Anaïs, **27**, 41, 133, 135, 237, 239, 240, 263

Anastasia, 24, **27**, 28, 31, 99, 117, 122, 147, 149, 151, 157, 188, 242, 243, 247, 256, 276, 281

Anastasios, 243

Anatolia, 276

Anatoly, 282

Ander, 180

Anders, 278

Anderson, 41, **130**, 252, 270, 286

Andi, 24, 27

Andra, 27, 92

Andre, 27, 29, 40, 49, 79, 81, 98, 114, 125, **130**, 131, 141, 147, 151, 185, 196, 220, 240, 265, 270

Andrea, 24, 25, **27**, 71, 94, 98, 106, 131, 136, 140, 148, 156, 194, 207, 245, 247, 264

Andreas, 28, 50, 95, 130, 151, 187, 206, 237, 242, 243

Andrei, 130, 282

Andres/Andrés, 25, 122, 130, 131, 151, 189, 255

Andrew, 18, 30, 55, 75, **130**, 131, 187, 194, 227, 270, 271, 286

Andromeda, 238

Andy, 25, 27, 70, 130, 157, 180, 270

Ange, 27

Angel, 27, **131**, 147, 148, 172, 220, 222, 254, 255, 260, 267

Angela, **27**, 78, 90, 204, 213, 267, 285

Angelia, 25, 27, 34, 42, 122, 247, 267

Angelica, 22, 23, 24, **27**, 35, 38, 40, 43, 55, 58, 92, 109, 122, 125, 129, 156, 193, 247, 254, 267

Angelika, 27

Angelina, **27**, 67, 87, 122, 224, 247, 267

Angeline, 21, 22, 27, 59, 89, 248

Angelique, 27, 141, 149, 151, 237, 240, 267

Angelita, 89

Angelo, 85, 108, **131**, 185, 245, 266, 280

Angie, 27, 70, 210, 267, 284

Angus, 88, **131**, 179, 184, 230, 271, 280

Ani, 27, 28

Anika, 24, 28, 192

Anisa, 261

Anita, **27**, 39, 81, 106, 119, 147, 153, 161, 162, 186, 197, 207, 212, 220, 254, 282

Aniya, 186, 254

Aniyah, 220

Anja, 140, 215, 241

Anke, 241

Ann, 28, 54, 68, 69, 92, 143, 195, 198, 200, 267, 282

Anna, 18, **28**, 41, 53, 100, 174, 215, 224, 227, 267, 285

Annabel, 14, 26, 28, 129, 180, 182, 207, 224, 231

Annabella, 28, 56, 199, 216, 224, 247

Annabelle, **28**, 32, 41, 267

Annalise, 27, **28**, 29, 224, 267

Anne, 24, **28**, 93, 154, 169, 173, 186, 195, 267, 269, 285

Anneliese, 28, 241

Annetta, 84, 103

Annette, **28**, 116, 125, 146, 172, 201, 240, 258, 259, 267

Annie, 27, **28**, 86, 159, 162, 164, 171, 173, 202, 224, 243, 267

Annika, 23, **28**, 68, 74, 90, 116, 163, 196, 206, 247, 267, 278

Annmarie, 81

Anouk, 240

Ansel, 249

Ansley, 92, 171

Anthea, 33, 41, 192, 208, 234, 287

Anthi, 53, 243

Anthony, 18, 67, **130**, **131**, 187, 273, 286

Antoine, 42, 51, 52, 130, **131**, 172, 218, 220, 240

Antoinette, **28**, 90, 220, 240, 248, 270

Anton, 28, 34, 41, 64, 66, 72, 82, 92, 96, 107, 131, 136, 140, 163, 199, 209, 242, 273, 282, 287

Antonia, **29**, 44, 64, 89, 145, 157, 167, 209, 213, 245, 247, 267, 270, 285, 287

Antonin, 131, 282

Antonina, 88, 245, 270, 281

Antonio, 58, 60, 91, 106,

122, **131**, 140, 174, 183, 185, 189, 193, 200, 245, 255, 273, 280, 286
Antonios, 243
Antony, 31, 40, 61, 65, 104, 131, 157, 193, 237, 277, 280
Antwain, 131
Antwan, 80, 131, 218, 220
Antwon, 131
Anwen, 230
Anya, 23, **29**, 60, 78, 88, 97, 98, 101, 101, 127, 187, 247, 256, 281
Aoife, 23, 56, 58, 100, 157, 204, 230, 262
Apollo, 67, 127, **131**, 175, 188, 238, 239, 262, 277
Apollonia, 30, 237, 276
Apple, 238
April, 26, **29**, 31, 33, 46, 63, 65, 68, 117, 137, 165, 179, 232, 265, 279
Aquila, 74, 193, 227, 247
Arabel, 29
Arabella, 28, **29**, 30, 67, 247, 287
Arabelle, 29
Araceli, 100, 254
Aracely, 99
Araminta, 29, 101, 119, 234, 237, 247
Aramis, 239
Arcadia, 16, 99, 260
Arch, 132, 190, 244
Archer, 15, 25, 83, **132**, 140, 158, 199, 204, 250, 270, 287
Archibald, 44, 64, 146, 158, 181, 230, 249, 270
Archie, 34, 53, 49, 51, 54, 56, 84, 85, 87, 88,

106, 132, 133, 142, 163, 165, 191, 244, 270
Ardell, 275
Arden, 83, 140, 142, 145, 153, 154, 222, 236, 252
Ardith, 145, 188
Are, 132
Arely, 26, 254
Aretha, **29**, 220, 247, 263, 284
Ari, 29, 30, 46, 53, 81, 89, 119, **132**, 170, 247, 256, 266, 287
Aria, **29**, 63, 72, 87, 172, 247, 260
Ariadne, **29**, 64, 80, 188, 195, 237, 262, 276
Ariana, 23, 25, **29**, 168, 220, 245, 247
Ariane, 54
Arianna, 29
Aric, 22, 26, 77, 156, 180
Arieh, 132
Ariel, **30**, 35, 46, 69, 97, 101, 132, 142, 150, 170, 189, 222, 245, 246, 247, 255, 263, 264, 280
Arielle, 30, 38, 40, 81
Aris, 94, 243
Aristotle, 239
Arkady, 282
Arleen, 30
Arlene, **30**, 98, 101, 113, 148, 151, 156, 159, 161, 282
Arley, 222, 252
Arlie, 30, 216, 243
Arline, 30, 182
Arlis, 155, 222
Arlo, **132**, 146, 189, 191, 244, 266
Arly, 30, 78
Armand, 28, 49, 255
118, 130, **132**, 166, 175, 240, 249, 266

Armando, 55, 91, 122, 132, 166, 183, 245
Armani, 30, 238
Armida, 257
Armin, 31, 166, 242
Arnaldo, 132
Arnaud, 132
Arne, 132, 278
Arnie, 132
Arno, 132, 242
Arnold, **132**, 162, 193, 197, 283
Art, 132, 270
Artemas, 157, 180, 227, 237
Artemesia, 30
Artemis, 29, 30, 31, 127, 262
Artemisia, 27, 29, **30**, 67, 101, 133, 141, 209, 237, 247
Arthur, 24, 28, 44, 56, 85, 128, 129, **132**, 154, 159, 165, 183, 187, 214, 249, 270
Artie, 30, 132
Artis, 198, 270
Artur, 132, 242, 282
Arturo, 132, 204, 255, 270
Arvid, 278
Arvil, 257
Arvilla, 257
Aryan, 258
Aryanna, 29
Asa, 62, 155, 204, 227, 247
Asante, 201, 217
Ash, 30, 132
Ashanti, 21, **30**, 193, 217, 220
Asher, 46, 56, 82, 101, 113, 116, **132**, 142, 161, 166, 170, 173, 227, 247, 287
Ashlee, 30, 146
Ashleigh, 30

Ashley, 18, 26, **30**, 175, 222, 279

Ashli, 30

Ashlie, 30

Ashly, 30

Ashlyn, **30**, 38, 136, 139, 163, 169, 195, 210, 225

Ashlynn, 30

Ashton, **30**, 31, 49, 78, 84, 103, 118, 121, **132**, 148, 169, 170, 176, 179, 206, 208, 212, 214, 222, 236, 252

Ashtyn, 30, 102

Asia, **31**, 48, 100, 106, 186, 212, 220, 265, 274

Asma, 261

Asmara, 274

Aspen, **31**, 37, 43, 76, 106, 112, 113, 119, 150, 151, 183, 196, 199, 207, 210, 233, 269, 274

Astrid, **31**, 62, 66, 104, 133, 154, 157, 167, 182, 215, 224, 237, 241, 278

Atara, 22, 111, 168, 184, 226

Athanasia, 243

Athanasios, 243

Athena, **31**, 46, 66, 67, 118, 123, 133, 147, 151, 176, 184, 203, 212, 216, 237, 242, 243, 262, 265

Athina, 31

Atlanta, **31**, 274, 287

Atom, 128, 238, 239

Atticus, 67, **133**, 141, 166, 208, 237, 263, 266

Auberon, 67, 235, 237

Aubree, 31

Aubrey, 23, 30, **31**, 32,

47, 76, 89, 113, 116, 127, 130, 132, 133, 137, 138, 142, 144, 147, 149, 159, 167, 169, 194, 207, 214, 215, 222, 252, 265

Aubrie, 31, 160

Audie, 31

Audra, **31**, 40, 107, 108, 180, 197, 248, 279

Audrey, **31**, 139, 143, 145, 186, 193, 199, 206, 265, 285

Audry, 31

Augie, 133

August, 22, 57, 93, 131, **133**, 146, 157, 203, 207, 209, 232, 249, 260, 271

Augusta, 22, 31, **32**, 93, 126, 130, 134, 147, 181, 201, 203, 248, 276

Augustine, 222

Augustus, 51, 130, 133, 191, 212, 237, 249, 271

Aura, 238

Aurea, 22, **32**, 35, 90, 128, 160, 162, 212, 247, 276, 287

Aurelia, 25, **32**, 72, 93, 104, 119, 126, 130, 183, 248, 276, 287

Aurelio, 255

Aurora, 22, **32**, 41, 111, 182, 187, 198, 205, 208, 212, 237, 262, 285

Aurore, 240

Austen, 133

Austin, 25, 40, 63, 72, 76, 90, 111, 118, **133**, 143, 151, 173, 236, 252, 266, 274

Austyn, 133, 206

Autumn, 16, 27, 31, **32**,

49, 57, 60, 69, 113, 115, 134, 165, 232, 260, 265

Ava, 31, **32**, 57, 61, 63, 67, 83, 89, 94, 96, 126, 128, 129, 148, 151, 154, 161, 168, 175, 182, 194, 200, 204, 224, 256, 265

Avalon, 131, 175, 238, 270

Averil, 33, 75, 101, 128, 137, 146, 168, 178, 237, 276

Averill, 33

Avery, 31, **32**, 38, 48, 71, 127, 128, 129, **133**, 135, 136, 139, 141, 143, 145, 149, 151, 155, 163, 182, 186, 194, 222, 252, 265, 266

Avi, 22, 33, 101, 120, 132, 166, 192, 247, 256

Avigail, 21

Avis, **32**, 44, 66, 97, 126, 150, 155, 157, 160, 189, 191, 198, 208, 248, 256, 265

Avital, 122, 168, 170, 226

Aviva, 22, 26, 30, **33**, 113, 120, 157, 170, 192, 246, 247, 287

Avraham, 127

Avril, 23, 29, **33**, 240

Axel, 32, 55, 111, 126, 127, **133**, 154, 157, 163, 192, 203, 237, 278

Axelle, 240

Ayana, 23, 33, 77

Ayanda, 217

Ayanna, **33**, 68, 77, 217, 220, 247

Ayden, 128, 171, 225

Ayla, 121, 225

Aylin, 169, 202, 225
Ayo, 217
Azarel, 227
Aziza, 261
Azriel, 122, 168, 227
Azure, 33, 45, 120, 232

Babette, 57
Babs, 33
Bailee, 33
Bailey, 33, 36, 40, 62,
  72, 76, 108, 113, 116,
  118, 133, 138, 138,
  142, 169, 188, 207,
  208, 211, 212, 222,
  224, 225, 250
Baird, 37, 55, 135, 228,
  230
Bakari, 15, 217
Baldwin, 252
Balin, 236, 277
Balthazar, 227, 280
Bambi, 238
Bannon, 78, 236, 252
Barak, 168, 227
Baraka, 217
Barb, 33
Barbara, 33, 39, 61, 71,
  91, 102, 199, 202, 268,
  282
Barbie, 33, 97
Barbra, 33, 259
Barclay, 215, 252
Barker, 250
Barnabas, 30, 94, 133,
  166, 227, 237, 270
Barnaby, 33, 133, 134,
  146, 227, 235, 237,
  270
Barnard, 277
Barney, 133, 244, 263,
  270
Baron, 29, 42, 92, 123,
  134, 196, 236, 239
Barrett, 42, 54, 108, 134,
  150, 252, 287
Barron, 134, 252, 270

Barry, 36, 43, 45, 50, 75,
  86, 103, 113, 116, 134,
  138, 160, 177, 259,
  270
Bart, 42, 71, 110, 134,
  270, 284
Bartholomew, 119, 133,
  134, 149, 180, 227,
  237, 270
Bartley, 134
Barton, 105, 148, 252,
  270
Bashir, 261
Basia, 47, 185, 281
Basil, 22, 136, 141, 155,
  158, 162, 235, 249
Basim, 261
Basma, 261
Bastien, 204, 240
Bathsheba, 226, 238
Batt, 134
Bay, 33, 37, 79, 83, 125,
  165, 168, 174, 209,
  228, 232
Baylee, 33, 36, 137, 138,
  176, 206, 285
Baxter, 150, 250
Baz, 108, 134, 216, 228,
  270
Bea, 33
Beatrice, 14, 33, 35, 41,
  45, 51, 52, 59, 64, 85,
  90, 93, 125, 133, 134,
  141, 143, 154, 175,
  203, 209, 234, 240,
  248, 270, 280
Beatrix, 29, 33, 64, 67,
  128, 129, 133, 141,
  146, 149, 157, 187,
  195, 234, 237, 276,
  287
Beatriz, 33, 91, 100, 254
Beau, 38, 42, 79, 109,
  134, 147, 199, 205,
  210, 228, 233
Beauregard, 88, 237
Becca, 106

Beck, 134, 136, 165, 228,
  252
Beckett, 134, 140, 181,
  252, 263
Becky, 34, 75, 103, 106,
  110, 210, 259, 267
Belina, 276
Belinda, 34, 46, 109,
  116, 134, 178, 247,
  284
Bell, 29, 154
Bella, 29, 34, 53, 61, 66,
  67, 81, 94, 224
Belle, 28, 34, 41, 44, 56,
  70, 82, 93, 94, 115,
  124, 126, 131, 132,
  159, 164, 194, 196,
  199, 224, 287
Ben, 21, 40, 46, 70, 88,
  94, 110, 134, 135, 164,
  270
Benedict, 14, 25, 33, 38,
  41, 59, 64, 72, 80, 90,
  91, 103, 108, 119, 119,
  133, 134, 157, 170,
  180, 198, 237, 270,
  280
Benita, 35
Benito, 255, 263
Benjamin, 18, 42, 75,
  105, 111, 123, 129,
  130, 131, 135, 148,
  173, 187, 191, 192,
  204, 227, 270, 271,
  286
Benji, 135
Bennet, 135
Bennett, 130, 134, 135,
  145, 168, 171, 182,
  188, 213, 252, 270,
  286
Bennie, 221
Benno, 135, 242, 244,
  270
Benny, 35, 244
Benton, 270
Berenice, 62, 227

Berkeley, 222, 252
Bernadette, 35, 108, 240, 282
Bernadine, 132
Bernard, 51, 116, **135**, 144, 154, 159, 164, 166, 172, 186, 187, 188, 201, 213, 249, 270, 283
Bernardo, 95, 280
Bernhard, 186, 242
Bernice, 96, 103, 158, 181, 214, 227, 275
Bernie, 135, 165, 244
Berry, 134, 257
Bert, 49, 51, 87, 128, 133, 135, 159, 166, 200, 244, 270
Berta, 34, 101
Bertha, 34, 60, 155, 166, 241, 275, 285
Berthold, 242
Bertie, 34
Bertram, 22, 44, 54, 62, 93, 104, **135**, 143, 145, 155, 158, 203, 207, 214, 242, 249, 270, 271, 280
Bertrand, 44, 59, 90, 104, 135, 240, 270, 272, 277
Beryl, 63, 101, 104, 162, 180, 195, 222, 248
Bess, **34**, 38, 53, 61, 84, 87, 88, 94, 99, 118, 133, 175, 190, 211, 243, 267
Bessie, 34, 54, 88, 243
Beth, **34**, 53, 70, 78, 85, 86, 108, 134, 146, 171, 177, 246, 267, 284
Bethan, 61, 163, 230
Bethany, **34**, 40, 71, 83, 96, 99, 109, 115, 116, 122, 137, 141, 170, 183, 227, 264, 267
Bethel, 180, 184, 226

Beto, 200
Betsy, **34**, 53, 62, 259
Bette, 35, 53
Bettie, 35, 164
Bettina, 44, 241, 267
Betts, 35
Betty, **35**, 53, 84, 151, 161, 267, 282
Bettye, 35
Beulah, 34, 130, 226, 275
Bevan, 236
Beverley, 35, 109, 205
Beverly, 33, **35**, 91, 102, 104, 113, 148, 206, 282
Beyonce, 220
Bianca, 30, **35**, 60, 95, 102, 141, 156, 162, 170, 181, 185, 193, 204, 244, 245, 267, 280
Bibi, 35
Bijou, 27, 238
Bilal, 110, 261
Bill, 51, 71, 108, 147, 161, 215, 270, 283
Billie, **35**, 50, 222, 243, 267
Billy, 103, 113, 215
Birch, 79, 80, 83, 120, 125, 165, 232
Birdie, 243
Bishop, 123, **135**, 239
Bjorn, 278
Blaine, 59, 110, **135**, 143, 149, 152, 176, 196, 212, 228, 277, 286
Blair, **35**, 51, 65, 81, 135, 138, 222, 228
Blaise, 29, 37, 54, 122, **135**, 176, 185, 228, 240, 277
Blake, 37, 67, 69, 101, **136**, 138, 142, 145, 150, 179, 228

Blanca, 35, 86, 198, 199, 254
Blanche, **35**, 41, 58, 190, 195, 207, 240, 248
Blane, 135
Blaze, 30, 67, 105, 172, 187, 196, 239
Bliss, 64, 135, 238
Blossom, 238, 243
Blue, 80, 239
Bo, 77, 105, 134, 233
Boaz, 22, 122, 168, 170, 227, 247
Bob, 84, 103, 161, 200, 272, 283
Bobbi, 81, 105, 108, 284
Bobbie, 33, 35, 222, 268
Bobby, 73, 110, 200
Bond, 33, **136**, 163, 228, 277
Bonita, **35**, 259
Bonnie, 35, **36**, 73, 96, 99, 103, 115, 162, 214, 232, 259
Bonny, 36
Booker, 218, 263
Boris, 101, **136**, 282
Borya, 136
Boston, 66, 123, 183, 236, 274
Boyce, 257
Boyd, 177
Brad, 34, 43, 47, 64, 70, 120, 121, 124, **136**, 148, 178, 210, 211, 270, 284
Brade, 136
Braden, 38, 69, 76, 77, 78, 88, **136**, 139, 225, 235, 236, 270
Bradford, 47, 136, 198, 252, 270
Bradley, 24, 27, 35, 36, 82, 83, 94, 98, 116, 122, 123, **136**, 150, 161, 214, 252, 265, 270

Brady, 30, 31, 32, 79, 89, 103, 115, **136**, 160, 194, 200, 225, 252, 266, 270
Bradyn, 136
Braeden, 69, 136, 235
Braedon, 235
Braiden, 136, 235
Bram, 37, 86, 93, 107, 127, **136**, 209, 215, 237, 241, 242, 270, 287
Bran, 137
Branden, 137
Brandi, 36, 220
Brandie, 36
Brandon, 18, 25, 30, 34, 37, 44, 46, 51, 80, 94, 99, 110, 122, 124, **137**, 175, 178, 203, 236, 265
Brandt, 105
Brandy, **36**, 46, 97, 279
Brannock, 129, **137**, 145, 158, 178, 230, 277
Brannon, 57, 112, 236, 252
Branson, 142, 215, 233, 236, 252
Brant, 35, 84, 112, 137, 144, 228
Braxton, **137**, 138, 170, 176, 252
Brayden, 16, 136, 225, 235
Braydon, 136, 235
Breanna, 36, 77
Breanne, 36
Bree, 36, 109, 228, 268
Breeze, 238
Brenda, **36**, 43, 45, 102, 113, 201, 208, 230, 259, 265
Brendan, 34, 37, 71, 92, 98, 109, **137**, 145, 157, 230, 236, 265, 266

Brenna, **36**, 93, 128, 136, 138, 139, 146, 170, 190, 230, 265
Brennan, 31, 33, 36, 76, 77, 84, 87, 89, 96, 106, 109, 124, 133, **137**, 146, 151, 163, 176, 177, 178, 179, 230, 236, 250, 252, 266
Brent, 31, 36, 46, 57, 64, 77, 78, 81, 95, 97, 115, **137**, 138, 142, 148, 161, 228, 279
Brenton, 37, 79, 121, 134, 236
Bret, 137, 180
Brett, 24, 39, 40, 65, 74, 75, 77, 80, 78, 83, 95, 109, 117, 121, 136, **137**, 144, 146, 150, 152, 153, 179, 210, 228, 265
Brevin, 218
Bria, 117, 119, 268
Brian, 25, 26, 29, 36, 43, 63, 64, 65, 70, 76, 78, 96, 127, **137**, 156, 170, 178, 194, 230, 265, 266, 279
Briana, 36, 137
Brianna, 18, 25, 29, **36**, 37, 88, 220, 247, 268
Brianne, 36, 46
Brice, 38, 41, 75, 84, 111, 114, 121, 134, 138, 139, 148, 176, 196, 211, 228, 240, 277
Bridger, 78, 233, 250
Bridget, **36**, 70, 82, 93, 98, 136, 137, 177, 194, 202, 205, 210, 230, 264, 268
Bridie, 36, 257
Brigham, 181, 252
Brighid, 36
Brighton, 274

Brigid, 36
Brigit, 36
Brigitta, 241
Brigitte, 36, 125, 240
Brisa, 186, 254, 268
Britany, 37
Britney, 37, 263
Britny, 37
Britt, 35, **36**, 37, 77, 84, 136, 158, 174, 180, 209, 222, 228, 278
Britta, 36, 182, 256, 276, 278
Brittanie, 37
Brittany, 30, **37**, 42, 120, 268, 274, 279
Brittini, 37
Britton, 236
Brock, 84, 97, 112, **138**, 138, 144, 147, 170, 179, 210, 252
Broder, 271
Broderick, 29, 137, 192, 207, 230, 252, 271, 272, 287
Brody, 36, 55, 78, 84, 103, 117, 118, 134, 137, **138**, 144, 145, 152, 163, 169, 179, 184, 198, 202, 222, 252, 271
Brogan, 55, 83, 137, 153, 154, 209, 210, 230, 252
Bronson, 42, 236
Bronwyn, 61, 107, 137, 230, 237
Brook, 37, 99
Brooke, 35, **37**, 59, 69, 80, 101, 137, 142, 145, 150, 152, 157, 160, 183, 205, 228, 264
Brooklyn, 37, 87, 136, 138, 183, 210, 274
Brooklynn, 37
Brooks, **138**, 228, 286
Brown, 258
Broz, 130

Bruce, 39, 43, 51, 59, 68, 73, 75, 83, 102, 103, 112, 113, 118, 134, **138**, 148, 152, 160, 177, 208, 214, 259

Brunilda, 275

Bruno, **138**, 194, 200, 242, 244, 245, 277

Bryan, 46, 82, 93, 97, 117, 137, 205

Bryanna, 36

Bryant, 74, 96, **138**, 169, 177, 190, 196, 208, 212, 214, 252, 266

Bryce, 33, 36, 78, 111, 113, 118, 121, 136, **138**, 142, 215, 216, 228, 230, 233, 274

Brycen, 69, 138, 228

Bryn, 36, 37, 153, 158, 162, 176, 215

Brynn, 14, **37**, 53, 88, 106, 110, 112, 135, 136, 149, 202, 210, 228, 230

Brynna, 36

Brynne, 37

Bryson, 21, 68, 69, 87, 136, **138**, 147, 179, 195, 212, 236, 252

Bubba, 50, 233

Buck, 57, 132, 171, 184, 233, 244

Buckley, 252

Bud, 244

Buddy, 35, 50, 105

Buffy, 53, 263

Buford, 214, 275

Burdette, 257

Burke, 136, 138, 184, 200, 229, 252

Burl, 275

Burley, 258

Burnell, 275

Burton, 107, 144, 164, 205

Buster, 138, 200, 244

Butch, 35, 123, 203, 258, 259

Byron, 40, 57, 114, **139**, 212, 213, 236, 266, 286

Cabot, 181, 252

Cade, 38, 67, 78, 106, **139**, 160, 229

Caden, 68, 136, **139**, 169, 225, 235, 236, 275

Cadence, **37**, 63, 66, 87, 169, 260

Cady, 37, 188

Cael, 86, 88, 110, 124, 133, 135, 139, 176, 256, 287

Caesar, 127, 141, 239

Caetano, 255

Caiden, 139

Cait, 37

Caitlin, 15, **37**, 46, 74, 94, 128, 137, 140, 145, 150, 178, 205, 225, 229, 230

Caitlyn, 74, 77

Caitlynn, 37

Cal, 139, 142, 171, 174, 229, 271

Cale, 117, **139**, 148, 158, 229

Caleb, 14, 21, 43, 47, 63, 83, 90, 96, 101, **139**, 143, 154, 156, 160, 167, 168, 173, 175, 182, 192, 205, 209, 215, 224, 226, 227, 271

Caleigh, 38, 225

Cali, 37, 38

Calista, 23, **37**, 113, 247

Calla, 26, **37**, 38, 79, 83, 86, 94, 95, 123, 165, 232, 256, 287

Callahan, 252

Callie, 25, 37, **38**, 39, 72, 88, 118, 243

Callum, 83, **139**, 146, 179, 185, 230, 271, 287

Calum, 139

Calvin, 105, 109, **139**, 271, 273, 286

Cam, 38, 139, 140, 271

Camden, 37, 68, 94, **139**, 169, 230, 236, 271, 274

Cameron, 14, 15, 24, **38**, 98, 111, **140**, 145, 151, 195, 222, 230, 260, 271

Cami, 38

Camilla, 21, 37, **38**, 42, 58, 59, 73, 104, 129, 140, 144, 169, 180, 234, 276, 285, 287

Camille, **38**, 41, 42, 47, 53, 60, 65, 73, 91, 114, 131, 148, 155, 162, 185, 193, 196, 240, 269, 285

Camillo, 245, 280

Cammie, 38

Campbell, 31, 92, 132, **140**, 192, 197, 200, 252, 271, 287

Camron, 24, 37, 171, 236

Camryn, 30, **38**, 139, 149, 169, 176, 225

Candace, 22, **38**, 73, 161, 208, 264, 268

Candice, 38, 40, 75

Candida, 268

Candido, 257

Candis, 38

Candy, 38, 42, 134, 268, 284

Canton, 236, 274

Canyon, 16, 113, 232, 233, 239

Caoimhe, 100, 230

Cap, 141
Caprice, **38**, 79, 260
Cara, 38, 74, 79 81, 94,
   96, 116, 117, 119, 137,
   148, 167, 199, 202,
   256, 264
Carey, 252
Cari, 40
Carin, 74
Carina, 38, 44, 74, 91,
   119
Carissa, **38**, 134, 247, 268
Carl, 28, 41, 56, 64, 66,
   91, 92, 108, 109, **140**,
   142, 163, 173, 180,
   183, 184, 195, 198,
   202, 283
Carla, 34, **39**, 47, 60,
   107, 120, 177, 210,
   222, 245, 268, 284
Carleen, 42, 268
Carleton, 38, 65, 140,
   154, 191, 202, 206,
   235, 252
Carli, 120
Carlie, 39
Carlito, 140
Carlitos, 140
Carlo, 29, 31, 59, 81, 85,
   92, 93, 107, 115, 140,
   142, 156, 185, 245,
   286, 287
Carlos, 61, **140**, 142,
   174, 183, 189, 254,
   255
Carlotta, 268
Carlton, **140**, 143, 144,
   191
Carly, **39**, 40, 67, 152,
   179, 268
Carlyle, 118, 190
Carma, 257
Carmel, 39, 184, 226,
   269
Carmela, 50, 84, 89, 130,
   131, 138, 146, 185,
   200, 245, 268

Carmelo, **140**, 245, 272
Carmen, 22, **39**, 86, 89,
   160, 185, 197, 222,
   254, 268
Carmine, 138, 200, 244
Carol, **39**, 51, 52, 54, 71,
   73, 99, 202, 259, 268,
   282
Carole, 39, 71, 108
Carolina, **39**, 88, 90, 96,
   98, 147, 182, 209, 215,
   224, 233, 268, 274
Caroline, 31, **39**, 44, 55,
   73, 75, 87, 123, 129,
   143, 145, 149, 164,
   168, 171, 188, 191,
   192, 196, 204, 206,
   224, 268, 278, 285
Carolyn, **39**, 48, 68, 75,
   83, 102, 177, 201, 259,
   268
Carolynn, 39
Carrie, 31, 39, **40**, 70,
   144, 268, 279
Carroll, 39, 183, 222
Carson, 21, 23, 30, 32,
   40, 84, 87, 89, 103,
   108, 133, 134, **140**,
   141, 144, 163, 165,
   182, 186, 195, 207,
   222, 230, 236, 252,
   266
Carsten, 37, 86, 136,
   140, 236, 242, 266,
   287
Carter, 32, 43, 94, 104,
   106, 125, 136, 140,
   141, 145, 165, 166,
   167, 168, 188, 194,
   199, 251, 266
Carver, 15, 251
Cary, 79, 102, **141**, 147,
   259
Carys, 37, 61, 215, 230
Casandra, 40
Case, 141
Casey, 36, 37, 39, **40**, 51,

74, 116, 117, 121, 134,
   141, 144, 146, 170,
   205, 210, 222, 230,
   233, 265, 279
Cash, 145, 169, 210, 229,
   233
Casimir, 104, 237, 282
Cason, 236
Caspar, 141
Casper, 21, 22, 33, 97,
   118, **141**, 170, 177,
   181, 182, 189, 203,
   209, 249, 263, 277
Caspian, 239
Cass, 40, 141
Cassandra, 24, 27, **40**,
   51, 92, 122, 196, 247,
   262, 264, 268, 270
Cassey, 40
Cassia, 37, **40**, 232, 247,
   268
Cassidy, 15, **40**, 43, 48,
   63, 77, 94, 105, 113,
   137, 142, 144, 145,
   147, 163, 169, 179,
   194, 196, 197, 207,
   233, 252, 268
Cassie, **40**, 70, 75, 268
Cassio, 280
Cassius, 101, 123, **141**,
   149, 175, 209, 237
Cat, 41
Catalina, 32, 39, **41**, 56,
   88, 198, 208, 224, 237,
   254, 274
Catarina, 254
Cate, 75
Caterina, 131, 245
Catharine, 41
Catherine, 28, **41**, 75,
   89, 93, 154, 165, 173,
   174, 186, 195, 213,
   215, 268, 285
Cathleen, 141
Cathy, 43, 48, 75, 123
Catie, 41
Cato, 280

Catrina, 75, 116
Catriona, 58, 75, 114, 137, 230
Cayden, 16, 139
Ceara, 77
Cece, 105
Cecelia, 159, 215
Ceci, 41
Cecil, 45, 103, **141**, 143, 152, 155, 162, 195, 235, 249, 266
Cecile, 25, **41**, 54, 72, 82, 85, 90, 118, 132, 143, 175, 194, 214, 215, 239, 240, 248, 268, 287
Cecilia, 26, 28, **41**, 86, 89, 127, 144, 164, 185, 193, 213, 268, 276, 285
Cecily, **41**, 54, 128, 129, 200, 224, 234, 276, 287
Cedric, 82, 131, **141**, 151, 161, 172, 177, 212, 220, 237, 272
Cedrick, 116, 141
Ceil, 41, 268
Celeste, **41**, 43, 53, 60, 148, 183, 240, 268, 285
Celestine, 41, 49, 240, 248
Celia, **41**, 45, 54, 64, 81, 100, 115, 155, 156, 170, 199, 268, 280, 285, 287
Celine/Céline, 38, **41**, 114, 240, 268
Cesar, **141**, 170, 193, 204, 255
Cezar, 141
Chad, 26, 29, 36, 43, 46, 63, 97, 115, 120, **142**, 146, 170, 279
Chaim, **142**, 247
Chamique, 205

Champion, 239
Chance, 16, 27, 31, 49, 56, 59, 63, 69, 72, 97, 106, 110, 115, **142**, 187, 229, 260
Chancellor, 251
Chandler, 24, 36, 54, 76, 96, 121, 133, 137, **142**, 149, 222, 251
Chandra, 80, 279
Chanel, **42**, 238, 279
Chanelle, 42
Chantal, **42**, 51, 110, 131, 148, 185, 205, 220, 240, 276
Chantel, 42
Chantelle, 42
Chapman, 251
Chardonnay, 238
Charis, 38, 237, 287
Charisma, 238, 260
Charissa, 38
Charisse, 220
Charity, **42**, 52, 102, 184, 217, 224, 232, 265, 287
Charleen, 42
Charlene, **42**, 47, 69, 220, 259
Charles, 28, 41, 44, 52, 53, 59, 89, 93, **142**, 154, 159, 161, 173, 174, 179, 200, 215, 271, 283, 286
Charleston, 271, 274
Charley, 34, 54, 51, 65, 85, 94, 99, 142, 163, 164, 244
Charlie, 28, 42, 57, 82, 86, 100, 109, **142**, 159, 198, 209, 222, 271, 283
Charline, 42
Charlotte, 38, **42**, 59, 72, 114, 124, 159, 169, 195, 215, 224, 234, 234, 269

Charlton, 271
Chas, 42
Chase, 25, 32, 43, 101, 136, 138, **142**, 145, 229
Chasity, 42
Chassie, 42
Chastity, **42**, 230, 231
Chauncey, 162, 195, 252
Chava, 246
Chavela, 66
Chay, 142
Chaya, 46, 107, 116, 142, 155
Chayton, 16, 75, 125, **142**, 147, 236
Chaz, 77, 119, 142, 229, 271
Checo, 204
Chela, 61, 89
Chelle, 96
Chelsea, 37, **42**, 74, 124, 265, 274, 279
Chelsey, 42
Chelsie, 42
Chente, 213
Chepo, 174
Cher, 42, 43
Cheri, 42, 113, 134, 151
Cherie, 35, **42**, 125, 284
Cherise, 279
Cherish, 260
Cherryl, 43
Cheryl, 36, **43**, 102, 116, 208, 259
Cheryle, 43
Chesley, 271
Chester, 58, 63, 64, 96, 101, **143**, 152, 214, 249, 271
Chet, 143, 271
Chevonne, 114
Cheyanne, 43
Cheyenne, **43**, 98, 111, 112, 113, 145, 147, 199, 207, 210, 233, 274

Chiara, 15, 40, 77, 93, 156, 161, 245, 287
Chick, 142
Chima, 217
China, 274
Chip, 259
Chloe, 18, 21, 43, 55, 60, 63, 69, 94, 114, 126, 128, 129, 139, 141, 145, 156, 161, 167, 168, 173, 182, 192, 211, 224, 234, 234, 256, 265
Chris, 40, 43, 83, 85, 120, 124, 143, 171, 197, 268, 271, 284
Chrissy, 43, 175, 268, 279
Christa, 64, 78, 144, 241, 268
Christabel, 33, 54, 234, 237, 248, 287
Christal, 97, 268
Christen, 78
Christi, 43
Christian, 18, 44, 95, 129, 143, 192, 236, 265, 271
Christiana, 23, 43, 58, 115, 247
Christiane, 43, 51, 241, 268
Christie, 43, 121
Christina, 22, 43, 57, 71, 75, 106, 123, 173, 194, 206, 268, 279, 285
Christine, 43, 73, 80, 107, 144, 146, 149, 171, 177, 189, 207, 240, 268, 279, 284
Christobal, 143
Christophe, 143, 240
Christopher, 18, 27, 43, 70, 71, 96, 115, 143, 170, 171, 265, 271
Christos, 50, 243
Christy, 40, 43, 70, 95, 142, 279

Chucho, 172
Chuck, 45, 103, 142, 259, 271
Chuy, 172
Cian, 176
Ciara, 23, 77, 139, 149, 151, 160, 230
Ciaran, 178
Cicely, 41
Cicero, 239, 280
Cielo, 254
Ciera, 176
Cierra, 113, 119
Cilla, 105
Cinda, 44, 46, 86, 96, 268
Cinderella, 238, 268
Cindi, 44
Cindy, 44, 46, 48, 49, 75, 83, 86, 108, 113, 124, 178, 197, 200, 210, 259, 268, 284
Cinnamon, 80, 238
Citali, 99, 254
Claire, 31, 39, 42, 44, 129, 163, 167, 168, 175, 193, 199, 211, 213, 240, 285
Clancy, 222, 230, 252
Clara, 25, 28, 44, 52, 56, 64, 83, 115, 130, 132, 153, 154, 156, 159, 165, 167, 175, 181, 183, 202, 209, 224, 248, 265
Clare, 44, 72, 145, 149, 180, 189, 196, 211, 285
Clarence, 58, 96, 123, 129, 143, 156, 249, 266
Claribel, 248
Clarice, 28, 33, 41, 44, 45, 56, 107, 124, 144, 159, 180, 187, 249, 265

Clarissa, 44, 74, 81, 138, 216, 247, 264
Clarisse, 44
Clark, 74, 98, 140, 143, 163, 182, 199, 207, 212, 283, 287
Claud, 143
Claude, 35, 44, 51, 54, 85, 90, 93, 101, 132, 136, 141, 143, 144, 155, 166, 184, 187, 240, 249
Claudia, 39, 44, 105, 241, 245, 285
Claudie, 44
Claudine, 275
Claudio, 143, 245, 280
Claudius, 280
Clay, 38, 143, 212, 229, 286
Clayton, 31, 39, 143, 144, 164, 186, 193, 214, 236, 286
Clem, 44, 172, 190, 271, 275
Clemens, 271
Clement, 22, 32, 35, 41, 54, 85, 90, 135, 141, 143, 203, 240, 249, 271, 277
Clementine, 44, 88, 158, 240, 249
Clemmie, 44
Cleo, 32, 34, 44, 67, 107, 126, 131, 133, 146, 155, 157, 160, 185, 190, 237, 256, 287
Cleon, 275
Cleopatra, 128, 131, 188, 238, 269, 276
Cletus, 275
Cliff, 34, 81, 134, 144, 259, 271
Clifford, 108, 115, 130, 143, 144, 162, 167, 249, 263, 271, 283

Clifton, 89, 140, **144**, 155, 159, 162, 163, 205, 215, 252, 271, 283

Clint, 38, 81, 97, 121, 137, **144**, 165, 174, 175, 229, 233

Clinton, 31, **144**, 170, 236, 252, 286

Clio, 44, 55, 66, 262

Cliona, 230

Clive, 104, **144**, 192, 229, 235

Clotilde, 257, 270

Clover, 232

Cloyd, 258

Clyde, 94, **144**, 181, 182, 194, 202, 213, 283

Coby, 139, 178

Coco, 57, 238

Cody, 42, 46, 120, 141, **144**, 212, 222, 233, 252, 266

Colby, 78, 132, 138, 142, **144**, 179, 225, 252, 271

Cole, 69, 96, 98, 101, 113, 136, 138, 139, 142, 144, **145**, 168, 169, 175, 179, 184, 192, 208, 211, 228, 229, 271

Coleman, 127, **145**, 182, 196, 211, 228, 252

Colette, 27, **45**, 102, 106, 119, 240, 259, 276

Colin, 23, 32, 37, 44, 59, 60, 71, 80, 92, 94, 95, 97, 109, 118, 137, **145**, 150, 152, 153, 157, 160, 183, 192, 203, 211, 230, 235, 236, 265, 271

Colleen, **45**, 61, 68, 113, 177, 230, 259, 265

Collin, 74, 145

Colm, 58, 100, 139, 153, 204, 230

Colman, 41, 145, 146, 153, 157, 213, 230, 236, 271, 277

Colt, 51, 105, 112, 134, 144, 145, 148, 199, 205, 229, 233

Colton, 15, 31, 39, 40, 43, 63, 98, 112, **145**, 147, 151, 207, 210, 215, 233, 236, 252

Columbus, 239

Con, 145, 146, 271

Conan, 22, **145**, 146, 202, 230, 236, 271, 277

Concetta, 140, 244, 245, 268

Conner, 145

Connie, 34, 36, **45**, 103, 110, 113, 116, 118, 121, 145, 146, 179, 208, 222, 259, 268, 271

Connolly, 15, 21, 191, 252

Connor, 38, 39, 62, 72, 77, 98, 108, 116, 128, 139, 140, **145**, 151, 153, 168, 182, 211, 230, 271

Conor, 49, 116, 120, 145, 163, 182, 230

Conrad, 29, 44, 59, 62, **145**, 146, 209, 249, 271, 280

Constance, 35, **45**, 62, 96, 108, 109, 151, 206, 232, 268, 282

Constantin, 104, 122, 124, 134, 191, 208, 212, 237, 271, 282

Constantinos, 243

Consuelo, 254, 268

Coop, 145

Cooper, 21, 48, 87, 94, 103, 106, 114, 136,

141, **145**, 167, 195, 207, 250, 251

Cora, **45**, 82, 108, 123, 129, 144, 154, 157, 224, 249, 268

Coral, **45**, 232, 268

Coralie, 240, 268

Corazon, 268

Corbin, 30, 38, 106, 139, **146**, 147, 152, 210, 211, 236

Cordelia, 33, **45**, 64, 90, 133, 135, 141, 146, 166, 181, 190, 191, 234, 249, 268, 280

Cordell, 271

Corey, 37, 40, 46, 68, 78, 120, **146**, 153, 225, 266, 279

Cori, 45

Corin, 83, 104, 117, 123, 192, 235, 236, 280

Corine, 41

Corinna, 29, 45, 65, 82, 179, 247, 268

Corinne, 44, **45**, 65, 155, 202, 240, 285

Corliss, 268

Cormac, 15, 58, 100, 114, 128, 137, **146**, 154, 178, 230, 277, 287

Cornelia, 143, 158, 207, 249, 268, 269

Cornelis, 146

Cornelius, 32, 51, 64, 82, 97, 127, **146**, 147, 237, 249, 271, 280

Cornell, 108, 146, 197, 271

Corny, 146

Corrie, 45, 268

Corrine, 140, 144, 182, 183, 220

Cortez, 220

Cortney, 46

Cory, 26, 36, 45, 112, 142, 144, 146, 285

Cosimo, 51, 146, 245
Cosmo, 146, 156, 237, 245
Coster, 251
Coty, 31, 42, 207, 233, 274
Court, 46
Courtney, 37, 42, 46, 76, 80, 117, 214, 220, 222, 252, 271
Craig, 39, 44, 48, 64, 83, 107, 108, 116, 120, 146, 171, 177, 178, 204, 210, 230, 284
Crawford, 88, 164
Creola, 257
Cris, 146
Crispin, 33, 59, 117, 123, 144, 146, 153, 208, 235, 236, 271, 277, 287
Crispus, 227
Cristal, 42, 46, 186
Cristina, 200, 285
Cristobal, 255
Croix, 201, 221
Cruz, 41, 56, 57, 85, 222, 255
Crystal, 46, 52, 120, 232, 260, 279
Crystie, 46
Cub, 168
Cullen, 40, 236
Currier, 251
Curt, 42, 48, 70, 71, 89, 103, 109, 110, 134, 146, 178, 183, 213, 271
Curtis, 28, 50, 105, 116, 119, 139, 146, 201, 207, 271, 280, 286
Cutler, 251
Cy, 147
Cyndi, 44
Cynthia, 46, 48, 67, 74, 102, 119, 122, 128, 146, 163, 197, 207, 259, 268, 270

Cyril, 22, 56, 61, 275
Cyrus, 120, 147, 167, 227, 249

Daan, 241
Dafna, 47, 142, 192, 246
Dafne, 47, 59, 262
Dagmar, 31, 241, 278
Dagny, 278
Dahlia, 26, 46, 58, 69, 104, 153, 184, 215, 232, 234
Daisha, 220
Daisy, 46, 61, 224, 232, 265
Dak, 147
Dakota, 16, 26, 43, 49, 98, 111, 113, 125, 147, 196, 222, 233, 273, 274
Dakotah, 147, 207
Dale, 46, 52, 59, 71, 81, 108, 110, 147, 162, 180, 201, 202, 203, 212, 222, 228, 282, 283
Dalia, 22, 26, 46, 48, 82, 132, 142, 166, 200, 246, 247, 265, 287
Dallas, 39, 147, 150, 207, 222, 233, 266, 274
Dallin, 236
Dalton, 33, 49, 62, 65, 76, 96, 103, 113, 116, 118, 147, 149, 166, 194, 207, 208, 214, 236, 252, 266
Daly, 225, 252
Damaris, 24, 46, 74, 91, 100, 141, 149, 156, 171, 180, 187, 195, 205, 208, 227, 237, 254
Dameon, 116
Damian, 22, 57, 98, 113, 115, 128, 147, 148,

152, 156, 157, 197, 237, 266, 277
Damiana, 115
Damien, 49, 53, 130, 147, 240
Damita, 220
Damon, 47, 79, 96, 106, 137, 147, 180, 205, 236, 262, 265, 266
Dan, 148, 271
Dana, 47, 60, 79, 86, 113, 121, 123, 136, 141, 147, 148, 200, 208, 210, 211, 222, 259, 284
Danae, 66, 94, 111, 123, 128, 208, 237, 243, 262
Dane, 148, 149, 176, 229
Danelle, 180
Dani, 47
Dania, 28, 150, 180
Danica, 281
Daniel, 18, 106, 111, 130, 131, 148, 149, 187, 189, 227, 265, 271, 286
Daniela, 23, 29, 39, 47, 53, 58, 71, 116, 144, 166, 196, 245, 247, 281
Daniella, 24, 47, 58, 81, 96, 103, 147
Danielle, 14, 25, 26, 46, 47, 55, 74, 78, 83, 100, 115, 153, 239, 240, 264
Danika, 185
Danila, 47, 93
Danita, 35
Danny, 45, 48, 118, 148, 208, 259
Dante, 27, 31, 33, 35, 49, 56, 82, 131, 148, 150, 161, 162, 181, 185, 218, 221, 245, 271

Danyel, 148
Daphne, 29, 47, 48, 50,
    56, 103, 104, 114, 132,
    150, 155, 192, 207,
    208, 234, 262, 285,
    287
Dara, 89, 93, 149, 202,
    230, 284
Darald, 257
Darby, 40, 49, 78, 102,
    108, 121, 158, 211,
    222, 230, 252
Darcie, 47, 210
Darcy/D'arcy, 47, 82, 89,
    92, 132, 197, 200, 222,
    252, 284
Daren, 50, 148
Daria, 47, 92, 107, 185,
    276, 281, 287
Darian, 33, 48, 49, 118,
    121, 148, 151, 176,
    221, 222, 236, 266
Darien, 76, 148, 214
Darin, 47, 136, 148
Dario, 15, 58, 115, 148,
    161, 192, 245, 277
Darius, 24, 30, 42, 49,
    90, 99, 111, 117, 148,
    149, 156, 197, 221,
    266, 277
Darla, 47, 113, 259
Darleen, 47
Darlene, 47, 152, 205,
    258, 259, 265, 282
Darline, 47
Darnell, 208, 221, 252
Daron, 148
Darragh, 230
Darrel, 148
Darrell, 36, 42, 45, 46,
    49, 102, 106, 125,
    148, 197, 259, 266,
    284
Darren, 24, 47, 48, 60,
    64, 68, 89, 112, 115,
    116, 120, 148, 177,
    211, 265, 266, 284

Darrian, 148
Darrick, 112, 116
Darrien, 117, 148
Darrin, 148
Darrion, 148
Darron, 148
Darryl, 50, 107, 148,
    153, 201, 213, 214,
    221, 284
Darwin, 148, 252, 263
Daryl, 148, 222
Daryle, 148
Dash, 149
Dashiell, 149, 209, 237
Dasia, 23, 26, 29, 75, 98,
    281
Dave, 149, 271
Daveth, 230
Davey, 259
David, 18, 48, 80, 90,
    148, 149, 189, 207,
    219, 227, 241, 271,
    286
Davin, 236
Davina, 83, 153, 179,
    247
Davion, 69, 77, 92, 221,
    271
Davis, 31, 66, 135, 143,
    143, 145, 149, 164,
    189, 193, 199, 202,
    213, 252, 271, 286
Davon, 221
Davy, 104, 149, 235
Dawn, 47, 60, 85, 117,
    120, 134, 149, 151,
    210, 211, 232, 284
Dawson, 37, 38, 57, 103,
    114, 142, 149, 160,
    163, 179, 236, 252,
    266
Dax, 229
Dayna, 47
Dayton, 31, 87, 139,
    149, 180, 236, 252,
    266, 274
Dean, 28, 70, 102, 103,

106, 122, 148, 149,
    171, 177, 191, 212,
    229, 259, 284, 286
Deana, 47, 48, 81, 116,
    121
Deandre, 221
Deane, 149
Deangelo, 221
Deanna, 48, 95, 148,
    247, 264
Deanne, 48
Deb, 48, 200
Debbie, 48, 78, 259, 268
Debby, 48
Debi, 48, 97
Deborah, 46, 48, 73,
    102, 149, 163, 226,
    259, 268
Debra, 48, 75, 259, 268
Declan, 48, 114, 149,
    178, 201, 202, 204,
    230, 277
Dedrick, 29, 79, 221
Dee, 48, 49, 50, 51, 103,
    105, 121, 149, 203, 259
Deena, 50, 151, 284
Deidre, 48, 202
Deion, 151, 180
Deirdre, 34, 48, 93, 114,
    177, 230, 284
Deja, 48, 121, 185, 220,
    256
Dejuan, 80, 221
Del, 48, 259, 271
Delaney, 40, 48, 77, 94,
    149, 152, 200, 252,
    268
Delano, 271
Delbert, 275
Delia, 45, 48, 249
Delilah, 46, 48, 81, 155,
    174, 226, 237, 263,
    268
Dell, 45, 49, 50, 190,
    243, 268
Della, 49, 54, 56, 84,
    105, 106, 162, 164,

165, 199, 243, 268, 287
Delma, 257
Delmar, 271
Delmas, 257
Delmer, 275
Delois, 257
Delores, 197
Deloris, 50
Delphia, 32, 45, 130, 199, 249
Delphine, 49, 119, 132, 135, 185, 240, 268, 287
Delta, 150, 199, 215, 233, 243, 268
Delton, 271
Demarcus, 221
Demetria, 50, 82, 201, 220, 276
Demetrio, 149
Demetrius, 46, 58, 122, 141, **149**, 208, 216, 221, 237, 277, 280
Demi, 50
Demitra, 50, 53
Demitrius, 51, 150, 151, 193
Denali, 274
Denis, 240
Denisa, 281
Denise, 39, 44, 45, 46, **49**, 50, 68, 73, 83, 108, 119, 122, 148, 177, 197, 240, 259, 265, 284
Dennis, 36, 39, 51, 59, 68, 73, 83, 89, 102, 110, 112, 115, 128, 138, **150**, 160, 192, 197, 259, 271
Dennison, 15, 29, 31, 140, 150, 164, 169, 207, 252, 271, 287
Denny, 150, 271
Denver, 86, 147, **150**, 233, 271, 274

Denzel, **150**, 221, 263, 271
Denzil, 150, 230
Deon, 31, 151, 221, 236
Deonte, 148
Derek, 24, 25, 34, 38, 40, 46, 47, 52, 55, 65, 71, 74, 75, 79, 94, 100, 116, 125, 136, 141, **150**, 153, 175, 210, 265, 266
Deric, 150
Dermot, 100, 146, 153, 158, 177, 230, 277
Derrell, 148
Derrick, 57, 63, 68, 76, 77, 78, 81, 83, 95, 98, 117, 137, 148, 150, 172, 177, 205, 272, 279
Des, 150, 271
Desdemona, 280
Deshawn, 212
Desi, 49
Desiderio, 271
Desirae, 49
Desiree/Désirée, **49**, 97, 98, 99, 119, 124, 131, 220, 240, 260, 279
Desmond, 79, 99, 141, **150**, 177, 185, 186, 212, 230, 237, 271
Despina, 50, 94, 243
Dessie, 49
Destin, 271
Destiny, 16, **49**, 56, 69, 97, 121, 220, 260
Detlef, 242
Dev, 150
Devan, 49
Deven, 49, 150
Devin, 36, 37, 38, **49**, 51, 72, 101, 109, 136, 142, **150**, 176, 182, 212, 222, 236, 265, 266, 273

Devon, 48, 49, 69, 74, 106, 148, **150**, 151, 169, 170, 185, 210, 212, 236
Devonta, 150
Devonte, 150, 205, 218, 219, 221
Devorah, 48
Devyn, 49, 145, 210
Dewayne, 221
Dewey, 87, 105, 153, 162, 164, 244
Dewitt, 159
Dex, 149, 150, 229, 271
Dexter, 47, 65, **150**, 190, 200, 208, 235, 251, 271, 286
Dez, 49 , 150
Di, 49, 50
Diamond, 27, **49**, 56, 67, 105, 119, 188, 196, 219, 220, 221, 222, 231, 232, 260
Diana, 50, 67, 73, 80, 90, 97, 128, 146, 149, 189, 207, 222, 262, 280, 285
Diane, 48, **50**, 51, 68, 75, 83, 89, 110, 112, 115, 122, 134, 138, 150, 153, 160, 207, 259
Dianne, 45, 50
Dick, 199
Didi, 48
Didier, 240
Diedre, 48
Diego, 25, 90, 131, **151**, 255, 277
Dieter, 242
Dietrich, 150, 242
Dilbert, 263
Dill, 151
Dillard, 275
Dillion, 236
Dillon, 39, 40, 76, 113, 119, 121, 144, 145,

147, **151**, 153, 207, 233, 236, 252
Dilys, 230
Dima, 151
Dimitra, 37, **50**, 75, 88, 95, 243
Dimitri, 23, 27, 29, 79, 102, 117, 118, 149, **151**, 157, 187, 237, 242, 243, 282
Dimitrios, 149, 151, 243
Dimos, 243
Dimple, 258
Dina, 22, 47, **50**, 89, 213, 246, 284
Dinah, **50**, 79, 170, 184, 226
Dineo, 217
Dino, 57, 60, 97, 134, 151, 210, 245, 259
Diogo, 151
Dion, 130, 131, **151**, 199, 221, 280
Dionne, 92, 284
Dirk, 42, 47, 60, 62, 150, **151**, 178, 242, 284
Dixie, **50**, 233, 243
Dixon, 252
Dmitri, 151
Dobbin, 200
Doc, 152
Dock, 56, 85, 103, 132, 159, 167, 184, 190, 194, 200, 244
Dodie, 51
Doe, 113
Dolly, **50**, 51, 106, 152, 188, 202, 233, 243, 263, 268
Dolores, **50**, 105, 253, 254, 268, 275
Doloris, 50
Dolph, 197, 203
Dom, 151
Domenic, 41, 151
Domenica, 245
Domenick, 51, 59, 80,

90, 119, 134, 151, 183
Domenico, 151
Domicela, 237
Domingo, 140, 151
Dominic, 37, 128, 147, **151**, 160, 175, 187, 201, 204, 216, 224, 277
Dominick, 27, 95, 122, 154, 168, 237, 272
Dominik, 201
Dominique, 42, 49, **51**, 151, 197, 205, 220, 221, 222, 240, 240
Don, 71, 75, 115, 127, 151, 183, 271
Dona, 51
Donal, 58, 139, 151, 230, 271
Donald, 30, 33, 35, 50, 61, 71, 73, 91, 108, 113, **151**, 159, 161, 200, 271, 283
Donatella, **51**, 102, 201, 244, 245
Donato, 47, 131, 245, 271, 272, 277
Donavan, 151, 271
Donell, 29
Donna, 28, 39, **51**, 68, 103, 108, 112, 134, 138, 172, 191, 197, 208, 259, 265
Donnell, 153, 221, 271, 284
Donnie, 70, 96, 121, 151, 259
Donny, 89, 151
Donovan, 38, 40, 48, 76, 87, 94, 107, 108, 112, 133, 137, 140, **151**, 152, 176, 196, 200, 252
Dontae, 148
Donte, 52, 148, 212, 218
Dora, **51**, 67, 119, 205, 249

Doran, 154
Dorcas, 172, 227, 275
Doreen, 259
Doretha, 148
Dori, 284
Dorian, 147, **152**, 236, 266
Doris, **51**, 101, 104, 153, 156, 166, 181, 182, 193, 262, 282
Dorman, 258
Doron, 62, 113, 247
Dorothea, 22, 33, **51**, 96, 144, 155, 249, 268, 287
Dorothy, **51**, 58, 92, 130, 135, 142, 144, 159, 162, 213, 268, 282
Dorrie, 51
Dorsey, 179, 180
Dot, 51
Dottie, 51, 268
Doug, 152
Dougal, 230
Douglas, 28, 36, 39, 43, 46, 48, 50, 51, 52, 75, 79, 93, 102, 103, 110, 112, 113, 115, 116, 119, 146, **152**, 163, 177, 191, 197, 207, 230, 259
Douglass, 152
Dov, 142, 166, 247
Dove, 65, 94, 102, 123, 165, 231, 232
Dovie, 54, 61, 159, 243
Doyle, 35, 50, 85, 93, 98, 104, 184, 252, 283
Drake, 21, 35, 48, 106, 132, 136, 137, 138, 139, 142, **152**, 168, 170, 198, 210, 229, 252
Draper, 251
Draven, 236
Dre, 130
Dree, 22

Drew, 23, 37, 39, 40, 42, **51**, 69, 71, 75, 84, 89, 116, 118, 120, 136, 137, 148, **152**, 211, 222, 229, 265, 271
Drucilla, 48, 134
Drusilla, 157, 227, 237
Duane, 36, 47, 61, 71, 93, 105, 113, 125, **152**, 153, 230, 259, 259, 283
Dublin, 123, 274
Dudley, **152**, 234, 235, 275
Duke, 57, 97, **152**, 153, 244, 259
Dulce, 62, 129, 131, 141, 151, 172, 183, 186, 201, 254
Dulcie, 54, 104, 117, 120, 144, 192, 234
Dumisani, 217
Duncan, 43, 64, 73, 88, 106, 135, 137, 139, **152**, 155, 162, 163, 185, 190, 236, 280, 286, 287
Dunstan, 117, 146, **153**, 235, 236, 266, 273, 277
Durante, 148
Durwood, 257
Dustin, 26, 30, 37, 40, 42, 46, 55, 57, 83, 117, 124, 146, **153**, 170, 171, 210, 236, 279
Dusty, 36, 77, 97, 105, 112, 153, 203, 279
Duwayne, 153
Dwain, 152, 153
Dwane, 152, 153
Dwayne, 148, 152, **153**, 201, 221, 284
Dwight, 27, 46, 61, 72, 86, 92, 146, 152, **153**, 197, 207, 259, 286
Dyan, 50

Dylan, 14, 18, 24, 25, 76, 98, 128, 133, 140, 143, 151, **153**, 156, 167, 182, 230, 230, 236
Dyll, 153

Eamon/Éamon/Éamonn, 38, 58, 100, 108, 114, **153**, 154, 157, 178, 230, 236, 266, 287
Ean, 158, 167
Earl, 57, 86, 119, **153**, 155, 159, 166, 181, 182, 197, 202, 221, 233, 283
Earle, 153
Earline, 275
Early, 257
Earnest, 156, 207, 214, 232
Easter, 135
Easton, 92, 102, 113, 149, 163, 179, 183, 236, 252
Ebenezer, 227, 263
Eboni, 52
Ebony, **52**, 80, 220, 232, 260
Echo, 22, 38, 128, 238, 262
Ed, 153, 154, 271
Eddie, 52, 110, 152, 154, 173, 244
Eden, **52**, 53, 63, 64, 87, 100, 104, 106, 114, 127, 132, 133, 154, 166, 168, 176, 204, 256, 260, 268
Edgar, 26, 41, 42, 64, 100, **153**, 165, 167, 193, 194, 213, 224, 235, 271, 277, 280
Edgardo, 153, 255
Edgerton, 252
Edie, 52, 77, 216, 268
Edison, 32, 129, **154**, 155, 162, 164, 188,

191, 211, 215, 252, 271, 287
Edith, 25, **52**, 56, 58, 92, 129, 153, **154**, 156, 159, 162, 164, 197, 214, 249, 268, 276
Edmond, 25, 32, 41, 54, 132, 154
Edmund, 32, 38, 56, 72, 85, 90, 134, 143, 153, **154**, 175, 203, 235, 249, 271, 272, 273, 277, 287
Edna, **52**, 56, 60, 61, 96, 268, 275
Edsel, 263
Eduardo, 154, 255, 271
Edward, 28, 41, 53, 57, 89, 93, 142, **154**, 161, 165, 198, 215, 271, 272, 273, 286
Edwin, 52, **154**, 167, 249
Edwina, 148, 275
Effie, 88, 177, 243
Efrain, 86, 255
Efren, 255
Egan, 145, 153, **154**, 157, 176, 230, 236, 287
Egon, 242, 277
Ehud, 227
Eileen, **52**, 69, 159, 162, 184, 214, 230, 265, 282
Einar, 278
Eirene, 66
Ekaterini, 243
Elaine, 30, **52**, 61, 73, 139, 147, 161, 172, 199, 200, 282
Elan, 22, 26, 33, 46, 192, 247
Elbert, 214, 223, 275
Elden, 104, 120, 236, 249
Eldon, 183, 188
Eldora, 54
Eldridge, 45

Eleanor, 24, 51, **52**, 72, 83, 85, 124, 135, 159, 164, 165, 175, 202, 209, 224, 249, 268, 269

Eleanora, 45, 51, 52, 119, 135, 199, 249

Eleazar, 180

Electa, 258

Electra, 22, 123, 127, 128, 175, 197, 238, 262, 268

Elena, **53**, 91, 131, 163, 174, 189, 195, 200, 213, 245, 254, 268, 281, 285

Eleni, **53**, 243, 268

Eleri, 230

Elgar, 277

Elgin, 45, 249

Eli, 32, 34, 53, 55, 56, 61, 67, 83, 88, 89, 96, 126, 127, 133, **154**, 155, 157, 173, 174, 182, 192, 194, 205, 209, 224, 227, 256, 266

Eliahu, 155

Elian, 255

Eliana, 23, 99, 161, 186, 247, 254

Elias, 37, 42, 83, 114, 147, 148, **154**, 155, 205, 216, 223, 224, 237, 243, 277, 278

Elida, 32

Eliezer, 171, 195, 227, 237

Elijah, 14, 21, 27, 63, 139, 154, **155**, 157, 160, 168, 184, 218, 221, 224, 227

Elin, 84

Elina, 24, 247

Elinor, 52, 90, 96, 98, 158

Elio, 245

Eliot, 139, 286

Elisa, 24, 81, 285

Elisabet, 53

Elisabeth, 53, 130, 285

Elise, 38, 44, **53**, 73, 185, 193, 202, 206, 211, 240, 268, 285

Elisha, 22, 24, 26, 142, 155, 217, 221, 222, 226, 227, 246, 247

Elisheva, 62, 113, 122, 195, 226, 227, 246

Elissa, 25

Eliza, 25, 34, **53**, 72, 85, 104, 114, 130, 134, 167, 171, 173, 174, 205, 224, 234, 269

Elizabeth, 18, **53**, 75, 169, 173, 174, 191, 227, 267, 268, 269, 285

Elkan, 33, 83, 165, 170, 236, 247

Elke, 136, 140, 209, 215, 241, 256

Ella, **53**, 56, 61, 64, 88, 89, 187, 224, 243, 268

Elle, 29, **53**, 54, 60, 133, 135, 148, 192, 196, 228, 256, 268, 287

Ellen, **54**, 64, 68, 74, 115, 143, 162, 179, 180, 186, 191, 195, 198, 203, 268, 282, 287

Ellery, 15, **54**, 65, 158, 192, 222, 287

Ellie, 52, 53, 54, 64, 268

Elliot, 99, 115, 135, 138, 150, 193, 196, 202

Elliott, 72, **155**, 266, 286

Ellis, 34, 41, 74, 82, 107, 129, 130, 144, 153, 154, **155**, 156, 162, 164, 167, 186, 201, 215, 252, 266, 283, 287

Ellsworth, 51

Elmer, **155**, 263, 274, 275

Elmo, 155, 263, 275

Elodia, 54

Elodie, 33, 41, 49, **54**, 55, 237, 240, 276, 287

Eloisa, 54

Eloise, 28, 32, 41, 44, 49, **54**, 63, 96, 132, 135, 240, 249, 268

Elon, 227

Eloy, 257

Elroy, 275

Elsa, 53, **54**, 62, 64, 66, 72, 83, 92, 96, 186, 241, 268, 278, 285, 287

Elsbeth, 53, 215, 241, 267

Else, 54, 192

Elsie, 24, 53, **54**, 87, 159, 243, 268

Elspeth, 83, 88, 129, 131, 179, 268

Elton, 236, 252

Elvira, **54**, 130, 166, 172, 202, 263, 275

Elvis, **155**, 263

Elwin, 275

Elyse, 53

Elza, 257

Em, 55

Emanuel, 32, 48, 156, 278

Emeka, 217

Emelia, 268

Emeline, 25, **54**, 249, 269

Emerald, 45, **55**, 80, 232, 260, 268, 287

Emeric, 54, 277

Emerson, 15, 51, **155**, 207, 249, 252, 266

Emil, 35, 101, 124, **155**, 242, 249, 278

Emile, 155, 240

Emilee, 36, 90, 176
Emilia, 26, 85, 130, 131,
    188, 245, 280
Emiliano, 26, 56, 99,
    186, 255
Emilie, 55
Emilio, 95, 129, 155,
    245, 255
Emily, 18, 55, 63, 105,
    111, 123, 129, 130,
    135, 168, 191, 192,
    204, 234, 268, 269,
    285
Emlyn, 15, 37, 55, 117,
    154, 160, 215, 222,
    230, 236
Emma, 18, 43, 54, 55,
    61, 73, 104, 133, 194,
    224, 265, 268, 278
Emmalee, 30
Emmaline, 54, 268
Emmanuel, 22, 27, 44,
    49, 58, 61, 107, 147,
    149, 156, 181, 185,
    188, 198, 218, 227,
    237
Emmet, 156
Emmett, 44, 59, 70, 156,
    157, 159, 170, 189,
    199, 249, 266, 286,
    287
Emmie, 55, 268
Emmit, 156
Emmitt, 145, 156
Emmy, 55, 243
Emory, 22, 32, 54, 56,
    59, 72, 104, 107, 120,
    195, 214, 222, 249
Endymion, 111
Enid, 98, 152, 162, 234,
    275
Enoch, 54, 213, 227, 275
Enos, 172, 227, 275
Enrico, 165, 245, 272
Enrique, 55, 62, 165, 255
Enzo, 44, 93, 146, 156,
    183, 244, 245

Eoghan, 154, 157
Ephraim, 184, 227, 237
Ephron, 227
Epifanio, 257
Erasmo, 257
Erasmus, 237, 277
Erastus, 227, 237
Eric, 25, 26, 70, 96,
    115, 137, 156, 170,
    178, 204, 207, 265,
    279
Erica, 26, 47, 55, 70, 78,
    98, 100, 115, 153, 171,
    203, 264, 265, 269,
    279
Erich, 62, 242
Erick, 156
Ericka, 55, 77, 177, 208,
    220
Erik, 74, 94, 152, 156,
    278
Erika, 55, 77
Erin, 25, 55, 74, 117,
    127, 150, 156, 157,
    170, 178, 204, 230,
    264, 265
Eris, 262
Erma, 132, 275
Ermintrude, 270
Ernest, 45, 52, 85, 96,
    101, 123, 129, 143,
    154, 156, 214, 249,
    271
Ernestine, 275
Ernesto, 156, 245, 255,
    271
Ernie, 156, 271
Ernst, 156, 159, 194,
    242, 271
Ervin, 144, 155, 221
Erwin, 275
Esme/Esmé/Esmée, 27,
    32, 33, 54, 55, 67, 84,
    86, 104, 126, 182, 237,
    256
Esmeralda, 55, 62, 129,
    131, 151, 189, 224, 254

Esperanza, 32, 41, 56,
    232, 254
Essence, 55, 56, 74, 97,
    186, 220, 260
Essie, 56
Esteban, 172, 207, 273
Estefania, 55, 115, 254
Estel, 257
Estela, 56, 254
Estella, 41, 48, 51, 56,
    118, 155, 157, 159,
    194, 249, 287
Estelle, 22, 35, 44, 51,
    56, 58, 82, 85, 86,
    90, 143, 166, 184,
    249
Ester, 56, 268
Esther, 44, 45, 52, 56,
    63, 97, 109, 128, 143,
    156, 166, 180, 190,
    199, 204, 206, 214,
    226, 246, 249
Estrella, 56, 254
Eternity, 131, 238, 260
Ethan, 18, 21, 63, 101,
    156, 189, 192, 226,
    227, 236, 273
Ethel, 22, 52, 56, 96,
    167, 190, 275
Ethelyn, 257
Etta, 56, 64, 84, 91, 132,
    184, 194, 243
Ettie, 56, 63, 64, 190
Euan, 157
Eudora, 249, 262
Eugene, 30, 50, 101,
    104, 136, 156, 159,
    188, 205, 213, 249,
    271, 283
Eugenia, 32, 162, 207,
    249, 276
Eugenie, 130, 141, 147,
    181, 240
Eula, 172, 194, 202, 213,
    214
Eulalia, 257
Eunice, 132, 152, 158,

182, 194, 213, 214, 227, 275

Eva, 28, 32, 44, **56**, 67, 83, 91, 100, 109, 152, 181, 209, 224, 230, 268

Evadne, 262

Evaline, 57

Evalyn, 57

Evan, 25, 55, 71, 99, 127, 152, **157**, 236, 265, 266, 277

Evander, 29, 83, 107, 129, **157**, 180, 195, 230, 237, 287

Evangeline, 28, 84, 97, 119, 122, 126, 134, 190, 191, 212, 237, 249, 268

Evangelos, 243

Evanthia, 50, 119, 242, 243

Eve, **56**, 59, 226, 256, 268, 285

Evelin, 57

Evelyn, 52, **57**, 124, 154, 161, 164, 175, 198, 224, 268

Evening, 38, 123, 135, 260

Everest, 16, 52, 239, 274

Everett, 29, 34, 80, 83, 119, 123, 124, 133, 144, 154, 155, 156, **157**, 167, 175, 209, 224, 249, 252, 266, 287

Everly, 54, 105, 181, 252

Evert, 136, 140, 242

Evie, 34, 56, 57, 59, 99, 106, 108, 167, 243, 268

Evita, 56

Ewan, **157**, 231, 236, 266

Ewell, 162

Ewen, 157

Exie, 257

Ezekiel, 155, **157**, 184, 216, 224, 226, 227, 237, 273

Ezell, 257

Ezequiel, 112, 255

Ezra, 34, 67, 127, 129, 133, 147, 154, **157**, 167, 173, 182, 190, 205, 206, 224, 226, 227, 238, 266

Fabian, 23, 27, 31, 58, 60, 82, 90, 91, 99, 103, 111, 117, **157**, 216, 242, 266, 277, 281

Fabien, 240

Fabio, 238, 245

Fabiola, 102, 112, 216, 254, 276

Fabrice, 42, 240

Fabrizio, 245

Fae, 34, 243, 256

Fairy, 258

Faith, 21, **57**, 65, 83, 114, 141, 145, 168, 173, 184, 215, 232, 233

Falco, 238, 277

Fallon, 55, **57**, 154, 157, 202, 205, 230, 265

Fannie, 166

Fanny, 50, 58, 243

Fantasia, 238

Farid, 261

Faron, 236

Farrah, 263, 265, 279

Farrier, 251

Fatima, 57, 110, 190, 261

Faulkner, 251

Fay, 107, 130, 152, 180, 184, 188, 202, 222

Faye, 105, 164, 182, 184, 195, 282

Federico, 159, 255

Felice, 57

Felicia, 24, 31, **57**, 98, 108, 123, 137, 247, 279

Felicita, 140, 245

Felicity, 37, 42, **57**, 58, 59, 60, 125, 149, 192, 196, 209, 232, 234, 265, 276

Felipe, 255

Felisha, 57

Felix, 25, 32, 59, 66, 99, 100, 126, 146, **157**, 175, 181, 182, 187, 193, 238, 266, 277, 286

Femi, 65, 217

Femke, 241

Ferd, 158

Ferdi, 158

Ferdinand, 21, 28, 44, 45, 124, 126, 134, 146, **158**, 191, 207, 238, 249, 281

Fergus, 58, 139, 204, 231

Fern, **57**, 63, 103, 119, 159, 232

Fernand, 240

Fernanda, 56, 254, 269

Fernando, 255

Ffion, 230

Fi, 58

Fidel, 255, 263

Fife, 22, 158, 231

Fifi, **57**, 72, 238, 240

Filomena, 104

Fin, 158, 195

Finbar, 231

Finian, 146, **158**, 178, 209, 231, 277

Finis, 257

Finlay, 23, 131, 158, 164, 177, 231

Finley, **158**, 191, 252, 287

Finn, 23, 37, 38, 53, 60, 66, 84, 88, 104, 106, 132, 139, **158**, 192, 202, 204, 229, 231, 278, 287

Finola, **58**, 100, 129,

137, 146, 157, 158, 178, 179, 230

Fiona, 58, 88, 117, 13, 139, 153, 162, 185, 196, 204, 211, 230, 234, 247

Fionnuala, 58

Fionola, 58

Flannery, 134

Flavia, 51, 128, 146, 156, 234, 237, 276

Fleta, 257

Fletch, 158

Fletcher, 91, **158**, 211, 251, 287

Fleur, 27, 33, 45, 55, 57, 65, 136, 232, 240

Flint, 79, 232, 260

Flip, 195

Fliss, 57

Flo, 58, 190, 268

Flora, 21, 25, 48, 57, **58**, 59, 66, 82, 86, 104, 107, 109, 163, 166, 182, 203, 232, 249, 262, 268, 276

Florence, **58**, 60, 155, 202, 249, 268, 274

Florian, 54, 59, 84, 122, 131, 135, 180, 183, 184, 187, 238, 240, 242, 277

Florida, 84, 243, 268, 274

Florin, 65

Florine, 158, 214, 275

Florrie, 58

Flossie, 58, 85, 243, 268

Floy, 257

Floyd, 22, 56, 61, 96, 98, **158**, 274, 275

Flynn, 132, **158**, 229, 252, 287

Fonda, 257

Forbes, 231

Ford, 252

Forest, 21, 37, 120, 133, 159, 207, 232, 249

Forester, 200, 251

Forrest, 45, 57, 95, 155, **159**, 186, 252, 286, 287

Forrester, 159

Foster, 21, 58, 82, 85, 86, 90, 93, 126, 132, 134, 154, 157, 158, **159**, 164, 194, 196, 211, 215, 249, 251, 266, 287

Fox, 38, 239

Foy, 257

Fran, 58, 159, 268

Frances, 51, **58**, 66, 69, 128, 129, 142, 144, 145, 154, 156, 162, 162, 164, 166, 181, 189, 198, 206, 213, 214, 249, 268, 282

Francesca, 23, 27, **58**, 60, 102, 162, 181, 185, 244, 245, 247, 268

Francesco, 245

Francie, 58

Francine, 42, 259, 268

Francis, 29, 51, 86, 91, 116, 135, 143, 156, **159**, 166, 181, 183, 249, 271, 276, 283

Francisca, 58, 254, 268, 280

Francisco, 122, 159, 195, 255, 271, 281

Frank, 66, 109, 128, **159**, 271, 283

Frankie, 58, 159, 221, 259

Franklin, 30, 33, 69, 91, 92, 103, 104, 108, 151, **159**, 161, 172, 186, 271, 283

Franz, 159, 242

Franziska, 241

Fraser, 65, 131, 159, 252

Fred, 129, **159**, 197, 271, 283

Freda, 49, 165, 194, 243

Freddie, 125

Freddy, 159

Frederic, 28, 41, 132, 159, 161, 240

Frederick, 41, 86, 92, 96, **159**, 161, 165, 179, 209, 249, 271, 272, 281, 286

Federico, 159

Frederik, 159

Fredrick, 89, 159

Freeman, 74, 155, 165, 202, 221, 252

Freya, 262

Freydl, 246

Frida, 278

Frieda, 61, 167, 249

Friedrich, 159, 242

Fritz, 88, 96, 109, 136, **159**, 194, 242, 244

Frost, 40, 55, 94, 165, 232

Gab, 58, 59

Gabby, 59

Gabe, 84, 160, 175, 271

Gabi, 58, 59

Gabriel, 21, 27, 49, 139, 143, **160**, 168, 171, 184, 191, 198, 216, 224, 227, 271

Gabriela, 22, 23, 27, 43, 47, **58**, 59, 92, 97, 99, 117, 156, 168, 171, 247, 281

Gabriella, 27, 58, 59, 60, 67, 151, 161, 245

Gabrielle, 58, **59**, 99, 101, 129, 183, 240, 264, 268

Gaby, 58

Gael, 23

Gaetano, 131, 245

Gage, 37, 67, 136, 139, **160**, 216, 229

Gaia, **59**, 67, 256, 262

Gail, 21, 50, **59**, 62, 71, 72, 75, 79, 89, 93, 162, 207, 259, 287
Gala, 59, 260
Gale, 59, 96, 183, 222
Galen, 133, **160**, 198, 210, 236, 238
Galilea, 122, 247, 254
Galina, 281
Gannon, **160**, 183, 184, 187, 236, 252
Gardner, 251
Gareth, 55, 129, 153, **160**, 168, 192, 231, 235, 287
Garett, 160
Garland, 91, 180
Garner, 194, 251
Garnet, 45, 232
Garold, 257
Garret, 112, 150, 160, 177
Garrett, 37, 59, 92, 93, 109, 113, 122, 137, 151, **160**, 161, 162, 211, 231, 235
Garrick, 25, 31, 108, 118, 123, 144, 160, 180, 197, 252, 272, 287
Garrison, 37, 40, 54, 142, 169, 252
Garry, 34, 46, 61, 89, 93, 96, 118, 121, 160, 179
Garth, 112, **160**, 183, 233, 238, 263
Gary, 42, 50, 51, 59, 68, 75, 83, 99, 112, 115, 128, 138, 150, **160**, 197, 259, 283
Gaspar, 141
Gaston, 49, 240
Gavin, 43, 60, 96, 98, 128, 145, 153, 157, **161**, 163, 182, 194, 201, 211, 231, 236, 266, 273
Gawain, 161, 231, 238

Gay, 259
Gayla, 50
Gayle, 36, 46, 59, 61, 68, 71, 90, 125, 153
Gaylon, 160, 233
Gaynell, 257
Geena, 60
Gem, 59
Gemma, **59**, 60, 61, 104, 123, 144, 146, 153, 160, 234, 245, 276, 287
Gen, 59
Genaro, 271
Gene, 30, 35, 69, 71, 84, 85, 91, 108, 110, 115, 151, 156, **161**, 182, 222, 271, 283
General, 239
Genesis, 49, **59**, 74, 97, 99, 121, 160, 260
Geneva, 25, 31, 54, **59**, 66, 89, 91, 116, 118, 123, 124, 212, 249, 274, 287
Genevieve/Geneviève, 28, 29, **59**, 72, 90, 119, 149, 157, 180, 207, 237, 249, 268, 276
Genie, 59
Gennadi, 282
Gennaro, 244, 245, 277
Genny, 59
Genoveva, 254
Geoff, 161
Geoffrey, 22, 24, 34, 38, 67, 80, 95, 98, 116, 123, 136, **161**, 171, 200, 208, 265
Georg, 242
George, 41, 83, 89, 93, 97, 109, 142, 154, **161**, 165, 198, 249, 286
Georges, 240
Georgette, 59
Georgia, 42, **59**, 66, 72,

91, 123, 124, 187, 222, 224, 233, 274
Georgiana, 59
Georgie, 59, 243
Georgina, 59
Georgine, 268
Georgios, 243
Gerald, 33, 35, 39, 61, 68, 71, 73, 91, 92, 102, 105, 108, 151, **161**, 202, 214, 259, 272, 283
Geraldine, 50, 193, 268, 275
Geraldo, 161
Gerard, 27, 45, 90, 106, 119, 125, 160, **161**, 172, 197, 213, 235, 240, 277, 283
Gerardo, 125, 255
Geri, 70
Germain, 172
Germaine, 60, 131, 185, 218, 222, 240, 268, 276
Gerold, 161
Geronimo, 172, 239
Gerri, 70, 268
Gerry, 45, 70, 161, 172, 222
Gert, 60
Gertie, 60, 243
Gertrud, 60
Gertrude, 60, 223, 241, 270, 275, 285
Gervase, 170, 238
Gia, **60**, 146, 192, 256
Giacomo, 245
Giancarlo, 23, 60, 162, 244, 245
Gianna, 14, **60**, 102, 129, 148, 162, 244
Gianni, 30, **161**, 162, 201, 245
Gib, 162
Gibson, 252
Gideon, 25, 42, 63, 72,

95, 102, 115, 117, 132,
155, **161**, 170, 171,
174, 184, 195, 198,
205, 206, 238, 287
Gidget, 238, 284
Gigi, 57, 60, 240, 268
Gil, 86, 162, 247, 271
Gilbert, 84, 89, 124, 135,
140, 143, 144, 145,
156, **162**, 162, 172,
201, 205, 214, 249,
270, 271, 277, 283
Gilberto, 162, 255
Gilda, 243
Giles, **162**, 175, 192,
235, 271, 277
Gilles, 162
Gillian, 58, 59, **60**, 71,
133, 152, 160, 162,
163, 196, 204, 211,
234
Gilly, 60
Gina, 39, 47, **60**, 71,
106, 107, 110, 148,
153, 245, 268, 284
Ginger, **60**, 70, 124, 171,
203, 232, 268, 284
Ginny, 59, 60, 124, 259,
268
Gino, 245
Gio, 162
Giorgio, 51
Giovanna, 23, 58, **60**,
201, 245, 247, 268
Giovanni, 15, 22, 35, 51,
60, 102, 124, 148, 156,
162, 244, 245
Gisela, 60, 241
Gisele, 60
Gisella, 65, 245
Giselle, 41, 49, **60**, 82,
100, 133, 135, 147,
197, 198, 239, 240,
254, 266, 268
Giulia, 60, 73
Giuseppe, 245
Gladys, 22, 34, 52, **61**,

96, 119, 167, 190, 230,
274, 275
Glen, 61, 125, 162, 163
Glenda, 47, 52, **61**, 62,
89, 93, 162, 213, 230,
259
Glendon, 32, 236, 283
Glenn, 27, 52, 54, 69,
73, 98, 113, 147, 152,
162, 191, 195, 201,
231, 259, 283
Glenna, 45, 98, 104, 108,
140, 183, 205, 206, 287
Glinda, 61, 65, 259
Gloria, 30, **61**, 73, 89,
91, 101, 161, 172, 202,
214, 266, 282
Glory, 61, 260
Glover, 251
Glyn, 61, **162**, 168, 212,
229, 231
Glynis, 61, 144, 160,
168, 184, 192, 230,
234, 237
Glynn, 32, 46, 162, 203,
213
Glynnis, 61
Godfrey, 152, 181, 235,
249
Golda, 34, **61**, 159, 246,
249
Golden, 135, 232, 260
Goldie, 61, 109, 167,
243
Gonzalo, 255, 281
Goran, 282
Gordie, 162
Gordon, 30, 51, 52, 84,
85, 93, 101, 104, 113,
143, 159, **162**, 183,
193, 213, 214, 283
Grace, 18, 28, 32, 53, 55,
46, **61**, 73, 86, 109,
114, 155, 224, 231,
232, 268
Gracie, **61**, 72, 86, 124,
243, 268

Graciela, **61**, 65, 91, 100,
122, 247, 254, 268, 287
Gracious, 220
Grady, 70, 91, 129, 155,
157, **162**, 164, 170,
196, 215, 252, 287
Graeme, 144, 162, 229
Graham, 41, 47, 53, 57,
58, 73, 103, 114, 115,
135, 138, 152, 155,
160, **162**, 189, 193,
196, 199, 231, 234,
235, 286
Grainne, 114, 230
Grania, 48, 58, 204, 230
Grant, 37, 44, 65, 139,
142, 145, 160, **163**,
179, 196, 199, 202,
229, 252, 286
Grayson, 137, 138, 149,
163, 176, 210, 214,
236, 252
Grazia, 245
Graziella, 61, 245
Greer, 36, 88, 203, 228,
252
Greg, 34, 60, 75, 78, 85,
117, 210, 271
Gregg, 68, 71, 107, 123,
146, 147, 177, 197,
284
Gregor, 136, 146, 163,
164, 179, 231, 271
Gregorio, 140, 245, 271
Gregory, 46, 48, 49, 50,
74, 122, **163**, 171, 207,
209, 265, 271
Greta, 31, 54, **62**, 64, 89,
241, 249, 278
Gretchen, 62, 66, 241,
266, 285
Greyson, 23, 35, 106,
163
Griff, 163
Griffin, 38, 58, 60, 76,
77, 95, 106, 107, 137,
140, 149, 152, **163**,

193, 196, 216, 231, 236

Griffith, 29, 37, 61, 84, 117, 163, 231, 252, 287

Grigori, 163

Grover, 54, 155, 166, 177, 263, 275

Guadalupe, 62, 95, 129, 172, 195, 222, 253, 255

Gudrun, 257

Güicho, 183

Guido, 163, 245

Guillaume, 240

Guillermo, 62, 255

Guinevere, 70, 94, 107, 237

Guiseppe, 245

Gulliver, 239

Gunnar, 28, 31, 36, 62, 84, 111, 140, 163, 169, 206, 242, 278

Gunner, 163, 197, 251

Günther, 242

Gus, 32, 54, 61, 65, 87, 88, 99, 105, 106, 109, 131, 132, 133, 163, 167, 184, 190, 244

Gussie, 32, 243

Gust, 257

Gustav, 278

Gustave, 49, 240, 271

Gustavo, 125, 255, 271

Guy, 143, 163, 167, 195, 198, 202, 277, 283

Gwen, 46, 59, 62, 81, 90, 124, 147, 152, 162, 177, 182, 183, 205, 212, 213, 259

Gwendolen, 62

Gwendolyn, 62, 103, 185, 188, 197, 230, 282

Gwyneth, 160

Hadassah, 62, 113, 226, 246

Haden, 165

Hadley, 130, 160, 179, 180, 196, 211, 252

Haia, 246

Hailey, 15, 62, 78, 79, 87, 165, 168, 186, 252

Haim, 142

Hakeem, 221, 261

Hal, 71, 72, 90, 98, 104, 106, 108, 118, 142, 163, 164, 165, 182, 191, 208, 283, 287

Hale, 147, 229, 283

Haleigh, 76, 88, 127, 137, 163, 169

Haley, 62, 133, 134, 142, 167, 212, 225, 266

Halia, 262

Halima, 261

Halina, 281

Halle, 173, 178, 192

Hallie, 34, 53, 61, 62, 72, 81, 129, 145, 149, 155, 166, 243

Halston, 239

Ham, 164

Hamid, 261

Hamilton, 154, 164, 252

Hamish, 88, 129, 164, 204, 231

Hamza, 261

Hana, 29, 47, 63, 168, 281

Hank, 165, 171, 259

Hanna, 63, 72, 164, 173, 189, 192

Hannah, 14, 18, 21, 55, 63, 101, 129, 139, 154, 155, 156, 160, 168, 204, 205, 224, 226, 266, 269

Hannelore, 241

Hannes, 242, 278

Hannibal, 209, 238, 263, 271

Hans, 242, 271, 278

Hansel, 84

Harald, 164, 278

Hardy, 59, 63, 107, 150, 162, 164, 188, 197, 233, 252

Hariett, 202

Harlan, 164, 165, 179, 188, 199, 252, 266

Harland, 164

Harley, 63, 84, 87, 105, 138, 176, 222, 252

Harmon, 159, 164, 194, 252

Harmony, 37, 42, 63, 72, 82, 94, 97, 99, 111, 260, 266

Harold, 52, 58, 128, 129, 156, 164, 166, 181, 249, 271

Harper, 134, 166, 251

Harriet, 22, 54, 56, 63, 85, 96, 98, 143, 144, 159, 164, 165, 166, 182, 203, 214, 249, 268

Harriett, 63

Harris, 92, 107, 134, 164, 182, 211, 214, 215, 252, 283, 287

Harrison, 28, 44, 73, 86, 87, 135, 143, 145, 149, 164, 171, 188, 196, 213, 252, 286

Harry, 28, 86, 109, 110, 115, 142, 159, 164, 165, 244, 271

Hart, 42, 165, 229, 232

Hartley, 54, 252

Harve, 165

Harvey, 165, 167, 190, 244

Haskel, 165

Haskell, 54, 82, 165, 166, 244, 247, 252, 266

Hassan, 110, 176, 261

Hassie, 257

Hattie, 63, 64, 243, 268

Hava, 132
Haven, 26, 31, 52, **63**, 72, 87, 94, 99, 110, 114, 171, 172, 176, 260, 287
Havilah, 226
Hayden, 78, 147, **165**, 167, 222, 224, 225, 235, 236, 252
Hayes, 36, 158, 174, 229, 253
Haylee, 62, 179, 225
Hayleigh, 62
Hayley, 62, 89, 112, 133, 142, 167
Haylie, 62
Hays, 79
Haywood, 164
Hazel, 57, **63**, 70, 109, 120, 164, 165, 170, 224, 232, 266
Heart, 238
Heath, 29, 65, 94, 118, 134, 137, **165**, 179, 205, 210, 229, 232, 279
Heathcliff, 239, 271
Heather, 26, 29, 46, 55, **63**, 65, 70, 78, 142, 170, 171, 232, 266, 279
Heaven, 27, 59, **64**, 97, 196, 238, 260
Heber, 257
Hector, **165**, 197, 198, 255, 262, 266
Hedwig, 257
Heidi, 47, 62, **64**, 116, 124, 211, 241, 279, 284
Heinz, 242
Helen, 24, 58, **64**, 66, 109, 128, 132, 159, 161, 164, 183, 198, 206, 214, 249, 268, 269, 282
Helena, 29, 41, **64**, 73,

85, 86, 131, 133, 153, 171, 189, 190, 193, 276, 280, 285, 287
Helene, 64, 93, 103, 144, 164, 189, 201, 240, 282
Helga, 136, 159, 241, 275
Helmer, 257
Heloise, 54, 240, 249
Hennie, 64
Henri, 165, 240
Henrietta, 21, 44, **64**, 124, 141, 203, 234, 249, 268
Henriette, 64
Henrik, 165, 242, 278
Henrique, 255
Henry, 21, 24, 28, 41, 45, 64, 83, 86, 89, 97, 109, 114, 132, 154, 159, 161, **165**, 168, 183, 214, 249, 271, 271, 286
Herb, 166
Herbert, 58, 103, 119, 132, **166**, 249
Heriberto, 255
Herm, 166
Herman, 52, 56, 58, 60, 85, 135, 154, **166**, 241, 249, 285
Hermann, 166, 242
Hermes, 97, 239, 262, 277
Hermia, 280
Herminia, 257
Hermione, 29, **64**, 94, 97, 101, 104, 134, 166, 237, 262, 276, 280
Hernan, 255
Hersch, 166
Herschel, 166
Herta, 257
Hertha, 257
Heshel, 166
Hester, 60, 124, 127,

130, 152, 158, 165, 166, 172, 213, 249, 263, 268, 275
Hestia, 262
Hettie, 56, 64, 94
Hetty, 268
Hezekiah, 227, 273
Hilary, 65, 81
Hilbert, 257
Hilda, 34, 52, **64**, 138, 166, 194, 275
Hilde, 64, 241
Hildegard, 241
Hildred, 257
Hildy, 64
Hillary, **65**, 79, 206, 222, 253, 266
Hillel, 62, 165, 227, 247
Hilma, 257
Hilton, 253
Hiram, 180, 184, 227, 249
Hirsch, 165, **166**, 246, 247
Hirsh, 166
Hogan, 253
Holden, 23, 95, 114, 140, 155, **166**, 200, 204, 236, 253, 263, 266
Holli, 65
Hollie, 65
Hollis, 54, **65**, 130, 158, 164, 192, 200, 222, 253
Holly, 24, 29, 36, 38, 42, 55, 63, 64, **65**, 70, 74, 84, 117, 136, 144, 150, 161, 165, 205, 210, 232, 264, 266
Holt, 136, 209, 253
Homer, 63, 65, 103, 155, 158, **166**, 194, 263, 275
Honey, 105, 238
Honor, 42, 59, **65**, 102, 136, 165, 232
Honoré, 33, 133, 232

Honorée, 65, 240
Hooper, 251
Hope, 38, 41, 44, 47, 53,
57, **65**, 67, 73, 115,
143, 149, 163, 167,
191, 193, 205, 232,
285
Horace, 22, 60, 82, 101,
143, 166, **166**, 184,
194, 202, 213, 249,
266
Horatio, 29, 64, 67, 101,
104, 133, **166**, 238,
281
Horst, 242
Hortencia, 257
Hosea, 69, 172, 180, 184,
227
Houston, 233, 253, 274
Howard, 84, 116, **166**,
189, 206, 283
Howie, 166
Hoyt, 233, 275
Hubert, 63, 82, 98, 143,
166, 249, 270
Hud, 167
Hudson, 63, 102, 106,
117, 149, **167**, 211,
253, 274
Huey, 167, 244
Hugh, 25, 38, 45, 52, 54,
57, 64, 85, 90, 124,
144, 153, 154, 155,
163, **167**, 175, 184,
235, 249, 277, 283
Hughes, 65, 253
Hugo, 25, 44, 67, 147,
157, 165, **167**, 240,
249, 255
Hulda, 257
Humberto, 255
Hunter, 15, 25, 40, 62,
84, 87, 98, 111, 113,
116, 118, 121, **167**,
173, 182, 207, 212,
222, 251
Hurley, 258

Hyam, 142
Hyman, 142

Iago, 263
Iain, 167
Ian, 37, 69, 79, 94, 99,
100, 118, 119, 126,
145, 157, **167**, 170,
173, 183, 231, 256,
265, 266
Ianthe, 262
Ibrahim, 190, 261
Icie, 258
Ida, 21, 22, 64, **65**, 87,
129, 138, 155, 167,
241, 249, 276, 278
Iesha, 23
Ifan, 157
Ifor, 168
Ignacio, 255
Ignatius, 238, 272
Igor, 101, 282
Ike, 34, 44, 65, 109, 152,
163, **167**, 168, 175,
190, 244
Ilana, 33, 113, 246
Ileana, **65**, 247
Ilene, 52
Iliana, 28, 46, 58, 65,
254
Ilias, 243
Iman, 65, 110
Imani, **65**, 185, 217, 218,
218, 220
Imelda, 263
Immanuel, 156
Imogene, 54, 249
India, 31, **66**, 77, 102,
111, 116, 196, 199,
220, 247, 274
Indigo, 239
Ines, 254
Inez, 22, 50, 155, 165,
194, 249
Inga, 64, 66, 192
Inge, 241, 278
Ingeborg, 257

Ingrid, 54, 62, **66**, 114,
206, 241, 285
Io, 256, 262
Ioannis, 243
Iolanthe, 237
Iole, 22, 126, 237
Ion, 65
Iona, 66, 82, 98, 164,
179, 191, 230, 249
Ione, 29, 32, 44, 48, **66**,
82, 83, 84, 86, 126,
128, 139, 157, 158,
160, 168, 177, 180,
183, 184, 189, 216,
237, 262
Ira, 87, 244
Ireland, **66**, 183, 274
Irene, **66**, 91, 116, 128,
130, 140, 153, 159,
164, 166, 181, 189,
206, 243, 262, 282
Irina, 66, 101, 281
Irini, 50, 53, 66, 243
Iris, 32, 39, **66**, 72, 88,
108, 150, 232, 262,
280, 285
Irma, 133, 158, 190, 194,
275
Irv, 167
Irvin, 221
Irvine, 167
Irving, 96, **167**, 244, 245,
275
Isaac, 21, 39, 44, 53, 57,
66, 73, 114, 156, **167**,
168, 173, 175, 184,
191, 227, 271, 273, 286
Isaak, 167
Isabel, 21, 39, 44, 53, 55,
66, 67, 73, 83, 139,
174, 194, 213, 224,
254
Isabela, 67
Isabella, 18, 27, 66, **67**,
101, 168, 204, 224,
245, 247, 248, 278,
280

Isabelle, 66, 67, 87, 114,
145, 240
Isadora, 67, 141, 149,
161, 166, 209, 237
Isai, 48
Isaiah, 29, 49, 65, 67, 69,
101, 111, 155, **168,**
171, 174, 198, 221,
224, 227, 271
Isaias, 66, 122, 149, 176,
188, 238, 277
Ishmael, 227, 238
Isidro, 255
Isis, 30, 31, **67,** 123, 127,
128, 131, 175, 187,
196, 201, 216, 237,
238, 262, 266
Isla, 230
Ismael, 261
Isobel, 66, 67
Isom, 257
Israel, 227
Istvan, 207
Itzel, 254
Iva, 21, 45, 65, 94, 107,
118, 147, 249
Ivan, 32, 53, 85, 91, 92,
98, 99, 107, 114, 148,
151, **168,** 175, 187,
201, 213, 277, 282,
286
Ivana, 281
Ivette, 125, 254
Ivor, 66, 83, 119, 153,
168, 213, 215, 231,
235, 238
Ivory, 45, 55, 232
Ivy, 32, 55, 56, **67,** 83,
111, 134, 154, 157,
167, 173, 182, 192,
201, 206, 216, 224,
232, 256, 285
Iyana, 220
Iyanna, 21, 30, 193
Izabella, 67
Izaiah, 171
Izetta, 257

Izora, 257
Izzy, 53, 66, 67, 168

Jabari, 21, 217, 221
Jabez, 74, 111, 122, 126,
168, 170, 227, 238
Jace, 139, **168,** 176, 216,
229
Jacey, 67, 79, 169, 225
Jack, 31, 53, 72, 74, **168,**
173, 229, 234, 244,
286
Jackie, 35, 45, 67, 118,
222, 259
Jackson, 15, 73, 87, 140,
141, **168,** 171, 236,
253, 271
Jaclyn, 67, 69, 74, 77, 79,
121, 124, 279
Jaco, 101, 168, 192, 247
Jacob, 18, 55, 63, 129,
168, 204, 226, 227,
271, 271, 286
Jacqueline, 50, **67,** 73,
99, 105, 122, 240, 285
Jacquelyn, 67, 220
Jacques, 240
Jacqui, 67
Jada, 52, **67,** 69, 76, 78,
79, 87, 94, 96, 100,
139, 169, 170, 220,
225, 256
Jade, 27, 32, 47, 49, 59,
67, 68, 69, 106, 121,
136, 138, 142, 160,
169, 172, 208, 211,
228, 232, 260
Jaden, 68, 78, **169,** 170,
195, 222, 225, 235,
236, 271
Jadon, 169
Jael, 86, 168, 226, 256
Jaelyn, 68, 225, 235
Jafar, 261
Jag, 169
Jagger, 23, 105, 155,
169, 184, 251, 263

Jaheim, 30, 221
Jaida, 69
Jaiden, 68, 169
Jaidyn, 68, 235
Jailyn, 68, 225
Jaim, 142
Jaime, 68, 169, 199, 222,
222, 255
Jaimie, 68, 105
Jair, 53, 97, 101, 168,
178, 229, 256
Jairo, 26, 107, 112, 118,
172, 255
Jakayla, 219, 220, 225
Jake, 25, 38, 46, 61, 70,
84, 98, 118, 154, 168,
169, 184, 205, 244
Jakob, 168
Jaleel, 261
Jalen, 16, 29, 67, 76, 79,
88, 136, **169,** 211, 221,
222, 225, 236
Jali, 217
Jalisa, 117, 180, 220
Jaliyah, 220
Jalon, 225
Jalyn, 68
Jalynn, 68, 225
Jamaal, 79, 80, 169, 176
Jamal, 110, **169,** 190,
193, 221, 261, 266,
271
Jamar, 221
Jamari, 30, 69, 193, 212,
221
Jamel, 272
James, 18, 41, 89, 142,
169, 173, 195, 200,
209, 215, 227, 265,
271, 272, 286
Jameson, 169, 253
Jamey, 84, 97, 117, 279
Jami, 68
Jamie, 40, 43, **68,** 70,
121, 142, 146, 169,
170, 210, 222, 279
Jamil, 23, 169, 261

Jamila, 23, 65, **68**, 169, 176, 205, 220, 261, 287
Jamin, 227
Jamison, 65, 127, 134, 169, 177, 196, 271
Jammie, 258
Jamya, 220
Jan, 68, 70, 75, 81, 86, 123, 173, 242, 268, 278, 284
Jana, 114, 202, 268, 281
Janae, 76, 179, 225
Janay, 117, 220
Jane, **68**, 173, 179, 198, 200, 268, 282
Janelle, 98, 106, 170, 172, 177, 208, 212, 220, 268, 269, 284
Janessa, 247, 268
Janet, 39, 54, **68**, 73, 99, 102, 138, 147, 162, 172, 177, 197, 201, 207, 259, 268, 282
Janette, 68, 69, 259, 284
Janice, 27, 51, 52, **68**, 71, 112, 150, 153, 259, 268, 282
Janie, 68, 110, 195
Janina, 68
Janine, 50, **68**, 109, 239, 268, 284
Janis, 46, 59, 61, 62, 68, 89, 90, 155, 287
Janiya, 220, 248
Janna, 256
Jannette, 69
Japh, 170
Japheth, 14, 40, 55, 166, 168, **170**, 195, 227, 238, 271, 287
Jaquan, 221
Jaquez, 221
Jared, 24, 25, 26, 34, 55, 69, 79, 81, 96, 109, 110, 127, 150, **170**, 171, 173, 175, 183, 227, 265, 266, 271

Jaren, 67
Jarett, 38, 138
Jarod, 170, 272
Jaron, 26, 30, 46, 91, 113, 116, 142, 150, **170**, 221, 236, 247, 266
Jarred, 170
Jarret, 30, 170
Jarrett, 49, 57, 71, 74, 89, 121, 124, 138, **170**, 177, 253, 266, 279
Jarrod, 40, 76, 81, 105, 170, 208, 253
Jarvis, 81, 98, **170**, 179, 233, 266, 279
Jase, 168, 170
Jasmin, 35, 67, 69, 106, 132, 145, 147, 150, 183, 220
Jasmine, 49, 56, **69**, 71, 115, 125, 156, 168, 173, 183, 220, 232, 260, 269
Jasmyn, 69
Jason, 40, 63, 70, **170**, 171, 262, 265, 271, 279
Jasper, 25, 28, 37, 44, 45, 59, 64, 66, 67, 70, 82, 86, 114, 123, 124, 141, 156, **170**, 185, 224, 232, 238
Javen, 225, 236
Javi, 170
Javier, 27, 55, 91, 141, **170**, 216, 255
Javon, 33, 77, 148, 221
Jax, 128, 168, 171
Jaxon, 64, 68, 69, 168, **171**, 172, 216, 236
Jay, 70, 78, 113, 116, 128, 168, 169, 170, **171**, 286
Jayce, 68, 69, 125, 168
Jaycee, 76
Jayda, 67
Jayde, 67

Jayden, 16, 68, 169, 221
Jayla, 16, 67, 68, **69**, 78, 136, 139, 220, 225
Jaylen, 24, 169
Jaylin, 68, 169, 225, 235
Jaylon, 169, 225
Jaylyn, 68, 225
Jaylynn, 68
Jayme, 68, 112
Jayne, 68, 259
Jayson, 170
Jaz, 69, 170
Jazlyn, 68, **69**, 171, 236
Jazmin, 30, 69, 148, 210, 212, 236
Jean, 35, **69**, 71, 84, 104, 173, 240, 268, 282
Jeanette, 30, **69**, 84, 152, 162, 191, 201, 203, 213, 268, 282
Jeanie, 69
Jeanine, 42
Jeanne, 45, 52, 69, 71, 85, 93, 119, 240
Jeannette, 69, 103, 240
Jeannie, 284
Jeannine, 68, 90, 105, 240, 259
Jed, 84, **171**, 174, 203, 216, 233, 271
Jedediah, 216
Jedidiah, 94, **171**, 227, 238, 271
Jeff, 48, 108, 169, 171, 271
Jefferson, 130, **171**, 182, 253, 271, 286
Jeffery, 171
Jeffrey, 27, 34, 43, 48, 73, 74, 76, 78, 96, 107, 120, 124, 137, 146, 161, 163, **171**, 204, 207, 209, 265, 271, 284
Jelani, 25, 65, 217
Jem, 69, 169, 171, 174, 216, 272

Jemima, 48, 50, **69**, 157, 226, 234, 263
Jemma, 59
Jen, 69, 70
Jena, 69, 74, 77, 117, 121, 148
Jenifer, 70
Jenna, 37, **69**, 71, 80, 94, 118, 134, 136, 145, 150, 157, 167, 169, 170, 183, 193, 211, 256, 264, 268
Jennie, 70
Jennifer, **70**, 170, 254, 268, 279, 279
Jennings, 164, 190
Jenny, 59, 68, **70**, 268
Jerald, 42, 45, 161
Jere, 256
Jered, 170, 272
Jeremiah, 168, **171**, 221, 272
Jeremy, 24, 25, 26, 27, 29, 43, 47, 55, 63, 68, 70, 75, 78, 94, 100, 115, 117, 142, 146, 153, 170, **171**, 174, 227, 265, 271, 272, 279
Jeri, **70**, 113, 268, 284
Jeriah, 227
Jerilyn, 268
Jermaine, 52, 76, 80, 116, **172**, 218, 221
Jermayne, 172
Jerold, 161
Jerome, 35, 39, 52, 90, 93, 109, 119, 125, 151, 161, **172**, 201, 221, 240, 272, 277, 283
Jerri, 70, 259
Jerrica, 268
Jerrie, 70
Jerrod, 36, 170
Jerrold, 35, 161
Jerry, 36, 70, 71, 73, 83, 89, 103, 161, 171, **172**, 179, 258, 259, 272

Jerusha, 69, 171, 172, 226
Jerzy, 185, 282
Jesper, 278
Jess, 70, 94, 99, 134, 172
Jessalyn, 268
Jessame, 268
Jessamyn, 268
Jesse, 70, 72, 75, 77, **172**, 214, 227, 233, 286
Jessenia, 205
Jessi, 70
Jessica, 18, 25, 30, **70**, 111, 127, 143, 171, 173, 174, 175, 264, 268, 279, 280
Jessie, 40, **70**, 172, 222, 268
Jessye, 70
Jesus/**Jesús**, 131, **172**, 174, 183, 227, 255
Jet, 172, 232
Jethro, 69, **172**, 227, 275
Jett, 27, 37, 56, 63, 67, 114, 171, 172, 188, 196, 229, 260
Jetta, 113
Jettie, 258
Jewel, **70**, 102, 133, 155, 207, 222, 224, 232, 260
Jewell, 55, 57, 70, 111, 123
Jezebel, 226, 263
Jill, 34, 39, 60, **70**, 71, 73, 86, 92, 124, 171, 178, 284, 287
Jillian, 37, 60, **71**, 106, 143, 236, 279
Jilly, 71
Jim, 36, 115, 169, 259
Jimena, 151, 172, 254
Jimmie, 244
Jimmy, 35, 50, 73, 103, 169, 172
Jiri, 282
Jo, 50, **71**, 72, 75, 92,

103, 115, 147, 152, 174, 203, 208, 214, 259, 268, 282
Joachim, 122, 172, 238
Joah, 37, 59, 97, 111, 227, 256, 287
Joan, **71**, 268, 282
Joanie, 71, 72, 259
Joann, 71, 161
Joanna, **71**, 72, 81, 115, 144, 148, 172, 187, 227, 268, 285
Jo Anne, 71
Joanne, 47, 68, **71**, 92, 124, 202, 259, 268, 282
João, 255
Joaquim, 172, 255
Joaquin, 27, 56, **172**, 255
Jocelyn, 34, 59, **71**, 127, 137, 145, 147, 150, 157, 163, 197, 236, 264, 268
Jocelyne, 71
Jodi, 47, 50, **71**, 210, 268, 279, 284
Jodie, 71, 81, 89, 121
Jody, 47, 70, 71, 72, 92, 120, 173, 174, 177, 210, 222, 284
Joe, 28, 35, 61, 68, 108, 142, 168, **173**, 174, 198, 244, 272
Joel, 44, 70, 81, 99, 106, 114, 116, 148, **173**, 185, 227, 286
Joelle, 131, 240, 268
Joey, 68, 71, 72, 120, 174, 222, 268, 284
Joffrey, 161
Johan, 28, 62, 206, 278
Johana, 72
Johann, 173, 186, 242
Johanna, 44, 66, 71, **72**, 171, 206, 241, 268, 278, 285

Johannes, 278
John, 18, 28, 93, 168, 169, 173, 174, 195, 226, 227, 271, 271, 286
Johnny, 35, 47, 173, 259
Jo Jo, 174
Jojuan, 219
Jolene, 42, 81, 284
Jolie, 53, 97
Jomar, 180
Jon, 34, 39, 86, 113, 171, 173, 259, 284
Jonah, 71, 73, 156, 163, 169, 173, 189, 192, 215, 227, 272
Jonas, 22, 34, 56, 81, 127, 157, 173, 205, 209, 224, 226, 227, 272, 278
Jonathan, 18, 25, 40, 135, 143, 173, 174, 227, 265, 273
Jonathon, 173
Joni, 70, 178, 284
Jonnie, 243
Jonty, 173, 235
Jordan, 25, 33, 62, 69, 72, 74, 76, 98, 101, 113, 116, 118, 151, 173, 190, 207, 208, 221, 222, 236, 253, 274
Jordana, 72
Jordie, 173
Jordy, 72
Jordyn, 37, 72, 132, 147, 169
Jorge, 161, 170, 255
José, 90, 174, 183, 227, 254, 255, 286
Josef, 66, 174, 242
Josefa, 41, 51, 59, 72, 82, 85, 104, 132, 145, 175, 248, 249, 268, 281, 287
Josefina, 72, 89

Joselyn, 268
Joseph, 18, 28, 53, 173, 174, 202, 215, 227, 272, 286
Josepha, 72, 119, 276
Josephina, 72, 91
Josephine, 41, 42, 52, 57, 59, 72, 83, 123, 124, 175, 206, 209, 222, 224, 268, 276
Josette, 72
Josey, 72, 174
Josh, 174, 226
Joshua, 18, 25, 80, 127, 171, 173, 174, 216, 226, 227, 265
Joshuah, 174
Josiah, 21, 90, 99, 121, 155, 161, 171, 174, 184, 189, 209, 221, 224, 226, 227
Josias, 174
Josie, 25, 38, 46, 61, 71, 72, 88, 118, 243, 268
Joslyn, 180, 236
Joss, 71, 96, 174, 175, 209, 222, 228, 229, 233, 287
Josue, 85, 99, 125, 141, 151, 172, 174, 255
Journey, 26, 49, 59, 63, 72, 74, 82, 87, 111, 172, 174, 187, 188, 193, 196, 219, 260, 268, 287
Jovan, 29, 79, 107, 110, 119, 212, 221, 282
Jovani, 101, 272
Jovanni, 162
Jovany, 162
Joy, 36, 72, 86, 95, 191, 232, 259, 287
Joyce, 33, 39, 61, 71, 73, 91, 101, 110, 152, 159, 161, 188, 199, 222, 282
Joycelyn, 218

Juan, 172, 173, 174, 183, 227, 254, 255
Juana, 254
Juanita, 255
Judah, 63, 66, 72, 91, 95, 113, 132, 155, 161, 171, 173, 174, 190, 205, 227, 287
Judas, 174
Judd, 160, 173, 174, 175, 233
Jude, 53, 58, 73, 74, 92, 110, 118, 135, 155, 174, 175, 176, 184, 202, 203, 209, 227, 229, 277, 287
Judge, 74, 135, 184, 239
Judi, 73
Judie, 73
Judith, 39, 52, 73, 83, 102, 201, 226, 259, 268, 282
Judson, 86, 199, 214, 253
Judy, 34, 36, 68, 71, 73, 103, 115, 160, 172, 179, 259
Jules, 21, 25, 33, 41, 54, 58, 73, 82, 85, 93, 104, 107, 118, 132, 143, 175, 239, 240, 249, 287
Julia, 28, 53, 55, 61, 73, 168, 195, 213, 213, 224, 241, 269, 278, 280, 285
Julian, 14, 21, 27, 28, 32, 39, 42, 44, 55, 67, 83, 87, 114, 128, 151, 154, 160, 168, 175, 188, 189, 194, 204, 213, 224, 235, 277, 286
Juliana, 27, 29, 47, 53, 67, 73, 122, 133, 135, 160, 164, 168, 248, 269, 276
Juliann, 73
Julianna, 73, 171

Julianne, 28, 67, **73**, 80, 264
Julie, **73**, 83, 107, 120, 124, 146, 171, 173, 177, 186, 204, 207, 240, 259, 269, 284
Julien, 175, 240
Julienne, 73, 240
Juliet, 47, 56, **73**, 91, 114, 135, 152, 162, 171, 182, 269, 280, 285, 287
Juliette, 28, 41, 73, 240
Julio, 106, 195, 198, 255, 286
Julissa, 25, 170, 255, 269
Julius, 22, 32, 34, 44, 45, 52, 56, 59, 61, 63, 72, 83, 90, 97, 109, 123, 133, 141, 153, 157, **175**, 181, 193, 194, 206, 209, 224, 249, 277
June, 35, 45, **74**, 90, 92, 108, 109, 163, 202, 222, 232, 282, 287
Junia, **74**, 180, 227
Junious, 257
Juniper, 80, 120, 232
Juno, 59, 262, 280
Jupiter, 123, 128, 131, **175**, 239, 262
Jurgen, 242
Justen, 175
Justice, 16, 26, 27, 31, 49, 52, 56, 59, 70, **74**, 82, 97, 123, 176, 216, 219, 220, 222, 260, 266
Justin, 30, 77, 78, 137, 143, 156, 170, 173, **175**, 178, 203, 236, 265, 266, 277
Justina, 74, 276
Justine, 22, 39, 42, 51, **74**, 190, 240, 266, 279
Justus, 26, 66, 72, 102,

102, 134, 157, **176**, 187, 188, 203, 227, 238, 277
Justyn, 175
Juwan, 180

Kabelo, 218
Kacey, 40
Kacie, 40, 225
Kade, 106, 168
Kadeem, 221
Kaden, 30, 37
Kadence, 37
Kadin, 139, 225
Kaela, 76
Kaelie, 96
Kaelyn, 68, 76
Kai, 28, 52, 53, 67, 100, 101, 132, 133, 139, 150, **176**, 178, 184, 192, 222, 229, 256, 278
Kaiden, 139
Kaila, 76
Kaile, 139
Kailee, 76
Kailey, 76, 77
Kailyn, 30, 76, 78, 149
Kait, 74
Kaitlin, 74, 236
Kaitlyn, 36, 37, **74**, 98, 143, 145, 153, 173, 176, 225, 269, 275, 279
Kaitlynn, 37
Kaitlynne, 74
Kaiya, 225
Kala, 77
Kale, 139
Kaleb, 24, 29, 32, 78, 88, 139, 169
Kali, 38
Kaliyah, 193, 220, 225
Kallie, 38
Kalliopi, 243
Kalyn, 76
Kamaria, 26, 65, 217
Kamea, 81

Kameron, 38, 77, 79, 88, 140
Kamil, 261, 279
Kamilah, 220
Kamryn, 38, 69, 178
Kane, 40, 62, 74, 76, 78, 79, 94, 112, 139, **176**, 178, 201, 208, 229, 231, 253
Kani, 218
Kara, **74**, 75, 77, 121, 141, 152, 178, 203, 204, 256, 264, 266
Kareem, 169, **176**, 218, 221, 261
Karen, 51, **74**, 102, 128, 149, 178, 186, 207, 259, 264, 266, 269
Karena, 74
Kari, 40, 43, 68, 74, 78, 269, 279
Karim, 176
Karin, 74, 89, 241
Karina, **74**, 147, 248, 269, 278
Karis, 38
Karissa, 38, 119, 177, 269
Karl, 54, 62, 92, 140, 186, 242, 286
Karla, 39, 177, 178
Karli, 39
Karol, 39
Karon, 74
Karren, 74
Karrie, 40
Karsten, 140
Karyn, 74
Kasey, 40, 109, 138, 141, 144, 147, 169, 177, 205, 269
Kasper, 141
Kassandra, 38, 40
Kassidy, 206
Kat, 75
Katarina, 269
Kate, 75, 129, 134, 138, 149, 215, 269, 285

Katelyn, 37, 74, 225
Katelynn, 76, 88, 179
Kateri, 75, 142, 269, 270, 276
Katerina, 28, 41, 50, 75, 151, 243, 281
Katerine, 75
Kath, 75
Katharina, 75, 224, 248, 280
Katharine, 75, 202, 280
Katherine, 53, 72, **75**, 111, 130, 269, 285
Kathi, 75
Kathie, 75, 258
Kathleen, 36, 39, **75**, 93, 110, 112, 115, 150, 152, 191, 229, 230, 259, 269
Kathlyn, 236, 269
Kathryn, 31, 38, 41, 75, 163, 179, 191, 195, 209, 215, 285
Kathy, 34, 74, **75**, 113, 149, 171, 197, 259, 269
Katia, 15, 29, 47, **75**, 97, 185, 269, 281, 287
Katie, 40, 70, 74, **75**, 81, 168, 172, 190, 193, 269
Katlyn, 74, 150, 225, 236
Katrina, 24, 38, **75**, 78, 79, 99, 116, 161, 179, 264, 269, 270, 279
Katy, 75
Katya, 75
Kay, 37, 46, 71, 74, **75**, 76, 88, 115, 182, 208, 212, 269
Kaya, 37, 225
Kaycee, 40
Kayden, 139
Kaydence, 37
Kaye, 59, 74, 75, 84, 228, 259
Kayla, 16, 18, 25, 62, **76**,

88, 96, 144, 173, 212, 220, 225, 269
Kaylah, 76
Kaylee, 76, 225, 269
Kayleen, 76
Kayleigh, 76
Kayley, 76
Kaylie, 76
Kaylin, **76**, 106, 176, 225, 236, 269
Kaylyn, 76
Kaylynn, 76
Kean, 176
Keane, 152, 158, **176**, 229, 231, 253
Keanu, 77, 81, 263
Keaton, 30, 118, 121, 138, 149, 163, 170, **176**, 207, 225, 236, 253
Keegan, 30, 38, 48, 68, 76, 94, 102, 137, 138, 139, 146, **176**, 178, 179, 231, 236, 253, 266
Keeler, 251
Keeley, 38
Keelin, 16, 55, 117, 176, 178, 209, 230, 236
Keely, 139, 225
Keenan, 37, 49, 76, 109, 119, 148, **176**, 177, 202, 221, 231, 236
Keenen, 176
Keir, 135, 154, 215, 229, 231
Keira, 79
Keisha, 52, 76, 80, 116, 117, 172, 220, 266, 279
Keith, 45, 49, 73, 78, 107, 113, 120, 124, 146, 149, **177**, 186, 191, 197, 204, 231, 284
Kelby, 225
Kellen, 236
Kelli, 43, 64, 76

Kellie, 76
Kelly, 36, **76**, 78, 79, 82, 106, 110, 120, 137, 148, **177**, 178, 209, 222, 230, 231, 264, 284
Kelsey, 42, 46, 62, 65, 76, 79, 113, 118, 119, 140, 190, 193, 200, 208, 222, 225, 253, 266
Kelsie, 76, 177
Kelton, 236
Kelvin, 48, 76, 93, 148, 177, 201, 208, 221, 231, 265, 266
Ken, 34, 121, 177, 272
Kenan, 227, 277
Kendal, 76, 177
Kendall, 51, 63, 66, 73, 74, **76**, 77, 78, 81, 84, 94, 103, 109, 127, 137, 146, 150, 170, 176, **177**, 200, 206, 222, 230, 231, 253, 272
Kendra, 74, 77, 99, 121, 141, 153, 177, 196, 208, 220, 264, 266, 279
Kendric, 177
Kendrick, 77, 170, **177**, 186, 196, 208, 212, 221, 231, 253, 265, 272
Kenia, 26, 48, 65, 77, 125, 148, 150, 212
Kenna, 94, 256
Kennedy, 14, 38, 40, 48, 76, 77, 87, 104, 106, 108, 176, 178, 179, 188, 195, 207, 222, 230, 231, 253, 272
Kennera, 137, 145, 158, 178, 276
Kenneth, 39, 50, 75, 93, 150, 152, **177**, 199, 207, 231, 272, 286

Kennith, 177
Kenny, 177, 259, 284
Kent, 39, 72, 79, 86, 134,
    147, 149, 151, 152,
    153, 177, 178, 197,
    259, 284
Kenton, 236, 253, 272
Kenya, 77, 176, 176,
    218, 220, 274
Kenyatta, 217, 221, 272
Kenyon, 68, 146, 236, 272
Kenzie, 37, 69, 76, 225
Keren, 246
Kerensa, 230
Keri, 76, 77
Kermit, 98, 158, 177,
    231, 263
Kerri, 77, 279
Kerry, 26, 76, 77, 81,
    107, 112, 115, 117,
    121, 177, 200, 205,
    208, 222, 230, 231,
    259, 284, 284
Kesha, 76
Keshawn, 193
Keshia, 76
Kevin, 36, 74, 76, 78, 82,
    96, 137, 156, 178, 204,
    209, 231, 265, 266
Keyshawn, 221
Keziah, 40, 157, 168,
    226
Khadijah, 261
Khalid, 23, 26, 57, 68,
    110, 112, 176, 185,
    221, 261
Khalil, 261
Kia, 77, 256
Kian, 225, 231, 236, 256
Kiana, 31, 69, 77, 81,
    148, 185, 202, 220,
    225, 248
Kianna, 33
Kiara, 77, 79, 94, 137,
    140, 150, 153, 158,
    201, 202, 202, 212,
    220, 230, 248, 276

Kiel, 121
Kiera, 77
Kieran, 114, 149, 176,
    178, 225, 231, 236,
    277
Kierra, 77, 225
Kiersten, 76, 206, 236
Kijana, 218
Kiki, 77, 97, 269, 278
Kiley, 78, 79, 127, 138,
    144, 146, 164, 176,
    182, 196, 198, 211,
    212, 214, 225, 253
Kilian, 75, 137, 157, 158,
    178, 231, 277, 287
Killian, 176, 178
Kim, 44, 48, 78, 171,
    178, 200, 222, 259,
    259, 269
Kimball, 15, 269
Kimber, 78
Kimberlee, 78
Kimberley, 78, 171, 204
Kimberlin, 269
Kimberly, 43, 76, 78, 95,
    96, 209, 264, 269, 284
Kin, 78, 188
King, 244, 260
Kingston, 102, 236, 274
Kinnia, 75, 146, 157, 276
Kinsey, 78, 181, 253
Kip, 134, 143, 177, 178,
    211, 284
Kira, 36, 74, 77, 78, 79,
    100, 112, 119, 139,
    168, 176, 256
Kirby, 284
Kirk, 136, 137, 151, 178,
    284
Kirsten, 78, 236, 264,
    278
Kisha, 76
Kit, 75, 143
Kitty, 75, 104, 109, 152
Kiva, 230
Kiya, 225
Kizzy, 220

Klaus, 192, 242
Kobe, 178, 216, 221, 256
Koby, 78, 178, 225
Kody, 144
Kofi, 218
Kohana, 75
Kolby, 23, 37, 114, 144,
    179, 222
Kole, 67
Kolton, 69
Konnor, 37
Konrad, 145
Korbin, 146
Korey, 146
Kory, 121, 146
Kostas, 53, 243
Koty, 147
Kourtney, 46
Kraig, 47, 77, 81, 112
Kris, 46, 70, 71, 78, 121,
    269, 284
Krissy, 78
Krista, 36, 76, 77, 78,
    146, 269, 279, 279,
    285
Kristal, 46, 121, 269
Kristen, 55, 75, 78, 83,
    153, 214, 236, 279
Kristi, 77, 269, 279
Kristian, 143, 222, 269
Kristie, 43, 78
Kristin, 43, 78, 269
Kristina, 43, 72, 78, 269,
    278
Kristine, 43
Kristopher, 143, 279
Kristy, 43, 97
Krystal, 46, 279
Krystle, 46
Kurt, 45, 120, 136, 177,
    178, 210, 242, 284
Kurtis, 31, 74, 105, 117,
    124, 170
Kwame, 26, 218, 221
Ky, 179
Kya, 178
Kyla, 69, 78, 139, 225

Kylan, 117, 225, 236
Kyle, 25, 46, 55, 74, 75, 77, 94, 157, 170, 175, 178, 203, 265, 266
Kylee, 74, 78, 136
Kyler, 30, 36, 69, 76, 78, 88, 112, 179, 253
Kylie, 16, 23, 67, 76, 78, 117, 169, 225
Kyra, 76, 78, 79, 120, 152, 163, 211, 216, 225, 256, 266

Laban, 227
Lace, 79
Lacey, 79, 83, 124, 192, 199, 225, 253
Lachie, 179
Lachlan, 131, 179, 231
Lacie, 79
Lacy, 35, 65, 79, 105, 150, 170, 179, 197, 214
Ladarius, 180
Laddie, 258
Ladonna, 125, 220
Laetitia, 82
Lafayette, 88, 125, 191, 202, 238
Laila, 81
Lainey, 79
Lakeisha, 76, 220
Lakesha, 76, 79
Lakisha, 80
Lamar, 170, 179, 233, 266, 286
Lamarr, 179
Lambert, 133, 270
Lamont, 179, 212, 272
Lan, 179
Lana, 23, 52, 79, 111, 212, 259, 287
Lance, 22, 35, 38, 57, 65, 70, 76, 78, 79, 80, 81, 95, 121, 123, 130, 137, 165, 179, 180, 204, 208, 229, 265

Lancelot, 239
Land, 179, 201
Landen, 23, 57, 68, 125, 160, 167, 169, 179
Lando, 239
Landon, 21, 23, 32, 38, 48, 72, 81, 106, 114, 132, 136, 144, 145, 147, 160, 169, 179, 180, 210, 236, 253
Lane, 36, 48, 84, 87, 111, 143, 145, 152, 179, 183, 199, 208, 210, 211, 214, 229, 233, 253
Laney, 37, 48, 52, 67, 79, 104, 180, 196, 211, 212, 225, 253
Langston, 253, 263
Lani, 23, 31, 81, 125
Laquita, 180
Lara, 24, 79, 151, 173, 179, 210, 264, 281
Laramie, 31, 233, 274
Larissa, 38, 44, 79, 111, 117, 150, 151, 177, 197, 212, 220, 248, 281
Lark, 16, 38, 79, 94, 111, 114, 118, 120, 165, 176, 199, 215, 228, 232, 260
Larkin, 78, 83, 117, 140, 145, 146, 181, 184, 199, 200, 209, 222, 236, 253
Laron, 79
Larry, 33, 39, 61, 68, 99, 172, 179, 201, 202, 214, 258, 259, 272, 283
Lars, 31, 62, 66, 179, 192, 209, 242, 272, 278
Larson, 142, 181, 236, 253, 272
Larue, 118, 179, 233, 243

Lashanda, 79
Lashaunda, 79
Lashawn, 79
Lashonda, 79, 220
Latasha, 80, 116, 220, 270, 279
Laticia, 82
Latif, 261
Latonya, 220
Latosha, 79, 80
LaToya/Latoya, 80, 172, 220
Latrell, 205, 221
Latrice, 220
Latricia, 270
Laura, 80, 106, 114, 186, 189, 195, 207, 235, 241, 269, 285
Laurel, 48, 50, 65, 73, 80, 95, 232, 264, 269
Lauren, 18, 25, 55, 69, 80, 94, 110, 137, 143, 156, 174, 175, 191, 203, 235, 236, 264, 269
Laurence, 28, 38, 90, 103, 108, 159, 161, 179, 281
Laurent, 240
Lauretta, 187
Laurie, 34, 48, 80, 85, 107, 110, 134, 197, 210, 269, 284
Lauryn, 38, 84, 133, 173, 179
Lavada, 257
Lavender, 26, 80, 232
Laverne, 181, 186, 187, 220, 275
Lavin, 222, 236
Lavinia, 14, 32, 80, 83, 180, 248, 249, 262, 269, 287
Law, 180
Lawrence, 52, 54, 69, 92, 109, 159, 162, 179, 186, 191, 195, 198, 203, 272, 283, 286

Lawson, 129, 130, 145, 180, 211, 236, 253
Layla, 23, 26, 57, 81, 112, 261
Layne, 179
Layton, 67, 225, 236
Laz, 179, 180
Lazar, 33, 149, 168, 180, 215, 238, 247
Lazaro, 180, 255
Lazarus, 101, 141, 166, **180**, 227, 238, 277
Lea/Léa, 65, **81**, 100, 119, 130, 143, 174, 193, 210, 240, 256
Leah, 44, 65, **81**, 98, 105, 111, 115, 127, 135, 167, 170, 171, 172, 173, 182, 185, 190, 191, 196, 205, 206, 226, 285
Leamon, 158
Leander, 29, 59, 66, 80, 84, 94, 119, 141, 157, **180**, 208, 238, 262, 270, 277
Leandro, 51, 180
Leann, 77, 81, 170, 202
Leanna, 79, **81**, 108, 248
Leanne, **81**, 203, 233, 284
Leatrice, 270
LeBron, **180**, 221, 263
Leda, 86, 262
Lee, **81**, 82, **180**, 181, 182, 195, 198, 199, 202, 203, 223, 229, 283
Lee Ann, 81
Leeroy, 181
Leesa, 83
Leia, 81
Leib, 247
Leif, 36, 79, 83, 108, 158, 160, 165, 179, **180**, 209, 210, 229, 238, 278, 287
Leigh, 35, 47, 77, **81**,

112, 115, 137, 144, 165, 179, 180, 199, 213, 228, 279
Leila, **81**, 110, 248, 261, 285
Leilani, **81**, 237
Leland, 164, 179, **180**, 253
Lem, 180
Lempi, 278
Lemuel, 50, **180**, 184, 227
Len, 181, 259, 272
Lena, 41, 53, 56, 64, **82**, 88, 89, 92, 100, 107, 124, 224, 241, 256
Lenard, 181
Lencho, 183
Leni, 82
Lennart, 181
Lennox, 80, 137, **181**, 184, 253, 272, 281
Lenny, 35, 181
Lenora, 44, 249, 269
Lenore, 164, 188
Lenox, 181
Leo, 21, 28, 45, 53, 56, 58, 65, 82, 86, 108, 109, 114, 115, 156, 157, 164, 175, **181**, 182, 187, 191, 193, 204, 224, 244, 272, 277
Leocadia, 94, 237, 276
Leola, 188, 194
Leon, 116, 130, 144, 180, **181**, 187, 188, 213, 221, 283
Leona, 51, 54, 61, **82**, 131, 141, 143, 144, 154, 166, 184, 249
Leonard, 58, 86, 101, 103, 132, 135, 164, 166, **181**, 186, 189, 193, 197, 206, 214, 244, 272, 283

Leonardo, 27, 60, 131, 162, **181**, 188, 193, 201, 244, 245, 272, 281
Leonato, 281
Leonel, 100, 172, 255
Leonid, 282
Leonidas, 243, 272
Leonie/Léonie, 82, 240
Leonor, 52, 54, 86, 180, 198, 249
Leontine, 240, 249
Leopold, 21, 32, 45, 93, 124, 130, 133, 141, 147, 158, **181**, 203, 212, 249, 272
Leora, 21, 25, 34, **82**, 97, 129, 143, 165, 166, 189, 190, 199, 204, 246, 249, 287
LeRoi, 181
Leroy, **181**, 221, 283
Les, 50, 259, 272
Lesley, 79, 82, 135, 186, 272
Leslie, 36, 48, **82**, 94, 173, 178, 194, 215, 223, 230, 264
Lessa, 23
Lessie, 41
Lester, 22, 34, 52, 56, 60, 61, 96, 103, 119, 158, 182, 190, 272, 275, 285
Leticia, **82**, 141, 220, 248
Letisha, 82
Letitia, 82, 270
Lette, 54
Lettice, 82, 234
Lettie, 82, 209, 243
Lev, 97, 192, 216, 282
Levar, 279
Levi, 14, 30, 102, 127, 154, 157, 168, 174, 175, **182**, 189, 190, 193, 204, 216, 224, 227, 233

Lew, 272

Lewis, 51, 54, 130, 143, 144, 159, 162, 181, 182, 183, 272, 283

Lex, 128, 129, 239

Lexi, 23, 24, 78, 138, 168, 211, 216

Lexington, 274

Lexus, 30, 238

Lia, 26, 32, 53, 60, 161, 245, 256

Liam, 43, 52, 67, 83, 94, 96, 100, 126, 128, 161, **182**, 215, 230, 231, 256, 266

Liana, 81

Lianne, 81

Libby, 53, 82, 143, 243

Liberty, 26, 74, **82**, 196, 260

Licha, 24

Lida, 75, 86, 96, 101, 256, 281

Liddy, 53, 86

Lidia, 86, 245

Lieselotte, 269

Lil, 83

Lila, 44, 48, 70, 74, **82**, 99, 100, 124, 132, 155, 159, 170, 182, 196, 205, 224, 256, 266, 287

Lileas, 83

Lili, 82

Lilia, 32, 83, 248

Lilian, 73, 83, 114, 153, 182, 196, 213

Liliana, 22, 27, 39, 73, **82**, 83, 90, 91, 111, 115, 124, 125, 172, 183, 204, 245, 248, 255

Lilias, 61, 66, **83**, 153, 157, 164, 166, 179, 230, 237, 287

Lilith, 48, 122

Lilla, 34, 224

Lillian, 28, 41, 57, **83**, 224

Lillias, 83, 158

Lillie, 28, 53, 83, 100, 109, 156, 162, 181, 211, 243

Lilly, 61, 83, 248

Lily, 21, 32, 46, 55, 57, 65, 66, 82, **83**, 87, 96, 104, 141, 154, 182, 187, 194, 205, 223, 224, 231, 232

Lin, 34, 83

Lina, 27, 82, 95, 155

Linc, 182

Lincoln, 73, 82, 86, 127, 132, 133, 171, **182**, 196, 202, 211, 264, 286, 287

Linda, 73, 83, 110, 115, 160, 179, 209, 259

Linden, 79, 80, **83**, 128, 142, 153, 232, 236

Lindsay, 46, 65, 68, 78, 79, **83**, 124, 138, 148, 153, 202, 214, 253, 279

Lindsey, 76, 83, 89, 150

Lindy, 34, 83, 95, 108

Linnaea, 83

Linnea/Linnéa, 80, **83**, 93, 104, 107, 184, 186, 187, 192, 237, 248, 278, 287

Linnie, 257

Linsey, 83

Linus, 64, 80, 97, 177, **182**, 262, 264, 277, 278

Linwood, 148

Lionel, 39, 84, **182**, 184, 203, 221, 272, 283

Lisa, 24, 39, 43, 53, 70, 73, 80, **83**, 120, 134, 284

Lisandra, 29, 61, 248, 255

Lisandro, 255, 273

Lisbeth, 28, 62, 84, 163, 267

Lise, 24, 28, 53, 83, **84**, 129, 136, 148, 162, 180, 209, 228, 240, 278, 287

Liselotte, 241

Lisette, 84, 240

Lissa, 25

Litzy, 255

Liv, 80, 101, 269

Livia, 82, 269

Livvy, 101

Liz, 53, 78, 110, 120, 134, 178, 284

Liza, 53, 83, **84**, 171, 174, 175, 203, 243, 269, 279

Lizbeth, 53, **84**, 216, 269

Lizette, 269

Lizzie, 88

Llewellyn, 231, 272

Lloyd, 52, 119, 155, 158, **182**, 188, 194, 275

Lockie, 179

Logan, 15, 30, 33, 36, 38, 40, 62, 72, 76, **84**, 87, 108, 112, 116, 121, 133, 137, 139, 140, 142, 145, 146, 150, 151, 152, 153, 167, 173, 176, 177, 179, **182**, 186, 188, 190, 196, 198, 200, 210, 211, 212, 223, 230, 231, 236, 253, 266, 285

Loïc, 27, 240

Lois, 51, 69, **84**, 189, 197, 227, 283

Lola, 50, 79, **84**, 138, 243

Lolita, 264

Lolly, 80

Loma, 257

Lon, 130, 179, 181, **182**,

183, 199, 208, 209, 212, 272, 283
London, 59, 66, 102, 183, 223, 236, 236, 271, 272, 274
Lonnie, 25, 152, 182, 195
Lonzo, 132, 167
Loraine, 85
Lorcan, 137, 145, 158, 179, 231, 236
Lorelei, 84, 237, 269
Loren, 80, 183, 223, 283
Lorena, 255
Lorene, 132
Lorenz, 179, 242
Lorenzo, 35, 44, 46, 58, 82, 89, 90, 120, 122, 124, 131, 162, 179, 181, 183, 193, 204, 244, 245, 255, 281, 286
Loreto, 57, 85
Loretta, 50, 69, 84, 105, 108, 116, 181, 182, 201, 213, 269, 283
Lori, 47, 50, 71, 80, 84, 85, 117, 269, 283, 284
Lorine, 180
Lorna, 98, 133, 148, 203, 205, 269, 283
Lorne, 92, 153, 179, 183, 259
Lorraine, 52, 84, 85, 93, 188, 205, 269, 283
Lorri, 85
Lotte, 36, 42, 85, 194, 241
Lottie, 42, 49, 51, 65, 85, 163, 243, 269
Lotty, 85
Lotus, 22, 232, 238
Lou, 85, 183, 184, 272
Loudon, 253
Louie, 56, 183, 244
Louis, 24, 44, 52, 58, 64, 66, 72, 91, 109, 115, 128, 132, 140, 159,

165, 167, 183, 214, 249, 272
Louisa, 22, 25, 29, 32, 38, 56, 85, 86, 93, 134, 141, 154, 159, 164, 203, 249, 276, 287
Louise, 58, 85, 86, 119, 143, 156, 166, 184, 240, 249, 269
Lourdes, 62, 85, 237, 255
Louvenia, 257
Lovie, 257
Lovisa, 85, 278
Lowell, 145, 148, 164, 180, 253
Loy, 257
Loyal, 239, 258
Loyce, 257
Loyd, 182
Loz, 179
Luc, 33, 41, 86, 185, 240
Luca, 60, 101, 125, 156, 161, 178, 186, 192, 245, 256
Lucas, 23, 27, 44, 80, 97, 99, 101, 145, 172, 183, 184, 205, 228, 265
Lucero, 255
Lucha, 86
Lucho, 183
Lucia, 44, 85, 86, 108, 131, 167, 173, 183, 185, 201, 245, 269, 276, 285, 287
Lucian, 101, 160, 238, 277
Luciana, 245, 269
Luciano, 60, 102, 183, 245
Lucie, 86
Lucien, 49, 240
Lucienne, 240
Lucile, 86
Lucilla, 86, 276
Lucille, 85, 86, 103, 156, 164, 179, 181,

188, 233, 240, 249, 269
Lucinda, 84, 86, 259, 268, 269
Lucio, 183
Lucius, 126, 162, 180, 183, 228, 238, 277
Lucretia, 237, 269, 270
Lucy, 28, 44, 53, 56, 59, 70, 82, 85, 86, 91, 110, 115, 142, 164, 181, 187, 193, 194, 224, 243, 269
Ludie, 257
Ludmila, 101, 281
Luella, 194
Luetta, 275
Luigi, 245
Luis/Luís, 140, 174, 183, 254, 255
Luisa, 60, 85, 146, 185, 200, 244, 245, 255
Luise, 85
Lukas, 28, 29, 47, 58, 75, 81, 95, 98, 99, 103, 110, 111, 116, 117, 166, 168, 183, 184, 201, 206, 282
Luke, 114, 145, 169, 175, 183, 184, 191, 226, 228, 229, 233
Lula, 56, 88, 109, 243
Lulu, 85, 132, 243
Luna, 30, 37, 59, 67, 86, 94, 118, 136, 199, 256, 262, 287
Lupe, 62, 86, 223, 255
Lupita, 62
Lurline, 275
Luther, 35, 41, 51, 63, 82, 93, 101, 108, 123, 130, 143, 144, 166, 184, 185, 187, 191, 195, 221, 249
Luz, 22, 39, 85, 86, 255, 256

Lydia, 26, 32, 41, 53, 85, 86, 100, 155, 171, 189, 194, 205, 206, 209, 224, 227, 285
Lyla, 82
Lyle, 51, 52, 84, 92, 98, 124, 183, **184**, 205, 208, 231, 283
Lyman, 253
Lyn, 37, 39, 223
Lynda, 61, 73, 83
Lyndon, 106
Lyndsay, 83
Lyndsey, 83
Lynette, 259
Lynn, 43, 62, 74, 78, 81, 83, **86**, 118, 123, 149, 177, 178, 228, 259, 284
Lynne, 45, 46, 50, 59, 86, 134, 191
Lyra, 59, **86**, 97, 101, 193, 216, 256, 287
Lyric, 29, 37, 67, 82, 87, 94, 187, 188, 196, 200, 216, 220, 238, 260
Lysander, 80, 281

Mabel, 34, 54, 87, 182, 202, 243
Mable, 56, 87, 190
Mabs, 87
Mac, 87, 146, 184, 272
Macaulay, 231, 272
Mace, 229, 239
Macey, 87
Maci, 87, 101
Macie, 87
Mack, 49, 56, 84, 105, 106, 107, 152, 165, **184**, 188, 233, 243, 244
Mackenzie, 15, 87, 98, 116, 182, 186, 207, 223, 230, 231, 250, 253, 272

Mackinney, 253
Maclean, 253
Macon, 274
Macy, 31, 60, 78, 79, 87, 94, 100, 132, 136, 138, 145, 149, 152, 160, 163, 166, 167, 176, 178, 179, 199, 204, 210, 211, 225, 253, 256
Maddalena, 51, 87, 88, 245, 248, 269
Maddie, 87, 269
Maddison, 87
Maddox, 93, 169, 181, **184**, 253
Maddy, 87
Madeleine, 87, 95, 240
Madeline, 24, 28, 39, 66, 87, 96, 114, 164, 224, 269
Madelyn, 24, 27, 88, 136, 149, 188
Madge, 87, 89, 103, 133, 163, 243
Madilyn, 38, 87, 236
Madisen, 87
Madison, 15, 18, 21, 72, 87, 111, 137, 163, 165, 167, 182, 186, 223, 236, 253, 269, 274
Madisyn, 87, 92, 160, 171
Madoc, 184
Madonna, 85, 238, 264, 269
Mads, 187, 278
Madyson, 87
Mae, 35, 49, 57, 65, 84, 85, **88**, 103, 105, 109, 144, 153, 167, 190, 232, 244
Maelle, 240
Maeve, 34, 37, 58, **88**, 139, 149, 158, 162, 175, 178, 194, 196, 201, 202, 204, 224, 230, 287

Magda, 88, 269
Magdalena, 48, 88, 227, 241, 255, 269, 278, 281
Magdalene, 74, 88, 104, 122, 124, 158, 183, 191, 249
Maggie, 25, 38, 70, **88**, 89, 269
Magic, 239
Magnolia, 88, 113, 125, 188, 232, 233, 269
Magnus, 31, 33, 37, 48, 66, 83, 84, 96, 122, 126, 129, 131, 157, 164, 180, 183, **184**, 186, 192, 194, 203, 212, 231, 238, 277, 278
Maguire, 253
Mahala, 26, 69, 125
Mahalia, 29, 30, 269
Mahlon, 69, 180, **184**, 201, 221, 227, 236
Mahogany, 232
Mai, 90, 91
Maia, 32, 43, 56, 88, 94, 101, 158, 187, 193, 256, 262
Maida, 158, 249
Maira, 248
Maire, 230
Maisha, 217
Maisie, 88, 89, 131, 164
Maj, 89
Maja, 278
Major, 29, 84, 99, 134, 135, 152, 199, 239, 244
Makaila, 88
Makayla, 16, 74, 76, **88**, 96, 225
Makenna, 94, 137, 138, 176
Makenzie, 87
Mal, 184
Malachi, 30, 81, 99, 155,

157, **184**, 221, 227, 238

Malachy, 158, 184, 231, 277

Malaika, 217

Malakai, 184

Malcolm, 58, 184, **185**, 189, 218, 221, 231, 264, 286

Malia, 77, 81, 116, 248

Malik, 31, 65, 68, 150, 169, **185**, 221, 261

Malinda, 95

Malka, 246

Mallory, 31, 32, 40, 65, 71, 74, 76, **89**, 96, 138, 143, 150, 188, 190, 214, 223, 253, 266

Mamie, 93, 109, 194, 200, 244

Mammie, 258

Mandy, 25, 97, 117, 142, 269, 279

Manny, 156, 166, 185

Manoel, 185

Manolo, 185

Manon, 91, 240

Manuel, 156, **185**, 195, 255, 277

Manuela, 165, 241, 269

Mara, 79, 81, 89, 91, 111, 116, 118, 121, 127, 143, 155, 174, 189, 193, 205, 226, 256, 266

Marah, 89

Maranda, 97

Marc, 24, 47, 48, 82, 94, 95, 96, 98, 117, 122, 136, 173, 185, 186, 265

Marcel, 42, 45, 45, 84, **185**, 240, 266, 277, 286

Marcela, 89, 92, 255, 281

Marcella, 29, **89**, 131,

138, 140, 200, 245, 248, 269, 276, 287

Marcelle, 45, 89, 240, 269

Marcellus, 82, 141, 146, 185, 238, 277, 281

Marcelo, 255

Marci, 89, 269

Marcia, 39, 42, 61, 68, 71, **89**, 153, 179, 201, 259, 269

Marcie, 42, 64, 89, 97, 279

Marco, 22, 35, 38, 46, 55, 58, 82, 91, 115, 124, 129, 131, 141, 148, 151, 170, 181, **185**, 189, 193, 198, 200, 204, 245, 255

Marcos, 39, 111, 140, 183, 185, 255

Marcus, 44, 71, 90, 92, 114, 115, 122, 123, 130, 150, **185**, 186, 190, 214, 218, 221, 286

Marcy, **89**, 121, 284

Marek, 47, 75, 97, **185**, 186, 277, 282

Margalit, 62, 113, 246

Margaret, 28, 41, 53, **89**, 92, 93, 142, 154, 159, 161, 165, 173, 174, 198, 203, 215, 222, 269, 285

Margaretha, 89

Margarita, **89**, 185, 197, 255, 285

Margarito, 257

Margaux, 90

Margery, 89, 90, 92, 140, 200, 214, 215, 269, 283, 287

Margherita, 89, 245

Margie, 89, 92, 244, 269

Margit, 31, 66, 84, 89, 131, 186, 187, 241

Margo, **90**, 121, 141, 200, 212, 259, 266, 287

Margot, 32, 54, 59, 62, 84, 89, 90, 92, 93, 179, 182, 183, 201, 213, 240, 241, 283

Marguerite, 28, 44, 51, 59, 89, **90**, 203, 220, 240, 249, 269, 276

Marguita, 89

Mari, 90, 91, 92, 151

Maria, **90**, 93, 91, 172, 174, 222, 227, 245, 254, 255, 269, 285

Mariah, 30, 89, **90**, 96, 113, 128, 147, 171, 174, 215, 224, 248, 266

Mariam, 103, 172, 255

Marian, 33, 54, 57, **90**, 92, 124, 134, 144, 154, 164, 167, 191, 214, 215, 266, 283, 287

Mariana, 25, 55, 58, 73, **90**, 95, 99, 103, 111, 117, 122, 131, 151, 181, 183, 188, 193, 248, 255, 276, 280

Marianna, 90

Marianne, 62, 73, **90**, 108, 119, 125, 197, 240, 283

Mariano, 130, 140, 245, 255

Maribel, 84, **91**, 114, 141, 150, 192, 199, 255, 287

Maribeth, 108, 109, 259, 267

Maricela, 248, 255

Marie, 66, **91**, 93, 130, 140, 159, 163, 164, 183, 227, 240, 283

Mariel, 28, 64, 91, 92, 107, 187, 241

Mariela, 61, 82, **91**, 95,

107, 124, 189, 248, 255, 287

Mariella, 91

Marieta, 91

Marietta, 31, 39, 41, 86, 89, **91**, 93, 150, 248, 274

Mariette, 91

Marigold, 232

Marilyn, 33, 35, 61, **91**, 104, 113, 159, 161, 283

Marilynn, 91

Marina, 24, 29, 44, 47, **91**, 107, 115, 148, 152, 168, 196, 198, 200, 201, 213, 245, 276, 280, 285

Marine, 240

Mario, 39, 53, 91, **185**, 186, 197, 200, 204, 222, 245, 255, 286

Marion, 45, 63, 85, 90, 98, 109, 123, 135, 143, 184, 211, 240, 249, 266, 283

Marios, 243

Marisa, 92, 109, 111, 125, 170, 183, 185, 200, 245, 248, 264

Marisela, 255

Marisol, 46, 61, **91**, 100, 106, 140, 196, 198, 255

Marissa, 25, 79, 90, **92**, 140, 248

Marita, 89

Maritza, 255

Marius, 65, 93, 185, **186**, 187, 238, 242, 266, 278

Marj, 92

Marjorie, 51, 84, 85, **92**, 103, 109, 214, 268, 283, 287

Marjory, 92

Mark, 48, 49, 70, 74, 80,

128, 137, 149, 171, 178, 185, **186**, 207, 226, 228, 259, 286

Markian, 282

Markie, 89

Markus, 28, 66, 89, 119, 163, 185, 186, 206, 242

Marla, 68, 147, 259

Marlee, 92

Marlena, 84, 92, 170, 279

Marlene, 91, **92**, 259

Marley, 92, 102, 105, 154, 160, 167, 169, 179, 184, 211, 253, 266

Marlin, 89, 105, 183

Marlo, 92, 210, 266, 284

Marlon, 80, 172, 221, 236

Marlowe, 92, 149

Marly, 92

Marlys, 203, 283

Marques, 80, 186

Marquis, 42, 49, 51, 105, 119, 120, **186**, 221, 239

Marquise, 49, 185, 186, 205

Mars, 131, 239, 262

Marseille, 274

Marsh, 186

Marsha, 89, 259

Marshal, 147, 186, 197, 260

Marshall, 52, 82, 100, 124, 159, 179, 185, **186**, 191, 203, 215, 251, 286

Marta, 92, 102

Martha, 64, 68, **92**, 93, 116, 132, 135, 143, 154, 156, 159, 166, 181, 193, 206, 227, 242, 249, 269, 269

Martin, 27, 140, **186**, 195, 213, 221, 283

Martina, **92**

Marty, 92, 110, 186, 210, 259, 284

Marv, 186

Marvel, 175, 196, 238, 239, 258

Marvin, 50, 93, 101, 113, 161, **186**, 188, 193, 221, 283

Mary, 41, 89, 91, **93**, 142, 169, 173, 174, 195, 200, 209, 215, 227, 269, 276, 285

Maryam, 97, 110, 190, 261

Maryanne, 259

Marybeth, 259

Marylyn, 91

Masha, 90, 281

Masika, 217

Mason, 57, 87, 156, 167, 168, **186**, 193, 194, 236, 250, 251, 266

Mateo, 25, 26, 60, 90, 91, 99, 151, **186**, 187, 255

Mathew, 187

Mathias, 33, 54, 55, 184, 186, 187, 278

Mathieu, 187, 240

Mathilda, 63, 93

Mathilde, 54, 93, 240, 278

Matilda, 22, 64, **93**, 125, 141, 154, 203, 249, 269, 270, 276, 278

Matilde, 278

Matt, 187, 272, 284

Mattea, **93**, 248, 287

Matteo, 23, 47, 60, 102, 161, 186, 192, 201, 245, 272, 273

Matthew, 18, 43, 71, 75, 105, 111, 130, 131, 143, 148, 185, 186,

187, 189, 226, 228, 272, 286
Matthias, 14, 30, 45, 64, 74, 128, 180, 182, **187**, 208, 228, 238, 242, 272, 277
Mattie, 92, 93, 244, 269
Maud, 85, 93
Maude, **93**, 101, 136, 146, 147, 155, 195, 249
Maudie, 93
Maura, 48, **93**, 145, 158, 177, 202, 266, 276
Maureen, 45, 75, 89, **93**, 116, 259
Maurice, 44, 125, 184, 187, 190, 221, 240, 272
Mauricio, 255
Maurine, 93
Mauro, 245
Maury, 187
Mav, 187
Maverick, 26, 59, 64, 74, 82, 98, 172, **187**, 196, 233, 239, 260, 272
Mavis, 84, 162, 183
Max, 25, 26, 41, 46, 55, 61, 66, 72, 73, 98, 99, 109, 110, 114, 168, 169, 187, **188**, 194, 224, 229, 244, 248, 272, 278
Maxie, 93, 132, 152, 244
Maxim, 58, 98, 99, 117, 133, 135, 151, **187**, 188, 201, 238, 272, 277, 282
Maxima, 141, 276
Maxime, 187
Maximilian, 23, 27, 31, 43, 101, 122, 134, 176, **188**, 204, 207, 216, 238, 256, 272, 277
Maximillian, 188
Maximo, 187, 255, 272

Maximus, 30, 99, 121, 187, **188**, 216, 239, 272, 277
Maxine, 85, **93**, 108, 188, 213, 283
Maxwell, 28, 47, 61, 87, 96, 101, **188**, 224, 253
May, 34, 72, 74, 87, 89, 93, **94**, 158, 199, 231, 232, 287
Maya, 23, 67, 69, 88, **94**, 118, 126, 140, 160, 173, 184, 192, 194, 194, 256, 266
Maybelle, 87, 244
Maynard, 207, 275
Mayra, 225, 255
Mazie, 88, 132, 167, 190, 244
McArthur, 272
McGuire, 188
McKay, 253, 272
Mckayla/McKayla, 88, 176
Mckenna, 38, 48, 76, 87, **94** 137, 140, 149, 168, 200, 253
Mckenzie, 87
Mckinley/McKinley, **188**, 202, 253
Meadow, 32, 37, 55, 57, 63, 66, 72, **94**, 111, 125, 187, 200, 232, 260
Meagan, 94
Meaghan, 94
Meche, 95
Meg, 71, 88, 89, 94, 178, 269
Megan, 30, 37, 80, 89, **94**, 100, 105, 110, 127, 137, 141, 150, 157, 167, 175, 178, 190, 203, 204, 205, 230, 236, 264, 269
Meghan, 57, 94
Mehitabel, 67, 69, **94**, 171, 226, 237, 268

Mekhi, 21, 30, 77, 125, 178, 193, 221
Mel, 26, 54, 94, 95, 188, 259, 269, 272
Melania, 94, 276
Melanie, 24, 82, **94**, 98, 122, 240, 264, 269
Melany, 94
Melba, 35, 164, 244
Melbourne, 272, 274
Meleia, 94
Melia, 22, 33, **94**, 248, 262
Melina, 50, **95**, 243, 248, 287
Melinda, 43, 48, 57, **95**, 108, 248, 269, 279
Melissa, 27, 63, 70, 78, **95**, 96, 170, 207, 248, 260, 264, 269, 279
Meliya, 94
Melly, 94
Melodie, 47, 95, 232
Melody, 26, 34, 60, 80, **95**, 134, 260, 269
Melton, 272
Melville, 272
Melvin, 186, **188**, 221, 272, 283
Melvina, 54
Melvyn, 188
Méme, 185
Mena, 104
Merce, 95
Mercedes, 62, **95**, 172, 195, 255
Mercer, 251
Mercury, 239, 262
Mercy, 16, 37, 42, 65, **95**, 102, 123, 129, 139, 205, 213, 232, 285, 287
Mere, 96
Meredith, 34, 38, 78, 82, 89, 94, **96**, 116, 161, 186, 188, 223, 264
Meri, 26, 96
Meriel, 98

Merit, 16, 42, 55, 63, 95, 207, 260
Merl, 188, 275
Merle, 182, **188**, 223, 233, 275
Merlin, **188**, 239, 264
Merrick, 253
Merrill, 205
Merritt, 21, 120, 155, 165, 175, 194, 249, 253, 287
Merry, 35, 45, 50, 72, 95, **96**, 232, 259
Mertie, 257
Mervin, 275
Mervyn, 231
Meryl, 65
Meta, 82, 89, **96**, 120, 159, 163, 192, 241, 256, 278
Meyer, 61, 244
Mhairi, 164, 230
Mia, 26, 32, 87, 90, 91, **96**, 167, 182, 256, 266
Mica, 96
Micaela, 96
Micah, 23, 26, 71, 74, 111, 115, 127, 173, 174, 182, **189**, 223, 227, 272
Michael, 18, 95, 106, 148, 149, 186, **189**, 194, 207, 209, 218, 226, 227, 228, 272, 286
Michaela, 39, 88, 90, **96**, 168, 216, 224
Michalina, 281
Micheal, 189
Michel, 102
Michela, 96, 245
Michelangelo, 239, 245, 272
Michele, 34, 43, 49, 90, 96, 107, 108, 146, 163, 171, 240, 284
Michelle, 27, 70, 78, **96**, 115, 137, 156, 170,

178, 209, 264, 269, 279
Mick, 188, 189
Mickey, 34, 96, 189, 223, 259, 272
Miguel, 140, 172, 174, 183, **189**, 255
Mika, 116
Mikaela, 88
Mikaila, 88
Mikayla, 33, 88, 96, 169, 179
Mike, 96, 189, 259, 272
Mikel, 189
Milagros, 86, 255
Milan, 123, 185, 274, 282
Mildred, 52, 60, **96**, 269, 275
Miles, 32, 38, 41, 43, 53, 56, 57, 60, 65, 67, 73, 94, 100, 104, 128, 133, 149, 155, 162, 163, **189**, 213, 266, 286
Milla, 38
Millard, 275
Miller, 150, 191, 215, 251
Millicent, 21, 44, **96**, 125, 249, 269
Millie, 26, 38, 54, 55, 96, 99, 163, 184, 244, 269
Milo, 32, 53, 55, 107, 118, 129, 138, 167, 181, **189**, 209, 238, 249, 266
Milos, 282
Milt, 189
Milton, 132, 166, 167, 181, **189**, 205, 219, 250, 275, 283
Mimi, 30, 90, **97**, 116, 259, 269
Mina, 62, 91, 96, 97, 100, 108, 124, 186, 241
Mindy, 95, **97**, 269, 279

Minerva, 64, **97**, 101, 188, 237, 249, 262, 269
Minnie, 69, 124, 244, 269
Mique, 98
Mira, 75, **97**, 110, 256, 266, 281
Mirabella, 122
Mirabelle, 287
Miracle, 64, **97**, 105, 219, 238, 260
Miranda, 22, 23, 30, 34, 40, 44, 91, 92, **97**, 109, 110, 122, 160, 183, 216, 248, 264, 269, 269, 280
Mirella, 245
Mireya, 118, 255
Miri, 97
Miriam, 26, 41, 62, 89, **97**, 99, 159, 190, 199, 206, 226, 246, 269, 285
Miryam, 97
Misa, 91
Mischa, 96
Missouri, 258
Missy, 92, 96
Misti, 97
Misty, 36, **97**, 112, 260, 279
Mitch, 103, 189, 190, 259, 272
Mitchel, 190
Mitchell, 73, 81, 105, 186, **190**, 202, 253, 272, 286
Mittie, 257
Mitzi, 93, 97, 259
Miuccia, 51
Mo, 93, 98, 190
Modesto, 85
Moe, **190**, 244
Mogens, 277
Mohamed, 190
Mohammad, 190

Mohammed, **190**, 261
Moira, 230
Moises, 100, 255
Mollie, 70, 88, 98, 110
Molly, 34, 55, 75, 81, 93,
   98, 118, 129, 168, 169,
   173, 190, 224, 244,
   269
Mona, 98, 105, 183
Monica, 27, **98**, 136, 264
Monika, 98
Monique, 49, 57, **98**, 99,
   131, 172, 218, 220,
   239, 240, 264
Monroe, 189, 190, 202,
   275
Monserrat, 56, 255
Monserrate, 237
Montague, 30, 238, 253,
   272
Montana, 26, **98**, 113,
   147, 207, 223, 233,
   272, 274
Monte, 50, 190, 259
Montgomery, **190**, 238,
   253, 272
Monty, 97, 141, 190, 272
Moon, 238
Mordecai, 62, 227, 247,
   272
Morgan, 14, 24, 36, 37,
   72, 74, 89, 94, **98**, 140,
   145, 150, 153, 161,
   173, 178, **190**, 211,
   223, 230, 231, 236,
   266
Morgana, 98
Morpheus, 127, 188, 262
Morrie, 190
Morris, 34, 56, 61, 167,
   187, **190**, 214, 246,
   272, 275
Mort, 272
Mortimer, 272, 275
Morton, 272
Mose, 56, 85, 86, 88,
   109, 126, 132, 159,

167, 189, **190**, 194,
   209, 244
Moses, **190**, 199, 217,
   227, 272, 286
Moshe, 247
Moss, 45, 190, 247, 272
Mossie, 258
Mozell, 257
Muhammad, 190, 261
Muriel, 62, 98, 131, 131,
   156, 164, 166, 205,
   214, 215, 230, 249,
   266, 283
Murphy, 82, 93, 100,
   139, 158, 164, 188,
   191, 207, 215, 231,
   253, 287
Murray, 61, 107, 133,
   275
Mustafa, 190, 261
Myles, 66, 112, 189
Myra, 52, 97, **98**, 108,
   161, 184, 205, 266,
   283
Myranda, 97
Myrl, 257
Myrna, 283
Myron, 275
Myrtle, 22, 34, 56, 61,
   96, 101, 155, 232, 275

Nadezhda, 281
Nadia, 23, 24, 75, 94,
   98, 111, 147, 157, 193,
   201, 248, 266, 281
Nadine, 85, 240, 275
Nadya, 98
Naima, 25, 261
Nakia, 116, 180, 217,
   220, 221, 223
Nallely, 99
Nan, 28, 71, 90, 99, 163,
   173, 180, 191, 212,
   269
Nancie, 99
Nancy, 28, 47, 68, 71,
   73, **99**, 103, 110, 161,

172, 177, 179, 199,
   201, 202, 259, 269,
   283
Nando, 158
Nanette, 45, 57, 97, 259,
   269
Nannie, 258
Naomi, 97, **99**, 100, 173,
   174, 226, 266, 285
Nap, 191
Naphtali, 227
Napoleon, 28, **191**, 212,
   238, 264
Narciso, 257
Nardo, 181
Nash, 149, 172, 229
Nasir, 261
Nat, 34, 99, 108, 171,
   190, 191, 244, 272
Natalia, 58, 60, 82, 90,
   91, 98, **99**, 111, 117,
   122, 124, 151, 157,
   204, 248, 255, 270,
   276, 281
Natalie, 18, 25, 41, 59,
   99, 191, 192, 196, 264
Nataly, 99
Natalya, 99
Natasha, **99**, 111, 120,
   131, 136, 220, 242,
   270, 279, 281
Nate, 175, 191, 272
Nathalie, 99, 100, 240
Nathan, 80, 81, 168,
   173, 185, **191**, 193,
   227, 236, 272, 273,
   286
Nathanael, 114, 115,
   156, 191, 216, 228
Nathaniel, 23, 39, 97,
   123, 129, 167, 171,
   183, **191**, 192, 204,
   204, 216, 227, 228,
   272, 273, 281, 286
Nautica, 238
Nava, 246, 256
Nayeli, 25, **99**, 254, 255

Nayely, 99
Nea, 83
Neal, 75, 81, 153, 191
Ned, 34, 104, 154,
    163, 191, 208, 244,
    272
Neeve, 230
Nehemiah, 184, 227
Neil, 50, 139, 146, 177,
    191, 231, 286
Neilson, 253
Nell, 34, 44, 49, 52, 56,
    85, 88, 99, 103, 106,
    118, 132, 136, 142,
    155, 162, 163, 164,
    167, 171, 184, 187,
    190, 191, 211, 214,
    244, 269, 287
Nella, 99
Nelle, 99
Nellie, 88, 99, 103, 103
Nelly, 108
Nelson, 144, 186, 191,
    253, 286
Neo, 218, 239
Neoma, 118
Nessa, 122
Nessie, 22
Nestor, 100, 255, 281
Netta, 28
Nettie, 28, 85
Nevaeh, 30, 64, 99, 220,
    260
Neve, 100, 112, 202, 228
Neville, 235
Newell, 140
Newton, 65, 148, 155,
    158, 188, 206, 211, 253
Nia, 65, 67, 77, 79, 100,
    126, 132, 150, 176,
    211, 217, 220, 230,
    256, 266
Niall, 23, 100, 157, 191,
    209, 231
Niamh, 23, 58, 88, 100,
    114, 230, 262
Nic, 100

Nicholas, 18, 55, 71, 75,
    105, 123, 129, 130,
    131, 135, 143, 145,
    173, 187, 191, 192,
    216, 243, 271, 272,
    277, 286
Nicholaus, 192
Nichole, 100
Nicholson, 15, 130, 164,
    192, 200, 253, 272, 287
Nick, 192, 272
Nickolas, 192
Nico, 23, 29, 46, 48, 60,
    88, 97, 100, 132, 150,
    156, 178, 192, 245,
    256
Nicodemus, 180, 228,
    238, 272
Nicola, 100, 102, 121,
    156, 234, 245, 269
Nicolas, 47, 59, 192, 240,
    255
Nicole, 25, 27, 47, 70,
    75, 77, 80, 98, 100,
    127, 203, 204, 239,
    240, 265, 269
Nicolette, 42, 51, 240,
    269
Niels, 62, 77, 120, 182,
    187, 192, 238, 242,
    278
Nigel, 192, 235, 266
Nikita, 42
Nikki, 36, 68, 98, 100,
    117, 121, 146, 269, 279
Niko, 86, 192
Nikolas, 192
Nikos, 15, 53, 192, 243
Nila, 206
Niles, 144, 192, 235
Nils, 83, 96, 184, 192,
    278
Nina, 68, 86, 97, 99,
    100, 157, 199, 256,
    266, 285
Nita, 27, 35, 163, 182,
    212

Noa, 55, 120, 246, 256
Noah, 55, 57, 63, 65, 94,
    126, 127, 139, 154,
    160, 167, 173, 192,
    227, 256, 266
Noam, 101, 113, 120,
    126, 166, 192, 247,
    256
Noble, 74, 239, 260
Noe, 41, 100, 240
Noel/Noël, 22, 41, 47,
    55, 67, 81, 88, 100,
    119, 185, 193, 199,
    240, 256, 286
Noelia, 255
Noelle, 38, 41, 53, 59,
    81, 99, 100, 111, 114,
    130, 152, 196, 240,
    265
Noemi/Noemí, 46, 61,
    91, 99, 100, 193, 198,
    226, 245, 255
Noémie, 100, 240
Nola, 48, 58, 88, 93, 107,
    139, 140, 146, 154,
    158, 180, 184, 185,
    191, 211, 249, 287
Nolan, 53, 141, 143,
    191, 193, 236, 266,
    286
Nona, 125
Nora, 41, 45, 52, 86,
    100, 115, 142, 224,
    230
Norah, 100
Norbert, 275
Noreen, 275
Norm, 193
Norma, 30, 50, 51, 101,
    113, 181, 186, 266,
    283
Norman, 50, 51, 104,
    108, 132, 156, 193, 283
Normandy, 274
Norris, 275
Norval, 34, 257
Nova, 238, 257

Novella, 258
Nuno, 255
Nunzio, 244, 245
Nyla, **101**, 125, 178, 220, 256

Oakley, 233, 253
Oceana, 127, 238
Océane, 240
Ocie, 257
Octavia, 195, 237
Octavio, 62, 255
Odalys, 255
Odell, 118, 158, 275
Odessa, 274
Odetta, 29
Odie, 257, 275
Odin, 262
Odion, 218
Odyssey, 238, 260
Oisin, 23, 230, 231
Okey, 258
Oksana, 281
Olaf, 192, 278
Ole, 278
Oleg, 282
Olga, 101, 136, 281
Olive, 58, 63, 93, **101**, 103, 141, 155, 232, 249, 269
Oliver, 14, 28, 29, 41, 42, 53, 57, 59, 61, 83, 86, 88, 100, 114, 123, 157, 175, 187, **193**, 223, 224, 235, 240, 277, 278, 281
Olivia, 18, 24, 63, **101**, 114, 128, 160, 175, 184, 224, 248, 269, 280
Ollie, 101, 193, 257
Olympia, 64, **101**, 149, 209, 237
Omar, 25, 57, 68, 106, 125, 141, 170, **193**, 221, 227, 255, 261
Omari, 21, 26, 77, 110, 150, 193, 218, 221

Omarion, 30, **193**, 221
Omer, 257
Onie, 257
Opal, 54, 57, 61, 101, 119, 120, 130, 155, 166, 194, 202, 213, 232, 275
Ophelia, 45, 249, 280
Oprah, 264
Ora, 194
Oral, 257
Orion, 31, 59, 67, 87, 121, 125, 127, 128, 131, 175, **193**, 216, 239, 262
Orlando, 46, 91, 102, 108, 122, 131, 141, 149, 151, 181, 183, **193**, 200, 201, 238, 245, 255, 281
Orlo, 257
Orly, **101**, 120, 192, 246, 256
Orpha, 257
Orpheus, 239, 262
Orval, 194
Orville, **194**, 214, 275
Oscar, 82, 130, 153, 165, 167, 185, **194**, 224, 255, 266, 278
Osheen, 230
Oskar, 194
Osten, 133
Osvaldo, 255
Oswald, 130
Otelia, 201
Otha, 257
Otho, 257
Otis, 29, 52, 158, **194**, 202, 213, 221, 275
Ottilie, 257
Ottis, 194
Otto, 49, 60, 61, 93, 103, 138, 155, 159, **194**, 242, 244, 266
Ouida, 257
Ova, 258

Owen, 26, 32, 55, 57, 61, 66, 83, 104, 140, 161, 188, 190, 192, **194**, 205, 224, 231, 236, 266
Oz, 247
Ozella, 257

Pablo, 195, 255
Packer, 251
Paddy, 194
Padraig, 194
Page, 101
Paige, 37, 69, 81, **101**, 120, 133, 136, 138, 142, 143, 145, 150, 151, 160, 163, 184, 199, 210, 211, 228
Palmer, 126, 159, 164, 165, 191, **194**, 266
Paloma, 46, **102**, 133, 151, 154, 161, 176, 216, 237, 287
Pam, 34, 102
Pamala, 102
Pamela, 28, 36, 46, 48, **102**, 103, 119, 152, 197, 259
Pamella, 102
Pandora, 209
Panos, 53, 243
Pansy, 195, 232
Paola, 35, 58, 60, 82, 85, **102**, 103, 148, 156, 157, 161, 162, 185, 204, 245, 266
Paolo, 195, 245
Paris, 42, 63, **102**, 122, 176, 183, 203, 223, 266, 273, 274, 281
Parker, 21, 31, 32, 33, 76, 77, **102**, 103, 106, 108, 114, 116, 132, 136, 147, 149, 160, 167, 169, 179, 186, **194**, 195, 200, 206, 211, 223, 251, 266

Parrish, 135, 253
Pascal, 238, 240, 271
Pasquale, 140, 245, 272
Pat, 102, 161, 194, 223, 269, 272
Patience, 42, 57, 102, 111, 157, 174, 209, 216, 224, 231, 232, 269
Patrice, 45, 80, 102, 109, 147, 198, 199, 201, 221, 240, 241, 259, 269, 270
Patricia, 33, 39, 52, 75, 99, 102, 103, 105, 152, 177, 199, 209, 259, 269, 270, 283
Patrick, 27, 43, 73, 80, 82, 106, 110, 122, 131, 189, 194, 207, 229, 231, 272, 272, 286
Patsy, 35, 50, 92, 102, 194, 244, 269
Patti, 102, 123, 259
Patty, 96, 102, 103, 104, 152
Paul, 28, 54, 68, 93, 119, 154, 162, 173, 186, 195, 199, 209, 228, 241, 281, 283, 286
Paula, 28, 36, 39, 102, 103, 106, 108, 113, 124, 134, 138, 146, 259, 266, 269
Paulette, 14, 240, 259
Paulina, 88, 103, 112, 255, 269, 280, 281
Pauline, 58, 61, 86, 103, 166, 187, 197, 240, 275
Pavel, 101, 185, 195, 281, 282
Pavlos, 243
Paxton, 92, 102, 137, 180, 207, 236, 253, 272
Payton, 30, 37, 38, 76,

87, 102, 103, 114, 136, 138, 146, 179, 194, 195, 225, 236, 266, 270, 272
Pearl, 35, 50, 56, 63, 87, 88, 101, 103, 165, 231, 232
Pearlie, 244
Pearline, 275
Pedrinho, 195
Pedro, 185, 195, 255, 281
Peerless, 105, 239
Peg, 89
Peggie, 103
Peggy, 71, 73, 99, 103, 115, 259, 269
Pelancha, 56
Pella, 77, 120
Pelle, 277
Pen, 103
Penelope, 103, 105, 109, 200, 262, 269, 285, 287
Penny, 45, 103, 104, 121, 178, 200, 215, 234, 259, 269
Pepe, 57, 174
Per, 278
Percival, 195, 234, 235
Percy, 141, 195, 249
Peregrine, 30, 42, 122, 238, 239
Perico, 195
Perla, 103, 129, 141, 255
Pernell, 183
Perry, 81, 195, 259
Pervis, 275
Peta, 256
Pete, 173, 195, 272
Peter, 115, 119, 146, 195, 195, 209, 228, 272, 286
Petra, 62, 72, 104, 118, 120, 124, 126, 135, 241, 249
Petrina, 281
Petro, 272

Petros, 50, 195, 243
Peyton, 31, 32, 68, 76, 103, 139, 141, 145, 165, 167, 195, 206, 222, 223, 236, 266
Phebe, 104
Phil, 104, 195, 272
Philip, 50, 102, 163, 169, 186, 195, 272, 286
Philippa, 69, 234
Phillip, 195, 197, 259
Phillipa, 192
Phillipe, 241
Philo, 97, 166, 182, 238, 249, 281
Philomena, 22, 64, 104, 124, 125, 130, 134, 146, 158, 207, 237, 249, 276
Phineas, 14, 29, 33, 94, 122, 133, 154, 170, 195, 205, 209, 227, 238
Phinehas, 195
Phoebe, 28, 34, 43, 47, 53, 66, 67, 88, 104, 142, 157, 167, 189, 205, 213, 224, 256, 266, 280
Phoenix, 26, 37, 63, 64, 66, 82, 87, 97, 111, 122, 187, 196, 216, 232, 233, 239, 274
Phyl, 104
Phyllida, 67, 104, 208, 234, 237
Phyllis, 35, 50, 51, 85, 104, 113, 151, 262, 283
Pierce, 26, 41, 45, 70, 73, 87, 88, 102, 104, 124, 134, 135, 175, 182, 196, 198, 205, 213, 224, 229, 287
Pierre, 195, 199, 241, 272

Piers, 36, 67, 104, 136, 144, 168, 196, 229, 235, 238
Piet, 195
Pietro, 195, 245
Pilar, 57, 85, 255
Pilot, 239
Pinchas, 195, 247
Pink, 258
Pinkie, 258
Pip, 103, 195
Piper, 23, 57, 79, 92, 102, **104**, 106, 126, 132, 135, 140, 145, 167, 198, 206, 213, 251, 266
Pippa, **104**, 144, 192, 234
Pita, 62
Polly, 93, 98, **104**, 110, 143, 163, 182, 195, 208, 269, 283
Porter, 39, 129, 155, 180, **196**, 211, 214, 224, 251, 287
Portia, 33, **104**, 133, 141, 166, 192, 237, 266, 280
Posy, 72
Potter, 251
Prada, 30
Prairie, 177
Precious, **105**, 238, 260
Pres, 196
Presley, 63, **105**, 155, 169, 223, 253, 264
Preston, 47, 65, 127, 143, 149, 163, 164, 168, 169, 190, **196**, 253, 286
Price, 16, 55, 134, 135, 260
Primitivo, 258
Primo, 245
Prince, 27, 64, **196**, 221, 239, 260
Princess, 105, 238, 260

Prisca, 105
Priscilla, **105**, 115, 227, 285
Prissy, 105
Prospero, 239, 281
Providenci, 257
Pru, 216
Prudence, 232

Queen, 238
Queenie, 152, 244
Quentin, 38, 41, 42, 47, 51, 53, 67, 81, 91, 98, 114, 138, 148, 152, 183, 185, 193, 196, 236, 241, 277, 286
Quiana, 77
Quin, 196, 197
Quincy, 106, 141, 150, 151, 177, **196**, 221, 253
Quinlan, 142, 231, 236, 253
Quinn, 29, 36, 38, 51, 63, 67, 84, 106, 116, 117, 137, 138, 139, 147, 148, 150, 176, 184, **196**, 198, 199, 223, 228, 229, 231, 253
Quint, 197, 211
Quinten, 197
Quintin, **196**, 197
Quinton, 22, 38, 49, 56, 73, 79, 119, 148, 150, 186, **197**, 212, 221, 236, 238

Rab, 200
Rachael, 105
Rachel, 55, 71, 75, 81, **105**, 106, 111, 127, 130, 131, 135, 148, 172, 173, 174, 184, 187, 189, 191, 216, 226, 266, 285
Rae, 49, 88, **105**, 106, 191, 244

Rafa, 198
Rafael, 198, 255
Rafaela, 14, 25, 29, 38, 72, 80, 83, 91, 93, 115, 119, 134, 248, 249, 287
Rafe, 198
Rafer, 77, 198, 272
Raffaella, 245
Raffi, 198
Raheem, 23, 205, 221
Raimondo, 198
Rainbow, 238
Rainer, 186, 242
Raisa, 281
Raleigh, 24, 88, 91, 274
Ralph, 101, 129, 153, 159, 164, **197**, 206, 283
Ram, 197
Ramiro, 100, 122, 255
Ramon/Ramón, 39, 50, 86, 89, 185, **197**, 198, 255, 286
Ramona, 86, **105**, 119, 124, 259, 269
Ramsey, 57, 88, 144, **197**, 253
Rania, 243, 261
Rand, 84, 165, 197, 229, 272
Randal, 197
Randall, 28, 43, 46, 48, 68, 102, 108, 109, 116, 122, 148, 150, **197**, 259, 272
Randi, **105**, 269, 284
Randolph, 86, 90, 103, 108, 119, 161, **197**, 249, 272, 283
Randy, 39, 44, 60, 70, 83, 105, 113, 120, 123, 134, 153, **197**, 203, 208, 259, 272, 284
Ranger, 38, 187, **197**, 199, 233, 239, 251

Ransom, 239, 258
Raoul, 198, 241
Raph, 198
Raphael, 44, 54, 73, 74, 85, 91, 161, 196, **198**, 201, 205, 227, 238, 277, 286
Raphaela, 276
Raquel, 24, 91, 98, 105, **106**, 140, 170, 174, 183, 197, 198, 255
Raquelle, 106
Raqui, 106
Rashad, 23, 68, 169, 176, 221
Rasheed, 221, 262
Rasmus, 278
Raul, 197, **198**, 255, 286
Raven, 30, 49, **106**, 115, 118, 119, 138, 142, 220, 231, 232, 236, 260
Ray, 51, 69, 74, 105, 130, 142, 166, 173, 180, 181, 184, 197, **198**, 223, 272, 283
Raya, 281
Rayburn, 272
Rayford, 272
Raymond, 31, 51, 57, 69, 84, 104, 105, 116, 128, 179, **198**, 203, 206, 214, 272, 283, 286
Raymundo, 198, 255, 272
Raynard, 272
Rayner, 272
Rayshawn, 272
Raz, 33, 101, 246, 247
Razia, 261
Rea, 106
Reagan, 21, 68, 77, 87, **106**, 223, 253, 264
Reamann, 198
Reba, 50, 99, 105, **106**, 107, 108, 118, 163, 174, 175, 184, 233, 244, 269

Rebecca, 43, 50, 80, 105, **106**, 131, 143, 148, 189, 194, 226, 267, 269, 285
Rebekah, 99, 106, 171, 216, 226
Rebekka, 106
Redmond, 198
Reece, 23, 87, 92, 104, 138, 152, 167, 179, 196, 198, 208
Reed, 199
Reenie, 93
Reese, 53, **106**, 117, 118, 119, 135, 139, 153, 196, **198**, 211, 216, 223, 228, 229
Reg, 198
Regan, 31, 60, **106**, 137, 139, 140, 144, 146, 147, 152, 153, 156, 165, 182, 201, 213, 236, 266, 280
Reggie, 60, 106, 198, 221, 259, 272, 284
Regina, **106**, 172, 183, 200, 212, 220, 259, 268, 276
Reginald, 45, 46, 82, 125, 125, 139, **198**, 200, 201, 212, 221, 272, 286
Regis/Régis, 22, 27, 33, 135, 160, 186, **198**, 238, 241, 272
Reid, 65, 112, 135, 138, 143, 149, 152, 155, 162, 163, 176, 179, 193, 196, **199**, 200, 202, 210, 229, 231, 253, 286
Reilly, 108, 200
Reina, 102, **107**
Rejoice, 220
Remington, 43, 63, 253
Rémy, 57, 241

Rena, 54, 163, 180, 249, 283
Renae, 220
Renata, 28, 47, 75, 88, 92, **107**, 115, 156, 245, 281, 287
Renate, 107, 241
Renato, 245
Rene/René, 66, 86, **199**, 241, 255
Renee/Renée, 49, 60, 73, 95, **107**, 125, 139, 148, 151, 171, 204, 210, 240, 284
Renita, 220
Reno, 233, 274
Resha, 166, 189, 246
Reuben, 32, 34, 88, 97, 100, 118, 131, 156, 165, 170, **199**, 204, 206, 227, 247, 286, 288
Reva, 49, 84, 106, **107**, 158, 162, 164, 191, 244, 287
Rex, 32, 46, 57, 72, 81, 90, 94, 104, 160, 163, 182, 198, **199**, 203, 208, 212, 213, 229, 288
Rey, 107, 198, 255
Reyna, 107, 118, 141, 189, 255
Reynaldo, 255, 281
Reza, 262
Rhea, 21, 25, 58, 86, 99, **107**, 118, 124, 132, 164, 189, 194, 201, 215, 249, 256, 262, 287
Rheta, 62, 198
Rhett, 111, 112, 139, 155, 165, **199**, 210, 211, 229, 233
Rhian, 55, 107, 160, 215, 230
Rhiannon, 22, 48, **107**, 140, 151, 230, 262

Rhoda, 51, **107**, 144, 164, 182, 197, 205, 227, 266, 283

Rhodri, 22, 231

Rhonda, 68, **107**, 148, 153, 183, 201, 220, 269, 284

Rhys, 37, 61, 198, 215, 229, 230, 231

Ria/Ría, 32, 90, 122, 256

Rianna, 109, 248

Ric, 156

Ricardo, 140, 199, 200, 255, 272

Rich, 199, 259, 272

Richard, 33, 35, 39, 52, 61, 68, 71, 73, 102, 108, 142, 151, 161, 177, **199**, 200, 202, 209, 272, 283, 286

Richie, 199

Richmond, 31, 59, 88, 113, 140, 154, 192, **199**, 206, 253, 272, 274, 288

Rick, 103, 118, 123, 141, 159, 177, 187, 194, 199, 200

Ricki, 26, 223, 269

Ricky, 44, 48, 197, 199, 210, 259

Rico, 97, 199, 245, 272

Rider, 94, 123, 132, 197, **199**, 288

Ridge, 117, 233

Ridley, 78, 197, 199, 253

Rikki, 105

Riley, 32, 46, 67, 77, 87, 104, **108**, 112, 127, 128, 133, 136, 140, 141, 145, 151, 161, 165, 169, 182, 182, 186, 194, 195, **200**, 201, 223, 230, 231, 250, 253, 266

Rilla, 244, 256

Rina, 91

Rio, 239, 256

Riona, 100, 145, 146, 153, 157, 158, 209, 230

Riordan, 154, 209, 231, 236

Rip, 203

Ripley, 78, 197, 223

Rissa, 79

Rita, 27, 69, 69, 71, 79, 89, 98, 101, **108**, 141, 153, 162, 214, 245, 283

River, 31, 42, 80, 82, 87, 94, 102, 111, 119, 125, 196, 197, **200**, 232, 239

Riviera, 238

Ro, 108

Rob, 200, 272, 284

Robbie, 42, 89, 108, 117, 200

Robert, 169, 199, **200**, 209, 215, 270, 272, 286

Roberta, 27, 69, 84, 105, **108**, 161, 197, 245, 268, 283

Roberto, 90, 185, **200**, 245, 255, 272, 286

Robertson, 200

Robin, 47, 70, 76, 80, 86, 102, 104, 107, **108**, 110, 120, 141, 147, 178, 197, **200**, 211, 223, 232, 235, 259, 266, 268, 272, 284

Robinson, 192, **200**, 253, 272

Robyn, 60, 65, 108, 112, 136

Roc, 27

Rocco, 84, 89, 138, 146, **200**, 243, 244, 245, 277

Rochelle, 81, 95, 105,

109, 116, 208, 212, 220, 227, 279, 284

Rocío, 107, 199, 255

Rock, 200, 239, 259

Rocky, 106, 200, 203, 244

Rod, 79, 97, 134, 151, 200, 201, 210, 259, 272

Roddick, 272

Roddy, 200

Roderic, 200

Roderick, 34, 122, 125, 139, 198, **200**, 208, 212, 221, 235, 272, 277, 286

Rodge, 201

Rodger, 201, 272

Rodney, 27, 45, 103, 106, 107, 148, 152, 198, **201**, 221, 259, 272

Rodolfo, 255, 272

Rodrigo, 35, 55, 90, 91, 103, 118, 151, 186, 200, 255, 281

Rogelio, 255

Roger, 34, 35, 39, 42, 52, 54, 61, 68, 73, 83, 89, 91, 93, 96, 99, 102, 147, 150, 172, 179, **201**, 202, 207, 258, 259, 277, 283

Rohan, 37, 66, 111, 139, **201**, 202, 221, 231, 236

Roisin, 230

Roland, 44, 69, 84, 89, 93, 103, 109, 135, 145, 156, 162, 172, 182, **201**, 213, 241, 283

Rolanda, 29, 220

Rolando, 61, 91, 193, 199, 201, 255

Rolf, 197, 203, 278

Rolla, 257

Rollie, 201

Roma, 107, 150, 184, 256, 269, 283
Romain, 241
Roman, 27, 29, 32, 58, 85, 111, 154, 168, 185, 187, 198, **201**, 238, 277, 282, 286
Romare, **201**, 221
Romeo, 41, 64, 122, 131, 196, **201**, 238, 245, 264, 280, 281
Romy, 77, **108**, 109, 269, 287
Ron, 110, 121, 202, 259, 272
Rona, 269
Ronald, 36, 39, 42, 47, 68, 71, 99, 105, 110, 172, 179, 201, **202**, 214, 272
Ronaldo, 202, 272
Ronan, 23, 32, 63, 149, **202**, 204, 231, 236, 266, 272, 277
Ronda, 107
Ronen, 247
Ronit, 246
Ronna, 50, 259
Ronnie, 45, 107, 123, 202, 223, 269
Roosevelt, 188, **202**, 253, 264
Rory, 32, 48, 93, 131, 139, 154, 177, 200, **202**, 204, 210, 223, 231, 233
Rosa, 92, 93, **108**, 109, 159, 163, 167, 180, 181, 191, 245, 249, 270
Rosalia, 276
Rosalie, 35, 84, 93, 104, 162, 240, 270, 283
Rosalind, 86, 90, **108**, 119, 197, 213, 270, 280, 283
Rosalinda, 108

Rosaline, 108, 280
Rosalyn, 108, 259
Rosamond, 181, 249
Rosanna, 31, **108**, 245, 248, 270, 287
Rosanne, 108, 116, 259
Rosario, 85, 223, 255, 270
Roscoe, 34, 54, 109, 133, 166, 172, 188, 194, **202**, 266, 275
Rose, 28, 44, 56, 57, 82, 91, 108, **109**, 114, 132, 140, 183, 186, 224, 232, 270
Roseanna, 108
Roseanne, 42, 93, 108
Roselyn, 270
Rosemarie, 92, 109
Rosemary, 35, 45, 61, 62, 69, 89, 92, 103, **109**, 159, 200, 232, 269, 270, 283, 287
Rosetta, 164, 183, 270
Rosie, 50, 104, 106, 108, 109, 165, 191, 198, 202, 244, 270
Rosita, 108, 270
Roslyn, 206, 283
Ross, 40, 65, 108, 144, 149, 199, **202**, 229, 229, 253, 286
Rowan, 57, 58, 67, 88, 107, 108, 117, 158, 178, 201, **202**, 231, 253, 277, 288
Rowena, 162, 188, 249
Rowland, 180, 199, 200, 201, 253
Roxana, 107, 109, 255
Roxanna, 34, 45, 82, 108, 109, 116, 150, 200, 248
Roxanne, **109**, 198, 267, 284
Roxie, 84, 105, **109**, 200, 243, 244
Roy, 50, 59, 66, 84, 86,

91, 92, 109, 124, 140, 153, 164, 181, 191, 197, **202**, 228, 233, 283
Royal, 196, 239, 260
Royce, 22, 32, 107, 123, 160, 198, 199, **203**, 212, 229, 229, 283, 288
Rube, 199
Ruben, 39, 44, 61, 100, 197, 198, 199, 200, 205, 255, 286
Rubin, 50, 180, 184
Ruby, 28, 46, 66, 86, **109**, 119, 123, 181, 202, 232, 244
Rudolf, 181, 203
Rudolfo, 203
Rudolph, 32, 54, 58, 61, 63, 72, 82, 93, 104, 118, 119, 135, 141, 143, 157, **203**, 249, 264
Rudy, 203
Rueben, 190
Rufus, 202, 275
Runa, 278
Rune, 36, 77, 84, 120, 229, 278
Rupe, 203
Rupert, 21, 22, 54, 64, 130, 135, 141, 153, 154, 192, **203**, 235, 249, 277
Russ, 70, 147, 203, 284
Russell, 92, 119, 139, 144, 162, 179, 191, 198, **203**, 214, 283, 286
Rusty, 60, 81, **203**, 233
Ruth, 24, 28, 51, 56, 64, 66, 89, 95, 97, 108, **109**, 128, 140, 153, 159, 161, 181, 190, 198, 204, 206, 215, 227, 283

Ruthie, 35, 109, 244
Ryan, 18, 24, 26, 30, 40,
    55, 74, 94, 100, 109,
    110, 117, 127, 137,
    141, 175, 178, 203,
    204, 223, 230, 231,
    236, 265, 266
Ryann, 69, 109
Ryder, 24, 54, 106, 199,
    200, 251
Ryker, 78, 160, 169, 184
Rylan, 68, 101, 106, 201,
    236
Rylee, 108, 200, 223
Ryleigh, 23, 68, 108
Rylie, 48, 68, 92, 102,
    106, 108, 114, 117,
    204
Ryne, 51, 77, 229

Sabelo, 218
Saber, 38, 239
Sabina, 65, 151, 180,
    183, 248, 276
Sabine, 43, 54, 140, 240,
    241
Sabrina, 40, 97, 109,
    116, 122, 140, 265,
    268
Sade, 110, 220, 264
Sadie, 95, 98, 109, 110,
    111, 127, 165, 190,
    194, 204, 224, 244,
    246, 270
Sadler, 251
Saffron, 238
Safiya, 217, 261
Saga, 77, 260, 278
Sage, 29, 31, 32, 52, 63,
    67, 72, 87, 97, 101,
    106, 110, 112, 114,
    139, 165, 168, 198,
    200, 208, 211, 216,
    223, 228, 229, 232,
    260
Sahara, 274
Saige, 139

Sailor, 251
St. John, 192, 235
Sakari, 75, 142, 278
Sal, 108, 110, 111, 244,
    270, 273
Salim, 262
Salina, 270
Sallie, 171, 244
Sally, 110, 111, 208, 214,
    270, 283
Salma, 186, 255, 270
Salome, 48, 84, 122, 149,
    168, 180, 212, 227,
    237, 240, 270
Salvador, 62, 85, 95, 255,
    273
Salvatore, 89, 245, 273
Sam, 21, 28, 41, 56, 82,
    88, 100, 109, 110, 110,
    115, 181, 187, 203,
    204, 248, 273
Samantha, 18, 80, 110,
    137, 173, 174, 175,
    216, 265, 270
Samara, 125, 270
Samir, 262, 273
Samira, 57, 68, 110, 190,
    248, 261, 270
Sammie, 110, 223, 244,
    244, 270
Sammy, 110
Sampson, 203
Samson, 48, 176, 203,
    227, 238, 273, 277
Samuel, 18, 42, 44, 53,
    61, 66, 73, 111, 135,
    167, 168, 174, 191,
    204, 213, 227, 234,
    273, 286
Sander, 129
Sandi, 110
Sandra, 23, 35, 40, 73,
    79, 83, 110, 112, 150,
    160, 172, 245, 259,
    270
Sandrine, 240
Sandy, 23, 24, 60, 110,

120, 129, 177, 223,
    259, 270, 273, 284
Sanford, 140, 188,
    273
Sanne, 136, 241, 242
Santesa, 270
Santiago, 56, 62, 103,
    172, 255, 273
Santos, 86, 255
Sapphira, 46, 74, 180,
    227, 237
Sapphire, 49
Sara, 47, 75, 111, 127
Sarah, 18, 53, 75, 81,
    105, 111, 130, 135,
    148, 168, 172, 174,
    187, 192, 204, 227,
    241, 270, 285
Sarahi, 23
Sarai, 89, 111, 155, 157,
    193, 227, 237, 266,
    270
Sargent, 126, 196, 201,
    239
Sarina, 111
Sasha, 23, 49, 111, 129,
    279, 281
Satchel, 264
Saul, 97, 182, 204, 227,
    247, 286
Saundra, 110
Savanna, 24, 31, 36, 37,
    40, 111, 112, 147, 210,
    248
Savannah, 39, 43, 49, 98,
    111, 113, 233, 274
Savina, 75, 128, 146,
    185, 276
Savion, 150, 193, 221
Savvy, 111
Sawyer, 40, 54, 63, 102,
    105, 113, 149, 167,
    200, 204, 206, 211,
    251, 266
Scarlett, 43, 98, 102,
    105, 107, 111, 112,
    155, 199, 201, 203,

215, 233, 237, 260, 264

Schuyler, 65, 206, 214, 253

Scot, 47, 50, 178, 204

Scott, 26, 27, 70, 73, 78, 83, 85, 112, 120, 146, 151, 177, 204, 210, 211

Scottie, 117, 284

Scotty, 71, 81, 92, 153, 204, 284

Seamus, 23, 149, 204, 231, 266

Sean, 27, 36, 47, 55, 94, 100, 115, 136, 137, 156, 173, 178, 203, 204, 205, 230, 231, 265

Seattle, 125

Seb, 204

Sebastian, 14, 27, 28, 57, 60, 67, 73, 87, 99, 101, 114, 147, 151, 171, 175, 188, 204, 211, 216, 234, 235, 258, 277, 278, 281

Sebastien/Sébastien, 204, 241

Sedona, 113, 197, 233

Selah, 29, 216

Selena, 55, 106, 111, 112, 118, 125, 170, 183, 185, 189, 204, 248, 255, 262

Selina, 61, 111, 151, 177

Selma, 202, 275

Senna, 83, 232

Serafina, 140

Seraph, 99

Seraphina, 51, 276

Serena, 23, 24, 74, 111, 117, 149, 152, 165, 204, 248, 276

Serenity, 42, 57, 59, 63, 64, 99, 110, 111, 121, 123, 216, 260

Serge, 204

Sergei, 204, 282

Sergio, 22, 82, 102, 125, 129, 141, 162, 170, 185, 204, 245, 255

Sergius, 204

Serina, 111

Seth, 80, 81, 127, 167, 170, 174, 204, 205, 227, 265

Severin, 238, 277

Severina, 237, 281

Severus, 277

Seymour, 219, 273, 275

Shadi, 75, 142

Shadow, 94, 97, 193, 239, 260

Shaina, 112

Shakira, 23, 68, 110, 111, 112, 169, 185, 193, 255, 261

Shalonda, 220

Shamar, 193, 221

Shameka, 220

Shamus, 204

Shana, 76, 97, 112, 266

Shane, 43, 81, 113, 125, 134, 137, 141, 144, 150, 199, 205, 210, 228, 229, 231, 233, 246, 265

Shani, 25, 217, 220, 246

Shania, 112, 207, 233, 264, 266

Shanice, 150, 180, 220

Shanika, 79, 80, 219

Shaniya, 193, 220

Shanna, 112, 117

Shannon, 29, 36, 57, 63, 68, 75, 76, 78, 81, 95, 115, 117, 125, 137, 165, 177, 205, 223, 230, 231, 266, 266, 279

Shanta, 116

Shante, 110, 220

Shantel, 42, 220

Shantell, 80

Shaq, 205

Shaquille, 205, 22, 264

Sharen, 112

Shari, 34, 112, 112, 113, 284

Sharif, 221

Sharla, 284

Sharleen, 42

Sharon, 39, 50, 68, 73, 74, 75, 110, 112, 115, 150, 160, 259, 269

Sharonda, 79, 80, 220

Sharron, 112

Sharyn, 112

Shasta, 57, 160, 233, 274

Shaun, 52, 75, 77, 78, 97, 112, 121, 204

Shauna, 112, 205

Shawn, 27, 29, 47, 68, 76, 79, 112, 142, 204, 205, 222, 223, 230, 279, 284

Shawna, 57, 112, 117

Shay, 112, 176, 204, 229

Shayla, 77, 81, 112, 170, 225, 248

Shayna, 112, 176, 225, 248

Shayne, 205

Shea, 40, 51, 101, 109, 112, 134, 138, 151, 152, 158, 207, 210, 211, 223, 228, 230, 253, 287

Sheena, 80, 279

Sheila, 36, 43, 45, 52, 103, 113, 134, 148, 201, 230, 259, 266

Shel, 205

Shelbi, 113

Shelbie, 113

Shelby, 33, 76, 98, 113, 116, 133, 144, 145, 147, 150, 151, 207, 208, 223, 253

Sheldon, 205, 283

Shell, 113

Shelley, 201, 259, 284

Shelly, 96, 153, 205, 213
Shelva, 258
Shem, 204
Shena, 113
Shenandoah, 88, 111, **113**, 125, 142, 233, 274
Sheree, 42, 220
Sheri, 85, 113, 177, 178
Sheridan, 15, 54, 134, 140, 181, 190, 192, 197, 200, 223, 253
Sherie, 42
Sherlock, 239
Sherm, 205
Sherman, 144, **205**, 253, 283
Sherrell, 43
Sherri, 113, 117
Sherrie, 113
Sherrill, 42, 43
Sherry, 42, 86, 103, 107, **113**, 259, 284
Sheryl, 43, 113, 118, 147, 177, 197
Shevaun, 114
Sheyla, 117
Shifra, 227, 246
Shimon, 113, 206, 247
Shira, 101, 246
Shirlee, 113
Shirlene, 275
Shirley, 30, 33, 35, **113**, 151, 283
Shlomo, 206, 246
Shola, 218
Shonda, 220, 279
Shosh, 113
Shoshana, 62, **113**, 115, 246, 248
Shoshanna, 113
Shoshi, 113
Shura, 23, 281
Shyanne, 43
Shyla, 112
Si, 205, 206, 244, 273
Sian, 23, 112, 229, 231

Sibyl, 141
Sidney, 116, 133, 152, 165, 167, 189, 206, 250, 253
Sidony, 33, 83, 133, 168, 192, 208, 234, 237
Siena, 66, 113, 118, 274
Sienna, 37, 40, **113**, 125, 196, 200, 216, 248, 266
Sierra, 16, 26, 31, 32, 43, 90, 98, 111, **113**, 115, 121, 136, 142, 145, 211, 215, 233, 248, 266, 274
Sigmund, 124, 242
Signe, 31, 180, 186, 192, 278
Sigrid, 31, 64, 184, 242, 278
Silas, 124, 147, 173, **205**, 224, 228, 273
Sile, 113
Silver, 80, 135, 232, 238
Silvia, 116, 193, 245, 255, 262, 280
Silvie, 116
Silvio, 131, 245
Sim, 258
Simeon, 48, 62, 83, 94, 111, 161, 170, 203, **205**, 206, 227, 238, 266, 273
Simon, 26, 28, 38, 53, 56, 61, 66, 72, 73, 81, 86, 99, 100, 104, 139, 189, 191, 204, 205, **206**, 213, 227, 228, 235, 273, 286
Simona, 65, 245, 281
Simone, 22, 27, 41, 42, 49, 91, 100, 110, **114**, 130, 141, 150, 151, 185, 220, 240, 266, 287
Simonne, 114
Simpson, 253

Sinbad, 22, 239, 273
Sincere, 30, 105, 239, 258, 260
Sindi, 217
Sinead, 58, 114, 230, 268
Siobhan/Siobhán, 57, 107, **114**, 149, 158, 230, 237
Sirius, 86, 193, 239
Sissy, 41
Skip, 96, 103, 259
Sky, 29, 63, 67, 87, 114, 169, 172, 176, 187, 206
Skye, 48, 52, 67, 74, 82, 110, **114**, 118, 160, 178, 184, 204, 216, 228, 260
Skyla, 68, 225
Skylar, 24, 37, 63, 76, 103, 106, 108, **114**, 142, 149, 165, 169, 195, 206, 210
Skyler, 30, 31, 40, 114, 138, 144, 194, **206**, 223
Slater, 251
Sloane, 35, 36, 37, 136, 158, 176, 179, 228
Sly, 207
Smith, 252
Soeren, 242
Sofia, 28, 53, 96, 114, 154, 163, 206, 243, 278
Sofie, 114, 278
Sojourner, 220, 264
Sol, 85, 190, 206, 244
Soledad, 255
Soleil, 42, 186
Solly, 206
Solomon, 27, 41, 64, 110, 127, 130, 190, 193, 199, 205, **206**, 224, 227
Sondra, 92, 125
Sonia, 47, 48, 50, 90,

114, 125, 139, 266, 281, 285
Sonja, 114, 278
Sonoma, 274
Sonya, 27, 62, 64, 114, 120, 125, 136, 284
Sophia, 14, 18, 32, 43, 53, 64, 67, 73, 87, 101, 114, 128, 133, 135, 167, 168, 175, 204, 224
Sophie, 26, 46, 57, 61, 66, 83, 98, 99, 110, 114, 139, 170, 175, 187, 189, 193, 204, 205, 223, 224, 231, 234, 240, 242, 244
Soren, 140, 236, 278
Sotiria, 243
Spence, 206, 229
Spencer, 41, 43, 92, 97, 98, 100, 109, 115, 123, 142, 143, 145, 155, 160, 163, 164, 186, 190, 193, 196, 206, 252, 253, 286
Spenser, 30, 206
Spike, 152, 239
Spiros, 243
Spring, 232
Stacey, 96, 115, 120, 136, 137
Staci, 77
Stacie, 115
Stacy, 26, 27, 40, 43, 47, 76, 115, 117, 177, 205, 223, 223, 279, 284
Stan, 206, 273
Stanford, 190, 206, 253, 273
Stanislaus, 238, 277
Stanislav, 281, 282
Stanislava, 281
Stanley, 103, 181, 189, 193, 206, 273, 283
Stanton, 32, 35, 90, 109, 119, 203, 206, 214, 253, 273, 283, 288

Star, 72, 105, 197, 216, 238, 260
Starla, 97, 284
Stasia, 27, 198, 287
Stavros, 50, 53, 243
Stefan, 28, 51, 62, 66, 68, 72, 74, 111, 119, 140, 163, 187, 206, 207, 242, 278
Stefania, 94, 115, 245, 248, 270, 281, 287
Stefanie, 115
Stefano, 245, 281
Stefanos, 206, 243
Steff, 206
Steffan, 55, 61, 206, 215, 231
Stella, 45, 56, 65, 82, 86, 110, 115, 123, 164, 224, 244
Stephan, 206, 207
Stephania, 53, 115, 115
Stephanie, 25, 27, 43, 47, 96, 98, 100, 115, 131, 143, 156, 171, 173, 187, 222, 265, 270
Stephany, 115
Stephen, 50, 80, 90, 106, 110, 128, 149, 163, 194, 195, 207, 228, 273, 286
Stephon, 110, 206, 212, 221
Sterling, 45, 55, 63, 120, 130, 171, 207, 232, 266, 286
Stetson, 113, 207, 233, 236
Steve, 118, 134, 206, 207, 259, 273
Steveland, 218
Steven, 43, 49, 73, 109, 113, 171, 177, 186, 189, 204, 207, 209, 265, 273, 284
Stevie, 39, 115, 223, 270, 279

Stewart, 119, 140, 163, 182, 197, 206, 207, 283
Stone, 25, 40, 55, 67, 94, 111, 113, 114, 119, 165, 232
Stoney, 97, 112, 284
Storm, 29, 106, 111, 118, 119, 232, 260
Stratton, 31, 274
Stuart, 90, 124, 125, 146, 153, 161, 195, 200, 207, 235, 286
Sue, 54, 68, 72, 73, 74, 75, 103, 104, 110, 113, 115, 116, 173, 208, 270, 283, 287
Suellen, 259
Sukie, 115
Sullivan, 23, 66, 207, 231, 253
Sully, 207
Summer, 32, 65, 67, 71, 95, 106, 114, 115, 119, 142, 232, 260, 266, 270
Sumner, 252
Sun, 49, 260
Sunday, 238
Sunny, 97
Sunrise, 238
Sunshine, 260
Susa, 115
Susan, 51, 74, 75, 83, 103, 115, 119, 128, 138, 149, 152, 186, 191, 195, 207, 259, 270
Susana, 105, 115, 116, 139, 169, 175, 185, 186, 190, 227, 285
Susanna, 71, 113, 115
Susannah, 14, 115, 116, 171, 198, 269, 270, 287
Susanne, 197
Susie, 115, 142, 159, 163, 244, 270

Suzan, 115
Suzann, 116
Suzanna, 115
Suzanne, 28, 45, 47, 86, 93, 115, **116**, 148, 258, 259, 270
Suze, 115
Suzette, 42, 68, 125, 153, 239, 240, 270, 284
Suzie, 116
Sven, 192, 278
Svetlana, 281
Sy, 207
Sybil, 65, 107, 180, 214, 249, 262, 267
Syd, 116
Sydnee, 116, 139
Sydney, 18, 33, 62, 66, 87, 102, 111, 114, **116**, 128, 147, 149, 186, 223, 274
Syed, 262
Syl, 116, 207
Sylvain, 241
Sylvan, 104, 277
Sylvester, 44, 96, 152, 158, 203, **207**, 249, 273, 277
Sylvia, 66, 108, **116**, 135, 142, 159, 183, 186, 189, 193, 206, 249, 283
Sylvie, 108, 116, 240, 287

Tab, 116
Tabby, 116
Tabitha, 34, 75, 96, **116**, 185, 210, 227, 265
Tad, 47, 50, 60, 71, 92, 136, 149, 178, 200, 208, 210, 235, 284
Taffeta, 238
Taft, 188, 229
Tahira, 261
Tai, 77, 139, 256
Tait, 208

Tal, 116, 120, 247
Tate, 176, 204, 208, 229, 253
Tali, 99
Talia, 23, 24, 66, 99, 101, **116**, 118, 170, 201, 246, 248
Taliyah, 220
Tallulah, 125, 237, 264
Tally, 116
Talmadge, 215
Talon, 106, 200, 232, 236
Talya, 116
Tam, 117, 231
Tamar, 74, 116, 122, 126, 161, 170, 203, 205, 227, 237, 270
Tamara, 27, 48, 60, 95, 114, **116**, 120, 121, 139, 209, 227, 248, 270, 284
Tameka, 116
Tamela, 220
Tami, 116
Tamia, 26, 33, 125, 220, 270
Tamika, 76, 79, **116**, 172, 205, 220, 270
Tamiko, 270
Tamir, 247
Tammie, 117
Tammy, 44, 85, 116, **117**, 270, 284
Tamra, 50, 134
Tams, 117
Tamsin, 117, 119, 129, 145, 146, 160, 230, 234, 236, 270, 287
Tamsyn, 117
Tanesha, 80
Tania, 117, 130, 147, 177
Tanika, 116
Tanisha, 217, 220
Taniya, 21, 220
Tanner, 33, 40, 113, 118, 133, 145, 147, 151,

207, 208, 211, 250, 252
Tanya, 79, 115, **117**, 137, 212, 266, 279, 281
Tara, 26, 29, 31, 55, 63, 65, 74, 78, 117, 142, 256, 266
Taras, 282
Tarian, 142, 236
Tariq, 23, 26, 33, 65, 110, 112, 169, 176, 185, 221, 262
Tarkin, 277
Tarquin, 29, 33, 123, 128, 180, **208**, 235, 238, 281
Taryn, 49, 109, 121, 148, 152, 190, 212, 236
Tarzan, 239
Tasha, 36, 52, 76, 80, 99, 105, 112, **117**, 121, 220, 270, 279
Tate, 102, 114, 121, 125, 160, 176, 198, **208**
Tati, 117
Tatiana, 15, 24, 27, 38, 77, 88, 91, 98, 99, **117**, 122, 148, 187, 188, 196, 248, 270, 276, 281
Tatum, **117**, 145, 169, 198, 208, 253
Tatyana, 117, 212, 220
Tavis, 55, 128, 168, 231
Tavish, 83, 164, 231, 238
Tawana, 220
Tawny, 279
Tay, 118, 208
Taya, 202
Tayla, 117, 225
Taylah, 117
Tayler, 208
Taylor, 15, 18, 37, 42, 72, 76, **118**, 133, 143, 144, 173, 207, **208**, 212, 223, 252
Tayo, 218
Teagan, 69, 117, 236

Teague, 79, 176, 209, 215, 229, 231
Tecumseh, 113
Ted, 35, 68, 71, 75, 103, 115, 154, 163, 191, **208**, 209, 273, 283
Teddy, 104, 208
Tee, 119
Tempest, 122, 123, 175, 197, 238, 260
Tennie, 257
Teo, 59, 77, 186, 208, 209, 256, 273
Teodoro, 273
Terence, 34, 109, 150, 192, 200, 208, 235, 284
Teresa, 27, 46, 48, 49, 80, 83, 90, 119, 149, 152, 163, 177, 186, 245, 270
Terese, 102, 119
Teri, 70, 71, 118, 120, 147, 177, 178, 284
Terje, 277
Terra, 55, 112, **118**, 256, 260, 270, 287
Terrance, 22, 38, 81, 116, 117, 161, 177, **208**, 212, 221, 265, 273
Terrell, 77, 172, **208**, 212, 221, 253, 273
Terrence, 48, 67, 73, 82, 198, 200, 208
Terri, 118
Terry, 43, 45, 73, 75, 86, 102, **118**, 119, 123, 134, 197, **208**, 209, 223, 259, 259, 270, 273
Tess, 25, 75, 98, **118**, 119, 129, 168, 169, 175, 182, 210, 244, 270, 287
Tessa, 31, 36, 39, 74, **118**, 210, 211, 256, 270

Tessie, 109, 118
Tevin, 51, 117, 236
Tex, 233
Thabo, 218
Thad, 134, 208, 284
Thaddeus, 119, 134, 134, 151, 180, **208**, 228, 238
Thalia, 31, 88, 91, 95, 111, 112, 113, **118**, 161, 248, 255, 262, 266
Than, 156, 173, 191, 273
Thanassis, 243, 273
Thandeka, 217
Thandi, 217
Thane, 229, 252
Thatcher, 252
Thea, 25, 46, 51, **118**, 249, 287
Theda, 25, **118**, 126, 266
Thelma, 22, 56, **119**, 166, 197, 275
Thelonious, 209, 238
Thelonius, 30, 67, 149, **209**, 272, 273
Theo, 44, 56, 63, 82, 84, 94, 99, 118, 120, 123, 131, 170, 181, 187, 189, 199, **209**, 224, 266, 273, 288
Theodora, 32, 104, **119**, 243, 249
Theodore, 24, 33, 64, 72, 124, 132, 133, 159, 175, 181, 207, **209**, 249, 273
Theophilus, 228, 238, 272, 273
Theresa, 45, **119**, 146, 155, 186, 195, 203, 209, 259, 285
Therese, 90, **119**, 125, 140, 161, 172, 207, 240, 270, 276, 283, 287
Theron, 22, 160, 183, 238

Theseus, 262, 281
Thibaut, 241
Thomas, 68, 153, 169, 173, 195, 199, 200, **209**, 228, 234, 273, 286
Thomasina, **119**, 237
Thor, 123, 128, 175, 239, 262, 278
Thora, 83, 93, 96, 120, 155, 184, 249, 278
Thulani, 218
Thurman, 150, 253
Tia, 29, 40, 46, 81, 102, 106, 118, **119**, 120, 127, 256, 270
Tiago, 255
Tiana, 42, 117, 148, 150, 176, 212, 220, 248, 270
Tiara, **119**, 260, 270
Tiarnan, 209
Tiernan, 114, 117, 145, 146, 153, 157, 178, **209**, 231, 236, 266, 288
Tierney, 181, 209, 253
Tierra, 118, **119**, 186, 232, 260
Tif, 120
Tiffani, 120
Tiffany, 42, 46, **120**, 279
Tilda, 93, **120**, 249, 270, 278
Till, 136, **209**, 215, 229, 242
Tillie, 85, 93, 194, 244, 270
Tillman, 252
Tim, 78, 89, 209, 273, 284
Tima, 57
Timmy, 209
Timon, 236, 281
Timothy, 27, 34, 43, 50, 73, 78, 80, 107, 108, 109, 116, 121, 161,

163, 171, 177, 186, 192, 194, 207, **209**, 228, 265, 273, 284

Tina, 43, 70, 83, 92, 108, 117, **120**, 122, 124, 146, 149, 178, 204, 210, 211, 283, 284

Tisa, 97

Titania, 280

Titus, 46, 228, 238, 281

Tobey, 210

Tobiah, 209

Tobias, 26, 42, 91, 102, 155, 168, 173, 174, 195, **209**, 224, 227, 273, 278

Tobin, 65, 92, 94, 121, 134, 209, **210**, 236, 253, 273, 288

Toby, 43, 47, 70, 79, 115, 121, 178, 209, **210**, 273, 281, 284

Tod, 112, 210

Todd, 34, 44, 47, 60, 78, 83, 85, 107, 108, 117, 120, 138, 177, 204, **210**, 211, 213, 283, 284

Tom, 209, 273, 283, 285

Tomas, 107, 131, 209, 282, 286

Tomika, 116

Tomiko, 116

Tommaso, 245

Tommie, 119, 221, 244

Tommy, 47, 71, 110, 172, 179, 195, 209

Toña, 29

Toni, 28, 29, **120**, 136, 270, 284

Tonia, 29

Tonio, 131, 273

Tony, 28, 48, 85, 120, 131, 171, **210**, 259, 273

Tonya, 117, 208, 220, 270, 279

Topaz, 65, **120**, 232

Topher, 143

Tori, **120**, 123, 270

Torquil, 168, 208, 231, 238

Torrance, 79, 116, 121, 221

Torrey, 205

Torsten, 31, 278

Tory, 105, 120, 223

Tosha, 117

Tova, 33, 36, 101, **120**, 126, 158, 166, 192, 246, 256, 266

Tove, 120, 132, 278

Toy, 258

Toya, 220

Trace, 31, 76, 98, 112, 114, **210**, 211, 229, 233

Tracee, 120

Tracey, 85, 120

Traci, 120, 148

Tracie, 120, 284

Tracy, 44, 115, 117, 119, **120**, 141, 144, 210, 223, 253, 284

Trae, 221

Travis, 22, 24, 34, 40, 47, 68, 77, 120, 136, 137, 153, 205, 210, 233, 266

Tre, 48

Tremayne, 79, 80, 180, 221

Trent, 79, 138, 142, 152, **210**, 229

Trenton, 24, 30, 36, 37, 132, 183, **210**, 236, 274

Tressa, 119

Trever, 211

Trevin, 210, 236

Trevon, 148, 212, 219, 221

Trevor, 32, 59, 60, 72, 76, 98, 110, 113, 115,

118, 128, 133, 137, 144, 145, 147, 150, 160, 178, 190, 210, **211**, 212, 231, 235, 266

Trey, 37, 119, 120, 179, 199, 208, **211**, 216, 229

Tricia, 33, 43, 77, 84, 97, 102, 117, **121**, 175, 270, 279

Trina, 47, 50, 60, 75, 89, 92, 112, **121**, 210, 220, 270, 279, 284

Trini, 121

Trinidad, 270, 274

Trinity, 16, 21, 30, 59, **121**, 188, 260, 270

Trish, 102, 121, 270

Trisha, 78, 117, 121, 144

Trista, **121**, 134, 279, 279

Tristan, 23, 29, 38, 47, 59, 60, 67, 92, 111, 121, 140, 151, 152, 196, 197, **211**, 235, 236, 241

Tristen, 211

Tristram, 104, 119, 208, 211, 235, 238

Triton, 22, 56, 86, 193, 239

Trixie, 33, 244

Troy, 44, 47, 60, 107, 117, 124, 148, 149, 210, **211**, 284

Tru, 121

Trudi, 121

Trudie, 121

Trudy, 60, 118, **121**, 141, 259, 270

Truman, 56, 107, 154, 158, 159, 164, 180, 194, **211**, 214, 215, 253, 288

Truth, 74, 239, 260

Tuck, 211

Tucker, 21, 36, 40, 84, 112, 114, 120, 121, 138, 146, 176, 179, 204, 207, **211**, 212, 252
Tuesday, 232
Turner, 171, 180, 182, 196, **211**, 252
Twan, 131
Twila, 32, 199, 203, 283
Twyla, 198
Ty, 75, 100, 118, 121, 142, 143, 168, 171, 210, **211**, 212, 216, 221, 229, 233, 273
Tyler, 15, 18, 30, 40, 49, **121**, 144, 173, **212**, 214, 223, 252, 273
Tylor, 212
Tyme, 87, 216, 239, 260
Tyne, 37, 79, 136, 138, 174, 208, 209, 215, 228
Tyra, 31, 48, **121**, 151, 196, 212, 220, 225, 256
Tyree, **212**, 221, 273
Tyrel, 212
Tyrell, 186, 208, **212**, 221, 273
Tyrese, 219, 221, 273
Tyron, 221, 272
Tyrone, 198, **212**, 221, 231, 273
Tyson, 79, 109, 138, 138, **212**, 236, 253, 273

Ulises, 255
Ulrich, 242
Ulysses, 31, 32, 126, **212**, 238, 262, 266
Uma, 264
Una, 230
Unique, 30, 238, 258
Urban, 257
Uri, 247
Uriah, 227

Uriel, 227
Ursula, 242, 280

Vadim, 282
Val, 122, 270
Valarie, 122
Valdemar, 278
Valencia, 29, **122**, 248, 270, 274
Valentia, 122
Valentin, 27, 49, 241, 282
Valentina, 27, 99, **122**, 161, 176, 187, 188, 208, 237, 270, 276, 281
Valentine, 30, **122**, 209, 223, 237, 239, 270, 281
Valeria, 24, 90, 95, **122**, 124, 129, 131, 172, 245, 248, 255, 270, 280
Valerie/Valérie, 50, 67, 94, 102, **122**, 128, 163, 198, 209, 259, 270
Valery, 122
Valia, 281
Valya, 122
Van, 46, 81, 90, 151, 157, 180, 182, 199, 203, **212**, 229, 283
Vance, 139, 195, **212**, 213, 229, 286
Vander, 157
Vanessa, 24, 27, 34, 40, 70, 75, 109, **122**, 137, 210, 220, 248, 265
Vanna, 60, 111
Vanni, 60
Vannie, 114
Vanya, 168
Vashti, 111, **122**, 170, 184, 227, 246
Vassilis, 243
Vaughan, 213
Vaughn, 61, 103, 193, 212, **213**, 229, 231, 253, 286

Vega, 86, 193, 239
Velma, 54, 144, 158, 166, 182, 190, 214, 275
Velva, 257
Velvel, 215
Velvet, 239
Venetia, 122, 220, 234
Venice, 102, **123**, 274
Venus, **123**, 127, 131, 175, 239, 262
Vera, 51, 58, 63, 101, **123**, 136, 166, 249, 266, 281
Verda, 257
Verena, 242
Vergil, 213
Verica, 281
Verity, 26, 40, 42, 65, 111, **123**, 232, 234, 287
Verl, 275
Vern, 182, 213
Verna, 132, 194, 213, 275
Verne, 54, 213, 275
Vernell, 275
Vernice, 275
Vernon, 84, 124, 132, 135, 144, 153, 166, 181, 186, 188, 201, **213**, 221, 283
Verona, 59, 274
Veronica, 22, 43, 98, 106, **123**, 131, 185, 269, 276, 285
Veronika, 123, 281
Versie, 257
Vesta, 257, 262
Vester, 257
Vet, 207
Vi, 123, 124
Vic, 213
Vicenta, 270
Vicente, 95, 172, 213, 255
Vicki, 36, 43, 70, 121, 123, 259
Vickie, 48, **123**
Vicky, 123, 147, 208, 270

Victor, 54, 73, 75, 86, 100, 165, 185, 194, **213**, 255, 286

Victoria, 18, 23, 39, 73, 101, **123**, 129, 135, 138, 143, 163, 168, 175, 192, 224, 234, 270, 285

Vienna, 274

Viggo, 278

Viivi, 277

Vikki, 123

Viktor, 185, 213, 282

Vin, 80, 213, 273

Vince, 50, 68, 125, 134, 183, 213, 273, 284

Vincent, 45, 185, 213, **213**, 241, 273, 277, 285, 286

Vincente, 213

Vincenza, 245

Vincenzo, 213, 245, 273

Vinnie, 213

Vinson, 273

Viola, 25, 32, 35, 56, 58, 82, 93, 123, 133, 146, 147, 162, 165, 239, 249, 280

Violet, 22, 41, 52, 59, 59, 63, 64, 66, 70, 72, 83, 88, 94, 95, 109, **123**, 124, 127, 132, 159, 165, 170, 175, 193, 224, 232

Violetta, 51, 119, 123, 190, 237

Violette, 44, 122, 123, 199, 240, 249

Virgil, 22, 35, 119, 141, 166, 181, 190, 194, **213**, 214, 249, 275

Virginia, 59, **124**, 125, 233, 249, 268

Vita, 96

Vito, 146, 200, 244, 245

Vittoria, 245

Vittorio, 245

Vitus, 75, 277

Viv, 124

Viva, 126, 155, 237

Vivi, 123, 124

Vivian, 57, 92, 116, **124**, 130, 135, 144, 162, 167, 179, 181, 191, 201, 203, 214, 223, 276, 283

Viviana, 23, 33, 51, 79, 82, 91, 115, 122, **124**, 181, 204, 245, 248, 255

Vivienne, 49, 124, 240

Vladimir, 101, 281, 282

Volker, 242

Von, 141, 150, 213, 229

Vonnie, 125

Vulf, 215

Wade, **213**, 229, 286

Waino, 257

Walden, 31, **213**, 253, 273, 274

Waldo, 34, 54, 63, 152, 264, 273, 275

Walker, 25, 34, 39, 46, 72, 104, 135, 145, 149, 163, 166, 188, 196, 211, **213**, 224, 252, 266, 273

Wallace, 51, 98, 143, **214**, 249, 273

Wally, 214, 259, 273

Walt, 214

Walter, 24, 58, 64, 66, 85, 92, 132, 156, 159, 161, 164, 166, 183, **214**, 249, 273

Walton, 150, **214**, 253, 273

Wanda, 105, **124**, 186, 188, 214, 220, 259, 266, 281

Ward, 74, 107, 143, 144, 163, 283

Wardell, 271

Warren, 31, 52, 69, 85, 92, 108, 162, 191, 203, **214**, 266, 283, 286

Washington, 26

Watson, 54, 164, 215, 253

Watt, 172, 229, 253

Wava, 257

Waverly, 253

Waylon, 233, 272

Wayne, 36, 47, 51, 68, 73, 92, 138, 152, 160, **214**, 233, 259

Weaver, 252

Webster, 54, 199, 252

Weldon, 148, 180

Wendi, 124

Wendell, 85, 90, 98, 105, 205, 283

Wendy, 44, 60, 62, 73, **124**, 153, 213, 284

Wenona, 125

Werner, 54, 242

Wes, 178, 214, 273

Wesley, 83, 120, 124, 141, **214**, 253, 273, 286

Westley, 42, 273

Weston, 30, 112, 121, 147, 166, 176, 212, **214**, 236, 253, 273

Wheeler, 252

Whisper, 239, 260

Whitman, 264

Whitney, 37, 42, 65, 79, 83, 120, **124**, 177, 214, 223, 253, 266, 279

Wilber, 214

Wilbur, 22, 96, 194, 213, **214**, 273, 274, 275

Wilda, 257

Wiley, 105, 106, 109, 126, 184, 233, 244

Wilfred, 194, 273, 275

Wilfredo, 255

Wilhelm, 215, 242, 273

Wilhelmina, 64, **124**, 181, 242, 249, 267, 269

Will, 38, 70, 88, 100, 215, 273
Willa, 32, 37, 59, 82, 90, 104, 107, 120, **124**, 129, 158, 189, 194, 214, 224, 249, 256, 267, 287
Willard, 96, 182, 190, 273, 275
Willem, 215, 270
William, 18, 53, 142, 154, 169, 173, 174, **215**, 270, 273, 286
Willie, 124, 214, 244
Willis, 52, 57, 63, 82, 90, 120, 123, 124, 154, 157, 184, 195, **215**, 249, 253, 270, 273, 283
Willow, 42, 57, 81, 94, 102, 104, 110, 113, 124, **125**, 167, 196, 200, 216, 232, 266
Willy, 215
Wilma, 51, 124, 152, 177, 181, 193, 275
Wilson, 29, **215**, 253, 273, 286
Wilton, 273
Win, 215
Windy, 258
Winema, 75, 113
Winifred, 21, 64, 96, 104, **125**, 195, 203, 207, 234, 249, 276
Winnie, 125, 133, 215, 244
Winona, 88, 112, **125**, 160, 179, 233
Winston, **215**, 253
Winter, 260
Wisdom, 239, 260
Wolf, 32, 86, 136, **215**, 238, 242
Wolfe, 215
Wolfgang, 242

Woodrow, 271
Woody, 233
Worth, 260
Wright, 252
Wyatt, 43, 67, 111, 126, 145, **215**, 233, 266
Wyn, 215
Wynn, 61, 157, 158, 174, 176, **215**, 229, 231
Wynne, 55, 215, 228, 230
Wynonna, 125

Xander, 23, 24, 129, 131, **216**, 273
Xandra, 23
Xanthe, 237, 262
Xanthia, 237
Xavier, 24, 25, 69, 102, 122, 135, 147, 151, 156, 157, 170, 171, 188, 197, **216**, 221, 241, 255, 258, 277
Xavy, 216
Xena, 239
Xia, 24
Ximena, 99
Xristina, 243
Xzavier, 216, 258

Yadiel, 99, 255
Yadira, 255
Yael, 192, 227, 246
Yaffa, 142, 166, 246
Yahir, 26
Yair, 247
Yakov, 168
Yann, 241
Yanni, 33
Yannick, 241
Yareli, 255
Yasmin, 23, 57, 69, 81, 169, 176, 190, 261, 269
Yasmine, 69, 112, 185
Yazmin, 102, 255
Yehuda, 174, 247

Yesenia, **125**, 170, 255
Yesi, 125
Yessenia, 125
Yetta, 257
Yevgeni, 156
Yitzhak, 246
Yolanda, 82, 106, **125**, 148, 198, 212, 220, 255, 259
Yolande, 125
Yoli, 125
Yosef, 142, 247
Yuliana, 255
Yusuf, 262
Yuval, 247
Yvette, 45, 107, **125**, 141, 183, 198, 199, 220, 240, 284
Yvie, 125
Yvonne, 27, 28, 102, 106, 124, **125**, 161, 220, 240, 259

Zach, 216
Zachariah, 14, 149, 157, 171, **216**, 227, 238, 273
Zacharias, 216
Zachary, 18, 23, 24, 34, 42, 76, 80, 97, 99, 110, 168, 174, 183, **216**, 227, 228, 265, 273
Zack, 34, 61, 72, 108, 216, 273
Zackery, 216
Zahra, 125, 261
Zaire, 77, 221, 274
Zak, 167, 216
Zakary, 216
Zalman, 206
Zander, 68, 125, 129, 216
Zane, 117, 151, 160, 168, 211, 215, **216**, 229, 233
Zaria, 30, 77, 92, **125**, 193, 220, 274

Zavier, 216
Zayne, 216
Zé, 174
Zeb, 126, **216**, 227, 273
Zebedee, 216, 228, 238, 273
Zebediah, 216, 273
Zebulon, 216, 273
Zechariah, 216
Zeke, 77, 157, 216, 273
Zelda, 97, **126**, 132, 177, 188, 237, 249, 266
Zella, 149, 157, 183, 209
Zelma, 257
Zena, 203, 237

Zenith, 30, 239
Zenobia, 237
Zev, 247
Zigmund, 257
Zilla, 94, 122, **126**, 155, 170, 184, 205, 216, 227, 237, 256
Zillah, 126
Zina, 220
Zinnia, 232
Zion, 16, 52, 92, 99, **216**, 260
Zipporah, 227
Zita, 276
Ziva, 246, 256
Zo, 130

Zodiac, 239
Zoe/Zoë, 43, 88, 94, 96, 100, 104, **126**, 133, 154, 161, 243, 256, 266
Zoey, 52, 126, 216
Zoie, 101, 126
Zoila, 257
Zola, 126, 191, 237
Zona, 257
Zora, 44, 104, **126**, 130, 201, 218, 220, 237, 287
Zorah, 126
Zvi, 192, 247, 256